Birmingham
1939-1970

HISTORY OF BIRMINGHAM

VOLUME III

Birmingham

1939-1970

BY

ANTHONY SUTCLIFFE

Lecturer in the Department of Economic History,
University of Sheffield

AND

ROGER SMITH

Lecturer in the Department of
Town and Regional Planning,
University of Glasgow

Published for the
Birmingham City Council by

OXFORD UNIVERSITY PRESS

LONDON   NEW YORK   TORONTO

1974

Oxford University Press, Ely House, London W1

GLASGOW NEW YORK TORONTO MELBOURNE WELLINGTON
CAPE TOWN IBADAN NAIROBI DAR ES SALAAM LUSAKA ADDIS ABABA
DELHI BOMBAY CALCUTTA MADRAS KARACHI LAHORE DACCA
KUALA LUMPUR SINGAPORE HONG KONG TOKYO

ISBN 0 19 215182 7

942.4

*Printed in Great Britain
by The Camelot Press Ltd, Southampton*

IN MEMORY OF
SIR HERBERT MANZONI

PREFACE

THIS volume could not have been written without the scores of people, in and outside Birmingham, who have generously provided us with advice, information, and practical aid during the last six years. There is no room to thank all of them here by name, but we should at least like to express our special gratitude to a number of individuals who have been intimately involved in the preparation of this volume. We can only hope that those whose names do not appear will accept this book, on which they have set their mark, as our thanks to them.

From the start of our task in 1966 we enjoyed the guidance of two steering committees. The Corporation of Birmingham, whose generous grant covered the full cost of our work, appointed a special subcommittee to advise us. We are grateful to its members—Aldermen Harry Watton, Mrs. Ellen Smith, Sir Francis Griffin, Neville Bosworth, Eric Mole, Ernest Horton, and the late Lionel Aldridge—for their interest and aid. Special thanks are due to two successive Clerks to the General Purposes Committee, Mr. R. D. Siddall and Mr. P. Booth, who metaphorically shepherded us through the Council House corridors, and were ever ready with invaluable counsel and assistance. At Birmingham University, which accepted the Corporation's commission to produce this volume, we were helped by a committee composed of Professors B. Cullingworth, J. A. S. Grenville, R. Hoggart, F. Lafitte, and the late Professor W. H. B. Court. The committee was chaired successively by Professors D. W. J. Johnson and R. H. Hilton, who have been a constant support. We have very happy memories of the School of History, which gave us an academic home and companionship for four years.

It was the policy of both these committees to allow us a free hand both in our investigations and in our conclusions. The blame for errors of fact and judgment must rest squarely with us. Much of our time was spent in the Birmingham Reference Library, where the local studies section became a second home. The staff of that section have made a special contribution to this volume, from Miss D. Norris and her successor, Miss D. McCulla, on the one hand, to the juniors on the other. We are happy that, before this book is published, the section will have moved into the spacious new premises which it has so long deserved. Our thanks are also due to Mr. Raymond Field, of the Public Works Department, and to Mr. G. M. Adams, Chief Librarian of the Birmingham Post and Mail Ltd., who obtained many of the illustrations which appear in this volume.

All the Corporation's senior officers have contributed, either directly or through their staff, to this volume, and it is perhaps invidious to single out individuals for special thanks. We will, however, take this risk by recording our special debt to three officers who have found the time to see us repeatedly during the period of our work, and to comment constructively on various drafts of the volume. They are Mr. R. F. H. Ross, Estates Officer; Mr. N. Borg, City Engineer, Surveyor and Planning Officer; and Mr. A. B. Neale, Corporation Statistician.

Dozens of Birmingham personalities willingly agreed to meet us for interview. We had hoped that all would be present to see for themselves how they had helped to shape this volume, but many, too many, have passed on meanwhile. In particular, we think of Sir Herbert Manzoni, the creator of modern Birmingham, who gave us so much of his time. Norman Tiptaft, whose hospitality we so frequently enjoyed, is sadly missed. And so are Wallace Lawler, William 'Teg' Bowen, and Victor Yates, who greatly extended our knowledge of Birmingham politics.

In the preface to Volume II of the *History of Birmingham* Asa Briggs regretted the lack of specialized monographs on aspects of the city's history. We were more fortunate; thanks to the Corporation's generosity we had the time and the resources to fill in some of these gaps by our own researches. We were ably assisted by two research assistants: Miss June Ward, who worked with us for two years, and Mr. Nicholas Tyldesley, who helped us on a temporary basis. Mr. K. Isaac-Henry generously allowed us to make use of his unpublished research on the history of comprehensive education in Birmingham. Yet, after four years' full-time work, and two years during which we have revised and added to our draft when our new duties away from Birmingham have allowed, we are still aware that we have merely touched on our topic. We have left many avenues unexplored, and many questions unanswered. The time has now come, however, when this volume, with all its faults and omissions, must be placed before its patrons, the citizens and ratepayers of Birmingham. We can do no better than borrow the words of a forebear, the author of *A Concise History of Birmingham* (1808):

Soliciting the indulgence of a generous Public towards those errors which, from the nature of works of this description, will sometimes creep in, unperceived, we throw ourselves on their candour, in the full confidence that our exertions to give amusement and instruction will plead in our behalf.

January 1973

ANTHONY SUTCLIFFE
University of Sheffield

ROGER SMITH
University of Glasgow

CONTENTS

LIST OF PLATES

TABLES*

* See also Statistical Tables, Appendix D

FIGURES IN TEXT

ABBREVIATIONS

Abstract	*City of Birmingham Abstract of Statistics*
A.R.P.	Air raid precautions
B.C.C., *Pro.*	Birmingham City Council, *Proceedings*
B.G.	*Birmingham Gazette*
Black	H. J. Black, *History of the Corporation of Birmingham*, vol. VI
B.M.	*Birmingham Mail*
B.M.O.H.	*Report of the [Birmingham] Medical Officer of Health*
B.P.	*Birmingham Post*
Briggs	Asa Briggs, *History of Birmingham*, vol. II
B.R.L.	Birmingham Reference Library
B.T.C., *Annual Report*	Birmingham Trades Council and Borough Labour Party, *Annual Report and Year Book*
B.W.P.	*Birmingham Weekly Post*
Econ.H.R.	*Economic History Review*
E.D.	*Evening Despatch*
H. of C. Deb.	*House of Commons Debates*
S.M.	*Sunday Mercury*
V.C.H. Warcks.	*Victoria County History of Warwickshire*
Y.B.	*Your Business*

I

INTRODUCTION

Birmingham is a wonderful place, when thoroughly comprehended, but this is not to be done by a glance.

The Builder, vol. vii, no. 346, 22 September 1849

WHEN the Birmingham Corporation commissioned a third volume of the History of Birmingham to cover the years 1939–1970, it created a unique opportunity to write the contemporary history of a thriving community at a crucial stage in its evolution. As part of a series whose previous volumes had already attained a high academic reputation, it would be able to present the city's recent history in a perspective stretching back to the very origins of the settlement. It would also, the Corporation hoped, constitute a major investigation into the condition and character of modern Birmingham.

Although this volume has some similarities to a social survey, we must make it clear from the outset that we have approached our task as historians. That is to say, we have been interested primarily in describing and explaining changes over time. By setting Birmingham's current problems in a time-perspective we may have shed fresh light on them, but to do so has not been our primary aim. On the other hand, we have tried to avoid the temptation, which often besets local historians, of portraying our city as unique and idiosyncratic. Modern Birmingham clearly exhibits more similarities to other British cities than differences, and we have tried to set its evolution in the context of urban society in the country as a whole. Yet we have endeavoured to identify and explain such differences as exist.[1]

The new volume raised difficulties as well as opportunities. The least daunting of them, perhaps, was the technical problem of adding a highly-concentrated third volume to a series that was already well defined as a wide-ranging survey over long periods of time. To devote several hundred pages to just thirty years meant that the book's structure, and the depth at which most topics were studied, would differ substantially from the previous contributions. Connected with this problem was the question of whether we should pursue some of the major concerns of the other two volumes, such as the dominant influence of nonconformity on Birmingham. We decided that it would be wrong to make Volume III conform to a pre-determined pattern for the sake

[1] When Birmingham is compared statistically with other 'major cities', these are (unless otherwise stated) the seven English provincial cities which had a population of over 300,000 in 1951 (Bristol, Hull, Leeds, Liverpool, Manchester, Nottingham, Sheffield), and Birmingham's biggest neighbour, Coventry (pop. 256,800 in 1951).

of continuity; instead, we have written a book that can stand alone as a study of a contemporary British city. The reader will certainly detect some discontinuity and overlapping, but the continuity of the main theme, Birmingham itself, should ensure that Volume III does not appear out of place even when read as part of the series.

The second major difficulty is common to the writing of all contemporary history. Although the need for time-perspective in historical writing is often overstated, the passage of time helps to ease the historian's task in many respects. We have faced an even more serious dearth of secondary works on Birmingham history than that lamented by Asa Briggs in his preface to Volume II.[1] More serious, our judgment may well have been distorted by too close an involvement in the events we have described. Yet contemporary research offers many valuable facilities to the historian. It allows him to meet and question many of the people whose actions he is trying to assess. These encounters are especially valuable to the historian of a local community, in which few notabilities leave papers or diaries, or write memoirs. As long as official records are open to the researcher, a city's history is perhaps better written shortly after events have taken place than after the lapse of several decades. And once his research is complete, the contemporary historian benefits from the comments of those directly involved in events in his account of what has taken place. Joseph Chamberlain, regrettably, is no longer here to point to such ignorance of nineteenth-century Birmingham as this volume may reveal; but Harry Watton and Sir Francis Griffin can, and will, identify any errors and failures of judgment that may mar our account of the last three decades. And so will any citizen of Birmingham who picks up this book. We have accepted this challenge and have found it a stimulus to accuracy and fairness.

We now come to a third problem, which cannot be dismissed so easily. Our terms of reference required us to produce a history of a small, well-defined area—the city of Birmingham. But Birmingham is more than just a city; it is the most important unit in one of the largest provincial conurbations in Europe, and the economic centre of the whole of the West Midland region. On the east and south Birmingham is bounded by agricultural land, but elsewhere it merges imperceptibly with neighbouring populated areas. Many people who work in Birmingham live elsewhere; some residents travel daily to work outside the city. Many Birmingham firms have branch factories outside the boundaries. So how can Birmingham be studied separately from the conurbation and even from the whole region? It can be argued, as has the City Council on occasions, that Birmingham is different in character and

---

[1] See Briggs, pp. v–vi, and Briggs's foreword to H. J. Dyos (ed.), *The Study of Urban History* (1968), p. ix.

interests from the rest of the conurbation. It also forms a single political unit, whereas the conurbation as a whole is composed of several independent authorities. But on the whole we accept that Birmingham should not be studied in isolation. Perhaps, even, the appearance of this volume will further strengthen the case for abandoning the traditional form of urban history based on biographies of individual cities.

Yet there is much that is positive in the study of a single city. The character of its people is easier to define than in a more amorphous conurbation, especially one so varied as the West Midlands agglomeration. More important, it is possible to associate politics, local decision-making, and general evolutionary trends much more closely than in the study of a broader area. Furthermore, we have not ignored the conurbation nor the region in so far as they influence Birmingham. We have shown how Birmingham's municipal affairs have become more closely interlinked with those of its neighbours, and how it has provided a growing range of services for them. But there is no denying that the region and the conurbation as portrayed in this volume are the product of Birmingham-based observation.

Within the limitations described so far, we have set out to write what is essentially a social history of Birmingham. We are interested in the people of the city, how they live and work and enjoy themselves. But we have not tried to produce 'total' history—an account of everything that goes on in Birmingham.[1] Features that are essentially national, the same everywhere in the country, are only touched upon. We have concentrated on those aspects of the city's life that are essentially urban, and those that are substantially influenced by the people who live and work in Birmingham.

One limitation of our work must be openly admitted. In attempting a sober assessment of Birmingham's recent history we have tried to steer clear of all subjectivism and impressionism. In so doing we are open to the criticism that we have failed to capture what is sometimes described as 'the spirit of Birmingham'. We can reply only by stating our contention that facts, in so far as they can be objectively determined, must form the basis of all historical writing. If we were to try to re-create the reactions and emotions of Birmingham citizens we would be in danger of extrapolating from our own personal feelings to the community as a whole, or of oversimplifying opinion in a city whose numerous and varied component parts admit of no valid generalization. So we have been cautious. We have hesitated to identify changes in public opinion unless we have voting figures or Gallup polls to support us; we have sought similar firm evidence before alluding

[1] For a critique of the type of 'total' urban history which treats a city in isolation from other cities and from the general urbanization process, see S. G. Checkland, 'English provincial cities', *Econ. H.R.*, 2nd series, vol. vi, no. 1, 1953, pp. 195–203.

to variations in public tastes. Perhaps our readers will still find that we have been too cautious, too matter-of-fact. We can only crave their indulgence. Their imagination, we believe, is just as valid as ours, and we will not impose our personal view of Birmingham on them. If we have succeeded in providing a sound foundation on which our readers may more firmly base their own subjective assessments of the city and its people, we shall be happy.

The organization of a book of this nature raises its own special problems. As historians we wish to create a feeling of movement through time, yet a purely chronological, year-by-year approach would be highly confusing. We have therefore chosen to isolate key themes of Birmingham's development, such as politics, population change, and entertainments, and to study their evolution in separate chapters or sections over our whole thirty-year period. The war years, however, were in many respects an exceptional episode, and so we have decided to confine the war's more ephemeral aspects to a separate chapter. Unfortunately, Britain's second city does not easily allow itself to be split into the neat categories which suit the historian's convenience. We provide frequent cross-references, but we are aware that readers do not take kindly to being forced to jump backwards and forwards. So we have sometimes provided certain basic information in more than one chapter. Repetition inevitably results on occasion, and may annoy those who wish to read the book at one sitting. Again, we must seek their indulgence in the interests of those who will consult the volume only on topics which are of direct interest to them.

The contents have been arranged in the following way. After a brief historical introduction (which now follows), we deal first with the exceptional circumstances of wartime—the blitz and its effects, and the mood of adventurous replanning induced by the war. Those aspects of Birmingham's life in the years 1939–45 that were not direct products of the war are studied in the following chapters, which cover thematically the whole of the period 1939–70. Two chapters deal with the city's political structure and the powers of the Corporation, and with the restriction of Birmingham's growth. Then follows a central core of three chapters covering fundamental factors in the life and environment of the city; industry and commerce, demography, and housing. After two chapters on social life and entertainments, four major sub-topics are examined: education, Commonwealth immigration, utilities, and the visual environment. The volume closes with an assessment of where Birmingham stood in 1970.

Birmingham has always been a city of rapid change. But some of the changes in the thirty years which followed the outbreak of the Second World War were among the most fundamental in Birmingham's whole history. The city centre and nearby slum areas were pulled down and rebuilt on a scale unparalleled in Britain; new roads transformed whole districts and revolutionized the city's pattern of communications. Birmingham trades flourished, and almost the whole population enjoyed a prosperity unknown before the war. Far outstripping Britain's other major cities, Birmingham became a centre of high mass consumption second only to London. These changes had bad effects as well as good; the needs of the residual minority of poor were sometimes ignored by the more prosperous majority, and materialism was prominent in all sections of Birmingham society. Yet in many other ways Birmingham changed little during these three decades. Its population and social structure remained almost static, and although its industries produced far more in 1970 than they had in 1939, there was little structural change in their character and in the number of people they employed.

Partly responsible for these static features in Birmingham's evolution was the city's declining power to shape its own destiny. Political decisions affecting Birmingham were made increasingly in Whitehall; and it was the central government which determined that the city should stop growing and that no new industries should enter it. More and more boardroom decisions were made outside the city as Birmingham firms were absorbed into national and international combines. These outside forces also affected other big provincial cities, so that Birmingham came increasingly to resemble them in many aspects of its life and structure. Even so, Birmingham in 1970 still differed from such cities as Leeds, Manchester, and Liverpool. Most of these differences were products of the city's development before 1939.

At the end of the Middle Ages Birmingham was a market town of more than local importance, but its industries were no different from those of most other settlements of its size.[1] Two centuries later the town had become the centre of a thriving metal industry.[2] This transformation resulted from the migration of iron manufacturers from the Staffordshire coal outcrops to the Tame valley, where water power was available for forges and mills. Birmingham, which lay near the valley, was especially attractive to those migrants because of its commercial standing and freedom from gild restrictions. In the eighteenth century the demand for metal goods increased in Britain and abroad, and the town's industries grew more diverse. Colonial expansion encouraged Birmingham to become a gun-making centre, and skills developed in this trade were utilized to make a wide range of brass toys, buckles, and buttons. From these simple beginnings grew the

[1] See R. A. Pelham, 'The growth of settlement and industry *c.* 1100–1700', *Birmingham and its Regional Setting* (British Association, 1950), p. 160.

[2] D. E. C. Eversley, 'Industry and trade 1500–1880', *V.C.H. Warcks*, vol. vii, p. 82.

precious metal and jewellery trades.[1] But skill was not always associated with Birmingham products, and it gained a reputation, not always unjustified, for producing shoddy goods. It was not until a high standard of workmanship was set by engineers, such as Boulton at his Soho manufactory, that Birmingham's name began to be associated consistently with quality. The standard of Birmingham jewellery improved with the foundation of the Assay Office in 1775, and that of guns with the opening of the Proof House in 1813.[2]

As the skills of Birmingham artisans developed, the less prosperous industries left the town. The cruder metal-working trades were lost to the Black Country, which acted almost as a colony, feeding Birmingham with processed raw materials and semi-manufactured articles. The departure of these primary trades allowed Birmingham to attract growing numbers of artisans and entrepreneurs.[3] But Birmingham's hegemony over the Black Country was not limited to the industrial sphere. During the eighteenth century the town was also becoming the financial and commercial capital of the West Midlands. Much of the capital for Black Country coalmining and iron-smelting was raised by Birmingham ironmongers. This role was further strengthened as Birmingham became the focal point of nationwide canal, and later railway, systems. The railway boom, in its turn, brought about the foundation of the Birmingham Stock Exchange.

By 1850 Birmingham's position as a major metal-working centre was assured, and from then onwards its development was a natural progression as the range of metal goods needed in a rapidly accelerating industrial society expanded. But in order to keep abreast of this changing market Birmingham entrepreneurs and artisans had continually to readapt their methods and products. They accepted this challenge and Birmingham developed a tradition of innovation. This adaptability permitted the rapid development of medium and light engineering trades from the 1880s. Birmingham's traditional skills were now turned to producing the presses, lathes, and other precision tools which were in increasing demand.[4] Local manufacturers were also eager to use new metals as soon as they became available. During the last quarter of the nineteenth century they made full use of steel; in the first years of the twentieth they began to utilize aluminium, which greatly broadened the range of hollow-ware goods.[5]

[1] G. C. Allen, *Industrial Development of Birmingham and the Black Country 1860–1927* (1929), p. 25.

[2] M. J. Wise and B. L. C. Johnson, 'The changing regional pattern during the eighteenth century', *Birmingham and its Regional Setting*, pp. 161, 179; Allen, *Industrial Development*, p. 33.   [3] Allen, p. 25.

[4] M. J. Wise and P. O. N. Thorpe, 'The growth of Birmingham 1800–1850', *Birmingham and its Regional Setting*, p. 215.

[5] Allen, *Industrial Development*, pp. 292–5.

Birmingham's wealth of engineering skills and ability to produce steel tubes made it an ideal environment to nurture the bicycle, motorcycle, and motor car industries. Although the British cycle trade was born in Coventry, by the end of the 1880s it was firmly established in Birmingham. The subsequent development of the motor industry in Coventry created a demand for component parts which Birmingham was happy to satisfy. Initially, Birmingham-produced components were of metal only, but Dunlop soon opened a factory in the city to manufacture rubber tyres. The newly-established electrical industries were also stimulated by motors, and the General Electric Company and Joseph Lucas were among the major firms founded in the city during this period. So when Herbert Austin converted an old factory at Longbridge for car manufacture, much of Birmingham's economy was already dependent upon an industry which was to play such a key role in its twentieth-century economic development.[1]

This ability to innovate, attract new industries, and develop new techniques and products freed Birmingham from the worst consequences of economic depressions. The 'great depression' of the 1880s, for instance, had an unhappy effect on some of the older Birmingham industries, such as brassfounding, but the advancing engineering industry soon took up the slack.[2] In the 1920s and 1930s Birmingham experienced periods of depression, but the gearing of its economy to growth industries such as motors and electrical goods allowed it to recover more rapidly than many other areas.[3]

Until the middle of the nineteenth century the bulk of Birmingham output came from small workshops owned or rented by master craftsmen employing a handful of skilled artisans. These workshops remained a common feature of the city, but from the 1870s the factory system was firmly established and extended in the town. As a result, capital, which had previously been subordinate to skill in Birmingham, came to be of paramount importance, while the level of skill required in many processes fell.[4] The growth in size of production units was accompanied by amalgamations of firms, beginning in the middle of the nineteenth century and quickening in pace during the twentieth. Typical of these expanding concerns was the Birmingham Small Arms Co., which sprang from an amalgamation of small arms firms in 1854. In the 1880s, when the gun trade was depressed, B.S.A. turned to bicycle manufacture. Rapid expansion and innovation soon allowed the concern to produce cars and then tools. Not content with buying up

[1] Allen, pp. 292 ff.   [2] See Allen, Chapter iii.
[3] Royal Commission on the Distribution of the Industrial Population, *Memorandum of Evidence Submitted by the Corporation of Birmingham*. Cmd. 6153, 1939, ev. no. 10.
[4] See esp. B. M. D. Smith, 'Industry and trade 1880–1960', *V.C.H. Warcks.*, vol. vii, pp. 140–208.

Birmingham firms, B.S.A. began to purchase companies in other towns.
The most notable of them was the Coventry firm of Daimler, acquired
in 1910.[1] Such amalgamations allowed some Birmingham firms to
become the kingpins of great national enterprises. One such merger
was that of Cadbury Brothers with J. S. Fry and Sons of Bristol in
1919.[2] More frequently, however, Birmingham companies were themselves absorbed into consortia that had not originated in the area.
The Birmingham munitions firm of George Kynoch, for instance, came
to be absorbed into one of Britain's largest companies, I.C.I., via the
I.C.I. Metals Division.[3] Other city firms were incorporated in the
massive Tube Investments combine. Nevertheless, small factories and
workshops continued to make a major contribution to Birmingham's
economic life even as late as 1970.[4]

Industrial changes had a major influence on Birmingham's topo-
graphy. As large production units grew up, they moved away from the
centre, and the new large-scale industries settled from the very first
in the suburbs. The older, non-expanding, labour-intensive industries
remained huddled in the central areas, hemming in an increasingly
cramped central business district.[5] Most of the new factories clustered
along the major railways and canals, in two major industrial corridors.
One extended from the town centre to the north-west, following the
Birmingham–Wolverhampton canal. The second, and more extensive, corridor ran to the north-east. It followed the Fazeley canal
through Aston, where it forked into two. One fork turned eastward
along the Derby railway line to Bromford. The other veered towards
the north-west, following the Tame valley canal. It was here, at
Witton, that the great Kynoch and G.E.C. factories stood. In addition,
two narrower tongues of industry stretched away from the city centre.
One ran to the south-east along the Warwick canal and the Birmingham–
Oxford railway; the largest single works in it was B.S.A.'s at Small
Heath. The second tongue followed the Worcester canal and Bristol
railway through Stirchley and Bournville, where George Cadbury
built his factory, to Longbridge, where Herbert Austin developed his.[6]

During the inter-war years further industrial districts developed,
generally at a radius of three to five miles from the city centre. Their
location was largely influenced by a shortage of cheap sites, for the
newer factories now needed acres of land. They were also affected by
the Corporation's town planning schemes, which reserved certain
areas for industry after the early 1900s, and excluded it from growing
residential areas like Quinton and Harborne. The result was the almost

[1] Smith, pp. 153, 157; Allen, *Industrial Development*, p. 358.
[2] Smith, p. 161.   [3] Smith, p. 158.   [4] Smith, p. 160.
[5] Wise and Thorpe, 'Growth of Birmingham', pp. 222 ff.
[6] Wise and Thorpe, especially map on p. 223.

complete industrialization of the Tame valley through the city, from Perry Barr in the north-west to Bromford and Castle Bromwich in the east.

Birmingham's prosperous industries made it a magnet for population. Growth was particularly rapid in the nineteenth century. The area of the borough, which contained 71,000 persons in 1801, held 401,000 eighty years later. Population also expanded in the suburban areas, which had strong economic and social links with Birmingham. The combined populations of Balsall Heath, Harborne, Saltley and Little Bromwich, for instance, rose from 7,000 to 94,000 between 1841 and 1911. Owing to these increases, and extensions of the borough boundaries, Birmingham grew to be England's largest provincial city by the 1930s, with a population in excess of one million. Much of the nineteenth-century growth was the result of immigration, but the influx slowed after the First World War. During certain years in the 1930s more people left the city than arrived, and the population continued to rise only because of the excess of births over deaths. Between 1931 and 1934, when the depression was at its height, there was a net loss of 8,000 migrants. It took the rearmament drive of the later 1930s to reverse this trend, producing a net gain of 17,000 persons during the last five years of the decade.[1]

As Birmingham's population grew, its centre of gravity shifted away from the inner districts. There is some evidence to suggest that the population of the central areas of the city was declining as early as 1891, and there can be little doubt of this trend after 1911. This fall, interrupted only by the First World War, has continued ever since. After 1918 it was accelerated by the development of big private and municipal estates on the outskirts of the city.[2]

During the first half of the nineteenth century the influx of population into Birmingham had resulted in the rapid building of cheap working-class houses. Most were three-storey back-to-backs, with three rooms and a cellar. Often they were grouped into courts or adjoined workshops. Privies were shared by several families, and water was obtained from communal standpipes in the yards.[3] Despite growing local and national criticism, back-to-back building for the working classes continued until 1876, when the Borough Council made it illegal. Most of these houses survived until the 1930s, despite the demolition of a number of them for railways and industrial expansion. During the 1930s the Corporation demolished some 8,000 back-to-back

[1] See G. Walker, 'The growth of population in Birmingham and the Black Country between the wars', *University of Birmingham Historical Journal*, no. 1, 1947, p. 160.

[2] W. Taylor, 'Migration in Birmingham 1931–47', *Birmingham and its Regional Setting*, p. 263.

[3] Bournville Village Trust, *When We Build Again* (1941), p. 52; Margaret Tomlinson, 'Secular architecture', *V.C.H. Warcks.*, vol. vii, p. 17.

houses, but 30,000 more remained standing. Some of them were improved by landlords, prompted by the Corporation,[1] but living conditions in nearly all remained totally inadequate.

Between the 1860s and 1914 the old, central areas were encircled by a new band of housing. Some of these houses, built before 1876, were indistinguishable from dwellings in the central areas. But most were of the two-storey tunnel-back type, with individual back yards, which became general after the reform of the building by-laws. Built in terraces, they were designed to make maximum use of land. The parlour opened on to the street; beyond were the living-room and the scullery, with internal running water. There were three bedrooms and an outside W.C. Some refinements of design had been introduced by 1900, but densities remained high. Most of these houses were occupied by prosperous artisans. But Birmingham's expanding middle class was also forced to move out of the centre. As early as 1760 there were a few large houses on the western fringes of Washwood Heath, as well as in Aston and Saltley. These mansions formed the cores of much more extensive upper-class developments during the nineteenth century.[2] These areas consisted of large detached and semi-detached houses with room for a number of servants. But, extensive though some of them were, all were engulfed sooner or later by the expanding districts of industry or workers' housing. Only in Edgbaston, on the Calthorpe Estate, were the upper classes secluded from the productive forces that were creating the city's wealth. The 1,560-acre estate, founded towards the end of the eighteenth century, was protected by strict leasehold control from the advances of unsympathetic developers. In places it adjoined the very core of the city, yet it preserved the atmosphere of a leafy, opulent suburb. Most of the houses on the estate were built during the nineteenth century, but some were added between the world wars, together with a number of blocks of luxury flats.[3]

In the inter-war years a third ring of housing developed, containing nearly ninety per cent of the dwellings built in Birmingham between 1920 and 1938.[4] Most of these houses were built by the Corporation, which planned its new estates to provide as sharp a contrast as possible with the older working-class areas. All the houses had large gardens, and overall densities were extremely low, with about twelve houses to the acre. Further estates were developed by speculative builders, especially in the 1930s. Most of their houses were semi-detached, with three bedrooms. Although overall planning standards were not as good as those of the municipal estates, these dwellings were more

---

[1] See the annual *Reports* of the Birmingham Medical Officer of Health.

[2] C. R. Elrington and P. M. Tillott, 'The growth of the city', *V.C.H. Warcks.*, vol. vii, pp. 12, 19.

[3] Elrington and Tillott, p. 13.   [4] *When We Build Again*, p. 52.

satisfactory in almost every way than the tunnel-backs. The outer ring also contained a few early, planned garden suburbs, the most important of which were George Cadbury's Bournville and J. S. Nettlefold's Harborne Tenants estate. Also to be found in the outer ring were some upper-middle-class areas, such as parts of King's Heath and Harborne, and a few very old houses in engulfed villages like King's Norton and Northfield.[1]

These housing developments must have reduced overcrowding in Birmingham. It seems certain that between the 1840s and the 1860s rapid immigration greatly overtaxed the supply of housing, and the small size of the back-to-back houses must have caused chronic over-crowding. The tunnel-backs alleviated this pressure, but the biggest improvement resulted from the building of new estates between the wars at a time when immigration was very low. Nevertheless, serious overcrowding remained, as the official survey of 1936 showed.[2] At this time some 8,000 families were overcrowded under the not-too-rigorous standards of the 1935 Housing Act. Most were in the central areas, but nearly a quarter lived in municipal houses in the outer ring.

Birmingham's distinctive social and economic structure had done much to shape the character of its politics. The absence of a strong landed class and the multiplicity of small masters made it a strong radical force in the early decades of the nineteenth century. Yet the small scale of its industries and high social mobility prevented the emergence of a bitter class struggle between employers and employed. After playing a prominent role in the great reform agitation, which united merchants, masters and artisans, Birmingham was only partially sympathetic to Chartism, which embodied a strong element of class conflict. As the nineteenth century wore on the Liberal party strengthened its hold on the town, and working-class organization was stunted. The Liberal caucus, perfected by Joseph Chamberlain and his associates in the 1860s, dominated Birmingham politics.[3]

In the 1880s this Liberal hegemony began to break down. As Birmingham's industrial structure was converted from small workshops to factories, the workers lost much of their identity of interest with the employers. Many middle-class people also sensed this alienation, and wavered in their allegiance to a Liberal party which seemed prepared to make increasing concessions to the workers. So Joseph Chamberlain's break with Gladstone over Ireland in 1886 actually helped him to retain his hold over Birmingham. By moving ever closer

[1] A. Pevsner and A. Wedgewood, *The Buildings of England: Warwickshire* (1966), pp. 143, 192, 201; Elrington and Tillott, p. 20.
[2] City of Birmingham Public Health Department, *Report by the Medical Officer of Health on the Overcrowding Survey* (1936).
[3] See Briggs, pp. 164–99.

to the Conservatives, he and his Liberal-Unionist followers were able to regain the loyalty of many middle-class voters who had begun to desert the Liberal Party in the 1870s and 1880s. Yet, by continuing to advocate certain radical policies, especially at municipal level, Chamberlain retained the support of a majority of the working class, who benefited from the rapid expansion of engineering and allied trades from the 1880s. Trade unionism was weak in these newer industries and deferential in the older trades, and the Labour Party had little electoral success until the 1920s. Even then the city's prosperity and the immense prestige of the Unionists, who were still led by members of the Chamberlain family, prevented Labour from establishing more than a foothold in Birmingham.

Unionist strength in Birmingham was partly founded on the prestige and enlightened policies of the Unionist-controlled City Council. After the incorporation of the borough in 1838 the council had for some years to share powers with the existing improvement commissioners, but in the 1850s it at last obtained wide authority to act for the general good of the town. In the 1860s and 1870s the council came to be dominated by Chamberlainite radicalism which municipalized the water, gas, and later, electricity and transport services. The town centre was transformed from the 1870s by a municipal improvement scheme centred on Corporation Street, and Chamberlain and his followers radically improved educational facilities after 1870. In the 1880s the council became more cautious; it did little, for instance, to provide public housing until after 1918, but it remained very receptive to new ideas. The town planning schemes pioneered before 1914, under the 1909 Town Planning Act, shaped a better environment for Birmingham, and after the war the council more than made up for its previous inactivity in housing. The city was now so large that municipal services could be organized with rare efficiency, and Birmingham retained its pre-war reputation as 'the best-governed city in the world'. But the Chamberlainite pioneering spirit was by now accompanied by a marked respect for economy which the national economic difficulties of the 1930s reinforced. Meanwhile the Unionists' hold over the Birmingham working classes weakened; half the Birmingham parliamentary seats fell to Labour or I.L.P. candidates in 1929. Labour's cause suffered a severe setback in the 1930s, and the party remained in a small minority in the City Council. Yet by the end of the decade there were indications that the working masses were again beginning to stir. The most dramatic of these portents was the huge municipal rent strike in the summer of 1939.

The civic improvement drive in the second half of the nineteenth century had provided Birmingham with many of the social and cultural amenities that had been neglected in the town's rapid growth. But the massive boundary extensions undertaken from the 1890s again created an overall dearth of amenities. The city became so large that many people had difficulty in reaching the centre, whose adequate expansion was restricted in any case by a tight ring of factories and slum houses. Extra amenities such as shops, libraries, and cinemas were slow to grow up in the suburbs where low residential densities threatened their economic viability. The high wages paid in industry made it more difficult than in less prosperous cities to find enough personnel for these services. Birmingham's size also prevented many citizens from attaining an overall sense of community, especially in the newly-annexed areas. During the 1930s many citizens began to question the way in which the city was developing, but no full reappraisal was made. Clearly, Birmingham was reaching a major turning-point, but it was still uncertain whether the city would summon up the will and direction to reassess its destiny completely. Yet within a few years the stimulus for such a reappraisal had suddenly been provided, by a second war with Germany.

II

BIRMINGHAM *VERSUS* HITLER:
1939–1945

AT 11.15 a.m. on Sunday, 3 September 1939, a Birmingham man addressed the British nation. For that man, Prime Minister Neville Chamberlain, his brief wireless announcement of the declaration of war on Germany ended two decades of fervent hope in the establishment of permanent peace in Europe. For his native city it heralded the end of an era, the end of eight decades in which the Chamberlains and their friends had guided Birmingham through an age of unprecedented growth, prosperity, and good government. Within a few months the Chamberlain government was to resign. Soon after, Neville Chamberlain would be dead. With his passing the name of Chamberlain virtually disappeared from Birmingham's affairs. Meanwhile, the conflict which Neville had striven so long to avoid was already transforming the face and character of his native city. Peace would eventually return, but after six years of war Birmingham would be very different from the city which these latter-day Medici had done so much to create.

The Second World War's direct effects on Birmingham were much more marked that those of the First. Parts of the city were destroyed or seriously damaged by bombs, many of its citizens were called away to fight and their places in factories and offices were taken by newcomers from outside the city. Many of Birmingham's children and young mothers were driven away to safer areas; most of its industrial production was concentrated on munitions. Yet from the point of view of its direct effects alone, the war was just a passing episode in the life of Birmingham; as soon as peace came, the city would return to normal. Of course, there would be serious problems, such as the rebuilding of thousands of houses. Moreover, the loss of thousands of citizens on the field of battle and on the home front would not quickly be forgotten. But the war also had important indirect effects on Birmingham; it influenced social and economic trends which had already been present before the war, and altered, though sometimes only very marginally, the features and character of the city and its people. These indirect results of the war were often less striking at the time than the direct, but many of them were more lasting. War, for instance, accelerated changes in industrial production methods, encouraged trade union membership, altered people's daily habits, and led to greater sociability and better standards of health and diet.

Even more subtle was the war's influence on the psychology and ideology of many Birmingham citizens. Almost all individuals and groups showed themselves more willing to plan ahead, and to make concessions to conflicting interests. Many believed they could see signposts to an ideal society, and they were eager to take their first steps on that road. They learned to think big; individualism and localism were alike eclipsed. Within Birmingham the war undermined class barriers and engendered a fuller sense of community; meanwhile the city felt a greater identity with other towns and with the nation as a whole.

It is because the Second World War affected Birmingham in these so different ways that it cannot be considered solely within the time-span of 1939 to 1945. Yet so exceptional were wartime conditions that it would also be wrong to treat the war as a mere six years in the steady evolution of the Birmingham community. This chapter, therefore, attempts to describe the wartime events and changes which had a direct effect on the city, together with those indirect results which were prominent during the war years. Those effects which influenced the post-war evolution of Birmingham are only summarized, and we shall return to them in later chapters in the context of the general development of Birmingham over the three decades.

Birmingham under fire

Shortly after one o'clock on the morning of 9 August 1940 a lone German bomber droned through the east Birmingham skies above a darkened city. Its crew were probably looking for Fort Dunlop or the Nuffield shadow aero factory, but eventually they lost patience, released their bombs, and headed for home. Thus it fell to a quiet suburban street in Erdington to suffer Birmingham's first casualties and damage by enemy action. Rescue workers from the A.R.P. depot at Spring Lane were quickly on the scene; they found one man dead and six people wounded. At three minutes past two the city's air raid sirens sounded the alert, but no more planes appeared and the all-clear followed just after half past two.[1] So began the Birmingham blitz.

Most Birmingham citizens had recognized for some years that the city would be a prime target for enemy bombers in the event of a new European war. Already during the First World War Birmingham's industries had made a major contribution to the might of the Empire.[2] The city had taken, then, a further step away from the labour-intensive, small-scale production of light metal goods, which had been

---

[1] A.R.P. Committee minutes, 19 August 1940; article by Martin Davies in *B.M.*, 2 August 1965. Unless otherwise stated, casualty figures are those reported by the Medical Officer of Health to the Casualty Service Sub-Committee of the A.R.P. Committee.

[2] See Briggs, pp. 214-19.

its staple in the nineteenth century, towards mechanized, mass production, and assembly work. The motor industry and its allied trades,
in particular, had been stimulated by the first motorized conflict. After
the war, the motor trade had gone on growing, and more and more
Birmingham firms, in accordance with the local tradition of interdependence, came to be associated with it. As Europe staggered towards
war in the 1930s, it was obvious that Birmingham would again have a
major role to play in hostilities. But a new war would bring dangers as
well as opportunities. Above all, would a big concentration of war
industries in Birmingham prove dangerously vulnerable to aerial
attack?

The Government began to worry about bombing in the early 1930s.
In 1934 the Air Council prepared a classification of safe and unsafe
areas in Britain. The south and south-east were classed as 'dangerous',
and the north as 'safe'—a distinction which coincided with the Government's policy of encouraging employment in the Special Areas, which
were designated in the same year, 1934. Birmingham was placed in an
intermediate zone, 'unsafe' and 'not free from danger'.[1] So there
seemed to be good reasons for diverting new armaments production
away from Birmingham, both in the interests of strategic safety and of
national employment policy. But the case for allowing expansion to go
ahead in Birmingham and its area was even stronger. Its labour force
and managements had a reputation for adaptability, and could be
expected to tackle the problems of munitions production more effectively than those of the Special Areas. The production of motors and
the assembly of both vehicles and aircraft would be even more important in a new war than they had been in 1914–18, and as Birmingham
and Coventry were the main centres of the motor trade outside London,
they could hardly be left out of war production plans. Admittedly,
Birmingham did not produce aircraft in peacetime, but car assembly
workers could easily adapt to fuselage construction, and motor engine
plants, like that of Austin's at Longbridge, could well switch to producing aero engines. Moreover, Birmingham was close to important
aero engine works at Coventry and Derby. So the Government decided
that it had no alternative but to plan for an important expansion of
munitions production at Birmingham. The organization of the production of most war items could be left to the initiative of Birmingham
firms; the aero industry, on the other hand, had to be imported into
the city under Government direction.

In 1935 the Government decided on the rapid expansion of the
military aircraft industry and financed the construction of additional
plant known as 'shadow factories' to build engines and airframes.
These factories were to be managed by existing motor concerns, near

1 William Hornby, *Factories and Plant* (1958), p. 286.

Sir Herbert Manzoni

Bomb damage near a primary target. John Bright Street and New Street Station, 21 November 1940.

Aftermath of a conflagration. The eastern end of New Street, 10 April 1941. After clearance of rubble, this became the 'Big Top' site, used for exhibitions to promote the war effort.

whose works most of them were sited. Several were built in Birmingham and Coventry, and until 1938 all but one of the shadow factories producing engines had been built in these two cities. From the summer of 1938 most of the new factories approved were sited in the 'safe' area, but a second group of aero factories was later authorized in Coventry and Birmingham. With aircraft factories being built in Birmingham from scratch, little extra danger was involved in allowing the expansion there of the engineering section of the armaments industry, which was already deeply rooted in the city. Extensions were approved, for instance, to B.S.A. at Small Heath for munitions production. On the other hand, when totally new explosive and weapon factories were set up, they were normally located in the 'safe' area of the country.[1]

Work started on the Rover shadow factory at Acocks Green in October 1936, and production of aero engine parts began there in July 1937. Rover built another shadow factory at Solihull, and the concern's other works in the Birmingham area were adapted to the production of aero engines and airframe parts by the early months of the war.[2] Austin's were able to build their shadow factory near their motor works at Cofton Hackett, and the first aircraft was completed there in June 1938.[3] The third and last unit in the shadow factory scheme for the Birmingham area was provided by the Nuffield Organization (Morris cars) which in 1938 bought a large site at Castle Bromwich, near Fort Dunlop, for an airframe factory. Although Nuffield already had a small works in Birmingham, the new factory was a major departure for the Oxford-based firm, and its choice of site had clearly been dictated by the easy availability of skilled labour and components in Birmingham. The decision was welcomed by Lord Austin, by the City Council (which owned the land) and by the engineering unions in the city.[4] 'We are laying the foundations of an entirely new and great industry for the city', exulted Wing-Commander Wright, Unionist M.P. for Erdington,[5] and indeed, a factory employing twelve to fifteen thousand people was not to be sniffed at while the unemployment rate in the city was still unusually high.[6] This, the largest shadow factory in Britain, was managed by Vickers from May 1940.[7]

The shadow factories brought new work to Birmingham, but they also brought an even greater danger of air attack. Yet only a fraction of the vast sums expended on munitions factories was devoted to the

---

[1] Hornby, pp. 288–95.

[2] H. B. Light, *Ninety Years of Industrial Progress and Outstanding Achievement: Short History of the Rover Company Ltd.* (1967), p. 14.

[3] *B.M.*, 31 May 1938.

[4] See *E.D.*, *B.P.*, 28 May 1938; *B.M.*, 30 May 1939; *E.D.*, 31 May 1938.

[5] *E.D.*, 31 May 1938.   [6] See editorial in *B.P.*, 1 June 1938.

[7] Hornby, *Factories and Plant*, pp. 220, 395.

protection of the civilian population against bombing. The contrast was a significant one; the shadow factories were built with Government money, but, until shortly before war broke out, air raid shelters had to be paid for by the Corporation. In the event, as we shall see, enemy air raids were not disastrously heavy and the Birmingham civil defence system stood up to them adequately enough. But in the later 1930s the Government was anticipating daily raids by hundreds of heavy bombers immediately on the outbreak of war, and it tried to prod Birmingham and other cities into taking air raid precautions on a comparable scale.

The City Council was extremely unsympathetic to the needs of civil defence. Until as late as 1938 or even 1939 optimistic (or short-sighted) council members could argue that Birmingham was not in danger of attack because it lay outside the range of bombers operating from bases in Germany. The City Council had become extremely economy-conscious during the 1930s, partly at the Government's encouragement, and it was unwilling to undertake major air raid precautions on its own initiative. So it waited to be ordered to act by the Government; and it expected (as did most other local authorities) to be given extremely generous grants for everything it did.

Neither of the major parties in the City Council had any natural inclination to prepare for war. The Unionists, who dominated the Council, were confident that Neville Chamberlain's appeasement policy would preserve the peace and so render all precautions unnecessary.[1] The Labour minority expressed no confidence at all in Chamberlain's policies, especially from 1938 onwards, but they none the less opposed local preparations for war. Apart from their natural inclination to oppose measures introduced by the Unionist majority, they feared that air raid precautions would be the thin end of the wedge in a greater regimentation of the working class. They also argued that money spent on them could be more usefully devoted to other services. So until war actually broke out in September 1939 the air raid precautions taken in Birmingham were the result of somewhat half-hearted Government pressure, and the unappreciated efforts of a small number of council members and officials who were sensitive to the approaching danger.

On 9 July 1935 the Home Office issued its first circular on Air Raid Precautions. It invited local authorities and private employers to cooperate with the Government in setting up an A.R.P. organization, and called on the public to volunteer for duties and to learn the

---

[1] Of course, Chamberlain had his critics even among Birmingham Unionists. The most prominent was L. S. Amery, M.P. for Sparkbrook, who quoted Cromwell in urging Chamberlain's resignation in May 1940. See L. S. Amery, *My Political Life*, vol. iii (1955).

rudiments of protection.[1] In October 1935 the City Council set up an *ad hoc* committee to deal with the circular. This Air Raid Precautions Committee was finally elected as a standing committee of the City Council in March 1938.[2]

In November 1935, just one month after the establishment of the new committee, Norman Tiptaft was elected Unionist councillor for Gravelly Hill ward. A man of great energy and enterprise, he had already behind him a long career in Birmingham politics and industry. Tiptaft took a special interest in the new committee and in civil defence problems. In 1936 he visited France and Germany to study air raid precautions, and in November 1937 he became chairman of the A.R.P. Committee.[3] From this time on he bore a greater responsibility for the defence of Birmingham against air attack than any other single member of the Council.

Until the summer of 1938 little progress was made in civil defence owing to what Norman Tiptaft later described as 'public and private apathy'.[4] However, a start was made on training air raid wardens and an embryo Auxiliary Fire Service was set up. Then, in July 1938, the City Council at last received clarification and confirmation of the generous Government grants that would be available under the Air Raid Precautions Act 1937.[5] Any remaining doubts were dispelled during the Munich crisis in September, when members of the public began to volunteer for service in greater numbers. The A.R.P. Committee welcomed this change, but soon found itself under attack on new grounds. Previously it had been criticized for wasting the City's money; now it was to be pilloried for not doing enough.[6]

Although the City Council gave more positive support to the organization of civil defence after Munich, it still took meticulous precautions against any wasting of the ratepayers' money. As early as May 1938 the Finance Committee had ruled that as much A.R.P. expenditure as possible should be charged to the revenue account, because it would create no capital assets for the city.[7] The inevitable result of this decision was that the Council hesitated to sanction any expenditure on A.R.P., because it placed an immediate burden on the rate fund. Even during the international crisis of March 1939, when civil defence arrangements were accelerated both locally and nationally, Alderman S. J. Grey, chairman of the Finance Committee, told the City Council: 'The international position does not mean a blank

[1] T. H. O'Brien, *Civil Defence* (1955), p. 56.
[2] Black, p. 25. It was renamed as the Civil Defence Committee in 1942.
[3] Norman Tiptaft, *The Individualist* (1954), pp. 163–4, 167–8.
[4] Tiptaft, p. 168.   [5] Black, p. 35; O'Brien, *Civil Defence*, pp. 106–7.
[6] In August, for instance, the Birmingham Communist Party issued a duplicated pamphlet calling for more effective measures.
[7] B.C.C., *Pro.*, 9 January 1940, p. 97 (Finance Committee).

cheque for A.R.P.—not even for petty cash.'[1] And although the A.R.P. Committee was kept on a tight rein, attacks were still being made in the Council on its 'extravagant' expenditure, even after the war had begun. A strong body of public opinion supported these criticisms, and the A.R.P. Committee realized that it still had to be circumspect in its efforts to protect the city.[2]

Despite these charges of 'extravagance', A.R.P. were far from complete by the time war broke out. Fire precautions, fortunately enough, were among the more advanced. They were based on the assumption that 1,000 fires might be started within the city in a few minutes, a threat which, happily, never materialized. Steps were taken to lessen the danger to the water supply, which was especially vulnerable because most of it reached the city by the Elan aqueduct. Armed guards were posted on the aqueduct, and schemes were prepared for a partial flooding of the River Rea, and to raise the water level in the canals, in order to provide alternative sources of supply.[3] An agreement was also made with Coventry Corporation to interconnect the water supplies of the two cities.[4]

Probably the best organized and staffed service was that of the air raid wardens. It was partly as a result of this high degree of readiness that the wardens were often given tasks for which they were not entirely fitted, such as the education of the public in anti-gas measures. At other times, when they were not given arduous tasks to carry out, the wardens often complained that they were bored, and that extra training should be arranged. Internal dissensions were more pronounced in this service than in any other, and it was partly in order to provide stronger leadership that the wardens were placed under the control of the Chief Constable in April 1939. The wardens welcomed this appointment at first but it did not completely eradicate muddle and indecision.[5]

The plans made for the casualty service were very comprehensive, though their execution was handicapped by shortages of volunteers and equipment. Thirty-two first-aid posts were set up to prevent the flooding of hospital facilities by slightly injured people, and this provision was found during the raids to be more than adequate for the numbers requiring treatment.[6] Twelve mobile units were established

---

[1] *Town Crier*, 17 March 1939.

[2] A.R.P. Committee minutes, 10 November 1939; *B.P.*, 16 October 1939.

[3] Unpublished account of Birmingham civil defence (communicated by Town Clerk's office), p. 32. See also Black, pp. 50–2.

[4] B.C.C., *Pro.*, 6 June 1939, p. 627 (Water Committee). Similar arrangements were made in 1940 with the East Worcestershire and South Staffordshire Waterworks Companies (ibid., 4 June 1940, p. 427).

[5] 'A Warden', *A.R.P.: The Wardens' Service in Birmingham* (1941), pp. 8–9.

[6] Tiptaft, *The Individualist*, p. 179. A total of 3,684 casualties were treated at the first-aid posts, and 3,009 in hospitals.

for use at the scene of serious incidents. In order to take some of the pressure off the hospitals during big raids, it was later decided to establish casualty annexes in the basements of Lewis's department store in the city centre and Ansell's brewery at Aston Cross. Both proved highly effective, but were not ready for use until early 1941. A fleet of over five hundred improvised ambulances, and of private cars for the less seriously injured, was slowly built up, but the state of readiness of vehicles and their crews was still inadequate in the last weeks of peace.

One field of A.R.P. that was fully organized by September 1939 was the air raid warning system. But it had a number of unsatisfactory features, which were already causing some concern. Some sirens were electrically operated by remote control, but the great majority were ordinary factory sirens and hooters. When the first full test of the sirens was carried out, many people complained that they could not hear them.[1] The number of independently controlled sirens was subsequently increased, but the system was bitterly criticized in some areas during the first weeks of the bombing.

Work went ahead on providing a report and control system, which had been planned in outline in 1938. Birmingham decided to site the main control centre in a strengthened part of the Council House, and by July the Home Office had agreed to the City's plans for underground buildings, five of which would serve as divisional control and report centres, and five as report centres only. At about the same time a new chain of command was established, after the Lord Privy Seal had recommended that local authorities should appoint without delay an Emergency Committee and an A.R.P. Controller. The Emergency Committee, to control the day-to-day running of the city in wartime, was appointed in April 1939, and the Town Clerk, Sir Frank Wiltshire, was made A.R.P. Controller.[2] In the same month, a local nobleman, the Earl of Dudley, was appointed by the Home Office as Regional A.R.P. Commissioner for the Midlands, with headquarters in Birmingham and wide powers to coordinate civil defence forces throughout the region.[3]

Although civil defence administrative arrangements had been made adequate by the summer of 1939, and recruiting was approaching a satisfactory level, the extent of shelter protection was still totally insufficient. Shelters, the most costly element in air raid precautions, had been ignored by the Government and the City Council until it was nearly too late. The almost complete absence of adequate shelter protection in Birmingham did not attract public attention until the

[1] *B.M.*, 3 February 1939.
[2] B.C.C., *Pro.*, 4 April 1939, p. 456 (General Purposes Committee).
[3] Black, p. 24. See also O'Brien, *Civil Defence*, pp. 175–86.

Munich crisis in September 1938. The A.R.P. Committee had given
some thought to the matter and a survey of basements in the more
populous areas of the city began in August 1938. The work was
accelerated during the four days of crisis, and the Public Works
Department provided shelter for 10,000 people in basements, which
were strengthened where necessary. Three miles of trenches were
hurriedly excavated to accommodate about 20,000 more people.[1]
It was possible, once the crisis had passed, to adopt more settled and
economical policies, but from this time onwards the provision of
shelters was greatly accelerated.

Previous to the Munich crisis the Government's shelter policy had
been based on the belief that the safety of the civilian population
could best be assured by dispersal. Most citizens would have to shelter
in their own homes.[2] Such a policy certainly made sense in suburban
areas, where the density of population was lower and the risk of attack
very slight, but it had no relevance to the inner and middle rings of
Birmingham with their high concentration of both factories and population. The City itself was well aware of the danger, and its efforts
to provide protection in the summer of 1938 were concentrated on these
areas. After Munich public opinion began to demand some form of
universal protection, and in December the Government took an
important step in this direction by announcing a scheme to provide steel
garden (Anderson) shelters free of charge to the poorer inhabitants of
vulnerable areas. This innovation did not fundamentally alter the
principle of dispersal, but the Government also promised to provide
steel fittings for strengthening basements, and more positive help in
the provision of public shelters. Local authorities were encouraged
to maintain, reconstruct, and extend the trench systems dug at the
time of Munich.[3]

Although the Government's initiative was welcomed in Birmingham,
there was a danger that the best protection would be given to the least
vulnerable areas of the city. Anderson shelters could easily be erected
in suburban gardens, and, at a pinch, in the back yards of most of the
tunnel-back houses in the middle ring. But for the back-to-back houses
of the inner ring some other protection was necessary. The City was on
the horns of a dilemma. Should it concentrate on erecting Anderson
shelters, which would protect the great majority of the citizens but
neglect those who were most in need? Or should it try to create some
effective protection in the central areas, even though the Government
would bear only part of the cost, and sufficient labour and materials
might be hard to obtain? And should there be any attempt to provide

[1] Black, pp. 45–6.   [2] O'Brien, *Civil Defence*, p. 170.
[3] O'Brien, pp. 170–1, 187–9.

bomb-proof shelters, even though the Government had decided that they would create more problems than they solved?[1]

The A.R.P. Committee studied a number of schemes for bomb-proof shelters at about this time, but they were so costly that the Government refused to provide subsidies. Public opinion in the city was also generally opposed to them on grounds of expense. So no concrete proposals were made to the City Council. Meanwhile, the first Anderson shelters were being erected. By October 1939, 82,000 shelters had been provided, and it was claimed that they afforded protection for 410,000 people —nearly half the total population. Many back-to-back houses were equipped with Morrison shelters—steel cages capable of resisting a collapsing building. Anderson shelters involved the City in hardly any expense and made few demands on Public Works Department personnel, as they were normally erected by the householders themselves. A much greater strain was placed on the City, and on its relations with the Government, by the public shelter programme. By February 1939 some ten miles of trenches had been built or planned, sufficient to protect 50,000 people. Subsequently attention was switched, on Home Office advice, to providing shelter in strengthened basements, and steady progress was made in the last months of peace. In October the A.R.P. Committee claimed to have provided public shelters for about 90,000 people.[2]

Although these efforts had resulted in the provision of some sort of protection for about half of Birmingham's population by the time war was declared, the City's own share in the achievement was minimal. Four-fifths of the protection was in the form of Anderson shelters supplied free by the Government. Well over half the places provided by the City were in trenches, and several thousands more were in a car park under St. Martin's Tollmarket which had not been designed as a potential shelter, and later proved to have serious shortcomings. Undoubtedly, the Government should have been more generous in its grants to local authorities, as many council members lost no time in pointing out. But the City Council's lack of urgency and even hostility to civil defence was the root cause of the inadequacy of shelter protection, as of other branches of air raid precautions. If Birmingham had been heavily bombed on the outbreak of war, as most people expected it would be, the results would have been disastrous.

Fortunately, the long months of the 'phoney war' allowed nearly all the services to be brought up to scratch, with greatly accelerated recruiting. Particularly helpful was the new cooperative attitude of the Labour group in the City Council. After the Munich crisis Labour had stopped condemning civil defence precautions as unnecessary and had

[1] O'Brien, pp. 190–2.
[2] B.C.C., *Pro.*, 17 October 1939, p. 1050 (A.R.P. Committee).

begun to attack them as inadequate. These criticisms were one aspect
of a general assault by Labour on the National Government and the
Unionist majority in the City Council, which brought inter-party
relations in Birmingham to their most hostile state since the early 1930s.
The climax of this energetic attack by Labour was the municipal
rent strike in the summer of 1939, when tens of thousands of municipal
tenants withheld their rent in protest against the Estates Committee's
plan to introduce what amounted to a differential rent scheme. The
strike was organized by a non-party body called the Birmingham
Tenants' and Residents' Association, but it was fully supported by a
number of leading members of the Labour group, in association with
prominent members of the Birmingham Communist Party. The strike
ended after some weeks in a complete victory for the tenants, and the
rent scheme was abandoned.

The Unionists bitterly resented Labour's part in this raucous
agitation.[1] In retaliation, they refused on the outbreak of war to let
trade union members sit on key committees, on the ground that they
could not be relied upon to act responsibly. For the same reasons, they
refused to allow Labour any representation at all on the Emergency
Committee. They soon realized, however, that this quarrel could only
weaken the Council's war effort and accentuate dissension within the
civil defence movement. A partial truce was reached when Councillor
Walter Lewis, a senior and respected Labour member, was admitted
to the Emergency Committee in December 1939. The other restrictions
on Labour members were removed when Churchill formed his coalition
government with Labour in May 1940, and inter-party cooperation
was thenceforth complete. Meanwhile, unrest within the wardens'
service had been largely eradicated by the establishment, in October
1939, of a new chain of command including a civilian Chief
Warden.[2]

The outbreak of war led to a welcome acceleration in the provision
of air raid shelters. For the first time some thought was given to the
problem of providing domestic shelter protection, other than Anderson
shelters, in the inner ring. The City Council decided to strengthen
one cellar in five where houses were equipped with them, and to build
communal surface shelters for the remainder. Yet, despite the large

---

[1] Not only had bitter personal attacks been launched against the chairman of the
Estates Committee, Theodore Pritchett, but the ceremony to mark the opening of
Birmingham's fifty-thousandth municipal house, which took place during the strike,
was disrupted by Labour council members who conducted a symbolic 'funeral' of
the municipal tenant on a neighbouring building site.

[2] B.C.C., *Pro.*, 17 October 1939, p. 1053 (A.R.P. Committee). Some wardens had
complained that under the Chief Constable's command they had become merely a
branch of the police service. The Chief Constable was reappointed as Chief Warden
in early 1942, when all the fuss had died down.

number of shelter places now available, many people in the city, including most Labour members of the Council, were worried about the standard of protection provided. The demand for deep shelters was particularly strong in London,[1] but it was echoed in Birmingham by the Borough Labour Party, the Communist Party, and some sections of the Trades Council. At first these attacks were headed off by Councillor Walter Lewis (Labour), the leader of the Labour group and president of the Trades Council. As a member of the A.R.P. and Emergency Committees he was associated with the Corporation's policy, and often expressed his scepticism of the value of deep shelters. But other members of the Labour group took an active part in the campaign for deep shelters, which grew stronger after the early raids.

The campaign for deep shelters built up partly because of Labour annoyance at the frustration of most of the group's attempts to claim a bigger share in the running of the city during the early part of the war. But there was also much honest concern over the standard and amount of shelter protection. The Anderson shelters, whose floor was normally below ground level, proved distressingly liable to flooding during the winter of 1939–40. Moreover, the public shelter programme was still far from its target in the early summer of 1940. While the domestic shelter programme was largely complete, thanks to the Anderson shelter, only two-thirds of the target figure of public shelters had been provided.[2] This shortage of public shelters need not necessarily have caused alarm, in view of the Government's policy of encouraging the greatest possible dispersal of the public during raids. However, when enemy attacks on Birmingham began in August 1940 the reaction of many citizens made nonsense of the official policies. Aware that domestic shelters offered no protection against a direct hit, they sought refuge in the nearest public shelter.[3] It was feared that direct hits on public shelters might cause intolerably high casualties, and lead to even stronger demands for the provision of deep shelters. There was also a serious health risk where shelters were occupied by large numbers of people night after night, for they had been designed to afford protection only for short periods, and were seriously affected by damp, dirt, and vermin. The Emergency Committee considered preventing people with domestic shelters from using public ones, but decided that such a regulation would be unenforceable, especially as many people who were entitled to private shelters had still not been provided with them.

So when the bombing began on that night in August 1940 Birmingham was much better prepared than in September 1939 to face the onslaught. News of the first raid spread rapidly by word of mouth. The press could provide little enlightenment, for fear that the *Luftwaffe's*

[1] See O'Brien, *Civil Defence*, pp. 190–2.   [2] B.C.C., *Pro.*, 23 July 1940, p. 632.
[3] B.C.C., *Pro.*, 15 October 1940, p. 703 (Emergency Committee).

confidence in its navigational aids would be increased if it received local confirmation that its aircraft had bombed the right city. The *Birmingham Mail* made a brief reference to a raid on 'a Midland town', but with no further details. The major talking point was whether or not the sirens had sounded before the bombs fell. Most people thought that they had not, but some were prepared to give the sirens the benefit of the doubt because they had already proved to be inaudible in certain parts of the city.

Many in the city must have been surprised by the small scale of the attack. Although nearly a year had gone by without any raids, dispelling the gloomy pessimism which had affected many people in September 1939, it was still expected that if German bombers ever reached Birmingham, their attacks would be heavy. Yet for nearly three weeks after the first raid the *Luftwaffe* restricted its efforts to a few minor attacks, using a handful of bombers. They did more good than harm, by allowing the civil defence services to perfect their organization. Then came the first serious test.

On the night of 25/6 August the bombers, which had previously concentrated on the east of the city, changed their tactics and raided the city centre.[1] Twenty-five people were killed, and the Market Hall was burned out. Although this raid was still on a relatively small scale, it brought home the reality of air attack to the thousands who worked in the city centre, and the Market Hall fire gave a timely warning of the speed with which conflagrations could develop. After another attack, on the night of 26/7 August, this first series of raids petered out. In the city it was 'business as usual', except that city centre cinemas were now opening at 10 a.m., and no programmes started later than 6.30 p.m. Public houses had suffered only a slight drop in business, and many big stores were pooling their resources to repair display windows with composite sheeting.[2] An air of optimism prevailed in Birmingham. An air raid victim told Mrs. Churchill, on a visit to the city: 'Though our houses are down our spirits are still up.'[3]

Perhaps it was the failure of its night raids, which had been directed almost exclusively against industrial targets, which led the *Luftwaffe* to experiment with daylight raids on the city. Above all, the enemy wanted to restrict aircraft production, yet the Austin aero factory at Cofton Hackett had so far escaped unscathed, and hardly any damage had been done at Fort Dunlop and the Nuffield shadow factory at Castle Bromwich. In the late afternoon of 27 September 1940, Fort Dunlop was attacked and a number of casualties were caused.[4] Then, on 13 November, the Austin aero factory was attacked in daylight, and six

---

[1] *B.M.*, 5 August 1965. None of the fifty bombers which took part in this raid was shot down (Basil Collier, *The Defence of the United Kingdom* (1957), p. 209).
[2] *B.G.*, 20 September 1940.   [3] *B.G.*, 15 October 1940.
[4] Sir Ronald Storrs, *Dunlop in War and Peace* (1946), p. 37.

employees were killed and twenty-five injured.[1] Meanwhile, sporadic night attacks took place in September and October. In four raids during September only sixteen people were killed, and after the night of 28 September the city enjoyed a respite of more than two weeks. This temporary lull apparently encouraged many people to stop using their shelters, for when the bombers suddenly returned on the night of 15 October they killed fifty-nine people and seriously injured forty-three others. Lighter raids took place on the next three nights, and again on 20 October. A much larger effort was reserved for the following week, during which the Empire music hall was burned out, and nineteen people were killed by a single bomb in a Sparkbrook cinema. But raids during the early part of November were light and infrequent. As the all-clear sounded on the morning of 19 November, after a raid which had killed fifteen people and injured only nine, many in the city must have slept soundly, believing that at least another week would elapse before the next light raid. No one could have guessed that within a few days the city would lie in greater peril than at any other time during the whole of the war.

The destruction of the centre of Coventry on the night of 14 November was the first sign that the main weight of the enemy attack had shifted from London to the Midlands. German radio proclaimed that other cities would soon be *coventriert*. Birmingham gave considerable help to its neighbour on that night, and its personnel gained valuable experience which was shortly to help them in their home city. When the sirens sounded on the night of 19 November, a force of 350 bombers was approaching Birmingham.[2] To counteract the jamming of their navigation beams, the *Luftwaffe* had by now formed pathfinder groups to drop incendiaries on the principal targets. The pathfinders themselves used a special beam which could not then be jammed, and which had made possible the successful attack on Coventry.[3]

Almost the whole of Birmingham experienced incidents in the raid, which went on for most of the night. Nearly 600 fire pumps, of which 100 came from outside the city, fought 338 serious fires.[4] B.S.A.'s Small Heath factory suffered its worst damage of the war, when the New Building was hit by high-explosive bombs, and completely burned out, killing nearly fifty workers who had been sheltering behind blast walls on the ground floor.[5] In the city as a whole, there were more casualties than in any other raid, and some 400 people were killed. On 20 November Birmingham carried on almost normally, and although

---

[1] Austin Motor Company Ltd., *How Longbridge Spanned the Years of War* (1946), p. 50.

[2] Black, p. 89; S. C. Leslie, *Front Line 1940–41* (1942).

[3] W. S. Churchill, *The Second World War* (1948), vol. ii, p. 343.

[4] *E.D.*, 23 September 1944; *B.W.P.*, 11 June 1968.

[5] Donovan M. Ward, *The Other Battle* (1946), pp. 46, 59.

the bombers returned during the night, the effectiveness of the fire services kept the number of serious fires down to one. The following night was completely undisturbed, and the civil defence and fire services were able to reorganize and repair their equipment without interruption. A panel of experienced fire officers from other cities arrived in Birmingham to advise and assist the City's own fire-fighting units.[1] This brief respite may have been of crucial importance in view of what was to come.

On the night of 22 November a force of 200 aircraft attacked the city. Although the force was considerably smaller and the casualties fewer in number[2] than on the night of 19 November, considerably more dislocation and damage seem to have been caused. Over 600 fires were started, and Tyseley and Saltley were particularly badly hit.[3] A B.S.A. dispersal factory at Tyseley caught fire and their Small Heath works was again set alight, and complete evacuation was ordered. The neighbouring Warwick and Birmingham canal, from which water was being drawn for fire-fighting at many points in the city, reached a dangerously low level, but supplies held out long enough for the B.S.A. fires to be brought under control.[4] Many other fires, which had sprung up in all parts of the city, went unchecked for lack of water. High-explosive bombs fractured three of the large gravitation mains feeding the general distribution system, and the situation was aggravated by the considerable local damage which had been done to the distribution system by the 19 November raid. Three-fifths of the city was deprived of mains water, forcing the fire services in many areas to rely even more heavily than usual on the canals, and to neglect fires in areas which were too far from such sources of water for temporary links to be set up. Some relief was afforded by the inter-connecting mains with neighbouring water authorities, which were immediately brought into operation.[5]

On the following day the Birmingham press, while admitting that the attack had been heavy, naturally made no reference to the water situation. The population were used to temporary local water cuts after raids, and could be allowed to remain unaware that most of the city was without supplies. It was estimated the Elan trunk main would take five days to repair, and Captain B. A. Westbrook, temporary chief of the Birmingham Fire Services,[6] reported that another heavy raid on

[1] B.W.P., 11 June 1948.   [2] 113 people were killed, and 470 seriously injured.
[3] E.D., 16 September 1944; Basil Collier, writing in B.M., 30 October 1957.
[4] Ward, The Other Battle, pp. 46, 57–8.
[5] B.W.P., 11 June 1948; B.C.C., Pro., 5 June 1945, pp. 460–1 (Water Committee).
[6] The Chief Officer of the Birmingham brigade sent in his resignation on 22 November after the heavy raiding had revealed serious deficiencies in the service. Westbrook substantially re-organized it in the following few days (H. Klopper, The Fight Against Fire: The History of the Birmingham Fire and Ambulance Service (1954), pp. 89, 91).

the following night would be disastrous. A company of Royal Engineers was detailed to blast fire breaks in rows of buildings in the city centre if an incendiary raid developed. Sixty pumps were rushed to Birmingham from London and other areas in readiness, though with three gravitation mains expected to be out of action for at least five days, the water shortage was a far more crucial factor than the number of pumps available. Yet, as so often during the war, the *Luftwaffe* failed to follow up its advantage and on the night of 23 November its attack shifted to Southampton. Apart from a pinprick raid which killed three people on the night of 28/9 November, Birmingham was not attacked again in any strength until 3 December.

In its December raids on British cities the *Luftwaffe* concentrated more exclusively than ever before on attempting to burn down city centres, which were empty at night and where it was difficult to organize fire watchers in sufficient numbers. Pathfinders aimed to drop incendiaries on the city centre, and later waves of bombers dropped high-explosive bombs on the fires.[1] On the night of 3/4 December fifty bombers raided Birmingham, killing thirty-six people and seriously injuring sixty.[2] Tiny raids on the following two nights did little damage, and the city thus enjoyed a brief respite until the enemy made a big effort on the night of 11 December. Then, in what proved to be the longest raid of the war,[3] 200 bombers attacked the city. Fortunately, the number of fire watchers on duty was greater than ever, and few of the fires were allowed to develop as beacons for the raiders.[4] However, as so often happened in the first raid after a lull, the casualty figures were depressingly high, with 263 people killed and 245 seriously injured.

Once again, the *Luftwaffe* failed to follow up its success, and switched its attack to the ports. Birmingham remained almost unmolested until April 1941, apart from a fairly heavy raid in March when the fire watchers were again very effective.[5] Then, on the night of 9/10 April, Birmingham underwent its last really heavy raid of the war. 650 high-explosive bombs and 170 sets of incendiaries were showered on the city by a force of 250 bombers, killing or injuring 1,121 people.[6] The raiders concentrated on the city centre and industrial areas. Severe damage was done to many churches, which the fire services had to regard as expendable when industrial and residential buildings were in danger. The most significant destruction was wrought in the city centre, where

---

[1] *Front Line*, p. 87.

[2] Black, p. 89. It was quite a short raid by Birmingham standards—only four hours (*B.M.*, 4 December 1940).

[3] It lasted for over thirteen hours, from about 6.30 p.m. to 7.30 a.m. (*E.D.*, 12 December 1940, 16 September 1944).

[4] *B.M.*, 12 November 1940; *B.G.*, 13 November 1940.

[5] *B.P.*, 12 March 1941.   [6] Black, pp. 88–90; *E.D.*, 16 September 1944.

a fire at the corner of New Street and High Street got completely out of control and a serious conflagration developed, destroying many neighbouring buildings.[1] At one point it was feared that the Royal Engineers would have to carry out their plan to blast fire breaks. Another conflagration destroyed numerous buildings on the east side of the Bull Ring, and at the same time the Prince of Wales Theatre in Broad Street was burned out, and 'finished for good and all', according to the managing director, Emile Littler.[2]

For once, the *Luftwaffe* tried to follow up its success by raiding on the following night. But they came in considerably less force, and no really serious fires broke out. Yet much concern remained about the ease with which conflagrations had developed on the night of 9/10 April. At the Council meeting on 6 May 1941 Councillor Albert Bradbeer (Labour) called for a private meeting of the Council to receive a special report from the Fire Brigade Committee on fire service operations on the night of 9/10 April. The Unionists too were sufficiently worried to allow Councillor Bradbeer's amendment to be carried.[3] The special meeting was held on 29 May, when reports were heard from the chairmen of the A.R.P. and Emergency Committees, as well as the Fire Brigade Committee. The Council accepted that the civil defence services had generally worked well, but called for some form of regional committee to supervise the operation of the National Fire Service, into which the Birmingham brigade had recently been incorporated.[4]

Fortunately, the enemy had now almost shot his bolt. A few more raids were made in the spring and early summer, but after July shorter nights and improved defence measures caused the *Luftwaffe*, already distracted by Germany's attack on the Soviet Union, to abandon its campaign against Birmingham and other cities. Yet already Birmingham had received a greater weight of high-explosive bombs—1,800 tons—than any other city except Liverpool–Birkenhead and London.

For over a year Birmingham remained free from attack, and, as time went on, many citizens came to believe that they would be undisturbed for the rest of the war. They would probably have been right if the increasing severity of R.A.F. attacks on German cities had not led Hitler to order reprisal raids on Britain. After the failure of the 'Baedeker raids' on historic towns in early 1942, the attack was switched to industrial centres. Some warning of what might be in store was given by a lone raider which bombed Birmingham in daylight in July 1942, and on the night of 27 July a force of sixty or seventy aircraft, the

<hr>

[1] *B.W.P.*, 18 June 1948. The site was later used for exhibitions and entertainments which took place inside a large marquee, and came to be known as the Big Top site.
[2] *B.M.*, 17 April 1941.
[3] B.C.C., *Pro.*, 6 May 1941, pp. 332–3 (General Purposes Committee).
[4] B.C.C., *Pro.*, 29 May 1941, pp. 361–3 (General Purposes Committee).

largest to attack Britain for many months, bombed the Birmingham area. A few lighter raids followed before the end of the month, and many people were killed because they failed to take shelter. But the July raids, which involved heavy losses in aircraft, turned out to be the *Luftwaffe*'s last fling. Birmingham remained completely undisturbed until a short hit-and-run raid on 23 April 1943, and from then to the end of the war no further aircraft attacked the city.

During the blitz Birmingham people were very confused about what the *Luftwaffe* was really trying to do, and the press did not help by referring frequently to the German bombing as 'indiscriminate'. After the war, however, it became clear that the enemy had set himself clearly defined objectives, but had never enjoyed the physical and technical resources necessary to achieve those objectives.

The scale and character of the attacks on Birmingham were determined to a very large extent by the pre-war development of the *Luftwaffe*. Whereas Bomber Command was built up as a long-distance strategic bombing force, in the belief that hammer blows at an enemy's factories and cities would sap his strength and bring a quick end to any war,[1] the *Luftwaffe* was developed as a tactical support arm for the army, and came to include a high proportion of single-engined dive bombers, twin-engined fighter bombers and light bombers. For most of the war the *Luftwaffe*'s heaviest land bomber was the Heinkel He 111, which had only two engines, and whose long-range bomb load was little more than one ton.[2] Indeed, until early 1938 the Germans had not even made contingency plans for an air offensive on Britain, and in May 1939 a study carried out by the *Luftwaffe* general staff concluded that an air attack on the British economy could not be decisive.[3]

Hitler hoped that Britain would sue for peace after Dunkirk, and ordered a large-scale air offensive only when he realized that it might be necessary to invade. Although the strategic study of May 1939 had discounted any possibility of a knock-out blow, it had suggested that the British aircraft industry would be the most vulnerable target. So Birmingham found itself in the front line right from the earliest days of the raids in the summer of 1940. The *Luftwaffe* raided the south of England by day in great strength, in order to destroy R.A.F. fighter forces in the air or on the ground, and to paralyse aircraft factories. Daylight raids on the West Midlands would have involved heavy losses, so the *Luftwaffe* made a number of night attacks. The raids on

---

[1] For an account of the development of this strategy, see C. Webster and N. Frankland, *The Strategic Air Offensive* (1961), vol. i.

[2] Peter Fleming, *Invasion 1940* (1957), p. 225.

[3] Hans-Adolf Jacobsen and Jürgen Rohwer, *Decisive Battles of World War II: The German View* (1965), pp. 75–6.

Birmingham in August and September 1940 were clearly aimed at the industrial concentration in the east of the city, in the Tame valley, where important factories such as Fort Dunlop, Moss Gear, and the Nuffield shadow airframe works were situated. Although most of the bombs missed their targets and fell on residential areas, only the incompetence and not the barbarity of the enemy was to blame.

After September the *Luftwaffe* changed its tactics. The failure of the daylight raids on the south forced the enemy to recognize that the R.A.F. could no longer be knocked out, and so there was no further point in directing night raids exclusively against aircraft factories. At this time the R.A.F. had no effective night fighters, and Bomber Command attacks on Germany were still of little significance. It was no surprise, therefore, when the raiders returned to Birmingham in October after a short lull, that they should aim mainly at the central areas. The raids now developed into a more general attack on industry, presumably in the hope of wearing down the British economy, and damaging the morale of the civilian population in the process. In Birmingham, industrial establishments clustered thickly around the fringes of the city centre, and throughout the central wards. Although the *Luftwaffe* raiders aimed primarily at industrial targets, as their briefings show,[1] they were aware that if their bombs missed the factories they would fall on the densely populated housing areas nearby, and so would not be completely wasted.

Although the late-1940 raids had some limited success in restricting production, and the enemy suffered only very slight losses, it was clear to both sides that they could not decisively reduce Britain's ability to carry on the war. As time went on, the *Luftwaffe* gradually changed its tactics once more, and, while factories continued to suffer, the raiders concentrated more and more on trying to burn down the city centre. Although city centre conflagrations had no effect whatever on industrial production, they might have induced alarm and despondency in the civilian population, and weakened the confidence of Britain's allies in her ability to continue the war. The city centre was an ideal target in that it combined the highest concentration of tall buildings in the city with a very low population. The civil defence authorities had continual difficulty in finding enough wardens and fire watchers for the central area, a fact which was probably well-known to the enemy. Later, in 1941 and 1942, as British fire raids on German cities grew heavier, the *Luftwaffe* became even more eager to set British city centres alight as a spectacular reprisal.

Concentration on the central areas, necessary though it may have seemed to the *Luftwaffe* strategists, was in some ways a mistake. The

[1] See collection of maps, aerial photographs, and briefings in the Imperial War Museum.

Disorder in High Street, Saltley, 17 May 1941. Birmingham industry presses on in the background.

Strikingly well-dressed citizens inspect bomb damage in Erdington New Road, 15 April 1941. The fur coats may reflect the difficulty of obtaining replacements for less hard-wearing garments during the war.

Alderman Byng Kenrick

expansion of Birmingham's industries before 1939 had taken place mainly on the fringes of the city, in the north-east, north-west, and south-west suburbs. Here, along the Tame valley, and in the Selly Oak, Northfield, and Longbridge areas, lay the largest and most modern works. The bombed central sector, although it contained such important factories as Morris Commercial Cars at Adderley Park and B.S.A. at Small Heath, also contained a large number of declining or non-expanding industries such as jewellery and sporting gun manufacture. The number of firms operating there was still further reduced during the course of the war by the Government's policy of concentrating non-essential production in a small number of units. So, by 1941, after the more important firms had dispersed much of their production,[1] the amount of damage that could be done to the economy by knocking out industrial activities in the central area had been minimized.

The premises of the Austin Motor Company and the Austin Aero Company at Longbridge and Cofton Hackett were not bombed at all during the whole war, apart from one abortive daylight raid. At Fort Dunlop, although the plant was bombed on several occasions, the failure to concentrate on its destruction meant that damage could be repaired almost immediately.[2] On the other hand, Fisher and Ludlow, the metal pressings manufacturers, with several Birmingham works, lost 400,000 of their 1,000,000 square feet of floor space during bombing in 1940. Dispersal was said to have been very successful in limiting the effects of the worst attacks.[3] Apart from the aero firms, most concerns had only one or two dispersal units, but one notable exception was B.S.A., which manufactured Browning guns in twelve separate units near Birmingham.[4] Dispersal was not unwelcome to the firms affected; it was a rapid means of expansion, and was economical in building resources and labour.[5]

Where munitions production could not disperse from the central areas the raids sometimes achieved spectacular, if only temporary, cuts in production. B.S.A. suffered most among the munitions firms.

[1] On Government instructions, Birmingham's major munitions firms had made plans to disperse their production at the start of the war, but no moves were made until heavy raiding began in October 1940. Then, the Government ordered the more important firms to shift as much of their production as possible to dispersal units.

[2] Storrs, *Dunlop in War and Peace*, p. 35.

[3] Birmingham Chamber of Commerce, *Journal and Monthly Record*, January 1941, p. 14.

[4] William Hornby, *Factories and Plant*, pp. 205–6; Ward, *The Other Battle*, pp. 63–9. Austin Aero had ten dispersal units in addition to that at Elmdon, but nearly three-quarters of its total labour force worked at the main Cofton Hackett plant (figures supplied by Personnel Department, British-Leyland works, Longbridge).

[5] Hornby, pp. 205–6. Serck was one firm which saw dispersal as a means of increasing production rather than of escaping attack (Serck Radiators Ltd., *War Record 1939–1945* (1946)).

D

Their Small Heath works was badly bombed on several occasions
before production had been fully dispersed, and the Prime Minister
himself became alarmed in January 1941.[1] In most cases, hurried
repairs and dispersal soon helped to restore production to its former
levels. Even B.S.A. was able to increase its production of Browning
guns from 894 in December 1940 to 3,750 in March 1941.[2] And other
factories in the central areas, some of them of even greater strategic
importance than the B.S.A. works, do not appear to have suffered the
same misfortunes. Serck Radiators Limited, whose main works in
Warwick Road, Tyseley, lay just a few hundred yards from B.S.A.'s,
suffered damage in 1940, but production was not held up. Yet destruction of the works would have been of infinite benefit to the enemy, for
all the radiators and oil coolers fitted to Spitfires and Hurricanes during
the Battle of Britain were made exclusively by Serck. The S.U. Car-
burettor factory, which was the only producer of aircraft carburettors
at the time of the Battle of Britain, was not hit until November 1940,
by which time plans for dispersal had been finalized.[3]

These experiences tend to confirm the generally accepted contemporary view that the loss of production was slight. In September 1940
an American observer estimated the total loss of output in Birmingham
at about 5 per cent,[4] and in November Swedish newspapers published
reports from their correspondents that the raids had had an insignificant
effect on war production.[5] Damage to general services was usually
quickly repaired so that production could continue; electricity, for
instance, was usually made available to damaged factories by alternative routes before the factories themselves were again in a position to
take a supply.[6] In all, ninety-nine factory premises were totally destroyed and 184 were so seriously damaged that demolition was
necessary. A total of 2,301 industrial premises were destroyed or
damaged in some way, excluding broken glass. Post-war estimates of
the loss of output in Germany during Allied raids, for which more
information is available than for Britain, are extremely low. Webster
and Frankland, for instance, suggest that the national loss of production
in Germany might have been in the order of one per cent for every
15,000 tons of bombs dropped in area raids. On the other hand, a
relatively high loss might have been suffered in heavily bombed towns.
In the case of Hamburg, it has been suggested that the dropping of
8,600 tons of bombs in one series of raids led to a total direct and

[1] Churchill, *The Second World War*, vol. iii, p. 644.
[2] *B.S.A. Group News: Centenary Issue*, 7 June 1961, p. 39.
[3] Ernest Fairfax, *Calling All Arms* (1945), p. 96.
[4] *B.M.*, 5 September 1940.   [5] *B.P.*, 29 November 1940.
[6] B.C.C., *Pro.*, 3 July 1945, p. 626 (Electric Supply Committee). For instances of
the effect of raiding on railway services, see C. I. Savage, *Inland Transport* (1957),
p. 199.

indirect loss of 3·6 months of production.[1] Such conjectures tend to support the estimate of neutral correspondents that production loss in Birmingham, which was much more lightly raided than most German cities, was never more than a few per cent.

There remains the question of damage to residential property. The officially quoted figure for the number of houses so seriously damaged that they could be considered a total loss was 12,391.[2] On the other hand, the damage figures reported to the Emergency Committee are very much lower, giving a total of 4,601 houses destroyed or so seriously damaged that demolition was necessary. The latter figure is more in keeping with the impressions of contemporary observers, who reported that damage was never immediately obvious to strangers and had to be looked for.[3] Even in the central redevelopment areas, which lay fully in the main target zone, the amount of serious damage was seen, once the dust had cleared, to be relatively small. In Duddeston and Nechells for instance, which lay next to a goods yard, a gas works, and a power station, all of which were marked as primary targets on German maps, only 170 buildings were made irreparable by bombing, out of 6,800 houses and a large number of factories and other buildings in the area. The City Engineer had to face the fact that even after the bombing, his slum clearance task was still almost as great as it had been in 1939; '. . . this factor has not materially facilitated the reconstruction of the area.'[4]

On the whole, the Birmingham public took the raids calmly, despite the widely-held belief, encouraged by the press, that the enemy was deliberately bombing residential areas. Even in the heavily-bombed areas of back-to-back housing in the inner ring, violent hatred of the enemy, when it occurred, was usually only a temporary reaction.[5] When an independent candidate in the Kings Norton by-election of 1941 made a demand for terror attacks on German cities the main plank in his platform, he lost his deposit and was nearly beaten into third place by a pacifist candidate.

The absence of any serious bitterness against the raiders may in part have been due to the relatively small scale of the attacks. Although sixty-three separate raids were made, only four destroyed completely more than 100 houses, and only three demolished more than ten factories. The civil defence services reported a total of 5,129 high-explosive bombs dropped during the whole war, of which 930 did not explode. In addition, there were forty-eight parachute mines, of which sixteen did not explode.[6] The *Luftwaffe*, then, dropped one high-explosive

[1] *The Strategic Air Offensive*, vol. iv, pp. 482–3.
[2] Black, p. 89. The total number of dwellings in the city was about 275,000.
[3] See e.g. *B.P.*, 27 September 1944 (editorial).
[4] B.C.C., *Pro.*, 17 July 1943, p. 451 (Public Works Committee).
[5] See e.g. Gwendolen Freeman, *The Houses Behind* (1947), pp. 7–8.   [6] Black, p. 88.

bomb for every ten acres of the city's area. Many thousands of
incendiaries were also dropped, but their threat was mainly to
property, not to human life. They caused 4,863 fires, which amounted
to roughly one fire for every two hundred residents. Of these, 3,984
fires were classified as small, requiring only one jet and minor apparatus.
Medium fires, requiring between two and ten jets, numbered 791.
Only eighty-seven fires were serious (ten to thirty jets), and the number
that developed into major fires or conflagrations was no more than
eleven.[1] Yet compared with other British provincial cities these figures
are extremely high. Well over 2,000 people lost their lives in the city,
and 3,000 were seriously injured. Many of these casualties were men
and women whose loss could ill be afforded: wardens, rescue workers,
fire fighters. On the other hand, Birmingham's ordeal was relatively
insignificant when compared with that endured by most large German
cities, not all of which were important industrial centres, later in the
war.

The relative lightness of the raids fortunately vindicated the City
Council's air raid shelter policy, which would have been totally inadequate if Birmingham had suffered raids half as heavy as some of
those made later by the R.A.F. on German cities. There was no mass
slaughter in the public shelters, the highest number of casualties caused
by any hit on a shelter being about twenty.[2] Most of the high-explosive
bombs dropped, with the exception of the notorious landmines, were of
relatively low calibre, and many exploded next to surface shelters
without injuring those inside. A direct hit, however, could have caused
havoc, as the A.R.P. Committee well knew, and their policy of dispersal
to small shelters was eminently sensible. Although many people
obviously liked to congregate in public shelters, others dispersed themselves voluntarily, by leaving the central areas each evening to spend
the night with friends or relatives in the suburbs.

Because most of the enemy raids were very light, the great majority of
citizens were inconvenienced rather than materially affected by them.
As they often went on all through the night, people got very little sleep,
especially when in public or private air raid shelters. As we have seen,
Anderson shelters were cold and nearly always damp. Public shelters
were not much better from this point of view, but they had other drawbacks too. A number of disturbances were caused by drunks and row-
dies, and the A.R.P. Committee had to appoint marshals to control
some shelters. The cleaning of shelters proved to be almost impossible
during the raids, for the regular users left mattresses and bedding in
them all day, gathering dust and dirt, yet effectively preventing the
cleaners from carrying out their duties. In October 1940 the A.R.P.

[1] Black, p. 89; unpublished account of Birmingham civil defence.
[2] *B.G.*, 26 September 1944.

Committee introduced new measures to improve ventilation and make cleaning more effective. All shelters were sprayed with disinfectant daily, and more seats were installed, many of them spectators' benches presented by sports clubs. Wherever possible, special units were reserved for women and children, and a start was made on installing bunks.[1]

Despite these improvements, the general level of health of Birmingham citizens deteriorated considerably in the winter of 1940-1, which, to make matters worse, was exceptionally cold. In the first months of attack in 1940 there was an increase in the number of deaths at all ages from respiratory diseases, and in the number of notifications of pneumonia. The Medical Officer of Health reported that this trend was 'not improbably associated with the frequent use of shelters, with all their difficulties of crowding, of stagnant atmosphere, and of extremes of temperature'.[2] In 1940 he noted a higher infant mortality rate, owing mainly to the heavy incidence of bronchitis, pneumonia, and other catarrhal infections, which he ascribed partly to 'shelter life'. This high rate continued into 1941.[3] Although domestic shelters were often cold and damp, the Medical Officer of Health was convinced that the public shelters were a much more serious danger. There was also a marked drop in the birth rate, from 16·4 in 1940 to 15·5 in 1941, which may have resulted partly from the disruption of normal life caused by the raids.

Other unpleasant trends resulted from the general disruption of the city's life caused by the raids and the precautions taken against them. The education of nearly all the city's children, whether in evacuation or not, was at first seriously dislocated.[4] Many also suffered from a lack of parental care. So many children were out of school that the rate of juvenile crime, especially vandalism, rose sharply.[5] With so much damage to be seen around them, many children could see no objection to having some fun by perpetrating a little more. Both the blackout and the more pressing preoccupations of the depleted police force helped them to get away with it. There was an increase, too, in more serious crimes, encouraged by similar factors. The blackout also caused a sharp increase in motor accidents.

Despite the vicarious excitement which the raids could occasionally provide,[6] people became very bored. Not only did they find it hard to

[1] B.C.C., *Pro.*, 15 October 1940, pp. 703-5 (Emergency Committee); pp. 723-5 (A.R.P. Committee).

[2] *B.M.O.H.*, 1940.

[3] The number of deaths under the age of one year per thousand live births rose from sixty in 1939 to seventy in 1940, and fell only to sixty-nine in 1941.

[4] See below, pp. 333 ff.   [5] See below, pp. 270 ff.

[6] This may appear to the reader to be a particularly tasteless comment, but the collection of readers' recollections of the raids published from time to time by the Birmingham press suggest that many people's lives were considerably enlivened by the bombing.

attend cinemas and sporting events owing to transport difficulties and the risk of being caught out in a raid, they even had problems in reaching a branch library to borrow books, which later in the war were to while away many a long hour.[1] Radio-listening was impossible for most people when in air raid shelters, for few people owned battery sets, and evenings were tedious when, as often happened, the alert was sounded as early as 6 or 7 p.m. Yet boredom and fear did not make people turn to religion; churches were as hard to reach as other public buildings. Many of them lost all their glass in the early raids, and dwindling congregations shivered through abbreviated services.[2]

But the raids had some good effects too. People became more concerned with the welfare of others, more eager to help. They became more sociable, even on the new estates which often had been so unfriendly before the war, and where air raid wardens had been difficult to recruit because people were used to minding their own business. The raids also helped to break down class barriers; middle-class people came into contact much more with workers, in city-centre public shelters, in public transport, and in contacts with A.R.P. personnel. Even though the working-class districts of the centre were more heavily bombed than any others, the newspapers implied that the suburbs, too, were equally hard hit.

Of course, people could see differences in the extent of damage when they moved about the city, as many now had to do more frequently. Yet movement was in itself encouraging to the growing sense of civic unity. In travelling to new places of work, or in 'trekking' out of the city to avoid the heaviest raids, working people obtained a fuller knowledge of their own city, and of the different ways of life that existed within it. Some people involuntarily assisted in the solution of the city's slum problem. Conscription and the evacuation of children made it easier for wives and mothers from the central areas to go to live with friends and relatives on the periphery. Other families moved out of the slums specifically to avoid the bombing, and never returned. Although they contributed to an increase in overcrowding in the outer districts, they were partly responsible for the fact that some 4,400 back-to-back houses had become void by the end of the war.[3] The tens of thousands who remained behind in the slums improved their conditions by their own efforts. They became more health-conscious, more prepared to listen to official advice on how to keep well, more aware of the greater hazards of infectious disease that resulted from the bombing. Industrial ailments, such as oil dermatitis, were also kept under control by careful precautions, despite the large number of inexperienced people in

[1] See below, pp. 287 ff.   [2] See below, pp. 256 ff.
[3] City of Birmingham Public Health Department, *Report by the Medical Officer of Health on the Housing Survey* (1947), p. 11.

industry.[1] People became more cleanly,[2] and with the help of official advice and free health-giving foods they looked after their children better. So after the big increase in infant mortality in the abnormal conditions of 1940 and 1941, the rate dropped to well below the pre-war level in 1942. By the end of the war it had sunk to two-thirds of the level of the early 1930s, partly as a result of the large-scale immunization against diphtheria begun in 1940, with which nearly all parents had been eager to cooperate.[3]

Birmingham industry and the war effort

We must now turn from the raids and their results to look at the general changes that were taking place in Birmingham during the early years of the war. One aspect of the city's life that was greatly affected was, of course, industry.

The shadow factories had to overcome a number of early difficulties of organization and labour relations,[4] but they had a clear advantage over other Birmingham munitions factories in that they were brand new, and faced no problems of conversion or adaptation.[5] They also had the advantage of full order books, thanks to the Government's early concentration on aircraft manufacture.[6] Many other Birmingham firms found that contracts for terrestrial munitions were few and far between in the early months of the war. The lack of military activity during the early part of the 'phoney war' persuaded the Government that the war would be a long one and that it might be decided more by economic exhaustion than by force of arms. Birmingham's industry was therefore enjoined to strengthen its export drive to help pay for the economic blockade which, it was hoped, would slowly strangle Germany. But shortages of materials, the loss of skilled labour to war work,[7] and transportation difficulties dogged these efforts.[8] Unemployment continued at a disturbing level until the autumn of 1940, and Birmingham

[1] See e.g. Ward, *The Other Battle*, p. 173.

[2] This inference is based on the sharp increase in the use of public baths in 1940 and 1941. Of course, this rise must also reflect the difficulty of heating water for baths at home, but the fact that high attendances continued into the early 1950s suggests that the early stages of the war saw a real increase in the frequency of bathing.

[3] Black, p. 250.

[4] See, for instance, criticism by Labour M.P.s of organization at the Austin shadow factory, in *H. of C. Deb.*, 5th series, vol. cccxliv, cols. *2119-21*, 8 March 1939.

[5] For the operation and production of the Austin shadow factory, see *How Longbridge Spanned the Years of War* (1946).

[6] See A. J. P. Taylor, *English History 1914-1945* (1965), pp. 411-13.

[7] See, for instance, *B.M.*, 6 May 1939 for early complaints about 'poaching' of labour by munitions firms. The Air Ministry set up a committee to study this problem in the winter of 1939-40 (P. Inman, *Labour in the Munitions Industries* (1957), p. 320).

[8] Best and Lloyd, for instance, were uncertain of being able to continue until the first of a series of big war contracts (Best and Lloyd, *Production for War and Peace* (1946), p. 5. B.R.L. 576153).

firms with Government contracts did not begin seven-days-a-week production until May 1940, when the Ministry of Supply issued a general call for higher output.[1] As late as July it was reported that very few firms were working night shifts.[2] It was fortunate, at least, that air raids did not take place on Birmingham until the late summer of 1940, giving the city's industries time to carry out partial reorganization without interference.

Many Birmingham firms, whose normal products were far removed from armaments, re-adapted themselves. Cadbury's set up Bournville Utilities Limited, which made a direct contribution to the country's military needs. At its peak of production 2,000 people were employed, and plant and personnel that before the war had been making chocolate were now making aeroplane parts, rockets, respirators, and other munitions. Cadbury's were also able to give accommodation to other firms involved in the war effort such as the Austin Motor Company, as well as the Ministries of Works and Food.[3] This ability to adapt existing skills to new demands, which had played such a vital part in the earlier development of the city, also proved crucial in smaller concerns. The skills of the jewellers and silversmiths, for example, were used to make component parts for radar equipment, rifles, and aeroplanes.[4] In all areas of the city's economy productivity increased. The electrical industry improved both its methods and products as demand increased for more sophisticated radio parts.[5] These advances were paralleled in the wire and alloy trades. Even the button industry had to update its traditional techniques in order to meet the unprecedented demand for military insignia.[6]

The traditional interdependence of Birmingham firms was strengthened by new administrative institutions in which the trade unions often played an important part. In July 1940, when the national Emergency Services Organization was formed to help damaged aircraft factories resume production as quickly as possible, the Birmingham area formed a distinct unit in the system, with a supervisory panel composed of local industrialists, trade union representatives, and administrators.[7] This later became known as the Birmingham Reconstruction Panel, and its work in organizing the repair of damaged factories of all types

[1] B.P., 27 May 1940. Owing to lack of Government contracts, half the employees of the Wolseley works in Birmingham had to be laid off on the outbreak of war (Fairfax, Calling All Arms, p. 106).

[2] B.C.C. Pro., 23 July 1940, pp. 632-3 (General Purposes Committee).

[3] Bournville Utilities, A War Record (1945), pp. 1-4.

[4] Adie Bros. Ltd. (1946); Birmingham Jewellers' and Silversmiths' Association, Arms and the Jeweller (1946).

[5] See e.g. Best and Lloyd, Production for War and Peace, p. 5.

[6] Industry in the West Midlands: The Official Handbook of the West Midlands Industrial Development Association Ltd. (1954), p. 11.

[7] E.D., 16 November 1940.

was highly praised.[1] To make the most of limited reserves of machinery in a situation of rapidly changing production, firms began to exchange machine tools. Early in the war the Ministry of Supply set up the Midland Tool Control Committee which, in July 1941, set up a mutual aid exchange for machine tools. Operated through weekly meetings of manufacturers, it had organized 40,000 exchanges or loans between Midland manufacturers by May 1942, by which time the idea had been adopted throughout the country.[2]

Full use of available plant was ensured through the Midland Regional Production Board.[3] Shortly after the Board was reconstituted in July 1942, in order to take account of changing conditions of production activity, the Birmingham District Production Committee was appointed to keep track of production within the city.[4] A further sub-division took place in December when the Committee divided the Birmingham area into five sectors, each with its own committee of experts to advise manufacturers.[5] Industrialists and trade unionists worked together at all levels of this organization. From January 1943 a central source of information was provided by the new Regional Capacity Office of the Midland Region of the Ministry of War Production.[6] Individual firms also extended their services in the interests of greater collective efficiency; in February 1940, for instance, Commercial X-Rays Limited, of Harborne, installed an industrial radiology plant for the inspection of aircraft castings, which previously had been inspected in London.[7]

Although many of Birmingham's small firms had always relied on interdependence for their survival, any amount of cooperation could not save the weaker of them in war conditions. Even before concentration of non-essential industries was adopted as Government policy, the smaller of city firms were being squeezed out of business. In June 1940 the inaugural meeting was held in Birmingham of an organization called Associated Smaller Manufacturers, and many complaints were heard there from firms with machinery standing idle owing to the shortage of Government contracts.[8] Firms not engaged on war work were often severely hampered by rationing of raw materials and by the Limitation of Supplies Order.[9] In March 1941 the President of the Board of Trade announced a policy of deliberate industrial concentration, affecting some ninety industries, which was intended to bring about the closure of many of the less efficient factories. First reactions among industrialists in Birmingham suggested that concentration would not greatly affect city firms, which, whether large or small, were for the

[1] See e.g. *B.M.*, 2 September 1942.   [2] *B.G.*, 23 July 1942.
[3] *B.P.*, 22 July 1942.   [4] *B.M.*, 17 October 1942.   [5] *B.G.*, 15 December 1942.
[6] *E.D.*, 7 January 1943.   [7] *B.P.*, 20 February 1940.   [8] *B.M.*, 26 June 1940.
[9] Toy firms, for instance, were limited to a mere fifteen per cent of their normal production, and much of this was devoted to supplying games for the Forces (*B.G.*, 24 October 1942).

most part engaged in war production.[1] But they were being over-optimistic. Many branches of Birmingham industry were affected by concentration—the jewellery industry, with its numerous tiny firms, in particular.[2]

As we have seen, manpower was not a serious problem in the early months of the war, except for certain types of highly-skilled engineering labour. But towards the end of 1940 a national shortage of labour was developing in step with the expansion of the armed forces and the munitions industries. The shortage became serious in the Birmingham area earlier than in most other cities,[3] for not only was it a key munitions centre, but its pre-war unemployment rate had been lower than that of most parts of the country. So there was less slack to take up. Three possibilities were open to Birmingham industry in its search for extra manpower; the dilution of the existing skilled labour force, the recruitment of new labour from the local population, and the importation of labour from other areas. All three were tried during the war. As early as March 1938 the leaders of the T.U.C. had agreed to relax craft restrictions in the engineering industry.[4] Thanks to the maintenance of good relations between the trade unions and the Government, and, in Birmingham, between the unions and the employers, dilution took place without causing the same conflicts as during the First World War. Many firms set up their own training schemes to prepare employees for transfer to more skilled work, and the Education Committee provided help, for instance, by organizing evening courses for foremen at the Technical College.[5] Some unemployed workers were retrained from early 1940 under a Government scheme which was operated from three centres in Birmingham.[6]

Dilution and retraining inevitably produced a shortage of unskilled labour, which was noticed in Birmingham as early as January 1941, ahead of most other areas.[7] One reaction to this problem was a reinforcement of efforts to persuade women to take up industrial work. As early as October 1940 the Ministry of Labour had organized a two-week campaign in Birmingham, with the full support of the Lord Mayor, to recruit women for munitions work.[8] The City Council had done all it could to help, by expanding its school meals services, and

[1] B.M., 5 March 1941; Birmingham Chamber of Commerce, Journal, May 1941, pp. 249–50.
[2] See complaint by the Unionist M.P., Walter Higgs, about the effect of concentration on the jewellery trade, in H. of C. Deb., 5th series, vol. ccclxxix, col. 1861, 14 May 1942. For an account of one large jewellery firm's adaptation to war conditions, see Adie Bros, Ltd. Even Adie's had to close one of their two factories.
[3] B.P., 8 May 1945. [4] Taylor, English History, p. 413. [5] B.P., 8 May 1945.
[6] B.M., 20 February 1940. A man could be brought up to semi-skilled level in thirteen weeks (E.D., 3 March 1941).
[7] W. K. Hancock and M. M. Gowing, British War Economy (1949), p. 292.
[8] B.G., 26 October 1940.

participating in a Government scheme to set up day nurseries. Many firms made it possible for women to work part-time—here again, Birmingham was in advance of most other areas.[1] But these efforts had to be further strengthened in the early months of 1941. In January, the Ministry of Labour opened one of its Birmingham training centres to women as well as men; by March women were being trained at all three centres in the city. Yet still not enough women came forward. It was suggested that middle-class housewives looked down on factory work, and influential members of the community were asked to do their best to create a contrary impression.[2] In August and September a massive campaign was organized in Birmingham to attract more women workers, but it failed to reach its target, producing only 6,500 definite offers by women.[3] There were some complaints that not enough was being done for women; there were not enough day nurseries, and the Minister of Labour, Ernest Bevin, suggested that Birmingham employers were bad at looking after girls who came to work in Birmingham from other areas.[4]

As time went on, more and more pressure was put on women to contribute to the war effort. Compulsory registration of women at employment exchanges began in April 1941, and all were eventually interviewed to see if they could be better employed. At the same time, women's status within industry was improved. Complaints had been made that women were unable to obtain jobs that corresponded to their qualifications and ability,[5] but by the end of 1942 a new grading system had been introduced into the engineering trades which removed much female frustration.[6] Great publicity was now being given in Birmingham to the deeds of women workers; in September 1942 Evelyn Duncan, a capstan lathe operator, was fêted when she broke the 'world shell production record' for the second time.[7] By September 1942 the number of women working in Midlands munitions industries had increased by 150 per cent since 1939, while the total labouring force had increased by 65 per cent.[8] Yet the total female working

[1] *B.P.*, 8 May 1945.

[2] *B.P.*, 13 September 1941; *B.M.*, 6 June 1941. In 1942 Mrs. Elvira Martineau, a former Lady Mayoress, took up factory work to set an example (*B.G.*, 20 November 1942).

[3] *B.M.*, 30 August 1941; *B.G.*, 15 September 1941.

[4] *B.G.*, 3 April 1941; *B.P.*, 13 September 1941.

[5] See e.g. Theodora Benson, *Sweethearts and Wives: Their Part in War* (1942), p. 23.

[6] *B.P.*, 14 December 1942.

[7] Women often proved to be quicker workers than men (Ward, *The Other Battle*, p. 170).

[8] *B.M.*, 3 December 1942. At Morris Commercial Cars the number of skilled and semi-skilled women workers doubled between late 1941 and late 1942, while the total of men remained unchanged. There were over ten times as many skilled or semi-skilled women in this works as unskilled women (figures communicated by Morris Commercial Cars).

population of the country as a whole increased by less than half between June 1939 and June 1943.[1] In June 1943 efforts switched in Birmingham to attracting older women to factory work, and house-to-house canvassing campaigns were conducted for the first time.[2]

Extra hands were also sought among juveniles and handicapped people. Demand for juvenile labour began to increase in 1941,[3] and the Corporation's Youth Employment Service did its best to help. Successful efforts were made to retrain disabled and handicapped men and women, and to find them suitable jobs.[4] S.U. Carburettors even employed blind people as inspectors, their sense of touch proving more accurate than the eye for some jobs.[5] Ireland was also tapped as a source of labour. In 1940 so many Irish were taking up jobs in Birmingham that E. W. Salt, Unionist member for Yardley, complained in the House of Commons that it was unfair to let them take the jobs of British servicemen when they themselves were not liable for call-up.[6] If any other Birmingham industrialists shared these scruples they soon suppressed them. In 1941 firms such as I.C.I. and Austin's were among the first in the country to send recruiting agents to Eire, and in 1942 the Ministry of Supply followed their example by organizing large-scale recruiting there.[7]

Despite all these efforts, there remained a general shortage of labour in Birmingham almost until the end of the war. Even voluntary schemes were important enough to attract attention in the press. Towards the end of 1941, for instance, a Moseley resident, F. C. Hallewell, set up a volunteer labour squad organization, and by February 1942 he had over 300 part-time workers on his books, most of them non-manual employees or students. Wherever possible they were allocated to factories, mostly for Sunday work. Two months later over one thousand people had volunteered, and the movement had doubled its strength again by the end of the year.[8]

Another important source was labour directed from other parts of the country. Most directed workers, many of them women, came from the depressed areas—Tyneside, South Wales, and Scotland. At first there was a high wastage rate among these transferred workers, partly owing to the lack of welfare facilities pointed out by Ernest Bevin.[9]

[1] *Monthly Digest of Statistics*, December 1946.
[2] *B.P.*, 12 February 1943; *E.D.*, 20 September 1943.
[3] *B.M.*, 30 December 1941.   [4] *B.G.*, 16 September 1944.
[5] Fairfax, *Calling All Arms*, p. 96.
[6] *H. of C. Deb.*, 5th series, vol. ccclvii, cols. *2221–2*, 29 February 1940.
[7] H. M. D. Parker, *Manpower: A Study of War-Time Policy and Administration* (1957), p. 339.
[8] *E.D.*, 24 February 1942; *B.M.*, 6 March 1942, 8 April 1942; *B.P.*, 10 September 1942.
[9] *B.G.*, 3 April 1941.

Many workers, arriving in Birmingham with nowhere to stay, never presented themselves for work and eventually returned home. To ensure a welcome for new arrivals, the Ministry of Labour set up reception desks at the two main Birmingham stations early in 1941, an example which was followed in other parts of the country.[1] The girls were often in poor shape when they arrived—and they seem to have made the same impression on Birmingham residents as had the city's evacuees on people in country districts.[2] But their condition improved in time. Many married local men and stayed on in Birmingham after the war.[3] Most firms followed the Ministry of Labour's advice and greatly expanded workers' welfare facilities.[4] Canteens were made obligatory in factories employing more than 250 people, but many employers recognized their utility sufficiently to arrange entertainments and dances in them, especially during breaks in the night shift.[5] Some Birmingham firms provided their workers with sun lamp treatment to keep them fit.[6] Austin's made a big contribution towards the cost of a War Workers' Club in Northfield.[7] And by 1943 a number of rest homes for over-strained factory workers were being set up in the Birmingham area.

The cumulative effect of all these efforts to encourage people to work in war industry, combined with industrial conscription, was to increase Birmingham's production to an unprecedented level. By the last months of 1944, 47 per cent of the rationed population of Birmingham was at work—a record unequalled in any British city of comparable size.[8] The total of those working in the munitions industries was estimated at 400,000, over one-third of the city's total population.[9] Some 5,500,000 square feet of new factory floor space was built in the city between 1938 and the end of 1944.[10]

This rapid industrial expansion could not have taken place without a large measure of harmony between managements and employees. Birmingham was by no means free of industrial disputes during the war, but there were few actual strikes.[11] Many causes of friction in the

---

[1] Parker, *Manpower*, pp. 396–7.   [2] See below, pp. 333–4.

[3] Ward, *The Other Battle*, p. 169; *B.P.*, 8 May 1945. In 1944 about one worker in fifteen at the Austin Motor Company had been directed from other parts of the U.K. or imported from Eire. The Eire contingent made up the very great majority of this group.

[4] *The Times, British War Production 1939–1945: A Record* (1945), pp. 52–3. See also *Hymatic in War and Peace* (1946), p. 14. B.R.L. 663055.

[5] H. V. Potter, 'Welfare in industry', *Chemistry and Industry*, no. 38, 17 September 1955, p. 1174; *B.P.* 27 May 1940; Fairfax, *Calling All Arms*, p. 115.

[6] *B.M.*, 27 November 1939.

[7] *B.P.*, 3 August 1942. The Lord Mayor referred to this gift as an example of 'enlightened self-interest'.

[8] *B.P.*, 31 October 1944.   [9] Black, p. 24.   [10] *B.P.*, 31 October 1944.

[11] B.S.A. was especially strike-free, owing mainly to the enlightened policy of the management (see Ward, *The Other Battle*, pp. 165–7).

new munitions plants, such as union recognition, and rates and conditions of war work, were ironed out before the war began; the Austin shadow factory, for instance, was largely untroubled by disputes after its one really big strike in 1938.[1] Wages were very high in the Birmingham armament industries. Engineering wages were often inflated by piecework and merit bonuses paid on top of the minimum rates, and aircraft factory wages had to be even more generous in order to attract labour from the highly-paid motor industry. Earnings in Midland shadow factories were among the highest in the country, often reaching up to double the basic time rates. Sometimes bonuses could be astronomical; in one airframe factory in 1942 the average bonus earned was 372 per cent of the basic rate. The shadow factories could pay these wages because of their immense resources and the great demand for aircraft, and in Birmingham and Coventry they exercised an inflationary influence on wages throughout the engineering sector. The Government considered ways and means of reducing high wage levels in the Midlands, but never made any serious attempts to do so.[2]

Efforts to increase productivity were made not only by the managements, but frequently by joint production committees representing both sides. The managements of many smaller firms already had close contacts with their employees, and some larger concerns, such as Cadbury's, Kalamazoo, and Boxfoldia, had developed organs of management–worker cooperation long before the war. But most of the munitions firms had to start from scratch. Very few joint production committees were set up early in the war, owing to distrust on both sides,[3] but when the trade unions threw their full weight behind the drive for increased production after the invasion of Russia,[4] they took the initiative in proposing the establishment of these committees. In October 1941 the Birmingham Trades Council organized a production conference, during which Alderman A. E. Ager, district secretary of the A.E.U., called for joint production committees to be set up in all Birmingham factories, as requested by the Ministry of Labour and the Select Committee on National Expenditure.[5] Support for the idea came from the Birmingham Chamber of Commerce, which agreed that the committees must have more than nominal powers.[6] But there was still

[1] The strike involved 5,100 workers and lasted from 29 August to 7 September (*Ministry of Labour Gazette*).

[2] Inman, *Labour in the Munitions Industries*, pp. 319–25. For average wages over the whole country in each industrial group, see Central Statistical Office, *Statistical Digest of the War* (1951), pp. 204–5.

[3] Alderman A. E. Ager (Labour) criticized the lack of cooperation in local industry in strong terms in October 1941: 'While I believe there has been this cooperation nationally, there has been very little cooperation locally' (*B.P.*, 2 October 1941).

[4] See below, pp. 47–8.

[5] Birmingham Trades Council, *Annual Report*, 1941–2, p. 12; *E.D.*, 2 October 1941.

[6] Birmingham Chamber of Commerce, *Journal*, October 1941, p. 505.

strong resistance from many managements, and in March 1942 Emmanuel Shinwell, M.P., criticized Birmingham munitions firms, with the notable exception of B.S.A., for obstructing proposals for joint production committees.[1]

Official support, however, was growing; in January 1942 the Midland Regional Board of the Ministry of War Production added its voice to the call for joint production committees. By June a large number were in existence, and they were said to be working well.[2] In October 1942 a Birmingham District Joint Production Committee was set up to handle problems concerning the whole city. The number of factory joint production committees eventually rose to about 500.[3] They frequently took the initiative in internal plant affairs to such an extent that the employers tried to restrict their activities.

Many of the more politically-minded workers saw the joint production committees as a step towards workers' control. In January 1942 the Birmingham Trades Council passed a resolution demanding workers' ownership and control of industry, and in March a resolution was passed at a production conference organized by the Council demanding legislation to force all firms to set up joint production committees. As a result of the conference, a production liaison committee was established to allow Trades Council and shop stewards' representatives to examine production problems and the work of the joint committees. However, the liaison committee was dissolved when a new body, the Birmingham District Trade Unions' Production Committee, was set up at the request of the T.U.C. to coordinate the joint production committees.[4] Furthermore, some managements saw the value of workers' criticism and comments; Dunlop, for instance, were among the first firms in the country to set up a suggestions box scheme, which they found to be very valuable.[5]

The success of the joint production committees reflected the general willingness of Birmingham organized labour to cooperate fully in expanding munitions production. From the early months of the war the Birmingham Trades Council, ignoring the objections of its Communist element, had followed the Borough Labour Party in giving its support to the war effort. It had made some show of reluctance nevertheless, and had called for compensatory concessions from the employers. The Council had also expressed doubts early in the war about military and industrial conscription, to which it did not formally agree until June 1940.[6] Then Hitler's invasion of the Soviet Union

[1] *B.G.*, 26 March 1942. His source of information was the Birmingham and District A.E.U.
[2] *B.M.*, 24 June 1942; *B.P.*, 16 July 1942.
[3] John Corbett, *The Birmingham Trades Council 1866–1966* (1966), p. 152.
[4] Birmingham Trades Council, *Annual Report*, 1942–3, p. 8; 1943–4, p. 64.
[5] *B.M.*, 20 May 1944.   [6] Corbett, *Trades Council*, p. 149.

removed all remaining suspicions that the working class had been dragged into a capitalists' war, and in August 1941 it pledged unqualified support to the British and Allied Governments. It immediately convened a conference of union leaders, shop stewards, and Labour and Cooperative Party representatives to discuss how maximum war effort could be maintained.[1] Soon afterwards, the Council and shop stewards' organizations threw themselves into the campaign for a second front, which was, they argued, the only policy that would stimulate the workers to maximum effort.[2]

With both local and national trade union leaderships virtually committed to a policy of cooperation with the employers and the Government, and with rapidly changing conditions in many plants, the initiative in relations with the employers passed from the full-time union leaders into the hands of the shop stewards, just as it had during the First World War.[3] By 1942 the shop stewards had organized themselves on a city-wide basis, and were taking the initiative in contacts with the employers and with politicians. In November 1942, for instance, the Birmingham munitions shop stewards sent a deputation to the Regional Production Committee to offer a 50 per cent increase in aircraft production as long as certain changes in the industry were speeded up, and provided that the shop stewards were allowed to help in attracting more women workers, and in improving the quality of works propaganda designed to increase production.[4] Sometimes they ran foul of their employers; in March 1942 two shop stewards were dismissed by a Birmingham firm for, so they claimed, criticizing bad management. Other shop stewards lobbied Midland M.P.s about the sackings, and attempted in vain to see Ernest Bevin. A serious dispute was averted only by the forebearance of the Birmingham and District organization of the A.E.U., which held back from industrial action in the interests of the war effort.[5] But sometimes the shop stewards were able to bring workers out on strike without union approval. In November 1942, for instance, several thousand workers came out unofficially for several days at a Birmingham plant, in protest against the dismissal of three workers.[6] Thanks to employers' recognition, union membership greatly increased during the war, especially in the engineering industry where it had been relatively low before 1939.[7] But the main beneficiaries were the shop stewards, not the official union leaderships.

[1] B.P., 4 August 1941.   [2] B.G., 9 May 1942.
[3] See, for instance, the report of a debate in the Trades Council in B.G., 6 July 1942, in which some delegates attacked the union leaders for being too far removed from the working classes.
[4] B.M., 13 November 1942.
[5] See Birmingham press, 10 March–30 March 1942.   [6] B.G., 23 November 1942.
[7] See H. A. Turner, Garfield Clack, and Geoffrey Roberts, Labour Relations in the Motor Industry (1967), pp. 192–4.

Municipal policies and planning for peace

The work of the City Council, like that of industry and other Birmingham institutions, was concentrated from an early stage in the war on making the fullest possible contribution to the war effort. Most of the Corporation's services were even more crucial in war than they had been in peacetime, but cuts were made wherever possible. Reductions in manpower often restricted services, and in some cases, such as street lighting, war conditions made the provision redundant. Nevertheless, most rate fund services carried on normally as far as possible; capital investment schemes, on the other hand, were almost all interrupted. Nearly all work on houses, roads, and public buildings ceased shortly after war broke out. The Council was allowed to proceed only with schemes which were essential to the war effort, such as the provision of new electricity generating capacity. Consequently, the Corporation's outlay increased only slowly during the war, despite the heavy load of the civil defence services.

During the First World War matters had been very different; the Corporation had frequently taken the initiative in organizing the life of the city on a war footing, for instance, by establishing rationing arrangements.[1] This time the central Government, either directly or through its regional organizations, took over most of this responsibility, and even took certain essential services such as the fire brigade out of the City's hands. Other services, such as hospitals and ambulances, were rigidly subordinated to regional and national requirements. The City Council accepted the principle of external control in this great emergency, but its imposition often caused friction, and a long series of disagreements lay behind the apparently trivial dispute with the Regional Civil Defence Commissioner, the Earl of Dudley, in 1942. Dudley had arranged the programme of a royal visit to Birmingham without consulting the Corporation. The Lord Mayor, Norman Tiptaft, was furious, and the City Council supported him by sending a strong complaint about Dudley to the Home Secretary.

In contrast to the general picture of retrenchment, a few very important municipal services, such as British Restaurants[2] and day nurseries, were either created or greatly extended during the war.[3] In nearly all these cases, however, the City Council acted on Government instructions, and received massive subsidies, which frequently

---

[1] See Briggs, p. 206; Reginald H. Brazier and Ernest Sandford, *Birmingham and the Great War* (1921).

[2] See Black, pp. 65–7. For an account of the opposition of the *Birmingham Post* and private caterers to the British Restaurants, see Tiptaft, *The Individualist*, p. 201.

[3] The majority of these services were related to the welfare of children. See Richard M. Titmuss, *Problems of Social Policy* (1950), pp. 506–17.

E

covered almost the whole cost of the services.[1] Consequently, when Government grants were withdrawn or reduced after the war, the services virtually collapsed. Such, for instance, was the fate of the wartime day nurseries.

It was partly because the City Council had to restrict its activities to essential services that the number and role of voluntary bodies expanded. Not only did the war create extra needs, but people were happier to give up their time to voluntary activity. Despite longer hours of work, people generally had more time on their hands owing to the restriction of entertainment and holiday possibilities, and civil defence propaganda made them more amenable to public service. It also seems very likely that the income of voluntary bodies grew during the war. Most citizens were earning more and had less to spend it on.[2] Much of their surplus was diverted into national savings, or gambling, but the success of the national wartime appeals, such as the Spitfire Fund, and local appeals like the Lord Mayor's War Relief and Victory Funds, suggests that more money was also being devoted to charity than before the war.

New voluntary organizations appeared almost immediately on the outbreak of war. A group of Birmingham Quakers founded the 'Friends Hospital Aid' in the second week of September 1939, and a few days later a Christian Service Corps was founded in Harborne.[3] More official in character was the Lady Mayoress's Depot, which opened in November 1939.[4] This was a revival of an organization first set up during the First World War, and it concentrated on providing clothing and other necessities for destitute or bombed-out citizens. It depended almost entirely on voluntary women workers, and cooperated closely with the national women's organization, the Women's Voluntary Service, which had opened an office in Birmingham in January 1939. By 1941 the W.V.S. had 5,000 active members in the city, and was cooperating very closely with the Corporation, a situation which did not always obtain in other local authority areas.[5] Other voluntary organizations which worked closely with the City, especially during the raids, were the Birmingham Citizens' Society, and the Citizens' Advice Bureaux, thirty-two of which had been set up in Birmingham by August 1939.[6] Most of these voluntary organizations found that pressure on their services dropped after the raids, but the approach of victory

---

[1] One exception was the child care service, which had to be expanded during the war on local initiative owing to the increase in demand (Black, pp. 324–5).

[2] For national figures of personal income and expenditure, see *Statistical Digest of the War*, pp. 200, 203.

[3] *B.P.*, 16 September 1939; 27 September 1939.

[4] [Helen C. Vaudrey], *The Lady Mayoress's Depot, Birmingham 1939–1945* (1952).

[5] *B.P.*, 18 March 1941; Titmuss, *Problems of Social Policy*, p. 299.

[6] *B.P.*, 12 August 1939.

brought new problems which produced a voluntary, as well as an official, response. The year 1945 saw, for instance, the foundation of the Birmingham Resettlement Advice Bureau, for demobilized servicemen, and the Birmingham Marriage Guidance Council, which reflected the strain that war had imposed on family life.[1] Much voluntary effort was also devoted to social activities such as War Workers' Clubs, and to the officially encouraged expansion of youth activities which took place during the war.

Although the City Council grew more dependent on the Government for both finance and instructions during the war, it began in 1941 on its own initiative to plan for the post-war reconstruction of Birmingham. This planning operation was at first a purely mechanical reaction to the damage caused by the blitz, but it took on a more positive character after the entry of the U.S.S.R. and the United States into the war made it seem likely that defeat could be avoided. Reconstruction meant a lot more than repairing war damage; it meant catching up on the backlog caused by several years of inactivity in house building and other new capital projects. It also meant replacing equipment and installations worn out during the war, when normal renewal and even maintenance had been almost impossible. But even more than this, reconstruction involved looking at problems afresh, planning for the new needs and standards which had been recognized during the war, and planning to make use of the spirit of social harmony and self-sacrifice that had grown up.

All the Council committees drew up plans, and we shall look at some of them in later chapters. For a time, however, it seemed possible that the most significant plans were those being made by a completely new committee, the Reconstruction Committee, which was set up in February 1942.[2] The Reconstruction Committee was the brainchild of the new Lord Mayor, Norman Tiptaft, who, after master-minding the city's civil defence arrangements, now wanted all post-war planning to be placed under a single direction. Thanks to the influence given him by his Lord Mayoralty (which, owing to some of the stormy events that marked its course, was known to councillors and officials as the 'Norman Conquest') Tiptaft persuaded the Council to set up the committee, and became its chairman. At first the new committee aroused great opposition, with the Unionist Theodore Pritchett among its biggest critics, but it produced a series of sensible reports which convinced many in the Council that it was doing a useful job. Some of the committee's work was very advanced—for instance, it commissioned a pioneer social survey of a suburban area as a guide for post-war

---

[1] *B.G.*, 17 April 1945; *C.S.C. Review: The Birmingham Christian Social Council Quarterly*, no. 7, May 1946, p. 1.

[2] B.C.C., *Pro.*, 3 February 1942, pp. 54–61 (General Purposes Committee).

housing and community provision. But other committees resented its interference and attempts to take over their own plans. In 1944 the Public Works Committee led a successful campaign to cut the Reconstruction Committee down to size, and it was wound up in the following year.[1] The committee, it was true, *had* interfered, and Norman Tiptaft's impatient manner had not endeared him to his fellow chairmen. But coordination of plans, as later became clear, would have been a great advantage. By the end of the war so many committees had prepared ambitious schemes that the cost of carrying them all out was much more than the City could afford, yet no order of priority had been established.

Fortunately, this lack of coordination was largely compensated for by the quality of the planning undertaken by the separate committees, and notably by the Public Works Committee. Moreover, a broader perspective was provided by a number of outside bodies interested in reconstruction. The most influential was the West Midlands Group on Post-War Reconstruction and Planning,[2] but existing bodies such as the Civic Society, and professional associations like the Birmingham and Five Counties Architectural Association, also took a keen interest in post-war problems. And these elite organizations were just part of a great wave of rethinking in which the general public took part at all levels. With more time to think, and more to think about now that the struggle for national survival had brought certain realities home to them, people began to discuss passionately the future of post-war Britain. Brains trusts and mock parliaments abounded; even the proceedings of regimental forums, published in the Birmingham press, had their influence on public opinion. The Education Committee of the Birmingham Cooperative Society organized open forums on post-war problems from as early as 1941, and they were addressed by such influential speakers as C. E. M. Joad, J. B. S. Haldane, Stephen King-Hall, and Bishop Barnes.[3] The predominantly middle-class Birmingham Central Literary Association had begun to discuss social reform even earlier, in March 1940.[4] Some discussion and study groups were set up specifically for this purpose; for instance, the Eleven Study Group, founded in September 1942 as the result of an advertisement in the Birmingham press.[5] Young people were particularly interested; we find, for instance, a youth parliament set up in 1941 by the Princess Alice Orphanage,

---

[1] B.C.C., *Pro.*, 25 July 1944, p. 493 (General Purposes Committee). See also Tiptaft, *The Individualist*, pp. 187–201, 220, 226–8.

[2] See below, p. 123.

[3] Education Department, Birmingham Co-operative Society, *Shaping the Future* (1942), B.R.L. 563132. For Bishop Barnes, see below, p. 265.

[4] *Central Literary Magazine*, June 1940, p. 78.

[5] Eleven Study Group, 'The causes of international war and their cures' (1945), p. 3 (B.R.L. 586818).

and a civic week organized by Olton Convent School in 1943.[1] Some of these manifestations were ephemeral, but others, like the Kingstanding youth parliament, set up in 1941, survived long after the war.[2]

It was this atmosphere which the Labour Party turned to its own advantage both nationally and in Birmingham. Not only did Labour, by building up its organization and continuing its propaganda during the war, gain the allegiance of many voters who had not been committed to the party before 1939, but by strengthening its links with the expanding trade unions it improved its hold on the working-class vote. These methods were especially successful in Birmingham where the growth in trade union membership was greater than average, and where a big section of the inflated pre-war Unionist vote was not ideologically committed to the Conservative Party.[3] Labour also made its presence felt by giving practical help to people. The Joint Emergency Committee, set up by the Borough Labour Party, the Co-operative Party, and the Birmingham Trades Council in 1939, was especially active in finding accommodation for bombed-out people, as well as calling for better official provision for them.[4] The Birmingham Unionists, who had wound up their organization when the war began, could compete with Labour in none of these respects, although their traditionally liberal attitudes were strengthened by the war. By the end, their policies were indistinguishable in many respects from those of Labour, and unlike the national Conservative Party they did not start to water down their proposals for social reform in 1944 and 1945. But their forward-looking views made little impact on the electorate because their opponents had by far the more effective propaganda machine, and they were embarrassed and weakened by the national Conservative Party's increasingly ambivalent attitude to reforms that had been proposed and widely accepted during the war, such as the Beveridge recommendations on social security. In Birmingham, Labour rammed home their advantage by increasingly violent attacks in the City Council from late 1943. Although Labour raised mostly national issues, on which they wanted the Council to express an opinion and, in some cases, to make recommendations to the Government, the Unionists were annoyed and embarrassed. Loyalty to the national party made them oppose Labour over most of these issues, which allowed their opponents to pin the label of 'reactionary' on them, even though most

---

[1] 'The Young Democrat' (B.R.L. Birmingham Periodicals, 1/1); *Civic Week at Olton Convent, 13-17 December 1943* (B.R.L. 549542).

[2] [Bryan H. Reed], *Eighty Thousand Adolescents* (1950), pp. 57-8.

[3] See below, pp. 75ff.

[4] It was reorganized, under the title of the Birmingham Council of Labour, in 1942. The rehousing of people made homeless by the bombing had been one of the less satisfactory aspects of the City Council's handling of the emergency.

Unionists proved themselves to be anything but reactionary when local matters were discussed.

Labour's growing assault on the Unionists was intended mainly as a tactical expedient, but it coincided with, and to some extent reflected, a general growth of social and political conflict in the last years of the war. This conflict resulted partly from growing boredom and war-weariness; people just could not keep up an effort that had reached its peak in 1941 and 1942. The spirit of self-sacrifice and conciliation also suffered.[1] While hoping that the best aspects of wartime society would be preserved, people, parties, firms, and trade unions nevertheless began to take up their own individual stands. Of course, they had never completely abandoned these positions, even in 1940 and 1941. But individualism became more and more prominent towards the end of the war. It was reflected not only in the growing number of strikes in Birmingham and other areas, but in the jockeying-for-position by firms planning their changeover to peacetime production, the growing disagreements between local authorities and the Government, the statements made by politicians with an eye to a future election, and the claims and counter-claims of special interests such as servicemen and munitions workers for favourable treatment after the war.

As the war drew to an end the contrast became increasingly marked between the ambitious plans made for the future and the worn-out state of Birmingham, its people, and of the country as a whole.[2] Machinery and equipment of all kinds were in an advanced state of deterioration by 1945, especially those that had not been directly essential to the war effort. The city's dwellings were in a poor state, for hardly any maintenance work had been done for six years, and repairs to war damage had often been rudimentary. The roads were full of ruts and potholes, tired trams clattered over distorted tracks, and bus breakdowns were legion. Even Birmingham industry, which had been much more favoured than other departments of the city's life in terms of new equipment and the new methods associated with it, could not face the future with confidence. On the whole, the war had strengthened the large firms and, for the most part, weakened the smaller concerns. Enforced dispersal had shown many firms that they could operate successfully with widely separated production units, and they were consequently more willing to expand outside the city after the war. But much obsolete machinery remained in use, and even new equipment had frequently been over-used and under-maintained, so that it was completely run down by 1945. Despite the difficulty of obtaining labour, the Government's success in encouraging and forcing

[1] See e.g. Donald Brook, *Writers' Gallery* (1944), p. 119.
[2] An interesting contemporary study of this growing disenchantment is to be found in [Mass Observation], *The Journey Home* (1944).

women, young people, and workers from other areas into service in Birmingham industry had spared the big munitions firms from a serious labour crisis. In addition, their workers had been prepared to work longer hours, and they were normally encouraged to do so by the managements, to whom money was usually no object on war contracts. So there still remained at the end of the war much inefficiency and under-use of labour. Indeed, Birmingham industry took a much more realistic (and pessimistic) view of its post-war prospects than did Birmingham local government.

Birmingham's reconstruction plans were much more ambitious and advanced than those of other cities, especially in respect of slum clearance and roads. But when the war ended Birmingham's future was linked much more closely than before with that of the whole country. National planning, in one form or another, had come to stay. Birmingham's grandiose plans were a product of the city's exceptional dynamism, but the question was, would this dynamism be given its head after the war by the central Government? The answer proved to be, on the whole, that it would not. Much of the enthusiasm for the future generated during the war in the city and the nation was dispelled during the long years of economic difficulties which followed. Birmingham's City Council found it almost impossible even to start major projects for at least five or six years after the war because the Government still had to repress local authority investment in order to build up the economy's productive capacity. Even when expenditure *was* authorized, as it was for housing, progress was held up by national shortages of labour and materials. Enthusiasm for communal action and social reform might have been maintained if, as in Germany, rapid economic progress had been made. But as it was, such steps towards greater social control as were taken after 1945, mainly by the new Labour Government, were often associated in the public mind with drabness and inferior standards. As a result, many of those elements of social harmony and cooperation which had survived until the end of the war (and they were substantial) withered during the first years of peace. Individualism, though cloaked to some extent in a veneer of socialism and overall planning, again came to the fore. When economic conditions began to improve in the 1950s, they were accompanied by even greater manifestations of individualism, both nationally and in Birmingham. Progress became associated with competition instead of cooperation; the private purse was again given priority over public expenditure.

True, the growth of the economy in the 1950s at last made it possible for Birmingham to undertake some of the vast schemes planned during the war. But how long had they been delayed! Without the period of reflection allowed by the war, and the immense concentration of minds and activities that war had stimulated, projects such as the inner ring road and the central redevelopment areas might have lacked some of their grandeur and unity of conception. The sweeping powers to carry them out might not have been granted by Parliament if the war had not made it necessary to subordinate all private interests to the public good. But there can be little doubt that substantially similar schemes would have been planned in any case, war or no war. The powers to carry them out would probably have been acquired progressively, just as they had been before 1939. When we find, for instance, that more slum houses were demolished in the eight years before the war than in the same period after it, not accounting for the six years in between during which the only slum clearance was being done (and inefficiently at that!) by Hitler, the war's effects on Birmingham appear somewhat less than beneficial. Much of the progress made in the 1950s was merely the belated execution of schemes which, but for the war, would have been completed long before.

Seen in this light, the war was essentially what people had feared in 1939—something alien, disruptive, something that could only do harm. In the event, people's fears of immediate dire evil were proved to be exaggerated. At the time, the war caused more inconvenience than injury, more decay than destruction. But because it was largely superficial in its effects it failed to bring about a major social revolution which might have allowed real progress to be made after the war towards a way of life which had been glimpsed by almost everyone in 1940 and 1941. And it so weakened Birmingham and the nation that both came out of the war worse off than they had been before, less able to face the future than they would otherwise have been. So it is that much of the rest of this book will tell the story, not of how Birmingham moved on after 1945 to new heights of happiness and achievement but of how it struggled to recover from the heaviest blow history had ever dealt it.

III

BIRMINGHAM GOVERNMENT
AND POLITICS

As the clouds of war lifted in 1945, the pages of the Birmingham daily press began to fill with details of the City Council's ambitious plans for a brave new Birmingham. Few readers could have concluded, on the evidence of these reports, that power to carry out the schemes lay anywhere but firmly in the hands of the Birmingham Corporation. Wartime controls and restrictions on Birmingham's freedom of action had been accepted as necessary to victory, but there seemed no reason why most of them should not be removed in peacetime. Yet even before 1939 Birmingham had not enjoyed sole control of its own destiny. An almost uninterrupted growth in central Government influence over local authorities, since the mid-nineteenth century, had already produced what Asa Briggs described as 'a close working partnership' between Birmingham and Westminster.[1] This central influence was reinforced by the war, and became even stronger in some respects after 1945. The achievement of a consistent standard of local services had been a growing Government objective since the nineteenth century, and spending restrictions on local authorities in the interests of the national economy were foreshadowed in the inter-war years. After 1939 the Government refined and reinforced its efforts to achieve these aims, and set itself further goals. These were to limit the growth of Britain's largest cities, and to redistribute industry for the benefit of the depressed areas.

The tools of central direction were legion. All local authority powers and functions rested on parliamentary sanction, and could be revoked or extended without reference to those who exercised them. Extensive powers of supervision were built up by central departments during decades of changing legislation. More subtle were the central Government's financial aids to local authorities, whose own tax base was weak and inflexible. These three categories of control—legislative, administrative, and financial—had all been present before 1939, but during and after the Second World War they were further developed. In combination, they substantially restricted local authority initiative. On occasion, even the central Government worried that its overall control was undermining the very *principle* of local government, and took certain counter-action. The most important of these measures was the 1958 Local Government Act, which radically reformed the subsidy system in order to allow local authorities greater freedom to allocate

[1] Briggs, p. 343.

their resources. Yet in the absence of major changes in the local taxation system, and given the persistence of other central influences and controls, this Act did little to strengthen local authorities' real independence.

As a large and prosperous city with vigorous industries, Birmingham found itself particularly restricted by central Government policies during the years 1939–70. In this chapter, therefore, we shall first of all examine the balance of power between Birmingham and Westminster in order to define the sphere of influence of local municipal politics. Within this framework we shall study the roles and motivations of Birmingham politicians, parties, and pressure groups. We shall see that changes in the extent of local authority initiative are not without influence on the nature of the political process within Birmingham. Another important influence on that process is a movement of public opinion away from the communalist ideals of wartime towards materialism and individualism. This movement appears to be associated with the steady growth in the prosperity of most sections of the Birmingham community from the early 1950s. Its major effect on the City Council is to restore the pursuit of economy to the position which it had so often held before 1939, as one of the major guiding principles of municipal affairs.

Birmingham and the central Government

In 1939 the body most directly responsible for the well-being of Birmingham was still, clearly, the City Council. The Council had originated at the incorporation of the Borough of Birmingham in 1838, and subsequently had absorbed the functions of a number of other local administrative bodies, among them the improvement commissioners, the poor law guardians, and the school board. It had also extended its geographical area of control by a series of boundary extensions which greatly multiplied the extent of the original borough. But Birmingham never became a city-state; indeed, the growth in the powers and functions of the Council reduced rather than increased its independence from the central Government.[1] In order to achieve a uniform standard of local government provision throughout the country, the Government encouraged municipal authorities to assume all administrative functions within their boundaries, thus creating a situation in which central control was easier to exercise. This uniformity did not become a major feature of central Government policy until the later nineteenth century, but thereafter, and especially after the upheaval of 1914–18, much progress was made towards its realization.

Central control could be exercised in three major ways. In certain cases Parliament could pass legislation directing local authorities to

[1] See W. J. M. Mackenzie and J. W. Grove, *Central Administration in Britain* (1957), pp. 404–5.

pursue a particular course of action, or to refrain from certain activities; but a more subtle method was to provide subsidies for local government services. Not only did the offer of a specific subsidy ensure, in almost every case, that the service envisaged by the Government was established, but the financial contribution allowed the central Government to influence the local running of the service. This influence, at first vague and ill-defined, gradually developed into a series of tight controls of local standards, practice, and expenditure. Local authorities usually resented the interference, but welcomed the financial contribution.[1] Birmingham was no exception. Like other local authorities, its major source of revenue was the taxation of built property, a system which dated, in its modern form, from the early nineteenth century. The tax was easy to assess and collect, but it was not an effective way of ensuring that a steady proportion of the wealth generated in an area was diverted into the local coffers. It was a regressive tax; that is to say, it fell most heavily on those who were least able to pay it.[2] Moreover, the evolution of the taxable (rateable) value of built property did not directly reflect changes in the wealth of the area, so that the rate of taxation in inflationary conditions had normally to be increased each year. Opposition to such increases could be very great, especially as many occupiers of property, who were liable to pay the rates, often did not share fully in general increases in the wealth of the area. Only the central Government could have remedied this situation, by reforming local taxation, but it chose to help only by increasing its subsidies, thus further restricting local authority independence.[3] In Birmingham, City councillors liked to believe that the size of their city gave it more independence from the central Government than smaller authorities enjoyed, but this view was largely chimerical. No local authority, however large, could escape the erosion of its freedom of action through the combined effects of statutory limitations, central financial support, and administrative controls. From the Government's point of view the bigger the local authority, the more important that it should conform to the national pattern.

[1] J. M. Drummond, *The Finance of Local Government: England and Wales* (rev. ed., W. A. C. Kitching, 1962), p. 22.

[2] See H. V. Wiseman, *Local Government in England 1958–69* (1970), p. 158.

[3] It is only fair to point out that the traditionally accepted picture of a decline in local independence linked to the growth of central grants and controls was being questioned in the early 1970s, notably by Noel Boaden in his *Urban Policy-Making* (1971), see esp. pp. xiii, xiv. However, support for the contention that payment of grant leads to more central control was still overwhelming, particularly among those with direct experience of local financial administration. See e.g. A. H. Marshall (former City Treasurer of Coventry), *Financial Administration in Local Government* (1960), pp. 15–16; International Union of Local Authorities, *Local Authorities and Culture: The Role of Local Authorities in Adult Education* (1956), p. 19; N. P. Hepworth (Assistant City Treasurer of Manchester), *The Finance of Local Government* (1970), esp. p. 14.

In 1939 Birmingham was already heavily dependent on the Government for financial support.[1] Government grants as a proportion of the Corporation's overall turnover were quite small, but it would be misleading to consider turnover alone. The Corporation's trading activities —housing, agriculture, gas, electricity, transport, and water—all had extensive revenues derived from service charges, but all except housing were completely self-contained, receiving little or no income from the rates and making no contribution to the rate fund. Leaving the trading departments on one side, we find that in the last full year before the war, 1938–9, the total of Government grants towards non-trading activities equalled just over half the City's income from the rates. Even when non-trading charges and general income are added to the rate fund total, Government grants still amounted to nearly one-third of the Corporation's overall revenues (excluding trading undertakings).

Nearly half (45·7 per cent)[2] of the funds provided by the Government took the form of specific grants—contributions to the cost of individual services calculated on a percentage basis. The services most dependent on Government financial support in 1939 were air raid precautions, elementary and higher education, and police. All of these, together with housing, obtained about one-half of their revenues from the central Government. Nevertheless, the City Council still enjoyed considerable independence of action, compared to the position in which it was to find itself after 1945. The proportion of its total income contributed by the Government had risen only slowly since 1918, and the great majority of the Corporation's services received only a minor Government contribution, or no contribution at all. The Corporation's financial position, like that of other local authorities, had been weakened by the Local Government Act of 1929, which in the hope of reviving the economy had exempted 75 per cent of the value of industrial and commercial premises from rate taxation, but some compensation was provided by the same Act in the form of a general, or 'block', grant. This grant varied from one authority to another according to expenditure and needs, and was not allocated to specific services.[3] In 1939 the block grant to Birmingham amounted to 14·7 per cent of the total cost of services financed from the rate fund. Moreover, the City Council still retained almost complete freedom to borrow for capital schemes.

The Corporation's independence was radically reduced during the

---

[1] Statistical information on Birmingham's finances is drawn or calculated from *General Statistics and Epitome of the City's Accounts*, unless otherwise stated.

[2] Excluding housing and other trading undertakings. If housing is included, the proportion of specific grants rises to 56·1 per cent.

[3] D. S. Lees, etc., *Local Expenditure and Exchequer Grants: A Research Study* (1956), pp. 4–5.

Second World War.[1] New burdens, such as civil defence, were placed on local authorities at a time when their rate income was stable or declining, owing to war damage and the high number of vacant properties. Consequently, the Government felt obliged to pay a very high proportion of the cost of these new services. Moreover, the emergency services had to be of the same standard everywhere, especially in the big cities, and the Government exercised a very stringent control over their establishment and operation. In some cases, municipal services were taken entirely out of local control in the interests of national security, so that they could be more effectively organized. Tight control was established, too, over capital schemes to prevent local authorities from allocating finance, men, and materials to projects that were unnecessary for the war effort. Emergency Government powers to direct labour and control supplies of materials had a similar effect. Local government staffs were in many cases reduced by order of the central Government, and unnecessary services and activities were abandoned.

The reduction of services and the abandonment of most capital schemes greatly reduced the burden on local finances. Large sums were spent on the emergency services, but because they were financed principally out of Government funds, the amounts spent on them from rate revenue were, at least in the later years of the war, normally less than the savings made on other services. In Birmingham, the City Council found itself able to build up unaccustomed surpluses. Much of these sums was used to redeem stock and to build up balances, but the Council was not legally able to make use of all the money, since it had no powers to set up a reserve capital fund.[2] So in 1943 it decided to reduce the rate poundage. Consequently, by the end of the war income from Government grants was almost as high as that from the rates, and in 1944–5 these grants made up 37·98 per cent of the total revenue of the Corporation, excluding trading undertakings. Although Government grants were reduced overall in the last two years of the war, mainly owing to a big fall in civil defence expenditure, they continued to make up a much higher proportion of the Corporation's revenue than before the war. The excess of total rate revenue over total grants increased between 1944 and 1948, but then it fell again, and from 1951 to 1956 income from grants actually exceeded rate revenue. Although rate income again overtook the total of Government grants from 1957, the total obtained from the rates in the later 1960s was still only about one-sixth higher than the sum of Government grants. And the gap

[1] See [West Midland Group], *Local Government and Central Control* (1956), pp. 1–6.
[2] B.C.C., *Pro.*, 14 March 1944, p. 166 (Finance Committee). Powers to establish a capital fund were not obtained until after the war, by the Corporation Act of 1946.

between them was again narrowing owing to reforms in the subsidy structure under the Local Government Act 1966.[1]

Although the high proportion of Government grants during and after the war clearly restricted local autonomy,[2] it is important not to exaggerate its effects. The Government hesitated, once parity between rate and grant income had been established, to increase the proportion of grants still more, for the advantages of such a step in terms of control were likely to be offset by a reduced local awareness of the need for economy.[3] In any case, post-war governments were prepared to use more direct means of control.[4] The first post-war Labour Government maintained the firm direction of municipal borrowing and spending on capital account that had been established during the war,[5] and controls over materials and labour continued to restrict the activities of most local departments. Minimum standards of service were imposed by the Government in more and more cases.[6] When the central Government began to allow bigger expenditure on capital schemes in the late 1940s and early 1950s, it laid down rigid cost standards to safeguard the larger contribution that it was now making to many of these projects. And the services on which the major part of this capital outlay was authorized, housing and education, were in fact functions in respect of which the central Government had *chosen* the local authorities to act as the agents of an integrated national policy.[7] Furthermore, certain services and undertakings were incorporated into national structures;

---

[1] H. V. Wiseman, *Local Government in England 1958–69* (1970), p. 163; Hepworth, *Finance of Local Government*, pp. 98 ff.

[2] For figures showing that British local authorities derive a generally lower proportion of their income from local sources than those of other countries, see International Union of Local Authorities, *Local Government Finance and its Importance for Local Autonomy* (1955), pp. 16–19.

[3] See Lees, etc., *Local Expenditure*, pp. 282–3. The proportion of local authority expenditure met by Government grants had risen from 28·9 per cent in 1938 to 40·6 per cent in 1952, but it then stabilized, and by 1963 it had fallen back slightly to 39·9 per cent (Committee of Inquiry into the Impact of Rates on Households (Allen Committee), *Report* (Cmd. 2582, 1965), p. 18). It rose again, however, from 1967.

[4] For detailed descriptions of the relations between Government departments and local authorities, which reveal the Government's marked eagerness to intervene in local affairs, see Sir Gilmour Jenkins, *The Ministry of Transport and Civil Aviation* (1959), esp. pp. 123–39; Evelyn Sharp, *The Ministry of Housing and Local Government* (1969), esp. pp. 24–38; Sir Frank Newsam, *The Home Office* (1954), pp. 35–79. For a general account of progress towards centralization after the war, see D. N. Chester, *Central and Local Government: Financial and Administrative Relations* (1951).

[5] For a discussion of the reasons for the strict control of local authority borrowing maintained by post-war Governments, see Institute of Municipal Treasurers and Accountants, *Local Authority Borrowing* (by N. Doodson, etc.) (1962), pp. 13–16. Without these controls, local authority capital investment would almost certainly have been substantially greater.

[6] Lees, etc., *Local Expenditure*, pp. 4–5.

[7] This point is made in Jean-Pierre Martin, *Les finances publiques britanniques 1939–1955* (1956), pp. 115–57.

and Birmingham, with its massive trading departments, was affected more than most local authorities by these changes. Electricity and gas production were nationalized in 1948 and 1949, and a big non-trading service, that of hospitals, was incorporated into the National Health Service in 1948, together with a number of other health and welfare services. Some consolation was afforded by the return of the fire brigade to municipal control in the same year. Yet in this and other cases where the Birmingham City Council took on, or resumed, an additional duty, it and other local authorities nearly always fell into greater dependence on the Government by demanding specific subsidies to help them carry the extra burden. The Birmingham Fire Brigade, for instance, had received a specific Government grant of 0·33 per cent of its net expenditure in the last full year of peace, 1938–9. In the first year in which it was back in the hands of the Corporation, 1948–9, it received a grant of 10·95 per cent, and the Government's contribution eventually stabilized at 25 per cent of net expenditure. In addition, new grants were instituted after the war for the local health service and the children's service, calculated on a basis of 50 per cent of net expenditure.[1] Consequently, the total of specific grants was even higher than during the war; in 1948–9 they accounted for 38·78 per cent of the total cost of rate fund services, compared to 35·22 per cent in 1944–5, and 25·34 per cent in 1938–9.

As we have seen, the Local Government Act of 1929 attempted, with some success, to increase the Government contribution to authorities in accordance with their needs. It was recognized subsequently, however, that a further contribution should be made to authorities with limited rate resources.[2] This step was taken by the Local Government Act of 1948, which replaced the old block grant by an Exchequer equalization grant, designed to help county and county borough councils whose rateable value was below the national average. During the first full year of this new arrangement, Birmingham received less in grants than in the last year of the old system (£945,183 instead of £1,327,966).[3]

[1] Black, p. 129.

[2] See J. R. Hicks and U. K. Hicks, *Standards of Local Expenditure: A Problem of the Inequality of Income* (1943), esp. pp. 47 ff. This study showed that rich areas tended to spend more than poor ones, because they could do so without imposing a crushing rate poundage burden on the ratepayers.

[3] But Birmingham received rather more in Exchequer equalization grant than many cities, because its rateable value per head of weighted population was relatively low. Nottingham, Sheffield, Leeds, Manchester, and Liverpool all had average rateable values higher than Birmingham's (Lees, etc., *Local Expenditure*, pp. 292–3). See also Inst. of Mun. Treasurers and Accountants, *The Effects of the Local Government Act, 1948, and Other Recent Legislation on the Finances of Local Authorities* (1949), pp. 18–21. For an explanation of the failure of rateable values to reflect Birmingham's prosperity in the 1930s and 1940s, see J. R. Hicks and U. K. Hicks, *The Incidence of Local Rates in Great Britain* (1945), p. 21.

However, Birmingham achieved an overall saving because the new grant was introduced at the same time as hospital and public assistance services were transferred to the State.[1] On the other hand, the old block grant had included some degree of compensation for losses incurred as a result of industrial derating, whereas the new grant did not. A further blow dealt by the 1948 Act was the abolition of the rating of nationalized railway, canal, and electricity hereditaments. Although an annual Government grant was made in lieu of these rates, it was calculated on the basis of the total rateable value of each area, and bore no relation to the actual loss sustained by individual authorities.[2] Birmingham, with its big concentration of these hereditaments, lost on the exchange.

The effect of these reforms was to produce a greater equality of expenditure among local authorities.[3] But there remained slight flaws in the system. Firstly, it was generally agreed that still more account should be taken of the differing needs of local authorities.[4] It was also recognized that local authorities were becoming too dependent on the central Government, and that, in particular, they were not being encouraged sufficiently to plan ahead. The next important step towards remedying these defects was taken in 1958. The Local Government Act of that year replaced the Exchequer equalization grant by a rate deficiency grant related solely to the average rate product of local authorities per head of population.[5] It also introduced a new general grant, which was intended to raise the proportion of general grants-in-aid from less than one-sixth to nearly two-thirds of the total of Government grants to local authorities. The general grant was to be fixed in advance for a short period of years, thus encouraging local authorities to prepare forward estimates of expenditure. A number of important specific grants were discontinued, including those to most education services, local health services, and the fire brigade. As a further step towards encouraging local autonomy, the derating of industrial and freight transport hereditaments was reduced from 75 per cent to 50 per cent, and in 1961 it was abolished completely.[6]

The abolition of industrial derating was welcomed in Birmingham. Its effect, when combined with that of the progressive re-evaluation of domestic properties, was to make Birmingham's rateable value per head of population as high as, or higher than, that of other large cities. As a result, Birmingham did not qualify for rate deficiency grant under the new Act. So the 1958 Act's overall effect was to reduce slightly the proportion of municipal income provided by the central Government.

[1] Black, pp. 129–30.   [2] Black, p. 146.
[3] Lees, etc., Local Expenditure, p. 284.   [4] Lees, p. 285.
[5] See J. M. Drummond, The Finance of Local Government (rev. ed., 1962), pp. 112–15.
[6] Drummond, pp. 115–19.

Alderman Francis (later, Sir Francis) Griffin

Alderman Harry Watton (right) and Richard Crossman, Minister of Housing, at the official inauguration of the Druid's Heath Estate in 1965. Crossman's decision to allow Birmingham to build outside the boundary, at Chelmsley Wood, was crucial to the City's spectacular housing performance in the later 1960s.

Moreover, the abolition of most specific grants gave the City Council greater freedom in the allocation of resources to municipal departments. In 1961 Birmingham was one of the first authorities in the country to set up a Priorities Committee to plan capital expenditure, and after a few years the new committee extended its activities to the planning of outlay on revenue account.

These were important reforms, but they strengthened Birmingham's autonomy only marginally. Government controls of capital investment, which was a major determinant of the development of local services, remained in force. So did the numerous departmental controls. More important still, in the absence of a complete reform of local taxation, the new grant structure could not fail to put greater pressure on the rates, and strengthen the hand of those who favoured economies of municipal expenditure.[1] Indeed, the City Council had opposed the new system before it became law, on the ground that the abolition of specific grants would hamper the development of the social services, especially education.[2] It is significant that during the early years of the new grant system pressure for stabilization of the rate poundage was stronger than ever in Birmingham, and there are signs that expenditure on some services, particularly education, had to be restrained.[3] On the other hand, central controls and local pressures did not prevent Birmingham's civic outlay from rising appreciably, in step with other authorities, during the 1960s.[4] The Local Government Act 1966 took some of the pressure off the domestic ratepayer by incorporating a domestic rate relief element into the grant structure, and economy faded slightly as a political issue in Birmingham in the later 1960s. Inevitably, however, the effect of this new grant was again to increase the proportion of Birmingham's revenues provided by the central Government. This was an ominous trend in view of the Government's intention, declared in the 1966 Act, to control the inflation of local government outlay by relating grants to 'a desirable level of local expenditure'.[5]

The extension of direct and indirect central Government control over the Corporation's administrative activities did not mean that the functions carried out by the City were restricted; on the contrary, in many cases they were increased at the Government's design. As long as local authorities could be made to act consistently, they were the most suitable agents for a wide range of governmental functions.[6] So

[1] See Wiseman, *Local Government*, p. 166.
[2] B.C.C., *Pro.*, 8 October 1957, pp. 402–13 (Finance Committee).
[3] See below, pp. 358–61.
[4] See A. E. Holmans, 'The role of local authorities in the growth of public expenditure in the United Kingdom', in A. Cairncross (ed.), *The Managed Economy* (1970), pp. 154–5.
[5] Wiseman, *Local Government*, pp. 166–7.   [6] See ibid., pp. 3–7.

F

Government-inspired extensions of the City's administrative responsibilities did little to increase its independence from Westminster. However, the Corporation also had the opportunity to
extend its powers and functions on its own initiative, by obtaining
special legislation. Before 1939 the City Council had made frequent
use of this facility, which, especially in the nineteenth century,
had allowed it to build up the Birmingham Corporation into one
of the most powerful in the country. In contrast to Government-
imposed duties, the powers obtained by special legislation frequently
extended the Corporation's independence and initiative, for Whitehall
had little reason to interfere in administrative processes that were
unique to Birmingham.

After the war several more Corporation Bills were presented to
Parliament, and in some cases the City Council sought to obtain
powers which would have substantially increased the authority of the
Corporation, especially in respect of control of property and the extension of trading activities. However, the Council came up against serious
obstacles.[1] Even within Birmingham opinion was no longer unanimous
that a powerful Corporation was desirable. Before the war the massive
Unionist majority in the Council had begun to have doubts about the
principle of municipalization, on which so many of the Council's
decisions had been based since the time of Joseph Chamberlain. During
the war, however, they set these doubts aside for a time, and by 1945
they seemed to be very much in harmony with the thinking of the
Labour minority, which had always wanted to see much greater
municipal control over the city's life. Consequently, the two parties
were almost completely united during the mid and later 1940s in the
promotion of public works and slum clearance schemes, which involved
a larger step towards municipalization than any that had been taken
since the 1870s. But this agreement began to fade away after the war,
and in the 1950s the Conservatives, now reduced to a minority in the
City Council, began to campaign against some of the further extensions
of powers desired by Labour. Now although only a simple majority was
needed in the Council to approve the propriety of promoting a Corporation Bill, it was always preferable to obtain unanimity, with a view to
convincing Parliament that the requested powers were desired by *all*
interests in the locality. Unanimity was especially important in the
1950s and early 1960s, when a Conservative-dominated House of
Commons and House of Lords could be expected to look critically at
proposals which did not have the approval of Birmingham Conservatives.

[1] For a general account of the difficulties faced by local authorities in extending
their powers, see J. G. Bulpitt, *Party Politics in English Local Government* (1967), pp. 1–20.
The courts' tendency to pronounce against local authorities in *ultra vires* cases is
examined in R. M. Jackson, *The Machinery of Local Government* (1959), pp. 234–5;
C. A. Cross, *Principles of Local Government Law* (1966), pp. 6–17.

In some cases, it is true, clauses were inserted in Corporation Bills after being approved by majority votes, but the odds were so strongly against their being incorporated in legislation that the Labour group nearly always tried to reach some agreement with the Conservatives. Such compromises nearly always weakened the powers applied for.

Even with the approval of the minority group in the City Council, Corporation Bill clauses faced an obstacle course which frequently brought them down before they reached the House of Commons. They had to be approved by a town's meeting of electors, after which one hundred signatures sufficed to demand a poll of the whole electorate which could reverse a decision of the town's meeting. Obviously, a minority group in the City Council had a good chance of packing the meeting with its supporters, and of campaigning successfully to have a disputed clause rejected again at the poll. But so low were the usual attendances at meetings, and turnouts at polls, that outside pressure groups were frequently able to have clauses rejected even when the Council was united in their support. In the 1950s the most effective of these pressure groups was the Birmingham Ratepayers' Alliance, led by a local businessman and, later, estate agent, Gregory Prescott.[1] This organization was much more strongly opposed than most Conservative council members to extensions of municipal powers, and it was successful in having a number of clauses struck out of Bills which the Conservatives had approved. Consequently, many more clauses were rejected or substantially modified locally than were turned down by Parliament—with a few notable exceptions,[2] only the more innocuous and technical clauses normally reached Westminster.

So restrictive was this procedure on the Corporation that the City Council took a national lead in the early 1950s in trying to persuade Parliament to abolish it. In July 1953 the Town Clerk was asked to raise the question at the next meeting of the Law Committee of the Association of Municipal Corporations, of which he was a member. The committee agreed that a change in procedure was necessary, especially in relation to town's meetings and polls. In May 1954 a joint committee of the Lords and Commons was set up to study the matter, partly as a result of the efforts in the House of Commons of the Labour M.P. for Yardley, Henry Usborne, and George Wigg, Labour M.P. for nearby Dudley.[3] After hearing evidence from a number of authorities, including Birmingham, the joint committee reported in May 1955 in favour of abolishing town's meetings and polls. Shortly

[1] Prescott's biggest success was to force the Corporation to suspend its free travel scheme for old-age pensioners in the early 1950s, by obtaining a court ruling that the scheme was *ultra vires*. See H. C. Swaisland, 'Birmingham', in W. A. Robson and D. E. Regan (eds.), *Great Cities of the World* (1972), p. 209.

[2] e.g. see below, p. 68.

[3] *H. of C. Deb.*, 5th series, vol. dcii, col. *781*, 4 March 1959.

before, Woodrow Wyatt, a former Birmingham M.P., had introduced a Town Polls Bill to achieve much of what the City Council wanted, but it was dropped at the dissolution of Parliament later in the year.[1] Despite the joint committee's recommendation, the Government showed no sign of being prepared to give time to a Bill on town's meetings and polls in the new Parliament. The Corporation urged the Birmingham M.P.s to deal with the matter by a Private Member's Bill, but for four years none of them was successful in ballots for the right to lay such a Bill before the House of Commons. Wing-Commander Eric Bullus, M.P. for Wembley North, was able to introduce such a Bill in February 1957, but it did not go beyond its second reading. It was not until March 1959 that Henry Usborne drew a winning ticket in the ballot. With the support of several other Birmingham Labour M.P.s, he moved a resolution to abolish town's meetings and polls on 20 March 1959, but it was talked out after a long filibuster by a Birmingham Conservative M.P. and former City councillor, Harold Gurden.[2] Gurden's intervention must have led the whole House to ponder on how far some sections of Birmingham Conservatism had deserted the Chamberlainite tradition. This was the last serious attempt to push a Bill through on this subject, and in 1970 Corporation Bills still had to obtain approval from a town's meeting and, if required, a poll. In the 1960s, however, the matter was of less moment, because the Labour majority virtually ceased its attempts to extend the Corporation's powers in the areas that had been contested in the previous decade by the Conservatives or by outside interests. And the Conservatives, in power from 1966, did not reverse their previous attitude on these matters.

Despite its defects, the Corporation Bill procedure allowed the City Council to extend its powers significantly in a few important areas. Most of these new powers were not as damaging to property and business interests as those that were strongly opposed and usually rejected in the 1950s. In some of these cases Birmingham's example resulted in the passing of national legislation to make the powers available to all local authorities. Among them were the management of slum houses until their demolition, the operation of a free-travel scheme for old people, the establishment of smokeless zones, and the control of multi-occupation. When related to the whole range of the Corporation's activities, these extensions of powers might appear minor, but in view of the difficulty in obtaining *any* new powers not previously envisaged by the central Government, they were an extremely important achievement. In all these cases in which Birmingham was able to take the lead, however, the city's political parties were in agreement, and a great

[1] B.C.C., *Pro.*, 6 November 1956, pp. 462–4 (General Purposes Committee).
[2] *H. of C. Deb.*, 5th series, vol. dcii, cols. 771–837, 20 March 1959.

preponderance of opinion within the city supported the proposals. Such extensions of powers could be based only on a consensus.

In addition to its loss of some functions and much initiative to the central Government, Birmingham found it more difficult after 1939 to act independently of other local authorities in the West Midlands. Here again, the central Government occasionally intervened, to encourage inter-authority cooperation and, in some cases, to set up regional institutions.[1]

Although the organization of local government into regions was first suggested by the Fabian Society, in 1905, Westminster took no positive steps in this direction until Britain was divided into twelve civil defence regions just before the Second World War.[2] These regional organizations were much criticized by local authorities, including Birmingham, and although some of the Royal Commissions and study committees set up during the war favoured the retention of some form of regional body, at least for planning, practically nothing was done after the war to this effect. The Government shied away from local government reform,[3] which would almost certainly have involved some form of regional organization, and left it to local authorities to make their own arrangements when they needed to cooperate on a regional basis. Such arrangements, however, were often unsatisfactory, and from the mid-1960s the Government began more actively to encourage regional economic planning, and the organization of some local government functions into regional units.

In 1964, the Labour Government divided the country into economic planning regions. From the following year nominated councils of local politicians, administrators, experts, and representatives of a variety of interests, were set up to give advice on policies affecting each region. Many local authorities were worried by the establishment of these non-representative bodies, even though they had no executive powers, but the Government, convinced of their importance, indicated that it might eventually be possible to make them elective as part of a general reform of local government.

Birmingham was dragged along very unwillingly in this progress towards greater regional organization, at least until 1969. Although it had fully accepted before 1939 that its boundaries should not be extended much further, if at all, it considered that it was a large enough local government unit to operate effectively on its own. It told the

[1] See Brian C. Smith, *Regionalism in England* (1964), and *Regionalism in England: Its Nature and Purpose, 1905–65* (1965).

[2] F. E. Ian Hamilton, *Regional Economic Analysis in Britain and the Commonwealth: A Bibliographic Guide* (1969), pp. 9–11.

[3] See Arthur Marwick, *Britain in the Century of Total War: War, Peace and Social Change 1900–1967* (1968), pp. 397–401.

Barlow Commission in 1938 that it was totally separate in character
and interests from the rest of the West Midlands conurbation.[1] It had
more trouble than most city authorities with its regional civil defence
commissioner, Lord Dudley, and it resented the practical steps taken
during the war towards regional organization, such as the reform of the
fire service. Its objections were partly based, of course, on the unrepre-
sentative character of wartime regional organization,[2] and it was
prepared to participate in post-war regional planning as long as the
application of a national plan to the West Midlands was carried out by
a regional body representing local authorities.[3] A step in this direction
was taken in 1945 when the Midlands Joint Town Planning Advisory
Council, which had originally been set up in 1923, was reconstituted
as the Warwickshire, Worcestershire and South Staffordshire Advisory
Planning Council.[4] But, fundamentally, the City Council was worried
by the danger that Birmingham, the largest and most dynamic urban
unit in the West Midlands, might be held back in any regional organization by less forward-looking authorities.

This concern became very obvious after the war, when the first
practical steps were taken towards regional planning. When West
Midlands local authorities met in 1949 to consider the major proposals
of the regional plan drawn up by Sir Patrick Abercrombie, it became
clear that there were certain differences between them, and Birmingham
and the others agreed that it was 'neither necessary nor desirable' to
set up a single planning authority for the area, as Abercrombie had
proposed.[5] By now, the Government had lost interest in setting up
regional representative bodies, and the matter was allowed to drop.
In the 1950s Birmingham played a full part in the organizations set up
to try to make overspill policy work, but the difficulties encountered
here were an indication that the post-war atmosphere of cooperation
had largely been dispelled.[6] Negotiations were carried on with a
severely practical end in view, and the authorities involved were clearly
more concerned with the protection of their own interests than with the
rational and harmonious development of the region.

If Birmingham had been prepared to give a lead towards the establishment of a more positive form of regionalism, the other authorities
might perhaps have followed. On the other hand, they might have

[1] Royal Commission on the Distribution of the Industrial Population, *Memorandum
of Evidence Submitted by the Corporation of Birmingham*, para. 1.
[2] A council representing local authorities in the Midlands civil defence region had
been set up when the regional A.R.P. organization was established, but it was a
purely advisory body (B.C.C., *Pro.*, 6 June 1939, p. 608 (A.R.P. Committee)).
[3] B.C.C., *Pro.*, 9 March 1943, p. 268 (Public Works Committee).
[4] B.C.C., *Pro.*, 6 February 1945, p. 103 (Public Works Committee).
[5] B.C.C., *Pro.*, 26 July 1949, pp. 358–9 (Public Works Committee).
[6] See below, pp. 134 ff.

interpreted any such move by Birmingham as a threat to their independence. Birmingham Corporation, for its part, hesitated to put forward proposals or to criticize existing arrangements for fear of provoking Government-imposed changes which might restrict its independence and authority within the city area.[1] Some leading members of the City Council, such as Alderman Bowen, Alderman Bradbeer, and, in the 1960s, Alderman Sir Frank Price and Alderman Dark, were prepared to support regionalism in theory, and Birmingham participated willingly in regional bodies which were set up to achieve defined practical ends, such as the regional crime organization built up from the 1950s, and the regional sports council founded in 1965. But the City Council as a whole took a very unfavourable view of any reforms which might have threatened Birmingham's independence, or what was left of it. The two party groups were agreed on this point, and the Council was able to present a united front.

Whenever it was asked after the war to make proposals or to submit evidence to Government committees or commissions on local government, the Council's main priority was to defend the City's boundaries and administrative structure against any threatened change. In this aim it was almost entirely successful. The post-war local government boundary commission, which recommended in 1948 that local government units should be made larger, and that the administration of the conurbations should be unified, left Birmingham alone after receiving evidence from the Corporation claiming that the City was already a large and efficient unit. The commission recommended that Birmingham should be an all-purpose authority, under the title of 'county', and that the Black Country county boroughs should be united in another new 'county', to be called Stafford South. The City Council was pleased that the commission had accepted its submission that Birmingham was separate and distinct from the rest of the conurbation. In any case, it knew that the proposals would not be put into effect in the near future, and in fact they were soon pigeonholed and forgotten.[2]

There was no further threat to Birmingham's status until the late 1950s when a new local government commission was set up. One of the areas to which it directed close attention was the West Midlands conurbation, but Birmingham again made it clear that it was happy with its present status and area, and would resent any interference. The City Council was relieved to learn, when the Government's proposals for the reform of local government were announced in March 1958, that Birmingham would not be affected directly.[3] How-

[1] See also Swaisland, 'Birmingham', pp. 236-7.
[2] B.C.C., *Pro.*, 4 May 1948, pp. 493-4 (General Purposes Committee); Marwick, *Britain in the Century of Total War*, p. 398.
[3] B.C.C., *Pro.*, 11 March 1958, pp. 796-807 (General Purposes Committee).

ever, the situation was soon transformed by Birmingham's decision to apply for an extension of its boundaries.[1] This move destroyed the tacit understanding which had been built up since the war, that Birmingham would not interfere with other authorities, but in return would expect to be left alone. Nevertheless, the City Council refused to recognize that there had been any basic change in its position, and in March 1959 it approved a reply to the local government commission questionnaire (which had been sent to all interested authorities), stating its case for the boundary extension, but otherwise claiming that all was for the best in the best of all possible worlds. It maintained that there was no lack of coordination in the local government of the West Midlands special review area which would justify the establishment of a joint board. Moreover, it stated that Birmingham had no evidence that would justify any general reorganization of local government in the area.[2] A City Council deputation met the local government commission in June 1959 and explained its reply to the questionnaire, apparently with some effect, for the commission's proposals for the West Midlands special review area, published early in 1960, left Birmingham untouched except for a few minor boundary adjustments.

The commission's main proposal was to make Solihull a county borough, and to merge the numerous local authorities in the Black Country into five large county boroughs.[3] The only recommendations affecting Birmingham's independent position were for the establishment of a joint board to deal with overspill problems, representing Birmingham and the five Black Country authorities, and for the creation of a single drainage board for each of the two main drainage basins, the Tame and the upper Stour.[4] Nevertheless, the City Council decided to object to almost every proposal which appeared to limit Birmingham's freedom of action, or which took land or population away from the city. It submitted that no useful purpose would be served by setting up a joint overspill board as proposed, and (sensibly) urged that, if such a body were to be set up the county planning authorities should be included. Although it was prepared to support the establishment of a new Tame drainage board, the Council objected to its being vested with powers any greater than those of the existing board, which allowed the Corporation extensive, effective control over the provision of drainage and sewerage within the city.[5] On all these points, Birmingham

---

[1] See below, pp. 140 ff.

[2] B.C.C., *Pro.*, 17 March 1959, pp. 993–1033 (General Purposes Committee).

[3] The commission recognized that there was a good case for a general authority covering the whole conurbation, but could see no way of avoiding its domination by Birmingham (T. W. Freeman, *Geography and Regional Administration: England and Wales, 1830–1968* (1968), p. 133).

[4] B.C.C., *Pro.*, 5 April 1960, p. 875 (General Purposes Committee).

[5] B.C.C., *Pro.*, 10 May 1960, pp. 1015–18 (General Purposes Committee).

obtained almost complete satisfaction, and the General Purposes Committee was able to report to the Council in July 1961 that the final proposals were 'reasonably satisfactory so far as Birmingham is concerned'.[1] Proposed transfers of land in Perry Barr and Quinton to other authorities were dropped, the joint overspill board was never set up, and even the new drainage board was established in accordance with Birmingham's wishes. The minor boundary changes that were finally approved came into effect in April 1966.[2]

By this time, Birmingham was about to face another round of negotiations over its future. These were associated with the new Royal Commission on Local Government set up by the Labour Government. Again, Birmingham presented evidence, in 1967, claiming that all was well, and that Birmingham should be left alone. This time, however, its advice was not entirely heeded. The commission proposed in 1969 that the three big conurbations—Merseyside, Selnec (Manchester area), and the West Midlands conurbation—should be governed by single metropolitan area councils, some of whose functions would be devolved to district councils, of which there would be seven in the West Midlands conurbation. Birmingham, with the addition of Sutton Coldfield and Solihull, would form one of the district council areas, but its council's powers would be very similar to those currently enjoyed by the Birmingham City Council.[3]

Both groups in the City Council were at first worried that these reforms would deprive Birmingham of some of its powers and independence. By 1970, however, the Government had succeeded in dispelling the Corporation's doubts. It even seemed for a time that by the mid-1970s a greatly enlarged Birmingham would be playing the leading role in the government of the whole conurbation, while retaining within its wider boundaries most if not all of the independence which it currently enjoyed as a county borough. But this Utopian vision had faded by 1972, after the Government had yielded to rich suburbanites and excluded Solihull from the planned Birmingham boundary extensions.

So the City Council faced reorganization, planned for 1974, with much of the distrust which had characterized its attitude to local government reform ever since the war. Looking back, it might well have regretted that it had done so little to contribute positively to the elaboration of these new arrangements. On the other hand, it is significant that on no occasion since the war had the central Government

---

[1] B.C.C., *Pro.*, 25 July 1961, p. 262 (General Purposes Committee).

[2] B.C.C., *Pro.*, 1 February 1966, pp. 617–18 (General Purposes Committee).

[3] Royal Commission on Local Government in England 1966–9, *Report* (1969), vol. i, pp. 161–70. These proposals were substantially modified by the Conservative Government elected in 1970.

questioned Birmingham's size, and to this extent Birmingham was proved right in its defence of the *status quo*.

Size was important to Birmingham because it contributed substantially to that feeling of power and independence which helps to explain why the City Council did not recognize any need to band together with other urban authorities in the West Midlands. The city's great size almost certainly helped to make its municipal services more efficient, as the Government recognized.[1] But did it also help the Corporation to get its own way with the Government, as council members often claimed? In those cases where Birmingham obtained special legislation to deal with problems which were particularly serious in the city, the Government was clearly happy to stand back and let the Council of so large a city deal with those problems as it thought fit. But such occasions were few. So arduous and uncertain was the process of obtaining special legislation that the City Council more frequently tried to establish its independence by claiming special exemptions and privileges from Government departments. Owing to the close central control which had been established over many municipal departments, the argument that Birmingham deserved special treatment because of its size and importance to the national economy had to be used very frequently, and it became somewhat threadbare. It would seem that in many cases Birmingham was able to have its own way more easily than would have been possible for a smaller authority,[2] but most of the time it did not get its own way at all, as later pages of this volume will make abundantly clear.[3] Sometimes size was a distinct handicap, when any concession made to Britain's largest provincial city would have been seized upon as a precedent by many smaller towns. It was partly for this reason that, for instance, the Government was so obdurate in its defence of the green belt against inroads by Birmingham in the later 1950s and early 1960s.

[1] The view that great size is generally associated with high quality of services has occasionally been questioned, but evidence collected so far is not conclusive. See e.g. Bleddyn Davies, 'Local authority size: some associations with standards of performance of services for deprived children and old people', *Public Administration*, vol. xlvii, summer 1969, pp. 225–48. Birmingham's specific claim that its great size helped it to provide efficient services was never questioned by academics or administrators.

[2] Mackenzie and Grove, *Central Administration*, p. 405.

[3] On the other hand, the Association of Municipal Corporations, to which Birmingham belonged, was frequently able to have its way over general issues affecting its members. Indeed, its strength and that of its sister organization, the County Councils' Association, have been held partly responsible for the Government's failure to reform local government after the war. See S. E. Finer, *Anonymous Empire: A Study of the Lobby in Great Britain* (rev. ed., 1966), pp. 38, 132–3; also J. D. Stewart, *British Pressure Groups: Their Role in Relation to the House of Commons* (1958). For a (superficial) argument of the case that big cities normally get their own way with the central Government, see Bruce Miller, 'Citadels of local power', *Twentieth Century*, vol. clxii, July–December 1957, pp. 325–30.

Some of the Birmingham M.P.s did their best to even up the odds in struggles between the Corporation and the Government. They frequently interceded with ministers, raised local matters in the House, and accompanied municipal delegations. The Labour M.P.s, in particular, devoted much time to this work. Nevertheless, the influence of backbenchers was minimal, and few Birmingham M.P.s rose to ministerial positions where they had real power to favour their city. Even those who did achieve high office were always careful not to show undue favour towards the city, which, when all was said and done, housed only one-fiftieth of the population of the United Kingdom.[1] So although Birmingham council members had every reason to be proud of their city's great size, importance, and reputation in so many fields of municipal government, those qualities did not significantly weaken Westminster's tight hold over Birmingham's destinies.

The Birmingham political parties

The Corporation's declining independence and initiative substantially altered the character of Birmingham municipal politics. In particular, national influences on voting grew at the expense of local factors. However, the peculiarities of the municipal electoral system ensured that national voting trends were not always reflected by relative party strengths in the City Council.

One-third of the Birmingham City Council was composed of aldermen, elected by the Council for a six-year term. The other two-thirds was made up of councillors directly elected by the citizens. Each ward of the city returned three councillors, only one of whom came up for re-election at the annual municipal elections. In other words, it took three years to elect the whole councillor body. Similarly, only one alderman in six faced re-election by the Council in each year, so that it took six years to elect the entire body of aldermen. By a gentlemen's agreement, the parties normally did their best to see that their respective strengths in aldermen were proportional to the numbers of their councillors, but because so few aldermen came up for re-election it was not always possible to achieve this balance in a given year. In consequence of the stability which this system conferred on the City Council, party strengths within it were not immediately responsive to swings in municipal voting.

This unresponsiveness to the expressed preferences of the electorate was by no means an undesirable feature, for voting swings in the annual

[1] For an account of the (mostly vain) attempts of Birmingham M.P.s to influence the policies of Government departments in favour of the Corporation, see Anthony Sutcliffe, 'The British Member of Parliament and local issues', *The Parliamentarian*, vol. li, no. 2, April 1970, pp. 87–95. The Birmingham Conservative Party's growing preference for local candidates in the 1950s is examined in Peter Paterson, *The Selectorate: The Case for Primary Elections in Britain* (1967), pp. 67–9.

city elections were usually much more violent than in the less frequent
parliamentary polls. Turnouts were very low, and many of those who
used their votes did so more to express their opinion of the Government
of the day than to record a positive preference for a municipal party.
These trends in municipal voting, as we shall see, tended to become
more pronounced as our period wore on, with lower polls, more violent
swings, and greater conformity of local voting to the national pattern.
Owing to the peculiarities of municipal voting, the best indication
of the strength of a party's support in Birmingham is provided by the
percentage of the total poll which it obtains at a general election. Its
performance in municipal elections will usually oscillate around this
percentage.

During the inter-war years Birmingham was virtually dominated by
the Unionist Party, which had grown up on the basis of a partnership
between the Birmingham Conservatives and the Liberal-Unionists
who had followed Joseph Chamberlain after his split with Gladstone
in 1886. By the end of the First World War the Birmingham Unionists
had become an almost completely homogeneous political grouping,
indistinguishable on nearly all points of policy from the national
Conservative Party. At a municipal level, however, the Unionists
retained much of the progressive outlook of their Liberal forebears;
indeed, they were to claim with some pride after the Second World War
that Birmingham had been the most 'socialist' of the Conservative
local authorities.[1]

Progressive municipal policies alone would not have been enough to
keep the Unionists in power in the City Council and to keep their
M.P.s at Westminster, but the Unionists had other factors in their
favour. Thanks to the development of modern engineering and vehicle
assembly industries from the end of the nineteenth century, Birmingham
was more prosperous between the wars than most other large cities.
Even in the 1930s its unemployment rates were low. Living conditions,
too, were more satisfactory, despite the existence of thousands of
slums, than in the northern industrial cities.[2] Trade union membership
was restricted. Birmingham's older industries were often carried on in
very small units in which unionism could not normally flourish, whereas
the new engineering and assembly industries which made up an
increasing proportion of Birmingham's industrial activity were nowhere
highly unionized. Because the city covered such a large area, many
middle-class districts lay within its boundaries and the parliamentary
divisions were arranged in such a way that there was a strong middle-

[1] Unionist local election leaflets.
[2] In the 1935 general election Birmingham Unionist candidates attempted to make
political capital out of the relative good fortune of industry in the city (L. S. Amery,
My Political Life, vol. iii (1955), p. 181).

class vote in nearly all of them. A positive point in the Unionist Party's favour was that several Birmingham M.P.s, such as Austen Chamberlain, L. C. S. Amery, and Neville Chamberlain came to hold key Cabinet posts. Moreover, owing to the events of previous decades the position of the Liberal Party was very weak in Birmingham, and many of its former supporters voted for the Unionists.

Nevertheless, despite the strongly entrenched position of the Unionists, the Labour Party had begun to challenge them effectively in the 1920s. Labour candidates had been successful in municipal elections before the First World War.[1] In the general election of 1906 the Labour candidate in the Birmingham East division, Jasper Holmes, came within a few hundred votes of unseating the Unionist member, and Labour also did well in Bordesley. However, Labour support was severely cut in the first general election of 1910 when their candidates stood again in these two divisions, and they did not contest either in the new election at the end of the year. Nevertheless, Labour strength in the City Council increased from 1911 until the war, and owing to the growth of trade unionism in the munitions industries, Labour was in a much stronger position in Birmingham by the end of the war. In the general election of 1918 Labour candidates stood in seven out of twelve divisions, and obtained an average of 22·10 per cent of the poll in each contest. Although they obtained more votes than the Liberals, they failed to win any seats. However, Labour did not oppose a Coalition Labour candidate, E. Hallas, who was returned for Duddeston.

The 1920s saw a mounting tide of Labour success. In the general election of 1922 Labour obtained 30·96 per cent of the votes cast in Birmingham, and an average of 35·98 per cent in the eight seats they contested. Over the country as a whole Labour obtained a lower proportion of the total vote, 29·5 per cent. In the general election of the following year Labour maintained their position in Birmingham, with 30·34 per cent of the total poll, and 37·54 per cent in each seat contested. The Liberals, on the other hand, lost support badly and from now on they were nearly always to come bottom of the poll even in the few seats that they would dare to contest. The success of 1923 encouraged Labour to contest all the Birmingham seats in 1924, and they won 38·50 per cent of the total votes cast, compared to only 33 per cent, and 38·2 per cent of votes cast in seats contested by Labour, over the

---

[1] See Briggs, pp. 191–9. To achieve clarity in this brief survey, the appellation 'Labour' is used for a variety of candidates, including I.L.P., Co-operative, and Communist nominees, who represented the Birmingham labour movement in interwar parliamentary elections. The title 'Unionist' will normally be used for Unionists, Conservatives, Coalition Unionists, and National Unionists. In 1953 the Birmingham Unionists officially adopted the title 'Conservative', and after that date they will normally be referred to as such.

country as a whole. Only one seat, however, that of Kings Norton, was actually carried by Labour.

The Birmingham Labour movement did not really begin to batter down the gates of Unionism until 1929, when, strengthened by the events of the general strike and its aftermath, it again contested all twelve Birmingham seats, and won six of them. This time, Labour obtained 41·6 per cent of the votes cast in the city, which was again more than the national average of 37·1 per cent, and the average per contested seat of 39·3 per cent. Labour were helped by a strong Liberal intervention in eight constituencies, three of which were won by Labour, and by the extension of the franchise to young women. Clearly, too, the arrangement of the Birmingham parliamentary divisions, which previously had favoured the Unionists by splitting the large Labour vote into several constituencies where it could normally be outweighed by the Unionist support, had now backfired against them.

In view of the handicaps faced by Labour in Birmingham, they had put up a creditable performance, and by the late 1920s Birmingham was far from the Unionist stronghold which has since been enshrined in popular myth. Labour's strength in the City Council, which had to be built up slowly by dogged annual effort, lagged behind the parliamentary achievement, but by the end of the 1920s Labour members occupied nearly one-third of the seats. Now that the handicap inherent in the arrangement of constituencies had been overcome, and had in fact been converted into a positive advantage for Labour, it seemed that nothing could stop them. But they *were* stopped; in fact, two years after the triumph of 1929 they found themselves again with no parliamentary seats. In the general election of 1931 Labour candidates obtained only 26·7 per cent of the Birmingham poll, which was less than the national average of 30·6 per cent, and substantially less than the national average of votes cast for Labour candidates in seats contested by that party, 33 per cent.

Labour's failure in 1931 was partly the result of the high volatility of its support, which had been built up in the 1920s thanks to energetic work and the stimulating leadership of men like John Strachey and Oswald Mosley, but which did not have the same firm foundations as in more traditionally Labour areas. The depression and the formation of a National Government under Ramsay MacDonald had bitten deeply into many voters' new-found support for Labour. Trade union support, which had been very strong in the 1920s, now waned, not only owing to the depression, but also as a result of the effect of Ramsay MacDonald's actions on a Birmingham labour movement which was markedly left-wing. Moreover, circumstances had conspired against Labour to take away even that which they might have kept. The Liberals contested only one seat in 1931, leaving the Labour candidates to bear the full weight of the Unionist onslaught. And the arrangement of constituencies was once again to Labour's disadvantage, for despite the success of 1929, they had no strongholds in the city.

The election result added to the demoralization of the Birmingham labour movement, which reached its nadir in the first half of the 1930s.[1] Cooperation between the trade unions and the Labour Party was at a low ebb, and seats began to be lost in municipal elections. In the general election of 1935 Labour made a recovery in Birmingham, winning 34·5 per cent of the votes cast, compared to a national average of 37·9 per cent. This level of support was higher than Labour had enjoyed in the early 1920s, but it was not enough to win them back any seats; in the absence of a Liberal intervention they would have needed at least 45 per cent to do that. Nevertheless, the result was encouraging for Labour, and in the later 1930s their morale returned. Cooperation with the trade unions, whose membership was now expanding rapidly, was improved. Labour adopted a more aggressive attitude in municipal politics, which culminated in its overt support of the huge municipal rent strike in 1939, in association with the Communists and other sympathizers. However, Labour's representation in the City Council, which had been slow to reflect the drastic reduction in Labour support at the beginning of the decade, failed to follow the upturn in party fortunes in the later 1930s. In fact, seats continued to be lost until 1938, when the Labour group sank to a membership of twenty-two, about one-fifth of the Council.

Although Labour support was clearly building up again slowly in the later 1930s, the party would have been hard put to it to win any seats if a general election had been held in 1939 or 1940. At two by-elections in Birmingham divisions, in 1937 and 1939, strong Labour candidates had increased their percentage of the poll over 1935, but not enough to come anywhere near unseating their opponents. Moreover, in both cases the total of votes cast for Labour was the same as in 1935, and the sharp fall in the Unionist vote could be attributed to apathy among their supporters. In any case, the Unionist organization was far from apathetic; it retained the efficiency and enterprise which had once typified Joseph Chamberlain's Liberal caucus, and it enjoyed massive financial support from the Birmingham middle classes and industrial firms. Had it not been for the war, the Unionist position in Birmingham would certainly not have been eroded so easily.

To say that the Birmingham Unionist Party gave up the ghost during the war would be an exaggeration, but it certainly lost much of its spirit and confidence in itself. The resignation of Neville Chamberlain

[1] For an attempt to prove conclusively that the Birmingham working class was markedly less inclined to vote Labour in the 1930s than that of London, see John Bonham, *The Middle Class Vote* (1954), pp. 160–1.

from the premiership in 1940 left the Unionists in a position which they had not experienced for half a century, where none of their members held a leading position within the national Conservative Party. Neville's brother, Austen, had died in 1937; L. C. S. Amery and Geoffrey Lloyd held only minor office during the war. The other Birmingham M.P.s were completely in the background. Opposition to the Government's foreign policy had partly undermined Neville Chamberlain's position in Birmingham in the last months before the war, but the total discrediting of this aspect of his work by the early 1940s dealt a severe blow to the strength of his party in Birmingham.

The party also weakened itself after the electoral truce[1] had been established in 1939, by giving up all campaign work, and letting its organization run down.[2] Birmingham Unionists believed that everyone's energies should be devoted to winning the war; they certainly devoted theirs to that end, though, in view of their political hold over Birmingham, they could afford to do so. Labour, however, placed a different interpretation on the electoral truce.[3] At a municipal level the Birmingham Unionists moved a surprisingly long way towards the left in their policies and political attitudes during the war, and co-operated more closely with Labour members of the Council than they had normally done in the 1930s. The Birmingham M.P.s were less influenced by this wartime trend towards socialism, although even some of the more right-wing of their number, such as Walter Higgs and Patrick Hannon, expressed less reactionary views than before the war. This Unionist move to the left at first made it difficult in some respects to distinguish between Unionist and Labour, and so Labour may have gained in respectability in the eyes of uncommitted electors. This was a change from the 1930s, when Labour had seemed very much on the left wing in Birmingham politics. Furthermore, when the Conservative national leaders hesitated to give unqualified assurances towards the end of the war that they would introduce the major social reforms envisaged in official documents such as the Beveridge Report, the Unionists in Birmingham lost the ability to convince the electorate that they would pursue the reformist policies on which they and Labour had seemed to be agreed during the middle years of the war. This unfavourable impression was reinforced by some of the Birmingham M.P.s before the election of 1945, when they again expressed views which most citizens had come to regard as reactionary.

It would be wrong, however, to suggest that the cause of the Labour landslide in Birmingham after the war was an abdication by the

---

[1] See Black, pp. 104–5.
[2] See e.g. Birmingham Unionist Association, *A Bulletin* (28 October 1939) (B.R.L. 507769).
[3] See G. D. H. Cole, *A History of the Labour Party from 1914* (1948), p. 378.

R. E. (Dick) Etheridge, works convenor at Longbridge, addresses a meeting of Austin workers in September 1947.

Austin engine-assembly workers protest against short-time working at Longbridge in April 1970. In the background can be seen the giant multi-storey car park used to store completed vehicles.

Birmingham in the 1960s

Reproduced by permission of Geographers' A-Z Map Co. Ltd. Based upon the Ordnance Survey Map with the sanction of the Controller of H.M. Stationery Office. Crown Copyright reserved.

Unionists. The war years saw a massive extension of trade unionism in Birmingham industries, especially in engineering and vehicle assembly. More women worked in industry than ever before, and although a large proportion of them did not become union members, they were brought into closer contact with the labour movement.[1] Links between the unions and the Birmingham Borough Labour Party were greatly strengthened,[2] and plans were laid from the early years of the war for the eventual victory of socialism in peacetime. The Borough Labour Party, taking advantage of the common wartime desire for greater social justice, extended its canvassing, public meetings, and membership drives as soon as the worst raids were over. Party organization, guided first by Harry Wickham and later Jim Simmons, was greatly strengthened.[3] Several policy discussion groups brought together a number of men who were to be prominent in Labour post-war politics.[4]

From 1943 Labour began to campaign openly on issues which seemed likely to dominate the next general election, and the Labour group in the City Council began to raise issues of policy (many of which did not concern the Council) in order to publicize Labour policies, and to force the Unionists into taking an opposing stand. Even more important, however, than Labour organization and tactics was the fact that as a result of the war the division of opinion in the Birmingham electorate came to conform more closely to that of the whole country. Although Labour were not as weak in pre-war Birmingham as has sometimes been assumed, they were certainly weaker than in most industrial cities. During the war, however, trade union membership came to resemble more closely the national pattern, and with full employment everywhere Birmingham workers could no longer be so easily convinced by the Conservatives that they were significantly better off than those in other areas. In any case, the national swing to Labour during the war originated partly from working- and lower-middle-class prosperity, which the electorate wanted to see maintained, and Birmingham was one of the areas which enjoyed a high level of affluence as a result of inflated earnings in the munitions industries. In other respects, too,

[1] Greater political consciousness among Birmingham women was noted by Norman Tiptaft in *I Saw a City* (1945), p. 94.

[2] Birmingham's election liaison organization between the Labour Party and the trade unions, which was maintained after 1945, was almost unparalleled elsewhere (D. E. Butler, *The British General Election of 1955* (1956), p. 224).

[3] The best account of the organization and fortunes of the Borough Labour Party before and during the war is Robert Hastings, 'The Labour movement in Birmingham, 1927–1945' (Birmingham University M.A. thesis, 1959).

[4] For an account of the work of these groups, including the well-known 'Loonies', see *B.M.*, 25 January 1963; *B.W.P.*, 22 May 1959; Vivian Bird, *Portrait of Birmingham* (1970), pp. 173–4.

G

the war almost completely destroyed what was left of Birmingham particularism; the national press was read more avidly, and national radio programmes and cinema newsreels were heard and seen by more Birmingham people. The sensation of overwhelming danger in the first years of the war produced a common, national reaction which was never completely lost, and local loyalties and variations of public opinion were greatly attenuated. So in 1945 the Birmingham vote in the general election reflected national divisions more closely than on any previous occasion. Labour obtained 53 per cent of the poll in Birmingham compared to 47·8 per cent in the country as a whole, and the Unionists took 39 per cent (40 per cent in the whole country). The Liberals and the Communists were completely out of the picture in Birmingham and in most other areas.[1] In Birmingham, Labour won ten out of thirteen seats, for despite a change in constituency boundaries and an increase of one in the number of divisions, most of the city constituencies still contained a balance of working-class and middle-class districts.

After their success at the general election, it was inevitable that Labour would make sweeping gains in the municipal elections of November 1945, the first to be held for six years. This was one of the rare occasions on which more than one-third of the councillors came up for re-election. In addition to those who would have finished their three-year term of office in 1939, all those members who had been co-opted to fill vacancies during the war had to retire. A further factor in Labour's favour was the assimilation of the local government franchise to the parliamentary franchise, under the Representation of the People Act 1945. Previous to this Act, only householders and their spouses had been allowed to vote in local elections, a situation which gave a slight advantage to the Unionists, and partly accounted for their generally better performance in municipal than in parliamentary elections before the war. In Birmingham the Act added nearly 150,000 voters to the local government register, most of whom were lodgers or young unmarried people living at home. It can fairly be assumed that a majority of them were more favourably inclined to Labour than to the Unionists.

Although Labour did even better in the municipal than in the general election, obtaining 56·20 per cent of the votes cast, their thirty-seven gains were not enough to give them overall control of the City Council, and they had to agree to share the chairmanships of committees with the Unionists. But in the following year, although they polled fewer votes than in 1945, mainly owing to the electorate's early disillusionment with the new Labour Government, they won

[1] See R. B. McCallum and A. Readman, *The British General Election of 1945* (1947). The swing to Labour in Birmingham, 23 per cent, was much greater than in any other city, though London and Leeds both registered swings of over 17 per cent.

enough seats to take full control. They now took all committee chairmanships. Public opinion, however, continued to swing heavily against the Government, owing to the shortages and inconveniences involved in the transfer of the national economy on to a peacetime footing. While the Government could plan ahead and face short-term unpopularity with equanimity, Labour municipal parties had to bear the full brunt of the electorate's displeasure at annual elections. Moreover, because it would have required at least three years of brilliant electoral success to build up a big majority in the City Council, Labour were not in a strong position to repel such an assault. So when the Unionists obtained over 53 per cent of the poll in 1947, they deprived Labour of their overall majority, and once again took over the chairmanships of certain committees. There was no contest in the following year owing to the transfer of the municipal elections from November to May,[1] but in 1949 the Unionists, with 54·77 per cent of the poll, took overall control, which they held until May 1952.

Although the City elections always recorded much lower percentage polls than general elections,[2] and so generally produced very marked fluctuations in voting patterns, Labour support was clearly in decline in Birmingham in the later 1940s. But although the Unionists hoped that their successes in 1947 and 1949 indicated a return to the situation of the 1930s, they were disappointed. In fact, by the time of the general election in 1950, Birmingham had moved back towards Labour, whose candidates obtained 51·8 per cent of the poll, rather less than in 1945, but still more than the national Labour poll of 46·1 per cent. The Unionists did slightly better than in 1945, obtaining 42·6 per cent, at the expense of minority parties.[3] They also won a seat from Labour, partly as a result of major boundary changes in all but two of the Birmingham divisions in 1948. This gain gave them four out of thirteen Birmingham seats.

In 1950 the situation was complicated by the intervention of ten Liberal candidates. These Liberals had clearly taken most of their small total of votes from the Unionists, for in the general election of

[1] Under the Representation of the People Act 1948.

[2] See D. S. Morris and K. Newton, 'Turnout in local elections: Birmingham, 1945–1969', Birmingham University Faculty of Commerce discussion papers, series F, no. 8 (1970). Turnout in Birmingham has corresponded very closely to that in other large cities since the war, confirming the dominant influence of national factors on local elections. The decline of turnout since the late 1940s provides some support for the hypothesis that the local elector feels increasingly that council affairs are not of great importance to him.

[3] The Birmingham swing to the Conservatives, 2·4 per cent, was lower than in any other major city except Nottingham (also 2·4 per cent). London and Leeds, which had been the only two major cities to register a swing to Labour similar to that of Birmingham in 1945, now swung strongly (4·8 per cent and 7·6 per cent) to the Conservatives (H. G. Nicholas, *The British General Election of 1950* (1951), p. 313).

the following year, when only one Liberal stood in Birmingham, the Unionists were able to increase their share of the poll to 46·9 per cent, whereas that of Labour rose only slightly, to 52·5 per cent. Nevertheless, Labour still did better than in the country as a whole, where they polled 48·8 per cent, and they were able to hold on to all their Birmingham seats. With their support in the city almost back to its level of 1945, Labour had every reason to feel pleased with their performance. The results of the municipal elections, however, presented a different picture. In the contests of 1950 and 1951 Labour obtained only 46·01 per cent and 40·97 per cent of the poll, mainly because Labour supporters were less willing to turn out to vote in local elections than were Unionist sympathizers.[1] These performances were inadequate to regain control from the Unionists.

Fortunately for Labour, the Conservative Government elected in 1951 was so unpopular in its early years that Labour support in city elections greatly increased from 1952, primarily because of protest voting and abstentions by erstwhile Unionist supporters. This movement allowed Labour to resume control of the Council in 1952, and in the next two years they managed to increase their overall majority to thirty-two, their highest ever. However, it is significant that their share of the poll declined from a record 57·07 per cent in 1952, when the unpopularity of the Conservative Government was at its height, to 45·53 per cent in 1955. By this latter year the Conservative Government had overcome its early difficulties, and in preparation for the general election had already allowed the electorate, in the form of tax reductions, some of the fruits of the hard years behind them. The marked prosperity of Birmingham's industries helped the Conservative cause in the city, and in the general election of May 1955 the swing to the Conservatives there (2·6 per cent) was more pronounced than in the country as a whole.[2]

Even so, Labour still maintained a narrow majority of the votes cast in Birmingham (49·91 per cent). The Conservatives, with 49·48 per cent, found that the new constituency structure set up in 1954 worked against them, for they were victorious in only four out of the thirteen Birmingham divisions. A further blow to the Birmingham Conservatives was dealt by the policies of the re-elected Conservative Government.

---

[1] It is also possible to argue, of course, that the city election results reflected the popularity of the *local* policies and achievements of the parties. We maintain, however, that Birmingham municipal elections have been dominated almost entirely by national issues (see A. R. Sutcliffe, 'Campaigns and policies: aspects of Birmingham municipal politics 1939–1966', History of Birmingham Project Research Paper no. 15, esp. pp. 68–71).

[2] The Birmingham swing was exceeded in only two other large cities, both of them in the Midlands—Coventry (5·3 per cent) and Nottingham (4 per cent) (D. E. Butler, *The British General Election of 1955* (1956), p. 184).

The post-election economic restrictions, followed by the Suez invasion in 1956 which caused severe unemployment in Birmingham, destroyed any possibility that the Conservatives might take control of the City. Their share of the municipal poll had been 51·89 per cent in 1955, but for the next few years it dropped to well under 50 per cent. It did not begin to revive again until towards the end of the decade, when the Conservative Government was again preparing for a general election.

The general election of 1959 was almost a repeat performance of 1955. After incurring unpopularity by rigorous anti-inflationary measures during their early years of office, the Conservatives removed these restrictions as the election approached. Birmingham was now even more prosperous, unemployment was minimal, and the difficulties of the mid-1950s were forgotten. The Conservatives managed to increase their vote in the city to 50·89 per cent, compared to a national average of 49·40 per cent, and despite the handicap of the constituency structure, they won a total of seven seats, reducing Labour's representation to six. However, the swing away from Labour was much smaller in Birmingham than in the country as a whole, and Labour candidates obtained 47·88 per cent of the poll in the city.[1]

Now that the Conservatives were stronger in Birmingham than at any time since before the war, they seemed to have a good chance of taking control of the City Council. But once again the three-year election process of the councillor body foiled them. In 1959 they obtained 47·43 per cent of the poll, and in the following year, with a low turnout betraying the apathy of many Labour supporters, their share was 55·10 per cent. But in 1961, with the Conservative Government again unpopular in the country, they could manage only 47·41 per cent. This performance was nevertheless enough to deprive Labour of a working majority, and the Conservatives were able to claim a share of chairmanships. But overall control eluded them, and in 1962 a poor Conservative performance, in which they obtained only 40·70 per cent of the votes cast, allowed Labour to resume overall authority. Labour strengthened their position further in 1963 and 1964.

Encouraged by the marked national unpopularity of the Conservative Government in the early 1960s, which was confirmed by opinion polls and by-election results, the Labour Party had high hopes of winning the next general election. The Government, with defeat staring it in the face, held on until almost the last possible moment, and the election was not held until October 1964. Yet in the last weeks before the election Conservative support revived unexpectedly, and although a big swing to Labour took place, the Conservatives took

[1] However, the Birmingham swing to the Conservatives (3·3 per cent) was much larger than that of any other major city (D. E. Butler and Richard Rose, *The British General Election of 1959* (1960), p. 218).

43·4 per cent of the national poll. Labour, with 44·1 per cent, obtained a majority of only a few seats in the House of Commons. In Birmingham Conservative support was eroded less than in most places; they took 48·3 per cent of the votes cast in the city, compared to 50·89 per cent in 1959, and Labour remained in second place, with only 47·0 per cent.[1] Nevertheless, the constituency boundaries still favoured Labour and helped them to win seven seats.

This result was a severe disappointment to the Labour Party in Birmingham. It had been obvious during the 1950s that Conservative support in the city was increasing, but this had appeared to be a national trend, and Labour strength was never seriously undermined. The City Council Labour group had taken steps to counter the right-ward trend in municipal voting by modifying its policies to suit owner-occupiers and the more affluent sections of the working class.[2] National Labour policy, under the leadership of Gaitskell and later of Wilson, had moved in a similar direction. Yet the 1964 city result, which differed more from the national result than that of any other general election since the war, suggested that Birmingham was again beginning to establish itself as an exception to the general rule, a Conservative working-class city. Among the explanations put forward were the influence of the issue of coloured immigration in Birmingham,[3] and the affluence of the Birmingham worker.[4]

The Conservatives were encouraged sufficiently to launch their

---

[1] The low swing to Labour in Birmingham was repeated throughout the West Midlands, which strengthened the common assumption that the explanation lay in the prosperity of the area. See e.g. Peter G. J. Pulzer, *Political Representation and Elections in Britain* (1967), p. 117. Concern about coloured immigration among West Midland electors may also have played its part, though the issue was raised by few Birmingham candidates. See below, pp. 394 ff.

[2] See below, pp. 101 ff.

[3] Butler and King conclude that the immigration issue played some part in the Conservative gain at Perry Barr, but it apparently did not substantially influence results in other Birmingham divisions (D. E. Butler and Anthony King, *The British General Election of 1964* (1965), p. 291). The Sparkbrook campaign, in which the immigration issue was never raised, is described in Alan Shuttleworth, 'Sparkbrook', in Nicholas Deakin (ed.), *Colour and the British Electorate: Six Case Studies* (1965), pp. 54–76.

[4] The theory that the allegiance of workers to the Labour Party had been weakened by higher living standards has been substantially undermined by recent research work (see e.g. John H. Goldthorpe, D. Lockwood, F. Bechhofer, J. Platt, *The Affluent Worker: Political Attitudes and Social Behaviour* (1968)). Nevertheless, there is some evidence that the more prosperous sections of the working class have become more instrumental in their attitude to the Labour Party, and therefore are less willing to support it unquestioningly (see *The Affluent Worker*, pp. 73–82). For a development of this point, see David Butler and Donald Stokes, *Political Change in Britain: Forces Shaping Electoral Choice* (1969), pp. 95, 104, 121–2. For a study of the motivations of those members of the working class who habitually vote Conservative, see Eric A. Nordlinger, *The Working-Class Tories: Authority, Deference and Stable Democracy* (1967).

biggest assault in years in the City Council, where they had virtually established a consensus policy with Labour in the early 1960s. Their share of the municipal poll had already improved to 44·66 per cent in May 1964, and thanks to the early difficulties of the Labour Government, it shot up to 56·10 per cent in 1965. In the following year the Conservatives did less well, owing to a resurgence of the Labour Government's popularity, but their 49·90 per cent of the poll was enough to give them a clear majority in the City Council for the first time since 1952. In subsequent years the actions of the re-elected Labour Government proved so unpopular that the Conservatives were able to score massive victories at the municipal elections, and they reduced the Labour group to the smallest it had ever been since before the war. Not until 1970 was Labour able to win any wards back, and the Conservatives remained in firm control until 1972.

Meanwhile, the general election of 1966 had done much to dispel, briefly, the gloom of the Birmingham Labour movement. The big swing to Labour in the city that had been expected in 1964, but had not materialized, now took place. Labour obtained 53·6 per cent of the poll, easily their best performance ever, and the Conservatives dropped to 41·6 per cent, which had been their level in 1945. Labour candidates were victorious in nine out of the thirteen divisions. The Conservative share of the poll was close to the national average of 41·9 per cent; Labour did considerably better than in the country as a whole, thanks mainly to the relative weakness of the Liberal party in the city.

The explanation most frequently put forward for the high Birmingham Labour vote was that the electorate had followed its previous practice of showing its gratitude for the city's prosperity by supporting the Government of the day. It seemed unlikely that the result represented any resurgence of loyalty to Labour's socialist ideals, for the Government's economic difficulties had forced it to adopt policies very similar to those of its predecessor. In short, the result did not entirely contradict the evidence which suggested a steady rightward movement in Birmingham voting since the early 1950s.[1] Nor did the result of the general election of June 1970. The national swing to the Conservatives was repeated almost exactly in Birmingham, where Labour obtained 48·90 per cent of the votes cast. Although the performance was rather better than Labour's 1964 achievement, it was so inferior to the result obtained

---

[1] Between 1950 and 1964 Birmingham swung by over 6 per cent to the Conservatives, more than any other major city. Bradford and Stoke-on-Trent were the only towns in the country to record a similar swing (D. E. Butler and A. King, *The British General Election of 1964* (1965), p. 291). The fall in Labour's share of the major party vote in the West Midland conurbation between 1945 and 1966 was exceptionally high. See Pulzer, *Political Representation*, p. 119.

in 1960 that it made that latter year, and not 1964, stand out as the exceptional election of the decade in Birmingham. Most observers associated the Conservative success in 1970 with the Labour Government's poor economic record. The issue of coloured immigration, which was raised forcibly in the Black Country, may have influenced some Birmingham voters even though it was hardly mentioned in the city.

So Birmingham entered the new decade with that most unusual combination, a Conservative City Council in partnership with a Conservative Government. Although this union was not destined to last beyond May 1972, when the Conservatives lost their majority in the City Council, it crowned the spectacular Conservative resurgence in Birmingham, a revival the origins of which lay back in the mid-1950s. We shall see later in this chapter that the Conservative revival had important consequences for Birmingham municipal politics. But first of all we must attempt to explain that revival.

The inevitable fluctuations in voting at parliamentary elections, and the even bigger swings in city contests, often masked long-term trends. To make these movements clearer we have converted some of the data to graphic form. Figure 1 shows changes in the Labour vote at general elections between 1945 and 1970 in Birmingham and other large cities. It indicates that Labour enjoyed significantly less support in pre-war Birmingham than in other large cities. By 1945 Labour had rallied, and the increase in their vote brought Birmingham more closely into line with the other cities. Yet even in 1945 six cities recorded a stronger Labour vote than Birmingham's; only in Nottingham and Liverpool did the party do less well. From 1945 until the end of the 1950s Labour support tended to fall everywhere, although there was a brief recovery in 1951. In Birmingham the Labour vote declined by 7 percentile points between 1945 and 1959, less than in Bristol, Coventry, and Hull, but the same as in Sheffield, and more than in Leeds, Liverpool, Manchester, and Nottingham. Consequently, by 1959 only Liverpool recorded a lower Labour vote than Birmingham.

During the 1960s Labour made a marked recovery in the large cities, with an especially good performance in the general election of 1966. Birmingham shared in this recovery, but Labour support there remained weak in comparison with the other cities. In 1964 the Labour vote in Birmingham was the lowest of all the cities, while in 1966 and 1970 only Bristol dropped lower. So in comparison with other large cities, support for Labour in Birmingham was always relatively weak, except during the late 1940s and early 1950s, when it occupied a median position.

Labour's support in Birmingham appears even weaker if it is related

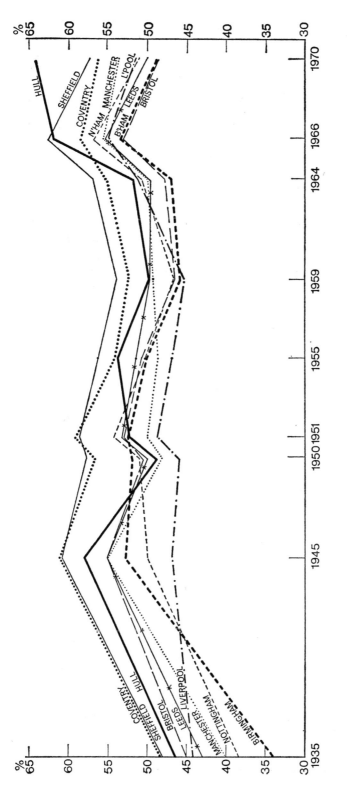

Figure 1 Labour candidates' share of total votes cast at general elections in Birmingham and other large cities, 1935–70

to social class. In many of the large cities, as in the country as a whole, the working classes tended to decline as a proportion of the total population after 1945. In Birmingham, on the other hand, this proportion remained roughly constant.[1] One might therefore reasonably have expected Labour's share of the vote in Birmingham to *improve* in comparison with other cities; its failure to do so suggests a major desertion of the Labour Party by the Birmingham working classes. An attempt to indicate the extent and timing of this desertion has been made in Figure 2. The result is far from satisfactory because accurate breakdowns of social composition are available only in census years. We have therefore related the Labour vote in 1945, 1950, 1951, and 1955 to the 1951 census, that in 1959 to the 1961 census, and the vote in 1964, 1966, and 1970 to the 1966 census. We have also made a comparison between the 1955 election results and the 1961 census, so Figure 2 shows two slightly differing results for 1955.

Further complications are caused by changing social classifications in the censuses,[2] and by the high proportion of indefinite occupations recorded in some cities in the 1961 census. In order to obtain from the 1961 and 1966 censuses a figure approximating to social classes III, IV, and V (skilled, partly skilled, and unskilled occupations) as defined in the 1951 census, we have distributed military personnel and indefinite occupations (groups 16 and 17) among the other occupational groups, and summed the totals of groups 5, 6, 7, 8, 9, 10, 11, 12, 14, and 15. By dividing Labour's percentage of the poll at each general election into the percentage of the total population belonging to social classes III, IV, and V a *very rough* indication can be obtained of those classes' propensity to vote Labour. The calculation produces a series of index figures which have been graphed in Figure 2. The lower the index figure, the greater is the propensity of social classes III, IV, and V to vote Labour. Figure 2 confirms the slow erosion of the Birmingham working classes' loyalty to the Labour Party from the mid-1950s. They maintained a median position in relation to the other big cities between 1945 and 1955, but by 1959 only the Liverpool working classes were less inclined to vote Labour than Birmingham's. In 1964 the Birmingham Labour vote, in relation to the size of its working classes, was by far the lowest of the big cities. It showed a slight improvement at the next two elections, but in 1970 the Birmingham working classes were still the least inclined to Labour of any large English provincial city, just as they had been before the war.

The effects of these changes on municipal voting in Birmingham are illustrated in Figure 3. Because low polls produce wild swings in city

---

[1] See below, pp. 215 ff.

[2] The significance of these classifications is explained below, pp. 215 ff.

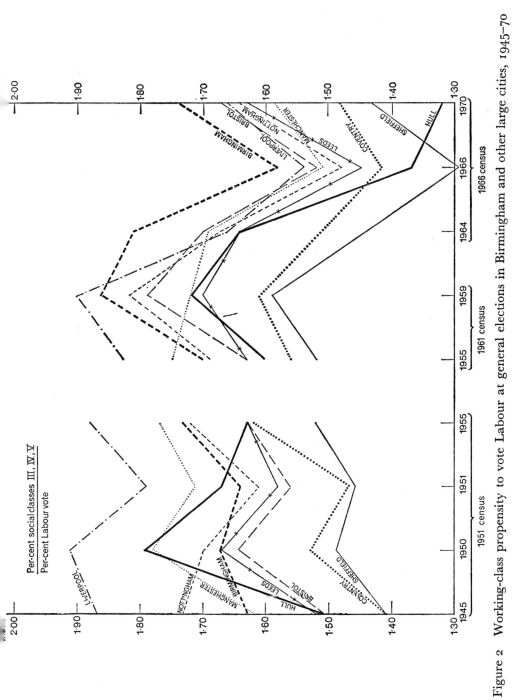

Figure 2 Working-class propensity to vote Labour at general elections in Birmingham and other large cities, 1945–70

elections, and because only one-third of the councillors are elected each year, we have calculated a three-year moving average for the years 1946–67, in order to emphasize long-term movements. To eradicate the effects of declining turnout we have used the percentage of the total electorate recording their votes in favour of each of the main parties, instead of the percentage of the poll. The graph shows that Labour support at municipal elections exceeded the Conservatives' for slightly less than half the period of twenty-one years covered by the moving average. The effect of anti-Government protest voting is obvious, but it is important to note that during periods of Labour Government the Conservatives did appreciably better in Birmingham municipal elections than did Labour during years of Conservative Governments. On this evidence, Labour's frequent feeling of insecurity during their long period of majority in the City Council, 1952–66, is perfectly under-standable. The Birmingham Labour vote was weak enough in parlia-mentary elections; in local contests, where a high proportion of working-class voters never bothered to go to the polls, it was a cause of serious concern.

Why was Labour so weak in Birmingham? We cannot provide a satisfactory answer to this question on the basis of the research under-taken for this volume, and as historians we must await the judgments of the political scientists. Yet it is tempting to guess that Birmingham's steady prosperity, reflected in high wages and low unemployment, was the major cause. Prosperity meant more material benefits for Bir-mingham workers, a high proportion of owner-occupied houses, great residential mobility within the city, and a high rate of immigration from outside.[1] All these changes broke up the traditional pattern of working-class life, and fragmented the older working-class communities, faster than in many other cities. Unlike Coventry, where similar changes were taking place, Birmingham had no strong tradition of Labour vot-ing; decades of industrial prosperity and enlightened Unionist admin-istration had seen to that. Yet the Coventry working classes, too, moved away from Labour after the war, and during the early 1950s this trend was more pronounced than Birmingham's. Birmingham did not begin to stand out until the late 1950s and early 1960s, when the effects of material wealth on working-class voting were compounded by a big influx of coloured working-class people from abroad. As far as one may judge, coloured people voted in much smaller numbers than their white counterparts, and they help to explain why the Birmingham

---

[1] We lack both the space and the expertise to discuss adequately the implications for Birmingham voting of the many explanations offered by political scientists and sociologists for the relative weakness of the Labour Party in modern Britain. The best general summary of the controversy is provided by David Butler and Donald Stokes, *Political Change in Britain: Forces Shaping Electoral Choice* (1969).

working-class Labour vote remained relatively low throughout the 1960s. But it is important to remember that the relative decline in Labour support had begun before coloured people had come to Birmingham in large numbers.

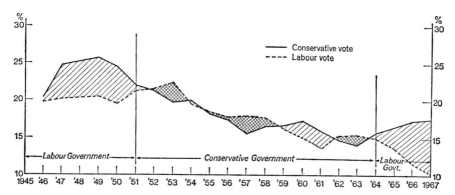

Figure 3 Percentage of Birmingham electorate voting for the two major parties at municipal elections, 1945–67: three-year moving average

If, as we have suggested, working-class support for Labour in Birmingham was on the wane from the mid-1950s, and if this decline was reflected more strongly in local than in national elections, it can hardly have failed to influence the municipal policies and attitudes of the Birmingham parties. It is to these policies and attitudes that we now turn.

Policies and issues in Birmingham municipal politics

Before 1939 city elections in Birmingham were fought predominantly on local issues. The Unionists claimed that local government was not a matter for party politics, an attitude which was reinforced by the official disinterest of the national Conservative Party in local affairs. In any case, the Unionists were in such a dominant position in Birmingham in the 1930s that they had no need to fight aggressive party-political campaigns in local elections. Labour, on the other hand, had traditionally seen local government as the key arena for the promotion of the socialist cause, and this attitude was reinforced when national power was torn from them in 1931 and they had little prospect of ever regaining it. Such was the national unpopularity of Labour that in Birmingham the party concentrated on municipal issues. Nevertheless, the results of municipal elections reflected, as we have seen, Labour's poor performances in the general elections of 1931 and 1935. Most people seem to have voted for the same party in both parliamentary and city elections.

The major intrusion of national issues into municipal elections did

not occur until after the war. During the war Labour had integrated
their local and national campaigning very closely, and this feature was
especially prominent in Birmingham where about half the prospective
parliamentary candidates had served on the City Council.[1] The massive
landslide to Labour in the 1945 general election ensured that this
intrusion of national politics into local affairs would continue. The
best way to ensure the election of Labour municipal majorities, or so
it seemed for a time, was to persuade the electorate that there was no
difference between national and local politics. In addition, now that
Labour had achieved national power, the party was no longer so
concerned about achieving socialism at a local level, for the job could
be done much more effectively by central direction. The prime task
of Labour councils would now be to carry out the orders of the Labour
Government. It was for these reasons that Labour campaigned in the
local elections of 1945 on the theme of 'Forge the Link'. The voters
were warned that the survival of Conservative local authority
majorities might hold up the measures promised by the new Labour
Government, which the electorate had so overwhelmingly supported.

In Birmingham, the Borough Labour Party's 1945 municipal campaign conformed to Labour's national strategy for the local elections.
However, so many positive plans had been made during the war for
the city's reconstruction that undertakings to carry them out were
very prominent in the campaign. The Unionists, for their part, continued to argue that national party politics should not intrude into
local elections, and urged the electorate to vote Unionist in appreciation
of the party's long record in Birmingham local government. But
although local matters were prominent in the 1945 campaign, the results
showed only too clearly that the national party-loyalties of the electorate had decided the issue.

Nationally, the Conservative Party was now in the same position as
Labour before the war, in that only in local government could the party
enjoy any form of power. So in 1946 the Conservative Party formally
re-entered the local government arena. This gesture was primarily
symbolic, and local Conservative parties still continued to stress local
rather than national issues when it was in their interests to do so.
However, the growing unpopularity of the Labour Government
tempted the Birmingham Unionists to claim with increasing force in
the later 1940s that a vote for a Unionist municipal candidate was a
vote against the Labour Government, and that a Unionist Council would
strive to nullify the more unpopular of the Government's policies.

By the later 1940s the pattern was established whereby a party which

[1] Experience of local government was a marked feature of Labour candidates
throughout the country in 1945 (McCallum and Readman, *General Election of 1945*,
p. 81).

was unpopular nationally would stress local issues in Birmingham municipal elections, while one whose national policies were popular would place them before the electorate to the exclusion of its local policies. This feature tended to become more pronounced as the years went by, because, as we have seen, local authority initiative was increasingly restricted, and so the number of issues on which the Council could itself take a decision was steadily reduced. Furthermore, the two major parties were very often in complete agreement on these local issues. In any case, a large section of the electorate had such a poor understanding of the workings of local government that to raise some of the more complicated issues would only have confused them.[1] Even those few local policies which did make an appearance in campaigns were usually discussed in a national context, simply because the availability of funds to execute them depended so much on Government economic policy.[2]

In only two areas did local affairs remain prominent in the campaigns and influence voting, though to a very minor extent. These were housing and municipal finance. Of these two, housing was the less important. It came to the fore from 1946 when house building in Birmingham got off to a very slow start after the war. At first the delay in Birmingham was no worse than anywhere else, and the Unionists used housing simply as a stick with which to beat the Labour Government. But by 1947 Birmingham's building performance was beginning to lag behind that of other areas, and housing became more and more of a *local* issue. With tens of thousands of families waiting for houses, the City Council's low building rate gave the Unionists an opportunity to win votes from working-class people who would otherwise have been inclined to support Labour.[3] This issue appears to have contributed marginally to the Unionists' successes in the elections of 1947 and 1949. It remained prominent in the 1950s and 1960s, but it was never again so influential as in the late 1940s. The building rate again dipped very

---

[1] See e.g. the depressing result of a poll undertaken by the Birmingham Municipal Officers' Guild to ascertain the extent of the public's knowledge of local government, in *Y.B.*, no. 118, May 1957, p. 3. But there is some evidence to suggest that voters are as ignorant about national politics as they are about local affairs. See Ian Budge, 'Electors' attitudes towards local government: a survey of a Glasgow constituency', *Political Studies*, vol. xiii, 1965, p. 389.

[2] Researches by Butler and Stokes suggest that in the early 1960s over 90 per cent of those voting in local elections voted for the party to which they felt closest at national level. Four out of five of those questioned said without hesitation that there were *no* local issues that concerned them, and the remainder mentioned matters that were more often the concern of the central Government than of the local authority (Butler and Stokes, *Political Change in Britain*, pp. 38–9). See also L. J. Sharpe (ed.), *Voting in Cities: The 1965 Borough Elections* (1967), pp. 319–20.

[3] See e.g. Birmingham Unionist Association, *Shameful Failure: The Housing Story 1945 to 1949* (1949).

low from the mid-1950s to the early 1960s, but by this time many more private houses were being built than in the 1940s. Moreover, housing had by now been eclipsed as the key local issue by finance.

Finance had been the most important issue raised in local elections before the war. The Unionists had maintained, especially in the 1930s, that economy was one of the most important features of local government. They claimed that Labour were spendthrifts, eager to waste the ratepayers' contributions on unnecessary schemes and services; only the Unionists had the sound business experience that alone could qualify a party to handle public funds. The Unionists pursued this line after the war, but until the late 1940s it was very subdued because, after a reduction in the rates during the war, the poundage was slow to rise simply because Government control of finance, materials, and manpower prevented the Council from developing its services and undertaking important capital schemes. Important savings were made in 1948 when certain services were transferred to the State, and the relative stability of the value of the pound meant that the cost of existing services rose only slowly. Consequently, as late as 1950–1 the rate poundage was still only 18s. 6d., the same as it had been in 1941–2.

This stable situation was transformed from the early 1950s. As the new Conservative Government relaxed controls, the economy began to expand rapidly, allowing local councils at last to carry out some of their plans for improvements. This growth was achieved only at the expense of the stability of the currency, and inflation rapidly increased local authority costs. By 1953–4 the rate poundage in Birmingham had been increased to 25s., and the ratepayers were beginning to grumble, even though they were still paying less rates in real terms than before the war. The rate poundage tended to rise especially fast in Birmingham because, as an area of almost static population, its total rateable value increased only slowly. Furthermore, the cost of local services was inflated by the needs of the large daytime population composed of people who worked or did business in the city but who lived outside, thus making no contribution to municipal finances.[1] The Conservatives now had an excellent opportunity to make use of an issue in which they had a traditional interest, and which might be expected to counter the depressive effect of Government unpopularity on their position in Birmingham. All householders had to pay rates; it was true that owner-

---

[1] See Committee of Inquiry into the Impact of Rates on Households, *Report* (1965), p. 55; Lees, etc., *Local Expenditure*, pp. 146, 148. In 1951 the daytime population of Birmingham was 6 per cent higher than the resident population, taking employed persons alone into account. The presence of people shopping and doing business in the city would have made the difference even greater. In 1952–3 Birmingham spent £3·58 per head of population on basic local services, compared to a county borough average of £3·28.

occupiers were usually more aware of them than private and municipal tenants, who paid each week through their rent instead of in a half-yearly lump sum, but this distinction was not a serious drawback to the Conservatives. The owner-occupiers tended to be Conservative supporters in any case; the main task in local elections was not to convert them, but to bring them out to vote, and an increase in the rates was likely to do just that. In Birmingham owner-occupiers were more heavily hit by rates in the later 1940s and early 1950s than in most other places; the average owner-occupier paid forty per cent more in rates than the average tenant, a much larger difference than elsewhere. The ratio of rate payments by owner-occupiers to their total expenditure was also higher than average, mainly because the spate of speculative building in the city between the wars and the cheap mortgages offered by the Municipal Bank had allowed more members of the lower income-groups to become home-owners than was usual elsewhere.[1] Since the transfer of the local elections from November to May in 1949, voters went to the polls shortly after the fixing of the rate poundage in March, so that the new rate was uppermost in their minds. Although the amount that had to be raised through the rates was largely beyond the control of the City Council,[2] the final decision on the poundage was made by the Council alone, and there were signs that the elector could be persuaded that if he used his vote to show that he wanted rate stability, the City Council had the power to give him his wish.[3]

The Conservatives began to launch heavy attacks on Labour over the finance issue in 1953, one year after they had lost control of the Council. At first Labour tried to ignore these attacks, claiming that money had to be found to provide the high standard of services that the city needed. But later in the decade they became increasingly worried about their declining popularity in the city, which was

---

[1] J. R. Hicks and U. K. Hicks, *The Incidence of Local Rates in Great Britain* (1945), p. 34. Even in the early 1960s, by which time rateable values in Birmingham had increased greatly from their artificially low post-war level, the average rate payment per domestic hereditament (£29·6) was higher than those of most other large cities, although it was exceeded by Manchester (£30·2) and Liverpool (£32·1) (Committee of Inquiry into the Impact of Rates, *Report*, pp. 233–5).

[2] Recent researches have suggested that the rate poundages in county boroughs are influenced only by the socio-economic structure of the town, and not by the political allegiance of the controlling group in their councils. There is no evidence that Labour control is associated with high expenditure (see F. R. Oliver and J. Stanyer, 'Some aspects of the financial behaviour of County Boroughs', *Public Administration*, summer 1969, pp. 169–84).

[3] For the great interest shown by local voters, especially Conservative voters, in economies of expenditure, and for confirmation that electors think about local politics in terms of immediate self-interest, see Budge, 'Electors' attitudes towards local government', esp. p. 391.

H

reflected in both local and parliamentary voting. Although a comparison of local swings in Birmingham with those in other towns and cities[1] suggests that even a major increase in the rate poundage by a Labour-controlled Council did not reduce the Labour vote by more than two or three per cent, the Labour leaders often assumed that rigid control of expenditure would help to restore their position. When Labour lost their working majority in the Council in 1961 they blamed the financial issue, and the group's subsequent efforts to control expenditure ensured that finance would remain an important bone of contention until Labour lost control of the Council in 1966. Despite their criticism of Labour's performance, the Conservatives in their turn were not able to stabilize the rates beyond their first year in office; in fact, they increased the poundage every year until 1970. However, these increases did them no harm politically, for the great unpopularity of the Labour Government outweighed any local bitterness against the continuing rise in the rates. In any case, Labour hesitated to base their municipal campaigns on an issue which was normally the province of the Conservatives. So municipal finance faded somewhat as an electoral issue towards the end of the 1960s.

It is not surprising to find, in view of the local government situation described so far, that the municipal policies of the Birmingham political parties were fundamentally very similar. Even before the war the Labour and Unionist groups had cooperated over many aspects of the Corporation's work. This cooperation was enhanced during the war, when the majority of Unionist Council members found themselves in growing agreement with Labour over the need for more social justice, a fairer distribution of wealth, and extended public control over the activities of individuals. Because plans were made then, and agreed by both sides, which laid down guide-lines for the development of many aspects of the city's life after the war, inter-party agreement on these practical issues survived for many years after hostilities had ended. An excellent example of the survival of a wartime consensus was education policy, where Labour remained loyal to the principle of selective education until the mid-1960s.[2] The Unionists, for their part, retained much of the more liberal outlook which they had assumed during the war. In any case, such was the Government's control over municipal policies after the war that there was much less to disagree over than before 1939. On the other hand, once the electoral truce had ended in 1945 it was inevitable that differences between the two parties should become more noticeable. Some of them were largely factious, mounted for the benefit of the electorate. But others were genuine disagreements of principle.

[1] See Sutcliffe, 'Campaigns and policies'.   [2] See below, pp. 340 ff.

In the late 1940s and early 1950s the major cause of the divergence between the policies of the two parties was a shift to the right by the Unionists. Their wartime move towards Labour had been the result of a very exceptional spirit of cooperation and social reconciliation that had then flourished throughout society. With peace restored and a Labour Government in power at Westminster, many Unionists grew disillusioned and returned to a more traditional Conservative stand. Labour also played their part in this estrangement. The wartime understanding did not prevent them from turning viciously on the Unionists in 1945 for their own electoral advantage. Labour also annoyed and disappointed their opponents by imposing rigid party discipline on their group in the council chamber. This the Unionists had never done. During and even before the war individual Unionist members had frequently voted with Labour. But from 1945 a genuine resentment against Labour tactics built up among the Unionists, who in turn hardened their party line on many issues.

A further factor in this estrangement was the disappearance from the Council of most of the respected Unionist members from influential Birmingham families such as the Beales, the Kenricks, and the Martineaus. Men from these families, such as Alderman Byng Kenrick, leader of the Unionist group until 1947, and Alderman Wilfred Martineau, Kenrick's successor as chairman of the Education Committee from 1943, normally enjoyed the respect of the Labour members for their liberal and humanitarian views.[1] Most of them were rich industrialists who had the time (or thought they had the time)[2] to devote to municipal affairs, and whose experience in running large organizations was a great help to the City Council.[3] But after the war many of these men left municipal politics. A high proportion of the councillors among them were defeated at the polls. Some of the older aldermen found that owing to the fall in the number of Unionist councillors, places could not be found for them when the time came for their re-election.[4] Others were forced to retire by their advancing age. Younger industrialists hesitated to stand now that the Unionist ticket

---

[1] See e.g. the fulsome tributes paid by Alderman Walter Lewis, one of the leading members of the Labour group, to Byng Kenrick, Wilfred Martineau, and members of the other Birmingham patrician families in *Alderman Byng Kenrick: Tributes and Appreciations on his Retirement as Chairman of the Birmingham Education Committee* (1943) (Birmingham University Institute of Education).

[2] Roy A. Church, *Kenricks in Hardware: A Family Business, 1791–1966* (1969), pp. 226–8.

[3] See D. S. Morris and K. Newton, 'Profile of a local political elite: businessmen on Birmingham Council, 1920–1966', Birmingham University Faculty of Commerce discussion papers, series F, no. 6 (1969), pp. 13–16.

[4] It has always been agreed by the parties in the City Council that the number of aldermen should be in proportion to the number of councillors of each party.

was no longer certain of obtaining them a seat, or of allowing them to keep it once won. Moreover, post-war industrial management was more competitive and demanding, and spare time for politics was difficult to find.[1]

By the early 1950s hardly any liberal-minded industrialists of the type which had guided the pre-war Council were to be found on the Unionist benches. Instead the Unionist group came to be dominated by white-collar workers and professional men and women—among them many solicitors, accountants, surveyors, and estate agents—and a smaller number of small manufacturers.[2] These professional people were the new leisured class, and their expertise was relevant to the massive building, slum clearance, property development, and public works programmes undertaken by the City Council from the early 1950s.

Nevertheless, the Conservative group always retained an important business element; the proportion of company directors, proprietors, manufacturers, and merchants, which had been 49·5 per cent in 1939, was still as high as 29 per cent in 1966.[3] The Conservative group never completely lost its liberal tradition, but closest to the hearts of many of its newer members were the interests of the Birmingham owner-occupier.

Despite these changes, the two party groups had few fundamental conflicts of policy until the very broad issue of finance came to the fore in the early 1950s. Over housing, the other big local issue, there was very little conflict of principle—both sides wanted to build as many municipal houses as possible; they disagreed only over which of them was better fitted to achieve this aim. During the 1940s the Unionists strongly defended the cause of local independence against encroach-

---

[1] This shortage of young entrants of sufficient calibre was reflected in the Conservative leadership's frequent appeals for more young people to enter local government, and the encouragement given to leading Young Conservatives to stand for election (see e.g. an account of the nomination of Anthony Dark, a leading Young Conservative in his early twenties, in *E.D.*, 11 February 1955). The Young Conservatives had been set up (as the Young Unionists) in 1945, and they provided a number of local election candidates from 1947 (see Birmingham Unionist Association, *Yearbook* (1948), pp. 6–7).

[2] See Morris and Newton, 'Occupational composition of party groups'. A somewhat unfavourable view of the effects of this change in social composition on the Conservative group is provided by Anthony Howard, 'The Chamberlain legacy', *New Statesman*, 7 August 1964, p. 170.

[3] D. S. Morris and K. Newton, 'Occupational composition of party groups on Birmingham Council, 1920–1966', Birmingham University Faculty of Commerce discussion papers, series F, no. 3, pp. 11–13. See also their 'Profile of a local political elite'. For an explanation of the current unwillingness of people of standing in a community to serve on local councils, suggesting that the amount of time involved is the biggest discouragement, see Roger V. Clements, *Local Notables and the City Council* (1969).

ments by the central Government, but abandoned this cry almost completely when their own party took power at Westminster in 1951. They also stressed increasingly the important role that private enterprise should play in rebuilding and in running the life of the city. In the 1950s and even more in the 1960s they turned against municipal trading, even though it had been created and maintained by their linear predecessors. Furthermore, the Conservatives never stressed the importance of improving social and cultural amenities to the same extent as did Labour, for such steps usually involved extra expense and sometimes intrusions into areas of activity which the Conservatives saw as belonging to private enterprise.

Other policy disagreements appeared in the 1950s largely as a result of Unionist loyalty to the policies of the Conservative Government. Differences appeared, for instance, over housing, when Labour wanted first a new town and later a boundary extension, while the Birmingham Conservatives repeated the Government's assurance that neither was really necessary.[1] But the fundamental cleavage was always finance. As living standards improved in the 1950s, the Conservatives felt able to drop or to qualify promises to extend or improve services, which they had made after the war as one aspect of their consensus with Labour. Instead, they stressed increasingly that full value for money should be obtained from all Corporation departments, and that municipal aid should be provided only for people in real need. Although these policies gave the Conservative programme an increasingly negative character, it was very much in tune with the views of their supporters and fitted in with the rightward movement of Birmingham political opinion in the 1950s and early 1960s.

Labour, as we have seen, began to worry in the mid-1950s about the erosion of their support at municipal elections. We have already suggested that the trends in municipal voting reflected changes in the relative popularity of the national political parties, and not their municipal performance in Birmingham. Most members of the Labour group recognized that national trends were more important than the local ones, but opinions differed as to the exact significance of local factors. Some senior members, such as Alderman Sir Joseph Balmer and Alderman Jim Meadows, were occasionally prepared to argue that even a big increase in the rate poundage did not significantly depress the Labour vote. But such views were not influential in the late 1950s and early 1960s, when the weight of opinion in the group favoured a more cautious approach. It has recently been suggested that local politicians tend naturally to over-estimate the influence of local issues on voting, and to under-estimate the electors' tolerance of controversial

---

[1] See below, pp. 139 ff.

policies.[1] This 'law of anticipated reactions' may not be of general application, but it certainly helps to explain why Labour were so easily convinced that high civic expenditure was responsible for the relative decline in their support.

Electoral expediency was not, however, the only influential factor. Labour might have sought extra support by appealing more specifically to the Birmingham working classes, who formed the great majority of the city's population. This would have been a risky step, for post-war experience had shown that a markedly lower proportion of the working classes than of the middle classes bothered to record their votes in municipal elections. Moreover, the number of Labour stronghold wards in the central areas had been reduced by the boundary reforms of 1949, and would fall again after further boundary changes in 1962. So there was a danger that the extra votes which Labour might attract by working-class oriented policies would be swamped by an irate middle-class reaction. There were, however, members of the Labour group who would have preferred such a course, and they were strongly supported by sections of the Borough Labour Party and of the trade unions. Their failure to persuade the group was partly the result of a marked tendency towards moderation among the group rank-and-file and, more significantly, among its leaders.

Although the Labour group retained a strong working-class element, its social composition was slowly moving closer to that of the Conservative group. In particular, the proportion of professional men and women within the group was steadily rising.[2] Boundary changes and the growth of municipal housing estates on the outskirts increased the proportion of Labour councillors who represented suburban districts. The effects of these two changes are very difficult to assess, but it is possible that they increased the proportion of Labour group members who were prepared to support moderate municipal policies.[3] It is much easier to identify changes of opinion among the group leadership, where age and experience together produced a tendency towards moderate views. Men like Alderman Bowen (group leader, 1950–2) and Alderman Bradbeer (group leader, 1952–9) had been left-wing socialists before and during the war, but by the 1950s several years of power in the City Council had convinced them that it was their duty

---

[1] See Roy Gregory, 'Local elections and the "rule of anticipated reactions"', *Political Studies*, vol. xvii, no. 1, 1969, pp. 31–2, 44–6.

[2] See D. S. Morris and K. Newton, 'The occupational composition of party groups on Birmingham Council, 1920–1966', and 'Chairmen and non-chairmen of Birmingham Council', Birmingham University Faculty of Commerce discussion papers, Series F, nos. 3 and 4, 1969.

[3] These influences have been investigated by Barry Hindess in 'Local elections and the Labour vote in Liverpool', *Sociology*, vol. i, no. 2, 1967, pp. 187–95; *The Decline of Working-Class Politics* (1971).

to govern Birmingham in the interests of *all* its citizens, and not just of the working classes. Alderman Harry Watton, who succeeded Bradbeer as leader in 1959, moved even further across the political spectrum. As late as 1953 his adulatory views on the Soviet system of society, except for its 'police-state aspects', were being quoted in the Birmingham press.[1] But as group leader, Harry Watton's main priorities were to run the city efficiently and economically, and to keep Labour in power at all costs, even if that meant making his group's policies almost indistinguishable from those of the Conservatives. Watton's successor, Alderman Sir Frank Price, elected as leader in 1966, had become a successful property developer during the early 1960s. All these men were highly effective group leaders who won great respect among their Conservative opponents and in the city. The extent of their support within the group is indicated by the fact that on only one occasion after the war did a challenger unseat a group leader at the annual leadership election.[2] However, no advocacy of left-wing socialist policies could be expected from the leadership.

The group leaders' authority and influence over Labour municipal policies increased during the 1950s and 1960s. Until the early 1950s the group leader had been a *primus inter pares* and changes of leadership had been frequent. This arrangement did not make for consistency and efficiency of administration, but its drawbacks were only intermittently apparent in the later 1940s while Labour was not yet firmly in the saddle. From 1952, however, Labour built up a clear majority and abandoned most of the remnants of its post-war consensus with the Conservatives. Consistent, far-sighted leadership now became essential. The group showed itself prepared to rally behind a leader who possessed such qualities and to retain him for much longer than had been usual in the 1940s. The first of this new type of leader was Albert Bradbeer (1952–9). But it was not enough for the leader to exercise more authority within the group; he also had to be given greater power to shape the Corporation's policies. A big step towards this end was taken in 1956, when the Labour group decided that the group leader should replace the Deputy Mayor as chairman of the General Purposes Committee,[3] and that the committee should be developed as the City Council's major coordinating and policy-making body.[4]

[1] *S.M.*, 19 July 1953.

[2] This was in 1959, when Watton was elected leader in a straight fight with Bradbeer.

[3] A first step in this direction had been taken in 1955, when Alderman W. T. Bowen, a former leader of the Labour group, retained the chairmanship of the General Purposes Committee after his term as Deputy Mayor had come to an end.

[4] The role of the General Purposes Committee had been expanding since the war; in 1953, for instance, it was given power to decide on an order of priorities for public works schemes, at the expense of the Finance Committee (B.C.C., *Pro.*, 16 June 1953, pp. 33–6 (General Purposes Committee)).

Bradbeer made extensive use of his new authority and influence, but it was left to Harry Watton (1959–66) to realize their full potential. Watton's ground for challenging Bradbeer for the leadership in 1959 were that the group needed an even stronger man to make its policies more realistic and consistent, and to revive its electoral fortunes. Devoting his full time and energies to the task, Harry Watton built up a personal influence over Birmingham's municipal affairs reminiscent of that exercised by Joseph Chamberlain in the 1870s. This extraordinary power and prestige in the City Council could not fail to strengthen Watton's influence over Labour group policies, and it became very difficult for dissidents to question his advocacy of rightward adjustments of traditional Labour policies.

The rightward movement in Labour group policies from the later 1950s was further encouraged by a similar movement within the national Labour Party under the leadership of Hugh Gaitskell.[1] Labour strategists were convinced, both by political scientists and by their own experience, that although the working class remained the key foundation of the party's support, the slow decline in the size of that class and the erosion of party loyalty among the more affluent workers would deprive Labour of all chance of power unless its policies were modified.[2] The Borough Labour Party was predominantly Gaitskellite in its views on national politics, and its moderate position was maintained by a highly centralized party machine built up by the secretary, Harold Nash. Nash's personal views were strongly Gaitskellite, and Harry Watton established a close partnership with him from 1959.[3] In Birmingham, however, the municipal Labour group moved much further to the right than did the national Labour Party under Gaitskell, and, later, Wilson. The extent of this movement was understandable enough on grounds of expediency, given that the rightward trend of opinion in Birmingham was apparently greater than in the country as a whole. Yet although it had enough support in the Labour group and the Borough Labour Party to ensure that it was never reversed, it inevitably created severe strains and tensions within the Birmingham Labour movement. Much trade union support was lost from the mid-1950s,[4] and the Trades Council grew increasingly outspoken in its

[1] See Stephen Haseler, *The Gaitskellites: Revisionism in the British Labour Party 1951–64* (1969).

[2] See e.g. Mark Abrams, 'Social class and British politics', *Public Opinion Quarterly*, vol. xxv, no. 3, 1961, pp. 342–50.

[3] 'Birmingham politics', *The Economist*, 7 February 1970.

[4] The proportion of trade union officials in the Labour group had been falling steadily since before the war. In 1930 they made up over one-third of the group; by 1966 they accounted for only 3 per cent of its membership (Morris and Newton, 'Occupational composition of party groups', p. 16).

criticisms.[1] Even large sections of the rank-and-file of the Borough Labour Party lost confidence in the group and its leadership. In 1950 the group and the Borough Labour Party had inaugurated an annual municipal policy conference, the first of its kind in Britain, in order to associate the rank-and-file more closely with municipal policies. By the end of the decade the conference had become predominantly an arena of conflict between party members and the group leadership. Even some members of the Labour group came out in revolt, the most serious incident being the opposition of several Labour councillors to the group's decision to abandon the general rate subsidy to housing in 1963. The leadership's answer to this disaffection was to tighten up group discipline and clamp down on all dissidence.

Although the majority of the Labour group strongly supported Harry Watton's decision to discipline the rent rebels, there were some murmurings, especially among the younger members of the group, in the mid-1960s. Watton's nickname, 'the Fuehrer', was not always affectionately used. Some newer members felt that too many major decisions were being made by Alderman Watton and a small group of confidants, the most important of whom were said to be the moderate Alderman Denis Thomas and Councillor Ernest Bond, chairmen of the Public Works and House Building Committees. Lack of electoral success encouraged these complaints, and if a serious illness had not effectively deprived Harry Watton of the leadership early in 1966, the next group election might well have done so. But Alderman Watton deserved the respect and admiration which he won in Birmingham. The Labour group needed firm leadership, especially during a time of strong Conservative challenge. Watton acted decisively on many occasions to reduce inter-committee friction, and he persuaded the City Council to establish clear priorities in the planning and execution of its policies. His group recognized that, by keeping Labour in power at a time when the redevelopment policies of the post-war period were beginning to come to fruition, Harry Watton gave Birmingham a prestige enjoyed by few other Labour municipalities. Even the Conservatives, who since 1947 had grown accustomed to an autocratic form of leadership under Alderman Sir Theodore Pritchett, paid grudging respect to Harry Watton.[2] So there was little to check the rightward drift of Labour's policies under Watton's leadership.

[1] For an analysis of the increasing estrangement of the trade union movement from the Labour Party, both locally and nationally, see Martin Harrison, *Trade Unions and the Labour Party since 1945* (1960), esp. pp. 343, 348. Yet in the early 1950s the Borough Labour Party had been renowned for its close cooperation with the local trade union and shop stewards' movements; this aspect of its work had been highly praised in the Wilson report on local Labour Party organization in 1955.

[2] The Conservative group leader had always enjoyed extensive authority, which normally included the right to make final decisions on matters of policy, and to

This drift to the right had to be rapid if it was to keep up with changes in Conservative policy. From as early as 1954 the Conservatives persistently demanded an enquiry into the means of municipal tenants, and the same year saw the formulation of their objections to the general introduction of comprehensive education, which Labour was considering at the time. A year or two later they began to attack 'unnecessary' municipal control of property and land, which they called 'socialism through the back door', even though the municipalization of real estate in the interests of good planning and better living conditions had been a key element in Unionist policy before and even since the war. This rightward movement by the Conservatives was accelerated as Labour began to make concessions to their point of view from about 1954, for it was not in their interests that the two parties should again become almost indistinguishable, as they had during the war. From 1958 the Conservatives began to urge not only that 'unnecessary' acquisitions should cease, but that existing assets, including city centre freehold sites, and the freeholds of municipal houses, should be sold wherever possible to private interests. From the following year they began to advocate the abolition of the general rate subsidy to housing.

Until the last years of the 1950s Labour tried to put off making major concessions to Conservative views by inviting support for their defence of the city's economic interests. Success in this field would be welcomed by all citizens, to whatever class or social group they belonged, and would not involve any abandonment of the interests of the working class. For instance, from about 1955 Labour built up its image as the defender of Birmingham industry. This move partly reflected the Corporation's growing involvement with industrial firms affected by central area development, which it did its best to re-locate by providing alternative land or premises. But Labour's defence of industry evolved further into a policy of promoting the city's economic development even to the point of expansionism. At first the Birmingham Conservatives were unable to support Labour's attempts to extend the built-up area of the city,[1] of which the Government disapproved, but they came round to doing so in the 1960s, and advocated such extension themselves after they took power in 1966. Another important aspect of Labour's desire to benefit all classes and interests was its 'New Birming-

[1] See below, pp. 143 ff.

---

nominate his successor and the deputy leader. These powers were codified in a document, known as the 'Charter', which was produced in 1957 by a committee set up by Alderman Sir Theodore Pritchett to study group organization. In contrast, the Labour group leadership had frequently changed hands until the early 1950s, and the annual election of the leader had occasionally been contested (this never happened in the Conservative group). Policy decisions, too, had been made by the whole Labour group.

ham' policy. It aimed to accelerate the rebuilding of the city by cooperating closely with private developers to stimulate the construction of shops, offices, and private houses, in addition to the dwellings built by the Corporation. Thus the city could be transformed to the benefit of all, but at no cost to the ratepayers.

In spite of Labour's partial rightward shift, and the emphasis placed on non-class policies,[1] the party ran into severe electoral difficulties in 1960 and 1961. As we have already suggested, these difficulties re-flected the national, not the local, political position, but Labour were panicked by them into a further move to the right. The first step was taken in March 1961 when Labour made drastic cuts in the rate estimates.[2] In May Labour announced plans to build houses for sale to people on the housing list, a partial concession to the Conservative demand for the sale of municipal houses and more private building. Also promised was a Priorities Committee to plan expenditure, some-thing which the Conservatives had wanted for years, but which Labour had previously claimed to be unnecessary. Another Conservative demand now accepted by Labour was for an independent organization-and-methods inquiry into the work of the Corporation. On the issue of comprehensive education, Labour stayed non-committal. But by far the biggest concession was made to the Conservatives in 1963, when Labour abolished the general rate subsidy to housing, making Birming-ham the first Labour-controlled municipality to take this step.

After the election of a Labour Government in 1964, the Birmingham Conservatives had good grounds to hope that anti-Government protest voting would return them to power in the City Council, regardless of their municipal policies. Nevertheless they developed, largely under the influence of their new leader, Alderman Frank Griffin,[3] a series of positive local policies. These included a fearless defence of the grammar schools, special measures to deal with the problems raised by Common-wealth immigration, a reduction in the number of multi-storey flats

[1] Voting trends in the 1950s suggested that the electorate was inclining increasingly towards policies of moderation. See Mark Abrams, 'Social trends and electoral behaviour', *British Journal of Sociology*, vol. xiii, 1962, pp. 228–42.

[2] The sharp rise in domestic rate payments in the early 1960s caused concern over the whole country, even though payments were still lower in real terms than before the war (see Committee of Inquiry into the Impact of Rates, *Report*, pp. 18, 137). In Birmingham, however, domestic ratepayers were largely protected from the drastic effects of the 1963 revaluation because the city contained so much industry, which was subject to big increases in rateable value (*Report*, p. 141).

[3] Alderman Sir Theodore Pritchett retired from the leadership in 1964. Alderman Griffin was a motor trader who later retired from active business life in order to devote himself fully to municipal affairs. His appointment as leader had been ex-pected to terminate the very close cooperation between the Conservative and Labour groups which had been engineered by Watton and Pritchett (see e.g. *B.P.*, 6 June 1964).

built, and greater scope for private enterprise. This last aspect of their policy included winding down the Building Department and the civic restaurant service and even handing over some bus routes to private operators. When they came to power in 1966 they put many of these new policies into effect, together with many of those which, like the sale of city centre freeholds and municipal houses,[1] they had advocated for some time.

After 1966 Labour found it difficult to maintain any consistent line of policy because their long rightward drift had deprived them of many of the principles on which they could base a policy distinct from that of the Conservatives. Their new leader, Alderman Sir Frank Price, who replaced the stricken Harry Watton just before the 1966 elections, substituted devolution of responsibility and internal democracy for Watton's more autocratic methods. Unfortunately, the Labour group had become used to firm leadership and its internal cohesion suffered. Price tried to encourage his dwindling followers to play a bigger part in the making and presentation of policy than Watton had allowed them, but in their demoralized state the result was a confusion of conflicting and uncoordinated statements.[2] Distinctive new policies did not emerge, and Labour contented themselves with making opportunist attacks on Conservative actions, and waiting for the national tide to turn.

No mention has been made so far of the policies of the minority parties because they were so unimportant.[3] Independents were rare as candidates and almost non-existent as members of the City Council; this was a feature not only of Birmingham but of all major cities, which were dominated by the big national parties. The Communists, although strong in the Trades Council, never obtained more than a very small minority of votes in municipal elections, and the Borough Labour Party always refused to make electoral pacts with them. Communist municipal policies, which were always very restrained, had no influence on the City Council. Fascist and racialist candidates attracted even less support, and they rarely stood at all in the city.

[1] The Conservative scheme for the sale of municipal houses attracted so much attention nationally that the Conservative Political Centre asked Alderman Griffin to write a pamphlet on the subject. See F. F. Griffin, *How to Sell Council Houses* (1967).

[2] For a more favourable view of Labour's policy-making and organization under Sir Frank Price's leadership, see 'How our cities are governed—Birmingham: a ferment of ideas', *The Statist*, 6 January 1967, pp. 15–16. Price's plans on becoming group leader are described in *B.P.*, 17 May 1966.

[3] An analysis of the fortunes of minor parties in Birmingham municipal elections is provided by D. S. Morris in 'Minor parties in Birmingham local elections', Birmingham University Faculty of Commerce discussion papers, series F, no. 7 (1969). For the national fortunes of the Liberal Party since the war, see Jorgen S. Rasmussen, *The Liberal Party: A Study of Retrenchment and Revival* (1965).

The only minority party to enjoy any success was the Liberal Party.[1] By 1939 Liberal representation on the City Council had dwindled to three, all of them aldermen. During the war Liberal stock revived to some extent when Paul Cadbury was coopted as a councillor to replace one of the Liberal aldermen. His interest in town planning made him a useful member of the Council, and his sensible views were always respected. But in 1945 and subsequent years the Liberal Party failed to make the same impact. The party's national eclipse was largely to blame, but Liberal municipal policies did not help. They were a curious mixture of individualism and collectivism, and for several years after the war the Liberals appeared to stand to the right of the Unionists.[2] After a series of severe reverses at the polls, the party completely gave up fighting local elections between 1951 and 1955. Then, under the influence of a dynamic new leader, Wallace Lawler, a plastics manufacturer of Irish descent, the Liberals again began to put up candidates.[3] The change of leadership involved a step down in the social scale, but Lawler was just the man to cultivate support in the central wards of the city, which the Liberals had previously ignored. Birmingham's policy of patching slum dwellings and managing them for some years before demolition[4] had created great discontent among the tenants of these houses, many of whom bore a grudge against the Labour-controlled Council for charging rents for sub-standard accommodation. These areas were fertile campaigning grounds for Lawler, especially now that Labour was toning down its appeal to the working class in order to seek a wider base of support.[5] Despite previous failures, Liberal candidates again began to stand in the suburbs too, owing to the dogged enthusiasm of party activists rather than any real hope of success.

Owing to its weak condition, the Liberal Party was not highly centralized like the two main parties, and candidates usually tailored their policies to suit their wards. With candidates standing in both the city centre and the suburbs, the result was a schizophrenic set of policies, which Lawler tolerated.[6] In the suburbs, the Liberals con-

---

[1] See Morris, 'Minor parties'.

[2] Rigid opposition to municipal trading, which was a major feature of Liberal policy in Birmingham in the late 1940s, reflected the high proportion of private traders in their ranks. At this time they were much more a party of small shopkeepers than either of their rivals.

[3] Lawler's political career had begun in 1944, when he founded a non-party ginger group, the Public Opinion Action Association (see Bird, *Portrait of Birmingham*, p. 152).

[4] See below, pp. 228 ff.

[5] This impression is supported by P. Davies and K. Newton, 'An aggregate data analysis of party voting in local elections', Birmingham University Faculty of Commerce discussion papers, Series F, no. 13, 1971, pp. 18–23.

[6] Exploitation of local dissatisfactions was a prominent feature of Liberal local election campaigning throughout the country. See Alan Watkins, *The Liberal Dilemma* (1966), pp. 108–9.

tinued to call for civic economy and the defence of private enterprise. In the centre, they preached a unique brand of communalistic populism. Consequently, when Lawler was elected to the Council in 1962, and was joined by more Liberals representing the central areas from 1966, it became clear that the party had no guiding political philosophy to present to the Council. Instead, the Liberals considered each practical issue in isolation, and their policies were often totally inconsistent. In some cases, such as their advocacy of self-build housing associations, they had a positive influence on the City Council; in others, such as their attitude to coloured immigration into the city, they fell out among themselves. In any case, their success was based mainly on the totally exceptional conditions prevailing in the central areas, and by the end of the 1960s it had become clear that without a national resurgence of the Liberal Party, they had no hope of becoming an influential force in the City Council. Wallace Lawler won the parliamentary division of Ladywood from Labour at a by-election in 1969, but lost it again at the general election of 1970. In the same year the Liberal advance in the municipal elections was held up, and the eclipse of the national Liberal Party in the general election boded ill for Liberal fortunes in Birmingham in the new decade.

Two major pressure groups

The City Council was the most important representative body in Birmingham, but it was by no means the only such body. A variety of pressure groups, large and small, are mentioned in this volume, and they must not be ignored as potential participants in the shaping of policies which affect Birmingham. Indeed, the Birmingham and District Property Owners' Association's strong negative influence on the extension of municipal powers has already been mentioned.[1] On the whole, however, pressure groups played only a minor role in Birmingham politics, as in other British cities. In Britain, in contrast to the United States, city interest groups can normally obtain adequate representation through the formal party structure, while city councils are powerful enough and representative enough to claim responsibility for taking all major civic decisions.[2] Nevertheless, throughout the years 1939–70 two major pressure groups, representing important interests, attempted to exercise a permanent, constructive influence on decisions affecting Birmingham. These were the Birmingham Chamber of Commerce and the Birmingham Trades Council—organized employers and organized workers. Both merit separate attention here, not so much because of their positive influence, which was minimal, but

[1] See above, p. 67.
[2] See K. Newton, 'City politics in Britain and the United States', *Political Studies*, vol. xvii, no. 2, June 1969, pp. 212, 215.

because of what their proceedings reveal about the nature of Birmingham politics.

(i) THE BIRMINGHAM CHAMBER OF COMMERCE

The Chamber of Commerce, founded in 1803, was Birmingham's principal representative of organized industry throughout the years 1939–70. Because political control of the destinies of Birmingham industry had come to reside principally at Westminster and Whitehall by the early years of our period, the Chamber devoted much effort to trying to influence central Government policies. However, the Chamber faced major obstacles to the realization of this ambition. In the first place, only about one Birmingham industrial firm in three was prepared to pay the subscription fee until the 1960s, when an expansion of the Chamber's services attracted several hundred new members.[1] The very great majority of member firms were of small or medium size. Very big firms and combines showed less and less interest in the Chamber as time went on, partly because they had no need of its technical advice and services, and partly because its work as a local pressure group was irrelevant to companies which felt strong enough to make their own representations to decision-making bodies, or which, having factories in several cities, did not feel a particular association with Birmingham. Such firms showed more interest in the work of the Federation (later, Confederation)[2] of British Industries or the National Union of Manufacturers, which had more influence on the Government than local or regional Chambers of Commerce.

The work of the big national employers' organizations did not of itself detract from the importance of the Chamber of Commerce. Although they maintained regional offices, they did not normally attempt to organize or to represent local or regional opinion.[3] So there was plenty of scope for the Birmingham Chamber of Commerce to carry out this function on behalf of the city and its immediate area.

The policy of the Chamber was decided by an elected council, which, on matters affecting Birmingham industry as a whole, took into account the views expressed by member firms. The Chamber's views

[1] Membership dropped very low during the war, totalling only 3,190 firms in 1945. Energetic recruitment campaigns had raised the figure to 4,146 by 1949, but it dropped under 4,000 again towards the end of the 1950s. But then membership increased again as the Chamber's services expanded from about 1959; in 1967 it totalled 4,521.

[2] The C.B.I. was formed by a merger of the F.B.I. and the N.U.M. in the early 1960s.

[3] The predominantly national role of the trade associations, which allows little scope for the representation of regional variations of opinion, is described in Leonard Tivey and Ernest Wohlgemuth, 'Trade associations as interest groups', *Political Quarterly*, vol. xxix, no. 1, January–March 1959, pp. 59–71. See also Allen Potter, *Organized Groups in British National Politics* (1961).

achieved a wide circulation through its monthly journal, the *Birmingham Chamber of Commerce Journal and Monthly Record*. Between the wars the Chamber had taken an increasing interest in national economic affairs, and was a strong advocate of protection and imperial preference.[1] In these years the Chamber's chances of exercising an influence on national policy were very strong, because of the prominence of Birmingham Unionist M.P.s such as Austen and Neville Chamberlain, and L. C. S. Amery, in the Conservative and National Governments which governed the country almost without interruption. The creation of protection for British industry by the Ottawa agreements of 1933 was strongly supported by the Chamber, although its direct responsibility for this change of policy was undoubtedly minimal. British industrial policy, even in the 1920s and 1930s, could not be decided by the needs of a single industrial area. In any case, whatever direct influence Birmingham might have enjoyed in the 1930s was lost after 1940, when the resignation of Neville Chamberlain marked the end of the city's ascendancy in parliamentary politics.

If Birmingham industry continued to prosper, it was not the result of policies guided or influenced by the Chamber of Commerce, but because of the city's importance, at first, as a munitions centre, and, after the war, as one of the spearheads of the national export drive. So important was Birmingham industry to the economic well-being of the whole country that it would have been fostered by the Government whether or not it had a strong Chamber of Commerce to further its interests. Nevertheless, the Chamber, recognizing that the Government could exercise a stronger control over local industry after the war than before, devoted most of its attention to national affairs. It remained strongly protectionist until after the war, but became a strong supporter of European free trade from the late 1950s.

From the 1950s the Chamber tried to strengthen its influence by building up links with nearby Chambers and claiming to represent the whole of the West Midlands region. In 1955 a conference was held of twelve Midland Chambers to discuss closer liaison, and in 1958 a close association was established between the Chambers of Birmingham, Wolverhampton, Walsall, and Dudley. Birmingham granted financial assistance to the other three Chambers. In 1964 a Midland regional group of Chambers was formed, in order to comply with the new regional reorganization of the Association of British Chambers of Commerce, and to facilitate cooperation with the regional economic planning structure planned by the Labour Government. Yet there were few signs that a regional approach substantially increased the Chamber's influence. Its repeated attempts to persuade the Government to

[1] This section leans heavily on Marsh, 'History of the Birmingham Chamber of Commerce', unpublished manuscript kindly made available by the Chamber.

A municipal flatted factory block, Lee Bank House, photographed on the point of completion in 1958.

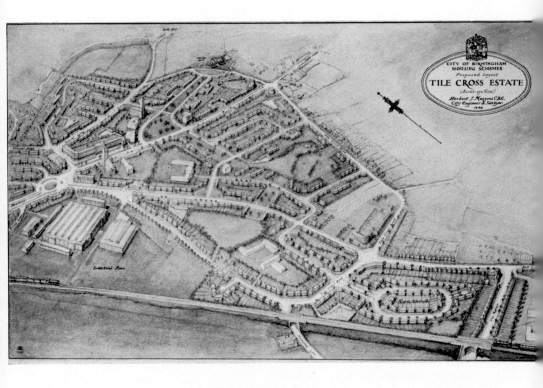

Two early post-war low-density housing estates, Tile Cross and West Heath.

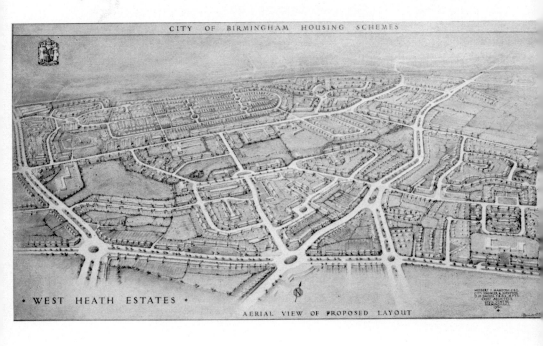

modify its industrial development certificate policy after 1945 to allow freer growth of local industry met with almost total failure. The declining attendance at meetings of the Council, which was first noticed after the war,[1] suggested that industrialists might be losing confidence in the effect of the Chamber's pronouncements on Government policy.

Even at a local level the Chamber of Commerce was not always accorded the respect which it thought it deserved, though it achieved rather more significant results than in its relations with the central Government, for the expenditure of rather less effort.[2] During the war it was not especially prominent in putting forward positive proposals for reconstruction,[3] but some of its members served on the advisory committees appointed by the City Council for this purpose. Instant agreement was reached in these discussions that Birmingham industry should be allowed to remain as prosperous as possible after the war. Although the City Council excluded it from any positive role in the drafting of the Development Plan, the Chamber was happy with the area of land zoned for industrial expansion. But it took strong exception to the state of uncertainty in which industrialists were kept in the early 1950s while the plan was under discussion, and argued that the Corporation should take the Chamber more fully into its confidence. The City Council recognized the justice of its case, and agreed to participate in a standing joint committee on trade and industry in Birmingham, in association with the Chamber and representatives of the Federation of British Industries and the National Union of Manufacturers.

The Chamber also had some influence over the City Council in ensuring the satisfactory re-location of industrialists displaced from the central redevelopment areas; in particular, the City Council came to accept the Chamber's view that it was more important to provide sites for firms to build their own premises than to erect municipal multi-storey factories for them. But the Labour majority in the Council ignored the Chamber's opposition, supported by the Conservative group, to the acquisition and renovation of sub-standard houses in areas zoned for industry. The Chamber was more successful in its opposition to a clause which the City Council wanted to insert in a Corporation Bill in 1954 to give it wide powers to acquire areas of bad layout and obsolete development; after strong attacks from the

---

[1] In 1950 the Articles were amended so that members who were absent from three meetings in one year lost their seats.

[2] The weakness of industrial pressure groups in British local politics is noted in Delbert C. Miller, 'Industry and community power structure: a comparative study of an American and an English city', *American Sociological Review*, vol. xxiii, no. 1, February 1959, pp. 9–15.

[3] Chamber of Commerce spokesmen maintained that the main task was to win the war (see e.g. *B.G.*, 4 May 1943).

Chamber, and bodies such as the Birmingham and District Property Owners' Association, the clause was defeated at a town's meeting and poll, and deleted from the Bill. In 1958 the Chamber again took part in a successful campaign to secure the rejection of a clause in a Corporation Bill which would have given the City Council power to use compulsorily purchased land for any purpose, no matter for what purpose it had originally been acquired. Other objectionable clauses, including one giving the Corporation power to make the provision of parking spaces a precondition of planning permission, were removed by a Select Committee of the House of Commons after the Chamber of Commerce had petitioned it to do so.

In the late 1950s, the Chamber declined to associate itself entirely with the Labour group's efforts to extend the city boundaries, which it considered to be a party-political matter. However, it tacitly welcomed the possibility of more space for industrial expansion within the city, for few of its members were willing to transfer their production away from Birmingham.[1] On the other hand, the Chamber openly supported the Corporation's plans to build an exhibition hall.

Another aspect of municipal policy which the Chamber fully supported, in association with organizations such as the Road Haulage Association, was the concentration on new road building and the provision of parking facilities in the city centre. Here again, the Chamber was not invited after 1945 to participate directly in the planning of the road programme, but the Corporation welcomed its support. For instance, the Chamber was invited to join municipal delegations which urged the Minister of Transport to allow an immediate start on the inner ring road in the mid-1950s. Moreover, the Chamber, and especially its junior branch, showed great foresight in calling from the early 1950s for the provision of a coordinated regional transport system using all existing means of transport. However, the Government and the elected authorities did not begin to take positive steps in this direction until the early 1960s. In contrast, the Corporation did its best to build up international air services from Elmdon airport, partly in response to requests by the Chamber.

More direct influence was exercised by the Chamber in the field of education. By occupying some of the numerous cooptable seats on the Education Committee, and serving as school and college governors, industrialists were able to exercise a personal influence on educational planning. Some of these members were appointed directly by the Chamber, and all of them were advocates of the Chamber's consistent policy, which was that technical education should be developed substantially to meet Birmingham industry's need for trained employees. This point of view was accepted by the Education Committee and the

[1] Birmingham Chamber of Commerce, *Annual Report and Accounts*, 1959, p. 2.

City Council, and as soon as it became possible in the 1950s to concentrate on technical education, Birmingham did so, achieving results which were paralleled in few other cities. The Chamber helped by encouraging industrialists to cooperate willingly and effectively in day-release schemes.

Before the war the Chamber had called repeatedly for economies of municipal expenditure. After 1945 it modified this demand, recognizing that local authorities no longer had much control over their own outlay. Instead, it began to call from 1953 for the reform of local government finance in order to allow authorities more choice in the services they provided. The Chamber maintained a firm opposition to the extension of all forms of municipal trading. It had much success here, for it was usually able to have clauses embodying new trading powers deleted from Corporation Bills.[1]

(ii) THE TRADES COUNCIL

Like the Chamber of Commerce, the Birmingham Trades Council[2] had to make up its mind whether to concentrate on national and international issues, where it could have very little influence, or on local affairs. Like the Chamber, it chose the former, despite the T.U.C.'s post-war efforts to persuade it to restrict its attention to local matters.

The Trades Council was considerably younger than the Chamber of Commerce, having been formed in 1866, but it was one of the largest provincial Trades Councils and claimed to have considerable national and local influence. Its meetings, attended by elected delegates of local union branches, were much larger than those of the Council of the Chamber of Commerce, and the attendance was often well over 150 in the early years after the war. Unlike the Chamber of Commerce, whose members became less and less interested in involvement with particular political parties, the Trades Council frequently linked its action to that of the Labour Party. However, its close ties with the Borough Labour Party did not always ensure harmony between the two, nor was the Trades Council, on account of its wider interests, consistently interested in the work of the local party.

During the 1920s the growing success of Labour municipal and parliamentary candidates in the city, and the general strike débâcle, had helped to strengthen support for political action among the Birmingham trade unions. But in the early 1930s the Trades Council withdrew much of its effort, and, in a local context, concentrated on industrial matters. Links with the Borough Labour Party were strengthened again towards the end of the 1930s, and they became very close

[1] Its big successes were in forcing the deletion of trading clauses from the Bills of 1953 and 1958.

[2] For a general history of the Trades Council, see John Corbett, *The Birmingham Trades Council 1866–1966* (1966).

during the war, when trade union support for the Labour Party both locally and nationally reached a new zenith.

After the war enthusiasm dwindled. The Labour Government and the new Labour majority in the City Council often disappointed the Trades Council. The first disagreement between the Trades Council and the Labour group occurred in 1946 when Labour refused to accept responsibility for squatters in army camps, against the Trades Council's wishes.[1] Communist strength in the Trades Council grew during the 1940s, and they and their sympathizers dominated it from 1943 till about 1950, and from about 1954 till 1962. The periods of Communist domination coincided with a growing disenchantment among both Communist and non-Communist Trades Council members with the actions of the Labour majority in the City Council. During these years, Communist influence was used by the Labour group of City Council members as an excuse for disregarding the Trades Council's views.

So despite its close links with a political party, the Trades Council had less influence on local decisions than did the Chamber of Commerce. Certainly the policies it advocated would have been more difficult and costly to apply than those favoured by the Chamber, which in their essentials amounted to the creation of a climate, and provision of facilities, which would allow private enterprise to flourish. The Trades Council, for its part, also wanted to see Birmingham industry prosper, and at times of high unemployment like the mid-1950s it advocated policies that differed little from those of the Chamber. But at other times its more socialist views were usually too much for the Labour group in the City Council, especially after the group's drift to the right had begun in the mid-1950s.

We can ignore the Trades Council's activities in respect of national and international issues, where it acted primarily as a debating society, for they had no relevance to Birmingham. Although only about one-third of its debating time was devoted to local affairs, it was in a much better position to influence these during and after the war than it had been before. Despite the growing strength of trade unions in Birmingham in the 1930s, their potential importance as a major agency in the shaping of community policy was not recognized until the war, when their cooperation was needed both to ease the running of the war economy, and to help organize local emergency arrangements. The number of public bodies on which the Trades Council was represented grew rapidly during the 1940s, and it acquired an enhanced public image of responsibility. This improved standing was accentuated by an increase during the 1940s in the representation in the Council of public and supervisory employees. A monthly newspaper, the *Birmingham Journal*,

[1] B.T.C., *Annual Report*, 1946–7, p. 8.

was launched by the Trades Council in 1946, after many criticisms by delegates of the Borough Labour Party's weekly *Town Crier*.

In the great majority of its resolutions on local matters, the Trades Council acted as a socialist voice of conscience for the Labour group in the City Council. It opposed municipal rent increases almost consistently, the only important exception being in 1963 when Alderman Watton, by a brilliant *tour de force*, persuaded it to approve the City Council's withdrawal of the general rate subsidy. It frequently called for better and cheaper public transport services, comprehensive secondary education, and the expenditure of more municipal funds on the arts. It believed that a high standard of social services was preferable to low rates.

In all of these matters the Trades Council was largely ignored, although one important exception was its call for free travel for old age pensioners in 1950.[1] Harry Watton, who was Vice-President of the Trades Council at the time, eventually persuaded the Labour group to adopt this policy. The group also agreed with the Trades Council on the need to encourage the arts. There was even one major success in influencing the Conservative group, which in March 1952 approved a new housing allocation scheme incorporating a number of modifications recommended by the Trades Council.[2] But the Council naturally devoted its major effort to influencing Labour's municipal policies, and members of the Labour group who were also members of the Trades Council found themselves increasingly isolated, as the 1950s wore on, among a mass of delegates who were hostile to many of Labour's municipal policies. However, the Trades Council fully supported the City Council's application for a boundary extension in 1959, in the interest of an improved building rate. It also supported clauses in Corporation Bills aimed to extend municipal powers; very often, of course, these were the same clauses that the Chamber of Commerce attacked. On the other hand, the Council echoed, though for different reasons, the Chamber's demand for the reform of the rating system. It wanted to allow the Corporation to increase its expenditure, not reduce it, and it campaigned in the 1950s for the abolition of industrial derating. Here, of course, it did not enjoy the support of the Chamber of Commerce.

There was some slight improvement in relations with the Labour group after the Communists lost control of the Trades Council in 1962, and internal quarrels in the Trades Council died down. However, the basic cause of the Trades Council's disenchantment with Labour had not been Communist influence, but a genuine concern shared by Communists and non-Communists alike at Labour's rejection of

[1] B.T.C., *Annual Report*, 1950–1, p. 8.
[2] B.T.C., *Annual Report*, 1951–2, pp. 14, 63.

traditional socialist policies. So the gulf still remained unbridged in the 1960s.

The Labour group, like the parliamentary party, courted danger by placing the loyalty of the trade unions at risk,[1] but it still considered that it had some justification for ignoring the views of the Trades Council. Not only could it argue that expressions of dissent were Communist-inspired, but it could also point to a decline in the interest of Birmingham trade union branches in the work of the Trades Council, dating from the early 1950s. After about 1950 the Trades Council's energies were dissipated by its failure to agree on whether to cooperate as far as possible with the Conservative Government and restrict itself to practical local issues, or whether to discuss national and international affairs. This quarrel, which was exacerbated by deep-seated political differences between Communists and non-Communists in the Trades Council, made it impossible to maintain the high level of interest and activity of the 1940s, and attendances at meetings began to drop.[2] The circulation of the *Birmingham Journal* remained low, and the paper lurched from one financial crisis to another. The Trades Council received as early as 1955 a rude indication of its declining municipal importance when the City Council failed to invite it to join a delegation to the Minister of Transport over the inner ring road, even though the Chamber of Commerce had been asked to attend.[3] Annoyance was expressed at a similar rebuff in 1961, when the Trades Council was excluded from a delegation to the Minister of Housing.[4]

Like the Chamber of Commerce, the Trades Council tried to play a regional as well as a local role from the 1950s, but without much success. Average attendance at meetings, which had increased from 106 in 1943 to over 200 by 1951,[5] had dropped to about seventy by the mid-1960s. Meetings obtained almost no coverage at all in the Birmingham daily press from the early 1950s, and one branch even suggested in 1957 that press facilities should be withdrawn unless reports were published.[6] So it is necessary to conclude that although the Trades Council was a very active pressure group, it had very little influence on decisions affecting Birmingham.[7] However, in one very important aspect it helped to influence Birmingham community attitudes. This was in the

[1] The *Birmingham Journal* did indeed assert that the Borough Labour Party's disarray was responsible for trade unionists' unwillingness to vote Labour at local elections (June 1960, p. 1).

[2] Corbett, *Trades Council*, pp. 156–7.   [3] B.T.C., *Annual Report*, 1955–6, p. 21.

[4] B.T.C., *Annual Report*, 1961–2, p. 8.   [5] Corbett, *Trades Council*, p. 144.

[6] This motion was defeated after the secretary, Harry Baker, had assured the Trades Council that its relations with the press were too good to be thrown away in this fashion (*Annual Report*, 1956–7, p. 13).

[7] The Sheffield Trades Council appears to have been equally without influence, for similar reasons, until the mid-1960s. See William Hampton, *Democracy and Community: A Study of Politics in Sheffield* (1970), pp. 75–6.

matter of coloured immigration. The Trades Council, despite occasional objections from some union branches, never deviated from its stand in favour of free entry into Britain for Commonwealth immigrants. Right from the early 1950s it urged local trade union branches to welcome coloured workers, and the great majority did so. Thus the Trades Council set an example in community relations, and by bringing coloured workers into the union structure it prevented the strife which might have resulted if large numbers of immigrants had worked for lower wages than equivalent white workers. There was a clear difference of attitude between the Birmingham Trades Council and other Trades Councils in the West Midlands, most of which came to favour immigration controls in the later 1950s.[1] The Birmingham Trades Council must receive some of the credit for the avoidance of serious racial conflict in the city.

This chapter has discussed some of the major aspects of Birmingham's political life during the years 1939–70. It has shown that power to secure the city's well-being was shared between the City Council and the central Government, and has suggested that the Government's share of that power tended to increase at the expense of the City Council's. We shall see in the following chapter how this shift in the balance of power virtually deprived Birmingham citizens of the right to decide the future size and functions of their own city.

[1] The Midland Federation of Trades Councils passed a resolution early in 1955 calling for control of immigration, against strong opposition from the delegates of the Birmingham Trades Council (B.T.C., *Annual Report*, 1955–6, p. 9).

IV

THE END OF EXPANSION: PLANNING STRATEGIES IN AN ERA OF RESTRICTED GROWTH

THE municipal boundaries of the city of Birmingham remained almost unaltered throughout the years 1939–70. This stability made an abrupt contrast with the rapid expansion of the city's area which began in the late nineteenth century and ended in the early 1930s. It was perhaps the most important single factor affecting Birmingham's development after 1939. The aim of this chapter is to explain how and why a policy of retrenchment replaced expansionism, and to examine its effects on the plans made during and after the war for the evolution of the city.

Even before 1939 the City Council had become aware that the local and national political climate was no longer favourable to Birmingham's further expansion. Until the early 1930s it had been an article of faith among the city fathers that sheer size was conducive to the prosperity and good government of Birmingham. This assumption had also been accepted by the central Government and even by many of the neighbouring communities which Birmingham had engulfed.[1] In the 1930s, however, the central Government began to show concern at the lack of expanding industries in the depressed areas, and at the strategic vulnerability of the large industrial cities.[2] The designation of the Special Areas in 1934 marked a substantial change of course towards the geographical planning of the national economy, and implied a deceleration of the immigration of people and industry into large cities like Birmingham. At about the same time, the neighbouring local authorities, some of whose populations contained growing proportions of people who had moved there to escape high rates and cramped living conditions in Birmingham, strengthened their opposition to boundary extensions.

The City Council accepted this new situation with good grace. It recognized the Special Areas' prior need for new industry, and it voluntarily toned down the efforts of the municipal Information Bureau, which had been set up in 1930, to attract firms to Birmingham.[3] The Corporation also accepted the implications of changes in the national housing subsidy structure in the 1930s, and concentrated its

---

[1] See Briggs, pp. 269–77.   [2] See above, p. 16.

[3] In the later 1930s the Bureau restricted itself mainly to providing general information, and to helping buyers to get in touch with Birmingham firms (J. T. Jones, *History of the Corporation of Birmingham*, vol. v, pp. 550–2; Black, pp. 654–6).

resources on slum clearance, rather than on increasing the total of dwellings in Birmingham.[1] At the same time, council members began to recognize the problems of providing adequate services and amenities in Birmingham's sprawling low-density suburbs, especially in a decade when capital expenditure was so severely restricted.[2] The introduction of industrial derating in 1929 meant that the accumulation of industry brought hardly any financial advantage to the Corporation. Moreover, informed public opinion within the city began to react against the old expansionist orthodoxy.[3] It was natural that the City Council, which had been in the van of town planning developments in Britain since the early 1900s, and which still retained within its ranks individuals from such families as the Cadburys and the Nettlefolds, which had long held advanced views on town planning, should recognize this movement of public opinion against unrestricted growth.

One symptom of the Council's changed attitude was its adoption of a green belt policy in the 1930s, when it purchased or accepted trustee-ship of large areas of land on the city boundaries for preservation as open space. By 1939 several thousand acres, mainly in the south and south-west, were under the Corporation's control, partly thanks to the generosity and cooperation of Cadbury Brothers Limited, which gave or sold large areas of land to the City Council. The Corporation entered into covenants in respect of most of this land to preserve it in perpetuity as open space.[4] In one instance, the City Council decided to preserve as open space land which it had purchased in 1930 for housing, but which it considered by the later 1930s to be too distant from the city centre. The Corporation also cooperated with neighbouring authorities to secure other areas against development.[5] Birmingham was almost the only provincial city to adopt so ambitious a green belt policy at this time.[6] It is true that the acquisition of these areas did not commit the City Council to the principle of an all-embracing, restrictive green belt; indeed, the City attempted to keep all its options open, and declared its opposition to any imposition of restrictions on growth by the central Government. But the Council's energy in securing these open areas was a clear sign of a movement of municipal opinion

---

[1] See below, p. 223.

[2] See e.g. Geoffrey Boumphrey, *Town and Country Tomorrow* (1940), pp. 21–3, quoting a Corporation official's criticism of the lack of amenities, and inaccessibility, of the new estates. On the other hand, because many people lived near their work, average journey times could still appear very low. See *When We Build Again*, pp. 64–5, 76; *City of Birmingham Education Committee, Report on Registration of Boys and Girls Order 1941,* July 1943, p. 13.

[3] See e.g. *B.P.*, 20 May 1938, editorial.   [4] Jones, pp. 337–8; Black, pp. 625–6.

[5] Royal Commission on the Distribution of the Industrial Population, *Memorandum of Evidence Submitted by the Corporation of Birmingham*, para. 61.

[6] *Conurbation*, p. 209.

towards some containment of growth.[1] In any case, the City Council
clearly recognized that the days of big boundary extensions had gone
for ever. The opposition of nearby local authorities strengthened as
time went on, for while the boundaries remained static from 1931, the
population of middle-class commuter suburbs outside the boundaries
steadily expanded. These middle-class communities were eager to
defend not only their own homes from annexation by Birmingham,
but also nearby agricultural areas which they regarded as essential
amenities. They certainly did not want to see them occupied by
working-class municipal tenants, who were part of the reason why
they had left Birmingham in the first place. These views penetrated
directly into the City Council through the growing number of Unionist
members who had homes in Solihull, Sutton Coldfield, and other
suburban or rural areas near the city.

The City Council's attitude towards the question of the optimum
size of the city in the late 1930s was embodied, though in a somewhat
indirect fashion, in its evidence to the Royal Commission on the
Distribution of the Industrial Population (Barlow Commission). The
major significance of this evidence does not lie in its strong demand for
the right to decide locally on the best size for the city, for such a reaction
was inevitable to a Royal Commission which might conceivably have
recommended the dismantling of sections of Birmingham's existing
industries. What shines through the somewhat defensive statement put
forward is the City Council's almost complete renunciation of expansionism. This renunciation was greatly strengthened during the
war years.[2] Again, this reinforcement resulted from a combination of
outside influences and pressures, and a movement of opinion within
Birmingham. The report of the Barlow Commission in 1940, accepted
in principle by the Government, called for the decentralization of
population and industry from the big cities, and the movement of
some industry to the Special Areas. The air raids convinced both the
Government and the City Council that the strategic dangers of the
concentration of industry had not been exaggerated, and emergency
dispersal arrangements for key firms worked so well that Birmingham
industry was no longer so resolutely opposed to decentralization as it
had been before 1939. The Corporation's determination to obtain the
best possible advice on post-war reconstruction led to the co-option of

---

[1] For further evidence of this movement of opinion, see e.g. B.C.C. *Pro.*, 10 January
1939, p. 59 (Public Works Committee); evidence of Alderman Harold Roberts
(chairman of General Purposes Committee) to the Barlow Commission, reported in
B.M., 19 May 1938.

[2] See e.g. statement of decision not to apply to the Local Government Boundary
Commission for an extension of the boundaries in 1946 (B.C.C., *Pro.*, 14 October
1947, pp. 1086–8 (General Purposes Committee)).

outside experts on committees and advisory panels, and the advice of local pressure groups was heard with interest and respect.

The most influential report of such a body was the Bournville Village Trust's *When We Build Again* (1941), which argued that Birmingham was already too big, and proposed the enforcement of a rigid green belt around the city boundaries, with one or more satellite towns some distance away to take surplus population.[1] Another important influence was that of the West Midland Group on Post-War Reconstruction and Planning, a product of the interest stimulated by the Barlow report, which was set up in January 1941.[2] Cadbury influence was almost as strong within this group as in the Bournville Village Trust, for the family provided two full members and one corresponding member, one of whom, Paul Cadbury, was honorary secretary. Financial support came from the Bournville Village Trust. The group also included a number of prominent academics, including Dr. Raymond Priestley and Professor P. Sargant Florence from the University of Birmingham, and some major local industrialists. Most important of all, it included the Unionist Alderman Sir Wilfrid Martineau, and the City Engineer, Herbert Manzoni. These two were the only representatives of Birmingham local government in the group until Paul Cadbury was invited to fill a Liberal vacancy on the City Council later in 1941.[3] Although the group was essentially a fact-finding body, not a propaganda institution, it made certain basic assumptions which appear to have been accepted by all its members. Among them was the premise that the conurbation was already large enough, and that redevelopment of existing defective areas should be given a high priority after the war. This point of view was certainly shared by Herbert Manzoni. The work of this group was well-known to the City Council long before its first reports appeared in 1944.[4] In addition, the Public Works Committee set up four advisory planning panels early in 1942, on to which outside experts and interest-representatives were co-opted, several of them from the West Midland Group. One of these panels was given the principal task of studying the 'limitation of the city', and although it did not completely rule out boundary extensions, its reports implied that the city's growth would be restricted or discouraged after the war.[5] Indeed, at that time and even until the late 1940s it was generally believed that the city would stop growing of its own accord, for accepted population projections

[1] Bournville Village Trust, *When We Build Again* (1941), pp. vii, 113, 120.
[2] West Midland Group on Post-War Reconstruction and Planning, *Constitution, Organization and Research Programme* (1946), pp. 2–5; *B.P.*, 23 May 1941. The Group was set up actually at the suggestion of Sir Montague Barlow (*ex inf.* P. S. Cadbury).
[3] *Conurbation*, pp. 5–8.
[4] *Reports on the Control of the Use of Land and the Administrative and Financial Problems of Town-Planning, with a Note on the Size and Function of Local Government Units* (1944).
[5] B.C.C., *Pro.*, 9 March 1943, pp. 258–9 (Public Works Committee).

assumed that the birth rate would return to the low level of the 1930s after the war, resulting in an actual *decline* of the population of Britain after 1950.[1]

Given these restrictionist influences, it is not surprising that the City Council's plans for the post-war reconstruction of Birmingham showed none of the outright expansionism which had been so fundamental a feature of its policies until the early 1930s. Herbert Manzoni presented a preliminary report on planning to the Public Works Committee as early as October 1941, and in March 1943 the City Council was given a long account of progress, and of the work of the advisory panels.[2] Other reports followed on specific planning problems, and although the probable necessity of some housing outside the city boundaries was already foreseen, hopes were high that much of it could be grouped in a satellite town or towns. Although the possibility of more peripheral housing was never explicitly ruled out, there was clearly no question of undertaking general extensions of the built-up areas. However, Government interference was still resented; the City Council remained unwilling to surrender control of the future size of the city to any regional organization, and expressed concern at suggestions that the Government might force some Birmingham firms to move out of the city after the war. It was reassured to some extent by the Minister of Reconstruction, Lord Woolton, who told a civic delegation in November 1944 that although Birmingham might be too big, it was unthinkable that any government should attempt to reduce its size.

Nevertheless, many council members continued to have misgivings. In January 1945 the Minister of Labour, Ernest Bevin, told Birmingham industrialists at a Town Hall meeting in his usual forthright manner that control of industry would be essential after the war.[3] In March of the same year the City Council expressed concern over the Government's Distribution of Industry Bill, which required prior notification to the Board of Trade of creations of industrial floorspace exceeding 3,000 square feet. The Council wanted to see that figure increased to 30,000.[4] Unionist and Labour leaders, supported by Paul Cadbury, joined in criticizing the Bill on the grounds that it would delay central area redevelopment and the replacement of obsolete factories.[5] Some of the speeches also reflected the views of Birmingham industrialists who saw the Bill as an intolerable restriction on their freedom to expand. Although the Government agreed to introduce certain modifications into the Bill, and the fuss in Birmingham died down after March, the City Council remained wary of the danger that restrictions on the size

[1] See e.g. *Conurbation*, p. 78.
[2] B.C.C., *Pro.*, 9 March 1943, pp. 258–72 (Public Works Committee).
[3] *B.G.*, 27 January 1945.
[4] B.C.C., *Pro.*, 13 March 1945, pp. 164–8 (General Purposes Committee).
[5] *B.M.*, 13 March 1945; *B.G.*, 14 March 1945.

of the city might be imposed from outside, instead of on the Council's own initiative, as it had always wanted. The Unionists now became much more prepared to listen to the Labour group, which was genuinely worried about the higher densities planned in the post-war housing and slum clearance programme announced to the Council in 1943.[1] In July 1945 the Council carried an amendment, proposed by Councillor Bradbeer (Labour), calling on the Public Works Committee to report on the possibility of acquiring land outside the city boundaries for a number of purposes, including housing and industry.[2] When Labour achieved a dominant influence in policy-making in November 1945, it took up where the Unionists had left off in defending the Birmingham industrialist against undue interference. Although the group was unwilling to take too strong a lead in opposing a Government formed by its own party, it supported a Unionist amendment in April 1947 calling on the Government to amend the Town and Country Planning Bill, which required Board of Trade approval for industrial developments, so that it should not apply to new buildings with a floor space of less than 10,000 square feet.[3]

This concern over the destiny of Birmingham industry might have lasted much longer if it had not soon become clear that the Government's bark was much worse than its bite. In November 1948 the Council carried a Unionist amendment calling on the Board of Trade to provide information on the number of Birmingham applications for new factories or extensions which had failed to secure industrial development certificates.[4] The Board of Trade refused, on the ground that applications were confidential, but a survey by the Midland Region office of the Federation of British Industries suggested that not a single firm had so far been refused permission to develop. So the Public Works Committee concluded that the section of the Town and Country Planning Act 1947 relating to industry 'has not, up to the present, had any serious effect upon the industrial development of the city'.[5]

With this reassurance on the effect of Government policy, the Council was able to proceed in some tranquillity to the preparation of the

[1] Labour had tried in vain to move a major reduction in planned densities in the Duddeston and Nechells redevelopment area in 1943 (B.C.C., *Pro.*, 27 July 1943, p. 462 (Public Works Committee)). Birmingham's high densities were also strongly criticized by the Town and Country Planning Association; see e.g. R. L. Reiss, 'Edinburgh, Plymouth and Birmingham: post-war proposals with an epilogue on density', *Town and Country Planning*, vol. xii, 1944, pp. 69–70; 'Big Seven' (editorial article), ibid., vol. xiii, 1945, p. 50.
[2] B.C.C., *Pro.*, 31 July 1945, pp. 720–1 (Public Works Committee). The City continued to purchase green belt land after the war; by 1950 it owned nearly 6,000 acres (*Y.B.*, no. 39, April 1950, p. 3).
[3] B.C.C., *Pro.*, 1 April 1947, pp. 534–5 (General Purposes Committee).
[4] B.C.C., *Pro.*, 9 November 1948, p. 91 (Public Works Committee).
[5] B.C.C., *Pro.*, 12 April 1949, p. 582 (Public Works Committee).

Development Plan for Birmingham, which was required of it by the Town and Country Planning Act 1947. It was fortunate to be able to consult two major studies of the conurbation which appeared soon after the war. The more influential of the two was the West Midlands Plan, which was commissioned in June 1946 by the Minister of Town and Country Planning from Sir Patrick Abercrombie and Herbert Jackson. The plan was completed in 1948, after Abercrombie's similar plan for Greater London. In the same year the West Midland Group's *Conurbation* was published. These two planning surveys had much in common. Both rejected the further peripheral growth of the conurbation, and advocated the establishment of a wide green belt around it. Both recognized that some control and dispersal would be necessary. They differed, however, in their attitude to the problem of overspill. The West Midland Group accepted a lower estimate of the future population of the conurbation than did Abercrombie and Jackson, and so was able to advocate the rehousing of all excess population from existing built-up areas on derelict and unused land *within* the boundaries of the conurbation. The West Midlands Plan anticipated that the population of the conurbation would continue to increase until the end of the century, and predicted that despite infilling within the conurbation, large numbers of people would have to move to new or expanded towns beyond the green belt. Both surveys agreed that Birmingham, as the most dynamic area of the conurbation, would generate a very high proportion of any excess population, and that some of its industries would have to move out. Moreover, great care would have to be exercised in allowing any new industries to enter Birmingham. However, both recognized that Birmingham was probably the most suitable location for certain industries, especially those using mass-production techniques, and those which had close links with industries already firmly established in the city, such as the vehicle industry. The West Midland Group estimated that the population of Birmingham would fall slightly by 1971 to about one million; Abercrombie and Jackson, on the other hand, projected a population of 1,210,883 by 1962. They recommended that the optimum population of Birmingham should be 990,000, which would involve an overspill from the city of some 220,000 people during the following fourteen years.

There was very little in the West Midlands Plan to which the City Council could take exception, especially as its main conclusions had been reached separately by the West Midland Group, which included Corporation representation. The Public Works Committee accepted the Minister of Town and Country Planning's recommendation that the West Midlands Plan should guide it in drawing up the city's Development Plan. At the Minister's request, the conurbation planning authorities met together in January 1949 to coordinate their plans, and set up a technical committee composed of their principal planning officers. This committee reported in June 1949 to a further meeting of the planning authorities, which accepted nearly all the major proposals of the West Midlands Plan. Their main proviso was that the plan's proposals for the redistribution of population and industry should be reconsidered with a view to the possibility of 'accommodating a portion of the anticipated increase in population of the area by higher densities and by extensions of certain urban units'. In addition, the meeting rejected Abercrombie's suggestion that a single planning authority should be set up for the whole conurbation, though it agreed that some form of joint organization was necessary.[1]

The Birmingham Public Works Committee accepted the conclusions of the meeting of planning authorities in so far as they related to the area as a whole, but later in the year it announced provisos to the West Midlands Plan's proposals for Birmingham. The committee wanted to ensure, first, that any redistribution proposals agreed by the conurbation authorities and/or the Government should have the prior approval of the Corporation, in order to 'safeguard the individual position of the City'. Secondly, it wanted to make sure that there was no exclusion of the possibility of accommodating surplus population and industry by the development of areas outside existing centres of population—in other words, it wanted Birmingham to retain the option of building a satellite town or out-city estate.[2]

In 1950 the Minister of Town and Country Planning made a slight concession to Birmingham's point of view when he recommended one million as a target population figure for the city, and overall the City Council was well satisfied with the course that events had taken so far. It was at this late stage in the preparation of the Development Plan that the Public Works Committee undertook, in addition to the statutory surveys required by the Town and Country Planning Act, an industrial survey to determine the availability of land for immediate or ultimate industrial use.[3] It also incorporated a new population projection published by the Registrar-General in 1950, which took account of the continuing high birth rate. This new material delayed the completion of the plan, and the Corporation obtained an extension of the period allotted under the Act for the preparation of Development Plans from 1 July 1951 to 30 June 1952. The City Council was told that 'the difficult issue of the future population size of the City and the problem of deciding how best the limited amount of available land can be used' was partly responsible for the delay.[4]

[1] B.C.C., Pro., 26 July 1949, pp. 354–9 (Public Works Committee).
[2] B.C.C., Pro., 4 October 1949, p. 536 (Public Works Committee).
[3] Black, p. 378.
[4] B.C.C., Pro., 24 July 1951, pp. 260–1 (Public Works Committee).

These clear indications that the Public Works Committee was considering fitting a few more gills into its pint pot were confirmed when a draft outline plan was presented to the Council in October 1951. It was based on a target population of 1,081,000, slightly less than the current estimated population of 1,112,340, but more than the target population of one million suggested by the Minister in 1950. The population was to be arranged in two density-rings; an inner zone with 75–120 persons to the acre, and an outer, with fifty persons to the acre.[1] Edgbaston would remain a low-density enclave with thirty persons to the acre. Coupled with these proposals was a recommendation by the committee that future boundary extensions should be ruled out completely: '. . . your Committee are firmly of the opinion that there should not be any extension of the existing boundaries.' The committee's readiness to take this stand resulted partly from its assumption that the problem of overspill would not arise until 1962, by which time the population would have risen to 1,170,120. Overspill would not become necessary until house building was concentrated in the redevelopment areas in the mid-1960s.[2] With the benefit of hindsight, this prediction appears somewhat ingenuous, for not only was it based on the assumption that the house-building rate would continue at a low level, thus retarding slum clearance, but it ignored the likely increase in demand for separate dwellings owing to the reduction in average family size. Indeed, a note of caution was introduced by the Labour group when the report was debated, and Councillor Denis Howell moved that the three basic principles of the plan—the target population, the density-rings, and the stability of the city boundaries—should all be subject to reconsideration should changing circumstances require it. These amendments were accepted by the Unionist majority.[3]

In November the Public Works Committee submitted the section of the plan which dealt with industry and employment. It proposed that the area zoned for industrial use during the twenty-year period of the plan should be 5,474 acres, an increase of 1,053 acres (23·8 per cent) over the area currently occupied by industry. It described this increase as 'severely limited', and explained that the Board of Trade had advised the Corporation to follow the guidelines in the 1948 White Paper on the distribution of industry. This White Paper had recommended that the industrial expansion of 'congested' areas, notably Greater London and Greater Birmingham, should be limited in accordance with the proposals of the Barlow Commission. In its practical advice to Birming-

[1] The West Midlands Plan had recommended three density-rings of 120, seventy-five, and fifty persons to the acre, but the Public Works Committee chose to work with only two in order to allow more flexibility in the planning of the inner zone.

[2] Total overspill was estimated at 60,000 by 1971.

[3] B.C.C., *Pro.*, 9 October 1951, pp. 335–43 (Public Works Committee).

Housing in the central redevelopment areas. Alma Terrace, Highgate, before and after renovation.

Housing in the central redevelopment areas. Linden Terrace, Monument Road, before and after renovation.

ham,[1] the Board of Trade had recommended that provision should not be made for the accommodation of any large, new enterprises within the city, and that the area zoned for expansion should be kept 'to a minimum consistent with the known needs of firms already in the City'. The Public Works Committee's report made clear that it was prepared to accept that new firms should not, as a rule, be allowed to enter the city, but it was concerned to ensure that adequate provision be made for the normal expansion of Birmingham firms and for the foundation of new ones by Birmingham citizens. Moreover, it wanted adequate space to promote the dispersal of industry within Birmingham from the congested inner districts, and to assure the re-location of firms displaced from the central redevelopment areas. The committee hoped that industrial dispersal would be approached with caution:

Bearing in mind the importance to its [Birmingham's] workers of the maintenance of opportunities of employment, the key position of the City's industries from a National point of view, and the inherent danger of a disturbance of the balance of the City's industries leading to a retrogression, the City Council feel that the question of dispersal of industry is one which should be approached with caution. The solution must be based on National policy, and the City Council appreciate that the particular problems of Birmingham's industry, i.e. the technical and commercial considerations involved, have been given due consideration by the Board of Trade.

Subject to these qualifications, the Public Works Committee recommended that the principle of industrial dispersal be approved by the Council. And so it was, together with the rest of the report, and without the moving of any amendment.[2]

In December 1951 the Council approved the sections of the plan which dealt with open space and recreational land. The West Midlands Plan had recommended that the area of open space per thousand inhabitants should vary from four to seven acres depending on the density-ring, and the Public Works Committee accepted this standard, adapted to the two density-ring arrangement. However, there was no prospect within the plan's twenty-year period of reaching this standard, which would have required the provision of 6,979 acres of open space. At that time Birmingham had only 3,527 acres, and by 1971 would have increased this area only to 4,929 acres. But the committee suggested that golf courses, the Lickey Hills, Sutton Park (!), school playing fields, allotments, and market gardens, all of which were either outside the city, or not technically scheduled as open space, should be included in the calculations. If they were so included, Birmingham actually exceeded the standard laid down by Sir Patrick Abercrombie.

---

[1] Board of Trade Advice Paper to Birmingham (no. 31, February 1951).
[2] B.C.C., *Pro.*, 6 November 1951, pp. 418–37 (Public Works Committee).

K

Moreover, the Council was assured that in the very long term Birmingham would build up the required total of 6,979 acres of open space. Of course, the committee was looking on the bright side; in fact, the open space allocation in the Development Plan had been pared down to a minimum to allow the accommodation of the high target population figure and the extra industrial expansion. School playing fields, in particular, were very badly provided for, and the Education Committee was warned that 1,900 acres out of its requirement of 2,550 acres would have to be sought outside the city.[1] The Council, however, approved this section of the plan, again without the proposal of amendments.[2] Shortly after, in January 1952, it approved the submission of the whole plan to the Minister of Housing.[3]

Although the City Council had recommended a generous allocation of land for industrial expansion, it had not done so directly at the behest of Birmingham industrialists. In fact, the Chamber of Commerce had been very hurt by its exclusion from the planning process and was still worried that the City Council might not respect the interests of Birmingham industry.[4] Discussions now took place between interested City Council committees and the Birmingham Local Industrial Committee, a body composed of the general purposes committee of the Chamber of Commerce, and representatives of the Midland Region council of the Federation of British Industries. The industrialists announced their general approval of the City Council's plans, but were worried that ignorance about redevelopment projects and the long-term implications of the Development Plan might affect particular firms. The Corporation promised to answer specific queries wherever possible. To deal with the more general implications of the plan, it was decided to set up a standing joint conference to represent municipal, industrial, commercial, and trade union interests.[5]

The public inquiry into the Development Plan was held in February 1954.[6] There were originally some 450 objections, mainly from owners or occupiers of property in areas zoned for purposes to which their property did not conform. Many of these objections were warded off by negotiation and only about 200 interests lodged objections at the inquiry. All of them were specific, detailed complaints; there was no opposition to the general principles on which the plan was based. The *Birmingham Post* suggested that the absence of fierce opposition was the result of Birmingham's pioneer planning work before the war, which had accustomed the citizens to the concept of planning more than in

[1] At that time, Birmingham had only 370 acres of school playing fields.
[2] B.C.C., *Pro.*, 4 December 1951, pp. 507–13 (Public Works Committee).
[3] B.C.C., *Pro.*, 8 January 1952, p. 629 (Public Works Committee).
[4] See above, p. 113.
[5] B.C.C., *Pro.*, 21 April 1953, pp. 882–3 (General Purposes Committee).
[6] Black, p. 380; *Y.B.*, no. 80, December 1953, p. 1.

other areas.[1] So it was left to the Minister of Housing to recommend any major changes.

In the event, the Minister's main criticisms of the plan centred on the amount of land allocated for industrial expansion. In April 1955 he told the representatives of Birmingham Corporation and the three neighbouring counties that a 23·8 per cent increase was too great in view of 'the already serious lack of balance between industry and housing in the City'.[2] The Corporation took strong exception to this view. It maintained that the City Council had made it clear, when the industrial section of the Development Plan was discussed in 1952, that Birmingham fully accepted that there should be a balance between the city's industry and the population that could be housed within its boundaries, that some firms (preferably those engaged in non-metal trades) would have to move out of the city, and that some enterprises should not be allowed in.[3] The Corporation had subsequently tried (in vain) to obtain powers through a Corporation Bill to control industrial premises vacated by firms moving to overspill areas, to ensure that they were not reoccupied by firms from outside the city. An increase of one-quarter in the area of industrial land was needed, claimed the Corporation, to ensure the adequate relocation of firms displaced from the central redevelopment areas and to allow for the normal expansion of Birmingham firms. An increase in industrial floorspace, it was asserted, did not necessarily imply an increase in the labour force. More space was often needed to set up mechanized production in the single-storey buildings preferred by industrialists, which might well employ fewer workers than older processes.[4] The Minister's counter-argument was that the large increase of industrial land was inconsistent with Birmingham's attempts to obtain powers to control industries coming into the city. A later Minister repeated this argument in a letter to the Corporation in May 1958, and predicted that the target population figure would not be realized until some industry had moved out of the city.

By now the problem had been greatly complicated by the initiation in the mid-1950s of an overspill programme, which the Development Plan had not expected until the 1960s.[5] It was clear that if industry did not move to the overspill areas, people would refuse to go to live in

---

[1] B.P., 3 February 1954.

[2] Joyce R. Long, The Wythall Inquiry: A Planning Test Case (1961), p. 36.

[3] These points were emphasized more strongly than in the somewhat cautious wording of the Development Plan at a press conference given by Alderman Griffith, chairman of the Public Works Committee, and in an article written by Herbert Manzoni. See B.G., and B.P., 3 January 1952.

[4] For a statement of this argument, see Manzoni's evidence at the Wythall inquiry, quoted in Long, Wythall Inquiry, p. 36.

[5] See below, pp. 134 ff.

them. Furthermore, the city was fast running out of building land. Again, the Development Plan had not foreseen this situation, because it had expected a lower rate of house building, and had not considered that a high rate of household formation might greatly increase the demand for accommodation even while the population remained stable. Although the Government made a generous contribution towards the cost of houses built by reception areas for Birmingham overspill, this and the Corporation's own statutory contribution were not enough to encourage the building of houses in any but ludicrously small numbers. The problem was further accentuated by the Government's growing tendency to argue that overspill was essentially Birmingham's responsibility.

The City Council's reaction to the Government's attitude was to make further efforts to control industry. Although the General Purposes Committee made it clear that it could not countenance any harassment of Birmingham industry to force some of it to leave the city,[1] it accelerated its programme of purchase of vacated industrial premises in order to prevent their occupation by undesirable firms. Of course, part of its aim in doing so was to provide accommodation for firms displaced from the central redevelopment areas, but this co-objective was perfectly logical because, as we have already seen, the City's whole industrial policy was based on the principle of providing more space and facilities for firms from the congested central areas.[2] Between 1957 and 1966 Birmingham spent about two million pounds on acquiring such premises—a higher proportion of its rate income than the L.C.C. and later the G.L.C. spent for the same purpose.[3] In October 1957 the Public Works Committee recommended, in view of the Council's policy 'to restrain the growth of population and employment potential in the City', that a clause should be inserted in the Development Plan to give some control of the use of industrial land, in addition to the power to refuse applications on planning grounds. What the committee wanted was power to stop the allocation of sites to 'new industries' in areas required for the re-location of badly-sited Birmingham firms, or by

[1] B.C.C., *Pro.*, 24 July 1956, pp. 280–1 (General Purposes Committee).

[2] The Labour municipal policy manifesto of 1957 stated that the purchase programme was intended to prevent the entry of 'new, undesirable industries'.

[3] We are grateful for this information to Mrs. Barbara Smith, Centre for Urban and Regional Studies. The site area of the premises so acquired between 1957 and 1966 totalled twenty-nine acres. A peak was reached in 1961, but more properties were being acquired each year in 1963–6 than in the later 1950s (*ex inf.* Estates Department). For other measures and methods used by the Corporation to discourage new firms from entering the city, and to encourage Birmingham firms to move to overspill areas, see Long, *Wythall Inquiry*, pp. 37–9. Of the seventy-two industrial premises vacated by firms moving out of the city in the late 1950s, the Corporation acquired thirty-five, of which it demolished twenty-six. The other nine were leased to firms from the central redevelopment areas (*Y.B.*, no. 150, April 1960, p. 1).

Birmingham firms which needed to expand. However, the committee thought that some land could be allocated to industries that were new in the sense that they were developed from scratch within the city. The Conservatives objected to the wording of this proposal, because it did not give sufficient prominence to the assurance that new firms developed by Birmingham citizens would be encouraged, in the tradition of the city. This criticism seemed to Labour to make sense and the committee's proposal was referred back.[1] At the next meeting it was passed in a new form, which stated that industrial land was intended 'mainly' for existing Birmingham firms, and not for enterprises from outside. Such land should 'mostly' be reserved for new industries created by Birmingham citizens, for the relocation of misplaced industry, and for industry which was cramped and/or outmoded.[2] This still left the problem of the reoccupation of existing premises, vacated by firms moving to overspill areas, by new concerns from outside the city. So in November 1957 the City Council *unanimously* approved the insertion of a clause in a Corporation Bill to give the City power to nominate tenants for industrial premises of over 5,000 sq. ft. vacated under overspill schemes. This power would have supplemented the Corporation's existing practice of purchasing such premises whenever possible. However, a town's meeting and poll in December 1957 and January 1958 rejected the clause. They also threw out a clause which had been rejected once before, in 1954, which would have allowed the Corporation to nominate tenants for residential premises vacated under overspill schemes.[3]

During the campaign for the Corporation Bill it was emphasized that the City Council wanted only to control new firms from outside the city, not to expel existing concerns. Leaders of the Labour group made it clear on several occasions that they were still not prepared for the Corporation to take the initiative in moving industry out of the city; moreover, the comments of some of them now suggested that they did not want any industry *at all* to move out.[4] This change of emphasis resulted partly from the increased level of unemployment in Birmingham since 1956, a factor to which Labour was particularly sensitive. A further contributing influence was the reduction of industrial derating in 1958 which substantially increased the amount paid in rates on industrial premises. At a time when the Labour group was coming under considerable pressure from the Conservatives to stabilize the

[1] B.C.C., *Pro.*, 2 October 1956, pp. 437, 446 (Public Works Committee).

[2] B.C.C., *Pro.*, 8 January 1957, p. 681 (Public Works Committee).

[3] *B.M.*, 19 December 1957; B.C.C., *Pro.*, 4 February 1958, pp. 692–3 (General Purposes Committee).

[4] See e.g. comments by Alderman Jim Meadows, chairman of the Estates Committee, in *E.D.*, 22 September 1958; speech by Alderman Albert Bradbeer at the Freedom of the City ceremony in May 1960 (B.C.C., *Pro.*, 7 May 1960, p. 983).

rate poundage, a higher industrial rate contribution was a windfall to be gratefully accepted. Moreover, a survey undertaken by the Chamber of Commerce suggested that the great majority of Birmingham firms had no wish to leave the city.[1] Finally, it would seem that the Labour leaders now became sensitive to a nagging fear that the industrial vitality of the city might be ebbing slowly away.

These considerations certainly contributed to the Labour group's decision to apply for a boundary extension at Wythall, which constituted the first major change since the war in the Council's general development policy for the city. But this decision was not influenced purely by Birmingham self-interest. It was also, in part, the result of a long series of frustrations in the city's overspill programme. It is to the history of overspill that we must now turn.

As we have already seen, by the end of the war the City Council and most sections of informed opinion in Birmingham had come to accept the principle of a restriction of the city's growth. But during the early years of peace the Government, in the interests of the export drive, had done little to restrict the natural growth of Birmingham's industries. Inevitably, industrial expansion attracted workers from other parts of the country and from abroad. In addition, earlier marriages, the decline in the average size of households, and the Corporation's ambitious slum clearance plans were piling up the odds against the successful application to Birmingham of a policy of growth restriction. In the late 1940s, however, the implications of these developments were not clearly perceived. The house building rate was so low that the land shortage, which had been clearly foreseen before the war, was not of immediate concern to the City Council. This problem did not begin to demand urgent attention until the early 1950s, when the Council was suddenly informed by its officers that all building land inside the city boundaries would be used up within some five years. Fortunately (or so it seemed at the time), the Town Development Act of 1952 allowed and encouraged large towns and cities to arrange for the transfer of excess population into houses built by nearby local authorities in return for a subsidy paid by the exporter.

Birmingham, of course, had foreseen the need to house some of its population outside its boundaries before the war, and the first discussions with Worcestershire County Council took place in 1945.[2] After the publication of the official West Midlands Plan in 1948, the possibility of housing the surplus population within the conurbation was

---

[1] Long, *Wythall Inquiry*, pp. 37–8; Birmingham Chamber of Commerce, *Annual Report and Accounts*, 1959, p. 2.
[2] Long, *Wythall Inquiry*, p. 75.

ruled out, despite the advocacy of the West Midland Group.[1] In December 1950 a memorandum from the regional office of the Ministry of Town and Country Planning, prepared by Abercrombie and Jackson, recommended as a general principle that overspill population should be housed in self-contained communities beyond the green belt.[2] At this stage it was still uncertain whether overspill would go to existing communities, as Abercrombie and Jackson had suggested, or whether one or more new towns would be established. Abercrombie had recommended in his Greater London Plan that new towns should be built for the capital, and a number had already been designated under the New Towns Act of 1946. However, the new Conservative Government was strongly opposed to the designation of further new towns from 1951, partly because of its desire to restrict capital expenditure, and partly because of the popular reaction against planning in general, and the defects of the new towns in particular, which followed the fall of the Labour Government.[3] Instead, it drew up the Town Development Bill, which became law in 1952. The Minister of Housing, Harold Macmillan, told the House of Commons: 'Broadly speaking, the purpose of the Bill is that the large cities wishing to provide for their surplus population shall do so by orderly and friendly arrangements with neighbouring authorities. . . . I want to make it clear that it is our purpose that all these arrangements should be reached by friendly negotiation and not imposed by arbitrary power.'[4] The Act also empowered the Minister to provide Exchequer help for town expansion schemes, but such assistance was intended to be enough only to get the schemes moving. In addition, exporting authorities were expected to make a small financial contribution to the receiving authorities.

The new Act was welcomed in Birmingham where it coincided with the final stages of the discussion of the Development Plan. The draft of the plan approved by the Council in 1952 anticipated that the total requiring public housing beyond the city boundaries would be 60,000 by 1971,[5] but the Council made it clear that it did not wish to seek an extension of the municipal boundaries.[6] The Act was attractive to the City Council because not only did it seem to make the Development Plan feasible, but it was also a cheap solution to the city's housing problem. Rateable value was lost, it was true, when houses were built

[1] For a comparison between the approaches of Abercrombie and the West Midland Group, see M. C. Madeley, 'A new town for the Midlands', *Town and Country Planning*, vol. xxiv, no. 144, April 1956, p. 198.

[2] Long, *Wythall Inquiry*, p. 60; B.C.C., *Pro.*, 24 July 1956, pp. 283–91 (General Purposes Committee).

[3] Madeley, 'A new town for the Midlands', p. 202.

[4] *H. of C. Deb.*, 5th Series, vol. cdlxvi, cols. 725–6, 25 February 1952.

[5] City of Birmingham, *Development Plan, Statement* (1952), p. 1.

[6] For a very clear statement to this effect, see H. J. Manzoni, 'The City's development plan reviewed', *B.P.*, 3 January 1952.

for Birmingham citizens in other districts, but this loss was compensated by the very low contribution made to the receiving authority for the provision of housing. Moreover, Birmingham industry would not be affected because it was anticipated that people moving to overspill areas would continue to work in Birmingham for some time.[1] Unfortunately for Birmingham, it soon became clear that a scheme which appealed to the City Council from a financial point of view was not likely to appeal to the receiving authorities, for precisely the same reason. Discussions held with the neighbouring counties of Warwickshire, Worcestershire, and Staffordshire from 1952 revealed from the start that finance was the main problem.[2] By the time the General Purposes Committee set up a special sub-committee to consider overspill, under the chairmanship of Alderman W. T. Bowen (Labour), in July 1954, agreement on the financial arrangements still had not been reached.

The new sub-committee decided to bypass the county councils and approach the district councils directly, but the counties took strong exception to this move. At this stage the Minister of Housing had to be brought in, and at a meeting between him, Birmingham, and the three county authorities, in April 1955, the acrimony which had resulted from Birmingham's actions was largely smoothed over. But the financial issue was left in the air. Birmingham was prepared to pay to receiving authorities the statutory rate fund contribution for each house for a period of ten years. The counties wanted it for fifteen years. The Minister undertook to see if he could close the gap, and he later announced that after ten years of payment of the contribution by the exporting authority, an extra Exchequer grant would be provided for any period during which an unduly heavy burden would fall on the rates of the receiving authority.[3] This arrangement was accepted by the City Council.[4] But it was still not enough for the receiving authorities. Some progress was made from July 1955 when Birmingham and the three counties agreed to set up a joint committee on overspill to decide which district authorities were the most suitable to receive it, and Staffordshire now proved especially cooperative. But many district councils meanwhile began to express doubts about the adequacy of the financial arrangements.[5] Nevertheless, some tentative overspill agreements were

[1] See, for instance, statement by Alderman Bowen reported in B.M., 10 June 1955.

[2] 'Towards a New Birmingham', Municipal Journal, vol. lxi, no. 3172, 4 December 1953, p. 2625.

[3] H. of C. Deb., 5th series, vol. cxl, cols. 43–5, 26 April 1955. The Minister also made it clear for the first time that Exchequer grants for water and sewerage schemes would be at the uniform rate of 50 per cent.

[4] B.C.C., Pro., 14 June 1955, pp. 35–9 (Public Works Committee).

[5] B.C.C., Pro., 24 July 1956, pp. 264–74 (General Purposes Committee).

made, and late in 1956 the City Council established an overspill register for housing list applicants who were prepared to leave Birmingham.[1] The Housing Subsidies Act of 1956 increased the Government's contribution from £22 to £24 per house per year, and the City Council agreed to increase its own annual contribution from £7 7s. to £8.[2] By July 1957 overspill agreements had been made with the ten receiving authorities, but only eighty-eight houses had become available.[3] And although the number of overspill agreements began to increase rapidly from then on, there was still no prospect that they would provide a full solution to Birmingham's problem. The position was now serious enough for the leaders of the Labour group to hold a special meeting with local Labour M.P.s in September 1957, at which Alderman Bradbeer announced that the City had come up against a brick wall in overspill.

The object of approaching the M.P.s was to bring greater pressure to bear on the Government to provide help for Birmingham. At the time it still seemed possible that the Government might be willing to designate a new town. The demand for a new town, which was formulated in the city with increasing precision in the 1950s, reflected an ambition which had been expressed in Birmingham since before the war. It was natural that public opinion in a city which had seen one of the first garden suburbs, Bournville, and had approved the development of municipal estates on garden-suburb lines, should be favourably disposed to the building of independent garden cities. Bishop Barnes was one of the many prominent citizens to support the idea in the last years before the war.[4] The Bournville Village Trust advocated satellite towns in *When We Build Again*. Norman Tiptaft was attracted by the idea.[5] But until the New Towns Act was passed in 1946 the new town, or 'satellite town' as it was usually called, was envisaged in Birmingham as a community to be developed entirely by, and to be closely linked with, the parent city. After the Act was passed interest waned in Birmingham, and support for the idea of a new town did not grow again until the deficiencies of overspill arrangements under the 1952 Act became obvious after the mid-1950s.[6] The advantages of a new town seemed at first to be predominantly financial, for a new town would qualify for very much greater Government help than town expansion and would therefore have a greater chance of success. But as

[1] *Y.B.*, no. 112, November 1956, p. 3.   [2] Long, *Wythall Inquiry*, p. 76.
[3] B.C.C., *Pro.*, 23 July 1957, p. 266 (General Purposes Committee).
[4] E. W. Barnes, 'Benefits of satellite towns', *Town and Country Planning*, vol. vii, 1939, p. 22.
[5] Norman Tiptaft, *I Saw a City* (1945), pp. 29–30.
[6] However, the call for a satellite town was first included in the Labour municipal election manifesto as early as 1950. At that time it was derided as a 'red herring' by the majority Unionist Party.

the 1950s wore on the industrial advantages of a new town attracted increasing attention. When some of the financial obstacles to overspill schemes were overcome from the mid-1950s, concern was diverted to the task of providing extra employment in the overspill areas, a problem which had at first been ignored.

The Board of Trade's advice paper to Birmingham in February 1951, in connection with the Development Plan, had suggested that much of the movement of overspill population would not be accompanied by industry because the receiving areas would not want it.[1] Similarly, the Town Development Act of 1952 completely ignored the question of employment. So Birmingham had some excuse for not facing up fully to the industrial problem at this early stage. It was agreed that some firms might have to move, but the Town Clerk, J. F. Gregg, made it clear in 1953 that '. . . every care is being taken to avoid unnecessary disturbance or restriction of "key" industries.'[2] At the time movement of industry did not seem crucially important, for Alderman Bowen and his colleagues still believed that many people moving to overspill areas would commute to Birmingham, and potential receiving areas had still not yet emphasized their desire for new industry. But the whole situation changed in the mid-1950s. In the first place, two potential receiving areas nearby, Sutton Coldfield and Solihull, from which daily travel to work in Birmingham would have been easy, made it clear that they did not want any Birmingham overspill.[3] Their attitude was hardly surprising in view of the fact that these select residential districts were occupied predominantly by middle-class business people who earned their livings in Birmingham but were horrified by the thought that the city proletariat might pursue them home at night. However, Birmingham had previously considered these suburbs as possible overspill areas, and when they were struck off the list the employment problem was made much more serious. Secondly, the rise in unemployment in the mid-1950s made most of the reception areas very wary of accepting extra population without equivalent employment.[4]

So from 1955 Birmingham began to make strenuous efforts to persuade industry to move to overspill areas. In July 1955 it set up a small joint committee on overspill, composed of the planning officers of Birmingham and the three counties, to study the movement of industry. It also established an industrial bureau to provide information for firms

[1] Arthur J. Day, 'Location of industry and population: post-war policy in the West Midlands' (Birmingham M.Comm. thesis, 1954), pp. 17–26.

[2] 'Towards a New Birmingham', p. 2625.

[3] B.M., 26 September 1956; B.P., 17 October 1956.

[4] See, for instance, Coventry's insistence in 1957 that industry should accompany any overspill from Birmingham (Long, Wythall Inquiry, pp. 89–90).

which might be prepared to move.[1] In 1957 it began to offer special inducements to Birmingham firms to develop in overspill areas, and, encouraged by the Minister of Housing, it announced its intention to try to reduce the volume of employment within the city by some 5 per cent.[2] But, as we have already seen, the City Council rejected the idea that any firms should be deliberately harassed to persuade them to move out; it did not wish to add to the difficulties of industry, 'which is the life blood of the city.'[3]

The City's efforts to provide employment in the overspill districts soon encountered two serious obstacles. The first was that the very great majority of Birmingham firms did not want to move out of the city. The second problem was that when a firm *was* prepared to move, or at least to set up a branch factory, it was under strong pressure from the Board of Trade to establish production in one of the development areas.[4] The new town seemed to the City Council to offer a partial solution to both these problems. Because it would be larger than most of the expanded towns, and would achieve a quicker rate of growth, Birmingham firms might be more willing to move to it. And because it would have generous Government financial support, the Board of Trade would be more likely to approve the industrial developments without which it could not be a success.

So Birmingham's demand for a new town grew stronger and stronger from the mid-1950s. In 1955 it received some encouragement when it became known that the Government was surveying potential new town sites in the West Midlands, and the Minister of Housing, Duncan Sandys, admitted at the end of the year that a new town had not been excluded from the Government's plans.[5] In the meantime, the Minister suggested that Birmingham should build its own 'new town' in the form of an out-city estate, and promised every support in such a venture except financial aid. A precedent existed in the Kingshurst Hall estate, which lay just outside the city boundary in Warwickshire, and which the City Council had decided to develop in 1953.[6] But when the Corporation tried in 1956 to acquire 600 acres of building land to the east of the city, its efforts came to nought because the area was in the

---

[1] B.C.C., *Pro.*, 24 July 1956, p. 281 (General Purposes Committee).

[2] B.C.C., *Pro.*, 12 March 1957, p. 883 (Estates Committee); *The Times*, 15 October 1957, editorial.

[3] B.C.C., *Pro.*, 24 July 1956, p. 281 (General Purposes Committee).

[4] For a report on the problems of persuading industry to move, see B.C.C., *Pro.*, 7 October 1958, pp. 464–6 (General Purposes Committee).

[5] Madeley, 'A new town for the Midlands', p. 202; *H. of C. Deb.*, 5th series, vol. dxlvii, cols. *985–6*, 13 December 1955.

[6] B.C.C., *Pro.*, 6 January 1953, pp. 657–8 (House Building Committee). The City had assured the Warwickshire County Council that this development would not lead to an eventual boundary extension.

proposed Warwickshire green belt.[1] The idea of developing an out-city estate beyond the green belt was unattractive to Birmingham, which argued that such a venture would amount to a full-scale new town, and should therefore be financed by the Government. Strong support for this view came from a new pressure group, the Midlands New Towns Society, which was founded in Birmingham in January 1956 by a number of interested laymen, many of them members of the university.[2] In May 1956 a deputation from the overspill sub-committee told the Minister of Housing that a deficiency of 36,000 houses already existed in overspill arrangements, and suggested that this was 'so large as to demand consideration of development on a new town scale'. In July the City Council, told that Birmingham's total overspill problem was now estimated at 221,000, gave formal support to the General Purposes Committee by approving the call for the creation of a new town, despite the Conservative minority's view that all other possibilities should first be fully explored.[3] But later in the year this request was turned down by the Minister.

By this time Duncan Sandys had obtained a reputation as a strong defender of green belts and a firm opponent of requests for new towns from cities like Birmingham and Manchester. So there was some optimism in Birmingham when he was replaced at the Ministry of Housing by Henry Brooke in January 1957. Another Birmingham delegation saw Henry Brooke in April, but he told them the same as Sandys would have done, that there was no chance of a new town for the city.[4] Another delegation in July, with M.P.s in support, got the same answer. In the meantime, the L.C.C. gave in to the Government and agreed to finance a big out-county estate itself, thus cutting the ground from under Birmingham's feet. Last, desperate efforts were now made to make the Minister change his mind; seven Birmingham M.P.s went to see him in December 1957, and the matter was raised again when the Minister visited redevelopment areas in Birmingham in March 1958. But all these efforts were proved vain when a letter from the Ministry on 22 April 1958 confirmed that Birmingham would have no alternative but to press on with its overspill schemes.[5]

This rebuff was the last straw for the leaders of the Labour group. They now saw a boundary extension as the only possible solution to Birmingham's housing problem, which had been aggravated since the early 1950s by a declining building rate caused by the shortage of

[1] B.C.C., *Pro.*, 24 July 1956, p. 274 (General Purposes Committee).
[2] See *Town and Country Planning*, vol. xxiv, no. 143, March 1956, p. 159; D. E. C. Eversley and D. M. R. Keate, *The Overspill Problem in the West Midlands* (1958), preface.
[3] B.C.C., *Pro.*, 24 July 1956, pp. 275–302 (General Purposes Committee).
[4] B.C.C., *Pro.*, 23 July 1957, p. 271 (General Purposes Committee).
[5] B.C.C., *Pro.*, 7 October 1958, pp. 466–7 (General Purposes Committee).

land within the city.[1] True, a boundary extension had never been explicitly ruled out by the City Council, and since the early 1950s the General Purposes Committee had frequently mentioned extensions as a possible last ditch solution if the overspill programme should fail.[2] But such statements were mainly intended to frighten the Government and the county authorities into making overspill work. It was clear that the Labour group much preferred overspill agreements, if they could be made effective, to a boundary extension. Alderman Bradbeer, the group leader, was a strong supporter of the new town proposal, and Alderman Bowen, a former leader, was actively involved in overspill negotiations. But the arguments in favour of overspill lost all their influence on the Labour leaders towards the end of 1957, as they faced the gloomy prospect that the City's housing and slum clearance programme would grind to a halt within a few years. When Alderman Bradbeer was put out of action by a serious illness at the end of the year, his deputy, Alderman Harry Watton, became acting leader of the group. Watton had not been directly associated with the overspill policy, and he was therefore free to take a fresh look at the whole problem. He did so.

After the Minister's visit to Birmingham in March 1958 the Labour group discussed the growing crisis and agreed in principle to apply for an extension of the boundaries to take in some 4,000 acres. The City Engineer, Herbert Manzoni, with whom the Labour leaders had established a very close working relationship, was asked to prepare a confidential report on the strength of Birmingham's case for an extension, and to suggest where the extension might take place. Manzoni was surprised at this turn of events, but suspected that the group might be seeking merely to put more pressure on the Government for the designation of a new town. Indeed, when he met the group officers with his report at the end of April, he told them immediately that although an application for a boundary extension might make sense as a political move, it was very unlikely to make a positive contribution to the land shortage because the Government was almost certain to turn it down. Not only was the Government's whole town planning policy firmly rooted in the defence of green belts, pointed out Manzoni, but Birmingham did not have a very good case for special treatment. It could not base its case on general housing deficiency because it did not have one;[3] the city's population was declining owing to the voluntary departure

---

[1] See below, pp. 229 ff.

[2] See e.g. B.C.C., *Pro.*, 24 July 1956, p. 274 (General Purposes Committee).

[3] Manzoni was not entirely correct here. In 1958 it was still not fully realized that the rate of household formation was a more important indicator of the demand for accommodation than the current total of individuals and households living in an area. In fact, Birmingham had a substantial housing deficiency, as was later made clear at the public inquiry (see below). Manzoni was always inclined to underestimate

of people to live outside the boundaries, and the Board of Trade's refusal to allow new industry to enter the city. It was misleading, he argued, to look at the number of applicants on the housing register, which grossly exaggerated the housing shortage. Alternatively, Manzoni went on, the City could base its case on the need to proceed rapidly with slum clearance, but the main objection here was that the Corporation had itself decided to build houses in large numbers for general needs instead of concentrating on slum clearance as he (Manzoni) had repeatedly advised. In any case, enough land was available to allow the present clearance programme to proceed for the next five or six years. So, concluded Manzoni: 'If you want to use the threat of extensions as a weapon it is a different matter, but if you really want an extension I am certain that you will need a far better case than the figures suggest.'

This was a discouraging report. But after discussion, in which Alderman Watton pointed out that the Labour group had already made up its mind, the group officers resolved to pursue an application for 2,500 acres of land outside the city boundaries. This was, however, much less than the group had at first wanted. So the scheme was already being cut down to a size which, even if accepted, would not provide as radical a solution to Birmingham's land problems as Labour had originally hoped. But the group leaders were now convinced that there was no alternative. Harry Watton had already been told in confidence that even if a Labour Government were to be elected in 1959 or 1960, it would be unlikely to designate further new towns in its first few years. So there was no point in waiting to see what happened at the general election.[1] Furthermore, the April letter from the Ministry of Housing, referring to rumours in the press that the Corporation might apply for a boundary extension to be considered by the proposed Local Government Commission, had pointed out that the Commission would not consider questions of land use. In addition, the letter reminded the Corporation that the Ministry had in recent years defended green belt land against development, and that as the neighbouring counties were about to submit their proposals for green belts,' . . . the Council . . . would be well advised to get the matter settled one way or the other without more ado by applying for planning permission for the development which they have in mind.'[2]

The Labour leadership now took the whole question before the General Purposes Committee. Discussions there were lengthy, owing to

[1] John Lewis, 'The man they call "the boss"', *B.P.*, 6 May 1965.
[2] B.C.C., *Pro.*, 7 October 1958, pp. 497–8 (General Purposes Committee).

---

general housing needs because he wanted to see the maximum effort devoted to slum clearance.

the total reversal of policy that was involved, and the Conservatives' previous opposition to boundary extensions. The committee decided in the early summer to apply for an extension, though the Council was not informed until October. However, the Minister had been warned officially by this time that Birmingham would probably apply for a 'small planned boundary extension'. The Council approved the application in principle. The Conservatives accepted the necessity for a limited extension, but objected to the implication that a general extension of the boundaries was desirable. But their amendment to this effect was negatived.[1]

Part of the reason for the long delay in making a definite decision seems to have been that the Labour group leaders still hoped against hope that the Government might be persuaded to designate a new town. The Birmingham Labour M.P.s, who were opposed to the extension of a city which they considered to be much too big already, certainly hoped as much.[2] Pressure also came from the M.P.s of neighbouring constituencies which were likely to be affected by boundary extensions, and notably from R. Moss (Labour, Meriden). As late as November 1958 the Birmingham Labour M.P.s were complaining that they were still unclear about the Labour group's attitude to the whole question of overspill, new towns, and peripheral expansion. But as time went on, and Henry Brooke refused to budge, the Labour group hardened in its determination to press for a boundary extension. So in March 1959 the City Council was asked to approve a definitive proposal for a boundary extension of 2,432 acres in the south-east at Wythall, in addition to a request for planning permission. This time there was strong Conservative opposition, and the proposal was carried by seventy-five votes to forty-seven.[3]

The Government's uncompromising attitude was now to bring about a shift of opinion within the Labour group towards a more overtly expansionist position. There can be no doubt that until the shortage of land began to slow down the building programme drastically in the later 1950s, Labour had been in favour of restricting the city's industrial growth to reduce pressure on housing. But by 1959 there were signs that the Labour leaders had a feeling of betrayal, and that they were tempted to overthrow the whole basis of the overspill programme in favour of peripheral expansion. As early as October 1958 the Council had been told that new towns might no longer be necessary if a boundary extension were allowed,[4] and an extremely

[1] B.C.C., *Pro.*, 7 October 1958, p. 504.

[2] See, for instance, intervention by Percy Shurmer, a former member of the City Council, in *H. of C. Deb.*, 5th series, vol. dxcii, cols. *208–12*, 22 July 1958.

[3] *Y.B.*, no. 139, April 1959, p. 1; B.C.C., *Pro.*, 17 March 1959, pp. 993–1033 (General Purposes Committee).

[4] *Y.B.*, no. 134, November 1958, p. 2.

strong statement in favour of expansion appeared in Labour's municipal policy statement for the elections of May 1959. Labour, the manifesto said, could not give way to pleas to restrict industry: 'Birmingham people are entitled to remain in Birmingham if they wish, and Birmingham Industry has a right to remain in the City it has done so much to make great.' Not only would a boundary extension allow redevelopment to continue, but it would 'enable much of our industry to remain within the city'. Moreover: 'It will enable the City to keep faith with the developers who are investing millions of pounds on development because they look upon the City as one with a prosperous future.'[1]

This hardening of expansionist opinion within the Labour group, in which Alderman Watton participated,[2] greatly complicated the issue to be faced at the public inquiry in July 1959. On the one hand, the area of land applied for was much too small to meet Birmingham's long-term needs if the overspill programme were abandoned, as a large section of the Labour group seemed to want. On the other, it was too large, and represented too sharp a break with previous policy, to be justified by the very modest case which the City had to make if it were to be able to refute accusations of expansionism. The City could be attacked on two fronts; that it did not really need the land in the short term, as it claimed; and that in the long term it would need much more, which it denied. The Corporation had taken Manzoni's advice, and had based its case primarily on its need to build an unusually large number of houses in the following few years to rehouse people displaced by slum clearance.[3] An extension, the City maintained, would not lead to an increase in the population of Birmingham; indeed, if it were granted, an equivalent area of land would be re-zoned as playing fields within the existing boundaries. Similarly, the area of land zoned for industry within the city would be reduced to compensate for new industrial development allowed at Wythall. But this case was so modest that, as became clear during the inquiry, if Castle Bromwich airfield were to become available for building during the next year or two, as seemed very likely, the short-term need would be almost completely satisfied. It was on this point that the hostile case of Warwickshire and Worcestershire rested—that Birmingham did not really need the land. The attack from the other front was mounted principally by the Midlands New Towns Society with the support of the Town and Country

[1] This policy statement was drafted by Ald. Jim Meadows, one of the Labour group's most outspoken expansionists. In view of the case that Birmingham was going to make at the public inquiry later in the year, it could have done with being toned down a little, but surprisingly no reference was made to it by opponents of Birmingham's proposals at the inquiry.

[2] See *S.M.*, 20 September 1963.

[3] For an exposition of Birmingham's case, see Long, *Wythall Inquiry*, pp. 1–34.

Planning Association. The society, which had enthusiastically supported Birmingham's application for a new town, now felt betrayed by the Council's change of course. Indeed, one of its original terms of reference had been 'to watch out for threats of encroachment on the Green Belt'.[1] Although the chairman of the society, Professor P. Sargant Florence, an expert on industrial location and a member of the Faculty of Commerce, Birmingham University, made an important contribution to the inquiry, the main assault on the Corporation was carried out by the honorary secretary, Dr. D. E. C. Eversley. Eversley was a man of wide academic interests, ranging from economic history to demography, who also lectured in the Faculty of Commerce. An active member of the Borough Labour Party, he had already contributed to municipal policy conferences, and had published a number of articles in the Birmingham press calling for lower residential densities and the decentralization of Birmingham industry.[2] Producing a series of figures to show that Birmingham's overspill during the following two decades would probably be well over 150,000 people, he accused the City of failing to take sufficient steps to prevent the growth of employment in Birmingham. He submitted, with characteristic bluntness, that the only alternatives were an energetic overspill policy fully supported by the Corporation and the Government, or almost limitless peripheral expansion.

Owing partly to Eversley's efforts, the inquiry was a complete disaster for Birmingham, despite valiant efforts by Manzoni and Watton to sustain a case which the City Engineer had warned might be inadequate. Even if their arguments had been watertight, the Minister of Housing would probably have been unwilling to reverse his policy on green belts, but their inconsistencies gave him an excuse for ignoring Birmingham's claims. The inspector's report, which reached the Minister in September 1959,[3] concluded that the Corporation was not justified in its claim that the Wythall land would allow it to meet all its housing requirements for the next twenty years. It suggested that some l'mited development at Wythall might be acceptable as a last resort if other arrangements failed, but maintained that an acceleration of the current overspill programme, possibly with more Government help, was both a desirable and a feasible solution. The Minister's rejection of the application, in April 1960, was based squarely on the inspector's report.[4] It called on Birmingham to renew its efforts to decentralize population and industry, and offered help in overspill negotiations. Its only sop to

[1] Eversley and Keate, *Overspill Problems*, preface.
[2] See e.g. *B.M.*, 20, 22 March 1957. See also below, p. 439.
[3] For a summary of the report, see Long, *Wythall Inquiry*, pp. 95, 102.
[4] See text in Long, pp. 105–13; B.C.C., *Pro.*, 10 May 1960, pp. 1000–7 (General Purposes Committee); *H. of C. Deb.*, 5th series, vol. dcxxi, col. 37, 5 April 1960.

the City was an indication that the development of part of the Wythall area, lying to the east of the Alcester Road, might be favourably considered at a later date.

With the request for a boundary extension disposed of, the Minister was able to go on in 1960 to approve Birmingham's Development Plan, subject to certain amendments. Most of these changes were minor, but three were major matters of policy. First, the Minister wanted, as the Council had expected, to reduce the area allocated to industry, from 5,474 to 5,236 acres. This represented an increase of some 18 per cent instead of 23·8 per cent. However, the Council was assured that this reduction would not affect the area made available to industry during the twenty-year period of the plan, for the original allocation had been intended to cover a period of fifty to sixty years. Secondly, the Minister wanted programmes to be drawn up for the clearance of houses in areas zoned for industry after 1971. Lastly, the Minister asked for a new estimate of overspill by 1971, for which the Public Works Committee proposed to use the estimate put forward at the Wythall inquiry. This came to 118,000 overspill for which the Corporation had responsibility; no estimate was given of voluntary overspill, but Alderman Watton had told the inquiry that it would be about the same figure, making a total of over 200,000.[1]

The Council agreed to accept all these amendments,[2] and the plan was approved by the Minister in December 1960. In view of all the ominous noises that had been emitted by the Ministry of Housing since 1955, the City Council had got off very lightly. If the Government had really wanted to restrict Birmingham's industrial growth, here was its chance to do so, but once again it left the task to Birmingham. Whatever the effect of the minor reduction of the industrial land allocation in the long term, it could do nothing to influence the evolution of the overspill problem over the next ten or even twenty years. It remained inevitable that Birmingham would have to make a further request for peripheral growth.

Meanwhile, the General Purposes Committee had immediately taken up the Minister's offer of help in accelerating overspill negotiations, and for a time it even looked as though all hopes of peripheral expansion had been abandoned. An article published in the municipal newsletter, *Your Business*, in April 1960 was optimistic about the future of overspill, suggesting that much industry had moved, or was moving, out of the city, and that new firms were not coming into Birmingham from outside.[3] But progress in negotiating firm overspill agreements remained slow, and in November Henry Brooke announced that he

[1] This was almost exactly what Sir Patrick Abercrombie had predicted in 1948.
[2] B.C.C., *Pro.*, 2 February 1960, pp. 774–5 (Public Works Committee).
[3] *Y.B.*, no. 150, April 1960, p. 1.

was considering possible sites for a new town, particularly in the neighbourhood of Dawley.[1] Yet, within a few months, the whole situation was again to be transformed.

The inspector's report after the 1959 inquiry had made it clear that the designation of a new town would not solve Birmingham's short-term problem. Although the increase of overspill subsidies in the 1961 Housing Act might be expected to accelerate progress, and the City had now been able to purchase Castle Bromwich airfield for housing, a major shortfall remained. So the Minister began to consider allowing Birmingham to build on the smaller area of some 600 acres at Wythall which had been pointed out by the inspector as a less undesirable site for development than the rest of the district, since it was already partly built-up. In August 1961 the Minister recommended the urgent implementation of overspill schemes at Redditch, Worcester, and Daventry, and gave his blessing in principle to a further application from Birmingham to build on the 600 acres at Wythall and to extend the city boundaries to include the area.[2] He also confirmed that a new town in the Dawley area of Shropshire was under consideration.

The City Council was delighted by this turn of events. Even the Conservatives could now support the proposal because it came from a Conservative Minister of Housing. But the Midlands New Towns Society and the affected county and district authorities were still irrevocably in opposition.[3] The course of the inquiry was essentially a repeat of that of 1959, although, with a much smaller area of land involved, Eversley's arguments carried even more weight than they had before. The inspector's report did not make a firm recommendation for or against the proposal, but the City Council was confident that the boundary extension would obtain Government approval since the Minister of Housing had been the first to suggest it. But unfortunately for Birmingham, when the inspector's report was laid on the Minister's desk, a different Minister was sitting there. Henry Brooke had been replaced as Minister of Housing by Charles Hill on 9 October 1961. Looking at the case with a fresh eye, Hill was impressed by the argument put forward at the inquiry that to grant the application would make only a minor contribution to the city's problem. The new Minister preferred to maintain the Ministry's previous position that the whole of the area should be preserved as part of the green belt. He also latched on to a fact which had emerged at the inquiry, that with its present land resources Birmingham could maintain its current

---

[1] *H. of C. Deb.*, 5th series, vol. dcxxix, cols. *808–9*, 8 November 1960.

[2] Long, *Wythall Inquiry*, p. ix; B.C.C., *Pro.*, 10 October 1961, p. 360 (General Purposes Committee).

[3] See Wythall Inquiry, 26 October–2 November 1961 (transcript of proceedings held by Town Clerk's Office).

building rate until 1966 at least.[1] So in February 1962 Hill turned down the application, and, in terms very similar to those used by Henry Brooke in 1960, called for an acceleration of the overspill programme with help from the Ministry.[2]

The Minister's decision caused consternation in Birmingham. There seemed little chance that the overspill programme could be accelerated as the Minister hoped. By the summer of 1962 only 1,567 houses had been built for Birmingham citizens in overspill areas.[3] Charles Hill was confident that Warwickshire and Worcestershire would do everything in their power to help Birmingham now that their green belt had been protected,[4] and in March his Ministry told the three neighbouring counties that two new towns and two major town development schemes were necessary in the immediate future. But a report by the Worcestershire Planning Committee in April 1962 stated that although the county would welcome the limited expansion of some towns, such arrangements would cater for only one-fifth of the total which the Minister thought the county should accommodate as its contribution to the conurbation's overspill problem.[5] In fact, most receiving authorities had begun to slow down their building programmes in 1961, even though they were far from reaching their targets. Partly to blame for this deceleration were high interest rates, high land prices, increased building costs, and the difficulty of providing sufficient industrial development. However, the City Council decided that a bigger financial contribution might provide more encouragement, and in July 1962 it increased its subsidy to receiving areas to £12 per house per year over fifteen years, in line with a similar increase in the Exchequer contribution under the 1961 Housing Act.[6] In November, the Council approved further financial and technical assistance for town development schemes, to help the district authorities meet certain capital costs, and to stimulate commercial and industrial development.[7] Meanwhile, the Minister of Housing had announced in May that a new town would be designated near Dawley. The City Council welcomed this decision, but added that it would favour the early designation of a second new town.[8]

At this stage another Government reshuffle produced a new Minister of Housing, Sir Keith Joseph, who took over from Charles Hill on

[1] Of course, Birmingham's building rate had been depressed by the land shortage.

[2] B.C.C. *Pro.*, 10 April 1962, pp. 899–903 (General Purposes Committee).

[3] B.C.C. *Pro.*, 24 July 1962, p. 229 (General Purposes Committee).

[4] *H. of C. Deb.*, 5th series, vol. dclv, cols. *143–6*, 13 March 1962.

[5] *B.M.*, 28 April 1962.

[6] B.C.C., *Pro.*, 24 July 1962, p. 230 (General Purposes Committee).

[7] B.C.C., *Pro.*, 6 November 1962, pp. 406–7 (General Purposes Committee).

[8] *Y.B.* no. 175, July 1962, p. 1; B.C.C., *Pro.*, 24 July 1962, p. 229 (General Purposes Committee).

13 July 1962. He did not make much impact on the situation until after the summer recess, but in the debate on the Royal Address on 1 November 1962 he told the House of the urgent need to increase the slum clearance rate in Birmingham, Liverpool, and Manchester. These local authorities could assume in planning their programmes, he promised, that land would be made available to them for rehousing. On 19 February 1963 the Minister told the House that the slum clearance needs of these cities were so great that there would have to be some building on nearby land. He announced his intention to designate a second new town for the West Midlands at Redditch, but said that if Birmingham found that still more land was needed to sustain its programme up to the 1970s, it should consult the neighbouring county councils and put proposals to the Minister. The City Council immediately passed a resolution welcoming the Minister's new approach to the problem and the designation of a new town at Redditch,[1] which, lying only a few miles from Birmingham, was more likely than Dawley to attract industry. The month of February also saw the finalization of a town development scheme at Daventry, Northamptonshire, on lines approved by the Council in November 1962, to be administered by a joint committee with Birmingham representatives.[2] This scheme amounted almost to the development of a new town by Birmingham out of its own resources, something which the Government had so often urged in previous years. But it was recognized that development would begin slowly until industry could be persuaded to move there, and industry always remained a limiting factor owing to the policy pursued by the Board of Trade (and, later, by the Department of Employment and Productivity) until the end of the 1960s.[3]

At the end of June 1963 the Corporation took up the Minister's offer of extra land, although without first consulting the county councils, and asked for the allocation of land for 20,000 dwellings in two areas—1,460 acres to the east of the city at Water Orton, and 278 acres at Kingswood Farm, adjoining the southern city boundary just to the west of Alcester Road, in the area originally applied for in 1958.[4] These proposals were discussed with Warwickshire and Worcestershire in October, and Birmingham made its formal application for the two areas in January 1964. This time, the City's case was based on overall housing deficiency, not on slum clearance requirements. A deficiency

[1] B.C.C., Pro., 12 March 1963, p. 798 (General Purposes Committee).
[2] B.C.C., Pro., 5 February 1963, pp. 724–6 (General Purposes Committee).
[3] B.M., 6 April 1963. For a recent summary of the restricting effect of Government industrial location policies on new towns and overspill developments, see evidence given by the Birmingham Chamber of Commerce and Industry to the Hunt Committee on Intermediate Areas, 8 May 1968.
[4] B.C.C., Pro., 5 November 1963, pp. 432–5 (General Purposes Committee).

of 39,000 houses was predicted for 1971, when the shortage would be worse than it had been in 1959. This problem was not being solved, the Corporation maintained, by existing methods or schemes.

A public inquiry into Birmingham's application, amended to take in 1,540 acres at Water Orton and 420 acres at Wythall, was held in May and June 1964. There was again strong local objection, but the counties' opposition was more muted, and the Midlands New Towns Society did not put up its usual barrage. In December 1964 the new Labour Minister of Housing, Richard Crossman, told the City that he would allow the development at Water Orton, but he again turned down the Wythall application.[1] The Minister defended his decision on the grounds that the Water Orton site was more suitable for the industrialized building methods that Birmingham would need to make rapid progress, and that it was undesirable to make inroads into the green belt at Wythall owing to the growth of Redditch a few miles to the south.

The City Council did not make the same mistake as it had in the case of Castle Bromwich aerodrome, where development had been unduly delayed,[2] thus giving the Government an excuse for not making further land available. Every effort was made to start building as soon as possible, and the master plan for the Water Orton land (Chelmsley Wood estate) was approved in March 1966.[3] Building began later in the year. In the meantime, Richard Crossman announced that he was considering further peripheral developments for Birmingham.[4] In December 1966 he warned Worcestershire that the assessment of the conurbation's housing needs made in the *West Midlands Study* (1965) had failed to foresee a gap in the early 1970s in the provision of land for housing. It would therefore be necessary to find additional land for 15,000 public-sector houses for Birmingham people, to be built between 1971 and 1975. To find suitable sites the Minister authorized a study of North Worcestershire, and in 1968 broad agreement was reached between the City and the county authorities for the building of 4,000 dwellings at Redditch, and 11,000 more in five areas lying to the south and south-west of the city. Some difficulty was caused by the fact that part of the land needed, to the west of Wythall, had been donated to the Corporation by Cadbury Brothers in 1937 for maintenance in perpetuity as open space.[5] But Cadbury's eventually withdrew their objections after the scheme had been modified to include more open space, and a public inquiry into the scheme was

[1] B.C.C., *Pro.*, 2 February 1965, pp. 579–81 (General Purposes Committee).
[2] See below, pp. 437–8.
[3] B.C.C., *Pro.*, 8 March 1966, pp. 777–8 (House Building Committee).
[4] See e.g. *H. of C. Deb.*, 5th series, vol. dccxxv, col. 237, 1 March 1966.
[5] See *The Expansion of Birmingham into the Green Belt area*, published by Cadbury Brothers Ltd. in September 1968.

held in 1969. Worcestershire County Council had misgivings about the proposals and opposed them at the inquiry, so that Government approval was delayed until after 1970.

It now seemed likely that even this extension of the city into North Worcestershire would not be the last. By 1966 only some 4,000 houses had been built for Birmingham in overspill schemes, and it seemed certain that overspill and new town arrangements could satisfy only a fraction of the conurbation's housing needs.[1] Very little industry had moved to the overspill areas, and the most successful developments were those in towns near Birmingham, such as Lichfield and Tamworth, from which the majority of overspill tenants commuted daily to work in the city. The Department of Economic Affairs' *The West Midlands: A Regional Study* (1965) foresaw an overspill of 500,000 people from the conurbation by 1981, but did not say how employment could be provided for them. When the study was referred to the West Midlands Economic Planning Council, the local authorities, feeling the need for some concerted action by elected bodies, formed the Standing Conference of West Midlands Planning Authorities. In 1967 the Economic Planning Council published its report, *The West Midlands: Patterns of Growth*, which envisaged a huge overspill policy, but provided no new ideas on how to make such a policy work. The report was partly rejected by the Government in 1968 on the ground that industrial movement would not be sufficient to support such overspill under current redistribution policies. Opinion in the regional office of the Ministry of Housing was now moving in favour of more general peripheral expansion of the whole conurbation, with the provision of industry in new suburban areas in order to limit expensive commuting. The Government, by 1968, was of the same opinion, and called for more study of commuter developments. The controlling Conservative group in the Birmingham City Council began to think along the same lines after it took power in 1966. Birmingham, they believed, could become the major employment centre for the whole of the West Midlands, if a more effective public transport system could be set up. And since the abolition of industrial derating in the early 1960s, such a role could bring the Corporation unprecedented revenues, which could be used to develop Birmingham's services to make it a more effective regional capital. However, this dream would take decades to come true. Ironically enough, several prominent members of the Labour group, notably Alderman Watton, Alderman Sir Frank Price, and Alderman Bowen, had joined the development corporations of the two new towns and the Daventry development committee in the early 1960s. They now found themselves defending the principle of

[1] See Barbara M. D. Smith, 'Industrial overspill in theory and practice: the case of the West Midlands', *Urban Studies*, vol. vii, no. 2, June 1970, pp. 189–204.

dispersal, which they had done so much to question, against the Conservatives, who had always advocated it when a Conservative Government was in power.

Despite the attractions of the expansionist dream, peripheral expansion was beginning to raise serious problems by 1970. Part of the agreement with the county authorities on which the Chelmsley Wood development had been based was that it should be a simple commuter estate, without industry, to prevent its generating a further demand for expansion within itself. And although a small amount of industry was subsequently included to provide work for women residents, it was by no means enough to employ all of them. So average household incomes at Chelmsley Wood were lower than on most municipal estates within the city, while rents and living costs, and travelling costs for wage-earners, were higher. The same result was expected in the North Worcestershire development.[1] So development costs, both constructional and environmental, had to be kept as low as possible. All these features increased the unattractiveness of peripheral developments, whose main drawback was that they were so far from the centre of a city which, being dependent almost entirely on motor buses for its public transport, took a long time to traverse. Only the provision of a rapid transit system and a new rent structure could make the out-city estates really attractive to municipal tenants.

The late 1960s saw some improvement in the rate of building in the new towns and overspill areas, but by the early 1970s they still had made only a marginal contribution to Birmingham's needs. By June 1971 nearly 9,000 houses had been built by receiving authorities in the city's fifteen overspill schemes, together with nearly four million square feet of industrial floorspace. These figures were impressive in themselves, but less so in comparison with the target figure of homes— 21,122—planned in the fifteen schemes. When one remembers that many of the agreements had originally been made in the mid-1950s, and that Birmingham Corporation was itself building some 9,000 houses *a year* in the later 1960s (thanks to peripheral expansion), the relative insignificance of overspill housing becomes more apparent. Nor were the new towns as yet making a spectacular contribution. Redditch housed 38,000 people by the end of 1971, but this was only 6,000 more than its population at the time of its designation as a new town seven years earlier. Telford (an extended version of the original Dawley new town) had 82,000 inhabitants, compared to a population of 70,000 on designation.[2]

---

[1] See City of Birmingham, Housing Management Department, *Land in North Worcestershire: Housing and Social Provision* (1969), pp. 2–6.

[2] Hazel Evans, 'Britain's new towns: facts and figures', *Town and Country Planning*, vol. xl, no. 1, January 1972, pp. 40–1, 51.

So by 1970 no fully satisfactory solution to Birmingham's land shortage had emerged. It its absence, the city's future size and functions remained uncertain. Perhaps local government reorganization in 1974 would integrate Birmingham's problem more fully with the conurbation's, and even lead to a definitive solution. Perhaps, like previous administrative changes, it would make no real difference to the city's concrete problems. But Birmingham could at least reflect that, whatever the trials and disappointments of the last three decades, they had taught it to face a difficult and uncertain future with equanimity.

V

THE BIRMINGHAM ECONOMY

BIRMINGHAM'S ethos and character have been determined to a very large extent by its industrial structure. Although the connection is not always a direct one, no understanding of the foundations of Birmingham post-war society is possible without full recognition of the importance of the city's role as the kingpin of one of Europe's greatest industrial regions. Yet any analysis of the city's industry is beset with difficulties great enough for Samuel Timmins, writing in the nineteenth century, to describe them as 'almost insuperable'.[1] Indeed, so diverse are Birmingham's industries that many local historians have done no more than catalogue the doings of individual enterprises, ignoring major trends and changes.[2] In this chapter, however, we shall concentrate on detecting overall features and movements, illustrated by the experiences of specific firms.

A second major difficulty is that the city does not form a complete economic unit. Although a distinction can be made between Birmingham's industrial structure and that of much of the Black Country, no such boundary can be drawn between Birmingham and Smethwick, or between Birmingham and Solihull. Nevertheless, we are concerned here with the economic history of Birmingham only, and the city will have to be studied largely in isolation from the rest of the conurbation and the West Midlands region. Birmingham on its own is certainly big enough to justify such a study, but it must be emphasized that the role and importance of the city's industries cannot, in the final analysis, properly be assessed until much more is known about the contemporary economic history of the whole conurbation and of the West Midlands region.

The industrial structure of Birmingham at the end of the Second World War

We have already seen how the Birmingham economy was affected by the Second World War, and how it returned to peacetime conditions in 1945 with a mixture of confidence and misgivings.[3] We can now go on to see how those forecasts were borne out by experience in the twenty-five years which followed the end of the war. However, in order to

---

[1] *The Industrial History of Birmingham* (1866), p. 208.

[2] Notable exceptions to this have been G. C. Allen, *Industrial Development of Birmingham and the Black Country 1860–1927* (1929); W. H. B. Court, *The Rise of Midland Industries 1600–1838* (1938); D. E. C. Eversley, 'Industry and trade 1500–1880', *V.C.H. Warcks.*, vol. vii (1964), pp. 81–139.

[3] See above, pp. 54–5.

assess with any effect the impact of the forces of change and stability within the Birmingham economy it is necessary to examine in some detail the city's industrial structure in the immediate post-war years. This picture will form a base line against which subsequent changes can be measured.

In making a quantitative assessment of the Birmingham economy immediately after the end of the war one is inevitably hampered by a shortage of accurate and relevant statistics. The Board of Trade figures, which categorize firms according to their principal activity or product, give the numbers employed in each group, but there is of course no necessary correlation between the capital or output of an industry and the numbers employed. The figures contained in the 1951 census are more informative in some respects than the Board of Trade figures for the same year, but they relate only to persons living in the city, whereas nearly 100,000 Birmingham workers lived outside the municipal boundaries at the time.[1] Much more satisfactory, therefore, are the figures showing the number of persons registered at the city's six labour exchanges in the census year of 1951.[2] Even here, however, two qualifications must be made. Firstly, the figures are only estimates. Secondly, the Birmingham labour exchange areas include part of Solihull as well as the city. Even so, any distortion which may result is likely to be less than that involved in using the census figures.

Table 1 gives the statistics according to broad industrial categories.[3] Column (a) of the table shows the number of persons working in each category, and column (b) expresses these figures as percentages of the total labour force. Column (c) shows the location quotient. A location quotient is obtained by using the formula:

$$\frac{\%\ employed\ in\ an\ industry\ in\ Birmingham}{\%\ employed\ in\ that\ industry\ in\ England\ and\ Wales} \times \frac{100}{1}$$

The quotient measures the extent of localization of an industry in Birmingham. A figure in excess of 100 means that there is a higher concentration of a particular industry in Birmingham than in the country as a whole. A quotient under 100 means that the industry is under-represented in the city. The figures for England and Wales used in the table are taken directly from the 1951 census, since at a national level the residential dilemma does not occur.

The figures show clearly that in 1951 a substantial majority of Birmingham's labour force worked in the manufacturing sector and that manufacturing industry was especially concentrated in the city. Vehicle manufacture, for example, employed 16·2 per cent of the total

[1] See also G. M. Lomas and P. A. Wood, *Employment Location in Regional Economic Planning: A Case Study of the West Midlands* (1970), pp. 26–7.

[2] *Abstract*, no. 2, p. 123.

[3] For a more detailed breakdown, see statistical appendix, table 1.

Table 1. The Industrial Structure of Birmingham Employment Area, 1951
(Estimated insured employees excluding ex-service persons not industrially classified)

	(a) *No. in* *labour force*	(b) *% of* *labour force*	(c) *Location quotient**
PRIMARY			
Agriculture, forestry, fishing	1,483	0·3	4
Mining & quarrying	145	–	–
Treatment of non-metalliferous mining products (except coal)	4,505	0·7	47
	6,133	1·0	10
MANUFACTURING			
Chemical and allied trades	12,175	2·0	100
Metal manufacture	29,245	4·8	185
Engineering, shipbuilding, electrical goods	81,355	13·3	168
Vehicles	98,703	16·2	345
Metal goods not elsewhere specified	72,698	11·9	541
Precision instruments, jewellery, etc.	12,983	2·1	300
Textiles	4,865	0·8	18
Leather, leather goods, fur	1,931	0·3	75
Clothing	6,987	1·1	32
Food, drink, tobacco	28,972	4·7	147
Manufacture of wood and cork	9,230	1·5	107
Paper, printing	12,315	2·0	87
Other manufacturing industries	19,847	3·3	275
	391,306	64·0	243
SERVICES			
Building and contracting	27,834	4·6	74
Gas, electricity, water supply	9,980	1·6	94
Transport, communications	27,857	4·6	61
Distributive trades	54,113	8·9	74
Insurance, banking, finance	10,534	1·7	85
Public administration and defence	17,282	2·8	35
Professional services	35,612	5·8	85
Miscellaneous services	30,316	5·0	54
	213,528	35·0	55

* Based on Census figures for England and Wales, 1951.
Source: Board of Trade, given in *Abstract*, no. 2, p. 123.

labour force in various ways; with 9·1 per cent concerned with the actual manufacture of motor vehicles and bicycles, and 4·8 per cent producing accessories. Engineering employed another 13·3 per cent of the labour force, and a further 11·9 per cent manufactured other metal goods. It is no surprise to find, therefore, that all these industries had very high location quotients in Birmingham. More surprising, however, are the low percentages of workers engaged in some of the other industries traditionally associated with the city. Particularly noticeable are the mere 2·9 per cent who worked in brass manufacture; the 2·1 per cent in the jewellery trade; 0·9 per cent in iron and steel tube manufacture; 0·7 per cent in the hollow-ware trade and 0·6 per cent battery and accumulator makers. Nevertheless these industries were strongly associated with Birmingham, not because they employed large numbers, but because they had high location quotients (1,450, 300, 450, 233, and 600 respectively). On the other hand, one of the industries traditionally associated with Birmingham, ordnance and small arms, had only an average location quotient (100), and employed a mere 0·3 per cent of the labour force.

It is nevertheless clear from the table that Birmingham was more than a simple concentration of metal working, engineering, and ancillary trades. The wood and cork industries, for example, had a location quotient in excess of 100, and thanks to the presence of Cadbury's the 'cocoa' industry's quotient was also high (567). But the city was under-endowed in the service sector. The only components in that area of the economy which had quotients in excess of 100 were civil engineering and building, gas production, and tramway and omnibus services. In other respects, the city appeared to enjoy less than its fair share of services, ranging from education to catering.

The sharp contrast between the numbers employed in the new engineering and vehicle industries, and in the traditional Birmingham occupations, was also reflected in their location and organization. The older industries such as jewellery and guns tended to remain clustered near the city centre and most of their production was carried on in highly interdependent small workshops which usually carried out single processes.[1] Other workshops near the centre produced component parts for the factories, and although these small units employed only a minor and decreasing proportion of the labour force, they contributed substantially to the smooth running of the Birmingham economy. Many of them found it easier than the factories to adapt to changing circumstances and demand, thanks partly to the high proportion of skilled labour which they employed.[2] Although some of these firms could be inefficient, their close proximity to one another reproduced in many respects the major advantages of a large-scale plant–physical

[1] Board of Trade Working Party Reports, *Jewellery and Silverware* (1946), p. 9; M. J. Wise, 'On the evolution of the jewellery and gun quarters in Birmingham', *Institute of British Geographers, Transactions and Papers*, vol. xv, 1951, p. 60; A. J. Bennett, 'Size and relations of firms in localized Birmingham trades' (M.Comm. thesis, Birmingham University, 1952), p. 47.

[2] This quality greatly impressed Jane Jacobs in her *The Economy of Cities* (1970), pp. 86–94.

juxtaposition of consecutive processes and auxiliary services.[1] Indeed, even in the 1960s many of these small firms were still being praised for their energy, adaptability, and inventiveness.[2] But the congestion and obsolescence of most of the workshop premises, many of which were located in the central redevelopment areas, were a substantial handicap.[3] Whatever vitality they retained, they were nevertheless the declining remnants of Birmingham's older industrial tradition.

Many of the growth industries of the late nineteenth century had moved to the middle ring and remained there ever since. Although their premises were generally much larger than those of firms which had stayed in the inner wards, the newest and largest factories were to be found on the outskirts of the city. The Austin Motor Works at Longbridge was particularly extensive, and its production techniques were among the most advanced in Europe. In 1946 it already covered one hundred acres and employed 17,000 workers. Division of labour was more extensive than in any other British factory, and between ten and twelve thousand of the labour force were each responsible for only limited technical operations.[4] Yet paradoxically even Longbridge, which was essentially an assembly shop, was dependent on smaller firms which supplied it with components. Although parts came from far outside the Birmingham area, most were made within ten miles of the factory.[5] Some of the suppliers were, it is true, other large Birmingham manufacturers, including Fisher and Ludlow, Joseph Lucas, Dunlop, and Girling. But the small city centre workshops also produced components. Even the gunmakers made motor parts when their own trade was slack.[6] Many of these firms also supplied motor vehicle manufacturers in other parts of the country, and it has been estimated that between 20 and 25 per cent of Birmingham's capital and labour were involved directly or indirectly in motor manufacture by the 1950s.[7] Nevertheless, owing to the presence of a great variety of firms not involved in the motor industry, Birmingham's industry could still be described as 'more broadly based than that of any city of equivalent size in the world.'[8] So the city benefited from the expansion of Britain's

[1] P. Sargant Florence, *Investment, Location and Size of Plant* (1948), p. 74. For evidence of generally high productivity among West Midlands engineering and metal working concerns, see West Midlands Economic Planning Council, *The West Midlands: An Economic Appraisal* (1971), p. 6. para. 2.22.

[2] See e.g. 'The booming Midlands', *The Cubit Magazine*, Autumn 1963, p. 6.

[3] B. L. C. Johnson, 'The distribution of factory population in the West Midland Conurbation', *Institute of British Geographers, Transactions and Papers*, vol. xxv, 1958, pp. 214–15.   [4] *Birmingham Journal*, vol. i, no. 2, 1946.

[5] *B.M.*, 21 April 1945; 'Austin Jubilee, 1905–55', *The Autocar*, July 1955, pp. 20, 22, 27, 36.

[6] Bennett, 'Size and relations of firms', pp. 28, 86.   [7] *The Times*, 8 May 1958.

[8] M. J. Wise,' On the evolution of the jewellery and gun quarters in Birmingham', *Institute of British Geographers, Transactions and Papers*, vol. xv, 1951, p. 66.

most dynamic post-war industry, motor manufacture, yet to an extent was cushioned against the worst effects of its periodic depressions.

National planning and the changing industrial structure, 1951–70

One of the key factors in Birmingham's continuing industrial vitality was its ability to adapt and to innovate, thanks to its farsighted management and its large supply of skilled labour. Since the turn of the century many new firms had come to the city to take advantage of the qualities of its workers, and in so doing had helped considerably to diversify its industrial structure. But it was precisely these processes that Government post-war industrial location policy threatened to nullify.[1] Of course the implementation of this policy came up against serious difficulties; especially when it came to preventing the expansion of Birmingham firms, or encouraging them to leave the city.[2] On the other hand, firms producing articles not associated with Birmingham's existing industries were generally kept out of the city. So it is easy to assume, as did many local industrialists and politicians, that Birmingham was becoming increasingly dependent on the motor industry, and that its industrial diversity was being restricted as some of its older trades died out. But what changes actually took place in the industrial structure between 1951 and 1966?

Estimates for these years are again hampered by the problem of place of work and place of residence, and further difficulties are raised by changes in the general classification. However, by using the special tables drawn up by the Registrar-General and set out in the *Birmingham Abstract of Statistics*[3] it is possible to discover the number of persons in each industrial grouping (used in Table 1) *working* in the City in 1951.[4] (These figures were not used to construct Table 1 simply because the numbers working in the sub-categories, and shown in the statistical appendix, Table 1, were not also given.) Similarly, the 1966 census published its industrial figures by place of work (unlike that of 1961 which gave its detailed industrial manpower figures only by area of residence). Unfortunately, we are prevented from making a direct comparison of the 1951 and 1966 figures because of a change in the general classification. It is, nevertheless, possible by a process of combining categories to make the 1951 figures comparable with those of 1966, with only a marginal error.[5] Table 2 shows the number of

[1] See above, pp. 120 ff.

[2] See Barbara M. D. Smith, 'Industrial overspill in theory and practice: the case of the West Midlands', *Urban Studies*, vol. vii, no. 2, June 1970, pp. 189–204.

[3] No. 5, 1958–9, table 8.

[4] These figures do not, however, enable one to break down the industrial categories further. See statistical appendix, table 1.

[5] Based on Appendix D of Census 1961, Industry Tables, Pt. 1. See statistical appendix, table 2.

Table 2. *Changing Industrial Structure of Birmingham, 1951–1966*
(Industrial categories of those in employment)

PRIMARY	Number				% work force	
	1951	*1966*	*Change*	*% change*	*1951*	*1966*
Agriculture, forestry, fishing	755	450	− 305	− 40·4	0·1	0·1
Mining and quarrying	265	160	− 105	− 39·6	—	—
	1,020	610	− 410	− 40·2	0·1	0·1
MANUFACTURING						
Food, drink, tobacco	23,047	21,760	− 1,287	− 5·6	3·7	3·4
Chemical & allied industries	6,811	8,280	+ 1,469	+ 21·6	1·1	1·3
Metal manufacture	33,860	27,830	− 6,030	− 17·8	5·4	4·3
Engineering & electrical goods, Ship-building, Engines, metal goods not elsewhere specified / Other manufacturing industries	178,689	175,550	− 3,139	− 1·8	28·6	27·2
Vehicles	94,504	77,580	− 16,924	− 17·9	15·1	12·0
Textiles	3,732	2,810	− 922	− 24·7	0·6	0·4
Leather, leather goods, fur	1,650	690	− 960	− 58·2	0·3	0·1
Clothing, footwear	7,789	2,600	− 5,189	− 66·6	1·3	0·4
Bricks, pottery, glass, cement, etc.	4,137	2,810	− 1,327	− 32·1	0·7	0·4
Timber, furniture, etc.	9,134	5,020	− 4,114	− 45·0	1·5	0·8
Paper, printing, publishing	11,942	12,500	+ 558	+ 4·7	1·9	1·9
Total manufacturing industries	375,295	337,430	− 37,865	− 10·1	60·2	52·3
SERVICES						
Construction	27,606	40,000	+ 12,394	+ 44·9	4·4	6·2
Gas, electricity, water	7,818	8,060	+ 242	+ 3·1	1·3	1·3
Transport, communication	34,081	34,130	+ 49	+ 0·1	5·5	5·3
Distributive trades	69,652	79,280	+ 9,628	+ 13·8	11·2	12·3
Insurance, banking, finance	11,173	17,250	+ 6,077	+ 54·4	1·8	2·7
Professional & scientific services	35,949	56,960	+ 21,011	+ 58·4	5·8	8·8
Miscellaneous services	41,348	53,650	+ 12,302	+ 29·8	6·6	8·3
Public Administration & defence	19,851	17,040	− 2,811	− 14·2	3·2	2·6
Total service industries	247,478	306,370	+ 58,892	+ 23·8	39·8	47·5

N.B. (*a*) Those persons whose industrial category is indeterminate have been omitted.

(*b*) The figures refer to persons *working* but not necessarily living in Birmingham Employment Area.

(*c*) Even by taking into account the qualifications made in (*b*), the changing classifications used in 1951 make the figures here incomparable with those in Table 1.

Source: 1951 figures from special table drawn up from the Census for the Birmingham Central Statistical Office and given in *Abstract*, no. 5, 1959, p. 68; 1966 figures are taken from 1966 Sample Census, Economic Activity Tables, Warwickshire, Table 3.

Table 3. Changing Industrial Structure of Birmingham, 1961–1970

	1961	*1970*	*change*	*% change*
Agriculture, forestry, fishing	978	677	− 301	− 30·8
Mining & quarrying	105	87	− 18	− 17·1
	1,083	764	− 319	− 29·4
Food, drink, tobacco	28,268	27,360	− 908	− 3·2
Chemicals & allied industries	13,738	8,456	− 5,282	− 38·5
Metal manufacture	29,637	32,006	+ 2,369	+ 8·0
Engineering & electrical goods	99,995	74,451	− 25,544	− 25·5
Ship-building & marine engineering	8	0	− 8	− 100·0
Vehicles	94,946	87,910	− 7,036	− 7·4
Metal goods, not elsewhere specified	82,198	74,253	− 7,945	− 9·7
Textiles	3,140	1,049	− 2,091	− 66·6
Leather, leather goods, fur	838	680	− 158	− 18·9
Clothing, footwear	4,322	2,449	− 1,873	− 43·3
Bricks, pottery, glass, cement	3,132	3,045	− 87	− 2·8
Timber, furniture	7,292	4,461	− 2,831	− 38·8
Paper, printing, publishing	13,324	12,672	− 652	− 48·9
Other manufacturing industries	18,413	17,545	− 868	− 4·7
	399,251	346,337	− 52,914	− 13·3
Construction	34,858	36,644	+ 1,786	+ 5·1
Gas, electricity, water	9,369	11,775	+ 2,406	+ 25·7
Transport & communications	23,555	20,032	− 3,523	− 15·0
Distributive trades	71,744	58,854	− 12,890	− 18·0
Insurance, banking, finance	14,664	22,996	+ 8,332	+ 56·8
Professional & scientific services	54,136	70,284	+ 6,148	+ 29·8
Miscellaneous services	44,324	40,140	− 4,184	− 9·4
Public administration & defence	13,351	14,883	+ 1,532	+ 11·5
	266,001	275,608	+ 9,607	+ 3·6

N.B. (*a*) Excluding persons not industrially classified.

(*b*) These figures are based on those for the Birmingham Employment Area.

Source: Board of Trade, given in *Abstract*, no. 6, 1960–1, p. 59; no. 15, 1970–1, p. 63.

M

workers in each amended industrial group in 1951 and 1966. The change
between these two dates, both absolutely and proportionately, is also
given, together with the percentages of the total labour forces.

Of course, one would not have expected a fundamental restructuring
of the city's industrial base in the few years between 1951 and 1966.
But there were some significant changes in emphasis. In most of the
manufacturing sectors (apart from chemical and allied industries,
parts of the metal working industries, and paper, printing, and publishing), there was a decline in the absolute and proportionate size of
the labour force. In other words, the manufacturing sector, including
many of the parts which had traditionally been associated with the
city, declined by some 10 per cent, in terms of manpower at least.
This reduction was accompanied by an increase of some 24 per
cent in the total labour force of the service sector. This increase
more than compensated for the fall in manufacturing employment, so
that there was a rise in the total number of jobs available in the city.

Because of the difficulty of comparability we would be wise to check
these general findings by examining a further source. Do we find similar
patterns if we study the labour exchange employment figures between
1961 and 1970, during which time there was no change in classification? If so, we may conclude that our general analysis based on Table
2 is correct. The figures in Table 3, based on labour statistics for 1961
and 1970, do in fact confirm that manufacturing industry contracted
slightly, whilst the service sector grew.[1]

It is tempting to assume that the contraction of manufacturing was
the result exclusively of Government policies, especially in view of the
almost complete absence from the city of industries such as man-made
fibres and chemicals, which greatly expanded nationally after 1945.[2]
Certainly Government financial incentives and control over industrial
development certificates can be regarded as the prime factor in persuading some of the major Birmingham firms such as B.M.C. and
Fisher and Ludlow to set up production in South Wales, Scotland, and
Merseyside.[3] But there are also grounds for arguing that the structure
of the city's economy in 1960 would not have been greatly different
without Government intervention. All the available evidence suggests
that Birmingham firms had little difficulty in obtaining industrial
development certificates for new floorspace within the city.[4] Outside
firms would have been discouraged from moving to Birmingham by

[1] See also Lomas and Wood, *Employment Location*, pp. 26–8.
[2] See *The Economist*, 2 April 1966.   [3] G. Turner, *The Car Makers* (1964), pp. 43–4.
[4] A survey undertaken by the Birmingham Chamber of Commerce at the end of
the 1960s found that 94 per cent of applications for industrial development certificates
by conurbation firms replying to the questionnaire had been approved, 88 per cent
of them without any modification (results quoted in Smith, 'Industrial overspill',
p. 194).

high land prices and the shortage of labour in the city. Many of the firms which moved part or all of their production out of Birmingham did so because they were short of space in Birmingham, or because they thought they could achieve greater efficiency elsewhere. Some of the bigger jewellery firms were moving for these reasons as early as 1946.[1] Many of the firms which moved out of the city did however remain within the conurbation.[2] A further cause of the contraction of Birmingham's manufacturing sector was the closure of a number of firms which could not adapt to changing market conditions. Several thousand workers were made redundant, for instance, by the closure of two large carriage and wagon works in the 1950s. Of course, some firms expanded physically within Birmingham, among them motor vehicles, light engineering, small tools and gauges, and rubber and plastic moulding. Between 1945 and 1970, 1,296 industrial building schemes were approved in the city, and overall production must have risen substantially through greater mechanization.

Although the overall decline in manufacturing employment was offset by the growth of the service sector, many service industries failed to expand. In some cases, such as domestic service, railways, cinemas, and coal dealing, a decline was only to be expected in post-war conditions. Yet in view of the fact that the general growth in the sector reflected an increasingly wealthy city's rising demand for services, and Birmingham's developing role as a regional capital, it is remarkable that even in 1966 the city was still under-endowed with services (see Table 2). It has sometimes been suggested that this under-endowment resulted from Birmingham's proximity to London,[3] but it is much more likely that it resulted from a shortage of available labour in an area of high manufacturing wages.[4] One of the biggest increases of service employment took place in the construction industry, reflecting the great volume of building undertaken in Birmingham and the whole of the West Midlands. There was also a big rise in the number of persons working in insurance, banking, and finance, and in a

---

[1] *Working Party Report, Jewellery*, p. 9; *Industry in the West Midlands* (1963), p. 19. See also the example of McKechnie, makers of copper sulphate, who moved voluntarily from Rotton Park to Aldridge in *The McKechnie Story* (1965), pp. 8–10; and Clifford Aero and Auto Ltd., who shortly after the war were forced to carry out their extensions at Stoke-on-Trent owing to building and labour difficulties in Birmingham (*F.D.*, 20 December 1946). The Birmingham labour shortage also persuaded J. B. Brooks and Co., makers of cycles and travel goods, to open a factory at Llanelly in 1948 (*E.D.*, 18 March 1948). For details of similar moves by Elkington and Co., electroplaters, and Copes, the button manufacturing firm, see *B.P.*, 23 January 1950 and *B.M.*, 14 April 1950.

[2] See also Lomas and Wood, *Employment Location*, pp. 143–4.

[3] *The West Midlands: A Regional Study* (1965), para. 66.

[4] See below, pp. 169 ff. See also A. G. Douglas Clease, 'The problem of personnel', *Bus and Coach*, October 1951, pp. 375–6.

wide range of professional services including law and accountancy. Employment in public administration, both local and national, also increased significantly. This growth was reflected in the extensive building of offices which took place, especially in the city centre and on the Calthorpe Estate.[1] A further increase took place in those branches which served the individual, such as garages and hairdressing. Nevertheless, the retailing sector declined, owing to the disappearance of numerous shops in the central redevelopment areas, and the shortages of shops in the new suburbs.[2] The expansion of service industries was subject to no control by the central Government until 1965, when a temporary ban on office building was applied to Birmingham. The local authority, for its part, encouraged the expansion of the service sector, especially during the late 1950s and 1960s, by readily making land available for new shops and offices.

Industrial Dynamics

The decline in manufacturing employment did not prevent very real economic progress in Birmingham between 1951 and 1970, and the rise in overall manufacturing productivity has been estimated at as high as 5 per cent per annum since 1945.[3] This increase was the result of a response by Birmingham industry to an expanding demand for its products. Most of this demand came from the home market, but exports increased in absolute terms and probably in proportionate terms as well. Certainly, the efforts of succeeding Governments to encourage exports were directed particularly at Birmingham manufacturers. In 1949, for instance, Harold Wilson, then President of the Board of Trade, maintained that: 'Exports of the kind of goods produced in Birmingham were enough last year to pay for half our imports of iron ore or all our imports of meat.'[4] Indeed, by the 1960s exports of metal and engineering products accounted for about 60 per cent of the total United Kingdom figure compared with 33 per cent between the wars, and by 1967 the West Midlands was the third most important exporting region in Britain.[5]

The increasing volume of exports from Birmingham was largely the result of the efforts of dynamic firms like the Austin Motor Company. Before the war British motor manufacturers had been discouraged from producing powerful cars by the domestic motor taxation structure, which put them at a disadvantage in export markets. But after the war the Government encouraged exports by deliberately restricting the home market, and the tax on horsepower was replaced by a flat rate

---

[1] See below, pp. 442 ff.   [2] See below, pp. 252 ff.
[3] 'The booming Midlands', p. 7.   [4] *Birmingham Journal*, vol. iii, no. 27, 1949.
[5] *The West Midlands: Patterns of Growth*, p. 13.

in 1948.[1] A year earlier Austin's had announced the first British car of completely post-war design, the A.40 Devon saloon, for which the chairman, Leonard Lord, personally led a sales campaign in the U.S.A. By 1949, 84,000 Austin cars had been exported since the war. After a slight check in the early 1950s, Austin exports began to rise again from about 1953, and the introduction of the Mini in 1960 allowed a further breakthrough into overseas markets. Other Birmingham firms' exporting successes, while perhaps less spectacular than Austin's, were equally valuable. Medium size and smaller firms were encouraged and helped to export by the Chamber of Commerce, whose conversion in the 1950s from a protectionist policy to one of support for Britain's entry into the European Common Market was highly significant of the outward-looking attitude of Birmingham industry.

Of course, those Birmingham products which sold well abroad were also in strong demand at home, and it was in an attempt to satisfy both markets that local firms made major improvements in productivity. They were also propelled in this direction by the shortage of labour in the city. The building of new factories, which was encouraged by the Corporation's redevelopment schemes, also helped. It has been estimated, for instance, that when firms moved into municipal flatted factories their productivity increased by as much as 18 per cent per worker.[2] Concerns which built their own accommodation probably realized even greater productivity increases. Some firms, such as Fisher and Ludlow, incorporated in new plant production techniques gleaned from visits abroad.[3] More new capital equipment was introduced into Birmingham industry after 1945 than at any other time in its history. Capital investment also depreciated more rapidly than before, so that machinery was being replaced at an ever-quickening rate. Smaller firms also improved their production methods. Abraham and Co. Ltd., for instance, manufacturers of glass gift ware, after making losses owing to overstaffing and poor quality products, reorganized to such effect that in 1966 they received the Queen's Award for Industry.[4] However, the most outstanding example of improved managerial techniques and automation, leading to higher productivity and output, is again provided by the Austin Motor Company at Longbridge. As soon as the war had ended, reorganization began to transform the factory, so that it maintained its position as one of the most highly mechanized plants in Europe. Automation was extensively employed

[1] A. Silberston, 'The motor industry', in Duncan Burns (ed.), *The Structure of British Industry* (1958), vol. ii, p. 23.
[2] *Industry in the West Midlands*, p. 19.
[3] Fisher and Ludlow, *A Hundred Purposeful Years* (1956), p. 34.
[4] *Sunday Times*, Magazine Section, 8 January 1967.

both in the manufacture of components and in the intermediate and final stages of assembly.[1] By 1950 a completely new car assembly plant was taking shape, making maximum use of electronic control for automatic selection, sequencing, and the feeding of parts on to the assembly tracks.[2] But the results of the revolution in flow techniques were most noticeable in the engine section. Much of the reconstruction at Longbridge was due to the work of Leonard Lord, who was recognized as one of the greatest production engineers of his generation. Lord had become first deputy chairman and joint managing director on the death of Lord Austin shortly before the war, and he was made chairman in 1945. When he retired in 1961, his dynamic policy was continued by his successor, George Harris.[3]

Increased productivity in Birmingham was encouraged by a number of voluntary organizations. One of the most significant was the Birmingham Productivity Association, founded by a number of progressive Birmingham manufacturers, educationalists, and trade unionists. Initially it aimed only to create a climate of opinion, by organizing meetings, staging conferences and exhibitions, arranging film shows and discussion groups, and setting up factory visiting schemes.[4] However, during the 1960s the Association began to work more and more closely with the Government. In 1962–3 it threw its resources behind the National Productivity Year Campaign. Of 500 local firms contacted, 47 per cent confirmed that the campaign had indeed assisted them.[5] In 1966, the Association was again active, helping in the Quality and Reliability Year.[6] Similar in its aims was the West Midlands Industrial Development Association. Founded in the early 1950s, it represented local authorities and Chambers of Commerce throughout the West Midlands.[7] Within Birmingham, the Chamber of Commerce also provided advice on productivity.

A further cause of increased efficiency has sometimes been said to be the absorption of many Birmingham firms into big national combines, and the expansion of others until they became the leaders of such groups. However, economists disagree about the extent to which these mergers improved productivity, and it would be wrong here to dogmatize about the issue one way or the other. Yet throughout the post-war period both vertical and horizontal links were made, and most of the major firms in the city pursued both these types of integration simultaneously. The most active proponent of this policy was the Birmingham Small Arms Company, which since the beginning of the

[1] *Birmingham Sketch*, vol. i, no. 2, 1957, p. 44.   [2] *Austin Jubilee*, p. 59.
[3] Turner, *The Car Makers*, p. 181.
[4] *Birmingham Productivity Association Annual Report*, 1957–8, p. 7.
[5] Ibid., 1962–3, p. 4.   [6] Ibid., 1966–7, p. 5.
[7] *Industry in the West Midlands. The Official Handbook of the West Midlands Industrial Development Association Ltd.* (1954), p. 7.

century had been buying up firms while their products were in demand, and selling them off when they ceased to be profitable. After the war the B.S.A.'s policy had two distinct objectives. One was to purchase supplying companies, and concerns which competed with the group's existing enterprises. The second was to create new companies to produce marketable lines developed by the group's research departments.[1] Bicycle production provided a good example of B.S.A.'s strategy. When there was a strong demand for bicycles after the war, B.S.A. extended production, using the whole of one plant, the Waverley Works. But when the bicycle boom ended in the late 1950s, the manufacturing interest was sold to Raleigh.

During the 1950s and 1960s there was also a quickening rate of amalgamation in the car industry. Austin's merged with the Nuffield organization to form the British Motor Corporation. By 1969, B.M.C. in turn had merged with Leyland to form British Leyland. Yet at the same time, these large firms were themselves absorbing smaller ones. Fisher and Ludlow, the body builders, were one of Austin's biggest acquisitions, after Fisher and Ludlow had themselves taken over many smaller companies. The chocolate industry was equally merger-orientated. Cadbury's, which had already merged with the Fry group before the war, purchased many smaller concerns after 1945 before being merged itself into the even larger Schweppes group in the late 1960s.

One effect of these mergers was to diminish the economic independence of Birmingham industry. Many decisions affecting the city's factories came to be taken elsewhere, with reference to the well-being of combines which often spanned not only Britain but the whole world. By 1970 this state of affairs had apparently produced no ill effects in Birmingham.[2] But there could be no certainty about what the future held in store.

Despite the expansion of the larger concerns, there was no marked fall in the number of small firms. Unfortunately, there are no figures for small workshops, but Table 4 shows that although the number of firms employing over 2,000 people increased by one, there was also an actual increase in firms employing less than a hundred. So even in the late 1960s there was still a preponderance of small firms in Birmingham.

A further aid to Birmingham industries after 1945 was the growth of the money market and financial institutions in the city. Although the larger concerns raised their capital on the London Stock Exchange, smaller companies needed to raise money locally. No issuing houses existed in Birmingham to provide this service until 1936, when G. R. Dawes founded Neville Industrial Securities. Few enterprises could be

[1] *B.S.A. Group News, Centenary Edition,* 7 June 1961.
[2] This may, however, be too optimistic a view. For a generally adverse picture of the effect of mergers see Gerald D. Newbould, *Management and Merger Activity* (1970).

Table 4. *Size of Birmingham Firms, 1952–1971*

Employing	No.	%	No.	%
	1952		*1971*	
2,000–	15	0·7	16	0·8
1,000–	38	1·7	34	1·7
750–	22	1·0	15	0·8
500–	39	1·8	27	1·4
400–	33	1·5	26	1·4
300–	40	1·8	38	2·0
200–	95	4·3	65	3·4
100–	264	12·0	157	8·2
11–	1,660	75·2	1,544	80·3

Source: *Abstract.*

assisted during the war, but in 1945 and 1946 Neville helped to float nearly one hundred companies.[1] This success was noted in London and in 1953 the Charterhouse Group of London merchant bankers opened a branch in Birmingham. In 1963 another firm of London merchant bankers, Singer and Friendlander, began to operate in the city, offering a wide range of financial services, including assisting with the floating of companies.[2] Six other London banks soon followed. But three years before their advent it had become apparent that Birmingham needed more issuing houses, and the city's financiers responded by establishing the Birmingham Industrial Trust with a capital of half a million pounds. Five per cent of this money was subscribed by Lazards, the London merchant bank, but the rest came from Midland institutions and individuals.[3] Amongst the more prominent Birmingham businessmen in this venture were Sir Evan Norton, Sir Charles Burman, and W. S. A. Russell. Nevertheless, many new companies still continued to be floated by the Birmingham brokers.

Birmingham had had its own stock exchange since the 1840s, and the number of companies quoted on it increased after 1939. The nationalization of railways, collieries, gas, and electrical companies was reflected in some temporary gaps in the list, but these were soon filled, and by 1967, 570 companies had their securities quoted in Birmingham, 200 of which were not even quoted in London. But 1967 saw the end of the Birmingham exchange. It was replaced by a new institution, known as the Midlands and Western Stock Exchange, formed by an amalgamation of the Birmingham, Nottingham, Bristol, Cardiff, and Swansea exchanges.[4] Although about £1,500,000 was the most that could be raised in Birmingham, there were distinct advantages in raising capital locally. Because they knew the local conditions, the Birmingham issuing houses could usually raise money more quickly, and on better

[1] B.P. *Review of Industry*, pt. ii, 29 January 1967, p. 28.
[2] *The Economist*, 4 May 1963.
[3] B.P. *Review of Industry*, pt. ii, 1967, p. 28.   [4] Ibid.

terms for the small firms, than the London houses. Transactions were
facilitated by the very close financial and commercial ties that the
Birmingham finance houses had with local industry.[1]

The post-war period also saw Birmingham grow as a regional banking
centre. The Bank of India, for instance, opened in the city in 1965 to
assist industrial and commercial concerns throughout the region, and
develop trade with the East, as well as help the immigrant Indian
population with their financial problems. In 1967 the Bank of London
and South America also opened a branch in the city. The chairman
commented that: 'It is our job to go where there is business'. Clearly
he felt that there was business in the West Midlands.[2]

Birmingham industry also benefited from a great improvement in
its communications with other parts of the country and of the world.
The opening of the London–Birmingham motorway in the late 1950s
was followed in the next decade by the completion of motorway
links to other major cities. The planned motorway system converged
on Birmingham just as the canals had done in the eighteenth century,
and in 1970 the city had still not felt the full benefits of its newly
favoured situation. Railway connections with London and the north
were also substantially improved by electrification in the mid-1960s.
Domestic and international flights from Birmingham Airport, reopened
to commercial use after the war, were steadily extended, though owing
to its small size and proximity to London, many services were uneconomic and the list of destinations was still a short one in 1970.
These improvements in transportation further enhanced Birmingham's
excellent position as a production and distribution centre. Public
transport within the city and the conurbation, on the other hand, did
not improve to the same extent, if it can be said to have improved at
all.[3] Even so, there is little to suggest that it reduced the commuting
ranges of workers living either inside or outside the city boundaries.

Earnings and the trade unions

Given the prosperity of Birmingham industry and the great shortage
of labour, it is clear that earnings were very high in the city. Unfortunately figures for Birmingham alone are hard to obtain. However,
there is no reason to assume that the city diverged substantially from
the regional pattern. The Inland Revenue's income census for 1959–60
showed that the average individual's income from employment in the
West Midlands region was 4 per cent above the average for the United
Kingdom, whilst the 1958 Census of Production registered a figure of
5·5 per cent above average. Family incomes were even higher. The
Family Expenditure Survey for 1961–3 showed that incomes per

[1] *The Economist*, 28 September 1963.
[2] *B.P. Review of Industry*, pt. ii, 1967, p. 26.   [3] See below, pp. 411 ff.

household in the West Midlands stood even higher than those of London and the south-east, and reached 13 per cent above the average for Great Britain. High family incomes can be partly explained by the shortage of labour and variety of industry in Birmingham, which both enabled and encouraged more women and young people to obtain employment than was usual elsewhere.[1] In fact, the growth in the number of women workers accounted for 70 per cent of the increase in the total employed in Birmingham between 1951 and 1966. But the number of women employed in manufacturing was falling, while that in the service sector was increasing. Table 5, which shows the percentage of married working women by age group, indicates that at all ages, on a proportionate basis, more Birmingham housewives were in employment than over the country as a whole. The percentage of working wives was also higher in Birmingham than the conurbation average.[2]

Table 5. *Percentage Occupied Married Females by Age Group,*
1961–1966

(a) *Birmingham*
(% employed wives to all wives in age group)

	15–24	25–44	45–64	65 +
1961*	50·1	43·7	44·2	7·1
1966	47·4	49·1	52·0	8·4

(b) *England and Wales*

	15–24	25–44	45–64	65 +
1961*	42·9	35·6	33·7	5·4
1966	44·1	42·4	41·8	5·7

* Non-single women (i.e. married, divorced, widowed).
Source: Censuses of Population.

The high earnings of individuals can be accounted for to some extent by the long hours of overtime worked in many shorthanded plants. But there is also every sign that basic wage rates were exceptionally high in Birmingham. All the industrial categories which had location quotients of more than 100 in Birmingham tended to pay high wages.[3] The shortage of labour in the city, which is reflected in its low

[1] Males employed per 1,000 employed females:

	Birmingham	England and Wales
1951	1,819	2,242
1961	1,777	2,079
1966	1,665	1,806

[2] Lomas and Wood, *Employment Location*, p. 119.

[3] Certainly if we look at the national wage rates of those industries which were well represented in Birmingham, we find that their level of wages tended to be high. For figures between 1955 and 1969 see Department of Employment and Productivity, *Statistics on Income*, no. 29, June 1969.

unemployment figures,[1] would alone have been enough to keep wages high.[2] But they were further inflated by the development of strong trade union organization from the late 1930s. This expansion of unionism in a city where it had previously been very weak was largely the result of the labour shortage, the growth of large firms which could no longer maintain the traditionally close relationship between management and labour in Birmingham, and the generation by the city's advanced industrial environment of labour leaders of high quality. So it is no coincidence that Austin's, where all three of these factors applied, saw a greater degree of union organization and pressure than any other Birmingham firm.

After the setbacks of the late 1920s and early 1930s, trade union strength in Birmingham did not begin to recover until the last years before the war, when the rearmament programme helped to reduce unemployment and raise wages. Most city unions registered increases in membership, but those of the general unions were the most marked. The Amalgamated Engineering Union, in particular, greatly increased its strength, which rose by 75·4 per cent in the years 1935-7 alone. About 2,000 new members were recruited each year until 1939, by which time the union's Birmingham district had over 12,000 members.[3] But there was still plenty of room for improvement, and union organizers complained that numerous non-unionists were still working in the Birmingham engineering trades. Nevertheless, the unions were largely successful in obtaining adequate conditions and wage rates in armament concerns, where new organization and methods were being introduced. Several successful strikes were held in the shadow aero factories from 1937, mainly over basic and piece rates.

During the war membership increased rapidly in most Birmingham plants as the employers conceded full union recognition, and some success attended efforts to recruit more women. The general unions, and the A.E.U. in particular, were the main beneficiaries, whereas the older, craft unions, such as the National Union of Gold, Silver, and Allied Trades, were adversely affected by the war. Within the general unions the shop stewards movement, which had already grown in strength before the war, was further reinforced. Shop stewards were prominent in joint production committees and in the numerous shop-floor

---

[1] The percentage of the Birmingham labour force unemployed, on average, over the years 1948-67, was 0·9 per cent. The corresponding United Kingdom average was 1·3 per cent. By 1970, however, this situation had been reversed, with rather higher unemployment in Birmingham than over the country as a whole.

[2] For evidence of consistently high engineering earnings in the Birmingham area, see K. Knowles and T. Hill, 'The structure of engineering earnings', *Bulletin of the Oxford Institute of Statistics*, vol. xvi, September–October 1954, pp. 272–328.

[3] Figures from A.E.U. reports in Birmingham Trades Council, *Annual Report and Year Book*.

negotiations which the rapidly changing conditions of wartime production involved. Although their powers were often resented by employers, and attempts to restrict them led to several disputes towards the end of the war, serious strikes were a rare occurrence during the hostilities.[1] Largely responsible for this harmony were the high wages paid in the engineering industries, which contrasted sharply with the relatively low rates paid in the 1930s. Other industries were forced to follow suit, transforming Birmingham into a high wage area, and giving the unions the upper hand in their relations with the employers.

After 1945 the unions, which had by now proved themselves capable of protecting their members and providing them with tangible benefits, were able to increase their membership still further. More women and young people were attracted into their ranks. Some employers tried to take advantage of the conversion to peacetime production by attacking union organization, and the power of the shop stewards in particular.[2] Yet no major strike took place over the shop steward issue until January 1950. And only one major strike, at the Dunlop Rubber Co. in December 1946, took place over a firm's refusal to negotiate directly with the trade unions. Such stoppages as did take place— and they were less frequent in the later 1940s than in the last months of the war—were almost all the result of unsuccessful claims for higher wages and piece rates. Apart from a big strike at Austin Motors over piece rates in August 1948, the motor industry did not figure prominently in the list of stoppages. But these years of apparent harmony resulted more from the T.U.C.-agreed policy of wage restraint than from local conditions. The growth of militancy among the shop stewards, the collapse of nearly all the joint production committees, and the domination of the Trades Council by Communists and their sympathizers, indicated difficulties to come. The union leaderships' support for wage restraint, and the multiplicity of unions in the big motor plants,[3] further strengthened the shop stewards, among whom Leonard Lord claimed to discern political agitators. Their militancy spread throughout the Birmingham general unions, and as early as February 1948 the area meetings of the A.E.U. and the T.G.W.U. declared their intention to press for higher wages, with strike action if necessary.[4] But owing to the near stability of the cost of living, and high earnings in the many Birmingham industries which added piece-

---

[1] Information on Birmingham strikes has been taken from the *Ministry of Labour Gazette* (later, *Employment and Productivity Gazette*). For national strike figures in wartime, see Central Statistical Office, *Statistical Digest of the War* (1951), p. 34.

[2] See B.T.C., *Annual Report*, 1946–7, p. 5; 1948–9, p. 7.

[3] In 1946 at least eleven unions had members in the Longbridge works.

[4] *B.G.*, 9 February 1948.

work bonuses to basic rates, this threat did not materialize until the early 1950s.

During the first years after its election in 1951 the Conservative Government adopted a conciliatory attitude towards the trade unions, and the annual total of days lost through strikes did not rise above two million until 1953. In engineering, however, and especially in the motor industry, the size and length of disputes (though not their number) began to increase rapidly. Several of the motor strikes resulted from the instability of demand for cars now that manufacturers were being allowed to produce more for the home market. Redundancies became frequent, and Austin's in particular caused anger among their workers by sacking shop stewards. The first serious strike over the victimization issue took place at Longbridge in June 1951, when over 10,000 workers were involved. An even bigger stoppage occurred at Austin's in 1953, when the management refused to take on a shop steward, McHugh, even though other redundant workers were being re-engaged. The strike, which lasted from 17 February to 4 May, was the biggest in Birmingham since the war, and the largest single-firm stoppage in the history of the motor industry.[1]

After the Austin dispute had ended, on terms by no means favourable to the strikers, serious motor strikes became a rare occurrence in Birmingham until the middle of the decade. Engineering disputes also remained infrequent. Indeed, until then Birmingham had been somewhat less affected by disputes than many other industrial areas. But all this began to change from 1956. While engineering strikes remained few in number, stoppages multiplied in the motor and associated industries. Three big disputes occurred in 1956 over redundancies, but this time the unions did not allow themselves to be manoeuvred into a showdown with the managements, as had occurred at Longbridge three years before, and their organization and militancy were strengthened.[2] In the following year, as production revived, the motor unions moved on to the offensive and four major strikes occurred, three of them after failure to agree on new basic and piece rates. In 1958 motor strikes declined sharply in severity over the country as a whole, but not in Birmingham—all the eight major stoppages there were in the motor and allied trades. Most resulted from wage claims.

[1] B.T.C., *Annual Report*, 1953–4, p. 10; H. A. Turner, Garfield Clack, Geoffrey Roberts, *Labour Relations in the Motor Industry* (1967), p. 242. For the Court of Inquiry report on the dispute, which criticized both sides for inflexibility, see *Industrial Courts Act, 1919. Report of a Court of Inquiry into the Dispute between the Austin Motor Company Limited and Certain Workpeople, Members of the National Union of Vehicle Builders*, Cmd. 8839.

[2] *The Clarion* (Organ of the B.M.C. Joint Shop Stewards Committee), vol. i, no. 1, January–February 1957, p. 2.

By now the motor industry had become as strike-prone as the traditionally vulnerable mining, shipbuilding, and dock sectors.[1] Between 1959 and 1961, twenty-three major stoppages occurred in Birmingham, all but two of them in motor and associated concerns. Nearly all arose from disagreements over pay and conditions. In the next two years the situation eased slightly but in 1964 there were eight major strikes, seven of them in the motor vehicle and components sectors. In the second half of the decade other areas of Birmingham industry became more liable to stoppages, and the proportion of serious motor disputes fell to about half of the total of big strikes. The strike rate fell sharply in 1966, but from then until the end of the decade it averaged about eight serious stoppages per year.

The extension of union membership after the war took the principal form of a massive reinforcement of the general unions. By 1967 the A.E.U. had eighty Birmingham branches, compared to thirteen before the war, and the T.G.W.U. had as many as 118 branches. But owing to the very size of these unions, much of the responsibility for negotiations with individual managements had to be further delegated to the shop stewards. This process was particularly advanced in the motor industry, where a number of unions enjoyed bargaining rights within each plant.[2] By the 1960s the workers had come to see the shop stewards' committees, and not their union branch or executive, as the real union when it came to negotiations with the management.[3] Consequently, many stoppages from the later 1950s were unofficial, particularly in the motor industry. As such, they allowed the Birmingham shop stewards to take advantage of the prosperity of local industry and the labour shortage, especially when negotiating piece rates. High earnings in the motor industry would have forced other local employers to increase their rates in any case, even without union pressure, but the wide distribution of stoppages throughout Birmingham industry in the later 1960s suggested that they were being forced even further along this path.

[1] See Turner, etc., *Labour Relations in the Motor Industry*; Graham Turner, *The Car Makers* (rev. ed., 1964), pp. 79–97; Henry Pelling, *A History of British Trade Unionism* (1963), pp. 210–56.

[2] For union distribution within B.M.C., see Turner, etc., *Labour Relations in the Motor Industry*, p. 195.

[3] See Turner, p. 222; remarks by Harry Baker, former secretary of the Birmingham Trades Council, in *B.M.*, 16 May 1966. As early as 1955 attendance at branch meetings had sunk to 10 per cent of total membership (*Birmingham Journal*, July 1955, p. 6; February 1957, p. 1). For a study of the extensive role of the shop steward in engineering industry, especially in the Midlands, see A. I. Marsh and E. E. Coker, 'Shop steward organization in the engineering industry', *British Journal of Industrial Relations*, vol. i, 1963, pp. 170–90. The importance of the shop steward is particularly emphasized in two articles on the development of trade unionism in Birmingham, in *Birmingham Journal*, May 1953, pp. 9–11; June 1953, pp. 9–11.

Economic fluctuations and the Birmingham economy

Labour relations in Birmingham were closely associated with the cycle of booms and slumps which afflicted the national economy after 1945. To what extent was Birmingham industry affected by these variations compared to the country as a whole? Table 6 attempts to answer this question by giving the numbers of unemployed and of unfilled vacancies in each June, as a percentage of the total labour force, for the city and the whole country. As the Birmingham economy was so dependent upon the motor industry, an index has also been provided of the total annual output of vehicles throughout the country. The most significant, and the least surprising, feature of the table is that local fluctuations moved in the same directions as national variations. In other words, when the country as a whole was doing well, then so was Birmingham and vice versa. Yet in time of expansion, the proportion of vacancies in Birmingham generally rose higher and the level of unemployment fell lower than the national rates. This suggests that when the country was well off, Birmingham did even better. And in years of national depression, the Birmingham economy was generally less seriously affected than most other areas, at least until the late 1960s.

It was often suggested that fluctuations in the Birmingham economy were determined by the health of the motor industry. Clearly, this sector had some influence, but Table 6 does not fully bear out the hypothesis. Unfortunately, car production figures for Birmingham alone are not available, but the national production figures do not show a good correlation with the rate of economic activity in Birmingham, especially in the 1950s. In the 1960s, it is true, rises in car output were usually paralleled in Birmingham by falls in unemployment and increases in the number of vacancies. On the other hand, it is more likely that the improvement of the city economy reflected the general prosperity of the country, which also caused the growth in demand for cars. As we have seen, Birmingham industry was still relatively diverse even in the late 1960s.

Between 1948 and 1968 we can detect four peaks of economic boom in Birmingham, in 1951, 1955, 1960, and 1965. There were correspondingly four troughs of depression in 1953, 1958, 1962, and 1967. We can relate the boom condition of 1951 to the gradual relaxation of early post-war controls and to the greater availability of raw materials. Especially useful for Birmingham was the greater availability of metal, but other industries benefited. During the early post-war years, for example, Cadbury's had been continually frustrated by the shortage of cocoa, but this obstacle was removed after 1950.[1] However, the post-war

[1] For examples of the restrictive effect on Birmingham industry of post-war materials shortages and power cuts, see e.g. *B.P.*, 31 January 1947; 25 February 1947; *B.M.*, 21 March 1947. See also the Chamber of Commerce report for 1946–7, in *Journal and Monthly Record*, May 1947, p. 323.

Table 6. Economic Fluctuations in Birmingham Employment Area

	% registered unemployed in June		% vacancies in June or nearest month		Index of cars manufactured in G.B.
	Birmingham	G.B.	Birmingham	G.B.	
1948	0·8	1·4	3·5	2·4	30
1949	0·5	0·9	2·4	1·8	37
1950	0·4	0·9	2·6	1·6	47
1951	0·3	0·9	2·8	2·2	43
1952	1·0	2·0	1·5	1·4	40
1953	1·1	1·3	0·9	1·3	54
1954	0·4	1·1	2·0	1·6	70
1955	0·4	0·9	2·6	1·9	81
1956	1·6	1·0	1·3	1·8	64
1957	1·0	1·1	0·8	1·3	78
1958	1·2	1·8	0·8	0·9	95
1959	0·9	1·7	1·5	1·0	107
1960	0·5	1·3	2·0	1·5	122
1961	0·9	1·1	1·1	1·6	91
1962	2·0	1·6	0·7	1·0	113
1963	1·8	1·9	0·9	0·9	146
1964	0·7	1·3	2·4	1·5	169
1965	0·5	1·1	2·7	1·8	156
1966	0·6	1·0	2·4	1·8	145
1967	2·1	2·0	1·5	1·1	141
1968	2·1	2·2	1·6	1·3	164
1969	1·7	2·2	1·7	1·4	155
1970	2·8	2·4	1·2	1·3	149

Source: Birmingham Abstract of Statistics.

period was never free from crisis or near-crisis and the boom broke in 1953, coinciding with the second post-war American recession. Yet towards the end of that year there was a private investment boom, helped partly by an 'expansionist' budget, and by 1955 the Birmingham economy was again forging ahead. After its re-election, however, the Conservative Government acted to reduce demand, and the Birmingham consumer industries were particularly affected. Motor car and motor-cycle production had already been considerably reduced when the Suez crisis of 1956 led to petrol rationing and a further drop in demand for vehicles. Recovery was slow in 1957 and 1958 owing to lack of confidence in sterling caused by growing inflation. But after the balance of payments and reserves had been restored to a healthy state, the Government again allowed home demand to grow, and by 1960 Birmingham was again enjoying very high employment. By 1962 Britain's economic growth was once more checked as the Government took measures to control inflation and the Birmingham economy consequently suffered. Once the inflation had been brought under control, growth again was encouraged until 1965. Then Birmingham suffered as the new Government attempted to correct the balance of

Mixed development at Millpool Hill, in the mid-1950s

Aston Villa players and mascot parade the F.A. Cup at Villa Park in 1957. The players (*l. to r.*) are Jimmy Dugdale, Les Smith and captain Johnny Dixon.

payments deficit which once more put the brake on growth.[1] This uncertain situation was maintained until the end of the decade.

As we survey the industrial post-war history of Birmingham, we can see many of those trends, which we first observed during the pre-war period, continuing and sometimes accelerating. Individual firms were becoming more efficient, amalgamations were continuing apace, and there was a further outward movement to the suburbs. Yet despite these changes, in many respects the industrial structure of Birmingham during the later 1960s was very similar to that of the mid-1940s. The distribution of manpower throughout industry tended to remain very similar. Birmingham remained essentially an engineering and metal-working centre throughout these years, and although the large concerns increased in size the small workshops still existed in profusion. There can be little doubt that the central Government's industrial location policies played some part in bringing this situation about, by preventing new industry from coming into the city and (perhaps) by discouraging the expansion of indigenous Birmingham firms. Yet in many respects the official policies merely reinforced existing features of the Birmingham economy. Many non-engineering firms from outside Birmingham had powerful reasons for not coming to the city. Wages were high, labour was scarce, there was much congestion on the main roads, and land prices were exorbitant. Nevertheless, many Birmingham firms, already implanted within the city, were reluctant to leave. Despite the economic disadvantages, Birmingham's pool of skilled labour, the inter-dependence of firms, and the prestige attached to the city's name, all operated to retain the majority of enterprises. But it should not be forgotten that the expansion and diversification of these firms could be restricted by the shortage of labour in the city, and the limited availability of industrial land and premises. So, despite a big increase in productivity during the post-war period, the overall effect of these market forces, social factors, and industrial location policies was to impose a general stability on the employment structure of the city.

Certain changes nevertheless took place. The manufacturing sector declined in terms of manpower, although this fall was more than compensated for by an increase in the number working in the service industries. The expansion of office employment was particularly marked. This growth in the service sector was generated by the expansion of local and national administrations, the vast building programme, and the increase in personal incomes which generated a demand for a whole range of personal services. The expansion of the sector was facilitated by the growing number of married women who were seeking employment.

[1] A. J. Youngson, *Britain's Economic Growth 1920–1966* (1966), pp. 179, 180–1, 192.

N

VI

THE CITIZEN BODY:
DEMOGRAPHIC STRUCTURE OF
BIRMINGHAM

DEMOGRAPHIC change in post-war Birmingham was a constant source of debate in which varying degrees of pride, suspicion, alarm, and even fear were expressed. Within this debate, fact and fantasy could become intricately mixed and confused. At a rational level a number of official and semi-official bodies argued in cogent terms that the city's population should be reduced, if only to keep housing and other social problems within manageable proportions and to prevent congestion from throttling the life of the city. This point of view was shared by the Bournville Village Trust, the West Midland Group, the Ministry of Housing, and even, at times, by the City Council. On the other hand, solid arguments could be put forward for tolerating population stability or even a modest increase. Such views were expressed by the Corporation at the Wythall inquiry of 1959 and at subsequent public inquiries held into applications for boundary extensions. The impracticability of curtailing all future economic growth and the harm which would ensue from any such efforts were pointed out, as was the natural reluctance of many citizens to leave Birmingham.[1]

These rational arguments were often supported or contested by more emotional considerations. Frequently in evidence was the belief, shared by some civic leaders and many citizens, that a growing population in some mysterious way added to Birmingham's prestige. Irrational in a different way were many of the arguments used to justify stemming or even reversing the inflow of coloured immigrants. It was often maintained that coloured immigration increased population pressure within the city. Even *The Times* rallied to this point of view in 1957, declaring: 'there is little point in dispersing present residents if expanding employment within the city attracts a continual flow of newcomers from further afield—even from Ireland and the West Indies.'[2] Yet by the early 1960s it had been proved beyond all doubt that Birmingham's population was actually falling. This decline was largely the result of the movement to homes outside the city boundaries of numbers of Birmingham citizens, many of whom continued to work within the city. Although the influx of overseas immigrants into Birmingham failed to cancel out this population loss, their presence was sometimes associated with defective social conditions

[1] See esp. Long, *The Wythall Inquiry*, ch. i.   [2] *The Times*, 15 October 1957.

in certain areas of the city. Because those moving out of the city often belonged to its more affluent strata, whereas most of the overseas immigrants were of low socio-economic status, some people continued to worry in the 1960s that social conditions were deteriorating.

The existence of this rich mythology relating to Birmingham's socio-demographic evolution adds to the relevance of a study of post-war changes in the city's population structure, which this chapter will attempt. Such an inquiry involves consideration of variations in population, and age and sex structures, over the city as a whole and in comparison with other cities. Within this overall picture we can investigate internal variations within Birmingham, and make some attempt to establish their causation.

Population change

The 1951 census showed that Birmingham had a population of 1,113,000 people, compared to 1,003,000 in 1931. Twenty years later, in 1971, the census gave a figure of 1,013,000. Between the 1951 and 1961 censuses the decline in the city's population was only a marginal 0·5 per cent, but over the next ten years it was as high as 6·3 per cent. This contraction of population was accompanied by an increase in the ratio of males to females, though at no time were there more men than women in the city. By 1966 the 1951 ratio of 922 males for every 1,000 females had risen to 973.[1]

That these changes were linked with the age structure of the city becomes apparent from the figures given in Table 1, section (a) of which shows simply the number of persons in each age group during each censal year. Section (b) gives these figures as percentages; whilst section (c) shows the number of males per 1,000 females in each age group.

It will be seen that the overall population decline was a direct consequence of the fall in persons aged under 15 and between 25 and 44. Such losses were not compensated for by the increase of persons in the other age groups. Turning now to the increase in the city's male–female ratio, it will be seen that this was caused by the growth in the proportion of males aged under 65, which more than compensated for the decline in the ratio of males amongst the population of 65 years and over.

[1] At the time of writing only the number of persons living in Birmingham in 1971, as shown by the census of that year, has been published. For the more detailed demographic data we cannot go beyond 1966. It should be noted, however, that the sample census of that year, according to the City Statistician's calculations, probably understated Birmingham's true population by 2 per cent. If this estimate were correct, the population of Birmingham in 1966 would be no more than 1,085,280, compared to the census figure of 1,064,000. If the higher of the two estimates can be taken as accurate, it would appear that the rate of decline of Birmingham's population was still accelerating in the later 1960s.

Table 1. *Age Structure of the Birmingham Population*

	Age Groups*				
	−14	15–24	25–44	45–64	65–
(a) *Numbers*					
1951	264,000	142,000	351,000	253,000	103,000
1961	258,000	163,000	294,000	280,000	112,000
1966	252,000	168,000	258,000	271,000	115,000
(b) % *of year's total population*					
1951	23·7	12·8	31·5	22·7	9·3
1961	23·3	14·7	26·6	25·3	10·1
1966	23·7	15·8	24·2	25·5	10·8
(c) *Males per 1,000 females*					
1951	1,035	854	1,006	869	651
1961	1,055	1,028	1,068	954	575
1966	1,060	1,046	1,079	977	564

* In this and subsequent tables, unless otherwise indicated, the raw figures are given to the nearest 1,000, whilst the percentages have been calculated from the precise figures.

Source: Censuses of Population.

Certainly, between 1951 and 1966 Birmingham had become an 'older' city, in that the percentage and absolute number of persons aged 65 and over during that period had increased. But this trend, and the increase in the proportion of males, were by no means unique phenomena; many other major industrial cities in the country had similar experiences. Manchester, Liverpool, and Sheffield all declined in numbers during this period, but at a more rapid rate. Their ratios of males also increased, although less markedly. All were becoming 'older', and yet were increasing their proportions of 15–24 year olds.[1]

To what extent did changes within the various districts in Birmingham conform to this general pattern? Before an answer can be attempted the feasibility of delineating internal districts must be discussed, although at the outset we must confess that we have been unable to solve the problem adequately. Birmingham, like other large cities, is composed of innumerable districts each with its own distinctive socio-economic composition.[2] But because they have not been fully defined (and even if they had, it is most unlikely that we should have the necessary statistical data for them) they cannot be used here.[3] Relevant figures are, however, available for each of the city wards, which themselves exhibit varying socio-economic characteristics.

[1] See statistical appendix, table 5.

[2] See M. B. Stedman, 'The townscape of Birmingham in 1956', *Institute of British Geographers, Transactions and Papers*, no. 25, 1958.

[3] For a highly successful attempt to delineate sub-districts of Birmingham based on unpublished census data, see John Edwards *et al.*, 'Social patterns in Birmingham 1966: a reference manual' (Centre for Urban and Regional Studies, 1971). This method cannot be used, however, to chart changes in such districts over time because of major modifications in the delimitation of enumeration districts from census to census.

An analysis on a ward basis is therefore a feasible proposition, although it may be objected that the wards are themselves too large for adequate analysis. Yet, for our purposes, there are too many wards. It is difficult, if we wish to describe internal population movements in very broad and general terms, to assess the position in each of some forty wards. In any case, it would be impossible to establish changes over our period as a whole, which must be our main objective, owing to major ward boundary changes in 1949 and 1962. Thus in order to bring out the more general internal changes, precise and detailed measurements will have to be sacrificed, and the wards will be grouped together. To do so we can employ the categories devised by successive Birmingham Medical Officers of Health who, by amalgamating wards, divided the city into three concentric circles—central, middle, and outer. At the beginning of our period the central wards contained Birmingham's oldest and most inferior housing, the legacy of the industrial revolution. The middle ring contained much of the city's growth between 1860 and 1918, whilst the outer ring contained the bulk of inter- and post-war building.

Unfortunately our problems do not end here. Owing to changes in ward boundaries in 1949 and 1962 the rings have had to be redrawn. The successive Medical Officers of Health were most anxious to preserve, as far as possible, the distinctive features of each ring, and they made their revisions accordingly. However, the size of the rings changed substantially in 1962, when the central wards grew from 3,500 to 4,000 acres, and the middle ring grew from 11,000 to 14,500 acres, while the outer ring shrank from 36,500 to 32,500 acres.[1] Although these changes make the drawbacks of employing a ring classification only too obvious, it is still the best classification we have if we wish to draw broad conclusions about internal population change. It can also be claimed that whilst it is undesirable to place too much reliance on internal population changes observed between, say, 1945 and 1966, much useful information can be gathered about changes between 1961 and 1966 because most of the 1961 statistics that we have are given for both the pre- and post-1962 wards. Having thus at least clarified our position on this technical matter, we can now proceed to examine demographic change within these rings.

Throughout our period each ring exhibited certain distinctive demographic features. In terms of population size the outer ring was by far the largest. In 1951, for example, with 637,000 residents, it held over half the city's population. The central wards were the smallest, with a population of 132,000 in 1951, while the middle ring housed 344,000 people. The central wards were characterized by a high proportion of males and children. The outer ring, in contrast, contained

[1] See statistical appendix, table 6.

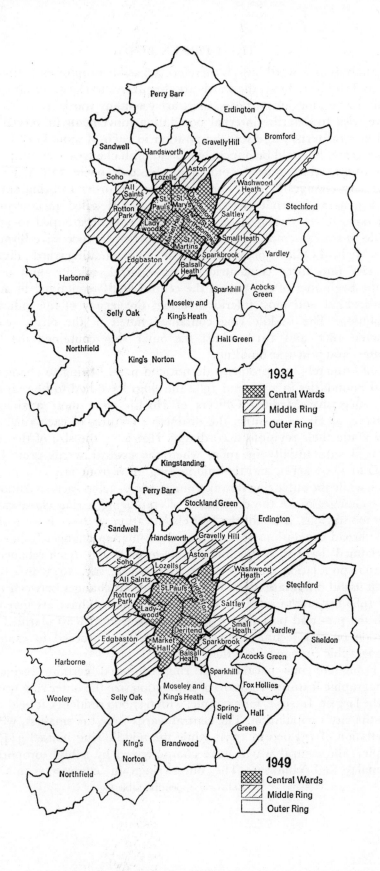

Figure 4   Changes in the definition of the three Birmingham rings, 1934 to the present

relatively few children, but a correspondingly higher proportion of middle-aged and elderly persons, as well as females. The demographic structure of the middle ring fell between these two extremes.[1]

These were the stable elements in the rings throughout the period. There were, however, changes, the most significant of which was the

[1] See statistical appendix, table 7.

extensive decline of population within the central wards. Between 1951 and 1961 (using the pre-1962 boundaries) it declined by 27·3 per cent, while between 1961 and 1966 (using the 1962 revised boundaries) it fell even more dramatically, in view of the shorter period, by 19·4 per cent. These are substantial movements by any standard and certainly between 1961 and 1966 they resulted in two other major demographic shifts in the central wards. The ratio of males grew from 1,028 per 1,000 females to 1,073 and the proportion of persons under 25 increased from 43·5 per cent to 46·9 per cent. The middle ring reflected this central ward pattern, but generally in a less pronounced form. Thus between 1951 and 1961, and 1961 and 1966, its population fell, but by only 3·7 per cent and 4·7 per cent respectively. Likewise, at least during the latter period, there was a slight increase in the ratio of males, and in the proportion of younger persons. In contrast to the two inner rings, the outer ring population actually increased by 6·7 per cent during the ten years following 1951 and thereafter held steady. There were few other changes in the demographic structure of the ring between 1961 and 1966.

We have now seen that during the post-war period, despite a rise in population in the outer reaches of the city during the 1950s, the overall Birmingham population fell. This reduction was mirrored in a substantial decline in the central areas of the city. However, it was the rise in the numbers and proportions of young males in the central wards and the middle ring that determined the changing sex and age structures in the city at large. Having thus described some of the major shifts in the demographic composition of the city, we must now set about explaining the factors which lay behind them.

Apart from a few exceptional years, since the beginning of the nineteenth century more births than deaths have occurred in towns and cities in the industrialized world. So when we find contemporary urban areas that are declining in numbers we can expect that gains from natural increase are being eroded by even greater volumes of persons moving away. We can easily demonstrate that this was the case in post-war Birmingham, by referring to Table 2 which analyses population changes by natural increase and net migration. The overall decreases in population between censuses are shown numerically and proportionately. The natural increases (calculated by subtracting the total number of deaths between censuses from the total number of births) are expressed as percentages. The differences between the overall declines and the natural increases represent the net numbers of emigrants (i.e. the excess of all emigrants over all immigrants). These figures, too, are expressed as percentages.

We can see that the marginal decline in Birmingham's population between 1951 and 1961 took place because the city's natural increase

Table 2. Population Growth of Birmingham and Selected Cities, 1951–1966

	Birmingham	Leeds	Liverpool	Manchester
1951–61				
Increase	−5,000	5,000	−45,000	−41,000
% increase	−0·5	0·9	−5·7	−5·8
% natural increase 1952–61	6·4	4·4	8·8	5·4
% net migration	−6·9	−3·5	−14·5	−11·2
1961–66				
Increase	−43,000	−6,000	−54,000	−63,000
% increase	−3·9	−1·0	−7·9	−9·5
% natural increase 1961–6	4·4	4·4	4·6	3·5
% net migration	−8·3	−5·4	−12·5	−13·1

Source: Censuses of Population and Registrar-General's *Annual Statistical Reviews*.

was 0·5 per cent of the 1951 population below losses from emigration. Between the periods 1951–61 and 1961–6 the average annual rate of natural increase grew from 0·6 to 0·9 per cent, but annual net emigration rose even faster, from 0·7 per cent to 1·7 per cent, with the consequence that the overall population of the city fell much more dramatically.

Table 2 also shows the position in the three other largest provincial cities of England. Relatively little separated Birmingham's rates of natural increase from theirs, especially between 1961 and 1966. Differences in their overall rates of decline were therefore caused by different rates of net emigration. Manchester and Liverpool were losing proportionately far more of their populations through migration than the other two cities, but Leeds was losing somewhat less than Birmingham.

Within Birmingham there were significant differences in rates of natural increase and migration and figures for the three rings are set out in Table 3.

While bearing in mind the warning that figures relating to pre-1962 boundaries cannot be directly compared with those tabulated for the post-1962 wards, it is clear that at least until 1966 and presumably in subsequent years, the rates of natural increase in the inner parts of the city were considerably higher than those in the outer reaches. But those factors working to increase the population of the central wards were completely undermined by the massive net emigration that was under way. Within the space of only five years, over a quarter of the 1961 population there had on balance moved out. The central wards contrasted with the outer ring, which between 1951 and 1961 was actually receiving on balance a trickle of immigrants. This immigration, given the relatively low rates of natural increase in the outer ring, contributed more than a little to the overall population growth there.

Table 3. Changes in Population in the Three Rings of Birmingham,
1951–1966

	Central wards	Middle ring	Outer ring
(a) *1951–61*			
Increase	−36,000	−13,000	43,000
% increase	−27·3	−3·7	6·7
% natural increase	11·9	5·6	5·6
% net migration	−39·2	−9·3	1·1
(b) *1961–6*			
Increase	−29,000	−18,000	4,000
% increase	−19·4	−4·7	0·6
% natural increase	6·5	6·4	2·4
% net migration	−25·9	−11·1	−1·8

Source: Special tables for ward population from censuses given in *Birmingham Abstract of Statistics*; figures on births and deaths in wards from the Birmingham Medical Officer of Health's *Annual Report*.

After 1961 the outer ring ceased to import population and experienced a slight net emigration, but as this was not more extensive than the ring's natural increase, the overall population held steady. It is more difficult to generalize about the middle ring because during the first period its demographic pattern, in many respects, bore a greater resemblance to that of the outer ring than to the central wards, whilst during the second period the reverse was true. Unfortunately we have no means of knowing whether these were fundamental changes or simply reflections of the redrawn ring boundaries.

We have now been able to isolate the relative importance of migration and natural increase in accounting for population change in post-war Birmingham. In our next two sections, we shall take this examination one stage further by looking at the causes of changes in natural increase and migration.

Natural Increase
(i) BIRTH RATES
The easiest way of measuring births is to calculate crude rates by expressing the number of births in an area for every 1,000 persons living there. Such rates in post-war Birmingham were normally one or two points above the national ones, although both the national and local annual figures tended to fluctuate in unison.[1] From 1945 Birmingham rates rose, reaching a peak for the whole period of 21·8 in 1947. Thereafter they fell steadily until 1955, when the lowest rate, 16·1, was recorded. This was followed by a further steady rise until 1964, after which they fell again. But if we were to isolate a general

---

[1] The figures are given in the statistical appendix, table 9.

trend between 1945 and 1967 it would be an upward one, although towards the end of the 1960s the rate again began to fall.

It might be surmised that this upward movement resulted from an increase in the marriage rate, causing a rise in the proportion of married women in the population. However, this hypothesis can be quickly discounted. In the first place the annual number of marriages per 1,000 population between 1945 and 1970 varied only between 8·4 and 9·5, whilst the general trend was one of quiescence. If we move on to examine the marriage rates amongst those whose civil status made them eligible, we find that between 1951 and 1970 the only major shift was in the younger marital ages of bachelors and spinsters. But this did not result in an increase in the proportion of married women in Birmingham, because, as we shall show later in this chapter, many of the emigrants from the city were younger married persons and their departure was responsible for a fall in the proportion of married women aged under 45 from 14·7 per cent of the adult population in 1951 to 12·3 per cent in 1966. So we shall have to seek reasons for the rising birth rates in the increased fertility of married women, rather than in an increase in their numbers. Changes in fertility can be established by calculating the annual number of legitimate births per 1,000 married women of fertile age (i.e. under 45). This shows that between 1950–2 the rate was 108, between 1960–2 it had risen to 136 and by 1965–7 to 145. Why this increase took place is not clear. Knowledge about contraceptive techniques was widely disseminated in Birmingham after the war, especially by the city's very active and energetic family planning association. Indeed, the first clinic to undertake work of this nature (named the Women's Welfare Centre) was opened in Birmingham in 1926, and as only the seventh to be founded in England it was very much a pioneering venture. It was fortunate in securing the patronage of Birmingham University and financial assistance from Sir John Sumner, both of which encouraged its growth.[1]

During the 1930s the family planning movement in Birmingham, as elsewhere, was attacked vigorously from some quarters. Some sections of church opinion in the city, supported by Dr. Newsholme, the Roman Catholic Medical Officer of Health, even objected, with more than a degree of passion, to a modest scheme whereby the local authority, under discretionary powers given by the Minister of Health, could set up clinics providing birth control advice to married women whose health would be endangered by further pregnancies.[2] Fortunately for such women, a full meeting of the City Council, prompted by Councillor Theodore Pritchett (Unionist), over-ruled Newsholme and the Public Health Committee, and two local authority clinics were set up, in the

[1] L. S. Florence, *Progress Report on Birth Control* (1956), pp. 13 ff.
[2] *B.M.O.H.*, 1934, p. 144.

Dudley Road and Selly Oak Hospitals. But valuable as the service was, its scope was limited and at the outbreak of war under a hundred women a year were being treated.

Meanwhile the bulk of the work in family planning was being carried on by the Women's Welfare Centre, renamed, in 1950, the Birmingham Family Planning Association. Before the war the clinic tended to advise only the poorest of the working classes. By 1948, with a growth in the social respectability of birth control, only half of the patients could be regarded as belonging to these social categories. The post-war patients also tended to be younger than had been normal before the outbreak of hostilities. Women coming to the clinic now wanted to control the size of their families from the beginning of their marriages, rather than to call a halt to excessive child bearing later in life.[1]

Steady progress was made in the work of the Association throughout the 1950s, but a further resurgence of energy during the 1960s resulted in the opening of numerous sub-clinics. The first had been opened in 1958, but there was a five-year gap until the second was opened in Handsworth. Thereafter, in quick succession, other clinics appeared in the central and middle areas of the city. Balsall Heath, Aston, Spark-brook, and Ladywood now all had their centres, thereby demonstrating that the association was still keenly anxious to help the poorer working classes. But other clinics were opened in more prosperous parts of the city, in districts such as Selly Oak, Northfield, Kings Heath, Kings Norton, and Bournville.

In view of this work, it is paradoxical that the birth rates amongst married women should have risen. We can be sure, however, that had it not been for the efforts of the Family Planning Association fertility rates would have been considerably higher. The work of the Association involved more than simply advising on the use of contraceptive techniques. It also organized a fertility clinic and a clinic for psycho-sexual difficulties. In many other respects, too, the Birmingham branch retained its earlier pioneering spirit. In 1960, for example, it was assisting in an extensive research project into oral contraceptives, whilst in 1966 a domiciliary service was set up, whereby doctors and nurses from the clinic visited patients in their own home if they were unable to get out.

During the 1960s the Family Planning Association was giving birth control advice to unmarried women. This type of advice was, however, provided on a much more extensive scale when the Brook Centre was opened. This development was not before time, as illegitimacy rates were rising in unison with legitimate ones. Between 1946 and 1950 the crude illegitimacy rate (illegitimate births per 1,000 of the total population) was 1·2 per 1,000. By the next quinquennium (1951–5) it

[1] Florence, *Progress Report*, pp. 19, 40.

had fallen to 0·9 per 1,000. Thereafter it rose dramatically from 1·3 in 1956–60 to 2·1 in 1961–5. By calculating the number of illegitimate births per 1,000 unmarried women aged 15–44 we have a much clearer picture of the 'real' position, but we find it very similar (although not identical) to our 'crude' pattern. In 1950–2, the average annual number of illegitimate births per 1,000 unmarried women of fertile age was 11·5. By 1960–2 the figure had more than doubled to 26·4. By 1965–7 it would appear that the rate had continued to rise, reaching 32·1. Birmingham was not, of course, exceptional in having increasing illegitimacy rates. The city was sharing in a wave of sexual 'permissiveness' that affected attitudes across Western Europe and America. It should be added, however, that Birmingham was receiving increasing numbers of young unmarried males, both from the United Kingdom and abroad. It would indeed be remarkable if such a situation did not have some effect on illegitimacy rates. This may account for the fact that, judged on crude rates, Birmingham tended to experience more illegitimate births than other major English industrial cities.[1]

Having described the overall trends in birth rates in Birmingham, we can now examine internal differences within the city. We can begin by looking at Table 4, which is divided into three parts. The first shows

Table 4. Changes in Birth Rates in the Three Rings of Birmingham, 1945–1970

		Central Wards	Middle Ring	Outer Ring
(a) *Births per 1,000 pop.*				
	1945–49	25·2	21·1	19·1
	1950–53*	23·3	17·1	14·8
	1954–58	24·0	18·2	14·8
	1959–61	25·1	23·0	15·7
	1962–66*	25·0	26·1	14·7
	1967–70	25·0	23·6	13·9
(b) *Births per 1,000 women aged 15–44*				
pre-1962 boundaries	{ 1951	103·3	75·1	65·8
	{ 1961	127·5	121·2	81·2
post-1962 boundaries	{ 1961	131·2	126·6	74·9
	{ 1966	137·3	136·2	74·4
(c) *Children under 5 per 1,000 women aged 15–44*				
pre-1962 boundaries	{ 1951	515	400	375
	{ 1961	589	449	342
post-1962 boundaries	{ 1961	576	420	334
	{ 1966	647	553	358

* Change in boundaries.
Source: Birmingham Medical Officer of Health's *Annual Reports*.

[1] See statistical appendix, table 10.

the crude birth rates per 1,000 population by ring. The second shows the number of births per 1,000 women aged 15–44 (the numbers of married women by ward in that age group on a ring basis being unknown). It will be apparent that neither of these methods necessarily reflects the fertility of married women, and a third calculation to assess birth rates, based on the number of children under five per 1,000 women aged 15–44, has been included. But the weakness of this method is that a ring with high child death rates will appear to have correspondingly lower birth rates. As we shall see later, such differences in mortality within the rings did occur. Thus none of the measurements we have devised for assessing fertility is completely reliable, but if the three sets of figures point in the same direction we may be reasonably confident of the accuracy of our findings.

Three significant points emerge from the table. The first is that the outer ring had the lowest birth rates, and they may even have fallen a little during the post-war period (though we cannot be certain because of the changes in the ward boundaries). The second point concerns the central wards. All the indications are that this area had the highest birth rates throughout the period, and they appear to have risen. Our final point is that whereas fertility rates in the middle ring lay between those of the other two rings, the rates of increase there were by far the most rapid. We have to attempt to explain, therefore, why birth rates were highest in the central wards, lowest in the outer ring, and rising most rapidly in the middle.

Throughout our period the central wards had the highest proportion of semi- and unskilled workers (Registrar-General's social classes IV and V) and some local evidence has been adduced to demonstrate that amongst these classes there was a great reluctance to use the more reliable methods of birth control, such as the cap or sheath. Greater faith was placed upon *coitus interruptus*, and hence one can hypothesize the higher birth rates![1] Conversely, because the outer ring contained the highest proportion of skilled workers and professional persons (Registrar-General's social classes I–III) who probably took a more 'responsible' attitude to family limitation, birth rates were at their lowest there.

We now have to explain the rising birth rate, which was experienced to a degree in the central wards, but much more extensively in the middle ring. Part of this increase must have been the result of the arrival of the Commonwealth and Irish immigrants, who settled predominantly in the middle ring. One recent study by the Corporation Statistician has suggested, however, that the West Indians did not share in responsibility for this increase. In Sparkbrook at least they did not appear

---

[1] Florence, *Progress Report*, pp. 110, 131.

to have a real fertility rate in excess of the indigenous population.[1] Support for this view comes from the Family Planning Association, which maintained that a high proportion of their clients were West Indians. On the other hand, the City Statistician's report provides figures which suggest that, in 1969 at least, the non-Irish Europeans (including the British) had lower 'real' fertility rates than all other ethnic groups in the city. In that year, out of 18,999 registered births, 6,703 were to women who had not previously given birth and 2,502 were to women who had previously given birth to four or more children. Forty per cent of the first-born children were born to parents both of whom were non-Irish Europeans. This figure contrasts sharply with the 27·5 per cent whose parents were Irish, 19·3 per cent whose parents were West Indian, and 22·7 per cent whose parents were Indian or Pakistani. Of the babies born to mothers who had previously had four or more children, only 7·2 per cent had non-Irish European parents. Again, there is a contrast with the 18·2 per cent born to Irish parents, 37·6 per cent to West Indian parents, and 24·9 per cent to Indian or Pakistani parents.[2] The implication of these figures is clear: the fertility rates of the overseas immigrants were higher than those of the rest of Birmingham's citizens. On the basis of this analysis it seems reasonable to argue that the rise in fertility suggested in the middle ring was due to the influx of overseas immigrants. It must, however, also be emphasized that any increase in the middle ring still did not bring birth rates there up to the level of the central wards, which if anything housed a slightly lower proportion of Irish and coloureds than the city as a whole.

Unfortunately, we do not have figures on illegitimacy by ring until 1964. However, it is no surprise to find that, between then and 1966, crude rates were at their highest in the central wards and middle ring (3·2 and 3·3 per 1,000 population respectively). The outer ring figure was 1·1.

To summarize our findings on birth rates, the crude rates in Birmingham had a propensity to rise, because there was an increase in the fertility of married women, brought about to an extent by the movement of overseas immigrants into the middle ring. This increase took place despite a most vigorous extension of the work done by the Family Planning Association in those areas. Perhaps its work was more effective in the outer reaches of the city where the social climate was more conducive to it. Certainly it was here that fertility rates were at their lowest. In the middle ring fertility rates were rising rapidly, yet by

---

[1] Corporation Statistician, 'Ethnic origins of Birmingham children born in 1969', para. 21. See also J. A. H. Waterhouse and D. M. Brabham, 'Inquiry into the fertility of immigrants', *The Eugenics Review*, vol. iv, esp. fig. 1, p. 14.

[2] 'Ethnic origins', table 4.

1966 they still had not reached the level of the central wards. The rising crude birth rates were also due partly to the increased illegitimacy rates, which were at their highest in the central and middle rings.

(ii) MORTALITY

During the post-war period the annual crude death rates in Birmingham (i.e. deaths per 1,000 total population) were somewhat below the national ones. Both fluctuated a little, but in unison. Yet the general trend was one of stability.[1] Between 1946 and 1950 the average Birmingham rate was 10·7; between 1951 and 1955, 10·9; 1956 and 1960, 11·1; 1961 and 1965, 11·2; and 1965 and 1970, 11·1. It is, therefore, tempting to infer from these findings that mortality can be seen as a constant factor in the city's history during this period. However, such an inference could be wrong. The weakness of the crude mortality figures is that they take no account of changes in the age structure of the population. As the Birmingham population was ageing (see Table 1), all other things being equal, one would have expected its crude mortality rates to have risen. That they did not do so requires comment.

Table 5 shows the age-specific mortality rates between 1951 and 1966. These are simply the annual number of deaths within a given age group expressed in terms of the total number of persons in it. The most obvious feature of the table is that, at each date, death rates were at their lowest amongst those aged 5–14, but then began to rise steadily in each of the succeeding age groups. Death rates were also relatively high amongst those under five. On the whole these rates tended to hold steady with only marginal improvements, except those of the sixty-fives and over, which fell quite dramatically.

Table 5. Age-Specific Mortality: Birmingham 1951, 1961, and 1966
(per 1,000 living)

	0–4	5–14	15–24	25–44	45–64	65–74	75 +
1951	6·4	0·5	1·0	2·1	12·1	46·2	129·1
1961	6·8	0·3	0·7	1·6	11·0	42·5	128·8
1966	5·5	0·3	0·8	1·8	11·4	42·0	115·6

How did the Birmingham experience compare with other great industrial cities? Part of the answer can be found in Table 6, which shows the standardized death rates of Birmingham and other great cities. Standardization, it should be explained, is a technique used by demographers to calculate death rates in given areas, as if they had the same age structure—that is, by removing any age differential bias.[2] At all dates the urban areas had higher death rates than the country as

[1] See statistical appendix, table 9.

[2] For a more detailed account see R. G. D. Allen, Statistics for Economists (2nd ed., 1951), pp. 115 ff.

Old people's cottages, and flats, on the Lyndhurst estate

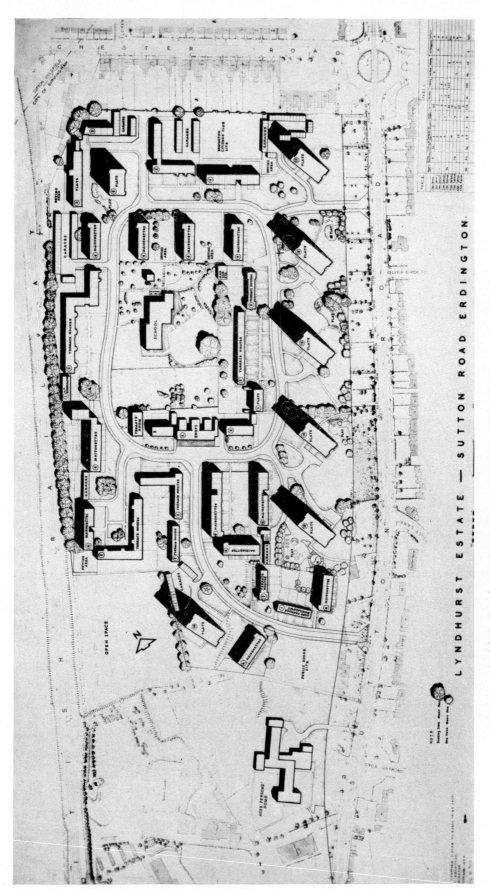

A high-density suburban estate. The Lyndhurst estate, Erdington,
planned in the late 1950s.

Table 6. Death Rates (Standardized to the Population of England and Wales 1951) in Birmingham and Selected Cities, 1951–1966

	1951	*1961*	*1966*
Birmingham	12·4	11·6	11·1
Liverpool	14·2	13·2	11·6
Leeds	13·3	11·8	11·3
Manchester	14·3	13·1	12·3
England and Wales	11·8	10·7	10·4

Source: Censuses of Population and Registrar-General's *Statistical Reviews*.

a whole. In this respect Birmingham was no different from other major cities. But in 1951 the Birmingham rates were somewhat lower than other comparable urban areas. Between 1951 and 1966, however, rates did not fall as extensively in Birmingham as elsewhere so that at the end of our period mortality in all the cities was comparable.

If we are to understand changes in mortality rates in Birmingham we shall have to examine changes in the deaths of infants. Infant mortality (i.e. the number of deaths of children under one year per 1,000 live births) is one of the major factors determining overall death rates. Deaths amongst infants have also been described as a crucial test of health services and social progress generally. To an extent adults are responsible for their own survival. The young child's life is entirely dependent upon the care of others. If, therefore, we are to attempt to measure social progress in Birmingham, we shall have to take cognizance of the number of deaths in infancy. The figures are given in Table 7

Table 7. Infant Mortality Rates

	Birm.	*Leeds*	*Liverpl.*	*Man.*	*Eng. & Wales*
1946–50	35	38	57	49	28
1951–5	26	29	33	32	27
1956–60	24	25	27	28	23
1961–5	23	24	26	29	21
1966–70	21	23	22	25	18

Source: As for Table 6.

which shows the infant mortality rates in Birmingham and selected areas in five-year groups between 1946 and 1970.

The general findings of this table bear a striking resemblance to our findings in Table 6. During the early post-war years infant mortality rates in Birmingham, whilst noticeably higher than those of England and Wales, were generally lower than those of other major industrial cities (and especially Liverpool and Manchester). There were substantial improvements in Birmingham in the late 1940s and early 1950s followed by more modest gains in the next decade. These trends were reproduced in the other cities, but their rates of improvement

o

were greater. Even so, by 1970 Birmingham's infant mortality rates
were still the lowest.

Having thus set out the infant mortality rates of Birmingham in the
national context, we can now examine internal differences within the
city. Table 8 shows the infant mortality rates within the three rings.

Table 8. Infant Mortality Rates within Birmingham
(Deaths per 1,000 births)

		Central Wards	Middle Ring	Outer Ring
pre-1949 boundaries	1945–9	53	40	34
1949–1962 boundaries	1950–4	34	28	24
	1955–9	30	27	21
	1960–1	29	23	21
post-1962 boundaries	1962–6	27	24	18
	1967–70	26	24	17

Source: Birmingham Medical Officer of Health's *Annual Reports.*

A glance at it reveals a pattern that will be familiar to urban historians
of earlier periods. The central areas of the city, which contained the
worst housing environment, had the highest infant mortality rates.
In 1931 the city's Medical Officer of Health attributed high infant
death rates in the central areas to a number of causes varying 'from
bad housing and overcrowding . . . to straitened conditions of life;
from bad landlords to bad tenants, and from diseases of the body to
warping of the mind.'[1] Even as late as 1970 much of this was still true.
In marked contrast, the outer ring, with its superior housing and its
more extensive upper-class social composition, had the lowest infant
death rates. But even taking into account the redrawing of the ring
boundaries, it is clear that this pattern was beginning to change.
Between 1945 and 1947 infant mortality rates in the central wards were
nineteen points above those of the outer ring. By 1962–6 only nine
points separated them. Between 1945 and 1970, there were improvements in all areas of the city, but they were most marked in the central
areas. Improvements in the outer reaches were more modest. Why was
this?

The overall improvement in each of the rings was due in part to the
more efficient medical and midwifery services and the general increase
in standards of living enjoyed throughout most social groups. But if we
look at the specific causes of death amongst infants we see that the
major improvements were made in those diseases which were most
closely associated with poor housing. Respiratory diseases, which were
responsible for eight infant deaths from every 1,000 births in 1946,
were responsible for only three twenty years later; deaths from diarrhoea
and enteritis fell from six to one and infective and parasitic diseases

[1] *B.M.O.H.*, 1931, Introduction.

also from two to one. We do not have an analysis of deaths by cause for wards, but we can be sure that the very rapid improvement in infant mortality rates in the central wards was due in part to the enormous slum clearance and redevelopment schemes that were being undertaken there, as well as to the rising standards of living enjoyed by most sectors of Birmingham society. However, in 1966 the central wards still contained the worst housing in the city, and infant mortality rates were still higher there than elsewhere.

It was not only the very young whose chances of survival improved. We saw in Table 5 that those of the older sections of the community did so too. There was certainly a decline in mortality from infectious diseases, such as influenza, as well as from tuberculosis. But to an extent gains here were undermined by an increase in mortality through cancer, strokes, and other heart diseases.[1]

During the 1930s and towards the end of the war death rates from tuberculosis had fallen. This trend continued despite the problems of post-war society. When the regional hospital board was set up in 1948 it established close cooperation with the Birmingham Health Committee[2] and by 1950 the board was providing more beds for tuberculosis patients. Meanwhile the local authority was using antibiotics and extending domiciliary treatment.[3] These measures helped to reduce deaths from tuberculosis and they help to explain why the age-specific mortality rates from the disease were much lower in 1951 than they had been in 1931.[4] It was not, however, until after 1956 that the rate of notified cases began to fall. Three factors account for this decline. One was the improvement in housing conditions in the central wards where the disease had been at its worst. The second factor was the extension of B.C.G. vaccination in the 1950s. The decline in notified cases quickly followed and death rates reached a very low level.[5] By 1966 death from the disease amongst the under-45s was practically non-existent, and even amongst persons over 64 the death rates were half those of 1931. The third factor, again, was the general rise in living standards in step with increases in real wages.

The authorities in Birmingham were continually worried about the danger that newcomers might bring the disease into the city. They were concerned at first about immigrant war workers. In the 1950s their attention switched to the Irish,[6] and then, in the 1960s, to Commonwealth immigrants. In all these cases there was some basis to their fears, although the public apprehension that sometimes accompanied the publication of figures was misplaced. It is true, for example, that

[1] See statistical appendix, table 11.
[2] *B.M.O.H.*, 1948, p. 112; 1950, p. 86.   [3] *B.M.O.H.*, 1951, p. 86.
[4] See statistical appendix, table 11.
[5] *B.M.O.H.*, 1958, p. 182.   [6] Ibid.

the Commonwealth immigrants had a higher proportion of infected persons than the indigenous population.[1] But it is also clear that they did not appreciably decelerate the downward trend in the incidence of tuberculosis. Thanks to the vigilance of the local doctors, most of the Commonwealth carriers of the disease were detected.[2] It is also most unlikely that such immigrants infected any of the indigenous population, although they may have infected other immigrants. This was mainly because the most infected group, the Asians, tended to live and work together and formed very few links with the host community.[3]

Influenza was becoming less of a danger to life in the city, especially amongst those over 65.[4] Deaths by other infectious diseases were generally restricted throughout our period to those under 15. Even here, death rates were improving largely because of the factors already examined. They were also responsible for the decline in nearly all age groups of deaths by respiratory diseases.[5] Some of this fall, however, was due to the policy, followed by the Housing Management Committee during the post-war period, of rehousing sufferers from bronchitis and asthma if they were living in unfit dwellings. The City also made great progress in establishing smokeless zones from the mid-1950s.[6] Nevertheless, the decline in age-specific mortality rates through tuberculosis and respiratory diseases in Birmingham was less pronounced than the fall in rates over the country as a whole. Furthermore, Birmingham registered a significant increase in deaths, especially amongst the over 44-year-olds, from cancer, heart diseases, and strokes.[7] These local increases followed the national trend, but the Birmingham rates were significantly higher. Clearly, the fall in Birmingham age-specific death rates reflected a situation in which the decline in deaths connected with slum conditions outweighed the increases caused by pollution and the stresses of modern society. But an urban community such as Birmingham was obviously less healthy than many others in England. The strain of city life and the survival of poor housing conditions in many districts maintained the declining diseases at a more virulent level than elsewhere, while the pace of modern urban life and atmospheric pollution in Birmingham accentuated those diseases that were increasing throughout the country.

As we have singled out housing improvements as a major cause of falling death rates in the city, we might expect to find the most significant falls, like those of the infant mortality rates, in the central areas. This assumption is borne out by Table 9 which shows the crude death

[1] T.B. sufferers 1966 per 1,000 pop. in national groups: England 0·36; Scotland 0·74; Wales 0·55; Ireland 1·18; Commonwealth 4·77; other foreign areas 1·85.
[2] B.M.O.H., 1958, p. 71.
[3] V. H. Springett, 'Tuberculosis in immigrants', Lancet, 1964, no. 1, p. 1094.
[4] See statistical appendix, table 11.   [5] B.M.O.H., 1958, p. 44; 1956, p. 323.
[6] See below, pp. 421 ff.   [7] See statistical appendix, table 11.

Table 9. Changes in Crude Death Rates in the Three Rings of
Birmingham, 1945–1970

	Central Wards	Middle Ring	Outer Ring
1945–9	13·9	12·0	9·6
1950–4*	11·4	12·7	9·5
1955–9	10·4	14·0	9·9
1960–1	10·9	12·9	10·5
1962–6*	10·8	12·9	10·2
1967–70	11·3	12·7	10·4

* Change in ward boundaries.
Source: As for Table 8.

rates in the three rings. Indeed, the table shows that by the 1950s the central wards no longer had the highest crude death rates, as this dubious claim to fame had been taken over by the middle ring. By the 1960s the outer ring and the central wards shared similar rates. But we must be wary with our interpretations. The low crude death rates in the central area reflected its youthful age structure; this means that if it were possible to standardize deaths on a ring basis we should probably find that the central wards would have had higher death rates than the middle ring. The decline in crude deaths in the central wards, we cannot doubt, was to an extent due to improvements in housing, but it also partially reflected the growing proportion of younger persons there. The middle ring, on the other hand, experienced little change in age structure and death rates, at least between 1961 and 1966, so we may suspect that age specific mortality changed relatively little there. A similar argument applies to the outer ring.

We began this section by asking why rates of natural increase changed in Birmingham. We were already aware from Table 3 that the average annual rate of natural increase in the city between 1961 and 1966 was more rapid than between 1951 and 1961. This we now know was because, although crude mortality rates remained constant, crude birth rates increased. We also noted that of the three rings the rate of natural increase was highest within the central wards. This was caused by declining crude death rates and high birth rates. The low rate of natural increase in the outer ring was the result of low birth rates which were not fully compensated for by the lower death rate there.

Migration

We have now examined some of the factors which determined the extent of Birmingham's natural increase, but it will be remembered that gains made here were undermined by an extensive exodus from the city. To understand this major influence on the size and shape of the post-war population we must familiarize ourselves with the inducements that drew people away. But once this has been done, we must also take into account the smaller, although still significant, immigration into the city.

(i) EMIGRATION

During the earlier history of Birmingham, the city's population grew partly as a result of boundary extensions into already populated areas, but mainly because industry attracted immigrants from outside the city. It is for this reason that post-war planners regarded the control of industrial expansion as essential if population growth were to be contained. True, the depression of the 1930s had produced a net out-migration from Birmingham but it was reversed towards the end of the decade when the armament drive gathered momentum. A net out-flow occurred again in the early war years, producing a net out-migration of 123,000 people between mid-1939 and mid-1941. These were mainly persons joining the armed forces, being evacuated, or seeking protection in the countryside.[1] An influx of war workers followed in 1941, and between then and 1944, 27,000 persons had been added to the city's population through net immigration. Most of these war workers were skilled men drawn from other parts of England, Scotland, or Wales. However, a substantial number of them came from Northern Ireland and Eire, although after 1943 the southern Irish were subject to wartime restrictions. The wartime demand for labour also drew in some migrants from the West Indies, although, unlike the Irish, most returned home when the hostilities had ended.[2] Yet over the war years as a whole the influx of war workers did not make up for the departures, and Birmingham lost 97,000 persons on a net basis between 1939 and 1945.

The increase in the number of Birmingham jobs after the war was not accompanied by a corresponding rise in population. This apparently paradoxical situation is explained by the growth of commuter belts around the city. The full extent of this development was not revealed until the publication of the 1966 sample census, but from that source we learn that of the 133,000 persons aged five and over who left Birmingham between 1961 and 1966 nearly three-quarters remained in Warwickshire, Worcestershire, or Staffordshire. Table 10 shows the main areas in which they settled. Some of these, like Solihull, adjoined the boundaries; others, like Water Orton, lay in the green belt itself or on its far side. Indeed, it has been estimated that the residential areas on the fringes of the West Midlands conurbation grew by 100,000 persons between 1951 and 1959, with four-fifths of them drawn either

---

[1] The figures are obtained from *City of Birmingham Annual Abstract of Statistics*, no. 1, p. 11.

[2] R. B. Davison, *West Indian Migrants* (1962), p. 2.

Table 10. Commuter Satellites around Birmingham

	Emigrants aged 5 and over from Birmingham 1961–6	Residence of commuters into Birmingham 1966
TOTAL NUMBER	132,510	150,840
	%	%
Warwickshire	26·8	42·2
Solihull	8·3	17·0
Sutton Coldfield	5·7	12·9
Meriden	6·0	7·7
Worcestershire	14·4	29·0
Warley	3·2	10·9
Staffordshire	25·0	25·8
West Bromwich	3·3	7·0
Aldridge	5·5	6·8

Source: Sample Census 1966; Workplace and Transport Tables, and Migration Regional Report; West Midlands Region.

from Birmingham, or the other older areas of the conurbation.[1]

One may fairly conclude that many of these emigrants of working age and in employment continued to earn their living in Birmingham because, as the table shows, the areas in which the city's former citizens settled were precisely the ones in which the city's commuters lived. But why did they not choose to go on living in the city, nearer their work? Here we must anticipate our chapter on housing. Broadly speaking, despite the increase in housing stock from 302,370 in 1951 to 325,320 in 1966, the city was unable adequately to accommodate its own labour force. In earlier days this situation would have resulted in overcrowding. But during the 1950s, with means of public and private transport readily available, voluntary overspill took place. A crude attempt can be made to quantify the extent of the housing shortage that would have occurred had there been no migration away from the city. As each marriage normally created the need for a further unit of accommodation, we can argue that the 157,000 marriages solemnized in the city between 1951 and 1966 resulted in a demand for a little under that number of houses or flats. Housing demand also came from slum clearance schemes. In the fifteen years following 1951 some 40,000 houses were either demolished or put to other use; so that some 40,000 families needed rehousing. We may guess, therefore, that internal demand created a need for perhaps 197,000 dwellings. The major source of supply, of course, was new building, and between 1951 and 1966, 63,000 houses were erected. A further source of supply was the release of houses through the deaths of solitary occupiers. It is

[1] *The Times*, 16 June 1959, quoting figures by D. E. C. Eversley.

difficult to measure this. However, we do know that in 1966 10·3 per cent of males aged 65 and over, and 24·9 per cent of females aged 60 and over, lived alone. By calculating 10·3 per cent of males who died at 65 and over and 24·9 per cent of females aged 60 and over between 1951 and 1966 we can estimate that 24,000 houses were released in this way. Thus altogether some 87,000 dwellings came on to the Birmingham housing market during our fifteen years, compared with a demand for 197,000. Crude as our calculations are, therefore, the magnitude of the imbalance of demand over supply is obvious. Consequently many families wishing to live in the Birmingham area were forced to move outside the city boundaries. Indeed, emigrants from Birmingham, at least in the years 1961–6, were predominantly young married people.[1] This emigration also had a noticeable effect on the social composition of the city's population.

We shall go on to show in a later chapter that the shortage of land within the city was responsible for the inadequate overall building programme.[2] The shortage also pushed up land prices, which had risen in some cases to £20,000 an acre by the end of the 1960s. This increase affected house prices generally so that the prospective house buyer found it advantageous to live in cheaper dwellings outside the city (where rates were also lower) especially if the saving could pay for a car to enable relatively easy access to the city centre.

Most of the houses built in Birmingham during our period were municipally owned. Consequently, a prospective municipal tenant was more likely than the would-be owner-occupier to find accommodation within the city, at least until the Corporation started building on a very extensive scale outside its boundaries at Chelmsley Wood, in the late 1960s. Since 1957 Birmingham had been making overspill agreements with other local authorities. By these arrangements accommodation was made available outside the city for Birmingham people on the housing waiting list. But such schemes were not wholly successful. Between 1957 and 1970, only 7,600 overspill houses were built compared with 43,000 provided by the Corporation of Birmingham. Nor were overspill arrangements popular with the Birmingham people, who were reluctant to leave their native heath. In the nine years from the inception of the schemes only 6,000 applied to go on the overspill register despite the length of the city's general waiting list, which still contained 38,000 applicants in 1966. A move away from the city usually meant a change in employment for the men and the loss of employment for the women. Wages were also normally lower outside the city, whereas rents remained high.[3] Indeed, in some cases the

---

[1] 72·2 per cent of the emigrants were or had been married and 63 per cent were aged between 15 and 44.
[2] See below, pp. 229 ff.   [3] *B.P.*, 9 November 1965.

overspill areas had no work available because of the Board of Trade refusal to grant industrial development certificates.[1] The overspill schemes were more successful if they were sufficiently near to Birmingham to allow commuting, but this involved the men in considerable travel costs, while still preventing many of their wives from obtaining work. The people leaving Birmingham thus tended to belong to those social groups which wanted and could obtain mortgages. They therefore contained a high proportion of professional and managerial persons (between 1961 and 1966 24 per cent of male emigrants were so occupied). Because the semi- and unskilled were less likely to leave, Birmingham was tending to become increasingly a working-class city.[2]

We demonstrated the extent of net internal migration in Birmingham in Table 3. The massive emigration from the central areas that we noted was clearly the result of the slum clearance schemes which, despite redevelopment, resulted in an overall decline of the housing stock. As the former inhabitants of demolished areas were often given accommodation in the outer ring of the city, we might expect to have registered a net immigration there. But this was not entirely the case. Although there was some net immigration between 1951 and 1961, the reverse was true during the succeeding five years, despite an increase in the overall housing stock. The reason for this net emigration was most probably to be found in children marrying, moving away from their parents and, if they purchased a house, settling outside the city. This exodus from the ring was greater than the inward movement of persons coming to live on the new municipal estates. The middle ring, too, was losing population through emigration but on a more extensive scale than the outer ring, although less so than the central areas. In the middle ring, as in the city as a whole, the demand created by marriage was not accompanied by a compensating increase in the housing stock. A further factor which encouraged emigration from the middle ring was the inconvenience and obsolescence of its houses. Many of the middle and upper-middle classes living in the large Victorian houses who could afford to leave did so, as did many of the working classes living in more modest dwellings there.

Of course we have simplified the migratory movements within Birmingham. Amongst the municipal tenants there was not always a natural outward progression from the central areas. The Corporation had a policy of buying up unfit properties in the central and middle areas with no immediate hope of demolition. If the original occupiers proved to be suitable tenants for the newer municipal properties, and could pay the higher rents, they were moved out. As central area properties were demolished, those displaced who were judged unsuitable for newer houses would then be put into vacated older dwellings.

[1] *The Times*, 23 October 1959.   [2] See below, pp. 215 ff.

Meanwhile, families from other areas of the city, if they had acquired sufficient points on the housing register, could move into some of the new houses and flats built in the central area redevelopment schemes. Furthermore, there was an additional, though limited, movement of population from the outer to the middle ring, caused by the relative cheapness of the late-Victorian houses there. This movement was facilitated in the 1960s by the willingness of the Corporation to grant mortgages on such properties. But even if these exceptions are taken into account, there was still an overall outward movement of population throughout the city.

(ii) IMMIGRATION

Although emigrants had outnumbered immigrants to Birmingham between 1951 and 1966, the 1966 census demonstrated that 46,480 persons aged five years and over had moved into the city within the previous five years from other parts of England, Scotland, or Wales. This figure understates the total number of newcomers to Birmingham, as it excludes the substantial number of immigrants born overseas who came to the city direct from their home lands. Thus, although we cannot be precise, it is clear that immigrants formed a substantial section of Birmingham's total population.

We can begin by examining the English, Welsh, and Scots in the city. Table 11 shows that the percentage of persons born in these

Table 11. *English, Welsh, and Scots in Birmingham's Population, 1951–1966*

	1951		1961		1966	
	no.	%	no.	%	no.	%
English-born	1,007,000	89·1	962,000	86·9	908,000	85·3
Welsh-born	25,000	2·3	22,000	1·9	20,000	1·9
Scots-born	13,000	1·2	13,000	1·2	12,000	1·1
	1,045,000	92·6	997,000	90·0	940,000	88·3

Source: Censuses of Population.

countries (including those born in Birmingham) and living in the city declined from 92·6 per cent in 1951 to 88·3 per cent in 1966. This decline was most marked amongst the English born, but the Welsh also fell by 5,000. It was the Scots, the smallest of the three groups, who contracted the least.

Fig. 5 shows the county of birth of all English and Welsh-born persons resident in Birmingham in 1951. The statistics are processed so that the number of Birmingham citizens born in each county is expressed per 1,000 of the county's inhabitants in that year. Such a map does not necessarily tell us which counties were the most important in providing Birmingham with new blood, but it does indicate something about the city's general sphere of attraction. Of course, by far the largest proportion of all residents (which includes the indigenous population) were born in Warwickshire (71 per cent). The rest of England and Wales fell into three main sectors. There were those counties where future citizens of Birmingham constituted more than 10 in every 1,000 of that county's population. These we can call counties of primary importance. Of secondary importance were those which provided between 5 and 9 Birmingham citizens per 1,000 population. Counties of tertiary importance fall below that level.

Up to 1951 counties of primary importance were found to the north of Warwickshire (Staffordshire), to the south (Gloucestershire and Oxfordshire), but especially to the west. Here was an extensive block of primary counties including those on the Welsh border and stretching into the northern, middle, and southern parts of Wales. The secondary counties included all those remaining in Wales and on the Warwickshire borders, with the addition of Somerset and Durham.

Birmingham's sphere of attraction in the middle of the twentieth century accords with what we know about the distribution of the birthplaces of immigrants into provincial towns one hundred years earlier. Immigrants then came mainly from districts surrounding the towns, their numbers growing fewer as the distance of their place of origin increased. This pattern is clearly discernible in Fig. 5 in 1951. However, as most of the immigrants in the city at that date had arrived during or before the war, we still have to decide whether such migratory patterns were present after the war when the volume of immigration contracted considerably. Unfortunately the 1961 and 1966 censuses do not give the county of birth of residents. Instead, in the 1966 census we are given the county of previous residence for all immigrants entering the city in the preceding five years. These figures are used to construct Fig. 6, which expresses the number of such immigrants according to the county of previous residence per 1,000 of all persons in that county in 1966.

Comparisons between our two maps are, of course, fraught with difficulties. Fig. 5 deals with *all* persons living in Birmingham, whilst Fig. 6 is based solely on persons aged over five who moved into the city during a period of only five years. Fig. 4 shows figures of birthplace, whilst Fig. 6 shows figures of previous residence. But, if we bear these discrepancies in mind, we can make some tentative suggestions about the changing pattern of origin of English and Welsh immigrants into Birmingham between 1951 and 1966. Throughout these years, of course, Warwickshire continued to be the major county supplying the city. The East Midlands also remained a major supplier. On the other hand, Birmingham was becoming less attractive to persons from the West Midlands (excluding Worcestershire and Warwickshire). Likewise, the appeal of the city for Welshmen, apart perhaps for those from

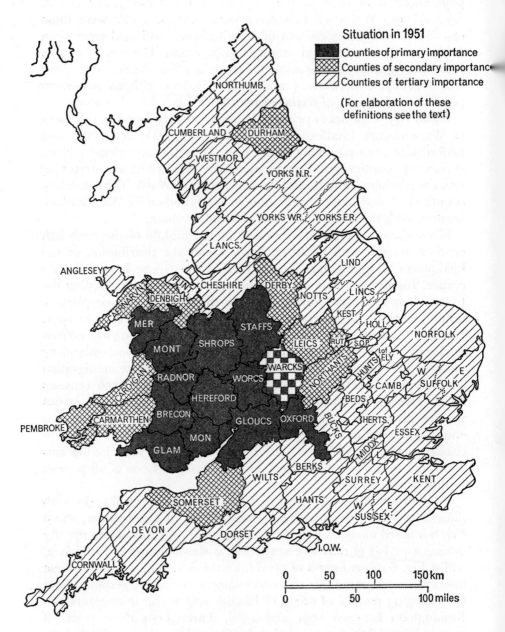

Figure 5   Birmingham's inhabitants by county of birth in 1951

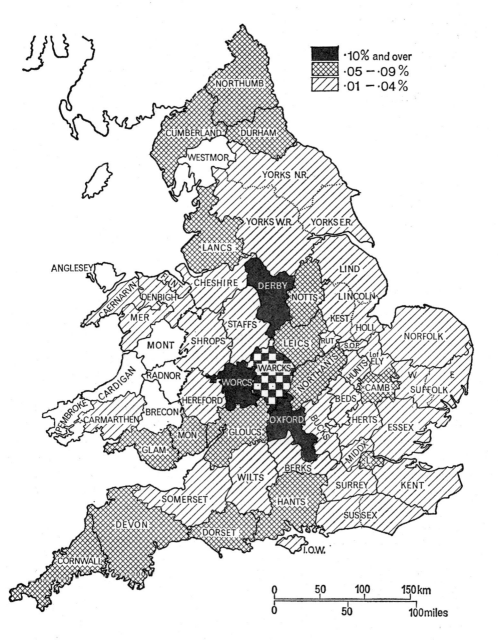

Figure 6   Counties of previous residence for all immigrants of five years' or
less duration in Birmingham in 1966

Glamorgan and Monmouthshire, appears to have diminished significantly. But in partial compensation Birmingham was becoming relatively more attractive to the non-industrial counties of the West Country and the far North. So it would seem that the traditional migratory pattern was beginning to break down.

Table 12 strengthens this conclusion by showing the regions from

Table 12. Region of Previous Settlement of Immigrants of less than 12 Months' Duration in Birmingham
(excluding immigrants moving into Birmingham direct from overseas)

Regions	1961		1966	
	no.	%	no.	%
Northern	300	1·9	620	3·5
North-West	890	5·5	1,250	7·2
West Midlands	9,050	56·2	9,290	53·2
South-East	2,490	15·5	3,110	17·8
Yorkshire	1,130	7·0	1,350	7·7
East Anglia	260	1·6	340	1·9
South-West	1,400	8·7	1,000	5·7
Wales I	420	2·6	400	2·3
Wales II	160	1·0	110	0·6

Source: Censuses of Population.

which came those who arrived in Birmingham during the two twelve-month periods before the 1961 and 1966 censuses. This is scanty evidence but it does support the view that the proportions of immigrants from Wales and the West Midlands were declining, whilst the proportion from much further afield, especially the north and north-west, was increasing.

These changes in the migratory pattern resulted largely from the growth of industry in the West Midlands and South Wales. During the 1920s and 1930s Birmingham's relative prosperity contrasted with much of the rest of the Midlands. By the 1950s and 1960s prosperity was much more evenly distributed throughout the area. This redistribution, combined with restrictions on economic growth in the city, meant that the indigenous West Midlanders could find ample economic rewards without necessarily moving into Birmingham.[1] Similarly the Board of Trade's policy of diverting industry to South Wales (sometimes from Birmingham) perhaps enabled a number of Welshmen, who otherwise would have emigrated, to find work in their own country.[2]

We might have been able to analyse the motives of immigrants more readily if we had some evidence on shifts in their age structure, marital status and occupation between 1951 and 1966. As it is, all we have are details of those English and Scots immigrants of five or less years'

[1] See, for example, *West Midlands: A Regional Study* (1965), esp. ch. ii.
[2] *The Times*, 15 October 1957.

duration in 1966. But at least we do know that they were likely to be younger than the emigrants, and more likely to be unmarried. There were also proportionately more unskilled workers among the immigrants.[1] Even so, we still do not know what changes had taken place in these features since the early 1950s.

The decline of the proportions of English, Welsh, and Scots-born in Birmingham meant of course that the city was becoming much more cosmopolitan. We can now turn to examine the increased proportion of overseas immigrants, including those from Northern and Southern Ireland. Their numbers in 1951, 1961, and 1966 are given in Table 13.

Table 13. Place of Birth of Overseas Immigrants into Birmingham, 1951–1961

A. *1951–1961*

(i) *Number*	1951	1961
West Indian	500	16,000
Pakistani & Indian	3,000	10,000
Rest of Commonwealth and Protectorates	3,000	5,000
Irish (N. & S.)	36,000	58,000
European foreigners	7,000	8,000
Non-European foreigners incl. USSR	2,000	3,000
	51,500	100,000

B. *1951–1966*

(i) *Number*	1951	1961	1966
Commonwealth	6,500	31,000	50,000
Irish (N. & S.)	36,000	58,000	57,000
Foreign	9,000	11,000	11,000
	51,500	100,000	118,000

(ii) % *of all overseas immigrants*	1951	1961
West Indian	0·9	18·0
Pakistani & Indian	6·3	10·0
Rest of Commonwealth and Protectorates	6·2	3·0
Irish (N. & S.)	69·4	58·0
European foreigners	12·7	8·0
Non-European foreigners incl. USSR	4·5	3·0

(ii) % *of all overseas immigrants*	1951	1961	1966
Commonwealth	13·4	31·0	43·1
Irish (N. & S.)	69·4	58·0	47·7
Foreign	17·2	11·0	9·2

N.B. In this table the raw figures are given to the nearest 500.

In 1951 there were 51,500; by 1961 this figure had risen to 100,000; and by 1966 it had reached 118,000.[2] In terms of the proportion of the whole Birmingham population the figures are 4·6 per cent, 8·9 per

[1] See statistical appendix, table 12.

[2] We should, however, remember that the 1961 figures for Commonwealth immigrants were under-enumerated. See Ceri Peach, 'Under-enumeration of West Indians in the 1961 census', *Sociological Review*, vol. xiv, no. 1, 1966, pp. 73–80.

cent, and 11·1 per cent respectively. Between 1951 and 1961 the average annual increase was about 5,000 per annum. Between 1961 and 1966, this figure fell to some 4,000 per annum.

The largest single nationality represented in the table, at all dates, was the Irish, whose numbers continued to increase until 1961. However, the proportion of Irish amongst the total overseas immigrant population fell from 69 per cent in 1951 to 48 per cent in 1966. This reduction was due to the increasing numbers of Commonwealth citizens who were coming into the city. In 1951 they constituted only 13·4 per cent of the overseas immigrant population. But between 1951 and 1961 they came into the city at an average rate of about 2,500 a year. Between 1961 and 1966 this figure increased to 4,000 a year, and by 1966 the Commonwealth immigrants constituted some 43 per cent of the overseas immigrant population.

Ideally we would like to break down these figures into individual Commonwealth countries. We can do so for 1951 and 1961, but not for 1966. However, we know that between 1951 and 1961 the West Indies provided more immigrants than India and Pakistan. By 1951 the Asiatic parts of the Commonwealth provided Birmingham with 6·3 per cent of its overseas immigrants, compared with under one per cent from the West Indies. By 1961 these proportions had changed to 10 per cent and 18 per cent respectively. Whether the West Indians were arriving in greater numbers than the Indians and Pakistanis after 1961 is as yet unknown.

Birmingham also had 9,000 other foreigners in 1951, all but 2,000 of whom had come from Europe. This group increased slightly in numbers during the 1950s, and then remained constant during the first half of the 1960s. In 1966 they made up less than 10 per cent of the overseas immigrant population.

In 1951 Birmingham had an overseas immigrant population only slightly higher in proportionate terms than Leeds, and on a par with Liverpool and Manchester. By 1966, however, Birmingham had a much larger proportion of such immigrants than any of the other three cities.[1] Clearly, Birmingham was becoming a major receiving centre for persons born abroad who wanted to settle in England.

From the evidence we have, we may picture the Irish or Commonwealth immigrant on his arrival as being typically a young unmarried male. This was certainly true in 1951, and it remained so in 1966. However, there were slight changes during our period. Between 1951

[1] % population born overseas	1951	1961	1966
Birmingham	4·6	8·9	11·1
Liverpool	5·3	4·6	4·1
Manchester	5·9	8·4	9·5
Leeds	4·1	4·5	6·7

Four-storey maisonettes in the award-winning Chamberlain Gardens, part of Ladywood redevelopment area, in the 1960s.

Alderman Sir Frank Price (*right*), leader of the Labour group and chairman of Telford Development Corporation, discusses the new draft plan for the enlarged Telford with its author, John Madin, in 1969.

and 1961 the ratio of male to female Commonwealth immigrants rose, implying that more single men were coming.[1] Thereafter the ratio fell, implying either that more single girls were coming or, more likely, especially in view of the 1962 Commonwealth Immigration Act, that more wives were joining their husbands. The fall in the proportion of women amongst the Irish, on the other hand, implies that the ratio of Irish bachelors coming to work in Birmingham was increasing.

Why were so many overseas immigrants coming into Birmingham? Undoubtedly, conditions in their various home lands were conducive to their departure. The West Indies, India, Pakistan, and Ireland, all predominantly rural communities, were facing growing populations and shortages of employment.[2] The Irish needed little capital to finance a journey to England. The West Indians were assisted by travel agents who provided credit; whilst the younger sons of Asiatic families were financed by their relatives. These emigrants from rural areas were attracted by the higher wages that were paid to the unskilled in the industrialized countries. And it was natural that Commonwealth subjects should come to Britain, especially after the McCarron Walter Act of 1952 tightened controls on West Indian immigration into the United States. In contrast, England allowed all Commonwealth immigrants free access until the Commonwealth Immigration Act of 1962.

Although there were factors which tended to expel population from the West Indies, Asia, and Ireland, they must not be over-emphasized. Indeed, recent research has suggested that no correlation exists between unemployment at home and the volume of emigration.[3] More important, perhaps, was the big attraction of Britain's demand for unskilled workers, which was especially strong in Birmingham. The indigenous population were moving into the well-paid jobs in the engineering and motor industries. They left a vacuum in the more unpleasant manufacturing processes and also in the service sector, especially in the transport and building industries. Of all overseas immigrant groups, the Irish were most strongly represented in the building trade. The West Indians tended to gravitate to transport, whilst the Asiatics could be found working indoors, for instance, as grinders or press cutters.[4] Some Asians also came to Birmingham simply to attend to the needs of their fellow countrymen by opening shops, running ware-

[1] *Females per 1,000 Males*

	1951	1961	1966
Commonwealth born	572	504	577
Irish born	814	804	714

[2] R. Desai, *Indian Immigrants in Britain* (1963), pp. 2, 7; O. Reilly, *A Worker in Birmingham* (1958), pp. 19 ff.

[3] Ceri Peach, *West Indian Migration to Britain: A Social Geography* (1968), ch. iii; J. A. Jackson, *The Irish in Britain* (1963), p. 105.

[4] J. Clews, 'The Irish Worker in English Industry with Particular Reference to the Birmingham District' (1962) (typescript), p. 20; Reilly, *Worker in Birmingham*, pp. 19 ff.; Desai, *Indian Immigrants*, pp. 2, 7.

houses, and handling Indian foods. Such enterprising immigrants also catered for some of the more distinctive needs of other overseas immigrant groups whose own people did not seem to have provided for themselves.

Throughout our whole period the bulk of the overseas immigrants took important but relatively menial work, and in many instances their qualifications were not utilized to the full. But from the 1960s, especially after the restriction of vouchers for Commonwealth immigrants, the proportion of professionally qualified persons increased. The same trend was to be found among the Irish, even though they were not subject to these restrictions.

The work taken by these overseas immigrants may have been relatively poorly paid compared with the wages earned by some of the highly-skilled indigenous population.[1] But they were still high compared with the earnings of very many of the indigenous British labour force. So why did not more of the English population move into Birmingham to enjoy this prosperity? Firstly, the English population was relatively reluctant to move, despite the promise of higher wages. We have already seen that the traditional catchment areas for Birmingham—Warwickshire and the adjoining counties, and South Wales—were becoming increasingly prosperous during the post-war period, thereby eradicating reasons for migration. The Birmingham housing situation also discouraged English-born immigrants. The chance of obtaining a council house was remote, and for the first five years it was completely out of the question. It was also difficult for an unskilled or semi-skilled worker to secure a mortgage sufficient to buy a modern or inter-war house in the outer ring or outside the city boundaries. The only other possible accommodation was a pre-1914 house to buy or rent, or a converted flat in one of the decaying Victorian upper-class houses in the middle ring. For many people, this prospect acted as a deterrent. But such factors did not affect the Commonwealth immigrants. They were primarily concerned with earning high wages even if living conditions were poor, and so were content to live in the middle ring, where distinctive areas of settlement evolved.[2] We can, therefore, now go on to see where in Birmingham these overseas immigrants actually settled. Table 14 quantifies this information by ring for 1961. Section (i) shows the absolute number of immigrants; section (ii) the percentage of overseas immigrants to the total population; and section (iii) their location quotient. This quotient is calculated from the formula

$$\frac{\% \text{ overseas immigrants in ring}}{\% \text{ immigrants in city}} \times 100.$$

[1] See below, p. 398.
[2] For a similar argument, see Peach, *West Indian Migration*, pp. 70–2.

*Table 14. Distribution of Overseas Immigrants within the Three Rings
of Birmingham in 1961*

	Ireland	British Caribbean	India & Pakistan	British E.W. & Central Africa, Malta, Cyprus & other C'wealth areas	Other Foreign	Total
(i) Numbers						
Central	12,000	3,000	3,000	500	1,000	19,500
Middle	30,000	12,000	6,000	2,000	5,000	55,000
Outer	16,000	2,000	1,000	2,000	4,000	25,000
(ii) % of population						
Central	7·8	1·7	1·9	0·5	0·7	12·7
Middle	8·0	3·1	1·6	0·6	1·4	14·7
Outer	2·8	0·3	0·2	0·3	0·8	4·4
(iii) Location quotient						
Central	150	113	211	100	70	141
Middle	154	207	178	125	140	163
Outer	54	20	22	75	80	48

Source: Special table in *Birmingham Abstract of Statistics*, taken from Census.

Any score in excess of 100 shows the extent of over-representation (or segregation) in a ring, whilst a score of under 100 shows the degree of under-representation.

The majority of Irish, West Indians, and Pakistanis settled in the middle ring. All three groups were very much under-represented in the outer ring, although the Irish had a greater degree of representation there than either the West Indians or the Asians. It is clear from the table that nearly all overseas immigrants, wherever they came from, settled either in the central or the middle areas of the city. The only point of difference between the various national and ethnic groups was the degree of dispersal within the rings.

Of course, this type of analysis is very crude and we are fortunate that a detailed study has been undertaken examining the areas of overseas immigrant settlement, based upon the 1961 census enumeration districts. According to this more detailed work, 'the pattern of Commonwealth immigrant settlement is seen to be a discontinuous ring of districts . . . surrounding the conurbation centre but at no point adjacent to it; these districts are in fact at least half a mile out from the centre.'[1] This belt could be further broken down into eleven clusters which contained only 9·4 per cent of the city's population, but 60 per

[1] P. N. Jones, *The Segregation of Immigrant Communities in the City of Birmingham, 1961* (University of Hull Occasional Papers in Geography, no. 7, 1967), p. 10.

cent of the Commonwealth immigrants.[1] This study demonstrated that these clusters were racially biased in their composition and that a process of segregation had occurred between West Indian and Asian immigrants.[2]

Having seen the position in 1961, we can now ask to what extent this pattern had changed between 1961 and 1966 after further overseas immigrants had come to live in the city. To help us do this, Table 15

Table 15. Changes among Overseas Immigrant Groups in the Three Rings of Birmingham, 1961–1966

	C'wealth-born	Irish-born	Others
(i) *Change between 1961 and 1966*			
Central Wards	+3,000	−2,000	−500
Middle Ring	+14,000	−3,000	−500
Outer Ring	+2,000	+3,000	+500
(ii) *% of total population 1961*			
Central Wards	4·1	7·8	0·8
Middle Ring	5·3	8·0	1·4
Outer Ring	0·8	2·8	0·8
(iii) *% of total population 1966*			
Central Wards	7·9	8·0	0·5
Middle Ring	9·6	7·6	1·4
Outer Ring	1·2	3·3	0·9
(iv) *Location quotients 1961*			
Central Wards	146	150	80
Middle Ring	189	154	140
Outer Ring	29	53	80
(v) *Location quotients 1966*			
Central Wards	164	151	50
Middle Ring	200	143	140
Outer Ring	25	62	90

has been constructed. It shows the increases or decreases in the numbers of such immigrants in each ring between 1961 and 1966, and their proportion of the total population, as well as their location quotients in 1961 and 1966. Most of the overseas immigrants who came to Birmingham during those five years settled in the middle ring although a number went to the other two rings. Yet there were some differences between the Irish and the Commonwealth immigrants. There was a net movement of Irish out of the central wards and the middle ring, and a corresponding movement by them into the outer ring. The location quotients suggest that the degree of segregation amongst the Irish was thus diminishing. In contrast, the Commonwealth immigrants do not appear to have moved so readily into the outer ring, and it would appear that their degree of segregation was increasing. This conclusion

[1] Jones, p. 12.　　　　[2] Jones, p. 17.

is supported by a detailed study of enumeration district data for 1966,[1] which suggests that although there is evidence of some limited dispersal of coloured immigrants between 1961 and 1966, the largest increases in numbers of coloured immigrants occurred in the concentric zone of immigrant occupation already evident in 1961. Although the districts of high coloured immigrant settlement increased in area, the proportion of coloured immigrants within these enlarged districts was higher in 1966 than in 1961. Moreover, the proportion of coloured immigrants increased most markedly in those areas where they were already most highly concentrated in 1961. The author predicted that this trend towards greater segregation would continue, and concluded:

Intensification has remained the dominant spatial process rather than a hoped-for dispersal and suburbanization. Movement [of coloured immigrants] to areas of post-1920 housing, whether private or municipal, is clearly not large enough to make any significant impact in comparison with the concentrations of the middle ring of the city. (. . .) It is thus not inconceivable that, if trends continue even in a modified form, the proportion of total coloured population in many of the clusters could at least *approach* a majority position in a relatively limited time span. It is this possibility which must be recognized and appropriate action taken to avoid the establishment of such a degree of segregation.[2]

We have seen that the main factor behind these trends was the availability of housing. Owing to the heavy overall demand for municipal housing and the operation of the points system, the majority of overseas applicants had not yet qualified for municipal tenancies by 1966. The relatively low basic wages of such immigrants and the insecurity of their work meant that mortgages on outer-ring private dwellings were very hard to obtain. Most immigrants settled for private rented accommodation, and this demand was partially satisfied by landlords who bought up large middle-ring Victorian houses and converted them into lodging houses and flats. But not all overseas immigrants lived in this way.[3] In 1961 many were found to be living in the small tunnel-back houses of the middle ring. The overseas immigrants frequently moved into houses vacated by the indigenous population as they moved to the outer ring, or outside the city. This movement was facilitated by the willingness of the Corporation to grant mortgages to these immigrants.[4]

Some writers have argued that the segregation of black immigrants

[1] P. N. Jones, 'Some aspects of the changing distribution of coloured immigrants in Birmingham, 1961–66', *Inst. of Brit. Geog. Trans.*, no. 50, July 1970, pp. 199–219. Similar conclusions are drawn in P. Davies and K. Newton, 'The social and political patterns of immigrant areas', University of Birmingham Faculty of Commerce discussion papers, series F, no. 11, 1971, pp. 20–2.

[2] Jones, p. 217.   [3] Jones, *Segregation of Immigrant Communities*, p. 21.

[4] J. Sibley, 'Immigrants in Aston', *Institute of Race Relations News Letter*, February 1966, p. 16. See also below, pp. 380 ff.

has largely been the result of municipal policy.[1] No direct evidence has been brought forward to support this case apart from the relatively low proportion of immigrants in municipal properties. But this is hardly proof. Most were ineligible for municipal houses on purely impartial grounds. Many did not have the necessary residential qualifications and others, especially those who had bought their own houses, could not legitimately be considered; neither could the single immigrants, who tended to live in lodging houses.

The local authority has also been accused of segregating its coloured population by restricting multiple dwellings to certain areas within the city. The Corporation used the Town and Country Planning Act of 1962 to define multi-occupation as 'a change of use' for which planning permission was necessary. This was backed up by a special Corporation Act passed in 1965 to limit the spread of multi-occupation.[2] Neverthe-less, a recent thorough study of Birmingham Corporation's implemen-tation of these powers concludes that: 'While it is difficult to prove or disprove any "racialist" tendency in Birmingham's use of its new powers, they do seem to be regarded as entirely preventive, rather than as a means of spreading more rented spaces more thinly.'[3]

We have already noted that the Irish, unlike the other major overseas groups, were assimilated much more readily into the outer ring. It is tempting to infer that they could move there because they were not subjected to colour prejudice. Indeed, some private builders deliberately kept their estates all-white, and house agents were often discouraging to coloureds.[4] But a more important factor contributing to the easier transfer of the Irish to the outer ring was their better position on the housing list, simply because many of them had been in Birmingham longer than most coloured immigrants.

Whilst housing was the major reason why overseas immigrants, but especially the non-Europeans, grouped together, we should not forget that in some respects they believed Birmingham to be an inhospitable city and so gathered together in a strange environment. Most wanted to live near to relatives, and sought to retain as far as possible their own distinctive culture. Before the 1950s the Irish had been subject to a degree of intolerance by the indigenous population. By the 1960s some of this dislike had switched to Birmingham's coloured citizens. The welfare officer for the Moslem Association even claimed that Birming-ham's coloured immigrants had often turned down accommodation on council estates because 'they did not want to cause trouble'.[5]

[1] e.g. J. Rex and R. Moore, *Race, Community and Conflict* (1967), pp. 26 ff.

[2] Elizabeth Burney, *Housing on Trial* (1967), p. 27.

[3] Ibid. See also below, pp. 379 ff.

[4] For reference to evidence of racial discrimination by estate agents in other parts of the country, see Peach, *West Indian Migration*, p. 90.

[5] *B.P.*, 22 August 1967.

Although there were shifts in the rates of natural increase in Birmingham, the major factor influencing demographic change was migration. From 1951 the city experienced a net emigration as families who were either unable to find accommodation in the city, or who disliked the inadequate central or middle ring houses, left to buy property outside the city boundaries. More and more of the Birmingham population chose to live in the commuter satellites that were growing up round the city. Yet we would be unwise to neglect the smaller, but important, inward movement of population. Families were leaving Birmingham either because they could find no accommodation, or because that which was available was inadequate for them. For the Irish, Asians, and West Indians who were coming to Birmingham, housing was of secondary importance. The main attraction of the city to them was the availability of employment there.[1] Such immigrants tended to be young and single, and many were prepared to live in very poor conditions in lodging houses. The married immigrants were willing to live in rooms, flats, or in the older tunnel-back houses in the middle areas of the city. In either case most of the overseas immigrants settled in the middle ring.

The changing social structure

It would be surprising if the substantial movements of population discussed so far did not affect the social-class composition of Birmingham. We can measure changes by using the classification adopted by the Registrar-General at various censuses. These are necessarily crude, and the revisions in the 1961 census add to the complications. Even so, they can be usefully employed, and have been used to construct Table 16. Part (a) is based upon the social classes used in the 1951 and 1966 censuses. Each person was ascribed to one of five social categories

Table 16. Social Structure of Birmingham, 1951–1966
(males occupied and retired)

(a) *Social Class*

	I/II	% III	IV/V
1951	13·7	59·0	27·3
1966	12·6	55·1	32·3

(b) *Socio-Economic Groups*

	1, 2, 3, 4 *13*	% *5, 6, 8, 9* *12, 14*	*7, 10, 11, 15* *16, 17*
1961	9·6	58·8	31·6
1966	9·9	58·4	31·7

[1] We are aware that our argument here conflicts with the views of K. Jones and A. D. Smith, who suggest that the availability of housing in areas of declining indigenous population may have exercised a strong influence on the settlement of coloured people, regardless of employment opportunities. See their *The Economic Impact of Commonwealth Immigration* (1970), p. 55.

according to his occupation; viz, class I, professional occupations; class II, intermediate occupations; class III, skilled occupations; class IV, semi-skilled occupations; and class V, unskilled occupations. These classes were selected so that 'so far as is practically possible, the category is homogeneous in relation to the basic criterion of the general standing within the community of the occupations concerned.'[1] For our purpose we have combined social classes I and II to form what we can call the upper and middle classes. Social class III, the skilled workers, has been left as it is and the social classes IV and V have been combined to represent the semi- and unskilled workers.

For the 1961 census this classification was dropped for local authority areas and in its place socio-economic groupings were employed. Seventeen categories were devised. Categories 1, 2, 3, 4 and 13 contain professional workers and employers, and correspond very approximately with our previous social classes I–II. Categories 5, 6, 8, 9, 12, 14 represent foremen, skilled manual workers, workers on own account, and non-manual workers (roughly our social class III). Categories 7, 10, 11, 15, 16, 17 represent those offering personal services, semi- and unskilled manual workers, agricultural workers, those in the armed forces, and those inadequately described. This group corresponds roughly to our previous social class IV–V.

The 1966 census re-adopted the five social categories on a national and regional level, but not at the level of local authorities. Fortunately, however, the Birmingham Corporation Statistician published special tables which make it possible to compare the social classes in 1951 with those in 1966. In addition, the sample census of 1966 gave the population of local authority areas by socio-economic groups, so that comparisons can be made between 1961 and 1966.

From the table we can see that there was a slight decline between 1951 and 1966 in the middle-class element of Birmingham's population, and a significant decline in the percentage of skilled workers. There was a corresponding, substantial increase in the percentage of semi- and unskilled. However, using the socio-economic group classification, it would appear that there was little or no change between 1961 and 1966. We can assume, therefore, that most of the changes in the social structure between 1951 and 1966 occurred during the first decade of the period.

How did the Birmingham situation differ from that of England and Wales, or of other major industrial cities? In 1951 Birmingham generally had a higher proportion of skilled workers than the nation as a whole and other cities.[2] Comparisons based on socio-economic groups

---

[1] A full list of occupations with their corresponding social classes can be found in *Census of England and Wales, 1951, Classification of Occupations* (H.M.S.O., 1956).

[2] See statistical appendix, table 8.

in 1961 and 1966 reveal a similar picture, although Birmingham's preponderance over other cities in terms of its proportion of skilled workers is less marked.

There are indications that the social composition of England and Wales was being altered between 1951 and 1966 by an increase in the proportion of social classes I/II, and a reduction in the proportion of social classes IV and V. There are also signs that this shift was occurring between 1961 and 1966.[1] This trend ran contrary to the movement noticeable in Birmingham. It would appear that over the country as a whole the extension of training and education allowed a higher proportion of persons to enter the top social classes. But the increased earning power of such persons in Birmingham enabled large numbers of them to move outside the city. Their places were taken by semi- and unskilled workers, many of them from abroad. Changes in socio-economic composition between 1961 and 1966 provide further confirmation of this trend. While the structure in Birmingham changed little between those two dates, the proportion of upper classes and skilled persons in the country as a whole increased.

How did Birmingham compare with other cities? Because we have no breakdown by social class in 1966 for the other local authorities, we will have to make do with changes in socio-economic groupings between 1961 and 1966.[2] Many towns, including Derby, Leeds, Liverpool, and Oldham, shared a general lack of change with Birmingham. But others, including York and Manchester, increased their proportion of professional and self-employed persons.

We can now move on to see how the various social classes and categories were distributed throughout the city. Although we cannot compare the social classes by ring between 1951 and 1966, owing to changes in ward boundaries, we can confirm from Table 17 that at both dates the central wards, in which housing was at its worst, had the highest proportion of semi- and unskilled persons, whilst the outer ring had the highest proportion of professional and skilled persons.

Table 18 shows the socio-economic structures of the rings in 1961 and 1966, so that we can have a further indication of changes in the internal social structure of the city. From the table we can detect an increase in the proportions of semi- and unskilled persons in the middle ring, where the overseas immigrants tended to settle. There were no appreciable changes in the other two rings, however.

We argued in our opening chapter that the economic structure of the

---

[1] In 1966 the social composition of England and Wales was: S.C. I/II: 19·3 per cent; S.C. III: 48·6 per cent; S.C. IV/V: 28·9 per cent; not known: 3·2 per cent. Compare these percentages with those in table 8 of the statistical appendix.

[2] See statistical appendix, table 8.

Table 17. Social Structure of Birmingham by Ring, 1951–1966
(males occupied and retired)

%

1951	I/II	III	IV/V	Unclassified
Central Wards	7·1	49·6	43·3	—
Middle Ring	11·1	58·9	30·0	—
Outer Ring	16·5	61·5	22·0	—
1966				
Central Wards	5·4	48·9	44·4	1·3
Middle Ring	10·9	51·2	36·7	1·2
Outer Ring	14·9	58·3	26·0	0·8

Table 18. Socio-economic Structure of Birmingham by Ring, 1961 and 1966
(males occupied and retired)

%

	1, 2, 3, 4, 13	5, 6, 8, 9, 12, 14	7, 10, 11, 15, 16, 17
1961			
Central Wards	4·0	52·3	43·7
Middle Ring	8·9	56·9	34·2
Outer Ring	11·5	61·6	26·9
1966			
Central Wards	4·3	51·1	44·6
Middle Ring	8·3	54·8	36·9
Outer Ring	12·0	61·9	26·1

Birmingham area during the nineteenth century determined the size of its population. During the post-war period the city economy was still responsible for attracting and holding the massive population in and around the city. Even so, during the 1950s and 1960s the city's industries were still experiencing a labour shortage, and some at least of the reasons for this shortage were to be found in the housing environment. The supply of houses coming on to the market was clearly inadequate to meet the need created by marriages and the slum clearance drives. The result was a movement of population out of the city. This general exodus was combined with a movement out of the inferior housing in the central and middle rings. There were, of course, still a substantial number of English-born migrants who came to live in the city, but the chances of getting modern accommodation must have deterred many. This discouragement did not, however, apply to the overseas immigrants to whom wages were of greater importance than housing.

The immigrants into Birmingham, both from overseas and from other parts of England, Wales, and Scotland, were typically young, male and unmarried, whilst the emigrants were typically in their late twenties, thirties, and forties, and married. Such a situation tended to increase the numbers of young persons (as was shown in Table 1) as well as the *proportion* of older persons. But the absolute number of persons over sixty-five also increased. This trend could not be attributed to migratory patterns, but rather to the growing longevity of the population (see Table 5). The exodus of married couples, combined with the influx of males, also explains why the city was becoming more male-orientated.

There were also variations in the demographic patterns within the three rings of the city. The central wards had the highest rate of natural increase, combined with the most extensive net emigration. The emigration was caused largely by the extensive slum clearance carried out there, whilst the high rate of natural increase was due to high birth rates, which counteracted the corresponding high infant mortality rates. Between 1961 and 1966, the middle ring, too, had high rates of natural increase and was receiving a large proportion of the overseas immigrants, although its population did not increase. Obviously, gains from these sources were being eroded by extensive emigration. Only in the outer ring, at least from 1961, did the rate of net emigration correspond more or less exactly with the low rate of natural increase, producing population stability.

VII

HOUSING IN BIRMINGHAM

THE quality of life enjoyed by most Birmingham citizens was not determined principally by the amount of money and effort expended on culture, sport, and transport, or even on health and education. Basically it was dependent on the quality of housing. Overcrowding, poor sanitation, and damp and decaying walls all demoralize and exhaust both physically and mentally, and induce a state in which only the most primitive of pleasures can be enjoyed. We have already suggested that the improved health of Birmingham people after the war was due even more to the creation of a better housing environment than to the advances made in social welfare and in medical techniques and services. Consequently, Birmingham's slum clearance and housing schemes must take precedence over all other aspects of the city's recent history.

Housing in Birmingham at the end of the Second World War

In 1945 the city already had much housing to be proud of in its inter-war municipal and private estates, and in the earlier Edgbaston and Bournville areas. In the middle areas of the city stood tens of thousands of terraced houses, built between 1870 and 1914, which, although unsatisfactory from the design point of view, were structurally sound and capable of serving for some decades to come. But in the central areas, which dated from before 1870, over 100,000 people still lived in totally inadequate conditions. The facts of the situation were brought home by the Public Health Department's Housing Survey of 1946, which revealed 81,000 houses without baths, 35,000 without separate W.C.s, and 29,000 built back-to-back.[1] Over half the houses in the central areas were built back-to-back, nearly two-thirds had no separate W.C.s, and over one-tenth were without internal water supplies. But the bad environment in the central areas was not caused by the structural deficiencies of the housing alone. Overcrowding was acute and the density of houses per acre was excessive. Mixed up among the dwellings were numerous factories, workshops, and warehouses. They replaced what light and air might otherwise have reached the houses by noise and smoke. Yet many of those who were forced to live

---

[1] City of Birmingham Public Health Department, *Report by the Medical Officer of Health on the Housing Survey* (1947). The Survey information was, in general, obtained by a call at each house, though in certain districts in which mansions were numerous, a questionnaire was posted in the first instance, followed up by a personal call where necessary.

in these grimy and crumbling slums worked wonders in making their homes comfortable and decent.[1]

Bad conditions were not confined to the central areas. A majority of the houses without baths were to be found in the middle ring, together with some back-to-back houses. Some of the older tunnel-back houses in the middle ring were showing signs of neglect, which had been accentuated by the depression and the war. Many of the larger detached houses there were already being deserted by the middle classes, and a growing proportion of the middle-class people who remained were old and impoverished.[2] Even the outer ring had some inferior dwellings, most of which were the remnants of older villages engulfed in the outward spread of the city. In addition, the outer ring had a high degree of overcrowding, especially in its municipal houses (see Table 1). This

Table 1. Overcrowding, 1946

	Number of overcrowded families	% of all families overcrowded	% of all municipal families overcrowded
Central Wards	1,000	3·3	4·2
Middle Ring	1,000	1·3	3·2
Outer Ring	4,000	1·9	5·6
Whole City	6,000	1·9	5·4

Source: 1946 Housing Survey.

overcrowding resulted partly from the rehousing in the outer ring estates of the most overcrowded central area families before the war, and partly from the spontaneous emigration of people from the centre during the war. Consequently, overcrowding in the central areas had declined substantially; the number of overcrowded families there fell from 4,411 to 1,209 between 1936 and 1946. There was also a marginal fall in the number of overcrowded families in the middle ring.[3]

The figures quoted so far understate, if anything, the inadequacy of Birmingham housing. Many houses had through-ventilation, running water, and separate W.C.s, yet were still unsuitable for decent living. Moreover, the 1936 overcrowding standard was extremely lenient. The West Midland Group in their study, *Conurbation* (1948), attempted to

[1] See Norman S. Power, *The Forgotten People* (1965), esp. p. 53; Gwendolen Freeman, *The Houses Behind* (1947), esp. p. 10.

[2] In 1951 10·9 per cent of the population of the middle ring was aged over 65, compared to 8·7 per cent in the inner ring and 10·1 per cent in the outer.

[3] The 1936 figures come from the City of Birmingham Public Health Department, Medical Officer of Health, *Overcrowding Survey of 1936*, and the 1946 figures from the *Report by the Medical Officer of Health on the Housing Survey* (1947). The city's three rings are those defined by the 1934 ward boundaries, and the overcrowding standard is that defined by the 1936 Housing Act. The number of overcrowded families in Birmingham fell from 8,390 to 5,754 between 1936 and 1946; but the number in the outer ring rose from 2,017 to 3,487.

provide much more realistic statistics. They argued that 63,000 houses in the city and Smethwick were ripe for demolition, and should have been condemned as insanitary under the Housing Acts. A further 45,000 would need replacing as soon as the worst property had been demolished. In other words, according to the West Midland Group, about one-third of the housing stock of Birmingham and Smethwick was unsuitable for habitation.[1] In addition, 17,000 families were living in rooms or shared houses in 1945. The Corporation was more conservative in its assessment of the overall problem. When it undertook a survey of housing conditions, as it was statutorily obliged to do, shortly after the war, it arrived at the figure of 51,000 unfit dwellings. However, the discrepancy between the Corporation's total and that of the West Midland Group is much smaller than might at first appear. It is not unreasonable to assume that at least one unfit house in six in the West Midland Group's figure was in Smethwick, not Birmingham, and the removal of Smethwick houses from the estimate would bring the number of dwellings urgently requiring demolition in Birmingham very close to the Corporation's total of 51,000. The Corporation had the power within certain limits to define the criteria of unfitness within its own boundaries, and could, therefore, have extended these criteria so as to include some of the further 45,000 houses whose demolition in the longer term was recommended by the West Midland Group. However, like most city authorities, Birmingham thought it advisable to restrict its estimate to a total whose demolition could realistically be planned for the foreseeable future.

Whatever the criteria, Birmingham was clearly faced with a gigantic housing problem at the end of the war. Nevertheless, conditions there were not greatly different from those of other major industrial cities. In 1951 Birmingham was, in proportionate terms, probably slightly less overcrowded than Liverpool and its houses were slightly better equipped with piped water, kitchen sinks, water closets, and other necessities. But Manchester, Sheffield, and Leeds all had a little less overcrowding, and generally a slightly greater preponderance of household amenities.[2]

House building and slum clearance in post-war Birmingham

After the war house building and slum clearance were more closely linked in Birmingham than ever before, for two reasons. Firstly, the rate at which clearance could proceed was dictated by the rate of supply of new housing, and by the City's allocation policies. But as available virgin sites in the city were used up, the building rate came to depend increasingly on the supply of cleared sites in the central areas. The

[1] West Midland Group, *Conurbation: a Planning Survey of Birmingham and the Black Country* (1948), pp. 87 ff.
[2] See statistical appendix, table 13.

result of this vicious circle was a rate of demolition and new building which always tended to decline until new areas of land became available on the fringes of the city in the 1960s.

By the time the Lord Mayor opened the fifty-thousandth municipal house to be built in Birmingham, on 20 June 1939, the city's overall housing deficiency had been almost overcome.[1] The number of appli-cants on the housing register had fallen to about 7,000, and in the 1930s the City, encouraged by changes in the Government subsidy structure, had switched its main effort from building for general needs to rehousing slum clearance and overcrowding cases. Between 1930 and 1939 some 8,000 dwellings were represented as unfit by the Medical Officer of Health, and most of them had been demolished before work was interrupted by the war.[2] In the later 1930s the City Council planned to accelerate the clearance programme, after the publication of its overcrowding survey in 1936. In 1937 the Estates Committee drew up a demolition schedule for the next six years, which required 23,400 new houses for slum clearance needs, and 3,524 for overcrowding cases. In December of the following year the City Council approved a five-year programme fo 25,000 dwellings, four-fifths of them for slum clearance and overcrowding.[3] But the City failed to face up fully to the fact that most slum-dwellers were unable to accept rehousing on suburban estates because of high rents combined with generally high living costs in the outer ring.[4] The Council decided, in December 1938, to build a large number of flats in the middle ring to house overspill from the redeveloped slum areas. However, opposition from Moseley residents to the Corporation's plans to build the first such flats in Alces-ter Road won majority support in the City Council.[5] Some council members, worried about the effect of municipal flats on property values in middle-class areas like Moseley, wanted to see the flats built solely within the clearance areas. But existing powers of acquisition were inadequate to ensure the speedy and effective redevelopment of slum areas without some decanting of population in the short term,

[1] For an account of municipal building in Birmingham before 1939, see H. J. Manzoni, *The Production of Fifty Thousand Municipal Houses* (1939). For a more exhaustive account of post-war building, see A. R. Sutcliffe, 'The production of municipal houses in Birmingham, 1939–1966', History of Birmingham Project Research Paper, no. 3.

[2] Sir Herbert J. Manzoni, 'Redevelopment of blighted areas in Birmingham', *Journal of the Town Planning Institute*, vol. xli, no. 4, March 1955, p. 90; *Y.B.*, no. 135, December 1958, p. 3.

[3] B.C.C., *Pro.*, 7 December 1938, pp. 55–76 (Public Works Committee).

[4] *Housing: A European Survey by the Building Centre Committee* (1936), vol. i, p. 114. For details of the higher cost of living found by suburban dwellers, see *When We Build Again*, pp. 87–8. In 1939 the Estates Committee stated that only 14 per cent of the slum-dwellers likely to be displaced over the following five years were prepared to move to the outskirts (B.C.C., *Pro.*, 4 April 1939, p. 487).

[5] B.C.C., *Pro.*, 10 January 1939, pp. 158–62 (Public Works Committee).

especially as many of the worst houses were in areas zoned for industry. No solution had been found to this impasse when the Minister of Health called for all demolitions to cease in October 1939. At the same time, nearly all building work came to a halt.

The war brought about a serious deterioration in Birmingham's housing situation. About 5,000 houses were totally destroyed by bombs, and nearly all the others deteriorated owing to minor damage and lack of maintenance. Many families left the central slum areas to live with friends or relatives in the suburbs. This exodus marginally facilitated the post-war task of slum clearance in that several thousand slum houses were left unoccupied at the end of the war, but overcrowding in the outer ring increased and the refugees, who still needed separate houses, simply added their names to the tens of thousands already on the housing register. The complete building standstill during the war, combined with high marriage and birth rates, allowed a serious overall housing deficiency to build up once again. During the war some relief was afforded by the official billeting scheme for transferred war workers, and by the requisitioning and reconditioning of unoccupied houses, which produced a total of some 1,200 dwellings. The City Council wanted to extend its requisitioning programme to meet post-war demand, but was held back by procedural delays and limited powers.

Although all new building was held up by the war, the bombing did not destroy enough slum houses to facilitate in any significant measure the task of clearance.[1] However, the war allowed the City time to plan its clearance operations more ambitiously and comprehensively than had been possible before 1939. It also created a climate of opinion which was favourable to the granting of extensive powers of acquisition to local authorities.

Before the war the only large clearance area to be designated in the central districts was Duddeston and Nechells (267 acres), and even here detailed redevelopment plans had not been drawn up. By 1941 the Public Works Department was working on plans for four more large areas, and the definitive Duddeston and Nechells scheme was approved by the Council in July 1943.[2] In the same year, the Government's newly established Ministry of Town and Country Planning began to study how adequate powers could be established to acquire large bomb-damaged areas. Herbert Manzoni, Birmingham's City Engineer, was appointed in June 1943 to an advisory panel considering this problem. He was at first horrified to discover that Birmingham's inner areas, which had not been seriously damaged in comparison with cities like Plymouth and Coventry, were not likely to benefit from the proposed emergency legislation. But he was soon able to persuade the

[1] See above, p. 35.
[2] Black, p. 382; B.C.C., *Pro.*, 27 July 1943, pp. 448–62 (Public Works Committee).

Demonstration of tenants of sub-standard houses owned by Birmingham Corporation outside the Housing Dept. offices in 1970. The 'Mr. Dark' named on one of the placards was Alderman Beaumont Dark, chairman of the Housing Committee.

panel that the problems of rebuilding slum areas were very similar to those encountered in blitzed districts, and that the opportunity to provide sweeping powers of acquisition should not be missed.[1] Manzoni's views received support from the Uthwatt committee on compensation and betterment, and the powers which Birmingham wanted were incorporated in the Town and Country Planning Act of 1944. Because Birmingham's redevelopment plans were by now much more advanced than those of any other city, it was in a good position to take advantage of the new powers before a post-war Government had second thoughts on the matter.

Shortly after the end of the war the City Council applied to the Ministry of Town and Country Planning for a compulsory purchase order for the five central redevelopment areas. The areas housed over 100,000 people in some 30,000 houses, over half of which were built back-to-back. They contained, as well as most of the city's really bad housing, nearly half the total overcrowding in the inner ring.[2] In addition to the houses, the City planned to take over some 2,650 shops and 2,300 commercial and industrial premises. After a public inquiry in July 1946, the Minister confirmed the order, with slight modifications, in June 1947. Although the Corporation had given assurances that clearance would begin immediately after the war, it admitted that the scheme would take some years to complete. Consequently, it requested, and received, permission to manage all the properties acquired in the redevelopment areas until their demolition.[3] Modernization was planned for all houses required to stand for more than a few years.

Once the central redevelopment areas were fully in the Corporation's control, there was no urgent need to begin clearance work. But Herbert Manzoni and the chairman of the Public Works Committee, Alderman Walter Lewis, were eager to begin as soon as possible. Progress depended, however, on the achievement of a rapid rate of building soon after the war. Unfortunately, Birmingham's achievement in this respect was to remain totally unsatisfactory for some years to come.

In July 1944 the Public Works Committee announced a tentative housing programme for the first year after the war. It estimated that 15–20,000 houses would be required to meet immediate needs; that is, to replace damaged houses and to overcome the deficiency that had

---

[1] Manzoni described his work on this panel in *B.P.*, 7 August 1963.

[2] City of Birmingham Public Health Dept., *Report by the Medical Officer of Health on the Housing Survey* (1947), p. 12.

[3] The right to draw rents, when combined with compensation of landlords at 1939 values, meant that acquisition cost the Corporation very little indeed. It was expected that revenue from the properties would cover five-sixths of the total cost of acquisition (£17,349,000). Net expenditure on acquisition would therefore be only £123,300 per year (B.C.C., *Pro.*, 4 December 1945, pp. 78–80 (Finance Committee)).

remained in 1939.[1] A target of nearly 5,000 was fixed for the first year, and the committee hoped that the whole programme could be completed in about three years, allowing a big transfer of resources to slum clearance. This high building rate would be achieved by the inclusion of a proportion of prefabricated and/or temporary houses, although the committee had doubts about the advisability of building large numbers of such structures. Unfortunately, the Government did not authorize a start on building until the summer of 1945, and even then shortages of labour and materials proved almost insuperable. So Birmingham was forced to accept a big allocation of Government-built temporary houses (prefabs), even though it had previously expressed reluctance to allow the erection of such an inferior form of accommodation in the city. And even the prefabs were delayed, partly owing to materials shortages, but partly, too, to the Corporation's reluctance to allow them to be built on sites earmarked for permanent houses. Only 325 temporary houses were completed in 1945, along with a mere six permanent houses. There was some improvement in the following year, when 1,475 prefabs and 413 permanent houses went up. Then the severe weather in the early months of 1947 brought building completely to a halt.

The slow progress so far had been caused almost entirely by materials and labour shortages that were beyond the control of the City Council. But it was itself partly to blame for discarding almost all non-traditional methods from its permanent building programme. The Labour group had never been entirely happy with the experimental steel and concrete houses built in Birmingham at the end of the war. So when it took effective control of policy in November 1945 it discontinued the experiments, arguing that the Government prefabs would meet the need for this type of house. This decision undoubtedly depressed the building rates when shortages of skilled labour and traditional materials such as bricks were unduly prolonged after the war.

Shortly after the end of the war the City Council had ordered a completely new housing survey of the city, to supersede the 1936 overcrowding survey. Ready early in 1947,[2] the new survey appeared to confirm that the overall housing deficiency, estimated at 7,000, was small enough to allow an immediate transfer of effort to slum clearance. That, at any rate, was the interpretation placed on the results of the survey by Herbert Manzoni. But the housing register maintained by the Estates Department gave an entirely different impression of the extent of the housing shortage. The number of names on the register had risen sharply from a few thousand in 1939 to nearly 32,000 in early

[1] B.C.C., *Pro.*, 25 July 1944, pp. 474–89.
[2] City of Birmingham Public Health Department, *Report by the Medical Officer of Health on the Housing Survey* (1947).

1942. At this stage the Estates Committee decided to discontinue the register, which was no longer of more than academic interest, but in July it opened a special register for Servicemen to ensure that they obtained priority after the war. This register contained 23,417 names by September 1945. In the meantime the ordinary register had re-opened, and the Council set up a points system to ensure fair allocation, while agreeing that three-quarters of all houses should go to applicants from the Service register.[1] This was all very well when the ordinary register contained just a few thousand names, as it did in 1945, but it rapidly began to catch up on the total of Service applicants. Early in 1946 the Service allocation was reduced to half, despite Unionist protests, allowing a 20 per cent allocation to special cases (over-crowding, ill-health, etc.), and 30 per cent to the ordinary register. A year later the Service register was abolished completely, although ex-Servicemen received extra points when they were transferred to the ordinary list.

By now the ordinary register contained over 50,000 names, but a high proportion of the small number of new houses had to be allocated to special cases. With so many people apparently waiting for homes, Manzoni's request for a big transfer of effort to slum clearance was ill-received by the Estates Committee. The pressure of public opinion had now begun to veer away from demanding the immediate demolition of slums towards requiring the housing of register applicants, who by now were more numerous than the families living in the designated slum areas. So all that Manzoni could do was to persuade the Estates Committee, in July 1947, to allocate one-quarter of all new houses for slum clearance.[2]

Such a small allocation was inadequate to allow a start on slum clearance while the building rate remained so low. A further obstacle which now began to annoy the City Council was the tight control which the Ministry of Health maintained over all local authority building, and which prevented Birmingham from planning ahead. By June 1948 there were nearly 65,000 names on the housing register, and special cases were still obtaining priority. In 1949 changes in the points system made it even more difficult for ordinary applicants to obtain a house, and a five-year residential qualification was established.[3]

By 1949 the housing shortage had been eased slightly by the rationalization of house building, and efforts to increase the number of exchanges and relets. A revision of the housing register in the summer allowed it to be reduced to 50,000 names, but the building rate was still so low that

[1] B.C.C., *Pro.*, 9 October 1945, pp. 775–6 (Estates Committee).

[2] B.C.C., *Pro.*, 29 July 1947, p. 1070 (Public Works Committee).

[3] B.C.C., *Pro.*, 1 February 1949, pp. 310–11 (Estates Committee). Persons who had *worked* in Birmingham for five years also qualified.

the Unionists made it the key issue in the municipal elections of May 1949, when they obtained a big majority. They immediately set up a joint housing conference, which soon confirmed that Birmingham's post-war building record was markedly inferior to that of other large towns and cities.[1] The blame was attributed mainly to shortage of labour, and the conference suggested various means of attracting more building workers and using them more efficiently.

Although the Public Works Committee did not accept all the conclusions of the housing conference, it agreed that more non-traditional houses should be built. It abandoned most of the local building firms which had fallen behind with their municipal contracts, and invited several big, national concerns, which had the organization necessary to build non-traditional houses on a large scale, to come to Birmingham. After some early teething troubles, this move proved very successful, especially as the Government was now allowing Birmingham more latitude in the planning of its housing programme. The number of dwellings completed rose from 1,227 in 1949 to 2,016 in the following year. By 1952 it reached a peak of 4,744, and the housing register had been reduced to some 43,000 applicants. But this progress was still insufficient to allow a big transfer of effort to slum clearance.

The postponement of demolition work after the war had placed a much greater emphasis on the modernization and repair of slum properties than had been envisaged during the war. But the plan was still to keep such work to a minimum; the Central Areas Management Committee announced in November 1947 that it intended simply '. . . to bring dwellings to the *minimum* standard of fitness attainable *under existing circumstances* and *so far as is practicable*, to arrange for such additional works to the houses as would be applied to them by a good landlord *under present conditions*.'[2] Consequently, the cost of initial repairs was estimated at only £30 per house. But by the spring of 1948 the committee had realized that most of the dwellings would have to remain standing for some years, and it began to repair more houses, and spend more on each of them.[3] Plans were drawn up to instal water supplies and W.C.s in suitable houses.[4] By the autumn of 1949 basic repair work had been done on some 12,000 houses, and a further 1,300 had been completely renovated.[5] Over 2,000 houses had been fitted with water supplies and W.C.s by 1952.[6]

[1] In 1948–9 Birmingham built 1·39 houses per 1,000 population, compared to the national average of 3·72. Its current production of permanent houses was less than half the average for other large towns (B.C.C., *Pro.*, 25 October 1949, pp. 573–600).

[2] B.C.C., *Pro.*, 10 November 1947, p. 35. The italics are ours.

[3] By October 1948 the average amount spent on each house had risen to £78.

[4] B.C.C., *Pro.*, 12 October 1948, pp. 1006–8 (Central Areas Management Committee).

[5] B.C.C., *Pro.*, 4 October 1949, p. 531 (Central Areas Management Committee).

[6] B.C.C., *Pro.*, 11 March 1952, pp. 869–70 (Housing Management Committee).

Meanwhile, a slow start had been made on demolition. No slum houses were pulled down at all until the summer of 1948, and by March 1949 only 270 houses had been demolished.[1] The 25 per cent allocation of new houses to displaced slum tenants was difficult to achieve because of the high priority given to special cases. There was some improvement in the early 1950s when the rate of clearance and re-housing was fixed at 1,000 families per year,[2] but high rents and living costs in the suburbs still discouraged many slum-dwellers from accepting new accommodation.[3] Instead they waited for the offer of an inter-war house. But the number of such re-lets now began to be reduced by another fall in the building rate.

The acceleration of the housing programme after 1949 rapidly reduced the City's reserves of building land. In 1950 and 1951 the Unionist-controlled City Council approved the acquisition of several hundred acres of medium and small sites, even though this left private builders with very little land for speculative developments.[4] In 1952 building at last began on cleared sites in the central redevelopment areas, but this could make only a minor contribution to Birmingham's housing shortage since only about half of the original residents could be rehoused in the redeveloped central areas. The City received an unexpected windfall of building land in the shape of the Kingshurst Hall estate, purchased from a private builder in 1952, but its area of 250 acres was too small to overcome the general shortage of land. Densities were increased on suburban estates, but this step was taken too late to produce more than a marginal easing of the land shortage. Flats took longer to build than houses, and many of the remaining sites were too small or inconvenient to allow rapid development. Consequently, the number of dwellings completed slipped back to 4,006 in 1953, and fell sharply to 3,005 in 1954. With further small sites becoming available from time to time, there was as yet no danger that new building would halt completely, and it was estimated that land for a further 6,000 dwellings would still remain at the end of 1956.[5] But a steady decline in the building rate could not be avoided.

Slum clearance did not suffer as badly from this deceleration as did the housing register, which reached a peak of over 70,000 applicants in 1958. The City Council's desire to clear the slums as quickly as possible was reinforced by its awareness that only the supply of sites in the central areas could prevent the building programme from coming to a virtual halt. Further, Government subsidy changes in the

[1] B.C.C., *Pro.*, 4 October 1949, p. 533 (Central Areas Management Committee).
[2] Manzoni, 'Redevelopment of blighted areas', p. 96.
[3] 'Towards a new Birmingham', *Municipal Journal*, vol. lxi, no. 3172, 4 December 1953, p. 2629.
[4] B.C.C., *Pro.*, 3 January 1950, pp. 900-1, 909 (Public Works Committee).
[5] B.C.C., *Pro.*, 10 January 1956, pp. 703-4 (House Building Committee).

mid-1950s encouraged all local authorities to concentrate on slum clearance. By 1957 displaced slum tenants were being allocated about 60 per cent of the total production of new homes.[1] But by now only about 2,500 new dwellings were being completed each year, and the renovation of slum houses had to be speeded up in the 1950s. In 1953 the Housing Management Committee persuaded the Council to agree to the provision of 'reasonably tolerable living conditions' in the remaining unfit houses.[2] This decision marked the City's final acceptance of the inevitability of its role as a slum landlord.

There was a danger that the expansion of the renovation programme would divert some of the City Council's attention away from immediate demolition. This danger was reinforced when the City's ownership of slum houses was extended even further in the mid-1950s. The Council had always recognized that the five central redevelopment areas contained only the hard core of Birmingham's slums, and after the war it slowly acquired further small zones of sub-standard housing. Unfortunately, the sweeping powers that had allowed the acquisition of the original five areas had largely been rescinded by the Town and Country Planning Act of 1947. In 1953 the Council sought special powers in a Corporation Bill to acquire areas of badly laid out and obsolete development, but the property owners' associations won majorities against this clause in the town's meeting and poll. But the Government now came to the aid of the City. Birmingham's repair and renovation techniques had caught its eye, and by the Housing Repairs and Rents Act of 1954 it allowed local authorities to acquire and recondition slum houses on the lines pioneered in the city. The Council hastened to make use of the new powers, just as it had after the war, and in February 1955 it decided in principle to acquire 25,000 sub-standard houses outside the central redevelopment areas at the rate of some 4,000 per year.[3] Complete renovation was planned, at a cost of £200 per house, because none would be demolished until the central redevelopment areas were completely cleared.[4] Because the new powers allowed the acquisition only of very small areas, the City Council compulsorily purchased (against strong Conservative opposition) certain additional areas to provide districts of convenient shape and size for redevelopment in due course. Even so, the new zones were considerably smaller than the five central redevelopment areas, around which they clustered.

By 1960 some 18,500 houses had been represented in the new areas, and 12,000 of them had come into the management of the Corporation.

[1] Y.B., no. 115, February 1957, p. 1.
[2] B.C.C., Pro., 13 October 1953, pp. 482–4 (Housing Management Committee).
[3] B.C.C., Pro., 1 February 1955, pp. 901–5 (Housing Management Committee).
[4] B.C.C., Pro., 12 July 1955, pp. 284–5 (Housing Management Committee).

Meanwhile, owing to deterioration, the total number of houses to be acquired in the new areas had risen to over 30,000. Some 3,000 of these houses had been reconditioned.[1] It had even been possible to demolish nearly 1,000 properties by 1963, by which time a total of over 6,000 had been reconditioned. By now, Birmingham's renovation techniques were speedy, effective, and economical. However, in all these respects they contrasted with the City's building programme, which by now was seriously delaying clearance work.

Owing to the extremely limited results of Birmingham's overspill arrangements,[2] the shortage of sites within the city had brought the rehousing programme down to a new low by the late 1950s. The total of dwellings completed dropped under 2,500 in 1958, and in each of the following three years it only just kept above the 2,000 mark. Owing to the persistence of the low building rate, Birmingham's housing organization was no longer as efficient as it had once been, and liaison between interested committees was no longer totally satisfactory. One symptom of this malaise was the long delay of four years before any building at all was started on the 350-acre Castle Bromwich airfield, which the City purchased in 1959, and which should have provided short-term relief to the land problem.[3] Consequently, the building rate was restricted to 2,500 or less until 1965. Some improvement resulted from changes in the administration of house building introduced after 1962 by the new committee chairman, Councillor Ernest Bond, but the building rate did not rise substantially until 1965, when it exceeded 4,000, thanks to the belated completion of large numbers of dwellings on the Castle Bromwich airfield. By now, Birmingham was beginning to make use of industrialized building methods which Labour, owing to its traditional fear of a lowering of standards, had previously shunned.[4]

From now on Birmingham made up for lost time in spectacular fashion. The Conservative Government had repulsed all its efforts to obtain building land outside the city boundaries, but in 1964 the newly-elected Labour Government immediately allocated 1,500 acres for an out-city estate at Water Orton (Chelmsley Wood).[5] With the promise of more land to come, the City Council was able to

[1] B.C.C., *Pro.*, 16 July 1960, p. 319 (Public Works Committee); 7 February 1961, pp. 815–16 (Housing Management Committee).

[2] See above, p. 151.   [3] See below, pp. 437–8.

[4] Industrial methods were first introduced in earnest in 1964, and by 1968 they, together with rationalized traditional methods, were responsible for 83 per cent of total housing production. According to the City Engineer, the big increase in the building rate from the mid-1960s would have been impossible without them (City Architect's Department press release, 2 April 1968). See also National Building Agency, *Housing Productivity in Birmingham* (1969).

[5] See above, p. 150.

put its housing machine into top gear. The number of dwellings completed rose from 4,725 in 1966, the year in which the Conservatives took control in the City Council, to nearly twice that figure two years later, allowing a massive reduction of the housing register. Under the chairmanship of Alderman Apps, the city's housing machine attracted nation-wide attention. Birmingham was now renewing itself faster than any other city in Europe, and although the building rate had fallen slightly by 1970, the short-term problems facing the City Council no longer concerned supply so much as rising costs, which inevitably resulted in higher rents.

The big increase in the building rate at last allowed the slum clearance programme to be accelerated. Indeed, that had been the major result hoped for by the Government when it granted building land outside the city in 1964.[1] Between 1955 and 1964 Birmingham had demolished only 16,005 houses in the central redevelopment areas and outside. But two years later this total had risen to 22,166, and the demolition rate accelerated even more after 1966.[2] By 1970 almost all of the original central redevelopment areas had been cleared and redeveloped on a scale unparalleled in Britain. And demolition was proceeding so fast in the newly-acquired areas that all the city's unfit houses were expected to disappear by 1975.

Building and demolition: a balance sheet

Although the Corporation was responsible for most of the demolition and building in Birmingham after the war, some was undertaken privately. A comparison of the 1951 and 1966 censuses indicates that 36,000 dwellings were lost to the city between these two dates, either through demolition or conversion to other uses. Corporation demolitions were responsible for nearly 24,000 of these; the others were pulled down or put to alternative uses by private initiative either because they were unfit, because the land was needed for new residential development, or because they had to be converted to industrial or commercial use. Most of these dwellings were very old, and it can be assumed that many were unfit for habitation, or on the point of becoming unfit. It is at least safe to say, therefore, that between 24,000 and 36,000 of the city's worst houses were demolished between the end of the war and 1966. After 1966 the number of municipal demolitions increased sharply and by the end of 1969 a further 14,000 unfit houses had been pulled down. Thus by the end of the 1960s the Corporation had demolished all but 13,000 of the 51,000 houses which it declared unfit shortly after the war. On the other hand, a considerable proportion of the 108,000 houses designated as unfit by the West Midland

[1] See e.g. *H. of C. Deb.*, 5th series, vol. dccii, cols. *1080–1*, 24 November 1964.
[2] See statistical appendix, table 14.

Group in Birmingham and Smethwick remained standing. Indeed, Birmingham's slum clearance progress was relatively slow until the mid-1960s. Birmingham pulled down more houses than any other provincial city, but it was also bigger than other provincial cities. Our estimate of the number of Birmingham houses demolished or put to alternative use between 1951 and 1966 amounts to 11·9 per cent of the total housing stock in 1951, and the percentage of demolitions by the Corporation on the same basis was 7·3 per cent. Both these figures were of course well above the equivalent rates for England and Wales as a whole (9·4 per cent and 5·4 per cent respectively), but they were lower than those of Leeds (15·3 per cent and 11·6 per cent), Manchester (23·3 per cent and 11·3 per cent), and Liverpool (19·5 per cent and 7·0 per cent).[1] However, when a higher building rate allowed Birmingham to demolish slums more vigorously after 1966, much of this lost ground was recovered. The nearest any other major city came to Birmingham's total of 14,000 houses demolished between 1967 and 1969 were Manchester with 12,500 and Liverpool with 9,500. Leeds demolished only 5,000 houses during these three years.

Birmingham's relatively slow clearance rate up to 1966 is largely explained by the City's relatively slow rate of municipal building. Although no other authority equalled Birmingham's 52,000 dwellings built within the city boundaries between 1945 and 1966, this total was only 18 per cent of the 1951 housing stock. Leeds and Liverpool both did better, with 20 per cent, and Manchester did considerably better, with 23 per cent. Here again, the year 1966 was a major watershed, for between 1967 and 1969 the City of Birmingham built the massive total of 25,000 houses (including 10,000 outside the city boundaries at Chelmsley Wood). This was substantially higher than the building rate achieved by any rival city during these years.

Within the city, building was most active in the central wards and the outer ring. Until 1961 more houses were built proportionately in the outer ring than in the central areas, but from 1962 this situation was reversed.[2] Of course, nearly all the building in the central areas was

[1] M. B. Stedman and P. A. Wood undertook a similar comparison of clearance rates for Birmingham and nine selected county boroughs over the years 1955–63. They found that Birmingham's clearance rate was higher than those of Bristol, Nottingham, Portsmouth, and Southampton, but lower than Leeds, Liverpool, Manchester, Newcastle, and Wolverhampton. See their 'Urban renewal in Birmingham', *Geography*, vol. 1, no. 1, January 1965, p. 9.

[2]

	1950–61 No. municipal houses built	% *1951 housing stock*
Central Wards	3,000	9·7
Middle Ring	3,000	3·3
Outer Ring	26,000	15·2
Central Wards	3,000	7·4

in the five central redevelopment areas. By 1967, 8,900 new dwellings had been built there, most of them in multi-storey blocks.

Private enterprise played a considerable role in new building in postwar Birmingham, even though most of the largest sites and many smaller ones were acquired for municipal housing. Housing associations and speculative builders erected some 20,000 dwellings between 1945 and 1966.[1] Expressed as a percentage of the 1951 housing stock, the Birmingham total of private dwellings built (6·6 per cent) is substantially below the average for England and Wales (18·1 per cent). This low proportion is not surprising in view of the priority given to municipal building. However, although Birmingham's total of private building in relation to the 1951 housing stock was lower than that of Leeds (11·2 per cent), it was much higher than that of Manchester (3·6 per cent), and Liverpool (3·8 per cent). In these last two cities only 15 private houses were being built for every 100 municipal houses; in Birmingham there were 38. These figures suggest that Birmingham's slow slum clearance rate until 1966 cannot be attributed solely to a shortage of land; if it had wished, the City Council could, perhaps, have held back private building by acquiring more land in order to give a greater priority to municipal housing. On the other hand, a reduction in the rate of private development would have brought about a much greater exodus of middle- and upper-middle-class people from the city than actually occurred.[2]

Most of the private houses were built in the outer reaches of the city, mainly on small estates, as the Corporation reserved nearly all the largest sites for itself. So short had land become by the early 1960s that considerable 'infilling' was taking place in existing developed areas. Very small plots of land were used for private housing, which in other areas might have been considered as totally unsuitable. Large areas were available for private housing in only a very few districts of the city. One of the most important of these was the Bournville Village Trust estate, and substantial numbers of houses were built for sale there, under the close supervision of the trustees. However, the Trust built, as a housing association, numerous houses for applicants from the municipal housing register in the 1940s and early 1950s, when few private building licences were available. Much new building, all of it private, took place on the Calthorpe Estate, in the middle ring district

[1] Housing associations normally received the full Government subsidy, in return for which they agreed to house applicants from the municipal housing register.

[2] See above, p. 215.

cont. from fn. 2, p. 233

	1962–6 No. municipal houses built	% 1961 housing stock
Middle Ring	1,500	1·5
Outer Ring	11,000	6·0

of Edgbaston. Between the end of the war and 1960 only about 300 houses were built on the estate, but rapid redevelopment of its older areas then took place. The City Council allowed this development in the interests of the city as a whole, but the Estate was required to raise its overall density, and was encouraged to lease certain fringe areas to the Corporation for municipal housing.[1] Some 1,500 private dwellings were built on the estate between 1961 and 1967, and it was largely as a result of this private redevelopment in the middle ring after 1960 that an upward trend in private building could be observed during the early 1960s.

The supply of accommodation was also increased by the conversion of houses into flats. The Corporation did relatively little of this, and between 1945 and 1966 it added only 700 flats to the housing stock in this way. Private enterprise did somewhat better by producing nearly 2,000 additional flats, mainly by converting large Victorian houses in the middle ring. And it may also be speculated that many more 'conversions' were undertaken unofficially, without approval of plans under the building byelaws, mainly to house the increasing number of coloured immigrants who were moving into the city.

The interaction of house building and demolitions until 1966 is shown in Table 2. The rate of increase in the housing stock in Birming-

Table 2. Changing Housing Stock: Birmingham and Selected Cities

(a) 1951–1966

	Housing stock		Houses built	Estimated demolition	Increase in housing	% increase
	1951	1966	1952–66	1951–66	1951–66	1951–66
Birmingham	302,000	325,000	59,000	36,000	23,000	7·6
Leeds	158,000	174,000	43,000	27,000	16,000	10·1
Liverpool	199,000	200,000	40,000	39,000	1,000	0·5
Manchester	204,000	193,000	37,000	48,000	− 11,000	− 5·4
England and Wales	12,389,000	14,977,000			2,588,000	20·8

(b) 1967–1969

	Total of new houses built, municipal and private 1967–9	Total of houses demolished by local authority 1967–9
Birmingham	21,000 (+ 10,000 at Chelmsley Wood)	14,000
Leeds	9,000	5,000
Liverpool	10,000	10,000
Manchester	9,000	12,000
England and Wales	—	—

ham was obviously not as great as in England and Wales as a whole. On the other hand, it was higher than in the other three large cities. This was because although Birmingham had a somewhat lower

[1] See below, pp. 457 ff.

municipal building rate, correspondingly fewer houses were demolished and a high proportion of private houses were erected.

When we come to examine the change in the housing stocks in each ring we find that between 1951 and 1961 the housing stock in the central wards declined by 28·6 per cent, and by 19·3 per cent between 1961 and 1966. The rate of demolition within these wards was far greater than the rate of rebuilding. Within the middle ring, the housing stock was constant between 1951 and 1961 and fell by only 3·9 per cent during the following five years. It was in the outer ring that the housing stock increased considerably, by 19·4 per cent in the first period and by 6·4 per cent from 1961.

Changes in housing conditions

The demolition of tens of thousands of houses and their replacement by new ones brought about a major improvement in Birmingham's housing environment. But in addition renovation also played an important role. As we have already seen, the Corporation took the lead here, and between 1947 and 1967 it improved 42,000 of the houses under its control. In many of these cases, only minor repair work was undertaken, but in others, water supplies were laid on and lavatories were fitted. As well as helping the Corporation to improve unfit houses, the Housing Repairs and Rents Act of 1954 benefited the private landlord, the private tenant, and the owner-occupier by empowering local authorities to make improvement grants. In Birmingham the owner-occupiers took more advantage of the Act than private landlords. By 1967, 13,000 grants had been made to owner-occupiers, while the landlords had obtained 6,000.

Although the censuses provide information on household amenities, it is not possible to make extensive comparisons between them. However, it is possible to compare changes in the numbers of houses with W.C.s and baths between 1951 and 1966. As Table 3 shows, a substantial improvement was brought about during these years.

Table 3. W.C.s and Baths by Households

Households without exclusive use of:

	W.C.		Fixed Bath	
	No.	*%*	*No.*	*%*
1951	72,000	22·2	149,000	46·1
1961	51,000	15·3	107,000	31·7
1966	36,000	10·8	83,000	24·9

Most of the improvement took place in the inner wards, where the Corporation owned 70 per cent of all dwellings by 1966. The City also enjoyed extensive powers, through general legislation and the Corporation Acts of 1946, 1948, and 1954, to compel landlords to make good certain specific faults, such as blocked drains and leaking roofs. When landlords failed to comply, the Corporation had power to carry out the work itself and send the bill to the landlord. The City made extensive use of these powers so that by 1970 housing conditions had been improved for 47,000 families. Yet because demolition was due sooner or later, none of the renovation work was sufficient to dispel completely the atmosphere of decay in the central areas.[1] Landlords and owner-occupiers often hesitated to spend money on their properties because they would soon be taken over by the Corporation for very little compensation. Many houses continued to deteriorate even after acquisition by the City and, as Canon Norman Power has shown, the break-up of old-established communities, the lack of security, and the constant demolitions all contributed to a growth of vandalism which led to further decay.[2]

Changes in basic amenities in the central wards in the 1960s are set out in Table 4. Although the increase in the proportions of dwellings

Table 4. Household Amenities in Central Wards, 1961–1966

	Without hot water		Without exclusive use of fixed bath		Without W.C.		Total households
	No.	%	No.	%	No.	%	
1961	32,000	76·7	33,000	79·3	18,000	43·1	42,000
1966	20,000	60·0	22,000	66·1	10,000	30·7	33,000
Decline	12,000		11,000		8,000		9,000

with such amenities as hot water, baths, and W.C.s was partly due to redevelopment, the table makes it clear that much of it resulted from renovation work. However, a surprisingly large proportion of inner-ring homes still remained without hot water and/or the exclusive use of a W.C. in 1966. Nevertheless these deficiencies must not obscure the significant improvements brought about by municipal action in many thousands of these older houses during the last years of their use.

Improvements of conditions in the inner wards were partly counter-acted by the decay of many of the older houses in the middle ring, as they fell into multi-occupation. As early as 1949 Alderman Roberts noted that 'what might be called the "Birmingham type of slum", the small back-to-back, which could be dealt with, was being superseded by . . . the "London type of slum"—a house which became a ruin.'[3] He was referring to the large Victorian houses which were structurally sound, but which were too large for single families, almost impossible to heat effectively and economically, and which lacked garage space. Occupiers who could afford their upkeep could also afford to move to more desirable properties, whilst those that could not were forced to

[1] See e.g. B.M.O.H., 1955, p. 19.   [2] The Forgotten People (1965), esp. p. 34.
[3] B.G., 25 January 1949.

stay, taking in lodgers or otherwise sub-letting.[1] Outside the Calthorpe
Estate, few of these larger houses were demolished and rebuilt although
many were converted, with varying degrees of competence and legality,
into flats to satisfy the demands of the influx of unskilled workers from
outside the city who could not afford to purchase properties, and who
had not qualified for a municipal house. As a result deterioration
continued as first of all the Welsh, the Scots, and the Irish came to live
in the middle ring, followed by the Indians, Pakistanis, and West
Indians.[2]

At the same time, many landlords, tenants, and owner-occupiers
made substantial improvements to the smaller, tunnel-back houses of
the middle ring. The results of improvement grants and the growing
popularity of 'do it yourself' are shown in Table 5, which gives the

Table 5. Household Amenities in the Middle Ring, 1961–1966

	Without use of or without exclusive use of:						
	Hot water		Fixed bath		W.C.		Total
	No.	%	No.	%	No.	%	households
1961	56,000	48·9	59,000	51·1	26,000	22·9	115,000
1966	41,000	37·0	49,000	43·7	21,000	18·9	112,000
Decline	15,000		10,000		5,000		3,000

number and percentage of households without the exclusive use of
certain basic amenities in the middle ring.

As there was relatively little rebuilding here, the decline in the
numbers of households without basic amenities reflects real improvements in the older houses.

Similar improvements were made in the outer ring (see Table 6),

Table 6. Household Amenities in the Outer Ring, 1961–1966

	Without use of or without exclusive use of:						
	Hot water		Fixed bath		W.C.		
	No.	%	No.	%	No.	%	
1961	25,000	14·2	15,000	8·5	7,000	4·0	176,000
1966	10,000	5·3	11,000	5·8	4,000	2·1	187,000

though there were still 10,000 houses here without hot water, and 4,000
without separate W.C.s, in 1966. However, the rate of improvement
here was much more rapid than in the middle and inner rings, mainly
because the older properties were usually in a better overall environment and were also less likely to be vested by the Corporation. So
landlords and owner-occupiers had much greater incentive to improve
their properties.

[1] A. G. S. Fidler, 'Slum clearance and redevelopment from the design and economic
point of view', a paper given at the Town and Country Planning Summer School,
Oxford, 1957, p. 4.
[2] B.M.O.H., 1961, p. 222.

Overcrowding

Improvements to the structure and fittings of dwellings cannot be considered in isolation from the density of their occupants. We have already seen that the potential demand for accommodation within the city was greater than the supply, but that the problem was partly resolved by voluntary emigration.[1] On the other hand, new immigrants were continually entering the city. What effect did these movements have on the adequacy of Birmingham's housing?

As has already been noted, the city's population fell in the post-war period while the housing stock increased. So there has been an almost unbroken reduction in the mean number of persons per dwelling. This trend was, however, temporarily reversed in certain areas. Immediately after the war, for example, the population rose somewhat as demobilization got under way, and the labour demands of the city's industries increased. House building took several years to satisfy the new demand and the mean number of persons per house increased from 3·8 in 1948 to 3·9 in 1950. Thereafter the figure began to fall, contracting to 3·3 in 1968.

Of course, such global figures can mask a much more complex situation, as is revealed by an analysis of each ring of wards. In the central wards both population and housing numbers were contracting rapidly. However, between 1950 and 1961 the housing stock declined more quickly than the population and the mean number of persons per house rose a little. From this we can infer that overcrowding, too, must have increased. But in the post-1962 period the central wards' population fell more rapidly than the housing stock and the mean number per house correspondingly contracted.

There was much concern in the city from the later 1950s that the overseas immigrants were increasing overcrowding. We now know that these immigrants did not add to the overall mean numbers of persons per house, but did they increase overcrowding in the area in which they predominantly settled, the middle ring? Again the answer is no. Between 1950 and 1961, according to the pre-1962 ward boundaries, the mean number per house in this ring fell steadily from 3·7 to 3·4, whilst between 1962 and 1967 (within the revised boundaries) it held steady at about 3·5. The number of overseas immigrants moving into the ring was clearly either equal to or slightly less than the number of the indigenous population who were leaving. It is difficult to draw firm conclusions from these figures, especially in view of the changes in the ring boundaries, but it at least seems likely that the incidence of overcrowding was not increasing in the middle ring. In the outer ring, on the other hand, the mean number per house declined steadily,

[1] See above, pp. 198–202.

from 3·7 to 3·4 between 1950 and 1961, and from 3·4 to 3·2 between 1962 and 1967. So here it seems certain that the incidence of over-crowding was falling.

These figures still remain vague, however, until they are related to the number of rooms per house and an analysis of household structures. Table 7 attempts to establish changes in household structure between

Table 7. Mean Household Size in Birmingham, 1951–1966

	1951	1961	1966
Mean no. household heads	1·00	1·00	1·00
Wives	0·87	0·82	0·78
Children	1·16	1·15	1·15
Family size	3·03	2·97	2·93
Non-family members	0·33	0·20	0·18
Household size	3·36	3·17	3·11

1951 and 1966 on the basis of certain assumptions. To estimate the mean number of wives per household it is assumed that all married women recorded in the various censuses were married to household heads. This is obviously untrue, but the degree of error involved is not prohibitively large. To arrive at estimates of the mean number of siblings living with the household heads, the assumption is made that all persons who were unmarried and aged under twenty-five were the children of household heads and lived with their parents. These figures are bound to be overstated, because of the young persons aged between fifteen and twenty-five who, as we have seen, were migrating into the city. The mean family sizes are estimated by summing the mean number of heads, wives, and children of each household. The mean number of non-'family' members is estimated by subtracting the mean family size from the mean household size. The mean household size is obtained by dividing the total number of households into the total population living in households.

If our estimates are reasonably correct, it is clear that the mean size of households was declining, because most of the component parts were also contracting. The mean number of wives was falling because, as the population was ageing, so the ratio of widowed persons increased. This ageing was also clearly an important reason why the overall mean family sizes were contracting. But why was there no corresponding contraction in the mean number of children living at home? If our estimates can be trusted, it seems likely that the answer lies in an increase in the mean number of children amongst household heads under forty-five. We have, unfortunately, no figures to demonstrate this directly, but the rising birth rate and contracting infant mortality rates after the war support such a hypothesis. The contraction of non-

B.S.A. cycles in the export bay, 1948

Motorcycle assembly at the B.S.A. factory in Small Heath, in 1971

Ladies (two of whom have apparently emerged from a nearby hair-dresser's) support a demonstration in favour of the ailing B.S.A. company, 14 October 1971.

family members sharing a household indicates that it was becoming easier for such persons to form a separate household of their own, as the reduction in the number of names on the municipal housing register would suggest.

Table 8 carries on the analysis by examining the mean number of

Table 8. *Mean Household Sizes in Birmingham by Ring,*
1951–1966
(a) *Mean Household Size*

		Post-1962 boundaries	
	*1951**	*1961*	*1966*
Central Wards	3·52	3·39	3·52
Middle Ring	3·35	3·02	3·05
Outer Ring	3·48	3·22	3·25

(b) *Number of children under 15 per household*

	1951	*1961*	*1966*
Central Wards	0·96	1·04	1·13
Middle Ring	0·76	0·69	0·77
Outer Ring	0·82	0·75	0·68

* Based on total population and not just population in households.

persons per household in each ring of the city. Unfortunately, we do not know the number of married women in each ring, so that we cannot attempt to analyse household structures. However, we can estimate the mean size of sibling groups by showing the mean number of children aged under fifteen per household in each ring.

The most significant point in the table is that the central wards had the largest household size and the middle ring the smallest. It would seem that the central wards achieved this position because of the large sibling groups that they had. Although infant mortality rates were higher there after the war than in the rest of the city, they did not significantly check the effects of the high birth rate. Between 1961 and 1966 the mean household size changed very little in the middle and outer rings of the city, but it rose substantially in the central areas. This increase was the result of a rising birth rate and declining infant mortality. Similar trends were in evidence in those years in the middle ring, and the mean number of children per household rose, though to a lesser extent than in the centre. Moreover, this increase had a less pronounced effect on the mean household size in the middle ring.

These findings on household structures can now be related to the changing ratio of persons per house. We have already seen that the mean number of persons per house was becoming smaller. This decline took place because although the number of households in the city increased from 323,000 in 1951 to 333,000 in 1966, this rise was more than matched by the increase in the total stock of dwellings and the mean number of households per house fell from 1·08 to 1·06. Even in

R

the central wards the increase in household size did not lead to a dramatic increase in the mean number of persons per house, and between 1961 and 1966 the number of households per house fell from 1·5 to 1·03. In the middle ring the mean number per house appears to have remained almost stable. Certainly after 1961 mean household sizes and the mean number of households per house (1·11) remained unchanged. In the outer ring the decline in household sizes and the small decline in households per house (1·02 in 1961 to 1·01 in 1966) brought about an overall decline in persons per house.

It would be useful to push the analysis one stage further and discuss the mean number of persons per room. Unfortunately, we are hampered by the Registrar-General's changing definitions. Thus, in the 1966 census rooms were defined as 'all living rooms, bedrooms, and kitchens'. In 1961 and 1951 a kitchen counted as a room only if it was regularly used for eating meals. We know, however, that the mean number of rooms per house in the city did not greatly change between 1951 and 1961 (4·8 and 4·9 rooms respectively) despite all the demolition and rebuilding which were undertaken during that decade. This meant that throughout the city in 1951 every person had an average 1·3 rooms, and that by 1961 this figure had increased to 1·4.

Although we cannot accurately assess changes in each ring, we at least know that the mean size of middle ring houses was the largest in the city, whilst that of the central wards was the smallest.[1] If we relate the population to rooms we find that little separated the mean number of persons per room in the middle and outer rings. The central wards, on this standard, were the most overcrowded.[2]

These figures provide every indication that generally the population was becoming less overcrowded. But this is not to say that all was well in the city on this score, for pockets of chronic overcrowding certainly existed. A survey conducted into lodging houses in 1961 revealed some appalling conditions. The average number of lettings in each house was a little over five, and about eleven persons were in occupation. A quarter of the houses were defective in management and about two-thirds were defective in facilities and amenities.[3] It would also appear that the number of lodging houses was growing in certain

[1] Rooms per House	1961	1966
Central Wards	4·21	4·96
Middle Ring	4·88	5·75
Outer Ring	4·66	5·39
[2] Rooms per person	1961	1966
Central Wards	1·19	1·37
Middle Ring	1·45	1·70
Outer Ring	1·42	1·73

[3] B.M.O.H., 1961, p. 234.

parts of the middle ring and it is clear that our overall ring figures have masked this particular aspect of the housing environment.

Since the 1920s and 1930s the large middle ring Victorian houses had begun to be converted into lodgings to meet the needs of the poorer, single immigrant. The researches of John Rex and Robert Moore have shed much light on this process in one of the major lodging-house areas, Sparkbrook.[1] Some of these lodging houses were owned by the indigenous population, while others were purchased by overseas immigrants. Often leases were short and normally it was not possible to acquire a mortgage from a building society on such property. This meant that money had to be obtained from more irregular sources at high interest rates on short-term loans. So the property itself had to yield a very high income. The landlord had to pack in as many lodgers as possible at high rents, whilst neglecting all but the most vital of repairs. Rex and Moore also argue that the landlords were satisfying a very real social need by housing people who for economic or racial reasons were not able to obtain alternative accommodation. Yet it would be naïve not to note that many of these landlords were exploiting their tenants in a most ruthless manner, and that many tenants were too intimidated to claim their legal rights.

Birmingham first attempted to control overcrowding as early as 1929 by making it illegal to multi-occupy a house without prior permission. However, the 1954 Housing Repairs and Rents Act repealed this local bye-law, so that it was no longer an offence to allow multiple occupation in a house without notifying the local authority. Powers to control overcrowding were restored by the 1957 Housing Act, but the City's Medical Officer of Health argued they were not as strong as the powers in the old bye-laws.[2] Further national housing acts in 1961 and 1964 gave local authorities powers to insist that adequate facilities were provided in lodging houses, by restricting the number of persons in occupation and securing a proper standard of management. The cumulative effect of these powers, combined with long hours of work by Corporation health visitors and inspectors, were responsible for marginal improvements in the living conditions of many people in Sparkbrook, Balsall Heath, Moseley, Handsworth, and Rotton Park.[3] At one stage so vehement was the purge on landlords that special afternoon sessions of the magistrates' court were held. But an out-and-out war on overcrowding was out of the question because of the extra strain that would be thrown on municipal housing resources. As there was clearly a need for lodging-house accommodation in Birmingham, the City Council could have relieved the problem of overcrowding in existing lodging houses by allowing more

[1] J. Rex and R. Moore, *Race, Community and Conflict* (1967).
[2] *B.M.O.H.*, 1957, p. 276. [3] *B.M.O.H.*, 1964, pp. 228, 238.

and more of the older Victorian houses to be used for multiple occupation. Such tolerance would have risked the environmental deterioration of other areas of the city. So the Corporation decided to restrict the spread of areas of multi-occupation. Initially this was attempted by utilizing the powers in the various Town and Country Planning Acts. The conversion of a house into flats was interpreted as a change in use, so that planning permission was required.[1] This procedure was slow and laborious, but it did help to check new areas of settlement. Much more effective in containing multiple occupation was the Birmingham Corporation Act of 1965. All houses in multiple occupation had to be registered, and permission had to be obtained for all new conversions to multi-occupation.[2] In many respects the Corporation regained the powers which it had lost in 1954.

Those who opposed the entry of black Commonwealth immigrants into Birmingham frequently used the example of the lodging houses to demonstrate that chronic overcrowding was the necessary consequence of that immigration. But this claim could be put into perspective by the 1966 census which revealed that only 2·8 per cent of the houses in the middle ring were multi-occupied, and that at the most only 1·7 per cent of all houses in the city had been converted into lodging houses. Even if these figures were understated, they help to confirm a point, which has already been made, that many of the overseas immigrants' families lived in houses vacated by the outward movement of the indigenous population.

So far we have discussed housing conditions in terms of accommodation and its occupants. However, a small but socially significant minority of the Birmingham population had no homes at all. Many people were made homeless by eviction from private rented houses, and their numbers were frequently swollen by those who came to the city to find work, but who were unable to find a place to live. The problem was not too serious during the war, because so many people had left the city, and billeting and requisitioning arrangements looked after the needs of war workers and their families. But after the war many returning servicemen, who had married Birmingham girls during the hostilities, found themselves without a home, and efforts to persuade local families to share their houses with them were largely in vain.[3] There was also a trickle of men, most of whom were single or who had left their families elsewhere, who came to find work in Birmingham. The problem was aggravated in the late 1940s by a large number of evictions, which had been held up during the war. By 1946 the number of homeless in the city was estimated at many thousands, and was said to be increasing at the rate of fifty per week.[4] The number of evictions

[1] B.M.O.H., 1964, p. 230.   [2] B.M.O.H., 1967, p. 228.
[3] E.D., 29 December 1945.   [4] B.M., 11 January 1946.

tended to increase, and by early 1948 it was claimed that there were fifteen of them a week.[1] The Estates Committee was able to provide permanent accommodation for only one-quarter of the evicted families, mainly in requisitioned houses.[2] Some of the other homeless were accommodated for a time in municipal hostels. Some Service families were housed in the hostels which had been maintained during the war for people whose homes were destroyed by bombs.[3] But a large surplus of homeless people remained and many of them, encouraged by the Communist Party, took over empty houses and Army camps in the city.[4] Despite Government pressure, the City Council at first refused to take responsibility for these squatters, but in 1948 it agreed to manage the occupied camps on behalf of the Ministry of Health, and the people in them were gradually dispersed.

Towards the end of the 1940s the ranks of the homeless were swollen by an increasing number of new arrivals, attracted by the promise of work in Birmingham's flourishing industries. Many were Irish, coming directly from Ireland or from northern districts of England which had a large Irish population but declining industries. The Council's decision to establish a five-year qualification for housing applicants in 1949 was an indication of the size of this influx. By 1950 the problem of the homeless was beginning to cause serious concern within the Labour Party, and in May Councillor Mrs. Crosskey (Labour) successfully moved an amendment calling on the Public Works Committee to establish the true extent of the problem, and to consider increasing hostel accommodation.[5] Later in the year the Council decided to set up a further municipal hostel, to make seven in all, and to establish a central bureau of lodgings.[6] But a scheme to convert some huts in Swanshurst Park to house evicted families fell through because the Ministry of Health objected to the planned separation of husbands from wives and children, and withheld its subsidy. By 1952, however, the Council was being assured that arrangements were now adequate, with most of the homeless families being relocated in sub-standard houses in the central redevelopment areas.[7] It would clearly have been unwise to make the arrangements too comfortable, because homeless families would have been attracted from other areas, and would have been deterred from seeking their own accommodation.

The matter was not raised again until 1956, when Councillor Mrs. Tomlinson (Labour) persuaded the Council to order a new inquiry into hostel accommodation.[8] Concern was now growing not only among

[1] H. of C. Deb., 5th series, vol. cdxlvi, col. 309, 5 February 1948.
[2] B.C.C., Pro., 27 July 1948, p. 941 (Estates Committee).   [3] E.D., 20 July 1945.
[4] E.D., 13 September 1946.   [5] B.C.C., Pro., 23 May 1950, p. 27.
[6] B.C.C., Pro., 5 December 1950, pp. 549–58 (General Purposes Committee).
[7] B.C.C., Pro., 11 March 1952, pp. 866–9 (Housing Management Committee).
[8] B.C.C., Pro., 7 February 1956, p. 755 (General Purposes Committee).

politicians, but in the churches and the voluntary welfare organizations, about the number of homeless, which was being increased by a large total of evictions.[1] But the City Council refused to depart from its previous policy and made it clear that it could not accept responsibility for every homeless family that turned up in the city, though it would provide temporary accommodation.[2] During the summer a massive campaign for better provision was mounted by the churches and such para-political organizations as Wallace Lawler's Public Opinion Action Association. The Council made some concessions by placing all accommodation for the homeless under the control of the Housing Management Committee, and increasing the number of 'half-way houses'—small living units with shared facilities.[3] Fortunately, the Rent Act of 1957 did not greatly increase the number of evictions, but the problem remained serious. By 1960 there were nineteen half-way houses, able to accommodate some 300 people, and five hostels for forty families of mother and children only. By now, the Housing Management Committee, despite its earlier enthusiasm, was limiting the number of half-way houses because it had adopted the practice of rehousing people from them in permanent houses, and did not wish this obligation to become any heavier. The committee had now made it a deliberate point of policy that cramped conditions in the hostels, and the separation of husbands from their families, should act 'as a deterrent to many non-genuine or undeserving applicants who report themselves as homeless.' Nevertheless, there was a marked increase in the number of families using hostels in the late 1950s.[4]

The situation continued to cause concern in the early 1960s. The number of hostels and half-way houses had to be increased, and by 1960–1 the total of people in hostels was over twice as high as in 1957–8.[5] But the growth in homelessness was not accelerated by the arrival of coloured immigrants, most of whom could find accommodation with friends or relatives. Only nine of the 642 families assisted in 1961–2 came from outside the British Isles; one-quarter, however, were of Irish origin.[6] The problem became even more serious as the Corporation stepped up its campaign against multi-occupation. But in the late 1960s a slow improvement took place as the increase in the building rate allowed more homeless people to be accommodated in sub-standard properties rather than in hostels or half-way houses.

[1] *H. of C. Deb.*, 5th series, vol. dlvii, cols. *105–6*, 31 July 1956.

[2] *Y.B.*, no. 105, March 1956, p. 2. See also *Picture Post*, 23 June 1956, p. 14.

[3] B.C.C., *Pro.*, 4 December 1956, pp. 559–72 (General Purposes Committee); *Y.B.*, no. 114, January 1957, p. 3.

[4] B.C.C., *Pro.*, 14 June 1960, p. 76 (Housing Management Committee).

[5] B.C.C., *Pro.*, 6 February 1962, pp. 799–809 (Housing Management Committee).

[6] *Y.B.*, no. 171, March 1962, p. 1.

The housing environment of Birmingham at the end of the Second World War clearly needed drastic improvement. The only consolation, if consolation it be, was that Birmingham was probably not much worse off in proportionate terms than other major industrial centres. By the end of the 1960s most of the very worst property in the central areas had been pulled down, and work had begun on demolishing property outside the five central redevelopment areas. By the end of our period the Corporation had demolished many of the houses it had designated as unfit after the war. In addition, many houses were improved by the local authority, private landlords, and owner-occupiers, with the support of national legislation.

Demolished dwellings were replaced by new buildings both in the outer periphery of the city, and on the spaces which had been cleared in the central areas. Although much municipal building replaced demolished slum houses, sufficient other municipal building was undertaken to provide houses for families on the city's general waiting list. This housing helped to relieve overcrowding in those households made up of more than one family. Indeed, on all the statistics we have examined, we have every indication that overcrowding was diminishing. Whilst the total housing stock was rising, household sizes were contracting. This trend was most marked in the outer ring, and we cannot be completely certain that a real reduction in the incidence of overcrowding was brought about in the central wards and the middle ring. We can, however, be confident that throughout these rings overcrowding was not generally increasing, although there were small patches in which it was getting worse.

Our overall picture of changes in the housing environment is an optimistic one. The numbers of overcrowded families and unfit houses were falling and this improvement was reflected in the decline in infant mortality rates in all rings. But the fact that the reduction in infant mortality was most marked in the central wards helps to confirm that they saw the most marked general improvements.

This chapter began with a comparison of the housing environment of Birmingham and other major cities after the war. It suggested that Birmingham was marginally better off than Liverpool and marginally worse off than Sheffield, Manchester, and Leeds. But how did they compare at the end of our period? Birmingham, as we would expect from an authority whose policy was to buy up unfit houses in such large numbers, had a very large proportion of houses in municipal ownership.[1] The 1966 sample census shows that in terms of household amenities, the city had the highest proportion of households without hot water apart from Liverpool, but was relatively well off in terms of households with fixed baths and inside W.C.s. Only Leeds was substantially better

[1] See statistical appendix, table 15.

provided with these amenities. There were indications that Birmingham was slightly more overcrowded than the other cities, as it had marginally the highest proportion of persons living at densities of 1·5 or more to a room. Yet in 1966 the Birmingham housing environment still differed only in detail from other major provincial cities. However, it may reasonably be assumed that, owing to the marked acceleration in Birmingham's building and slum clearance performance after 1966, a significant improvement in the city's housing environment had occurred by 1970.

VIII

SOCIAL LIFE AND AMENITIES

THE pattern of Birmingham's social life was profoundly influenced after 1945 by the massive transfer of population to the suburbs, and the partial redevelopment and repopulation of the central and middle ring districts. The old communities in the central redevelopment areas, which, despite their poverty, had often possessed a neighbourliness and friendliness unknown elsewhere in the city,[1] were almost completely destroyed. When slum-dwellers were dispersed to the suburban estates they were often depressed to discover an environment which did not encourage the type of social life which they had once known. Low-density housing reduced the number of chance encounters, and forced people to travel further to meet their friends. Many of the new estates were so far from the city centre that their residents could visit only rarely relatives who had remained behind in the older areas. Yet these drawbacks were only part of the picture. Many people in the new suburbs had not originated in the older areas of Birmingham, and so had no feeling of estrangement. Comfortable houses and large gardens encouraged people to stay at home after work, a tendency which was reinforced from the early 1950s by television. Birmingham men worked long hours, and after spending lengthy periods commuting from the suburbs to their work, they often had no desire to leave home in the evenings. Nor did their wives, more of whom had paid jobs than in most other cities. Consequently, many people in the city had long been accustomed to going to bed early, a tradition which survived long after 1945, and which still influenced Birmingham's social life in the later 1960s.[2] The middle classes never went to bed so early, but they were less socially inclined and were even further dispersed in low-density suburbs than the working classes.[3] In any case they constituted only a small proportion of the city's population.[4] Nevertheless, in such a large city, minority interests of all sorts had a chance to flourish. Birmingham was particularly rich in forms of social organization connected with its various ethnic and

[1] See e.g. Gwendolen Freeman, *The Houses Behind* (1947); Norman S. Power, *The Forgotten People* (1965).

[2] Many citizens complained that 8 p.m. was too late a start for BBC television programmes when the Midland service began in 1949, because their normal bedtime was before the end of the first main programme.

[3] These conclusions about working-class and middle-class sociability are based partly on Peter H. Wilmott and Michael Young, *Family and Kinship in East London* (1957), and *Family and Class in a London Suburb* (1960).

[4] See above, p. 215.

regional minorities. Until coloured immigrants began to arrive in large numbers in the early 1950s, the principal minority social unit was formed by the Irish.[1] The Commonwealth immigrants were even more eager than the Irish to maintain their traditional groupings and cultural activities, and by the late 1960s Birmingham's variety of sub-cultures outshone that of any other British city outside London. This social differentiation also had a strong topographical basis. In such a large city, many people felt a closer association with their immediate district and its inhabitants than with Birmingham as a whole. So this chapter can give only an incomplete picture of the city's rich and varied social life, which in any case is bound to escape our clumsy attempts at objective assessment and classification. We shall begin by looking at the habitat in which over one-third of the city's population had come to live by the 1960s, the municipal estates.

There had been many complaints before 1939 from both tenants and public figures about the lack of community spirit and amenities on the new estates.[2] The City Council had provided some encouragement for the foundation of community centres, but had done little directly to provide social amenities, or to plan the estates as social units. The result was a genuine discontent among many tenants, which was brought home to the City Council in 1939, first of all by the residents' unwillingness to volunteer for civil defence service, and then, in the summer, by the massive municipal rent strike. The problem was temporarily obscured by the war, which produced a much greater social cohesion in the suburbs,[3] but the demand for major improvements was not eradicated. Indeed, it grew stronger, for the municipal tenants had now found their voice. Tenants' discussions on how to make the estates more satisfactory to live in were encouraged by the Labour and Communist parties, which had played a key role in organizing the rent strike. They were also encouraged by the churches, which had done all they could to create a sense of community on the new estates.[4] In Kingstanding, whose lack of amenities had been notorious before 1939,[5] the local political parties and churches set up the Kingstanding and District Planning Council to prepare a plan for post-war social development. Similar steps were taken in the south of the city, at Highter's Heath and Warstock, where a conference

[1] See E. Robinson, 'The Irish in Birmingham' (Birmingham University B.A. thesis, 1969).

[2] See Briggs, pp. 235–6; Black, p. 314.

[3] Norman Tiptaft, *I Saw a City* (1945), p. 18.

[4] See for instance, *Billesley has a Church*, published by Holy Cross Church, Billesley Common, 1944.

[5] See Briggs, pp. 235–6; Geoffrey Boumphrey, *Town and Country Tomorrow* (1940), pp. 21–3.

of local bodies was organized by the Maypole New Citizens' Group.[1]

These tenants' and residents' associations obtained plenty of support from Birmingham's semi-official planning bodies. As early as 1941 the Bournville Village Trust suggested that community centres should be built on all the new estates with municipal assistance. The Trust also criticized the estates' single-class social composition, their great distance from places of employment, and their limited shopping facilities: '. . . they lack the essential integration of communal life without which no settlement of people can emerge as an organic social whole.'[2] It was partly with a view to improving social planning that the City Council asked the Birmingham and Five Counties Architectural Association to prepare a draft plan for the Shard End Estate in 1943. The scheme, which was ready by 1944, was based on a system of neighbourhood units, with full community facilities. Neighbourhood units were also incorporated in estate plans prepared by the Corporation, after they had been recommended to local authorities by the Ministry of Health's 1944 *Housing Manual*.[3]

It was clear that in the long run better community planning would make a substantial contribution to the quality of life on the housing estates. But the early post-war years brought frustration and disappointment. Building resources were so limited that they had to be concentrated exclusively on houses. So few new dwellings were available that wartime hopes of varying the social composition of estates by letting accommodation to upper-income groups could not be realized. Even the benefits that were to be expected from the creation of neighbourhood units in the new estates were slow to arrive. Resentment soon built up once again among municipal tenants, especially in the north of the city. In May 1947 the City Council passed a resolution, proposed by local councillors, calling for the provision of better amenities and public services in Perry Barr.[4] Some progress was now made here and on other estates in improving amenities by the provision of temporary shops, extended bus services, and better street lighting, but major amenity developments had to wait until the relaxation of

---

[1] *C.S.C. Review: The Birmingham Christian Social Council Quarterly*, no. 4, March 1945, pp. 1–3; Birmingham Communist Party, *Homes for Birmingham: The Communist Party Plan* (1945), p. 10.

[2] Bournville Village Trust, *When We Build Again* (1941), pp. 119–20.

[3] Birmingham and Five Counties Architectural Association Reconstruction Committee, 'Extracts from a memorandum on the planning of a typical housing development . . .', *The Architect and Building News*, vol. clxxix, 29 September 1944, p. 198. See also *Birmingham (Shard End) Compulsory Purchase Order, 1945: Tentative Layout* (B.R.L. 574626). For the final layout of the estate as it was completed in the 1950s, see 'Towards a New Birmingham', *The Municipal Journal*, vol. lxi, no. 3172, 4 December 1953, p. 2641.

[4] B.C.C., *Pro.*, 6 May 1947, p. 622.

building restrictions in the early 1950s. Then, the Corporation gave first priority to providing enough shops.

Little thought had been given to new shops before 1950, because housing progress was so slow, and commercial building licences were hard to obtain.[1] But in December of that year the House Building Committee accepted the City Engineer's suggestion that nearly one hundred shops should be built immediately, and even more scheduled for future estates. But after other committees had urged that an exhaustive survey be carried out, it became clear that many more new shops would be needed. Sheldon, for instance, had only one shop for every 228 residents, compared to a city average of one to fifty-six. Moreover, the Corporation was still following its pre-war policy of grouping shops in small clusters rather than major centres, so that traders had no local competition. As a result of this survey and the controversy it aroused, the Council decided in November 1952 to provide one shop for every hundred residents on new estates, and to group them in larger shopping centres. Nevertheless, it was agreed that no house should be more than a quarter of a mile from shopping, and that isolated general stores would be allowed where necessary. This new scheme provided for the construction of 341 shops, and although only a slow start could be made immediately, some 260 new shops had been completed by 1958.[2] Moreover, the Council was nearly always able to keep its promise, made in 1952, that shops would be ready by the time the first tenants moved on to a new estate.

Now that the shop problem was being dealt with, the Council was able to provide a further amenity, the tenants' club room, which had already proved successful in London and some of the new towns. A first batch of twelve was approved in 1954, and the first club room was opened in the following year. The initial programme was then extended, and progress was so rapid that nineteen rooms had been provided by 1962. Three years later there were twenty-eight of them.[3] One of the major reasons why the City Council pushed ahead so rapidly here was that it had been able to do little to provide full community centres. In the 1920s and early 1930s the City had left the provision of community centres to voluntary bodies, and although it later agreed to establish some centres directly, it had achieved very little by the time

[1] Only twenty-three shops were built on municipal estates between 1945 and 1952.

[2] B.C.C., *Pro.*, 4 November 1952, pp. 463–76 (House Building Committee); *Y.B.*, no. 69, December 1952, p. 2; B.C.C., *Pro.*, 1 July 1958, p. 309 (House Building Committee).

[3] B.C.C., *Pro.*, 5 January 1954, p. 680 (House Building Committee); 12 July 1955, p. 245; 4 July 1961, p. 205; *Y.B.*, no. 97, June 1955; Birmingham Council for Community Associations, *Annual Report*, 1962, p. 5; 1965, p. 6.

war broke out.[1] During the war the Council strengthened its resolve to provide adequate community centres,[2] and full Ministry of Education support was promised. However, building restrictions prevented any progress in the late 1940s. As late as 1949 it was still impossible to allocate even temporary huts for use as community centres.[3] Although the City Council continued its pre-war practice of making a grant to the Birmingham Council for Community Associations, the main handicap was not finance but the shortage of buildings, especially when the house building rate improved in the early 1950s. By 1954 the Birmingham Council for Community Associations was complaining that the shortage of facilities was again relatively as great as it had been in 1930.[4]

The new tenants' club rooms met part of the need, but hardly any full community centres were built by the Corporation until the 1960s. Rather more were provided by voluntary enterprise, though often in premises that were not entirely suitable. By 1965 there were twenty-one community centres in Birmingham, only a handful of which had been purpose-built by the Corporation.[5] In any case, much though these facilities were appreciated, they provided only a partial solution to the estates' community problems, which often stemmed from a feeling of isolation. In 1957 the new Lord Mayor, Alderman J. J. Grogan (Labour), who had once represented a suburban ward, launched a campaign to encourage those who lived on remote estates to play a full part in the life of the city community.[6] In 1959 the *Birmingham Mail* featured the plight of 'The Lonely Exiles of Kingshurst', who complained that amenities had been neglected there, and feared that the lack of social activities would result in trouble among the younger sections of the community. The Corporation promised that plans were now well under way to improve the situation, and announced a scheme to provide Birmingham's first municipal shop-on-the-corner on the Kingshurst Hall Estate.[7] The decline of the building rate in the last years of the 1950s gave the Corporation another chance to catch up in the provision of social facilities, and complaints faded away in the early 1960s.[8] They did not recur again in large numbers until the building rate started to increase rapidly in 1964. Then, despite the

[1] Briggs, pp. 235–6; *V.C.H. Warcks.*, vol. vii, p. 245. Up to 1938 the *total* Corporation expenditure on community amenities had been only £8,000 (Birmingham Council for Community Associations, *Annual Report*, 1938, p. 8).

[2] See e.g. B.C.C., *Pro.*, 1 December 1942, p. 48 (Reconstruction Committee).

[3] Birmingham Council for Community Associations, *Annual Report*, 1949, p. 2.

[4] Ibid., 1954, p. 6.

[5] Calculated from ibid., 1965.

[6] *Y.B.*, no. 119, June 1957, p. 2.   [7] *B.M.*, 16, 17 February 1959.

[8] A survey in 1963 of forty-three families who had recently moved to new municipal estates suggested that a high level of neighbourliness had developed very quickly (Fred Milson, *Families on the Move*, Westhill Paper no. 7 (1963), p. 3).

Council's good intentions, new residents at first found exactly the same conditions on the developing Castle Vale and Chelmsley Wood estates as had tenants in Sheldon just after the war. It seemed that no matter how good amenity planning was, there would always be some time lag before full provision was made. Very often there was nothing that the City Council could do; shopkeepers, for instance, sometimes refused to take up tenancies until estates were fully occupied. Telephone and postal facilities, always a major bone of contention, were entirely outside the Corporation's control. In the 1950s the Birmingham M.P.s fought a strenuous campaign in the House of Commons to obtain improvements, but the G.P.O. was not able to satisfy them until the early 1960s.[1]

Another aspect of suburban amenities that was beyond the City Council's control was the provision of places of entertainment. It could, and did, reserve sites for them, but their construction remained entirely within the province of private enterprise. As we have seen, suburban densities were too low to make places of entertainment readily accessible to large numbers of people, and estate dwellers were in any case less willing to seek entertainment outside their home than citizens in the older areas. So hardly any cinemas were opened in the suburbs after 1955, and many were closed.[2] Those that remained came to be patronized almost exclusively by courting couples; family entertainment was much cheaper in front of the television set.

The shortage of other forms of amenity placed a great strain on the suburban public houses. Their great size and comfort, and small numbers, were the result of an agreement made between the City Council and the Birmingham brewers at the turn of the century. Known as the 'fewer and better' scheme, it encouraged the brewers to give up the licences of obsolete and inadequate public houses in the inner ring slums on the understanding that they would be allowed to open a smaller number of bigger houses in the new suburbs. The Council encouraged them to provide a higher standard of service in their suburban houses than would have been possible in their older establishments, and prevented the proliferation of smaller public houses that might compete with them and force them to reduce their standards. The 'fewer and better' scheme made economic sense to the brewers because, with lower population densities and better living conditions in the suburbs, only a house that would draw customers from a wide area, without local competition, could be expected to return a profit. The City Council hoped that the scheme would reduce casual drinking, and it was not disappointed. In 1938 Birmingham had only 9·20

[1] See A. R. Sutcliffe, 'The tip of the iceberg: Birmingham M.P.s and local issues, 1939–1966', History of Birmingham Project Research Paper, no. 8.
[2] See below, pp. 293 ff.

licensed premises for every 10,000 residents, compared to a national average of 17·94.[1] Some newer areas were bypassed completely; in Acocks Green, for instance, there was no increase in the number of public houses after 1900, even though the population multiplied several times.[2] The 'fewer and better' scheme ceased to operate officially in the 1930s, but the Corporation could still control the provision of public houses on municipal estates by its allocation of sites. After the war a new system of licence exchange was introduced to compensate the brewers for the loss of public houses in the city centre and the central redevelopment areas, and its results were similar to those of the pre-war arrangement.[3] But in the 1950s competition from television made the brewers hesitate to build new houses, and the city suffered a net loss of public houses owing to demolitions in the central areas. By 1966 there were only 798 in Birmingham and Smethwick combined, compared to 975 in 1939.[4] This loss was, however, compensated by the growth in the number of clubs and licensed hotels and restaurants, which was especially rapid after 1960. This new development produced an increase in the total of licensed premises in Birmingham from 930 in 1960 to over 990 at the end of the decade, compared to 947 in 1939.[5]

The shortage of suburban public houses at least ensured that most premises enjoyed a big patronage, though some people who did not own their own motor cars found it difficult to reach them. So big were most of the houses that landlords could provide not only a great variety of accommodation in different bars, but rooms for private functions and club meetings. The brewers recognized that the social function of their suburban houses was quite different from those in the middle and inner rings. Robert H. Butler, chairman of Mitchell and Butlers, the city's biggest brewery, went so far as to claim in the early 1950s that public houses were 'an important educational factor in the life of the people'.[6] Indeed, by this time, plays, exhibitions, and lectures were being held in public houses. More important, perhaps, their meal facilities were greatly extended after the war, especially in the suburbs, which were almost devoid of restaurants. When skiffle and other forms of popular music played by semi-professionals developed in the 1950s, they were welcomed in the public houses. In fact, licensed houses increasingly took over from working men's social and entertainment

[1] Sir Patrick Abercrombie and Herbert Jackson, *West Midlands Plan* (1948), III.22.22.

[2] C. J. G. Hudson, 'The Story of Acock's Green', p. 14 (B.R.L. 752946).

[3] The scheme, based on the principle of 'barrelage', is described in *B.P.*, 17 April 1970.

[4] *Kelly's Directories of Birmingham and Smethwick.*

[5] City of Birmingham, *Reports of the Licensing Committee of the Justices.*

[6] Norman Tiptaft, *My Contemporaries* (1952), p. 54.

clubs, which had never been as strong in the Birmingham area as in the north of England.[1] Many social clubs in the inner and middle rings closed during the difficult years of the 1950s, and although those that survived enjoyed a great resurgence of popularity in the 1960s, only a few new ones were established in the outer suburbs. In fact, clubs and societies of all sorts seemed to obtain less support in the suburbs than in more densely populated districts. Apart from a slight increase in the number of gardening societies and bowling clubs after the war, the move to the suburbs appeared to bring about a reduction in club activities.[2] It was precisely because the new suburbs were a social desert that the churches came to see them as their principal mission ground.

Organized religion

Churchgoing and church membership began to decline in Birmingham, as in the country as a whole, from the turn of the century. The fall was accelerated by the First World War, and continued during the 1920s and 1930s. In Birmingham only the Roman Catholic Church strengthened its position, thanks mainly to the great influx of immigrants of Irish origin. The numbers of clergy also declined rapidly in most denominations, and by 1939 the churches no longer had the resources nor the manpower to minister to the whole community as they had tried to do in the nineteenth century.

Some churches hoped that the new war would strengthen the churches, by bringing about a national revival of faith. True, national days of prayer for peace attracted large congregations. But the emotions which they engendered were generally superficial, and they did not lead to a revival of regular churchgoing. Instead, the early months of the war actually reduced participation in church life.[3] Congregations lost their most active young men to military service; Sunday schools were disrupted by evacuation. Air raid precautions and the expansion of voluntary services of all types affected the churches indirectly because members who took on these extra duties could give less time to church work. Because of the blackout, evening services, which were often the best attended in wartime, had to be held in the afternoon during most of the year. Even greater disruption was caused by the actual raiding. Church buildings were given a very low priority by the fire services, and many were destroyed or very seriously damaged. Some churches were able to establish their own fire watching organizations, but

---

[1] *The Club Herald*, 20 June 1963, editorial.

[2] This conclusion is based on an examination of club and society entries in the *Birmingham Post Year Book*.

[3] See, for instance, T. N. Veitch, *A Vision of the Immediate and Future Work of the Church* (1940), pp. 6–7 (B.R.L. 513674).

Children at play in a redevelopment area, 1970

Old and new schools in Birmingham. Camden Primary School, photographed in 1961, and Welford Primary School, Handsworth, in 1973. The steeple-like ventilation shaft was a feature of most of Birmingham's older board schools.

most found that their able-bodied members were already responsible for the protection of industrial and domestic buildings. Even when churches escaped fire damage, their glass proved very vulnerable to blast, and cold and draughts severely reduced many congregations.[1] Attendances at central churches were particularly low, because so many of their members lived in the suburbs and found it difficult to travel about the city on Sundays. Towards the end, war-weariness further reduced people's willingness to participate in church life. So by 1945 nearly all the Birmingham churches were in a much weaker position than before the war.[2]

Fortunately, the restoration of peace brought about some improvement. The more active members were again able to concentrate on church affairs, and the repaired churches provided an outlet for the widespread demand for joint activity which characterized the grim years of anti-climax and austerity in the later 1940s.[3] True, there was no marked increase in church membership, but at least the steady decline of earlier years was halted. The churches' position was further reinforced during the 1950s as new building allowed the distribution of churches to correspond more closely to the new pattern of settlement within Birmingham.[4] More clergy became available, and the financial position of most denominations was strengthened. In the late 1950s and 1960s, however, a renewed decline in participation set in, resulting probably from the greater affluence of the population and a broadening of the choice of weekend activities.[5] Only the Roman Catholic Church, and some of the denominations appealing to Commonwealth immigrants, maintained their steady expansion. The locally-estimated Roman Catholic population of Birmingham rose from over 52,000 in 1940 to 103,475 in 1969, and the national Newman Demographic

[1] See, for instance, Stechford Methodist Church, *Newsletter*, spring 1941, p. 2 (B.R.L. 428777).

[2] For the experience of one church during the war, see *St. Paul's Church, Balsall Heath 1853–1953: the Story of the First Hundred Years* (1953), B.R.L. 635399. The Band of Hope was also severely weakened by the war. See Midland Band of Hope League, *Centenary Celebration: Souvenir Handbook* (1947), pp. 12, 19 (B.R.L. 589621).

[3] At Carr's Lane Congregational Church, for instance, attendances increased after the war. See Arthur H. Driver, *Carrs Lane 1748–1948* (1948), p. 90.

[4] For instance, the total membership of Methodist churches in the Belmont Row Circuit (E. and S.E. Birmingham), which sank from 1,803 to 1,547 between 1939 and 1946, had risen to 1,602 by 1958 (calculated from Belmont Row Circuit, *Plan and Directory*, B.R.L. 349878).

[5] The Birmingham Baptists suffered a particularly sharp decline in the 1960s. In 1968 their total membership was only 5,703 compared to 6,955 in 1939 (calculated from *The Baptist Handbook*). The Congregationalists appear to have suffered similar heavy losses, but the Methodists were less seriously affected (*V.C.H. Warcks.*, vol. vii, p. 433; *Methodist Conference Handbooks*). The number of communicants in Birmingham's six Presbyterian churches fell from 1,053 to 892 between 1961–2 and 1968–9 (calculated from Presbyterian Church of England, *Official Handbook*).

s

Survey put it somewhat improbably at twice the latter figure in 1962.[1] In fact, by 1970 the Birmingham Roman Catholics were stronger in terms of committed adherents than all the other churches together.

It is paradoxical, in view of Birmingham's strong non-conformist tradition, that the total of Anglican adherents should apparently have declined less after 1945 than that of dissenters. The Church of England maintained its position partly because it built more churches in new centres of population, and partly because, in a time of declining religious enthusiasm, it made fewer demands on its worshippers than did the free churches. By the late 1950s the Church of England appeared to be about equal in terms of active adherents to all the nonconformist denominations together. It was estimated in 1957 that the Birmingham nonconformist churches had a membership of no more than 30,000.[2] At the same time (1958) the Birmingham Anglican diocese recorded an Easter communicant rate of 34 per 1,000 population over the age of fifteen, which suggests that its total of active adherents in the city was between 25,000 and 30,000.[3] In 1962 the Easter communicant rate in the diocese was still 34 per 1,000[4] and although it probably fell subsequently, allegiance to nonconformist churches appears to have fallen faster.

Even before the Second World War the Church of England had taken a clear lead over the nonconformists in the redistribution of church provision within Birmingham, thanks mainly to its greater resources and authoritarian organization. Nevertheless, the diocesan authorities recognized that not enough new churches had been built in the suburbs. During the war the City Council strongly encouraged the planning of more churches by reserving sites and keeping the diocese fully informed of its building and redevelopment plans. In May 1945 the diocesan conference set up a commission to enquire into the needs of the diocese, and its report later in the year stressed the importance of providing for the new housing areas, and the urgency of obtaining new sources of finance.[5] It was to achieve these aims that the diocese inaugurated the Ten Year Forward Movement in the following year, under the chairmanship of the Ven. Michael Parker, archdeacon of Aston. But it was also emphasized that the movement was intended to bring about a

[1] Calculated from *The Official Catholic Directory of the Archdiocese of Birmingham*, 1940, 1969; for the higher estimate, which puts the proportion of Roman Catholics in Birmingham at 19·6 per cent, see A. E. C. W. Spencer, 'The demography and sociography of the Roman Catholic community of England and Wales', p. 64, in Laurence Bright and Simon Clements (eds.), *The Committed Church* (1966); John D. Gay, *The Geography of Religion in England* (1971), p. 225.

[2] *V.C.H. Warcks.*, vol. vii, p. 434.

[3] *Facts and Figures about the Church of England* (1961), p. 58. The Birmingham Easter communicant rate was considerably lower than in any other Anglican diocese.

[4] *Facts and Figures about the Church of England* (1965).

[5] Diocese of Birmingham, *Report of Commission of Enquiry* (1945).

general regeneration and reorganization within the church, and was not just a general appeal for money from the community at large.[1]

Although no bricks could be laid for some years, a few temporary church halls were erected in the later 1940s and the whole diocese, priests and parishioners alike, found a renewed unity and enthusiasm in the face of the challenge.[2] Public generosity produced large sums and in the early 1950s the Church Assembly, stimulated by Birmingham's ambitious plans, approved a new scheme of financial aid for the building of new churches.[3] Bishop Barnes, who had strongly supported the campaign, and whose good relations with the City Council had ensured full municipal support, retired in 1953, but his successor, Bishop Wilson, was equally interested in this aspect of the diocese's work. A former missionary, he continually emphasized the similarity between the Church's role in Birmingham and that in Singapore, where he had served for many years.[4] In 1956 Bishop Wilson launched a new public appeal, with a target of £1,200,000, for new churches.[5] Although private individuals made only minor contributions, Birmingham industry responded generously, and by early 1959 over £600,000 had been raised.[6] Churches and halls now began to be completed at more frequent intervals. In 1956 only one new church (at Shard End) and five dual-purpose buildings had been completed since the war; by 1959, three more new churches were in use, and three others were under construction.[7] Another public appeal was made in 1961, and by 1965 the combined appeals had raised a total of £1,254,000.[8] By now, however, the appeal's momentum was slowing down, and it was weakened by the general decline in church attendance in the 1960s. Nevertheless, the needs of most of the new areas, in terms of buildings at least, had been met by the end of the decade.

The Church of England's example was followed by such other Birmingham Protestant denominations as were strong enough to build new churches.[9] Like the Anglicans, they were helped by war damage

[1] Diocese of Birmingham, *Forward! The Journal of the Ten Year Forward Movement* (1946); *Forward Movement* (c. 1947).

[2] *Manchester Guardian*, 8 July 1949; *Diocesan Assembly, June 21–4, 1950* (Programme), p. 3 (B.R.L. 628891).

[3] See Church Assembly, *Report of the Committee on the Church in New Housing Areas* (C.A. 1024, 1952); *B.G., B.P.,* 12 June 1952; *B.P.,* 10 November 1961.

[4] *B.P.,* 19 June 1953.

[5] See *Circles without Centres—The Facts of the Case: The Bishop of Birmingham's Jubilee Appeal* (1956).

[6] *The First Three Years: The Bishop of Birmingham's Appeal* (1959), p. 2; *B.P.,* 16 March 1956, 4 June 1958. By 1958 only 11 per cent of the total raised had been donated by individuals.

[7] *The First Three Years*, p. 4.

[8] *Circles without Centres—The Second Mile: The Bishop of Birmingham's Appeal* (1961), pp. 2, 6–7; *B.P.,* 28 July 1965.

[9] See e.g. Methodist Conference, 1953, Birmingham, *Handbook*, pp. 38–9.

compensation to transfer central churches to the outskirts.[1] The Baptists, for instance, closed eight churches and built seven between 1939 and 1968.[2] But the free churches, on the whole, lacked the resources of the Church of England, and their appeals to public generosity were not so fruitful because of a smaller response from industry. Some of the new churches had to struggle to survive, particularly on the municipal estates, and most nonconformist denominations found increasingly that their main support came no longer from the artisanal districts of the middle ring, but from the middle-class suburbs. Some of the smaller denominations made no attempt to decentralize, preferring to retain a city-centre church which would be equally accessible to all of their scattered flocks.

The Roman Catholic Church also declined to join in the rush to build new churches in the suburbs. Its main strength remained concentrated in areas of the middle ring, such as Sparkbrook, whose population contained a high proportion of Irish. Such districts were not generally affected by slum clearance, and many Irish took a long time to qualify for municipal houses, partly as a result of the five-year residence qualification. Thanks to this population stability not a single Roman Catholic church or mission had to be closed between 1940 and 1969. Nevertheless, the first-generation Irish showed some tendency to disperse through the city in the 1950s and 1960s, while the indigenous Roman Catholic population grew rapidly. Eight new churches were built in the suburbs, and the number of Birmingham rural deaneries was increased from three to four in 1951 in order to meet the needs of the eastern suburbs.[3] Yet compared to the Protestant churches, the Roman Catholic archdiocese gave a very low priority to church building. Instead, effort was concentrated on the provision of schools.[4] As Archbishop Grimshaw explained in 1964: 'Our first anxiety has to be a dwelling place for our Lord of another sort. We have to ensure that the children of the next generation are formed into living temples of God. We have to put all our energy first into the building of schools, making do very often with church accommodation we should dearly love to replace but cannot while the heavy pressure of debt weighs hard upon us.'[5] This rejection of dispersal allowed the Roman Catholics to maintain teams of priests at their relatively few churches, instead of the solitary clergy who typified the local organization of the Protestant churches. In 1940 thirteen of Birmingham's thirty-three Roman Catholic churches were staffed by only one priest; in 1969 only twelve had only

[1] See e.g. *Together Travel On: Bristol Road Methodist Church, Northfield* (1956), B.R.L. 660495.
[2] Calculated from the annual *Baptist Handbook*.
[3] *The Official Catholic Directory of the Archdiocese of Birmingham.*
[4] R. H. Kiernan, *The Story of the Archdiocese of Birmingham* (1950), p. 50.
[5] *The Church of St. John Fisher, West Heath, Birmingham: Brochure, 31st March, 1964.*

one man, despite an increase in the number of places of worship to forty-five. Although the number of Roman Catholic priests in Birmingham did not keep pace with the rise in the Roman Catholic population, it increased substantially, from eighty-eight to 120, between 1940 and 1969.[1]

The success of the Roman Catholic Church[2] seemed to some to bring into question the methods of the other churches, and especially of the Church of England. Were they right to spread themselves evenly over the whole city, building a church or mission in every centre of population, without adequately considering the staffing problem, and the chances of attracting a congregation large enough to support each church? This question had in fact worried the Anglican diocese since the war, for it had always had a higher proportion of very large parishes, and fewer priests, than most other areas. Moreover, it had in Barnes a bishop who was not very interested in parish life and administration, and whose preference for men of high intellect occasionally led him to make appointments to working-class parishes which some of his clergy considered to be unsuitable. As early as 1945 the diocesan commission of enquiry stressed how serious was the manpower problem.[3] Partly to blame was the general poverty of stipends in the diocese, which was one of the poorest in Britain. When the diocesan conference discussed this problem in 1946, it emerged that thirty benefices in the diocese had an income of less than £400 a year, and most did not exceed £600.[4] The diocese attempted to improve stipends by means of mutual aid between parishes, and by taking advantage of the Church Commissioners' 'K' scheme, which doubled any amounts raised by parishioners in order to increase the stipend of the incumbent. By 1948 it had proved possible to increase the minimum stipend to nearly £500.[5] But there was still no significant improvement in the manpower position, and in November 1950 Michael Parker told the diocesan conference that the Forward Movement, of which he was still chairman, should be wound up because of the shortage of clergy. Some men, he said, were breaking under the strain, and the church could not expand at the circumference if it were not strong at the centre.[6]

After this scare, there were signs of improvement in the manpower position. Higher stipends and new vicarages began to attract more of the new ranks of post-war trained clergy who were beginning to emerge from the theological colleges. Plans were announced in 1951

[1] *The Official Catholic Directory of the Archdiocese of Birmingham.*

[2] The archdiocese was confident enough in 1960 to establish a Midland edition of the *Catholic Pictorial*, but it was forced to cease publication in January 1965. It was outlived by the Liverpool edition of the paper (*B.M.*, 2 January 1965).

[3] Diocese of Birmingham, *Report of Commission of Enquiry* (1945), p. 5.

[4] *B.G.*, 6 December 1946.   [5] *B.P.*, 4 June 1948.   [6] *B.P.*, 24 November 1950.

to help the bishop in the administration of the diocese by the appointment of residentiary canons.[1] Some new clergy were attracted to the
diocese from 1953 by the evangelical, liberal reputation of Bishop
Wilson. But these hopeful trends did not overcome the immediate
problem. At the diocesan conference in 1954, Michael Parker expressed
concern about the shortage of assistant curates for large parishes,
which still abounded in the diocese; there were still fifty-one parishes
with populations of over 10,000 which were staffed by only one priest.[2]
Bishop Wilson confirmed that the situation was still grave: 'Our
situation in Birmingham is, I think, more desperate than in any other
diocese in England.'[3] Birmingham's lack of a distinctive image, he
said, was partly to blame; most clergy wanted either a tough job in the
north or a soft living in the south, and the West Midlands was neither
one thing nor the other.[4] By 1958 the Birmingham diocese still had
fewer clergy per head of population than any other; it also had the
lowest proportion of Easter communicants, and a confirmation rate
lower than any diocese except London.[5] Meanwhile, however, stipends
were being substantially improved, and in 1964 the diocesan board of
finance was able to announce that they were now the best in the
country.[6] Nevertheless, the staffing position improved only gradually,
and in the late 1960s the shortage of clergy was still more acute than
in any other diocese.

It was partly in recognition of this shortage, and of the low attendances at many suburban churches, that the diocese started to build
smaller churches in the 1960s. Parishes were combined into larger
units for certain purposes, such as adult education schemes,[7] and in
1959 all parish magazines were incorporated into a standard parish
newspaper using syndicated material throughout the city, the *Birmingham Christian News*.[8] There was also a return to a policy of erecting
multi-purpose buildings, of which the influential Hodge Hill church,
opened in 1968, was an excellent example.[9] Here, the buildings were
designed to serve as a community centre as well as a church, and Hodge
Hill marked the full maturity of the policy of social provision followed
by the churches ever since the war.

[1] *B.P.*, 11 June 1951. Further help was provided by the creation of the suffragan
bishopric of Aston in 1954.
[2] The number of curates in the diocese had fallen from 178 in 1938 to only thirty-
eight ten years later (Angus Calder, *The People's War: Britain 1939–1945* (1969), p.
479).
[3] *B.M.*, 11 June 1954.　　　[4] *B.P.*, 9 June 1955.
[5] *Facts and Figures About the Church of England* (1961), pp. 14, 25, 55, 58.
[6] *B.M.*, 6 May 1954.　　　[7] *B.M.*, 9 September 1954.
[8] *Manchester Guardian*, 14 January 1959. Birmingham was one of the first areas to
launch such a church newspaper. Its success is described by its chief organizer, the
Rev. Nicolas Stacey, in his autobiography *Who Cares?* (1971).
[9] *S.M.*, 23 March 1969.

Because the Corporation's scheme for community amenities fell so seriously behind schedule in the 1940s and 1950s, the churches were often the first organized social units to appear in the new areas. They frequently took the initiative in organizing local community activities; at Quinton, for instance, in 1959, the Protestant churches and the local institute of further education jointly organized a summer festival. The Methodists revived their 'class' system (regular meetings of small groups of church members) in the new suburbs from the early 1950s, with a social as well as a religious objective. By the early 1960s the idea had proved so successful that it was being adopted by other local churches, and was beginning to spread beyond Birmingham.[1] Nevertheless, the churches often found that their social role declined as units of secular social organization came to be established. Despite being first on the scene, the churches were nowhere able to bring about a permanent revival of religious activity in the new areas.

The weakness of the Birmingham Protestant churches, and the liberal attitude of the Anglicans, stimulated a greater degree of cooperation between them than in many other parts of the country. From his appointment in 1924, Bishop Barnes established friendly relations with all the nonconformist denominations, and the gravity of Birmingham's social problems encouraged Anglican and dissenting clergy to work together in such ventures as the Birmingham Christian Social Council.[2] Inter-church cooperation in the work of church extension had also been established before 1939.[3] The war created a desire for even closer cooperation, and all the Protestant churches joined in sending 'factory padres' into the bigger Birmingham plants, and in organizing the General United Mission in 1942.[4] The announcement of redevelopment plans for the central areas provided a further stimulus to cooperation, and in 1945 the Church of England and the free churches were discussing the possibility of setting up a combined religious centre in Duddeston and Nechells.[5]

Wartime cooperation engendered a desire for more formal links between the Protestant churches. The efforts of Bishop Barnes and other leading clergy led in 1951 to the foundation of the Birmingham Council of Christian Churches, which was accompanied by the formation of local church councils.[6] Bishop Wilson carried on these

[1] B.P., 30 July 1962.
[2] See Guy Rogers, A Rebel at Heart: the Autobiography of a Nonconforming Churchman (1956), pp. 175–6.
[3] See e.g. Handbook of the Methodist Conference: Birmingham 1943, p. 9.
[4] V.C.H. Warcks., vol. vii, p. 429; C.S.C. Review, no. 8, September 1946, pp. 3–4.
[5] Norman Tiptaft, I Saw a City (1945), p. 88.
[6] B.P., 24 November 1950. For the foundation of one such local council, see K. A. Busia, Urban Churches in Britain: A Question of Relevance (1966), p. 124. By 1956 there were four local councils, and two more were about to be founded (Birmingham Council of Christian Churches, Minutes, 28 September 1956).

efforts; in 1954 he told a meeting of Birmingham Methodists that he was 'almost a fanatic about church unity'.[1] A number of joint missions and other activities were organized by the Council of Christian Churches, including an annual Christian Aid week of fund raising for an agreed project. Even the Roman Catholics began to join in discussions in the late 1950s and changes in the Vatican allowed them to move closer to the Protestant churches in the 1960s. The first joint service with Protestant and Roman Catholic representatives was held in 1968.[2] Cooperation at a local level was strengthened by the joint social service schemes inaugurated in the 1960s.[3] But the most effective steps towards unity were taken between the Anglican and Methodist churches. More progress was made in Birmingham than in most places, and when Anglican clergy were asked in 1969 to vote on the proposed national reunion of the two churches, Birmingham diocese recorded the second highest majority in favour—76 per cent.[4]

This move towards church unity was a welcome one, but most clergy were aware that it resulted partly from the decline in strength of the individual churches, except of the Roman Catholics who, significantly, were the least interested in cooperation. How effective, then, was the work of the churches, and what influence did they have on the life of the city?

By 1939 the churches had long since lost the strong moral influence over ordinary people which they had enjoyed in the nineteenth century. Many clergy had come to believe that they could exercise social influence only through their actions, and the inter-war years saw a series of attempts by clergy to bring about material improvements in living conditions. The Conference of Christian Politics, Economics, and Citizenship (COPEC), founded in 1924,[5] was joined in the early 1930s by the Birmingham Christian Social Council. This body was chaired for many years by the rector of Birmingham, Canon Guy Rogers, who made the parish church of St. Martin's into a centre for the preaching of the gospel of 'social salvation'.[6] But the Council did not make a strong impact on the life of the city during the 1930s; perhaps it might have achieved more if unemployment had been as serious in Birmingham as elsewhere. During the war the Council, and the churches in general, failed to establish a strong hold on public opinion, partly because the social reforms that they favoured were no different from those advocated by secular bodies. After 1945 the

[1] B.G., 11 March 1954.
[2] Birmingham Diocesan Ecumenical Commission, The Bulletin, March–April 1969.
[3] See Responsibility in the Welfare State (1961), p. 75.
[4] B.P., 18 June 1969.
[5] See E. Benson Perkins, So Appointed: An Autobiography (1964), p. 55.
[6] Rogers, A Rebel at Heart, p. 174.

introduction of far-reaching reforms by the central Government,[1] and the reduced role of local authorities, largely took the wind out of the sails of local religious pressure groups, and the Christian Social Council faded into obscurity for a time. The churches, aware of the need to build up their membership, returned for a while to personal evangelism. Bishop Barnes continued to make pronouncements on secular affairs, and he gave as good as he got in many a controversy right up to his retirement. Though his support for euthanasia and eugenics worried some people, Birmingham loved him for his humanity, independence, and healthy disrespect for established authority and precedent. His successor, Bishop Wilson, preferred to avoid the controversies in which Barnes had revelled, and he made few statements on secular affairs. Nor did he encourage his clergy to undertake political work, as Barnes had done. Nevertheless, the churches performed an important role in the 1950s by helping to ensure an amicable reception for coloured immigrants; this was perhaps their greatest post-war social achievement.[2] But in other fields they switched their efforts more and more to direct action, rather than to the moulding of public opinion.

By the early 1950s it had become clear that the Welfare State was not the millennium. Meanwhile, many clergy were becoming dissatisfied with personal evangelism which, although it had helped to stabilize church membership after the war, did not allow them to play an active role in society. Indeed, it was precisely because they wanted to play such a role that many of them had come to Birmingham in the first place. So in 1956 the Birmingham Council of Christian Churches decided to commission a survey of the operation of the social services, and the part played in them by the churches. The results of this survey, the first of its type in Britain, were published in 1961.[3] It concluded that the churches could usefully cooperate with voluntary bodies in providing 'neighbourly help', leaving more ambitious services to the public authorities. A number of such local service schemes were set up in the 1960s,[4] and by the end of the decade a few full-time social workers had been appointed.[5] Nevertheless, only modest results were achieved, and most schemes were set up in the suburbs where the proportion of churchgoers was high, rather than in the inner and middle rings where social needs were greater. Moreover, the churches' initiative did not significantly extend the statutory authorities' awareness of the true nature of social needs, as had originally been hoped.

---

[1] See Rogers, p. 217.

[2] See below, pp. 365 ff.

[3] *Responsibility in the Welfare State?: A Study of Relationships between the Social Services and the Churches in a City Suburb* (1961). The survey area was Longbridge.

[4] See e.g. K. A. Busia, *Urban Churches in Britain* (1966), pp. 87–8.

[5] See e.g. *Christian Aid News*, no. 2, June 1969.

Young people

The growing weakness of the Protestant churches greatly reduced their contact with, and influence on, young people in the city. It was estimated in 1950 that the churches were in effective and regular contact with only one-quarter of Birmingham's young people,[1] and although they later tried hard to improve their youth organization, this proportion had almost certainly sunk even lower by the end of the 1960s. Consequently, the organization of youth leisure-time activities became increasingly the responsibility of secular bodies.

Although the City Council had taken positive steps to help young people find employment since before the First World War,[2] the need to provide more than a school education and work for them did not become obvious until the 1930s. During that decade many school leavers were unable to find work, and spent most of the day on the street. The teenage gang became a common phenomenon, and aroused public concern. By 1939, however, youth activities had been greatly extended by the churches and other organizations. Scout and guide groups were expanded, and the number of boys' clubs rose to nearly one hundred.[3] So a firm basis already existed for the great expansion of youth activities which took place during the war. Most of the boys' clubs decided to carry on in wartime, and the churches concentrated on the needs of young people,[4] partly because of the decimation of their adult membership. From 1939 the Board of Education began to urge all local authorities to form youth committees, and Birmingham did so in 1940 by expanding and renaming its Juvenile Organizations Committee, which dated from 1918. Nevertheless, the City Council was unwilling to restrict the role of the voluntary bodies, and so it set up a youth council to coordinate their work with that of the Education Committee.[5] So Birmingham was well prepared to implement the Registration of Boys and Girls Order, 1941, which required every boy and girl of sixteen years of age to join a youth organization. Many young people who were not in contact with existing organizations like the scouts were catered for by the formation in 1941 of a Youth Service Corps. This was organized partly by official and partly by voluntary initiative, and by 1942 some sixty units, containing 2,500 young people, were in operation.[6] More flexible groups were set up for young people in the poorer districts of the city, who were often unwilling to cooperate in a highly organized body. One of the most successful was the Sher-

[1] Bryan H. Reed, *Eighty Thousand Adolescents* (1950), p. 42.
[2] See Briggs, p. 245.
[3] *B.M.*, 28 October 1939.
[4] *B.P.*, 14 September 1939.
[5] Black, p. 320; B.C.C., *Pro.*, 10 October 1944, pp. 532–41.
[6] Black, p. 322.

bourne Road Centre, Balsall Heath, which opened in May 1941.[1]

The success of the wartime youth movement made it appear essential to the Government, the City Council, and local bodies that a high level of youth organization be maintained after the war.[2] However, the level of activity inevitably dropped when wartime compulsion was abandoned. One of the biggest casualties, perhaps not surprisingly, was the Youth Service Corps, which had only two units in 1950, compared to sixty-one at the end of the war.[3] By 1949, it was estimated that nearly half the city's young people were attached neither to a youth organization nor to an evening institute.[4] The City Council nevertheless maintained its policy of encouraging voluntary organizations to provide for youth, rather than initiating extensive youth work of its own. This attitude was welcomed by the voluntary organizations,[5] and the Corporation showed itself eager to help whenever it could, for instance by making buildings such as civic restaurants available for use as youth centres.[6] As time went on, more and more boys' clubs were replaced by youth clubs which both boys and girls could join. Some of them were run by the larger Birmingham firms, such as I.C.I. Metals Division.[7]

Despite all these efforts, the youth organizations faced increasing difficulties, especially as the choice of commercial leisure-time activities widened in the 1950s. In the late 1940s it was estimated that unattached boys and girls spent about three evenings at home each week, with a further one or two evenings spent at the cinema.[8] The boredom of those evenings at home may well have forced many to join an organization. But after 1950 television was there to entertain them, and when industrial prosperity allowed them to earn high wages, a large number of coffee bars, clubs, and bars sprang up to cater for them. In the later 1940s very few young people frequented public houses,[9] but by the end of the following decade many pubs and bars in the city centre and in the suburbs catered almost exclusively for young people between the ages of about sixteen and twenty-five. Young people also devoted an increasing amount of their time from the later 1950s to the pursuit of

[1] *Youth in a City: An Account of an Experiment of Youth Service in its Initial Stages* (Board of Education Pamphlets no. 117, 1943).

[2] See e.g. Birmingham Youth Committee, *Handbook for Youth Leaders* (1945), p. iii (B.R.L. 568785).

[3] *Eighty Thousand Adolescents*, p. 90; B.C.C., *Pro.*, 7 October 1943, p. 538 (Education Committee).

[4] *Eighty Thousand Adolescents*, p. 67.

[5] This attitude, however, sometimes gave the impression that Birmingham City Council was not interested in youth. Denis Howell, for instance, complained in 1962 that the Birmingham youth service was the worst in Britain (*Birmingham Journal*, May 1962, p. 11).

[6] See e.g. *Y.B.*, no. 4, February 1947, p. 1.

[7] I.C.I. Ltd. (Metals Div.), *Apprenticeship Training in the Engineering and Building Trades* (1950), p. 15 (B.R.L. 610921).

[8] *Eighty Thousand Adolescents*, p. 129.   [9] Ibid., p. 47.

popular music, which eventually spread out of the clubs and dance halls into many of the public houses, thus strengthening their hold on the young. Young people also became more mobile as they acquired scooters, motorcycles, and cars, and by the late 1950s they were very willing to seek their entertainment in the city centre,[1] which was now attracting fewer of Birmingham's older citizens owing to the shift of population to the suburbs.

By now the Corporation was not providing much help to voluntary youth organizations. When the Education Committee's budget began to come under heavy pressure in the late 1950s, youth service expenditure was one of the easiest items to cut back. In 1958 a Ministry of Education report criticized the City's inadequate efforts to provide and assist youth clubs, and pointed to the serious understaffing of the youth service. The Education Committee was stung into action, and prepared an ambitious development scheme, including the appointment of a senior man as youth officer, and the provision of four municipal youth centres. But, although they accepted an increased financial contribution from the City Council, the Birmingham Association of Youth Clubs and the Birmingham Federation of Boys' Clubs attacked the Corporation's practical proposals as 'empire-building', and in the end they were dropped.[2] After this rebuff the Council lost a lot of its interest, and when the education budget came under even greater pressure after 1958 owing to the effects of the block grant, youth expenditure suffered badly.

With their limited financial resources, the youth organizations found it very hard to compete with the growing range of commercial attractions. Many church youth clubs were restricted to those who attended the churches that ran them;[3] others lost members because they maintained single-sex operation. Because young people were particularly dissatisfied with youth facilities in the suburbs, plans were made to create special accommodation in the city centre, like the abortive Shantasea complex planned for Smallbrook Ringway in the mid-1960s.[4] By 1970 none of these plans had been realized. Very successful, on the other hand, was the Midland Arts Centre for Young People, promoted by the City Council in Cannon Hill Park in the later 1960s. Other organizations flourished because they appealed to well-defined groups of young people and so could provide exactly the right

[1] See especially Fred Milson, *Youth at the Centre* (1965), B.R.L. 752753.

[2] Birmingham Association of Youth Clubs, *Report of the Development and Ideas Committee 1962*, p. 7.

[3] In 1962, twenty-seven of the eighty-one clubs affiliated to the Birmingham Association of Youth Clubs were church clubs. Their membership tended to fall as church attendance declined in the 1960s (*Report of the Development and Ideas Committee 1962*, p. 6).

[4] See Milson, *Youth at the Centre*, p. 2.

activities. One such club was the nationally famous Double Zero Club, founded by a young Anglican priest, the Revd. David Collyer (the 'Ton-Up Vicar'), for leather-jacketed motorbike riders.

Nevertheless, by the end of the 1960s that era in youth organization which had begun between the wars, when it was thought necessary to provide separate facilities for young people, was almost over. Earlier puberty and the greater independence and self-confidence brought by high wages were now allowing young people to spend their time in much the same way and in the same places as adults (until the adults moved elsewhere!). This trend was an unfortunate one for the voluntary youth organizations, which lost members.[1] On the other hand, it allowed the city centre to regain from the late 1950s its pre-war position as an entertainment focus, and it contributed substantially to the general increase in the number of places of entertainment, both public and private, in Birmingham from about 1958. There were signs, on the other hand, that the increase in juvenile crime was partly linked to the declining influence of youth organizations on young people.[2]

Crime

It would be rash to associate the increase in crime solely with the declining moral influence of the churches and the greater freedom enjoyed by young people. Serious crimes were always the work of just a tiny minority of the population of Birmingham. But it was a growing and/or a more active minority.

To provide a full account and analysis of changing crime patterns in Birmingham since 1939, and of their relation to crime prevention measures, is outside the scope of this volume. In the first place, the study of local variations in crime is handicapped by the varying practices of police forces in recording offences. Even in the late 1960s there were signs that Home Office attempts to standardize procedure had not been fully successful;[3] before the war, and even for some years after it, there was so much variation from force to force that comparative statistics often meant very little. Only in the later 1960s did it become possible to carry out meaningful comparative studies of regional or local crime rates. A further difficulty is raised by the lack of

[1] A survey carried out in about 1960 suggested that less than one-quarter of young people in Birmingham were attending clubs or other organizations (*Responsibility in the Welfare State* (1961), p. 41). Fred Milson suggested in 1965 that the youth organizations' claim to be in touch with one-third of all young people might well be a serious over-estimate (*Youth at the Centre*, p. 6).

[2] See *Chief Constable's Report*, 1958, p. 86. In that year the Lord Mayor promoted an inquiry into juvenile crime, and the Chief Constable called for more youth clubs.

[3] F. H. McClintock and N. Howard Avison, *Crime in England and Wales* (1965), p. 82. See also John R. Lambert, *Crime, Police and Race Relations: A Study in Birmingham* (1970).

information on changes in rates of crime over time in different districts within Birmingham. Recent work suggests that Birmingham corresponds to the pattern of other large cities, with a central 'criminal area' containing a high proportion of economically deprived people of low social class, and with a decrease in the incidence of crime outward towards the periphery.[1] But information is not available to establish changes in the character and extent of this 'criminal area' since 1939. These difficulties, finally, rule out any attempt to correlate changes in crime patterns with the evolution of Birmingham's social structure and living standards. Nevertheless, crime and efforts to control it are an important feature of the life of any city, and some account of them is needed here.

Before 1939 Birmingham was fortunate to have, so far as one may accurately judge, a lower incidence of crime than most big cities, and an efficient and well-manned police force.[2] Nevertheless, there was a rapid increase in the amount of crime in the late 1930s. The number of indictable offences known to the police rose from 5,006 in 1936 to 7,819 in 1939—an increase of well over half. It was partly to meet this challenge that the male establishment of the police force, which had not been changed since 1921, was raised from 1,587 to 1,887 in 1936. Over half of this extra strength had been recruited by the time war broke out, but meanwhile civil defence duties had placed a further load on the shoulders of the police.[3] When war broke out, the force was greatly reduced in strength, mainly as a result of national service. Fortunately, the police were able to call on the services of large numbers of special constables and other auxiliaries, so that the efficiency of the Birmingham force was not threatened. After the war, however, most of the auxiliaries and some of the regular officers left the force as soon as the revocation of wartime regulations allowed them to do so, and the maintenance of adequate numbers came to depend on the recruitment of new regular officers and the return of those who had been serving in the armed forces. But neither of these sources produced enough men.

During the war the incidence of crime in Birmingham continued the rapid upward trend of the late 1930s. The rise was particularly marked during the first three years of hostilities, and was almost entirely the result of an increase in the number of offences against property. It seemed likely that easy access to premises owing to damage, the blackout, the absence of many occupants, and the extra difficulties faced by the police in carrying out their duties, were largely to blame for this

[1] Lambert, *Crime, Police and Race Relations*, pp. 91–130, 281–91.

[2] Black, pp. 404–7; *Reports of the Police Establishment and the State of Crime in the City of Birmingham (Chief Constable's Reports)*. There were some indications that cities with high unemployment had the most crime during the 1930s (Hermann Mannheim, *Social Aspects of Crime in England between the Wars* (1940), pp. 139–40).

[3] Black, pp. 37–8.

increase.[1] There was also a big rise in the number of offences committed by juveniles, owing largely to lack of supervision and boredom.[2] Vandalism became very frequent. By the end of the war the juvenile problem had been partially solved by the provision of more youth activities, but the only possible solution to the adult crime problem seemed to be more efficient operation by the depleted police force. One of the biggest innovations was the introduction of short-wave radio into police operations, and the establishment of an embryo '999' system. This important step forward was a direct result of the war, which established an absolute necessity for quick communication between police cars and their headquarters. The first experiments were carried out in 1938 and 1939, and the full system was established on a permanent basis in the autumn of 1942. At this time the Birmingham force was well ahead of the rest of the country both in its wireless arrangements and in the facilities afforded to the general public.[3] The national '999' scheme, set up in 1946, was largely based on the Birmingham example. And the Birmingham force was always to maintain its position as one of the most technologically advanced in the country.

After the war the Birmingham crime rate remained at the high level which had been reached by 1942, but although there was a sharp increase in 1948, the general upward trend was only slight until the early 1950s. The incidence of crime remained less than in most large cities and many smaller towns. The Birmingham public were extremely cooperative and helpful to the police, and the Chief Constable maintained that the state of crime in the city was no cause for alarm, despite the big increase in offences since the 1930s.[4] This state of affairs made the force's recruitment difficulties a little too easy to ignore. Before the war, men had been attracted to the force in sufficient numbers in Birmingham because it offered secure employment and often permanent accommodation. But after 1945 full employment and the high wages paid in Birmingham's booming industries made police service less attractive, and not enough police houses were available even for the few new recruits attracted into the force, most of whom came from outside the city. The Watch Committee was able to obtain a substantial allocation of the new houses built by the Corporation,[5] but

[1] However, the number of crimes, including breakings, actually *fell* during the first weeks of the blackout (*B.P.*, 27 September 1939). For the encouraging effect of blackout conditions on crime see Hermann Mannheim, *War and Crime* (1941), pp. 130–3.

[2] See e.g. *Chief Constable's Report*, 1941, p. 7. See also *Youth in a City: An Account of an Experiment of Youth Service in its Initial Stages* (Board of Education Educational Pamphlets, no. 117, 1943), pp. 1–2. Investigations carried out in Birmingham and other cities suggested that the wartime employment of youths at high wages was not responsible for the increase in delinquency. See H. M. D. Parker, *Manpower: a Study of War-time Policy and Administration* (1957), p. 363.

[3] Black, pp. 41, 407; B.C.C., *Pro.*, 1 December 1942, pp. 40–1 (Watch Committee).

[4] *Chief Constable's Report*, 1945, p. 2.   [5] Ibid., 1946, p. 17.

the pay problem was more intractable. Birmingham was allowed to pay only the nationally agreed rate for police officers, a problem which was almost exactly the same as that faced by the Education Committee in recruiting teachers. However, from the late 1940s national pay awards brought about an improvement, though a short-lived one, in recruiting,[1] and from 1953 until 1955 the crime rate, which had been increasing slowly, suddenly dropped. The outlook was certainly bright in the mid-1950s. Birmingham's crime rate in 1955, at 1,043 per 100,000 population, was only slightly above the national average of 966, and was greatly exceeded by Liverpool, Manchester, Hull, and Coventry among the big cities. Only Bristol, with 777, had a crime rate substantially lower than Birmingham.[2]

This happy situation began to alter radically from the late 1950s. The Birmingham crime rate, after stabilizing in 1955, began to increase again from 1956, at a time when the strength of the force was starting to fall. Juvenile crime became especially serious, so much so that the Lord Mayor promoted an inquiry into the whole problem in 1958, and the Chief Constable called for more youth clubs and facilities.[3] Although the recruiting position improved slightly, it proved impossible to do more than maintain the existing size of the force, and by the end of the decade there were signs that the crime wave was getting out of hand. The detection rate, which had amounted to nearly half of all indictable offences in the mid-1950s, fell steadily from then on.[4] The courts became so overcrowded that the period between committal and trial lengthened appreciably, and because the justices were unwilling to remand untried people in custody for long periods, they allowed bail to many criminals who committed new offences while awaiting trial.[5] By 1960 the rate of indictable offences was twice as high as in 1955, and Birmingham was now as crime-prone as Manchester and Liverpool. The increase in crime continued, with only minor interruptions, during the 1960s, while the detection rate further deteriorated. In 1965 only 33 per cent of Birmingham's indictable crimes were cleared up—less than in any other British city.[6] And although Birmingham still saw fewer crimes per head of population than most large cities, it had caught up substantially on them since 1955, with a percentage increase

[1] In 1951–3 the Birmingham force's average daily strength in relation to population was lower than the county borough average, and lower than any other big city except Sheffield (D. S. Lees, et al., Local Expenditure and Exchequer Grants (1956), table 96).
[2] McClintock and Avison, Crime, p. 292.
[3] Chief Constable's Report, 1958, p. 6; Lord Mayor's Parlour, 'Enquiry into juvenile crime' (1958). The main conclusion of this investigation was that the development of youth organizations could do much to reduce juvenile crime.
[4] McClintock and Avison, Crime, p. 298; Chief Constable's Reports.
[5] Chief Constable's Report, 1960, pp. 58–9.
[6] McClintock and Avison, Crime, p. 298.

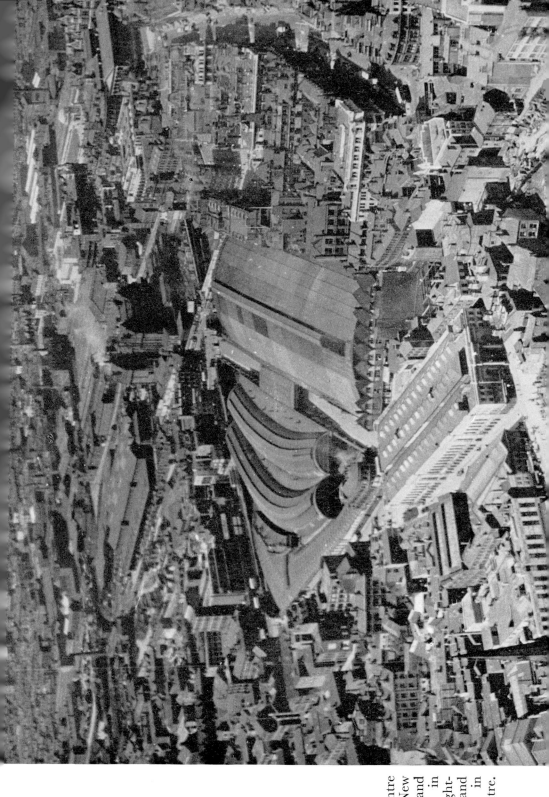

The changing centre of Birmingham. New Street Station and its surroundings in 1933. Note how tightly factories and workshops hem in the shopping centre.

The changing centre of Birmingham. New Street Station and its surroundings in 1969.

The inner ring road, entering the picture at the bottom right, snakes between the Rotunda and the Bull Ring Centre, past the partly rebuilt New Street Station, and on through Smallbrook Ringway past the Albany hotel. A sharp right turn at the roundabout takes it up the hill to the civic centre site, a wilderness of car parks and road-works, to the right of which stand the Town Hall and the Council House. Visible in the top right is the G.P.O. tower, which stands close to the northern section of the inner ring road, not visible in this picture. The main shopping district occupies the right-hand side of the view, between the Rotunda and the G.P.O. tower.

higher than any big city except Leeds and Nottingham, both of which
had also once been areas with relatively low crime rates.

It would be misleading to suggest that the undermanning of the
police force[1] was responsible for the increase in crime, but the low
detection rate, which was partly the result of the manpower shortage,
probably made Birmingham criminals more confident and ambitious.
Pay restrictions still hampered the Watch Committee's efforts to
recruit more men. As late as 1968 the Home Secretary was still turning
down Birmingham's requests for permission to pay an undermanning
allowance.[2] Yet an important by-product of this difficulty was that the
Birmingham force was encouraged to maintain its technical lead over
most other forces.[3] The most important innovation was the introduction
of a system of 'unit policing', using small cars to replace the policeman's
regular beat, from about 1964. The whole city was covered by this
system by 1967. The decreasing number of men engaged in foot duties
were all equipped with personal radio sets by the last years of the decade.
Unnecessary duties, such as control of parking, were handed over to
auxiliaries from the early 1960s, and by the end of the decade traffic
wardens were active throughout almost the whole city. Sophisticated
methods of traffic control were introduced to cut down point duty to a
minimum, and manual direction of traffic was rarely seen, even at the
inconvenient temporary junctions which were often set up at Birmingham's many road improvement schemes. Another step forward was in
the direction of regional cooperation. During the war the Watch
Committee strongly and successfully resisted the Home Office's somewhat half-hearted attempts to amalgamate the Birmingham force with
those of nearby county boroughs,[4] but after 1945 practical links with
other forces in the West Midlands were built up steadily. From the
mid-1950s the Birmingham and regional crime squads were developed
into a key weapon in the struggle against crime, and by the end of the
decade they had taken over a significant proportion of detection work
in the city.[5]

Nevertheless, despite this progress in techniques, it is clear that the
crime wave which set in from the mid-1950s placed a severe strain on
the Birmingham police force. The causes of this big growth in crime
cannot be discussed adequately here. The big rise in juvenile crime was
nation-wide. The increase in property offences was to be expected in
such a prosperous place as Birmingham; there simply happened to be
more stealable material lying around, and car thefts, for instance,

[1] See Institute of Municipal Treasurers, *Police Force Statistics* (annual).
[2] *Chief Constable's Report*, 1968, p. 9.
[3] For a general account of technical advances in police work after 1945, see T. A.
Critchley, *A History of Police in England and Wales 1900–1966* (1967), pp. 255–8.
[4] B.C.C., *Pro.*, 1 December 1942, p. 40 (Watch Committee).
[5] *Chief Constable's Report*, 1959, p. 67.

T

formed one of the fastest growing categories of crime. Prosperity and the growth of new forms of entertainment encouraged people to leave their homes more often in what had once been a stay-at-home, early-to-bed city. More people went away on holiday, and stayed away longer. Violent crimes, which had never been a feature of Birmingham, remained relatively few in number; in 1965 only Bristol and Sheffield had less violence among the big cities.[1] Many local people blamed coloured immigration for the crime increase but the Chief Constable denied this suggestion: 'The general standard of conduct of the very large coloured population in the city is highly commendable and causes the police very little concern.'[2] And recent research suggests that the coloured population continues to be more law-abiding than the non-coloured residents of areas favoured by immigrants.[3] Indeed, the Chief Constable was inclined to put the blame for a high proportion of offences, and especially of the more serious crimes, on people who had come to Birmingham to find work from other parts of the British Isles.[4] Although this contention is difficult to prove, there were certainly indications that, although the coloured immigrants committed relatively few crimes, much of the city's law-breaking was generated in the deteriorating areas occupied by a high proportion of newcomers to the city.

Sport and recreation

One of the biggest social defects of the deteriorating areas in the inner and middle rings was their shortage of open space and sports facilities. But this shortage reflected a more general under-provision in the city as a whole, which constituted a serious handicap to one of the most important of social activities, amateur sport.

Although Birmingham had become an important centre of amateur sport and physical education in the second half of the nineteenth century,[5] its sporting facilities were clearly inadequate in 1939. The movement of population to the suburbs, with their extensive open spaces, was slowly overcoming the problem, and industrial firms were very active in providing sports grounds. But there was still a severe

[1] McClintock and Avison, *Crime*, p. 84.

[2] *Chief Constable's Report*, 1958, p. 12.

[3] John Lenton, Nicholas Budgen, Kenneth Clarke, *Immigration, Race and Politics: a Birmingham View* (1966), p. 33; Nicholas Deakin, etc., *Colour, Citizenship and British Society* (1970), pp. 284–5; Lambert, *Crime, Police and Race Relations*; A. E. Bottoms, 'Delinquency among immigrants', *Race*, vol. viii, no. 4, 1967, pp. 359–83.

[4] *Chief Constable's Report*, 1958, p. 12. The Chief Constable diplomatically left his readers to decide from which part of the British Isles these newcomers might have originated; few in Birmingham would have been in much doubt at the time about what he meant.

[5] See e.g. Peter G. McIntosh, *Physical Education in England Since 1800* (2nd ed., 1968).

shortage of buildings for indoor sport, which were an important requirement in a city afflicted by a wet and windy climate. Many sports clubs were handicapped by the siting of their grounds on the city outskirts, distant from the homes of many of their members.[1] School playing fields, too, were concentrated in the suburbs, greatly limiting their use by the central schools. They were also recognized as inadequate in area. In these circumstances, it is not surprising that minority-interest sports such as tennis and squash were very badly catered for. However, some of the bigger sports clubs, such as the Bournville Athletic Club, had done much to incorporate minority interests in their activities by the 1930s. At Bournville, tennis, golf, squash, and badminton, all of which had been exclusive to the middle classes before 1914, were introduced or greatly developed between 1918 and 1939, during which time the membership of the club (which was not restricted to employees) doubled.[2]

The major effect of the Second World War was to weaken amateur team sports, because the age-group which provided the backbone of most teams became the main source of personnel for the Forces. Rugby was worse affected than most sports. Shortly after the outbreak of war all rugby matches were cancelled, and although they were resumed later on a scratch basis, many rugby clubs closed down for the duration of the war.[3] Soccer clubs were normally able to carry on, because the game's great popularity ensured that there was always a large reserve of potential players, but both teams and fixture lists were sadly depleted.[4] On the other hand, the increased demand for social contact during the war led to great extension of the social activities—such as dances, parties, and outings—organized by the sports clubs. This development, which continued for a time after the war, strengthened the interest of women in the life of the clubs.[5] The working of long hours of overtime created a demand for greater availability of sporting facilities on Sundays, and the Corporation withdrew its ban on organized Sunday-afternoon games in its parks in 1940. This new freedom was maintained after the war.[6]

The first years of peace saw a big growth in demand for sporting

[1] Sir Patrick Abercrombie and Herbert Jackson, *West Midlands Plan* (1948), III.20.21.

[2] *1896 and All That: Fifty Years of the Bournville Athletic Club 1896–1946* (1946), pp. 1–19 (B.R.L. 576158).

[3] Gerald Holmes, *Midland Rugby Football* (1950), p. 41; B. M. Bowker, *Sixty Years of Old Boys' Rugger: A History of Camp Hill Old Edwardians Rugby Football Club 1893–1953* (1953), pp. 25–6.

[4] *1896 and All That*, p. 19; *The Birmingham and District Works Amateur Football Association: Golden Jubilee Souvenir, 1905–1955* (1955), pp. 11–13 (B.R.L. 660209).

[5] See e.g. J. Elliott Ewing (ed.), *Pickwick Athletic Club, 1858–1958: Centenary Year Handbook* (1958), p. 101 (B.R.L. 661105).

[6] Black, p. 469.

facilities, which was encouraged by the Corporation. New clubs were founded, and in some cases inter-club organization was strengthened, often on a regional basis. For instance, in 1947 the Midland Club Cricket Conference was set up to coordinate all the main cricket clubs and cricket-playing schools, and the Warwickshire Table Tennis Association was founded. It was also in 1947 that the *Evening Despatch* sponsored the establishment of the Midland Cricket Federation, which was designed to coordinate the existing leagues on the lines of the well-known Yorkshire Federation. At that time Birmingham had seven major leagues and associations, several of which were composed of works teams.[1] Association football, on the other hand, was weakened to some extent by the effects of a slight decline of works football which occurred just before the war. The peak total of 205 clubs and 278 teams reached in the later 1930s by the Birmingham and District Works Amateur Football Association was never attained again, even in the late 1940s.[2] And although membership of all the city's sports clubs was certainly larger after the war than ever before, it nevertheless included only a small minority of the population, estimated at less than 5 per cent.[3]

Although the demand for sporting facilities continued to grow in the 1950s, team sports began to decline in relative popularity. This trend was caused partly by the factors which, as we have seen, restricted most other group activities from the early 1950s. But sports were particularly affected by pressure on reserves of building land, which led to the sale of a number of factory sports fields for housing. Other sports grounds were swallowed up by factory extensions. So after the membership of the Birmingham and District Works Amateur Football Association had reached a post-war peak of 173 clubs and 250 teams in 1951/2, a decline set in. By 1955/6 there were only 161 clubs and 235 teams, and the number of divisions had been reduced from twenty-one to nineteen.[4] The slow decline was not halted in the following decade; in 1967/8 the Association grouped no more than 187 teams in sixteen divisions.[5] Non-works amateur football also declined slightly in the 1950s, but it expanded to new heights in the following decade after the Football Association at last recognized Sunday football in 1960.[6] Until then Sunday football had been frowned on in Birmingham, although there had been for many years a flourishing organization called the Birmingham Monday League Sunday Section, which grouped seventy-eight teams in 1950/1. With the formation of new Sunday leagues, such as

[1] *Sports Argus Cricket Annual*, 1949, pp. 24, 27.
[2] *Birmingham and District Works A.F.A.*, p. 66.
[3] Norman Tiptaft, *So this is Birmingham* (1947), p. 97.
[4] *Birmingham and District Works A.F.A.*, p. 66.
[5] Birmingham and District Works Amateur Football Association, *Official Handbook*.
[6] P. G. McIntosh, *Sport in Society* (1968), p. 102.

the Birmingham Sunday Alliance, and the North Birmingham Sunday League, in the 1960s, the total of football teams playing in the city had reached some 1,075 in 1966/7 compared to only 842 in 1950/1.[1] The membership of older leagues also began to increase from the early 1960s, partly as a result of the switching of some fixtures to Sundays. The increase in the number of youth teams was especially marked, and as time went on the numbers of suburban teams grew while those from the central districts declined. Most of the games in these minor competitions were played on public pitches, and the flourishing condition of football in the 1960s clearly reflected the greater accessibility of parks and recreation grounds now that a high proportion of the population lived in the outer districts. The expansion of the Sunday game allowed many players to turn out for two or even more teams over the weekend, or to support a professional club on Saturday afternoons without forfeiting the chance of playing themselves. So both professional and amateur football in Birmingham benefited from the growth of Sunday play.

Other team sports were less able to benefit from a switch to Sunday fixtures. Cricket had always been played to a large extent on Sunday in any case; rugby and hockey remained faithful to Saturday in deference to the wishes of players and organizers. Certainly, as time went on, more cricket was played on Sundays and less on Saturdays, but this trend did not prevent a fall in the popularity of cricket; in 1956 only 215 adult cricket teams were playing in the city, compared to 291 in 1949.[2] Interest in hockey fluctuated greatly, without a clear trend towards growth.[3] Rugby remained a relatively unpopular game, largely because it was hardly played at all in Birmingham schools outside the King Edward grammar schools. In 1945 two Birmingham schoolmasters began a scheme to encourage elementary schoolboys to take up the game, and although it was deemed a success,[4] it did not make the game substantially more popular in the city in the long run. In 1966 there were still no more than twenty-five rugby clubs in Birmingham, eight of which were Old Boys' organizations. Only five industrial concerns had rugby clubs.[5] Yet, because so large a centre of population as Birmingham was bound to house some players of high quality, many of them originating from more rugby-minded parts of the country, some of the Birmingham clubs maintained a very high standard. The Moseley and Birmingham clubs, in particular, enjoyed national renown. It was for the same reason that Birmingham, though short of

[1] *Sports Argus Football Annual*; South Birmingham Amateur Football League and Combination, *Official Handbook*.
[2] *Sports Argus Cricket Annual*.
[3] J. Elliott Ewing, *Pickwick Athletic Club*, p. 77.
[4] Gerald Holmes, *Midland Rugby Football*, p. 44.
[5] *Midland Counties Rugby Football Handbook*.

athletics tracks and active participants, was able to maintain at least one famous athletic club, the Birchfield Harriers. Like Moseley rugby club, the Harriers were able to maintain the city's reputation in a sporting activity in which the vast majority of citizens showed little interest or desire to participate.

The growth of amateur football as more and more people moved to the suburbs helped to confirm that shortage of recreational facilities had greatly restricted sporting activities in the older areas of the city. The area available for team sports was sharply reduced during the war because many parks and recreation grounds were used to grow food. Parts of others were used for prefabricated emergency housing in the early years after the war. When peace came it took several years to restore the cultivated areas to full recreational use. Grassing-down had been completed by the late 1940s, but the turf needed some time to become firm enough for sport. Consequently, even as late as 1950 the Corporation had considerably fewer football and cricket pitches available than before the war,[1] and in that year the City Council passed a Labour amendment calling attention to the city's inadequate sports facilities.[2] But improvement was already under way as the turf matured, and the area available for recreation increased greatly in the early 1950s. The Corporation was slow to lay out new public recreation grounds until the later 1950s,[3] but in the following decade well over twenty new grounds were opened, mostly on new housing estates. Inevitably, the inner areas of the city were still somewhat short of recreational space, but the Parks Department made the fullest use of the area available by encouraging teams to play on suburban pitches so that the parks could be freed for more general recreation. The popularity of some sports declined after the war, allowing a reduction in provision. The number of cricket pitches maintained by the Corporation was thus reduced by 40 per cent between 1951 and 1968, and there were only 246 municipal tennis courts in this latter year, compared to 425 before the war. These reductions allowed the Parks Department to make provision for minority sports within its existing recreation areas, and facilities for athletics, Gaelic football, baseball, netball, and volleyball were greatly extended between 1945 and 1970. Demand for some minority sports, such as hockey, fluctuated during the period, and in such cases the Parks Department tried to be flexible. The department made spectacular provision for the soaring popularity of golf, and by 1970 had opened seven full-size municipal golf courses and twenty-two putting greens. This magnificent achievement far

---

[1] Black, pp. 469–70.

[2] B.C.C., *Pro.*, 4 April 1950, p. 1295 (Parks Committee).

[3] Birmingham's first new public recreation ground since the war was opened early in 1959 (*Y.B.*, no. 137, February 1959, p. 3).

outshone the efforts of most other industrial cities in providing for golf. The Corporation made little or no provision for those growing minority sports, such as squash, which required expensive indoor installations, but private clubs and firms met some of this need.

The increase in the popularity of golf was so rapid that by 1970-1 as many Birmingham citizens were playing golf on municipal courses as were playing football on municipal pitches.[1] Nevertheless, the increasing popularity of parks football after the war, as Sunday play became more common and works soccer declined, put growing pressure on the municipal pitches. In the 1960s they were being used to capacity at weekends, and many pitches were also played on several times during the week. Wear was a major problem, and playing areas often had to be restricted in order to allow the turf to recover. This factor was partly responsible for a fall in the number of municipal pitches from a post-war peak of 158 in 1951 to 145 in 1970. Certainly, the available pitches were being used much more intensively in the later 1960s than in the early years after the war, but the Parks Department recognized that more football space was needed, and hoped to be able to provide it during the 1970s.

One obstacle to the provision of extra public recreational space was the priority accorded by the City Council to extending the area of school playing fields. The Education Department went to great lengths, including acquiring land outside the city boundaries, and leasing parts of the Birmingham Racecourse.[2] But the overall shortage remained. In 1954 the Education Officer admitted that the city had only about 35 per cent of the school playing fields that it needed, compared to 25 per cent before the war.[3] A year later, the Trades Council passed a motion calling attention to the inadequacy of school playing fields in north Birmingham as 'a failure on the part of local administration'.[4] The Education Department did its best by transporting children over long distances to play games, and by making sports grounds serve for a variety of activities. But such expedients and palliatives could not provide a satisfying solution, and school sporting facilities remained substantially less than the Education Department's requirements in 1970.

Of course, the shortage of traditional recreational facilities did not

[1] In 1970-1, 321,489 daily round tickets were issued for the seven municipal courses, while 14,627 games of football were played on 145 municipal pitches. Assuming that all the matches were played by full sides, 321,794 individuals were involved, not counting match officials (information supplied by Parks Department).

[2] City of Birmingham, *Development Plan for Primary and Secondary Education* (1953), vol. i, pp. 4205-8; 'Racecourse as playing fields: successful enterprise of Wolverhampton and Birmingham', *Municipal Review*, May 1963, pp. 310-11.

[3] *B.P.*, 29 March 1954.

[4] Birmingham Trades Council, *Annual Report*, 1955/6, p. 15.

greatly affect the minority-interest sports which grew greatly in popularity after the war. Many of them, like judo and basketball, were carried on indoors, and their growth was made possible by the increase in the number of multi-purpose halls attached to new schools, churches, and institutes of further education. In view of the uncertainty of the Birmingham climate, indoor sports were bound to become popular once the premises were available for them. The number of badminton clubs, for instance, climbed from only two in 1950 to twenty-one in 1967.[1] Judo clubs had risen from none to twelve in the Birmingham area between 1945 and 1957,[2] and their number subsequently increased, with the addition of at least one karate club by the late 1960s. But table tennis remained by far the most popular of the Birmingham indoor games, with 300 clubs and 9,000 registered players in 1957.[3]

The Corporation played only an indirect role in encouraging these indoor sports. Apart from extensions to the premises of the Birmingham Athletic Institute, the City Council provided few purpose-built sports buildings. In 1970 Birmingham's only complete sports centre, containing a wide variety of facilities, was on the campus of Birmingham University, financed by Government money. This situation was not peculiar to Birmingham, however; other local authorities had done just as little.[4] Even swimming baths hardly increased in number in Birmingham, although they were substantially improved. Attendances at swimming baths fell during the war years owing mainly to the closure of a number of baths, but after 1945 they increased far above pre-war figures, thanks partly to the generalization of mixed bathing during the war, and the introduction of café facilities at some establishments. Greater use was made of them, too, by schools after the war. Growing demand for swimming during the winter months led to the abandonment at most baths of the pre-war practice of flooring them over in winter to allow for dances and entertainments.[5] But it proved impossible to fulfil the Baths Committee's wartime dream of providing one swimming bath for every 25,000 inhabitants, compared to one to every 60,000 before the war, even though the City Council approved the scheme in principle.[6] In the early years after the war priority had to be given to the provision of new washing baths, demand for which had increased during the war, and remained high into the 1950s. By 1954 it was reported that swimming facilities were being over-taxed in the summer months.[7] An ambitious new swimming bath at Stechford

[1] *Birmingham Post Year Book and Who's Who.*

[2] Central Council of Physical Recreation, West Midlands Region, *A Sporting Chance; Warwickshire* (1957), p. 38.

[3] *A Sporting Chance*, p. 49.

[4] See Wolfenden Committee on Sport, *Sport and the Community* (1960), pp. 36–40.

[5] Black, pp. 450–2.   [6] B.C.C., *Pro.*, 6 April 1943, pp. 336–40.

[7] *Y.B.*, no. 89, September–October 1954, p. 3.

was approved in principle in 1955, but its construction was long postponed owing to Government restrictions on capital expenditure, and it
was not opened until June 1962. In 1969 the total of swimming baths
open in Birmingham—eighteen—was only one higher than it had been
twenty years before. So it is hardly surprising that the rapid increase in
attendances in the early post-war years was not maintained. It did,
however, continue at a less spectacular rate and by 1968 the annual
total of attendances had risen to over three million, more than twice as
many as in the first year after the war. Owing to the failure to build
more than a few baths in the new suburbs, most of the city's swimming
baths were, in 1970, still concentrated in the inner and middle rings.
This at least meant that these areas, so deficient in most amenities, had
adequate provision of one major recreational facility.

The central and middle ring districts also benefited from the growth
of commercial sporting facilities from the late 1950s. Although public
billiard halls almost died out, their number falling from thirty-six in
1939 to only three in 1968, there was a big development of ten-pin
bowling from the late 1950s.[1] These establishments, of which there were
nine in the city by the mid-1960s, were concentrated on the outer
fringes of the middle ring and in the inner suburbs, mostly in converted
cinemas. They expected to prosper from their location in areas which
were short of social and sporting facilities, but where young people
were becoming increasingly affluent. Another commercial enterprise
of this type was the Silver Blades ice rink, which opened in the city
centre in 1964, with ten-pin bowling attached. After a few years
skating proved more durable than bowling, which people found
expensive and somewhat boring. By 1970 the number of bowling
establishments had dwindled to six.

Amateur drama

Amongst the general mediocrity of Birmingham community activity,
amateur dramatics stood out vividly. The amateur theatre had already
been flourishing in the city before the war, and one amateur 'little
theatre' company, the Crescent, performed regularly at its city centre
premises from 1932. Amateur dramatics received a further fillip from
the war. As early as October 1939 representatives of Birmingham
dramatic societies met to discuss what contribution they could make
to the war effort, and they received strong encouragement from the
Ministry of Information, which believed that they could help to raise
public morale.[2] The war encouraged participation in group activities
of all sorts. People became used to working together, and their sense of

[1] City of Birmingham, *Reports of the Licensing Committee of the Justices of the City of
Birmingham*.
[2] *B.P.*, 25 October 1939; *B.M.*, 31 October 1939.

drama was heightened by the war. They wanted exciting things to happen, and after the heaviest air raids had passed, many people sought satisfaction in the drama that they could create for themselves on the amateur stage. So we find the Highbury Little Theatre, Erdington, opening its doors in May 1942, after building work had been carried on by the players themselves since 1937.[1] In the same year the Crescent Theatre, which had been almost defunct during the raids, re-opened as a garrison theatre with special shows for the Forces.[2] Its membership increased so greatly during the war that it had to adopt a new constitution in 1946.[3] Smaller drama societies also flourished, and new ones were founded. In 1943 appeared the Birmingham Community Players, a drama society linked to the Birmingham Council for Community Associations.[4] The following year saw the foundation of the Hall Green Little Theatre Society, which after a few performances in hired premises, decided to build its own theatre.[5]

After the war amateur dramatics grew stronger than ever. Many people found the post-war years an anti-climax, and felt the need for self-expression more strongly than before.[6] The number of active societies increased rapidly.[7] By the end of the decade the total in Birmingham was estimated at between 150 and 200,[8] and it was suggested that some 5,000 people were actually engaged in amateur dramatics in Birmingham and its immediate vicinity.[9] In 1948 the members of the Birmingham Amateur Dramatic Federation set up the Birmingham and District Theatre Guild, which grouped both amateur and professional undertakings, and became the first provincial branch of the British Drama League. By the following year it had a membership of 191 societies and theatres.[10] Also in 1949 the British Theatre Exhibition, which was the first of its kind and the product of national post-war interest in all aspects of the theatre, was held in Birmingham. The little theatres expanded their activities, and in 1948 a new one appeared, the King's Heath Little Theatre, formed by an existing amateur dramatic society, the Curtain Players.[11] In the same year the Crescent Theatre,

[1] *B.P.*, 18 May 1942.

[2] *The Crescent Theatre* (1946), p. 3.

[3] *In the First Quarter: Being the Story of the Crescent Theatre, 1924–1949* (1949), p. 17 (B.R.L. 598840).

[4] Birmingham Council for Community Associations, *Annual Report* (1943), p. 2.

[5] *S.M.*, 10 June 1945.

[6] See, for instance, Hall Green Little Theatre, *Greasepaint and Girders* (1950), p. 4 (B.R.L. 626453).

[7] *B.C.C.*, *Pro.*, 10 October 1950, pp. 342–5 (General Purposes Committee).

[8] *B.G.*, 30 May 1949.

[9] *E.D.*, 30 November 1948. For an example of the ambitious work undertaken by many such societies, see Dunlop Dramatic Society, *Brochure* (1948–9), B.R.L. 640179.

[10] Birmingham and District Theatre Guild, *Annual Report*, 1949.

[11] See King's Heath Little Theatre, Programmes, leaflets, etc., B.R.L. 600181.

recognizing the demand for better training among its members, set up its own school of acting and stagecraft.[1]

Although amateur drama was not short of active participants, it was handicapped by a shortage of suitable premises. Very few societies were brave enough to follow the example of the Hall Green Little Theatre and build their own theatre with their own hands. City-centre accommodation was especially in demand now that the Theatre Guild was creating a more centralized pattern for amateur drama. In 1948, soon after its foundation, the Theatre Guild asked the City Council to provide it with accommodation, and after considering a number of premises the Council decided, in October 1950, to acquire a near-derelict cinema at Gosta Green.[2] But owing to financial and practical difficulties, and its own indecision, the City Council had still not begun the adaptation of the building in 1954, by which time the Theatre Guild had become so impatient that it made a formal complaint.[3] This at least prodded the Council into deciding that the premises were unsuitable for a theatre centre, and that they should be sold to the BBC as a television studio.[4] The Theatre Guild had no choice but to accept, reluctantly, the Council's compensatory offer of the Vestry Hall, Islington Row.[5] After the absolute minimum (£6,000 worth) of work had been carried out, the Vestry Hall opened as the Birmingham theatre centre in November 1957, nine years after the idea was first suggested to the Council.

It would be unfair to place all the blame for this delay on the City Council, whose generous attitude towards existing amateur theatres betokened a genuine interest in drama. The Crescent Theatre was especially favoured. After the theatre had been unable to take up offers of municipal interest-free loans in 1949 and 1954, the City Council leased it a new site and granted an interest-free loan of £25,000 in the early 1960s, when the site of the old building was needed for redevelopment. Building began in 1963, and the new theatre was complete by the summer of the following year. The Hall Green Little Theatre also benefited from two interest-free loans which helped the members to complete their building in 1960.[6]

This crowning achievement of the Hall Green players came at a moment when amateur drama was already feeling the impact of

[1] *In the First Quarter*, p. 15.

[2] B.C.C., *Pro.*, 10 October 1950, pp. 342–5 (General Purposes Committee). The premises were known either as the Delicia Cinema or the Birmingham Stadium. It is difficult to decide which title was the more inappropriate.

[3] *B.M.*, 20 October 1954.

[4] *T.B.*, no. 92, January 1955, p. 2. The Corporation suggested that use of the building for television would be more in the interests of the city.

[5] *E.D.*, 18 November 1954.

[6] See Hall Green Little Theatre, *The First Ten Years* (1960), B.R.L. 661889.

television and other pastimes. Against the brilliant Hall Green success must be set the more modest performance of the nearby King's Heath Little Theatre, which never realized its ambition of building its own premises. The number of societies affiliated to the Theatre Guild began to decline after reaching a peak of 203 in 1950.[1] In 1956 the total of affiliations was as low as 150, and although it subsequently rose slightly, it had again stabilized at about 150 by the later 1960s. Nevertheless, the survival of this very large core of stable societies indicated the continuing strength of amateur drama in Birmingham.

Cultural institutions

The great strength of Birmingham amateur dramatics stemmed partly from its appeal to all social classes, and partly, also, from the even distribution of societies over the whole city. So it is no surprise to find that older cultural institutions, which did not enjoy these advantages, declined after 1945. But it would be too simple to explain their eclipse in terms of the movement of many middle-class people out of the city. Birmingham's proportion of middle-class residents declined only marginally after 1945,[2] and in any case evening access to the city centre for persons travelling by car was probably easier in the late 1960s than it had been twenty years earlier. The explanation lies rather in a declining interest among the Birmingham middle classes in the older, more formal cultural institutions.

The Birmingham and Midland Institute, the city's most important cultural and intellectual institution since its foundation in 1854, was particularly afflicted. It had once had an important educational role, but this function was increasingly restricted as municipal further education expanded. By 1939 it was already predominantly a cultural club, whose premises could also be used by affiliated societies. Serious financial and organizational problems, which had begun in the 1930s, continued during the Second World War.[3] The air raids, naturally, reduced attendance at meetings, but there was no marked improvement after 1942, and the general decline continued after 1945. After a Ministry of Education inspection in 1951 had revealed the sharply reduced number of enrolments for the Institute's further education courses,[4] it was decided to abandon them almost completely as soon as the Corporation could make alternative arrangements. The Institute

---

[1] Birmingham and District Theatre Guild, *Annual Reports*. For a more encouraging picture of the state of amateur dramatics in the early 1950s see Paul S. Cadbury, *Birmingham—Fifty Years On* (1952), p. 80.

[2] See above, p. 215.

[3] Rachel E. Waterhouse, *The Birmingham and Midland Institute 1854–1954* (1954), pp. 180–1.

[4] Ministry of Education, *Report by H.M. Inspectors on Birmingham and Midland Institute, Inspected in the Spring Term 1951* (B.R.L. 626434).

continued to run its School of Music, whose importance for the West
Midlands the inspectors had recognized, but whose organization had
come in for some criticism from them. However, by 1956 the School of
Music was in such difficulties that the City Council passed a resolution
calling on the Education Committee to take full responsibility for
musical education in Birmingham.[1] The committee declined to take
immediate action, but the Institute itself decided to share the administration of the School of Music with an advisory council representing
local education authorities in the West Midlands. This new body was
set up in 1960, and it eventually eradicated the School's major shortcomings.

With its educational function now almost gone, the Institute tried
to stave off further decline by associating more closely with other
cultural institutions facing similar problems. In 1955 it merged with
the Birmingham Library, Margaret Street, and it was strengthened
by the affiliation of a number of important societies, among them the
Birmingham Natural History and Philosophical Society (1954).[2] But
the departure from nearby Edmund Street of a number of arts departments of Birmingham University in 1964 was a severe blow, and in
1965 the Institute's own premises were pulled down to make way for
the inner ring road. Although the Corporation reserved an alternative
site, first of all near Aston University, and later in the Civic Centre, the
Institute was severely handicapped by its move into temporary quarters
in Margaret Street. By 1970 the new buildings had still not been
started, and it remained uncertain whether new accommodation and a
promised new style of activity could revitalize the Institute.[3]

One of the major causes of the decline of the Birmingham and Midland Institute was the falling membership of its affiliated societies,
which meant that fewer people used its buildings. One such society was
the Birmingham Central Literary Association.[4] Limited by its constitution to 250 members, the Association's aim was to group a small but
highly active and well-educated number of people in meetings and
activities from which all would benefit. But as time went on the group
became smaller, less active, and, probably, less well educated. Until the
war the membership quota was almost completely taken up, and an
average attendance of over fifty in 1930–9 suggested that, unlike the
Birmingham and Midland Institute, the Association was still strong.
During the war the members acquired an enhanced social consciousness, and even extended this liberalism to their own organization by

[1] B.C.C., *Pro.*, 6 November 1956, p. 547.
[2] Waterhouse, *Midland Institute*, p. 142.
[3] By 1972 substantial progress had been made on the new buildings for the Institute.
[4] This section is based on annual editions of the *Report* of the Association, and its
magazine, *The Central Literary Magazine*.

allowing women to join in 1940. Nevertheless, membership and attendances plunged after the war; by 1951 the Association had only 139
members. By the early 1950s its *Magazine* was in serious financial
difficulties, and in 1954 it was decided to admit people under the age of
twenty-five as associate members. Nevertheless, membership dropped
to eighty-seven by 1960–1, and to about sixty by the end of the decade.
What kept the Association in being was its hard-core support; attendances at meetings stabilized at around twenty-five and the *Magazine*
continued to appear.

Efforts to attract younger people to keep up flagging membership
also characterized the Birmingham and Edgbaston Debating Society,
which had close links with the institutions described so far.[1] It had
once been an important training ground for Birmingham politicians,
including Joseph Chamberlain, but it began to lose this distinction,
and members, after the First World War. By 1939 it had only 199
members, and after severe curtailment of its activities during the war,
its membership had fallen to 161 by 1945–6. In the following year the
committee decided to abolish the entrance fee for persons under
twenty-five. This concession did not halt the slide in membership,
but as time went on young people made up an increasingly large
proportion of it. The efforts of a hard core of members ensured that it
was still an established institution in 1970. And at least one successful
politician emerged from its ranks. This was L. H. Cleaver, who was
still a member at the time of his election as Conservative M.P. for
Yardley in 1959.

In addition to the big, general societies, Birmingham was large
enough to support a great number of specialized groupings, many of
which appealed only to very tiny minorities. Generally speaking, the
wider their appeal, the more they declined after 1945, and the more
they came to depend on a hard core of members. The more specialized
societies, which did not necessarily meet in the city centre, appeared
to flourish and even to increase in number. The decline of the Birmingham Civic Society was typical of the larger groups. Founded in 1918 to
unite 'all citizens who desire to stimulate a deeper concern in the
beauty of their city', the Civic Society did some useful work in its early
years, when its advice was often heeded by the City Council. But it
frequently became bogged down in details, and it played only a minor
role in wartime replanning. After the war, when it still had over 250
members, it was involved in a few minor projects, but it found in the
1950s that it no longer had much influence over the Corporation,
when several buildings of historic interest were pulled down against its
advice in the city centre. Accustomed to work with the Corporation,
not against it, it made almost no effort to stir up public opinion in

[1] This section is based on the annual *Report of the Committee* of the debating society.

favour of better planning, and by 1970 it was almost totally moribund.[1]

A good example of the more specialized societies that developed after the war was the Birmingham Writers' Group, founded in 1946.[2] By 1955 the Group had about one hundred members. It even put out a short-lived literary magazine, the *Birmingham Bulletin*, in 1963–4.[3] Many of these smaller societies depended on newsletters rather than meetings for keeping members in touch. It was clearly with this type of organization that the future of society activities lay, and not with the big, general institutions.

Libraries, museums, art galleries

The decline of some of the older, elite cultural societies did not mean that interest in literature and the arts was fading among the great mass of the population. The level of that interest is of course difficult to assess, but it was reflected to some extent by the use made of library and museum facilities. In turn, of course, the use of these facilities depended on their maintenance and development by the Corporation, which bore almost sole responsibility for them.

The development of the city's public libraries, museums, and art galleries, like that of so many other of its services, was dictated by Government capital expenditure controls. Before the war Birmingham's library services had been dominated by the great responsibility of the Reference Library, and the lending libraries had left much to be desired. Public demand, however, was steadily increasing. By 1938–9 the annual total of books issued had reached a record four and a half million. The number of issues fell sharply during the first two months of the war owing to the blackout and restricted opening hours, but later growing boredom produced more borrowing, and the annual total rose to well over five million books by the end of the war.[4] This increase was halted in 1946–7, but a steady rise began again in 1950–1. By the late 1960s nearly ten million books were being lent each year.

Much of this increase reflected the growing leisure time and widening interests of Birmingham people, but it was facilitated by improvements in the library service, especially in the 1960s. The city's great area and low population densities were a serious problem for the lending-library service, because they made it difficult to provide branches within easy access of all residents. The Public Libraries Committee planned a number of new branch libraries after the war, but owing to capital

---

[1] Birmingham Civic Society, *The Work of the Birmingham Civic Society from June 1918 to June 1946* (1947); Black, pp. 636–7; Norman Tiptaft, *My Contemporaries* (1952), pp. 105–7.

[2] Birmingham Writers Group, *Newsletter* (B.R.L. 635406).

[3] B.R.L. 662631.

[4] Black, pp. 514, 520; *Notes on the History of the Birmingham Public Libraries 1861–1961* (1962), p. 12; B.C.C., *Pro.*, 4 June 1940, pp. 472–3.

and materials restrictions building could not be resumed until 1952. Even then, the first stage of the programme fell badly into arrear. In the late 1950s the Public Libraries Committee itself warned the City Council that borrowing in Birmingham could not be expected to reach the national average until more branch libraries were provided.[1] During the following decade provision was substantially improved as City Librarian Victor H. Woods, and, from 1965, William A. Taylor, concentrated on overcoming the deficiencies of the lending service. By 1961 three new branch libraries, supplemented by five temporary buildings, had been opened, and several more followed during the rest of the decade.[2] Shortage of staff, particularly of children's librarians, was at first a problem as the service expanded, but by 1970 a local training scheme had done much to overcome the problem of the children's libraries. Meanwhile, the libraries introduced a number of important labour-saving devices, for instance in book issues and the production of catalogues, in advance of most comparable cities. Book-ordering was centrally organized, resulting not only in the efficient allocation of expenditure but also in the wide variety of books available in branch libraries. Certain aspects of the service were greatly expanded. Children's libraries, in particular, were developed from the mid-1960s and contributed greatly to the increase in borrowing during the decade. Links with the school libraries service were extended and by 1970 the Public Libraries Department was sharing in the planning of schemes for integrated libraries and community centres.

This progress contributed greatly to a big relative increase of book-borrowing in Birmingham, which was well up to the county-borough average by the later 1960s. Expenditure on libraries also moved closer to the national average. During the early post-war years Birmingham had continued to spend less than other large cities on its libraries.[3] Even in the late 1950s the City was spending annually only 11·9 pence per head of population on books, less than half the amount spent by Liverpool, Manchester, and Sheffield, and considerably less than any other large city. Birmingham also had fewer library staff per head of population than any other large city except Leeds. During the 1960s, however, book outlay crept up year by year much closer to the county-borough average. Total expenditure on library services was still below average in 1970, but it was clear that the opening of the new reference and central lending library would increase it to well *above* the county-borough average during the 1970s.

The Reference Library housed a fine collection of books, but its old premises had long been totally inadequate. Its buildings dated from

[1] *Y.B.*, no. 125, January 1958, p. 1.
[2] *Notes on the History of the Birmingham Public Libraries*, pp. 12–14.
[3] *West Midlands Plan* (1948), III.17.15.

The inner ring road. Smallbrook Street in 1946. The bombed sites on the left-hand side of the road influenced the decision to begin work on the new road at this point.

The inner ring road. Smallbrook Ringway under construction, 1958. The shell of the Market Hall, later demolished, is visible in the distance.

The inner ring road. The completed Smallbrook Ringway, in 1969. The multi-purpose function of this, the first section of the ringway to be undertaken, reflects the original design for the road drawn up in the mid-1940s. It contrasts strongly with later sections which, especially to the north of the city centre, were built to urban motorway standards.

the 1880s, and had not been extended since 1909. So the increase in the book stock from 150,000 in 1900 to over 700,000 in the 1960s[1] caused serious problems. The City Council was told in 1939 that conditions in the library were 'chaotic', and that a new building should be provided 'at the earliest possible moment'.[2] In 1943 the Public Libraries Committee announced its hopes that a new library, which the Council had approved in principle in 1938, would be built 'immediately after the war'.[3] But these were vain expectations. The Public Libraries Committee continued to demand a new building, but they were put off by the City Council time after time. In 1956 the committee asked if there was any chance of building the new library in the next five years, but they were told to wait until the new master plan for the Civic Centre had been approved. By July 1958 the plan had been accepted, and the Libraries Committee now asked whether a new building could be put up within seven or eight years. The General Purposes Committee passed the question on to the City Engineer and the City Architect, asking whether a new library could be built within seven to ten years. The site allocated to the new library by the master plan was occupied by the old university buildings, and although it was thought in 1960 that they would be vacated by the end of 1961, the last university departments did not leave until 1964.[4] By this time, the City Council had decided, in October 1961, to defer the whole project by at least five years owing to Government capital restrictions. Although the Priorities Committee recognized the need for an early start on the library, and obtained the Council's approval for making a capital provision for it in December 1962,[5] further Government restrictions again held up progress. Fortunately, in the late 1960s work started on a nearby section of the inner ring road, for which the site of the old library would eventually be needed. So the City Council at last approved the building of the new library, and gave it sufficient priority in applications for loan sanction to ensure Government approval. Work began in 1969, and it was completed in 1973.

The operation of the Corporation's museums and art galleries presented fewer problems than did the libraries, for most of them were adequately housed, the size of their collections was not increasing rapidly, and they did not have to be sited all over the city. The only major new museum established after 1939 was the Museum of Science and Industry. The Museums Committee had formulated the intention long before the war of building a science museum, which would certainly not have

[1] *Notes on the History of the Birmingham Public Libraries*, pp. 9–11.
[2] B.C.C., *Pro.*, 6 June 1939, p. 652 (Public Libraries Committee).
[3] B.C.C., *Pro.*, 1 June 1943, p. 360 (Public Libraries Committee).
[4] B.C.C., *Pro.*, 5 January 1960, pp. 601–6 (General Purposes Committee).
[5] B.C.C., *Pro.*, 4 December 1962, p. 514 (Priorities Committee).

U

been out of place in one of Europe's major industrial centres. But slow progress in building the Civic Centre caused the scheme's postponement, even though suitable exhibits were steadily disappearing owing to the 'crying need' of somewhere to store them.[1] After the war the Newcomen Society, in association with the Birmingham Common Good Trust, launched an appeal for information on items of industrial interest, in the hope that they might eventually form the basis of a Midlands industrial museum.[2] In the following year, 1948, the Museums Committee decided to appoint staff and to acquire storage premises for industrial exhibits. In 1950 the museum was set up in a vacated factory in the city centre, and it was opened to the public in May 1951.[3] These premises, part of which dated from the 1840s, were of much historical interest, but they did not prove entirely suitable for their new purpose and in November 1960 the City Council approved a scheme to rebuild the whole museum.[4] Capital expenditure restrictions prevented a start until the mid-1960s, and the scheme was still only partly complete at the end of the decade. By 1972, however, the rebuilt and enlarged museum was fully open to the public.

Other new ventures undertaken after the war were the restoration and adaptation in the 1950s of Blakesley Hall, Yardley, as a museum of local history, and the restoration of Sarehole Mill, one of the area's few surviving water mills, in the 1960s. On the whole, however, new museums and art galleries came very low on the Council's list of priorities, and even the Sarehole Mill scheme was delayed for several years owing to strong opposition by the Labour group leader, Alderman Watton, to what he considered to be a complete waste of money. It was fortunate that the City had already acquired such an interesting variety of collections and premises before the war, and these existing resources were developed with great skill and enterprise. From 1945 the City Council began to follow the example of Manchester and other cities in making an annual grant to the art gallery for the purchase of works, which allowed it to catch up some of the ground lost to the Barber Institute of Fine Arts, on the university campus at Edgbaston. The Barber gallery, rarely visited by Birmingham citizens, still housed the finest art collection in the city at the end of the 1960s. The City's collection would have remained a relatively poor one if the foresight of the director of the art gallery in purchasing British pre-Raphaelite paintings before the war had not been so fully vindicated by the growing esteem in which this school came to be held after 1945. The director had originally advised the committee to concentrate on paintings of

[1] B.C.C., *Pro.*, 2 May 1939, p. 571 (Museums Committee).

[2] Newcomen Society, Birmingham Common Good Trust, *Interim Report 1948: Survey of Items of Engineering Historical Interest in the Midlands*, p. 3 (B.R.L. 598725).

[3] Black, pp. 440–1.   [4] *Y.B.*, no. 156, November 1960, p. 1.

this type because they were cheap, and might in the course of time come to be respected. By the time his prophecy came true, Birmingham art gallery had the finest collection of pre-Raphaelite paintings in Britain. But the gallery never had the resources to expand adequately the other sections of its collection. Moreover, the premises of the gallery, and of the museum in the same building, were somewhat cramped. However, good layout and organization did much to overcome this defect, while the art gallery coffee bar acted as a blessed haven for jaded researchers from the Reference Library and others with time on their hands.

IX

MASS ENTERTAINMENT

BIRMINGHAM's reputation as an entertainments centre has never rivalled its renown as a producer of industrial goods, nor is it likely that it ever will. An industrial city, if the products of its trades are sufficiently in demand, can export to the whole world, but the success of such commercial entertainments as it offers will depend solely on the demand generated in the city and its immediate region. In most British industrial cities that demand is limited, in both quality and quantity. The lack of a large middle class restricts the demand for quality, and the long hours worked in industry reduce the quantity of working-class demand. In those industrial cities which also act as major regional centres the relative lack of demand within the city is compensated by demand from outside, but Birmingham has always found it hard to develop to the full its potential as a regional capital. Many residents of the Birmingham region look to Wolverhampton or Coventry for their entertainment; others, especially in the western areas of the Black Country, find that Birmingham's eccentric situation renders it inaccessible.[1] So it was that throughout the years 1939–70 Birmingham appeared under-endowed in many aspects of commercial entertainments, and the lack of quality and variety in the entertainment provided were a constant cause of complaint. This dissatisfaction was not expressed solely by middle-class citizens; everyone had his own grouse, ranging from the extreme rarity of boxing title fights in Birmingham to the lack of frequent opera and ballet. During most of our period the correspondence columns of the city press frequently carried complaints that there was 'nothing to do' in Birmingham, and the occasional opinion surveys of the citizens' views of their own town suggested that they saw it as rather a dull place. And this was certainly the view of most people outside the city.

Before the picture becomes too bleak, two important features of Birmingham's entertainment life must be pointed out. Firstly, much local criticism took the form of comparing Birmingham with other cities half its size, and complaining if its entertainment facilities could be shown to be anything less than twice as good as theirs. This complaint was based on the assumption that entertainment quantity and quality are related directly to population size. But this premise is highly questionable. Many quite small towns can, for instance, support a flourish-

[1] For an analysis of Birmingham's relative accessibility from different parts of the conurbation, see J. N. Jackson, 'The regional functions and sphere of influence of Birmingham', in *Birmingham and its Regional Setting* (1950), pp. 323–34.

ing theatre, thanks very often to the special role of such a prestige institution in a small community. To argue from such examples that Birmingham should be able to support several theatres, or even an opera company, is quite unrealistic. Even the step from maintaining one theatre to maintaining two is a difficult one, for variety of choice removes the purely social attraction which a single theatre can exercise. Sometimes critics would vary their argument by comparing Birmingham unfavourably with London, and asking why a city one-tenth of London's size could not provide at least one-tenth of its entertainment facilities. They forgot that London was a national entertainments centre, whereas Birmingham did not even enjoy undisputed pre-eminence as the entertainment focus for the West Midlands. These malcontents were all loth to recognize that in real terms Birmingham offered a great deal—three thriving theatres, a resident symphony orchestra, several cinemas showing first release films, and two first-class football clubs. The second feature which must be stressed is that entertainment tended to improve during the 1939–70 period, and that the improvement was very marked during the last ten years and positively spectacular during the last five.

Whatever Birmingham's relative deficiencies in facilities, entertainment always played a positive role in the life of most citizens. With the decline of some forms of spontaneous social activity, charted in the previous chapter, places of entertainment grew in relative importance as a focus of social contact. Even the cinemas could play this part, and even when converted into bingo halls, as many were from the 1950s, the use of the term 'bingo *and social* club' was not without significance. Bingo, of course, appealed mainly to women, as one suspects the cinema did too. For the men, professional football offered an even clearer social identification with their fellow citizens and with their city. The thrilling chant of 'Birmingham . . .' which echoed round the terraces of St. Andrews in the 1960s must have reminded more than one spectator that he was a member of a single city community. Many an Austin worker would say that he lived in Longbridge, not Birmingham, but it was in Birmingham that even he would seek his entertainment if he wanted anything more than what his local cinema could provide.

Cinemas

Before the Second World War the cinema had become as strongly rooted in Birmingham as in any other major city in Britain. After 1945 it underwent many vicissitudes, but in 1970 it still maintained its joint role with football as the principal entertainer of the working masses. It is therefore appropriate to begin this chapter with an account of the development of the cinema in the city.

The history of Birmingham's cinemas between 1939 and 1970 has many similarities to that of the churches. Attendances at both declined dramatically, especially in the middle ring, where many establishments were forced to close. Most central establishments, however, survived, drawing people from all over the city and from outside. But there was one big difference between the churches and the cinema. The former expanded into the new suburban areas of Birmingham; but the cinemas made no attempt to follow their example.

By 1939 Birmingham was well provided with cinemas, especially in the central areas and in the middle ring.[1] An important centre of the British cinema since the early 1900s, Birmingham was the home of Oscar Deutsch's Odeon cinema chain and of the smaller Jacey circuit.[2] Between the wars numerous cinemas were built in the city centre, the middle ring, and the new suburbs. Like the new suburban public houses, the suburban cinemas were very large and few and far between for owing to low residential densities their catchment areas had to be very large indeed. So although cinema provision in the central wards was as high, or higher, than in most big cities, over the city as a whole it was relatively low.[3] This imbalance was already causing concern before 1939. In 1937, when five new cinemas were opened, the chairman of the Birmingham branch of the Cinematograph Exhibitors' Association warned that saturation point had been reached.[4] He repeated this warning in the following year, when three cinemas were opened, and the total of cinema seats in Birmingham reached 117,000.[5] The licensing justices showed that they too were aware of the dangers of over-provision in the inner and middle rings; in March 1938, for instance, they rejected an application to open a new cinema at Nechells on the grounds that the district was already adequately served.[6]

Although the Birmingham cinemas, in common with other public places of entertainment, were closed on the declaration of war, they were allowed to reopen a few days later.[7] The war proved to be a boom time for them. Theatrical and sporting entertainments were restricted, and suburban cinemas benefited from the difficulty of access to the city centre, especially at night. The cinemas had to close their doors early, at about 9 p.m., but they were allowed to open in the mornings, when

---

[1] See figures of cinemas in each ward in City of Birmingham, *Report of the Public Entertainments Committee of the Justices* (annual).

[2] The first Odeon cinema was built in 1930 at Perry Barr. The headquarters of the circuit, which was controlled by Birmingham's leading Jewish citizen, did not move to London until 1939 (*B.M.*, 18 August 1939).

[3] See Patrick Abercrombie and Herbert Jackson, *West Midlands Plan* (1948), table xcviii, III.19.13.

[4] *E.D.*, 14 January 1938.   [5] *E.D.*, 20 January 1939.

[6] *E.D.*, 21 March 1938.   [7] On 15 September 1939.

they were patronized by Servicemen on leave and by night workers, whose numbers greatly increased during the war. Sunday evening opening, which had first been allowed by the licensing justices in 1933,[1] was extended to Sunday afternoon. So the Birmingham cinemas were able to provide almost continuous entertainment, even during alerts.[2] They naturally benefited from a situation in which the normal timing of the city's social and economic life was completely upset. Most of them were lucky enough, even in the city centre, to escape serious damage.[3] The only Birmingham cinemas to close down were those that were actually bombed out of action.[4]

The cinema boom continued after the war, partly because of the lack of alternative entertainment, and partly because most people had now fully acquired the habit of filmgoing.[5] A series of bright comedies and musicals, most of them produced in the United States, helped to take people's minds off the dreary conditions of the early post-war years, and the drab Birmingham surroundings, which now looked gloomier than ever owing to bomb damage and lack of maintenance. No new cinemas could be built owing to building restrictions, but hardly any closed, even in the central redevelopment areas. In 1950 there were still eighty-six cinemas open in the city. Sunday afternoon opening was authorized by the licensing justices even after the war, despite protests from the churches, which feared a reduction in Sunday school attendance.[6] Yet within two or three years of the war there were signs that people were becoming more discriminating. In 1949 one Birmingham cinema manager suggested that, although there was no sign of a decline in attendance, people did not go regularly every week to the same cinema as they had done during the war.[7] Then in December of the same year, the BBC began to beam television programmes into Birmingham from its mast at Sutton Coldfield. At first the number of television sets in Birmingham grew only slowly,[8] and there were no cinema closures until 1953. Indeed, closure did not become frequent until 1957, by which time 265,000 television licences were held in the Birmingham postal area, and entertainment tax, introduced in 1954,

[1] Birmingham was the first city outside London to allow Sunday openings.
[2] See above, p. 27.
[3] In 1943 ninety cinemas were still licensed, compared to ninety-nine in 1939 (figures from *Reports of the Public Entertainments Committee of the Justices*).
[4] *B.M.*, 18 January 1946.
[5] See, for instance, *E.D.*, 20 December 1946: 'People have made a practice of visiting a certain cinema on certain evenings and in fact are so regular in attendance that they have picked on various favourite seats.'
[6] See *B.P.* editorial supporting Sunday-afternoon cinema, 18 October 1946.
[7] *B.G.*, 9 November 1949.
[8] In 1950 only 28,841 sets were licensed in the Birmingham postal area (which was larger than the city alone). The total rose to 72,416 in 1951, and to 136,260 in 1953 (City of Birmingham, *Abstract of Statistics*).

was becoming a crushing burden.[1] By 1960 the number of cinemas had fallen to fifty-four, and their decline continued as rapidly in the following decade, despite the abolition of entertainment tax in 1960. In 1968 only twenty-nine cinemas were open in the city. Many were converted into bingo halls to satisfy public demand for small-scale gambling, and to overcome boredom among housewives. A few were totally or partially converted for ten-pin bowling.[2] Fifteen of the smaller cinemas became garages.[3] Several more, beginning in 1959 with the Triangle, Balsall Heath, eked out a tenuous existence by showing Indian and Pakistani films at more or less frequent intervals.[4]

Nearly all the cinemas closed or converted to other uses lay outside the city centre—most of them, in fact, were in the central redevelopment areas and in the grossly overprovided middle ring. But the city centre cinemas, too, were severely hit by the decline in cinema attendances during the 1950s—a decline which does not appear to have ended until about 1964.[5] The provision of cinema seats in the city centre was not, however, excessive, partly as a result of its relatively small area. Moreover, the building of cinemas there had been artificially halted by the war and by post-war building restrictions. In 1949 there were still only six feature cinemas and two news theatres in the centre of Birmingham,[6] and none was subsequently closed except when the sites were required for redevelopment by the Corporation.[7] One completely new cinema, the Scala, was opened in Smallbrook Ringway in 1964, replacing the old Scala, demolished in 1960 for the inner ring road. It had two auditoria, the smaller of which was opened as a cinema club showing uncensored films in 1965. Other central cinemas were improved. The Broadway cinema, Bristol Street, was rebuilt and reopened as the Cinephone in 1956, specializing in continental films.[8] The Gaumont was converted for cinerama in 1963, and was followed shortly afterwards by the installation of a cinerama screen at the A.B.C., Bristol Street. The Odeon was refurbished in 1965. Most of these alterations and replacements involved a reduction in the

---

[1] *B.M.*, 6 February 1957. At the time, 1957 was considered to be a crisis year for cinemas (*Birmingham Sketch*, November 1957, p. 18).

[2] The first combined cinema-bowl was the Warwick, Acocks Green, converted in 1963.

[3] *Planet*, 19 November 1964.

[4] *B.M.*, 15 July 1959; *Planet*, 19 November 1964. For evidence on the frequency of cinema-going in the Midlands, suggesting that people went less frequently than in the north and the London area, see the Newspaper Society, *Regional Readership and Markets Survey* (1961).

[5] *Planet*, 19 November 1964.

[6] *Birmingham Post Year Book and Who's Who*.

[7] The Jacey news theatre in High Street, demolished in 1960, was not replaced despite its owners' declared intention to do so (*B.M.*, 10 March 1960).

[8] *Architectural Review*, vol. cxx, July–December 1956, pp. 327–8.

number of seats,[1] and in the 1960s the central cinemas concentrated on providing good quality films in comfortable and intimate surroundings.[2] They encouraged their customers to feel that they were enjoying a special night out—something which they would not obtain at their local cinemas. The two national cinema circuits, Rank and A.B.C., had by now abandoned weekly programme changes in their principal central cinemas, and allowed films to run for as long as they could attract an audience.[3] They were also prepared to allow films to build up runs in their secondary central cinemas if the demand justified it. By 1963 these policies seemed to be paying off, and the great success of *From Russia with Love* at the Odeon was symbolic of the resurgence of the central cinemas.[4] From 1965 a number of central cinemas experimented with late night shows, after a relaxation of restrictions by the licensing justices; but they were not very well patronized.

Although the central cinemas remained commercially successful, they failed increasingly to serve fully the needs of the city in the later 1960s. The West End cinema, and the A.B.C., Coleshill Street, demolished for municipal redevelopment in 1967 and 1969, were not immediately replaced, and pressure of demand increased on the remaining cinemas in the centre. One of them, the Gaumont, made a speciality of showing musical films, always popular in Birmingham, which were capable of making long runs. Audiences were maintained during these runs by coach parties drawn from all over the Midlands, and by the phenomenon of repetitive viewing.[5] Consequently, there were very few changes from week to week in the programmes of central cinemas, and the shortage of accommodation meant that quality films which were not certain to succeed commercially could not obtain a showing. Only the Scala had a policy of showing quality films, and it too fell for the temptation of allowing popular presentations to build up long runs. These deficiencies encouraged the growth in the 1960s of a demand for quality cinema.

Even before the war complaints had been numerous that the best films reached Birmingham late or not at all, and that the city's cinema catered for the lowest tastes.[6] Positive action to counter this situation

[1] The number of seats at the Gaumont was reduced from 2,000 to 1,200 in 1963. The Cinephone held only 608, and the Scala about 470 (*ex inf.* managers of Gaumont and Cinephone cinemas).

[2] But a scheme to convert the Odeon into two cinemas, considered in 1964, was not proceeded with (*B.M.*, 31 January 1964).

[3] The first film to enjoy a very long run in Birmingham was *South Pacific*, shown at the West End from September 1958 to July 1960 (*B.M.*, 1 February 1967).

[4] *B.M.*, 21 October 1963.

[5] Mrs. Alice Jackson, of Gravelly Hill North, saw *The Sound of Music* 130 times in two years between 1965 and 1967 (*B.M.*, 1 February 1967). This film ran on at the Gaumont until 1969.

[6] See, for instance, letter in *B.P.*, 2 November 1937.

took two forms: the development of film societies, and attempts to obtain the showing of quality films at commercial cinemas in the city centre.

The city's first film society, the Birmingham Film Society, was founded in January 1931 by a group of enthusiasts which included many well-known members of the university.[1] Its activities were curtailed in the early years of the war, but they began to expand again from 1944 as public interest in the cinema grew.[2] It was joined after the war by a number of local film societies, among them the Bournville Film Society, and by 1948 there were ten such groups in the Birmingham area.[3] These newcomers were partly responsible for a reduction in the membership of the Birmingham Film Society, which totalled only 400 in 1947.[4] The Society was further handicapped by the spread of Sunday opening, which deprived it of the use of a central cinema before 9 p.m. on Sunday evenings. But in 1952 the Society was able to persuade the Birmingham and Midland Institute to convert a lecture theatre into a cinema,[5] which allowed it to expand its activities considerably. After the demolition of the Institute buildings in the mid-1960s the Society moved to the Crescent Theatre. The other societies continued to flourish, although the early post-war growth in their numbers was not maintained. In 1969 there were still nine of them in Birmingham and Solihull.[6]

The success of the societies stemmed partly from the insufficient variety of films shown at commercial cinemas in Birmingham. For this reason, they were somewhat ambivalent participants in the almost continuous campaign for specialist, quality cinema in the city centre. Commercial promoters were discouraged from ventures which might have to compete with the societies; and the societies were similarly apprehensive of commercial competition, even though they professed to welcome any initiative which might improve Birmingham's cultural facilities. An early attempt to establish a repertory cinema in Birmingham similar to London's Academy cinema (1930) was made in 1931, when an Erdington man, John Stone, promoted a season of films in a central cinema. This venture failed owing to the small size of the audience. In 1937, Stone, confident that public appreciation of the cinema had risen in the intervening years, announced a plan for a permanent repertory cinema, for which he had this time obtained a leading distributor's backing. The Birmingham Film Society was not very optimistic about the project, suggesting that 2,000 customers a

---

[1] *Flashback: a Hundred Shows of the Birmingham Film Society, 1931–1948* (1948), pp. 5–6. The Birmingham society followed those of London (1925), Glasgow (1929), and Edinburgh (1930).

[2] *B.P.*, 8 November 1944.   [3] *Flashback*, p. 10.   [4] *B.P.*, 4 December 1947.
[5] *B.P.*, 15 March 1956.   [6] *Birmingham Post Year Book and Who's Who.*

week would be needed to maintain it—more than three times its own membership. They were right; Stone's plan never got off the ground. However, in the following year it was rumoured that the Academy cinema might set up a branch in Birmingham,[1] and later it seemed likely that the Marquis of Casa Maury, who ran the Curzon cinema in Mayfair, would open a repertory cinema in the city.[2] All these hopes were dashed by the war, but the growing interest in quality cinema during and after the war greatly strengthened the optimism of local supporters of a repertory cinema. The Birmingham Film Society, which had difficulty in hiring suitable premises after the war, now strongly supported the call for such a cinema.[3] It was endorsed in 1955 even by the Lord Mayor, Alderman Joseph Balmer, who suggested that the Corporation should build a civic cinema as well as a civic theatre.[4] However, the support of the Birmingham Film Society appears to have waned after it obtained suitable accommodation in the Birmingham and Midland Institute in 1952.

In 1956 it seemed that the need for a specialist cinema would be satisfied when the Jacey circuit opened its Cinephone cinema in Bristol Street. The owners announced their intention to show high quality continental films which until then had not been able to obtain a showing in Birmingham. During the early months they made some attempt to show such films, but they soon found that they could obtain bigger audiences for 'X' films of a pronounced sexual character, which quickly came to constitute the Cinephone's principal bill of fare. This left Birmingham cinema-lovers where they were before, except that their clear failure to give adequate support to quality films at the Cinephone made it unlikely that any more such experiments would be made. Declining cinema attendances in the later 1950s also reduced the proprietors' willingness to take risks.

The matter was not raised again until 1966, when the British Film Institute announced its intention to set up a Midland Film Theatre in Birmingham. It hoped to use the old Repertory Theatre in Station Street, as soon as the company was able to move out to the new repertory theatre. In the meantime, the Institute was negotiating for the use of the Scala during one week in every month.[5] However, plans were delayed when the City Council's General Purposes Committee refused to put up the sum of £549, requested by the Institute as a guarantee against loss.[6] For a time, Wolverhampton Council tried to encourage the Midland Film Theatre to move to Wolverhampton and the Birmingham scheme did not emerge again until January 1967, when the City Council offered a guarantee against loss of up to £200.

[1] S.M., 10 April 1938.   [2] B.M., 2 December 1938.
[3] See, for instance, letter in B.P., 17 September 1948.   [4] B.P., 10 February 1955.
[5] B.M., 22 February 1966.   [6] B.M., 17 September 1966.

Compton Cinemas reduced the rent asked for the use of the Scala, and
it was planned to begin operations in April.[1] But the starting date had
to be delayed, and by the summer the whole scheme was again in
ruins, with the Scala again unavailable. The irony of the situation was
that in 1967 the Scala had begun to show quality films, which enjoyed
such success that they were able to build up long runs. When *A Man
for All Seasons* had run for several weeks, the management realized
that it would be commercially damaging to them to interrupt runs
each month to allow the Midland Film Theatre to use the cinema.[2]
So the offer to the British Film Institute was withdrawn. However,
plans were announced later to open the film theatre in the Cannon
Hill arts centre, as soon as suitable premises became available there in
1972.

The success of the Scala's quality films did at least show that the
discrimination of the Birmingham public was growing and in early
1970 Jacey Cinemas began to show repertory programmes in their
news theatre in Station Street. This venture was moderately successful
for a time, but sex and violence had become the principal bill of fare
at the cinema by 1972.

The theatre

The experience of the cinemas suggested that city-centre establishments
could do well in spite of competition from other forms of leisure activity.
So how fared the theatres, which, with very few exceptions of which
the Aston Hippodrome was the most notable, were not to be found
outside the city centre?[3]

Although theatre proprietors had been worried by competition from
the cinemas between the wars,[4] the growing demand for city-centre
entertainment as living standards improved and working hours
shortened had allowed them to survive without closures. They were
helped by Birmingham's shortage of theatres; in 1939, with four
theatres and three music-halls, the city had one seat for every 97·4
inhabitants—a considerably higher ratio than Liverpool, Manchester,
Bradford, and Leeds.[5] But in order to survive the theatres had to concentrate on popular programmes, and the tawdry vulgarity which
had been a feature of the Birmingham theatre in the nineteenth century
was maintained, if not enhanced.[6] The pantomime season was longer

[1] *B.P.*, 5 January 1967.   [2] *B.M.*, 19 August 1967.
[3] See *V.C.H. Warcks.*, vol. vii, pp. 238–9.   [4] Ibid., p. 241.
[5] Patrick Abercrombie and Herbert Jackson, *West Midlands Plan* (1948), III.19.24;
City of Birmingham, *Reports of the Public Entertainments Committee of the Justices.*
[6] According to G. B. Shaw, Birmingham was 'notorious as the rottenest town on
the Number 1 circuit when anything but the vulgarest art of the theatre was concerned' before the Great War (quoted in Bache Matthews, *A History of the Birmingham
Repertory Theatre* (1924), p. 168).

in Birmingham than anywhere else, and could last for up to four months, sustained by the mass party bookings that would later create long runs for musical films.[1] Only the Repertory Theatre, founded by Barry Jackson in 1913, gave the city a reputation for quality productions. Largely to blame for the low standards of Birmingham programmes were the local audiences. They were said to be notoriously slow to recognize talented acting or writing.[2] Promoters, companies, and individual artistes were often unwilling to come to the city; the press officer of the Theatre Royal, for instance, once wrote: 'Indeed, many of the internationally famous artistes—and this goes for the music-hall profession also—loathe and detest coming to Birmingham. In their opinion, it has no social or theatrical life and very few amenities.'[3]

After enforced closure during the first few days of the war, the theatres, like the cinemas, benefited from the general shortage of entertainment. Many famous companies and individual actors chose to leave London because theatres there had to close before 6 p.m., and appeared in productions in Birmingham. Local audiences responded well, and by January 1940 theatre critics were expressing the hope that these new high standards would be maintained after the war.[4] These golden months came to an end in September 1940, when all places of public entertainment in Birmingham were required to close by 9 p.m., and during the air raids evening houses were very poor. Matinees, on the other hand, continued to be well attended, and the pantomime season was unaffected, even in the winter of 1940–1.[5] After the worst Birmingham raids ended in the spring of 1941, the situation returned nearer to normal, with both good and bad results. Evening performances were extended and were better attended, but restrictions on the London theatres were also relaxed, causing a sharp fall in the number of high-quality touring productions to reach Birmingham. Furthermore, two of the city's biggest theatres had been completely destroyed by fire—the Empire music-hall, in October 1940, and the Prince of Wales, in April 1941. Towards the end of the war, the high hopes of 1940 were fading away. The only remaining theatre which specialized in touring companies, the Theatre Royal, was heavily attacked by the *Birmingham Post* in 1944 for its superficial, unimaginative programmes, which consisted mainly of a long string of musical comedies.[6] The management replied that it was now unable to attract good touring productions; producers and managers had returned to their pre-war preference of starting tours in Manchester

[1] M. F. K. Fraser, *The Alexandra Theatre* (1948), pp. 71–2.
[2] J. C. Trewin, *The Birmingham Repertory Theatre, 1913–1963* (1963), p. 146.
[3] Letter in *B.P.*, 26 September 1944.
[4] *B.P.*, 3 January 1940; *Time and Tide*, 3 February 1940.
[5] *B.P.*, 3 September 1940; *B.M.*, 26 September 1940; *B.P.*, 21 May 1945.
[6] *B.P.*, 23 September 1944.

or Glasgow, and often took them off before they ever reached Birmingham.[1] When visiting the West Midlands, many companies
preferred Coventry to Birmingham.

Perhaps if more theatres had been available in Birmingham, the
growth in interest and knowledge in the theatre, which was generally
recognized at the time, might have built up firmer foundations. But
with the Alexandra concentrating on lighthearted productions to
distract its audiences from the realities of war,[2] the only home of serious
plays was still the Repertory Theatre. And, in fact, the Rep was going
through a very difficult time. Long-term plans were abandoned, and
selections could not be made more than one or two productions ahead.[3]
The theatre had had to close for a time during the air raids and the
company was kept together only by performing plays in the Birmingham
parks.[4] It did not return to the theatre until November 1942.

Although attendances continued at a high level in the early years
after the war, the general quality of productions remained low. Despite
the development of municipal bus services and the establishment of a
night service, the wartime habit of beginning performances early, at
around 7 p.m., was continued. Musicals continued to make up the
majority of touring productions; in the first three months of 1947, for
instance, Birmingham saw only three non-musical stage plays, compared
to seventeen in Manchester, twelve in Bradford, and six each in
Liverpool and Leeds.[5] So the Birmingham theatres could give little
encouragement to the interest in the serious theatre which had built
up during the war, and which now faded away or was diverted into
amateur theatricals. Owing to bomb damage, Birmingham's ratio of
theatre seats to population was now even lower than that of other
comparable cities. In 1948 it had one seat for every 132 citizens,
compared to 1:62 in Liverpool, 1:75 in Bradford, and 1:79 in Leeds.
Even Sheffield was better provided than Birmingham.[6] There was a
further deterioration in 1956 when the Theatre Royal, which was the
only theatre capable of adequately housing opera and ballet, was
demolished.[7] The other theatres also faced difficult times in the 1950s,
owing mainly to the growing popularity of television. The Aston
Hippodrome survived for a time by putting on strip shows, but by the
end of the decade it had been converted into a bingo hall. However,
the serious theatre, as a minority interest, was less seriously affected
than more popular entertainments by the spread of television and the
motor car. The Alexandra Theatre actually increased the serious
element in its productions after the war, and its manager, Derek

[1] *B.P.*, 26 September 1944.   [2] Fraser, *Alexandra Theatre*, p. 89.
[3] T. C. Kemp, *The Birmingham Repertory Theatre* (1943).   [4] Ibid., pp. 104–9.
[5] *B.M.*, 31 March 1947.   [6] *West Midlands Plan*, III.19.24.
[7] *B.M.*, 22 January 1955. It was replaced by a Woolworth's store and offices,
built by Jack Cotton and Partners, the Birmingham developers.

Salberg, made it a point of policy that there should be one prestige play for every three commercial productions.[1] He also reduced the pantomime season from seventeen weeks to twelve, although he still relied on it to finance other productions. Salberg's realistic and imaginative management from 1937 enabled the Alexandra to put aside its early blood-tub image and emerge as a worthy partner to the Repertory Theatre in providing a wide choice of entertainment. The Repertory Theatre, on the other hand, ran into financial difficulties in the 1950s and, as we shall see later, came to depend more and more on outside financial help. But it resisted the temptation, as did the other Birmingham theatres, to solve its problems by big price increases, and in 1957 its seats were still the cheapest of any repertory theatre in Britain.[2] The Hippodrome, which after the loss of the Theatre Royal was the biggest theatre in Birmingham, with over 1,900 seats, took over the Theatre Royal's role as the home of musicals and touring shows, and abandoned its earlier function as a music-hall.[3] But it faced the same problem as the Theatre Royal—shortage of good shows—and in the 1960s its owners seriously considered pulling it down.[4] However, it benefited from the increased demand for city-centre prestige entertainment towards the end of the decade, and in 1970 it was thriving. Unfortunately, the same could not be said of the other Birmingham theatres.

Although the Birmingham theatre made a much fuller contribution to the cultural and intellectual life of the city after the war than it had before, its economic position declined from the early 1950s. Even the Alexandra, which seemed to be pursuing a commercially successful policy during the 1950s, ran into serious difficulties in the following decade, when all three Birmingham professional theatres were at various times threatened with closure. Fortunately, the improved reputation of the post-war theatre in the city made the City Council better disposed towards supporting it. Modest though the Council's contribution was for many years, it was crucial in maintaining the theatre in Birmingham. It helped in three major ways: by encouraging commercial promoters to provide new theatres, by subsidizing existing theatres, and by making the major contribution to the building of a new repertory theatre.

The importance of the theatre was first brought home to many people,

---

[1] Fraser, *Alexandra Theatre*, p. 104; Norman Tiptaft, *My Contemporaries* (1952), pp. 170-1.

[2] *E.D.*, 4 February 1957.

[3] Both the Theatre Royal and the Hippodrome were controlled by the same circuit, Moss Empires. The Hippodrome changed its name to the Birmingham Theatre in 1964, partly in order to emphasize that it no longer regarded itself as a variety theatre.

[4] See below, p. 306.

including members of the Council, when the Empire and the Prince of Wales were destroyed in the air raids. In 1943 the Reconstruction Committee recommended that Birmingham should accept the growing view that local authorities should encourage the theatre.[1] It was at about this time that discussions first took place on the possibility of building a municipal theatre. As yet there was no suggestion that the Corporation should subsidize actual running costs, and its encouragement to the commercial theatre was to be limited to the reservation of city centre sites for theatre building. It seemed possible for a time that the Empire might be rebuilt on its old site in Snow Hill, but the Prince of Wales stood within the perimeter of the planned civic centre, and so would have to be rebuilt elsewhere. In July 1945 the Public Works Committee agreed in principle to offer a site on the corner of Hill Street and Smallbrook Street to the owner of the Prince of Wales, Emile Littler, for the reconstruction of the theatre. The site was on the line of the inner ring road, and the committee already hoped to create a 'theatreland' in this corner of the city centre, near the existing Hippodrome and Alexandra theatres. Unfortunately, when Emile Littler asked for the use of the site in 1948, none of the properties standing on it had been acquired, owing to the postponement of the inner ring road project.[2] The Corporation immediately took steps to negotiate their acquisition, but by the time the site was available Emile Littler was no longer able to undertake construction of the new theatre. Attempts were made to find another promoter, but it was not until 1956 that the City was able to lease the site, when Moss Empires wanted to build a replacement for their demolished Theatre Royal. The ground rent was fixed lower than would have been expected from a commercial development, because the Council was so eager to have the Theatre Royal replaced, after the outcry that had accompanied its demolition.[3] The leader of the Labour Group, Alderman Bradbeer, was a keen theatregoer and supporter of amateur dramatics, and so was his deputy, Alderman Watton. Moreover, the chairman of the Public Works Committee, Alderman Price, was an enthusiastic supporter of any scheme designed to improve Birmingham's entertainment facilities, and the creation of a 'theatreland' near Smallbrook Ringway was particularly close to his heart.[4] But their high hopes were soon dashed. When the Council approved the lease to Moss Empires it was hoped that the new theatre would be ready in 1958, but as the months dragged by no start was made on building and Moss Empires eventually had

[1] B.C.C., *Pro.*, 12 October 1943, p. 511.
[2] B.C.C., *Pro.*, 27 July 1948, p. 882 (Public Works Committee).
[3] B.C.C., *Pro.*, 2 October 1956, p. 443 (Public Works Committee); *Y.B.*, no. 111, October 1956, p. 1.
[4] *S.M.*, 22 May 1960.

Britain's first provincial underpass, at Birchfield Road, Perry Barr, before and after (1962) construction.

The inner ring road. This grade separated junction at Lancaster Place, terminus of the Aston Expressway, photographed in 1971, typifies the design standards applied to the sections of the inner ring road undertaken in the 1960s

to renounce all interest in the site.[1] They objected that the cost of the building proposed by the Corporation, which was intended to be consistent with the high standard of development established for the ringway, was more than they were prepared to finance. The Corporation now attempted to arouse Val Parnell's interest in the site, and even went so far as to offer to build the theatre itself and rent it to him.[2] These negotiations also fell through.

In view of the increasing financial difficulties of the city's existing theatres, the situation now looked hopeless. Yet the City Council kept up its search for a developer, which was all the more urgent now that the rest of the new Smallbrook Ringway was being lined with shops and offices. Advertisement of the site produced four firm offers from developers, but none of them was prepared to operate the theatre, which they wanted to lease back to the Corporation when built. Moss Empires were now consulted again, and expressed a willingness to operate the sort of theatre that two of the developers had in mind. Finance was still a problem, however, and in the end the Corporation had to agree to grant what amounted to the free use of the site. These terms were approved by the Council in January 1962, when it was hoped that work would start in the autumn.[3] The developer was Atlas Securities Limited, which at the time was building the Prince Charles Theatre (later, Cinema) in London. The agreement was well received in Birmingham although it had now become clear that if the new theatre were built, Moss Empires would close their Hippodrome theatre nearby.[4] However, further difficulties forced the scheme to be abandoned, and negotiations began again with other developers. Meanwhile, Moss Empires extensively modernized the Hippodrome in 1963, which suggested that they were no longer interested in building a new theatre. In 1964 Atlas Securities was taken over by Westcliff Properties Limited, which wanted to develop the site with more shops and offices than had been included in earlier schemes, and a smaller theatre, with 500 seats instead of 1,800. The A.B.C. cinema circuit also showed interest in building a combined theatre-cinema. But none of these ideas came to anything, and when the Conservatives took control of the Council, in May 1966, the site was still unlet. It seemed for a time that the Conservatives, in view of their pre-election promise to dispose of all sites 'unnecessarily' in the ownership of the Corporation, might lease or sell the site to the highest bidder for shops and offices. Alderman Simpson, chairman of the Public Works Committee, threatened as much within a few days of taking up his responsibilities.[5] But

---

[1] *Y.B.*, no. 127, March 1958, p. 2.   [2] *E.D.*, 10 September 1958.
[3] B.C.C., *Pro.*, 9 January 1962, pp. 670–2 (Public Works Committee); *Y.B.*, no. 120, February 1962, p. 1.
[4] *B.M.*, 5 January 1962.   [5] *B.P.*, 26 May 1966.

w

the Conservatives soon began to reveal a lively concern for the protection of entertainment facilities in the centre of Birmingham, and they pursued Labour's policy of trying to make a compromise arrangement with a developer. By 1970 the site was still vacant, but it had been sold to a private developer for a 'leisure centre', including a small theatre, and hopes were expressed that building work would begin during the year.[1]

Meanwhile, the dream of a large, new commercial theatre had emerged in a new form. In September 1967, Associated Television (ATV), which now controlled Moss Empires, asked the Corporation for the lease of a large site at the top of Suffolk Street, which had been earmarked since the late 1950s for a municipal exhibition hall.[2] ATV offered to include a theatre of 2,000 seats in this development, for use partly as a television theatre, but also for non-televised performances.[3] A month later, Moss Empires announced its intention to close the Birmingham Theatre (Hippodrome) in 1970.[4] Once again, it seemed that the precondition for the building of a new theatre was to be the closure of an old one. ATV, however, soon began to throw doubts on its own willingness to include a theatre in its new development, and in September 1969 it was announced that the Birmingham Theatre, now enjoying a welcome boom of attendances, would not close after all.[5] The final design for the ATV Centre did indeed include a television theatre, but in the early 1970s it was used only as a studio, not as a theatre in the wider sense of the word.

The Corporation's record in trying to ensure the provision of new commercial theatre accommodation in the city centre was a very creditable one. It was the reluctance of developers and impresarios to build and operate a new theatre, and not any lack of enthusiasm on the part of the City Council, that thwarted all the plans made through the years. The main discouragement to the provision of a new theatre was, until the early 1950s, building restrictions and materials shortages. Subsequently, it was the decline of attendances which resulted mainly from the competition of television. This decline led to a situation where the City Council was called upon increasingly to demonstrate its loyalty to the theatre by providing subsidies.

The origins of the municipal subsidization of Birmingham theatres are, like those of so many post-war developments, to be found in the years of the Second World War. Shortly after the Repertory Theatre reopened in 1942, its trustees applied to the City Council for financial assistance. The Council, recognizing that the Repertory Theatre was facing its gravest financial crisis since the 1920s, was well disposed to this

---

[1] B.P., 20 June 1969. Building was under way on this site by the summer of 1972.
[2] See below, pp. 452 ff.   [3] B.P., 9 September 1967.
[4] B.M., 3 October 1967.   [5] B.M., 18 September 1969.

request. The Education Committee suggested that a link between the theatre and the education authority might be of great benefit to the city's schools, and would justify a grant. The idea of such an association coincided with the broader concept of education which grew up in Birmingham during the war, and which was already reflected in plans for C.B.S.O. concerts for school children, in return for an extra subsidy.[1] So the City Council approved the principle of a grant to the Repertory Theatre in March 1943.[2] At first, however, the grant was a small one, and the Repertory Theatre's rapid recovery towards the end of the war and in the early post-war years made it less crucial. Moreover, it amounted to a payment in return for services rendered to education, and was not a general contribution to the theatre's running costs. The Council would have liked to do more, but it had no specific legal authority to provide a subsidy until the Local Government Act 1948 gave it wide powers to provide entertainments, spending up to the product of a 6d. rate. It immediately took advantage of the new Act by agreeing, in January 1949, to provide the Repertory Theatre with a financial guarantee against loss of up to £3,000 for 1949/50.[3]

The theatre had to agree to submit accounts to the Corporation, and to give the Corporation additional representation on its governing body. Subsequently, Alderman Bradbeer, the Labour group's principal theatre enthusiast, was appointed as an additional trustee.[4] In the following year, the Council renewed its guarantee, but felt unable to accede to a request for a grant of £1,000 to cover the cost of new curtains and carpets because the theatre had already built up a large capital reserve.[5]

In 1951 the Repertory Theatre, which had been forced to take up nearly all of the two previous guarantees against loss, and was still losing money, asked the City Council to increase the guarantee to £5,500. With the Conservatives now in control, there was perhaps rather more opposition to this request than there might have been under Labour, and it was turned down. However, the General Purposes Committee maintained its helpful attitude, and consulted with the director of the Repertory Theatre on ways in which attendances might be improved, and on other matters affecting the theatre's wellbeing. Although the Council could not agree to increase its guarantee, it converted the existing guarantee of £3,000 into a fixed grant of that sum.[6] This move led to an even closer association between the theatre and the City Council. Sir Wilfrid Martineau, a Unionist alderman,

[1] See below, pp. 314 ff.
[2] B.C.C., *Pro.*, 9 March 1943, p. 294 (Education Committee); Kemp, *Repertory Theatre*, p. 128.
[3] B.C.C. *Pro.*, 4 January 1949, pp. 177–8 (General Purposes Committee).
[4] Black, pp. 644–5.   [5] Black, p. 645.
[6] B.C.C., *Pro.*, 4 December 1951, pp. 498–9 (General Purposes Committee).

was made a director of the theatre, and the management was asked to include occasional productions of more general appeal to the public. By 1952 the theatre's financial position was improving, but the Labour-controlled Council decided in December to renew the grant of £3,000. At the same time, it asked for 'direct representation' on the board of directors.[1] This request was implemented after the Council had decided, in February 1953, to make an interest-free loan of £6,500 to the theatre, on condition that the board of directors would in future include two members of the City Council.[2] The annual subsidy of £3,000 was maintained throughout the 1950s, but the theatre put growing pressure on the Council for an increase owing to falling attendances and financial difficulties. In 1956 the Council approved the payment of an exceptional subsidy of £5,000, and agreed not to ask for early repayment of the interest-free loan, but did not increase the general grant.[3] However, in December 1959, it was decided to increase the grant to £5,000 a year.[4]

During the 1960s links between the Council and the theatre became even closer, as plans for the building of a new theatre, to be occupied by the Repertory Theatre's company, began to crystallize. In 1964 the Council's annual grant was increased to £7,000,[5] and in 1966, to £8,000.[6] In 1965 the directors asked the Council to appoint two further representatives to the board, and the Council agreed to do so in January 1966.[7]

A case could be made for subsidizing the Repertory Theatre because it was not a profit-making venture, and because it made a big contribution to the satisfaction of minority cultural interests in a city that was not very well provided for in this respect. It was quite another matter to subsidize the purely commercial theatre, and this possibility was not seriously discussed until the early 1960s. By this time, however, the Alexandra Theatre was beginning to have difficulty in keeping its head above water. It felt that because of its efforts to include a proportion of serious performances in its programmes, it could justifiably look to the municipality for help. Since the demolition of the Theatre Royal, the Alexandra had been the only theatre capable of taking opera and ballet—though it was so unsuitable that experiments had even been made with opera and ballet in the even more inconvenient Repertory Theatre. The Council was grateful to the Alexandra's management for inviting the Sadler's Wells Company to put on annual performances, and in 1964 it was persuaded to make a grant of £200 per week

[1] B.C.C., *Pro.*, 2 December 1952, p. 545 (General Purposes Committee).
[2] B.C.C., *Pro.*, 3 February 1953, p. 701 (General Purposes Committee).
[3] *T.B.*, no. 112, November 1956, p. 2.   [4] *T.B.*, no. 147, January 1960, p. 3.
[5] *T.B.*, no. 192, February 1964, p. 2.
[6] B.C.C., *Pro.*, 8 March 1966, pp. 738-9 (General Purposes Committee).
[7] Ibid., 4 January 1966, p. 548 (General Purposes Committee).

towards the cost of the Sadler's Wells visit.[1] This precedent was followed in subsequent years. In June 1965, when the theatre seemed to be in danger of closure, the Council agreed to make an interest-free loan of £30,000 to the Alexandra for certain repairs and improvements, on condition that the theatre continued its present policy, and did not introduce such novelties as variety shows, bingo, and striptease. The General Purposes Committee clearly stated that it would not be in the best interests of the city if the Alexandra were to close for lack of support.[2] The loan was intended to help the theatre to extend its main frontage and foyer to the inner ring road at Suffolk Street, as part of a new commercial development there, approved by the Council in March 1965.[3]

After starting work on this extension, which suggested that the management was optimistic about the future, the Alexandra ran into further difficulties. In October 1967 it announced that it might have to close in 1970 owing to heavy losses.[4] Now that the Conservatives were in control of the City Council, it seemed likely that they would maintain the view, which had frequently been expressed by some of their prominent members, that the commercial theatre should stand on its own feet. But when they were faced with the danger of losing yet another Birmingham theatre (it seemed likely at the time that the Birmingham Theatre would also close within two years) the Conservatives offered to take over the theatre and establish it as a non-profit-making organization similar to the Repertory Theatre. The City Council approved this proposal in October 1968.

This unexpected enthusiasm for the theatre on both sides of the Council grew out of its decision to build, at last, a new repertory theatre for Birmingham. Here again, the origins of this proposal were to be found in the Second World War. Until plans were finalized in the 1960s, three variations of the scheme had been under consideration. One was that the Council should build a new theatre, additional to the Repertory Theatre, to be used by touring companies. The second possibility, which gained more and more support as time went on, was that a new home should be provided for the Repertory Theatre, which was increasingly ill at ease in its old premises, even though they had once been the last word in design. The third proposal, which was not seriously considered after the early 1950s, was that a civic theatre should be provided for the city's amateur dramatic societies.

In October 1943 the Reconstruction Committee presented one of

---

[1] B.C.C., *Pro.*, 21 July 1964, pp. 196–7 (General Purposes Committee).

[2] Ibid., 15 June 1965, pp. 37–8 (General Purposes Committee).

[3] Ibid., 7 January 1964, p. 708; 9 March 1965, pp. 745–7 (Public Works Committee).

[4] *S.M.*, 8 October 1967.

its wide-ranging reports on the future of amenities in Birmingham. It had called Sir Barry Jackson into its discussions on the future of the theatres, and he had stated that he would like to see a municipal theatre built. He also promised to give all the help he could if such a scheme should be approved.[1] The idea of a municipal theatre was particularly dear to the Borough Labour Party, which had played an important part in the organization of amateur dramatics before and during the war. This enthusiasm was reflected by the Labour group, which was led at the time by Alderman Albert Bradbeer, himself a keen participant in amateur dramatics. It was Bradbeer who, in July 1946, moved in the City Council that a clause should be inserted in the next Corporation Bill to give powers to build a municipal theatre and arrange for entertainment there.[2] This proposal was carried without difficulty, and in the following year, when Bradbeer was Lord Mayor, he campaigned consistently for the realization of his dream.[3] But it was still unclear whether the Council wanted to build a theatre for the use of amateur societies, or a new professional theatre. There even seems to have been some confusion in Bradbeer's mind. The Birmingham press, led by T. C. Kemp, theatre critic of the *Birmingham Post*, showed some concern on this point. Kemp was the man who, in 1944, had led the attack on the Theatre Royal, and he urged that the city's prime need was for a new professional theatre. However, it soon became clear that there was no chance of building any sort of theatre in the short term. In the 1950s the City Council set about finding accommodation in the city centre for the amateur dramatic societies,[4] but it was made clear that these efforts in no way precluded the building of a professional theatre as soon as it became possible to do so.

Although the Labour Party's election manifestos frequently referred to its plans to build a civic theatre, it did not give the matter serious consideration until the end of the 1950s. By this time several other municipalities, among them Nottingham, had decided to build municipal theatres, and Arts Council grants to help them in such projects had become generous. Pressure built up within the Labour group to erect a theatre. When Bradbeer lost the group leadership in 1959 he was succeeded by a man who was equally enthusiastic about the theatre, Harry Watton. Watton applied his distinctive brand of enthusiasm and political skill to getting the theatre built, and it became one of his dearest ambitions. The building of a theatre fitted closely into the overall policies developed by the Labour group in the late 1950s which, now that material standards of living had risen, stressed the importance of culture and leisure in the life of the community. One of the main proponents of this argument was Alderman Frank Price, who during

[1] B.C.C., *Pro.*, 12 October 1943, p. 511.   [2] B.C.C., *Pro.*, 2 July 1946, p. 739.
[3] See, for instance, *B.G.*, 14 April 1947.   [4] See above, p. 283.

his years as chairman of the Public Works Committee (1953–9) had shown a particular concern for the wellbeing of the Birmingham theatre, and was prepared to support any improvement of the city's amenities. At this time, the Conservatives were calling on the City Council to economize, and might have been expected to oppose the idea of a theatre. However, as in the case of the exhibition hall, which they approved in 1958, the Conservatives smiled on a scheme which would clearly be of benefit to the city. After all, it was a case of capital expenditure, and it was mainly in the field of revenue outlay that the Conservatives wanted to see economies. Moreover, the understanding which had built up between the leaders of the two groups, Alderman Watton and Alderman Sir Theodore Pritchett, was enough to smooth over any difficulties that remained.

By this time, the Birmingham theatres had run into such difficulties that an additional commercial theatre was out of the question. In view of the problems faced by the Repertory Theatre, the obvious solution was to rehouse it in the municipally built theatre. In 1960 a conference was set up of representatives of the General Purposes Committee, the Repertory Theatre, and the Arts Council. It agreed that, despite the decline of public entertainment in recent years, there was every sign of a revival of interest in the arts.[1] However, a new type of building was needed, with a variety of facilities which could be used throughout the day, and including restaurants, bars, and a car park. The only disagreement within the conference arose over the siting of the theatre. The directors of the Rep wanted it to be in the Civic Centre near the other cultural buildings planned for the site. But the Public Works Committee wanted it to be near Smallbrook Ringway, in the 'theatre-land' which it had been trying for years to create there. The General Purposes Committee decided in favour of the Civic Centre site, but when the results of these discussions were reported to the Council in May 1961, the chairman of the Public Works Committee, Councillor Denis Thomas (Labour), went so far as to move an amendment referring the whole matter back for further consideration of the site. Although the Council accepted the General Purposes Committee's report, Thomas's intervention provided an ominous sign of dissension within the Labour group, which was later to develop into a dispute, not only over the siting of the new theatre, but over the fundamental question of whether it should be built at all. This quarrel was carried on entirely within the Labour group, and did not reach the ears of the general public. But it caused a serious deceleration of progress towards the building of the theatre.

The matter did not come before the Council again until January 1963, by which time a site had been earmarked for the theatre in the

[1] See B.C.C., *Pro.*, 25 May 1961, pp. 18–20 (General Purposes Committee).

Civic Centre, and an estimate of cost (£500,000) had been made. But the site could not be made ready until the end of 1964, and it was expected to take up to three and a half years to design the theatre and prepare for building. Work could not begin, therefore, until mid-1965. The Council approved the building of the theatre in principle, and accepted the full capital cost, less any contributions that might be made by the Repertory Theatre, the Arts Council, and other bodies.[1] In April 1964 the Council approved draft plans for the theatre in principle.[2] Although it was still hoped at the time to begin work in 1965, unforeseen events now became influential. The new Labour Government imposed heavy restrictions on capital expenditure, which made it more important than in previous years for the Labour group to establish clear priorities for its capital projects. This problem greatly strengthened the hand of those elements within the Labour group which were opposed to the theatre. Harry Watton's advocacy of the scheme would probably still have been enough to carry it through, but his illness early in 1966 removed him from a crucial Labour group meeting at which it was decided not to give the theatre main priority in asking for loan sanction. So Labour went out of office without definitely ensuring that the theatre would be built, and those who had been supporting the project for years quaked at the prospect of what the Conservatives might do to it in the name of their economy drive. Yet, here again, the Conservatives' pre-election bark turned out to be worse than their post-election bite. They gave the scheme clear support, while making vigorous efforts to obtain further financial contributions from non-municipal sources. In 1968, shortly after deciding to acquire the Alexandra Theatre, they at last approved a start on work on the repertory theatre, for which loan sanction had now been obtained. Building began early in 1969, and by 1972 the new theatre was open and flourishing.

Civic entertainments

The City Council's willingness to encourage the serious theatre grew out of its promotion of more popular entertainments. It became involved in this field of activity for two main reasons. Firstly, it positively desired to supplement the city's somewhat limited provision of commercial entertainment by providing its own. Secondly, it enjoyed a strong influence over commercial entertainment because it owned a high proportion of the suitable public buildings in the city.

Before 1939 the City Council had not taken a strong interest in entertainment.[3] Private enterprise catered for most needs, and, in any

[1] B.C.C., *Pro.*, 8 January 1963, pp. 605–10 (General Purposes Committee).

[2] Ibid., 14 April 1964, pp. 881–3 (General Purposes Committee).

[3] For details of musical entertainments in the parks, which were initiated in 1936, see Black, p. 471.

case, the Corporation had insufficient powers to promote or subsidize entertainment on a large scale. But during the war a big demand built up for entertainment and social activity. In many cases all the Council had to do was to be cooperative, for instance by making schools and the Town Hall freely available for public dances.[1] But it was also encouraged by the Government to organize entertainments itself, in order to keep war workers happy during their summer holidays. The result was the Brighter Birmingham Campaign, which was repeated annually with great success from 1942 until the end of the war. A variety of entertainments were provided, mostly in the city's parks.

Although interest in summer entertainments declined at the end of the war when people found it easier to go away for their holidays, the Council decided to continue them. Both party groups were committed to making Birmingham a more interesting place to live in, and by now semi-permanent facilities had been provided in several parks, notably in Cannon Hill Park. By the late 1940s, however, the performances were making heavy losses, and they soon had to be restricted to Cannon Hill Park only. Meanwhile the Corporation had acquired much wider powers to promote entertainments under the Local Government Act of 1948, and in the summer of 1954 it held its first Festival of Entertainments. Like the wartime offerings, the festival aimed to entertain the majority of the citizens, and had no cultural pretensions. Adjudged a success, the festival was repeated annually, with a steadily increasing proportion of popular events. Nevertheless, by the end of the decade it was losing money heavily, and the press began to campaign for its replacement by an arts or music festival like Coventry's, which had been launched in 1958.[2] The City Council retorted that Birmingham, with its all-year-round programme of concerts and plays, would not support such a festival. Half-hearted attempts were made from the early 1960s to raise cultural standards, but the Corporation was never prepared to face the big losses that might have resulted from the engagement of really well-known (and expensive) orchestras and performers. Opera and ballet were however performed concurrently in the Birmingham theatres, which cooperated increasingly in the festival, especially after the city's entertainment machine had been tuned up to peak fitness during the World Cup in 1966. Nevertheless, the annual festivals never arrived at a satisfactory formula. If they made a loss, they were heavily criticized, especially by the Conservatives; but if they made a profit, the argument was that no subsidy or guarantee against loss was needed.[3] The City Council was, however, happy to

[1] In 1945 over 1,600 temporary licences were issued for dances in schools, compared to only ninety-one in 1938 (City of Birmingham, *Reports of the Public Entertainments Committee of the Justices*).

[2] *B.M.*, 3 October 1959.   [3] See e.g. *B.M.*, 11 November 1961.

organize totally self-supporting entertainments, which increased in number and success as public demand grew in the 1960s. A revival of entertainments in the parks took place, thanks largely to the flair and imagination of Alderman Frank Price, now chairman of the Parks Committee. In addition to events such as firework displays and jazz festivals, the Corporation launched a highly successful annual venture, the Cannon Hill Park Tulip Festival, in 1960. These events, which Birmingham organized with great talent, had contributed greatly to making the city a more interesting place in which to live by the end of the 1960s.

The C.B.S.O.

One of the strongest arguments against organizing an annual Birmingham festival similar to the Edinburgh festival was that music, one of the major elements in any such event, was provided throughout the year by the City of Birmingham Symphony Orchestra. And just as no festival could be held without Corporation support, neither could the orchestra have survived without municipal aid.

From the later eighteenth century until the First World War, the Birmingham Triennial Music Festival had given Birmingham a national reputation in the field of music which was not paralleled in any other aspect of the city's cultural life. But the festival, interrupted by the war, was not revived after 1918. Consolation for the loss of the festival was provided by the formation of a symphony orchestra in 1919, with the active encouragement of the City Council. At first the orchestra was a part-time affair, but its standards improved considerably in the 1930s, when its audiences markedly increased.[1] Its financial position, however, was never very secure, even though the City Council made it an annual grant of £2,500 from 1935. The Second World War placed it in difficulties for a time, but it continued to give concerts, which proved extremely popular, under the title of the City of Birmingham Emergency Orchestra. By 1943 it had proved itself such an asset to the city that the Council agreed to establish its annual grant on a more permanent basis in return for special children's concerts and school visits.[2] But this scheme could not work satisfactorily until the orchestra was established on a permanent basis. In 1944 the City Council helped it towards permanency by voting an annual grant of £7,000, in addition to the payment for services to education, which amounted at the time to £7,500.[3]

[1] V.C.H. Warcks., vol. vii, p. 243.
[2] B.C.C., Pro., 2 February 1943, pp. 99–100 (General Purposes Committee).
[3] Black, pp. 639–44; B.C.C., Pro., 2 May 1944, pp. 345–6 (General Purposes Committee).

For a short time after hostilities ended, public interest in classical music remained at its high wartime level. In the 1945–6 season the Town Hall was frequently full for concerts,[1] something that had been rare before 1939. Then a slow decline in attendances set in.[2] In 1949 the management committee, fearing that the great frequency of concerts was to blame for the average attendance of only just over a thousand, reduced their number and slackened its efforts to introduce new or little known works.[3] Lower prices and popular programmes were introduced in an attempt to attract an audience from outside the restricted Birmingham middle class.[4] Even experimental lunchtime concerts were tried.[5] The Council provided help by increasing its general grant and payment for services in 1948. But all these efforts were in vain. By 1952 the orchestra was in such dire straits that even a merger with the Bournemouth Symphony Orchestra was considered, until the idea was turned down by Bournemouth.[6] That such a merger should be even suggested caused some shock in Birmingham and in April 1952 Alderman Bradbeer (Labour) moved an amendment calling on the General Purposes Committee to consider ways of maintaining the orchestra in its existing form.[7] The amendment was carried, and in June 1952 the General Purposes Committee proposed an interest-free loan of £20,000 to the orchestra.[8] Some Unionist members objected, but having encouraged the orchestra to set up a full-time establishment, and appointed representatives to its management committee, the Council was morally obliged to continue its assistance. The interest-free loan was approved, and the Birmingham Council asked for contributions from other West Midlands local authorities. But only paltry offers of support were received.

In December 1952 the Council had to increase its general grant from £11,000 a year to £21,000, and took the opportunity of appointing further members to the management committee.[9] Then, a national pay award to musicians forced the Council to increase its grant to £25,000 in February 1953.[10] On both of these occasions the Education Committee was authorized to make greater use of the orchestra and to pay higher fees, but these increases were not so high as those in the general grant. This discrepancy meant that the Council moved from a position where most of its payment to the orchestra was for services

[1] City of Birmingham Information Dept., *City of Birmingham Orchestra* (1947), p. 7.
[2] *T.B.*, no. 15, February 1948, p. 2; no. 23, November 1948, p. 2.
[3] *T.B.*, no. 30, June 1949, p. 1.
[4] *T.B.*, no. 34, November 1949, p. 4; no. 38, March 1950, p. 1.
[5] *T.B.*, no. 41, June 1950, p. 1.   [6] *T.B.*, no. 63, May 1952, p. 2.
[7] B.C.C., *Pro.*, 8 April 1952, p. 925 (General Purposes Committee).
[8] B.C.C., *Pro.*, 17 June 1952, pp. 59–69, 80 (General Purposes Committee).
[9] B.C.C., *Pro.*, 2 December 1952, pp. 536–43, 559 (General Purposes Committee)
[10] B.C.C., *Pro.*, 3 February 1953, pp. 698, 706 (General Purposes Committee).

rendered, to one where it was predominantly giving general support under the Local Government Act of 1948. This trend was dangerous in the long run, for the bigger the general grant, the stronger became the opposition of the voluble minority of councillors who believed that the orchestra should be run on a purely commercial basis. Indeed, after 1953 the Council voted only small increases in the grant, and in 1962 it was still only £30,000 a year. In 1963 the grant was increased to £35,000, but it was reduced again to £30,000 in 1966, as part of the desperate economy measures introduced by Labour in that year. This reduction placed the orchestra in such difficulties that the new Conservative majority had to approve a supplemental grant of £20,000 in July 1966. In this field, as in so many others, the promised Conservative economies did not materialize and the annual grant was soon increased to £50,000. But by 1969 the orchestra was again in such trouble that it had to apply for a further increase in grant, and this time the Conservatives refused. Instead, they urged the orchestra to make a public appeal for funds, similar to those of the early 1950s, which had had some success. But there seemed little chance that the necessary sum could be raised, and in the summer of 1970 the very future of the orchestra appeared uncertain. However, once non-municipal sources of support had rallied to the orchestra the Conservatives, who had been seeking such an outcome, were happy to provide the extra finance necessary to keep the orchestra in being.

These financial difficulties continually restricted the work of the orchestra, and made it almost impossible to plan for the future. In the late 1940s and early 1950s, when the Council was generous with its grants, the management committee tried to improve the standard of the orchestra in the hope that it would make a major contribution to British music. Until about 1951 it remained to some extent a local or regional orchestra, engaging many local soloists and featuring Midland composers. Subsequently it began to use soloists of national renown. The standard of the orchestra undoubtedly improved, but it was never able to achieve the same national recognition as Manchester's Hallé orchestra. The conservatism of Birmingham audiences forced it to concentrate on popular works. Another severe restriction was the lack of a proper concert hall. Although the Birmingham Town Hall had been built in 1834 specifically to house the Triennial Music Festival, its acoustics were very bad, and its seating, despite frequent modifications, was no longer up to modern concert standards. The Labour Party occasionally announced long-term plans to build a new concert hall, but the City Council never seriously considered the idea. Not only did the Town Hall prevent the public from hearing the orchestra's music properly, but it did not contain enough seats to allow the orchestra to cover its costs if it engaged soloists of international repute or entertained well-known foreign orchestras. Temporary price increases on such major occasions often proved self-defeating.

The Town Hall

Of course, the Town Hall had to serve many other interests besides classical music. Because it was the only large public hall in the city, the Corporation was under a considerable obligation to keep it in a satisfactory condition, if not to replace it by a more modern hall, and to make it freely available to organizers of entertainment. On the whole, it fulfilled its responsibilities very well. The Town Hall was used for a variety of entertainments and functions during the war, and there was subsequently no restriction of its use, except in the case of all-in wrestling, which the Council considered to be unsuitable for such a dignified building. Jazz concerts, for instance, were frequently held there in the later 1940s, at a time when they were almost unknown in other cities.[1] Indeed, the Corporation's encouragement of jazz, and of local jazz ensembles, made an important contribution to the development of the idiom in Birmingham after the war. But the Town Hall's acoustics were often a problem. Its relatively small size was also a discouragement to some promoters and the larger Odeon cinema was occasionally used for stage shows. But the Town Hall really came into its own from about 1960 when a growing demand for high quality popular entertainment, especially among young people, coincided with the appearance of pop groups who organized their own amplification, and were not normally inconvenienced by poor acoustics. Despite some criticisms, the Corporation allowed the hall to be used for all-night jazz balls,[2] and generally did all it could to meet promoters' needs. The Corporation's Estates Department, which handled bookings, built up valuable experience of show business procedures, and was in turn able positively to promote the Town Hall as an entertainments centre.

If the Council could not build a new hall, it could at least modernize the old one. Indeed, the Town Hall's more frequent use after the war almost forced it to do so. But improvements were retarded and unsatisfactory to many. Owing to Government restrictions on capital expenditure, redecoration and the provision of adequate changing accommodation could not be carried out until the late summer of 1951.[3] Because this improvement was so modest, the Council had in 1955 to consider a further scheme, for the thorough modernization of the building. The project, which was expected to cost £100,000, was opposed by the Conservative group and the Chamber of Commerce,

---

[1] See Louis D. Brunton (ed.), *Jazz at the Town Hall* (1948) (B.R.L. 603089).
[2] *B.M.*, 22 August 1959.
[3] *B.M.*, 10 February 1951; *B.M.*, 24 August 1951; *B.M.*, 1 October 1951.

which claimed that it would be a waste of money in view of the long-term plans to build a new concert hall.[1] The scheme had to be post-poned in any case owing to economic restrictions in 1956. It was not considered again until 1959, after the General Purposes Committee had discussed, and rejected, a suggestion by a group of councillors that both the Town Hall and the Council House should be demolished and their sites leased for commercial development.[2] Then little more was heard of the plans until October 1960, when Alderman Stephen Lloyd (Conservative), who was actively involved in the city's musical life, successfully moved an amendment calling on the General Purposes Committee to submit a modernization scheme.[3] But once it became known that the Town Hall might be closed for twelve months during the work, strong opposition was expressed by many citizens.[4] Although it proved possible to re-phase the scheme, its scope was also restricted after some of the Labour group leaders had attacked the original plans as too ambitious.[5] Then loan sanction was delayed for some time, and it took several years to carry out the work. At the end of the 1960s the Town Hall remained a cold and uncomfortable building, deficient in many basic amenities. Another major improvement scheme was, however, undertaken in 1972.

Being aware of the shortage of buildings suitable for public assembly in the centre of Birmingham, but unable to build extra accommodation, the Corporation had to satisfy this need by the acquisition of existing buildings. Its main purchase was the Digbeth Institute, which had been on the point of closure, in 1955. After renovation in the following year, it was used mainly for public meetings and community association gatherings, but such was the pressure on central premises that it came to be used more and more for a variety of commercial entertainments. In 1957 it became the headquarters of the Midland Jazz Club,[6] and in 1959 the Estates Committee agreed to allow all-in wrestling there. Wrestling did not actually begin until 1964, but by this time the committee had decided to develop the building as a centre for a variety of recreations.[7]

Professional sport

The West Midlands Plan of 1948 revealed a general shortage of most cultural and social amenities in Birmingham. Facilities for spectator

[1] *B.G.*, 23 December 1955. Their view was supported by the *Birmingham Mail*. See *B.M.*, 23 December 1955, editorial.
[2] *B.M.*, 17 July 1959.
[3] B.C.C., *Pro.*, 4 October 1960, p. 378 (General Purposes Committee).
[4] *B.M.*, *B.P.*, 29 June 1960.   [5] *B.P.*, 12 July 1960.
[6] *E.D.*, 2 November 1957.
[7] *B.P.*, 6 March 1964; *B.M.*, 3 June 1964.

sports were not, however, among them. As a major industrial centre with a prosperous working class, Birmingham had been able to support a number of professional sporting institutions ever since the late nineteenth century. Like the music-hall, they provided ill-educated workers with entertainment of a rare quality, combining excitement, amusement, and the opportunity to participate by encouraging or jeering the performers. Association football was in 1939 by far the most important professional sport in the city. Not only could it be viewed by large numbers of people, which reduced the cost to each spectator, but the Birmingham teams seemed to represent the whole community in an unending struggle against the outside world. On most Saturdays the crowds could roar on one of the Birmingham sides to beat a team of foreigners from Manchester, Liverpool, or London. But when the Birmingham clubs played each other, the communities in conflict were no longer cities, but areas of a city the frenetic growth of which had engulfed a number of communities which always retained a special identity of their own. North Birmingham and the prosperous artisan classes of the middle ring were represented by Aston Villa. The club retained a curious aloofness from Birmingham, partly because Aston had remained an independent borough until 1891, but from the 1890s it began to attract supporters from all over the city. Many were drawn by the glorious name of a club that had won the F.A. cup five times before the First World War, and which in the early 1930s was represented by some of the best teams in its history. Birmingham City drew its supporters principally from the inner ring of slums, and from the municipal estates of the south and south-west. The club always resented playing in the shadow of Aston Villa, and it was never a very successful side, for the best local players were attracted to the rival club, and Birmingham City was always too poor to buy really good players from outside the West Midlands. But its ground had a friendly atmosphere, and its supporters showed a loyalty and enthusiasm that only an underdog can command. For the north-west of Birmingham the principal team was West Bromwich Albion, whose stadium lay a few yards outside the city boundary. This club, like Birmingham City, had a chip on its shoulder, for when the Birmingham teams were playing well it was almost ignored by the city press. Its crowds were usually smaller than those of the two Birmingham clubs, for it was too far away from the densely populated central areas. They were quiet, too, being composed largely of Black Countrymen, who were often more stolid and impassive than the more polyglot Brummies. Even the team's nickname, 'The Baggies', suggested an inability to move with the times, and their ground, The Hawthorns, retained an almost rural, *fin de siècle* atmosphere until after the Second World War.

Although football was Birmingham's main interest, there were

extensive facilities for other professional sports by 1939. The Warwickshire county cricket club had its headquarters at Edgbaston, a
magnificent ground where test matches were regularly played. There
was a flourishing racecourse at Castle Bromwich, and the city had
three tracks for greyhound racing. But professional boxing was less
well catered for, owing to the shortage of adequate halls.

Immediately on the outbreak of war all public sports stadia were
closed on the Chief Constable's orders. Unlike the theatres and cinemas
they were not allowed to resume operations a few days later. The Chief
Constable, acting fully within his powers, refused to take the risk of
heavy casualties at football grounds in the event of a surprise daylight
raid. The decision did not affect Aston Villa, which had decided to
close down for the duration of the war,[1] but Birmingham City was
eager to take part in the wartime league and cup competitions which
had hastily been arranged. Vehement protests were made in the press,
but the Chief Constable's only concession was to allow greyhound
racing to resume on a restricted basis.[2] Even the City Council,
encouraged by the Labour minority, protested, and several Unionist
M.P.s raised the matter in the House of Commons.[3] But the Chief
Constable remained adamant until the spring of 1940, by which time
Birmingham was the only city in Britain still without first-class football.
When he lifted his ban, the season was nearly over. In the following
season play was severely disrupted by the bombing, and the Birmingham City ground was itself badly damaged. Conditions did not return
to normal until the 1941–2 season, when a great renaissance of football
took place. Huge crowds came to watch the games, mainly because
other entertainment opportunities were so restricted, and even the long
hours worked by many citizens did not noticeably reduce attendances.

Big crowds, much higher than before 1939, were maintained after
the war. Aston Villa, which began operations again in the 1945–6
season, enjoyed an average home attendance of 40,000 or more from
1947 until 1950. Average crowds at Birmingham City were almost as
high, at well over 30,000.[4] But neither club was able to capitalize on
this support by achieving real success on the field. Birmingham City
remained rooted in the second division, and Aston Villa, although they
finished regularly in the top half of the first division until the end of the
decade, never came higher than sixth. Attendances at both clubs
began to drop in the 1950s. Birmingham City's enjoyed a brief revival
in the mid-1950s when the club was promoted to the first division, but
poor performances there resulted in a renewed decline from 1957.

[1] B.M., 13 October 1939.   [2] B.M., 16 October 1939.
[3] B.C.C., Pro., 5 December 1939, p. 47; H. of C. Deb., 5th series, vol. cccliii, cols.
726–7, 15 November 1939; vol. ccclvii, cols. 1515–16, 22 February 1940.
[4] Information on attendances has been supplied by the respective football clubs.

Hockley flyover, before (1963) and after (1968) construction

B.M.C. car stockpile at
Wythall, October 1966.

Aston Villa had little success in the 1950s, although in 1957 they won the F.A. cup for the seventh time in their history, but for only the first time since 1920. This success was no happy omen. In 1959 they were relegated to the second division. Although they won their way back even more quickly than they had after their first experience of relegation in 1936, and returned to the first division after only one season among the lower orders, they were never more than a mediocre side in the 1960s. In 1967 they were again relegated to the second division, and despite desperate reorganization and changes of manager, they dropped into the third division in 1970, for the first time in their history. They clambered back into the second division in 1971–2. Villa's decline gave Birmingham City their first ever opportunity to become the city's major club, but they were unable to take it. After a series of poor performances in front of declining crowds in the early 1960s, they sank into the second division in 1965, and despite frantic efforts, including a complete reorganization of the club, they failed to get back into the first division until 1971–2.

The decline in attendances at Birmingham clubs in the 1950s and 1960s was part of a national phenomenon. The growing availability of alternative forms of entertainment, increased personal mobility owing to the spread of the motor car, and inadequate accommodation at football grounds, all reduced the game's attraction. In Birmingham and other big cities the football grounds found themselves increasingly distant from the main concentrations of population as new suburbs grew up and the inner slum areas were demolished. So there was little that the clubs could do except improve ground facilities. Many clubs in other cities were unwilling to do even this, but the two Birmingham clubs and West Bromwich Albion all made substantial improvements by building new banks and stands, and providing covered accommodation, from the late 1950s. Aston Villa and West Bromwich Albion, which had access to nearby unused land, also provided off-street parking for their growing number of motorized spectators. Birmingham City was one of the first clubs in the country, after Coventry City, to provide special travel information and entertainment facilities in addition to football. Aston Villa carried out a reorganization on similar lines in the last years of the decade, after their own drop to a lower level of football. These efforts were not in vain; Birmingham's average attendances even in the second division grew to be higher than those of many a first division club from the mid-1960s. Even more spectacular was the size of Aston Villa's crowds after relegation in 1967. These high figures clearly reflected the strong demand for football in an area of the Midlands which had few successful teams; many people preferred to watch even low-quality play rather than stay at home on Saturday afternoons. But attendances cannot have been entirely unaffected by the

x

clubs' efforts to improve their facilities and stimulate loyalty among their supporters by the development of social clubs and travel schemes. Moreover, the Birmingham press gave city football all the encouragement it could.

Maybe the frenetic support of many spectators actually made it harder for the teams to play with calm and confidence, for they were always under such strong pressure to do well. An especially hysterical atmosphere developed on the terraces and in the columns of the Birmingham press from 1967, when both the Birmingham clubs were in the second division and the whole city (or so it seemed) was willing one of them at least to regain what was considered to be Birmingham's right as a great city to top-class football. But the causes of the decline of Birmingham football were to be found much further back than the 1960s. Aston Villa's last really good team broke up in the early 1930s, and relegation in 1936 showed that something was seriously wrong. Most doubts could be dismissed when the club returned to the first division in 1938, but Aston Villa never seemed able to adapt to a situation in which it was no longer one of the country's finest clubs. Management techniques remained out-dated, and the club seemed to assume that the best players would come to it without being sought out.[1] This approach did not become really disastrous until the abolition of the maximum wage and the granting of greater freedom to players to choose their clubs in the late 1950s. By this time Aston Villa no longer had the reputation to attract players nor the resources to tempt them. Moreover, the remarks of many of the players who declined to come to Birmingham suggested that the city did not appeal to them as a place in which to live. It was no longer enough to depend on young local players, for in the more competitive post-war era ambitious clubs had to draw their apprentices from all over Britain. Not only did local football fail to produce enough good players, but many good prospects were signed by clubs from other parts of the country.

Birmingham City's problems were very different from Villa's. There was no complacency here—there was no room for it. Although Aston Villa had declined from their pinnacle of old, they could still attract more support and good players than Birmingham City.[2] Even after the financial reorganization of the mid-1960s, which made Birmingham City a wealthy and efficient club by the standards of the second division, performances on the pitch did not improve in proportion. The club now had the resources to buy expensive players, but

---

[1] This attitude is reflected very clearly in Fred Ward, *Aston Villa* (1948), esp. p. 30. For direct criticisms of the Villa's complacency and bad organization, see Danny Blanchflower, *The Double and Before* (1961), pp. 51–70; Peter Morris, *Aston Villa: the History of a Great Football Club 1874–1960* (1960), esp. pp. 109–10, 200, 225, 247–8, 277.

[2] See Leslie Knighton, *Behind the Scenes in Big Football* (1949), pp. 109–23.

many did not come up to expectations, and others, unhappy in an unsuccessful club and a strange, unwelcoming city, soon left. It is impossible to go further in explaining the decline of Birmingham professional football up to 1970, but it certainly did not lie in any lack of interest among the citizens. Indeed, in 1970 the directors, managers, and players of the two city clubs appeared to have failed to grasp the opportunities offered by the existence of so great a reserve of loyal support. But success was just around the corner. Both Aston Villa and Birmingham City narrowly missed promotion in 1970–1, something which they put right in the following season, when Birmingham City also reached the semi-final of the F.A. Cup. There was every hope that the new decade would see a football renaissance in Birmingham.

The history of the Warwickshire county cricket club after the war was similar in many ways to that of the Birmingham professional football teams, except that public interest in the club's vicissitudes was much more limited. Even before the war cricket at Edgbaston had attracted fewer spectators than games in cities like Manchester, Sheffield, Leeds, and Nottingham.[1] The ground was close to the city centre, and very accessible to many of the middle-class residential districts that might have been expected to provide support. But the team had never been consistently successful, and amenities at the ground were admitted to be deficient by the club's official historians shortly after the war.[2] In any case, games which were carried on in daytime during working days of the week had little chance of attracting many spectators in a city where a very high proportion of the population had full-time jobs. Consequently, financial difficulties began to hit Warwickshire in the 1950s even before they affected the soccer clubs, and the financial reorganization which the club carried out to meet them set an example which Birmingham City and Aston Villa later followed. A major programme of ground improvements was also carried through, in advance of the football clubs, and to a much higher standard of comfort than they ever achieved. But lack of paying support remained a serious problem. Club membership was stable at around 10,000 by the 1960s, and the supporters' club, founded in 1953, had grown to 150,000 members by 1970. But the number of spectators could vary from year to year, depending on the weather and the success of the team, to a much greater extent than soccer crowds.[3] Even test cricket sometimes failed to attract large crowds to Edgbaston, and in the 1960s Birmingham lost the privilege of an annual test match, though many tests were still held there. So the Warwickshire club became one of the most enthusiastic supporters of Sunday cricket when it was authorized in the later 1960s.

[1] Edgell and Fraser, *Warwickshire County Cricket Club: A History* (1946), p. 147.
[2] Edgell and Fraser, p. 147.   [3] *Ex inf.* L. T. Deakins, general secretary, W.C.C.C.

Despite its financial problems, the club's post-war performances were creditable. A consistently successful spell in the late 1940s and early 1950s was crowned by the winning of the county championship in 1951. Subsequent performances were uneven, but the club went through another relatively successful period in the early 1960s, coming third in 1962 and second in 1964. By 1970 the Edgbaston ground was widely accepted as one of the finest in the country.

So far we have discussed professional spectator sports which still retained a major place in the life of the city in 1970. The destiny of horseracing in Birmingham was not such a happy one. The racecourse at Bromford Bridge, on the eastern boundaries of Birmingham, had been established in 1895, and it flourished until after the Second World War, with eight flat-race meetings a year and various National Hunt fixtures.[1] In the 1950s, however, it began to run into financial difficulties, and pressure from builders, both municipal and private, was hard to resist. In 1953 it reached an agreement with the Education Department to lease part of its site for use as school playing fields, and eventually it sold the whole area to the Corporation for housing. The racecourse closed down in 1966. Birmingham's three greyhound racing tracks, on the other hand, survived. Like the football clubs, their most successful period was after the war, when they were also used for speedway, whose brief heyday came in the later 1940s. During the following decade they were well patronized because they offered easier and more frequent opportunities for gambling than the racecourse. Towards the end of the 1950s, however, they came into competition with the growing mania for bingo, and after the Betting and Gaming Act of 1960 the spread of betting shops and gambling clubs very greatly reduced their popularity.

Broadcasting

With declining public participation in many aspects of sport and entertainment, as well as civic affairs, a heavier responsibility for entertaining and informing Birmingham's citizens fell on the newspapers, radio, and television, the last of which was itself partly responsible for that decline in participation. How well did they meet this challenge?

Before the war the Birmingham studios of the BBC had produced a complete daily radio service, but it was designed to meet the needs of the whole of the Midland region. Birmingham news, and programmes about Birmingham, were prominent, but the service was never specifically local. On the outbreak of the war the BBC's regional radio services were abandoned, and although an increasing number of programmes of Midlands interest were produced in Birmingham towards the end of the war,[2] national items predominated on both the

[1] J. Fairfax-Blakeborough, *A Short History of Birmingham Races* (1951), pp. 17–22.
[2] See *B.M.*, 7 December 1942; *E.D.*, 26 May 1945.

major radio services. After the war, the satisfaction of Birmingham's local needs was not helped by the permanent establishment of a 'Midland' region which included the whole of East Anglia. Television, which reached the Midlands in 1950, was organized on the same regional basis as radio but at first few items were produced in Birmingham. It was not until the late 1950s that the BBC Midland region began to provide an effective regional news service, when it came into competition with the newly-established ATV Midlands. This was an independent television company which served the region alone—although it transmitted a majority of nationally networked programmes. Serving a smaller area than the BBC Midland region, ATV set the pace in local news and programmes throughout the 1960s. Although local programmes reached large numbers of people, they were not screened at peak viewing times, and it seems likely that most citizens, even in the early 1970s, saw a Birmingham evening paper more frequently than a local television programme.

Although the regional role of the two television services was still expanding at the end of the 1960s, a need was felt in Birmingham and the nation as a whole for broadcasting facilities which could serve individual towns and cities. Towards the end of the decade the BBC announced plans to set up a number of local radio stations, but Birmingham City Council refused to give the required financial guarantee for a Birmingham station, claiming that the city was already adequately served by the regional programmes. In 1970 the BBC announced plans for a second set of local stations, for which no guarantee was requested, and Birmingham was included among them. Radio Birmingham was inaugurated later that year, but because it transmitted only on a VHF waveband, very few local people were able to tune in to it until 1972, when the BBC allowed all its local stations to transmit on medium wave.

Newspapers

The limited scope of local broadcasting allowed the Birmingham press to maintain its key role in the city's life. Birmingham was too close to London for any of its newspapers to aspire to a national role like that of the *Manchester Guardian* or the *Scotsman* but it supported a flourishing city and regional press. By 1939 most of the Birmingham newspapers were controlled by two major companies, the Birmingham Gazette Ltd., a member of the Westminster Press Group, and a city-based private company owned by Sir Charles Hyde. The Birmingham Gazette Ltd. was the stronger of the two. In addition to morning and evening daily papers, the *Birmingham Gazette* and the *Evening Despatch*, it published the *Sunday Mercury*, the only Sunday newspaper in the Midlands, and a sporting daily, the *Sporting Buff*. It also produced a

Saturday evening sports results paper, the *Sports Argus*. All its newspapers, according to their editors, maintained an independent political
standpoint, except the *Birmingham Gazette*, which was avowedly Liberal
in sympathies. Sir Charles Hyde's company published a morning paper,
the *Birmingham Post*, and an evening paper, the *Birmingham Mail*. Both
were avowedly Unionist in sympathy but the company's weekly paper,
the *Birmingham Weekly Post*, was politically independent. It was ironic
that the *Gazette*, which had been published almost continuously since
its foundation by Thomas Aris in 1741, and which had been a Tory
newspaper in the nineteenth century, should have become a Liberal
organ in the twentieth.[1] Less surprising, perhaps, was the conversion of
the *Post*, founded in 1857 as a Liberal daily, to Liberal-Unionism and
later to Unionism pure and simple after 1886. These political labels,
however, did not worry the readers very much, and the strength of the
rival newspapers—the *Gazette* sold nearly three times as many copies
as the *Post*—certainly did not reflect the relative strength of the
Liberal and Unionist parties in Birmingham. The Labour cause was
represented only by an ailing weekly paper, the *Town Crier*, which had
first been published in 1861 as a satirical magazine of Liberal allegiance.
The most politically committed of the Birmingham newspapers was
the *Birmingham Post*, which supported the Unionists locally and the
Conservatives nationally in its editorials and even in its news columns.
The *Birmingham Mail* appeared less attached to the Unionist cause
only because, as an evening paper, it devoted less space to politics and
more to the ephemera of local life. Politics intruded far less frequently
into the editorial columns of the *Gazette* and the *Despatch*, and their
news pages showed much less political bias in the selection of material.
Although the *Gazette* gave prominence to the Liberal case at election
times, it and the *Despatch* also gave far more coverage to the Labour
Party than did the two Unionist newspapers. All these publications,
except the *Town Crier*, had an important regional circulation, which
influenced their contents to some extent.

The size of all the Birmingham newspapers was reduced by newsprint restrictions during the war, and circulation was held to a fixed
maximum. But the strong demand for news during the war years
ensured that none of them ran into financial difficulties. Only the
Sports Argus was suspended, owing to the interruption of professional
sport. Even the weak *Town Crier* revived temporarily during the war,
after the Hon. Frank Pakenham had taken it over in 1938 to save it from
extinction. The future of the *Birmingham Mail* and the *Birmingham Post*
was placed in question when Sir Charles Hyde died in 1942, but local
control was maintained when the company was purchased by Lord

[1] For an account of this transformation, see H. R. G. Whates, *The Birmingham Post
1857–1957: A Centenary Retrospect* (1957), pp. 240–2.

Iliffe in 1943. Iliffe set up a public company, the Birmingham Post and Mail Ltd., but accepted Sir Charles Hyde's stipulation that the newspapers should pursue their traditional policy.[1]

Newsprint restrictions were maintained after the war until 1950, and the Birmingham press concentrated on producing more copies to satisfy a demand that had not been fully met during the war, rather than on increasing the number of pages in each issue. Now it was the turn of the Birmingham Gazette Ltd. to run into difficulties. Although it published several flourishing newspapers, it was severely handicapped by the relatively small circulation of the *Evening Despatch*—about 170,000. The Birmingham Post and Mail Ltd. could use the huge circulation of the *Birmingham Mail*—nearly twice as large as that of the *Despatch*—to subsidize the *Birmingham Post*. The Birmingham Gazette Ltd.'s problem was that it fell between two stools, for although the *Birmingham Gazette* sold some 100,000 copies each morning, this was not enough to make it financially independent, while little financial support could be expected from the *Evening Despatch*. In 1956 the Birmingham Gazette Ltd. was taken over by its rival. All its newspapers continued to appear except the *Gazette*, which was absorbed into the *Post*. Although the *Post*'s circulation benefited considerably from the change, rising from some 40,000 to nearly 90,000 in the late 1950s, it retained only about half the readers of the old *Gazette*, which had had a much greater popular appeal even than the new *Post*. By 1960 the readership of the *Birmingham Post* had sunk again to just over 75,000. The *Evening Despatch* continued to be published until 1963, when it was absorbed into the *Birmingham Mail*. It had been losing circulation steadily since the late 1950s. Again, the circulation of the combined newspaper did not reach the sum of its two constituent parts, but at over 400,000 it made the new *Birmingham Mail* one of the three biggest provincial evening newspapers in Britain.

In contrast to the dailies, the weekly papers published by the Birmingham Gazette Ltd. before 1956 continued to flourish after the merger. The *Sunday Mercury* even increased its circulation in the 1960s while the other Birmingham newspapers were losing some of theirs. In fact, it was the *Birmingham Weekly Post* which ceased separate publication in 1960 and merged with the *Sunday Mercury* after its circulation had fallen from over 43,000 in 1952 to a mere 24,000. Its popular appeal had always been limited, and its failure reflected an inability to attract new, young readers.[2] The *Sports Argus*, of course, had an assured circulation and future.

The reduction in the number of newspapers published in Birmingham in the later 1950s and early 1960s, and the concentration of those that remained under a single control, encouraged attempts by other interests

[1] Whates, *The Birmingham Post*, pp. 230–3.   [2] *Birmingham Sketch*, May 1960, p. 22.

to launch rival publications. A monthly magazine, the *Birmingham Sketch*, was launched by a national publishing group in 1957 and has continued ever since, though with a very small circulation. It reflected many aspects of the life of the city and the surrounding countryside, but concentrated on social gatherings—like a Warwickshire version of the *Tatler*. Less successful was the attempt by a group of Midlands weekly newspapers controlled by the former Birmingham Labour M.P., Woodrow Wyatt, to launch a weekly paper, the *Birmingham Planet*, in 1963. The *Planet* struggled to establish itself for a few years, and achieved the distinction of being the first Birmingham newspaper to print regularly in colour, but it was forced to cease publication in 1967. Another casualty, in the late 1950s, was an old-established weekly newspaper specializing in Birmingham local news, the *Birmingham News*, which had been one of a number of local newspapers published in the conurbation by the Birmingham News and Printing Company.

So by 1970 Birmingham was left with one morning, one evening and one Sunday newspaper, all published by the same company. The circulation of all of them, except the *Sunday Mercury*, had declined slightly during the 1960s, but none was in danger of collapse. However, the small circulation of the *Birmingham Post*, which totalled only 70,000 in 1970, was a cause of some difficulty to the Birmingham Post and Mail Ltd. Fortunately, it had never been the newspaper's policy to aim for a readership outside the Midlands,[1] so it was not over-stretched when the general decline in newspaper circulation set in in the 1960s. In view of the city's proximity to London, Birmingham was fortunate to retain such a flourishing local press.

There was a substantial change in the character of Birmingham's newspapers after the war. All became more popular in their appeal, including more illustrations and reducing weighty articles and lengthy news items to a minimum. Even the *Birmingham Post*, which saw itself as the city's quality newspaper, had to broaden its appeal from 1956 in an attempt to retain the readers of the old *Despatch*. The newspapers also became less politically committed.[2] Owing to the near eclipse of the Liberal Party after the war, the *Gazette* promoted the Liberal cause less energetically. The *Post* and the *Mail* were vigorously anti-socialist during the years of the Labour Government, but their tone moderated markedly in the 1950s as they sought, above all, to maintain their circulations. Indeed, they began to style themselves as 'independent' in politics. The *Post* became even more impartial after its merger with the *Gazette* in 1956, and left the *Mail* as the main Conservative standard-

---

[1] See Whates, *Birmingham Post*, pp. 238–9.
[2] Donald Read has suggested that provincial newspapers pursue a moderate conservative line in the hope of retaining the support of most shades of local opinion. See his *The English Provinces c. 1760–1960: A Study in Influence* (1964), pp. 249–50.

bearer in Birmingham. But even the *Mail* slackened its attacks on Labour from the late 1950s, partly because of the movement towards a party consensus on municipal affairs during these years. This trend was confirmed in 1963 after the *Mail*'s merger with the *Despatch*. In place of blind allegiance to Conservatism, the *Birmingham Post* began to crusade on a number of issues of public concern, without concerning itself with the attitude taken by the Conservative or any other party. One such issue was the integration of coloured immigrants, which the *Post* did all it could to encourage from the late 1950s, although it always supported immigration control. The *Post* also called for more overall planning of the city, and attacked Labour's advocacy of a flexible approach. It also strongly attacked the Conservative majority's decision to sell municipal houses in 1966. In the late 1960s, the *Birmingham Mail* began to move in the same direction, and early in 1970 it organized a vigorous campaign for more effective measures to integrate coloured immigrants.

The growing political impartiality of the Birmingham daily press compensated to some extent for the weakness of the Labour organs of public opinion. Despite its expansion during the war, the *Town Crier* began to encounter difficulties in the early years of peace. After the establishment of the *Birmingham Journal* by the Trades Council in 1946[1] it was no longer the sole organ of the Birmingham Labour movement, and it ceased publication in October 1951. The monthly *Birmingham Journal* seemed to be well-established by the early 1950s, but it ran into increasingly serious difficulties from the end of the decade. Although still in existence in 1970, its circulation, and its influence, were very small indeed.

The spread of local trivia through the columns of the Birmingham press did not lead to better reporting of local affairs than before the war. On the contrary, events such as City Council debates and munici-pal elections received less and less attention. Editorial comments were greatly restricted, and the correspondence columns of the *Mail* (though not of the *Post*) had come to contain numerous examples of rhetoric, prejudice, and inanity by the 1960s. On the other hand, much reporting of local and regional affairs, especially in the *Post*, was of a high standard, and the *Post*'s national news reporting was also impressive. Both news-papers maintained a large readership in the West Midlands outside Birmingham, and were a major support to the city's role as uncrowned regional capital. Moreover, the *Mail*'s coverage of local news was so dense that local weekly newspapers, of which there had been a few before 1939, had been rendered completely redundant within the city boundaries by the 1960s. However, we cannot help expressing the view, unreasonable though it may be in the face of commercial realities,

[1] See above, pp. 116–17.

that the Birmingham popular press could have done more to inform
and educate its public, especially in the late 1950s and 1960s. With radio
and television able to exercise only a limited influence on opinion and
activities within Birmingham, the press alone had the power to
counter apathy and ignorance in politics and the arts. But this was
a responsibility which it declined to accept, and whose existence it
even stubbornly refused to recognize.

The war and the post-war austerity years created a seller's market
for entertainment in Birmingham. With high earnings, a shortage
of goods for sale, and an unusually drab environment, all forms of
escapism were in much greater demand than before the war. But for a
long time no marked expansion of entertainment provision took place.
Building restrictions prevented the construction of new premises and
the repair of the more seriously damaged theatres and cinemas. Few
improvements were made to existing buildings and stadia; with long
queues for every event, they were not needed to attract the public.
The entertainment provided was aimed at the satisfaction of the greatest
possible number of citizens, and its quality was low. So the entertainment industry was highly vulnerable to competition from television
after 1949. Because of the city's low population density, many people
found major places of entertainment hard to reach, especially as they
were not numerous in the newer suburbs. Television encouraged people
to stay in their homes, most of which were becoming increasingly
comfortable.

The fall in attendances was, of course, a further discouragement to
improvements and new enterprises. Many establishments closed, mostly
in the over-provided middle ring. It was not until the later 1950s,
when public entertainment attendance had almost reached rock bottom,
that promoters began to improve their programmes and accommodation. Television had now lost some of its appeal, especially for
courting couples and young marrieds. Working hours were shorter, and
living standards higher, than at the beginning of the decade. More
people had motor cars which in the evenings allowed them to reach
the centre rapidly and they started going to bed later than the traditional
Midlands bedtime of 10 p.m. Facilities in the city centre were not
up to the standard that might have been expected in a city of Birmingham's size, but they at least provided an exciting environment
and a standard of luxury which the neighbourhood cinema could not
provide. So from the early 1960s city centre entertainment enjoyed a
revival, while the suburban cinema continued its decline, though
more slowly now that the least attractive houses had been closed. The
centre benefited, too, from the mushrooming of private dancing and
theatre clubs, many of them supported by various forms of gambling,

after the Betting and Gaming Act of 1960.[1] Many teenagers and single young people attended these clubs and a number of city-centre public houses which the brewers now began to promote as places of fashionable resort. The club boom reached the suburbs too, but efforts to establish ten-pin bowling as a major pastime there had suffered a setback by the end of the decade.

The revival of city-centre entertainment in the 1960s was restricted almost entirely to mass entertainment. The theatre and classical music remained in serious difficulties, although even here there was some revival in audiences towards the end of the decade. The continuing problems of the minority-interest activities helped to confirm that the revival of city-centre entertainments was the result of the reaction against television of a richer, more mobile working class, and the more sophisticated demands of young people emancipated by high wages. There was clearly less potential for growth in entertainments of interest to Birmingham's small middle class, which had never been completely won over by television, even in the 1950s. Despite the valiant efforts of the Corporation to encourage the arts, little working-class support could be expected while the general standard of education in the city remained so low. Yet even the city-centre mass entertainments had by no means reached their full potential by 1970. In the 1960s demolitions for the inner ring road reduced the already small number of cinemas there, and the delay in building a theatre and/or entertainment centre in Smallbrook Ringway was an ominous sign of promoters' and developers' lack of confidence. Sites were too expensive in the restricted central area for such projects to be undertaken lightly, and although many developers' schemes included cinemas in shopping precincts to attract the Corporation, such frivolities were usually abandoned once a lease of the site had been obtained. Birmingham still had not realized its full potential role as the entertainment centre of the West Midlands conurbation. Without a rapid transport system, its location on the east of the conurbation made it inaccessible to many, and its attractions were not sufficiently superior to Wolverhampton's for it to act as a strong magnet on the densely-populated north-west.

At any rate, the popularity of the city centre in the 1960s suggested that the City Council's policy of redeveloping the area and improving road access to it was proving a success. What was needed in the 1970s was a greater willingness by developers to take risks in providing new entertainment. With just a little more enterprise and imagination, Birmingham had the potential to become one of the liveliest cities in Britain.

[1] Nevertheless, Birmingham still had fewer clubs and restaurants with floor shows at the end of the 1960s than Manchester and Liverpool. Totals for large cities were: Birmingham 6; Liverpool 7; Manchester 12; Leeds 4 (*Stage Year Book*).

X

THE EDUCATION OF THE CITIZENS

WHATEVER the standard of its housing, communications, and other physical equipment, the character and achievements of any urban community depend ultimately on the qualities of its inhabitants. Enough has already been said to indicate the generally industrious and enterprising character of Birmingham's population. This chapter will attempt to throw some light on the quality of their intellectual equipment by examining the development of education in Birmingham during the years 1939–70. Of course, many residents were not the products of Birmingham's education system, having migrated to the city in adulthood. Even more would no doubt have maintained that their most useful capacities had been developed, not at school or college, but by direct experience in employment. Yet the education system was a crucial element of Birmingham's history throughout this period. The basic educational knowledge of the great majority of Birmingham citizens was acquired in city schools and colleges. As the heaviest single charge on the rate fund, education was recognized as one of the most important of the Corporation's responsibilities. Furthermore, the political aspects of education policy were sufficiently idiosyncratic to qualify it for consideration separately from other municipal activities.

The development of public education in Birmingham after 1939 was a story of steady progress under major handicaps. The members of the Education Committee, officials, and teachers made strenuous efforts to overcome the nineteenth-century legacy of slum schools and generally poor educational provision. Some of them gained national reputations in the process. The past, however, could not be wiped out overnight. Effort had to be concentrated on certain priorities: further education in the 1950s; secondary education in the following decade; and, from the later 1960s, primary education. It proved very difficult to modernize facilities in the central districts where population was declining at the same time as providing new schools to meet growing demand in the suburbs. Central Government restrictions were often a cause of frustration. So too were occasional major disagreements between the parties, and between individual members of the Education Committee, over education policy.

The inter-war years had seen a marked improvement in many aspects of Birmingham's education provision.[1] The Education Committee, chaired by Sir George Kenrick until 1922 and subsequently by Alderman Byng Kenrick, both of them nationally known educationists, was

[1] For an account of education in these years, see Briggs, pp. 236–48.

recognized as 'one of the most efficient organizations of its type in the country'.[1] Many of its decisions anticipated national education policies; for instance, it had already decided to separate primary and secondary education before the Hadow Report was published in 1926.[2] Yet by 1939 the committee had done very little to solve the problem of Birmingham's numerous slum schools. It had been forced to concentrate on building schools for the suburban areas, and had been held back by Government restrictions on expenditure in the 1930s. Moreover, it had been unable to give Birmingham the provision for secondary education that it needed, or even one that would have put it on a par with other large cities. Again, Government restrictions in the 1930s were largely to blame, but there was also a strongly held belief in Birmingham that apprenticeship was a sufficient education for many boys, and that the city did not need as many secondary schools as cities with a lower proportion of skilled employment. Both these problems were to continue to dog the Education Committee after the war.

By the late 1930s much of the gloom surrounding the future of Birmingham education since the economy cuts of the early 1930s had been dispelled. The City's expenditure on education increased by 13 per cent between 1935 and 1939, while its total outlay rose by only 9 per cent.[3] Some progress was made towards increasing the number of secondary school places[4] and in 1938 King Edward's High School moved from its old premises in New Street into spacious new buildings at Edgbaston. The announcement by the Government that the school leaving age would be raised to fifteen in September 1939 aroused some criticism in the City Council, but the great majority of members and the Birmingham press welcomed it.[5]

The Second World War broke out on the very day that the school leaving age was to have been increased. The inevitable abandonment of this reform was the war's first pernicious influence on education in Birmingham, but it was by no means the last.[6] All schools in the city were immediately closed, and numerous children were evacuated from the central districts, which the Government had designated as a high risk area.[7] Unfortunately, 30,000 children stayed behind, and were

---

[1] Briggs, p. 237.   [2] Briggs, p. 239.

[3] Calculated from City of Birmingham, *General Statistics and Epitome of the City's Accounts*.

[4] *B.M.*, 4 March 1944, editorial.

[5] Opponents of the reform were reassured by the Education Committee's promise that children going into 'beneficial employment' would still be allowed to leave school at fourteen. It was suggested that the proportion of such early leavers would be as high as one half.

[6] For a general account of the effect of war on education, see Gerald Bernbaum, *Social Change and the Schools 1918–1944* (1967), pp. 98–106.

[7] For a full account of evacuation, see Black, pp. 56–65.

rejoined within a few days by growing numbers of children and mothers who could see no good reason for staying in the reception areas. They added greatly to the problem of providing an education service in the non-evacuable, suburban districts. The City Council was unwilling to reopen schools there until they had been provided with shelters (mainly in trenches). Some schools resumed operations on a voluntary basis in October, but attendance could not be made compulsory until all of them were fully protected. In the central areas the Corporation set up a home teaching scheme, but it was not entirely satisfactory and several thousand children continued to roam the streets all day.[1] The Labour group wanted to have all the central schools reopened, but the Board of Education insisted that full protection be first provided. This took some time, but by the spring of 1940 many schools were open again, and it was estimated that only 8,000 Birmingham children were receiving no instruction at all.[2] All the neutral zone schools, including secondary schools, opened for the summer term, and shelters had been provided throughout the city by July.

When heavy bombing began in August 1940, and many children were evacuated for a second time, the Education Committee was able to keep most of its schools open. But such disruption was caused that many children were able to play truant with impunity. By March 1941 it was estimated that four children out of ten were playing truant,[3] and absenteeism remained high even after the raids.[4] Classes stayed over-crowded until the end of the war owing to damage and the shortage of teachers.

There can be no doubt that most children's education suffered from the war, as indicated by tests carried out on teenagers called up for national service in 1946 and 1947.[5] Yet in many ways the war was a time of progress in education. The provision of milk and school meals was greatly expanded, and dozens of nursery schools were provided to allow mothers to work in industry. The Birmingham public acquired a greater awareness of the importance of education, and Government proposals for educational reform, which culminated in the 1944 Education Act, were generally welcomed by the Education Committee, the City Council, and the press.[6] True, the Labour group complained

[1] B.C.C., *Pro.*, 4 June 1940, p. 449 (Education Committee).

[2] *H. of C. Deb.*, 5th series, vol. ccclxi, col. 782, 4 June 1940. At this time Birmingham was educating a much higher proportion of its children than Manchester, Leeds, and Liverpool, but less than Sheffield. Only 14,500 Birmingham children now remained in the reception areas.

[3] *B.G.*, 1 March 1941.

[4] In 1942-3 the average elementary school attendance in Birmingham was 84·5 per cent, compared to 88·9 per cent in the last year before the war (Richard M. Titmuss, *Problems of Social Policy* (1950), p. 416n).

[5] Titmuss, p. 409.

[6] See e.g. *B.M.*, 25 January 1944.

that the Government reforms would maintain inequality of educational opportunity, but its members continued to express respect for the Unionist achievement in Birmingham education before the war.[1] The two groups were in general agreement that the post-war development of education in Birmingham should proceed along lines similar to those established before 1939. In October 1945, the chairman of the Education Committee, Alderman Wilfrid Martineau (Unionist), stated that a major factor in plans for the future was 'the soundness of the present educational structure'. Unlike the L.C.C., which had decided on a whole new system of multilateral schools, Birmingham would continue with its present secondary structure of grammar, secondary modern, and technical schools. Experiments with new types of school, such as multilateral schools, would, however, be made in some areas of the city.[2] The Labour Party was perfectly happy with this approach, and after the elections of November 1945 the Labour group unanimously supported the re-election of Martineau as chairman of the committee. The change of majority would not, it was made clear, lead to any changes in education policy.[3] And this assurance was repeated after subsequent changes of control into the early 1950s.

The main lines of Birmingham's post-war education policy were embodied in the development plan which it was required to draw up under the 1944 Act.[4] Its various sections and amendments were approved by the City Council between 1946 and 1952, and it was accepted by the Ministry of Education in 1953. In the field of primary education its main innovation was to plan for the voluntary education of children under the age of five in nursery schools or nursery classes.[5] Secondary education was to develop in a variety of forms so that each child could receive an education suited to its 'age, abilities, and aptitudes'.[6] It was decided to maintain the current grammar school provision of about 15 per cent, although an increase was planned in the number of girls' places. The technical school provision would rise from 7 per cent to about 14 per cent, an improvement that seemed 'particularly desirable in view of the nature of much of the industry in the City.'[7] The remaining children, about 71 per cent, would attend secondary

---

[1] See e.g. *Alderman Byng Kenrick: Tributes and Appreciations on his Retirement as Chairman of the Birmingham Education Committee . . .* , 1943, p. 11 (Birmingham University Inst. of Education Library).

[2] *B.M.*, 26 October 1945. See also 'Development of secondary education: a Birmingham report', *Education*, 18 May 1945, pp. 716–18.

[3] *B.P.*, 13 November 1945.

[4] City of Birmingham, *Development Plan for Primary and Secondary Education*, 2 vols. (1953).

[5] City of Birmingham, *Development Plan for Primary and Secondary Education*, vol. i, pp. 4–5.

[6] Ibid., pp. 5–6.   [7] Ibid., p. 7.

modern courses.[1] Because of the decision to maintain grammar school provision at its somewhat low level, it appeared to be 'the wise and indeed the only practicable course to retain such schools in their present form' and to concentrate on providing new secondary modern and technical schools: 'This policy would aim at preserving all that is best in the past organization of Secondary Education, and at the same time developing newer types of Secondary Schools.' However, there was room for experiment in grouping schools of different types on the same site, in order to facilitate transfers and 'promote a greater social unity'.[2]

One of the first problems to be faced after the war was the rebuilding of damaged schools and the construction of new ones to meet the post-war bulge in the birth rate and the development of new housing estates. But for some time a large-scale building programme was out of the question. The Government approved twelve primary school building schemes in 1946, ten of them for suburban estates, but they were all particularly urgent.[3] Secondary school building was especially restricted, and only a few secondary modern projects were included in the 1947 building programme.[4] When the school leaving age was raised to fifteen in 1947, Birmingham had to build a number of temporary huts under the Ministry of Education's HORSA scheme.[5] Grammar school developments were also greatly restricted, and little could be done to overcome the serious shortage of girls' places. Government building restrictions began to ease towards the end of the decade, and by 1951 twelve new schools had been completed. Fifty-nine more had been altered or extended, and a total of 9,500 new primary and 1,000 secondary places had been provided.[6] The first schools built were of luxurious design, but by 1951 economies were being introduced owing to new restrictions on expenditure by the Ministry of Education.[7] Non-traditional methods were increasingly used in the early 1950s to speed up building.[8] By 1955, 121 out of 223 major building schemes planned since the war were complete, and fifty-eight more were in progress. Out of 190 minor schemes planned, 156 had been carried out.[9] The emphasis now had switched from primary to secondary schools, as the post-war bulge began to pass into them. By September 1958 half of the seventy-six new secondary schools planned after the war had

[1] The Ministry of Education had recommended that the proportion of secondary modern places should be 70–75 per cent.

[2] Ibid., p. 8.   [3] Black, p. 279.   [4] Black, p. 282.

[5] Black, p. 283. HORSA was an abbreviation of 'Huts on the raising of the school leaving age'. W. T. Benslyn, Education Committee architect, was strongly opposed to these huts, and experiments showed that permanent buildings of light construction could be built just as quickly (The Builder, 14 February 1951).

[6] Ibid.

[7] The Story of Post-War Schoolbuilding (Min. of Education pamphlet, no. 33), 1957.

[8] E.D., 13 October 1953; 'Focus on Birmingham', Education, 4 March 1955, p. 411.

[9] 'Focus on Birmingham', p. 403.

been opened.[1] There was also some use of temporary buildings. But by now the shortage of accommodation had largely been overcome, and the Education Committee found itself preoccupied by a more intractable problem, the teacher shortage.

Birmingham had not enjoyed a surplus of teachers before 1939, and, as we have seen, the size of classes greatly increased during the war.[2] The shortage was eased slightly when teachers returned from the forces in 1945 and 1946, but it grew serious again when the bulge began to hit the primary schools at the end of the decade. Birmingham's predominantly young population produced large numbers of children, and between 1946 and 1952 the city's school population increased by 27·5 per cent, while that of the country as a whole rose by only 19·3 per cent. The local birth rate continued at a high level even after the immediate post-war bulge, and over the years 1946–57 Birmingham's population of school age rose by 41 per cent compared to a national average of 35 per cent. By 1957 Birmingham needed eleven teachers for every eight that it had employed in 1946, merely to maintain the staffing standard of the latter year, which was totally inadequate when compared to the maximum size of classes laid down by the Ministry of Education in its 1951 grant regulations.[3] Unfortunately, Birmingham now found it much harder to recruit teachers than before the war. Then, it had been allowed to pay attractive salaries, and it had a country-wide reputation as a good employer.[4] So although it did not produce enough teachers for its own needs, it was able to import them from other areas and notably from South Wales.[5] Unfortunately for Birmingham, area salary weightings were abolished on the advice of the Burnham committee after the war, and the Ministry of Education refused all the City's subsequent requests for permission to pay an extra allowance.[6] The number of teachers rose from 4,200 in 1946 to 6,019 in 1957, but by the latter year the average size of a Birmingham junior class was 39·9, compared to a county borough average of 37·0.[7] Although Birmingham still retained its reputation as a good employer, the Birmingham Teachers' Association (the city branch of the N.U.T.) grew increasingly worried that quality would suffer. The turnover of

[1] E. L. Russell, 'Organisation of Secondary Education: Birmingham', *Education*, 5 December 1958, p. 981.

[2] For difficulties in obtaining teachers towards the end of the war, see *B.P.*, 1 April 1944; *B.G.*, 25 November 1944.

[3] E. L. Russell, 'Organisation of Secondary Education', p. 981.

[4] *Alderman Byng Kenrick: Tributes and Appreciations*, p. 25.

[5] 'Focus on Birmingham', p. 399.

[6] See e.g. statement by the Minister of Education, Sir David Eccles, in *H. of C. Deb.*, 5th series, vol. dxxxv, cols. *1102–3*, 9 December 1954.

[7] Ministry of Education, *Selected Statistics Relating to Local Education Authorities in England and Wales*. The only major city to have bigger classes than Birmingham was Hull.

Y

young teachers was rapid, especially among the women, and threw
a heavy load on the older teachers. Resignations owing to bad conditions and overcrowding multiplied from about 1948. In the mid-1950s
it was estimated that 70 per cent of the teaching staff had less than
seven years' experience.[1] A high turnover meant rapid promotion,
but as a result teachers often did not stay in one school long enough
to become fully committed to it and to allow the development of new
studies.[2] Now that Birmingham was unable to pay a special allowance,
teachers were reluctant to come from other areas because of the general
unattractiveness (whether real or imagined) of the city,[3] conditions
in the schools, and the difficulty of finding living accommodation.

So the Education Committee decided to seek more potential teachers
among Birmingham school leavers. Immediately after the war it set up
its first training college, in temporary accommodation, which it moved
in 1957 to purpose-built premises in Edgbaston. Later, in 1963, it
opened a day training college at Bordesley. By the mid-1950s about
60 per cent of the teachers trained in Birmingham remained in the
city to teach.[4] But Birmingham alone could never completely supply
its own needs in teachers. Fewer pupils stayed on at school beyond the
school-leaving age than in most other big cities, and the proportion
doing so was considerably lower than the average for all county boroughs. Consequently, the proportion of school-leavers entering training
colleges was much lower than elsewhere.[5] Birmingham's extremely
low number of girls' grammar school places was partly responsible for
its dearth of women teachers, which was much more serious than the
shortage of men. The relative unattractiveness of prolonged secondary
education to Birmingham children was usually attributed to the
multiplicity of well-paid jobs and opportunities for professional training
in the city, and high wage levels made teaching especially unattractive
from a financial point of view.

The Education Committee did more to attract teachers to Birmingham than issue attractive brochures;[6] it obtained special powers
through a Corporation Bill to set up the Martineau Teachers' Club
and Centre, opened in 1952. But such blandishments had only a
marginal influence, and when the teacher shortage became even
worse in the mid-1950s, Birmingham began to call on the Government

[1] 'Focus on Birmingham', p. 401.
[2] See e.g. B. M. Bowker, *Golden Hillock Boys 1910 to 1960: The History of a Birmingham School* (1960), p. 29.
[3] See e.g. the Minister of Education's comments on this score in *H. of C. Deb.*, 5th
Series, vol. dlv, cols. *674–5*, 28 June 1956.
[4] 'Focus on Birmingham', pp. 402–3.
[5] Ministry of Education, *Selected Statistics*.
[6] See, for instance, *Birmingham: Second City of Britain* (1957); City of Birmingham
Education Committee, *Teaching in Birmingham* (1959).

to fix a quota of teachers for each education authority, to stop teachers gravitating to attractive areas like the South Coast resorts. Maximum establishments for certain categories of women teachers had been in force since 1948, owing partly to pressure from Birmingham, and in 1956, after strenuous lobbying by the city M.P.s, the Minister of Education agreed to introduce a general quota system. Unfortunately, quotas were only a partial solution, as Birmingham's teacher shortage was largely a reflection of a very serious national shortage.[1] Between 1956 and 1959 Birmingham's total of full-time teachers rose only from 5,914 to 6,414. Four years later the total had risen only by a further two hundred. Although the employment of part-time teachers under a national scheme afforded some relief from 1959, Birmingham's average junior class was still bigger in 1963 than the national average for county boroughs. Among the major cities, only Liverpool had bigger classes. And only Bristol had a higher ratio of senior pupils to teachers.[2]

Happily, the situation was already beginning to improve, thanks to a steady increase in the national supply of qualified teachers—an indirect result of the expansion of secondary education in the 1950s. By 1966–7 the ratio of primary pupils to full-time teachers had fallen in Birmingham to 28·1, and of secondary pupils to 18·3.[3] The city was now slightly better off in these respects than the average county borough, and than several other large cities. In May 1968 it was announced that Birmingham might even reach its maximum authorized establishment in 1968–9, for the first time since the quota system was introduced in 1956.[4] In fact it failed to do so, but in 1969 the Education Committee considered itself to be so well provided with teachers that it could afford to decelerate their recruitment as an economy measure.

To overcome Birmingham's legacy of slum schools was another lengthy task. After the war the Ministry of Education wanted local authorities to concentrate on providing schools for the increased population of school age, rather than on replacing obsolete buildings. The problem was very similar to that created by the housing shortage; the first priority was to cater for those who had no accommodation at all. The Education Committee accepted this policy. After all, the population of the central areas was declining, so that overcrowding of buildings, at least, was not a serious problem in the central schools. Moreover, the quality of the teachers in these schools was often extremely high, for they attracted men and women who relished a challenge. In 1949 the Ministry of Education chose a Birmingham school, Steward Street Junior School, as an example of what could be done 'in an

[1] On the effect of the quota system, see Russell, 'Education in Birmingham', p. 45. See also E. L. Russell, *The Crucial Factor: The Supply and Training of Teachers 1960–1970* (1960).

[2] Ministry of Education, *Selected Statistics*.

[3] Institute of Municipal Treasurers, *Education Statistics*.   [4] *B.M.*, 23 May 1968.

environment which others might well have found discouraging'.[1]
Here the headmaster, A. L. Stone, had pioneered teaching methods
designed to help children in self-expression which were later widely
adopted throughout the country.

Of course, such brilliant successes did not make any less urgent the
provision of new schools in the central areas. Unfortunately, the postponement of central area redevelopment delayed the provision of new
school buildings. Very little was done until the mid-1950s, when
Birmingham still had 1,500 places in schools built before 1870, and
60,000 in schools built between 1870 and 1902. In May 1955 the Labour
group announced plans to make a start on improving slum schools,
after the relaxation of Government restrictions. Unfortunately, the
Ministry of Education cut back Birmingham's school building programme shortly afterwards in order to concentrate on the reorganization of rural schools, and the replacement of slum schools was particularly affected.[2] After talks with the Ministry, Birmingham was allowed
to continue its slum school programme in December 1955,[3] but the
first central school was not demolished until early in 1958, and the
school built to replace it was not planned to be ready until 1960.[4] It was
not until 1965 that the first secondary school was opened in a central
redevelopment area.[5] In 1967 some twenty-eight schools still remained
in use which the Education Committee had scheduled for closure shortly
after the war, most of them in the central areas. And the condition of some
of the older primary schools, such as the Highfield and Osborne schools,
was a matter of continuing concern to the Education Committee. However, increasing resources were switched to the central area schools after
the post-war bulge began to pass out of the secondary schools in 1961,[6]
and as the redevelopment of the central areas made more rapid progress. After coming to power in 1966 the Conservatives maintained
the effort to clear the slum schools, and by 1970 they had made considerable progress towards this end, thanks partly to the Government's
willingness to allow a high concentration of resources on the problem.

So far we have concentrated on material factors affecting the
quality of education. But what of the types of education provided?

[1] *Story of a School* (Ministry of Education Pamphlet, no. 14), 1949, p. 5. But these
teaching methods were not universally approved at the time in Birmingham. See
Councillor Jack Wood's (Labour) article in *B.G.*, 11 July 1950, claiming that 'fancy
teaching methods' were partly to blame for the decline in standards of literacy
detected by the Westhill College survey, *Eighty Thousand Adolescents*. Other members
of the Education Committee criticized such experiments, but Alderman Sir Wilfrid
Martineau was prepared to support 'free activity' teaching if it were done well.
[2] *E.D.*, 4 May 1955; 11 August 1955.
[3] *E.D.*, 19 December 1955.   [4] *B.P.*, 28 December 1957.
[5] *B.M.*, 3 July 1965. This was Duddeston Manor bilateral school.
[6] Russell, *The Crucial Factor*, p. 3.

This question leads us on to the whole problem of secondary education policy, which created much difficulty from the mid-1950s.[1]

The 1944 Education Act did not specify a tripartite division of secondary education into grammar, technical, and secondary modern schools, but such a system had been embodied in previous Government reports. It was generally understood at the time that the effect of the Act would be to establish a tripartite system, and the vast majority of local education authorities were prepared to reorganize along these lines. Only a few Labour-controlled areas, such as the L.C.C. and Middlesex, planned a large-scale system of comprehensive schools after the war. The Labour Government adhered to the tripartite system, although it was prepared to sanction experiments, especially in rural areas and districts of new housing. Indeed, the Labour Party itself was not united on the issue. Some sections of the party wanted to see a general system of multilateral or comprehensive schools,[2] an idea which had originated in the late nineteenth century,[3] but the parliamentary Labour Party did not come out firmly in favour of comprehensive schools until the mid-1950s.[4] Even then, it was not agreed on what type of comprehensive school was best, and the party's policy of fully comprehensive schools was not clearly defined until 1958.[5]

Given this uncertainty at national level, it is not surprising that the Birmingham Education Committee was able to agree on a tripartite system at the end of the war.[6] Labour members of the committee recognized that multilateral schools were an unknown quantity, and they were happy to accept the experimentalist approach which was sanctioned by both the main national parties.[7] There were some criticisms from within the Labour group of the details of the development plan, mostly on the ground that not enough comprehensive schools were included, but these comments generally came from individual councillors and did not reflect group policy. The plan included a total of four comprehensive schools, catering for 4·5 per cent of children reaching secondary school age, in districts where there had previously been little or no provision for secondary education. Two of them, Great Barr and Sheldon Heath, were to be fully comprehensive, and the other two were to be bilateral.[8] Plans were made in some cases for the

[1] I am indebted to Mr. K. Isaac-Henry for much of the information on which this section is based.

[2] Olive Banks, *Parity and Esteem in English Secondary Education* (1955), p. 133.

[3] Brian Simon, *Education and the Labour Movement 1870–1920* (1965), p. 201.

[4] See Labour Party pamphlet *Towards Equality* (1956).

[5] See Labour Party pamphlet *Learning to Live* (1958).

[6] Opposition to the tripartite system was expressed by F. G. Dolphin, president of the Birmingham Association of Teachers (N.U.T.) (*B.G.*, 11 February 1944).

[7] Plans for experiments with 'multi-type' schools were announced in Birmingham as early as March 1945 (*E.D.*, 26 March 1945).

[8] These two schools opened in September 1955 (*B.P.*, 22 July 1955).

grouping of different types of secondary school on the same sites, a system which, in Alderman Martineau's opinion, had many of the advantages of the multilateral school without the drawback of excessive size.[1] In 1956 the City Council approved a further comprehensive school for the south and south-west of Birmingham.

Meanwhile, however, dissension was beginning to grow up within the Borough Labour Party, which was influenced by a swing of opinion within the national Labour Party in favour of a general comprehensive system. The Borough Labour Party had at first accepted the development plan, and at policy conferences in the early 1950s the majority of delegates had demanded an increase in the number of grammar school places. But in 1955 the conference passed a motion proposed by the local branch of the National Association of Labour Teachers calling for the experimental grouping of schools on comprehensive lines, using existing buildings. This resolution signalled the start of a long battle between the Borough Labour Party and the Labour group. In 1957 a special policy conference was held on education, and motions calling for further steps towards comprehensive education came not only from the teachers but also from many ward associations. Further support came from the Birmingham Trades Council.[2] The Labour group now decided to put pressure on the Education Committee, and in October 1957 the City Council passed an amendment proposed by Alderman Bradbeer, leader of the Labour group, calling on the committee to consider abolishing the eleven-plus examination, providing more comprehensive schools, and extending the range of secondary modern courses.[3]

The Education Committee agreed to study the problem, and in 1959 it announced plans for a fairer eleven-plus examination. But it proposed no other substantial changes. The chairman of the committee, Alderman Jack Wood (Labour), told the policy conference in 1959 that there was no point in making plans for more comprehensive schools because they would not be approved by the Ministry of Education.[4] Furthermore, the committee had come to the conclusion that there was no longer any need for large comprehensives to strengthen sixth-form work, because so many secondary-modern pupils were now staying on voluntarily beyond the school leaving age. In any case, the committee

[1] *B.M.*, 29 November 1946. For a description of the first of these groups to be completed, see 'Birmingham's first "mixed education" experiment', *Municipal Review*, August 1959, pp. 434–5.

[2] See B.T.C., *Annual Report*, 1957–8, p. 10; 1959–60, p. 13.

[3] B.C.C., *Pro.*, 8 October 1957, p. 442. The Conservatives opposed this amendment and called for the retention of the selective system, with minor modifications.

[4] The Ministry had refused to sanction certain plans made by the L.C.C. and Manchester for comprehensive schools in the mid-1950s (Robin Pedley, *The Comprehensive School* (1963), pp. 44–5).

felt that sixth-form colleges were a better solution than comprehensive schools where any strengthening of sixth-form work was necessary. But the policy conference was unimpressed by these arguments, and again called for immediate steps towards a comprehensive system in existing buildings, despite Alderman Wood's prophecy that teachers would refuse to work under such conditions.

Resolutions passed at the municipal policy conference did not necessarily carry much weight, especially as the Labour group became increasingly disenchanted with the behaviour of the conference from the mid-1950s and ignored many of its recommendations. But the Education Committee itself was no longer so completely agreed on policy as it had once been.[1] Secondary education showed signs of becoming a party issue in the mid-1950s, and one or two Labour members who still favoured a bi-partisan approach sometimes ran into trouble with the majority of the Labour group. A serious quarrel blew up in December 1955 when the chairman of the committee, Alderman Mrs. E. V. Smith (Labour), resigned after it had been made clear to her that the majority of Labour members on the committee no longer had any confidence in her, owing to what they saw as her habit of siding with the Conservatives.[2] But her resignation did not solve the problem, and the Labour members of the committee continued to clash, both on personal grounds and over the issue of comprehensive education. In 1961 Alderman Watton vainly attempted to eradicate bickering among the Labour members by appointing as chairman Councillor Nigel Cook, who had never even sat on the committee. So divided were they three years later that Watton himself decided to prepare a confidential report on secondary education for submission to the group, even though he had little specialized knowledge of the matter. The Education Officer, Sir Lionel Russell, did not attempt to impose his personal views on the committee[3] which, owing to frequent changes of chairman, lacked firm leadership.

Nevertheless, the Labour members of the committee were steadily being won over to the comprehensive principle. So in June 1963 Sir Lionel Russell was asked to prepare a report on further educational development. This report was presented to the committee in March

[1] See, for instance, report of the Birmingham Trades Council representative on the committee, A. McCulloch, on efforts made by himself and others to obtain quicker progress towards comprehensive education (B.T.C., *Annual Report*, 1956–7, p. 55).

[2] Alderman Mrs. Smith's resignation followed her opposition to a decision by the Labour group that the two new comprehensive schools should be co-educational. She had been the unanimous choice of the whole committee for the chairmanship in 1952, in succession to Sir Wilfrid Martineau (*B.P.*, 23 May 1952).

[3] See, for instance, Russell's balanced analysis of the role that comprehensive schools might play in the future of Birmingham, in 'Organisation of Secondary Education', p. 985.

1965.[1] Meanwhile, the 1964 municipal policy conference had passed a motion calling for the full recognition of the comprehensive principle, and had been told by the chairman of the committee, Councillor Nigel Cook, that although the group now accepted the principle, it could be implemented only in the long term. The Russell report incorporated this new approach. It repeated previous arguments that comprehensive schools were no longer necessary to ensure an adequate sixth form, and that the problem of buildings and sites prevented the immediate introduction of a general comprehensive system. Instead, it suggested that there should be a smaller type of comprehensive school operating on a two-tier basis. One tier of schools (Junior High Schools) would take children between the ages of eleven and fourteen years, after which they would be transferred to Senior High Schools. This solution would allow the use of existing buildings, and would make it possible to abolish the eleven-plus examination. Sir Lionel also suggested a third possibility, the extension of GCE courses to all secondary schools, which had been the declared policy of the Education Committee since 1956. But, as he pointed out, this would not overcome the problem of selection.

During the preparation of the report, Councillor Cook had stated that if it recommended changes, the Labour group should have the courage to carry them out.[2] This resolve had worried the Conservatives, and Alderman Sydney Dawes, the Conservative spokesman on education, had begun to publicize his opposition to any generalization of comprehensive schools. And his views were firmly supported by the *Birmingham Post*.[3] But after considering the report, the Education Committee opted for Sir Lionel Russell's third proposal, the extension of GCE courses, as an interim measure, while the Education Officer was asked to draft *long-term* plans for a general reorganization on comprehensive lines. Alderman Jack Wood, a former chairman, actually opposed this compromise because it maintained both the tripartite system and the eleven-plus examination. It was also strongly condemned by the Labour municipal policy conference in March 1965. The Conservatives supported the extension of GCE courses, but were opposed to any long-term reorganization on comprehensive lines.

Meanwhile, a Labour Government had been elected. Before the general election the Labour Party had pledged itself to introduce a comprehensive system if it came to power, and the result was a circular

---

[1] Sir E. L. Russell, *Report on the Organisation of Secondary Education* (Russell Report) (1965), B.R.L. 743869.

[2] *B.P.*, 5 May 1964.

[3] See, for instance, editorial in *B.P.*, 28 February 1968. The defence of the grammar schools, and particularly of the two King Edward direct-grant schools, by the Birmingham press, dates from the early post-war period. See, for instance, editorials in *B.M.*, 6 October 1945, and *B.P.*, 23 July 1951.

from the Secretary of State for Education and Science to all education authorities in July 1965.[1] It requested all authorities to submit plans for reorganization along comprehensive lines if they had not already done so. Until then the Education Committee had refused to endorse the comprehensive principle partly because it had in the pipeline many new schools that were already committed to the tripartite system, and partly because many Labour councillors were not convinced of the merits of comprehensive education. These councillors still felt that the problem was mainly one of giving better educational facilities to working-class children, which they thought could best be achieved by increasing the number of grammar school places. Indeed, between 1956 and 1961 the proportion of grammar school places had risen from 16 per cent to over 25 per cent, which was enough to satisfy the great majority of Council members.[2] Until 1964 the committee had been able to use the Conservative Government's opposition to generalized comprehensive education as an excuse for pursuing its compromise policy, even though cities such as London, Coventry, and Bristol had found means of introducing comprehensive schools on a large scale. Although many Labour members of the committee had come to favour the comprehensive system by 1965, some of them supported the compromise solution in the interests of group unity, and because the Conservatives would have made political capital out of any suggestion that Labour opposed a plan to extend GCE opportunities to more children. There was also a strong awareness of the political danger of attacking the grammar schools at a time when Labour had a very narrow majority in the City Council. Councillor Meyrick Rees, a member of the Education Committee, tried to persuade the policy conference in March 1965 that every grammar school child carried four or five votes with him. 'Let us win these people over', he said.

This whole situation was transformed by the publication of the Department of Education Circular 10/65. It was immediately attacked by the Conservatives, and Nigel Cook himself did not appear very enthusiastic about it. However, Sir Lionel Russell was asked to accelerate the preparation of his report on comprehensive reorganization, which was presented to the committee in December 1965.[3] The plan proposed that the 116 county secondary schools should be reduced to sixty comprehensives, thirty-nine of which were to be all-through comprehensives. The voluntary aided schools and the two direct-grant schools of the King Edward Foundation were excluded from the plan.

[1] Dept. of Education and Science, *The Reorganisation of Secondary Education*, Circular 10/65, 1965.

[2] This increase resulted largely from the provision of extra girls' places.

[3] City of Birmingham Education Committee, *Report of the Chief Education Officer on the Reorganisation of Secondary Education on Comprehensive Lines* (1966).

This at least spiked the guns of those who were determined to defend the two King Edward Foundation schools at all costs, but who were not especially concerned about the other King Edward grammar schools, whose intake, like that of the city's other grammar schools, was already decided on eleven-plus results.[1] The Conservatives opposed the plan, but they generated very little heat about it—and some Conservative supporters later blamed Alderman Hall and Sir Edward Boyle, the Conservative shadow Minister of Education, for not giving a clear lead. The plan was approved by the City Council against Conservative opposition in February 1966, by sixty-nine votes to sixty-eight.[2] Although Nigel Cook pointed out that the reorganization would preserve the grammar schools in all but name, and would in any case take a long time to implement, some elements in the Birmingham Conservative Party, with the Brandwood Ward Conservative Association prominent among them, now began to call for stronger opposition to the plan. Meanwhile, Labour were very slow in obtaining approval for the plan from the Department of Education and Science, even though they were clearly in danger of losing control of the Council in May 1966.

So when the Conservatives took control, they were able to scrap the plan and prepare a new one. In March 1967 the Conservatives published a plan for the reorganization of both primary and secondary education, retaining the grammar schools but replacing the eleven-plus by a system of 'guided parental choice'. But after strong criticism by the teachers and also from within the Conservative Party, guided parental choice had to be dropped, leaving the eleven-plus examination intact. The Conservatives now began to come under strong pressure from the Labour Government, but they held firm. With numerous local education authorities coming under Conservative control from 1965, plans for comprehensive education were held up all over the country. The Labour Government promised legislation to *force* all authorities to adopt the comprehensive principle, but it failed to enact it before its defeat at the general election of 1970. The Birmingham Conservatives were delighted by the removal of the threat of Government coercion, but in the early 1970s it still seemed likely that this important matter would drag on for years without a definitive solution.

The Education Committee's original decision to adopt a tripartite system had been based on the principle that children should be given the type of education to which they were best suited, and that parents

---

[1] Sir Edward Boyle told the House of Commons that the position of the direct-grant schools was causing more concern in Birmingham than any other aspect of Government education policy (*H. of C. Deb.*, 5th series, vol. dccxxv, cols. *1472–3*, 3 March 1966.

[2] B.C.C., *Pro.*, 1 February 1966, p. 713.

should be given a wide choice of types of school.[1] The committee was prepared to accept a relatively low proportion of grammar school places because it planned to provide numerous places in new technical schools, which, it believed, were both essential and desirable in a big industrial city.[2] Like the grammar schools, these technical schools would cream off the best children from the primary schools. They were originally planned to provide 14 per cent of the total secondary places, compared to 16 per cent in grammar schools.[3] In March 1945, the Higher Education Sub-Committee of the Education Committee announced plans for six new technical schools, three homecraft schools, and one commercial school. Facilities for practical education were also to be improved in other secondary schools.[4] However, it proved very difficult to carry out these ambitious plans, and somewhat easier to expand the capacity of the grammar schools which were already well established by 1945. By 1957 only 2·5 per cent of eleven-year-olds leaving primary school were entering technical schools. This low proportion was partly explained by the fact that owing to shortage of accommodation, nearly half the intake of the technical schools was made at thirteen years and over, but even the proportion of fourteen-year-olds in technical schools was only 8·5 per cent.[5] In addition, some technical intake went into comprehensive schools, and by the late 1950s it was already clear that most new technical places, as well as new grammar places, would be provided in comprehensive or bilateral schools, and not in separate institutions.[6] By the mid-1960s the curricular distinction between grammar and technical schools had become much less marked.[7]

The failure to provide a large number of places in technical schools reinforced local demands for more grammar school places. As early as March 1944 the *Birmingham Mail* pointed out that grammar school provision in Birmingham was low when compared with most other cities: '... judged by any reasonable modern standard, our local provision for advanced education is very inadequate.'[8] It returned to this theme in 1949, claiming that grammar school places were 'fewer, very many fewer, than a city of the size and wealth of Birmingham should afford'. It went on: 'The fact is that Birmingham has never offered to its children the number of secondary (and, for that matter,

[1] See *B.P.*, 6 March 1945. Variety was considered to be one of the most attractive features of Birmingham's system. See e.g. Russell, 'Organisation of Secondary Education', p. 981.

[2] The demands of industry were a major factor in the decision to expand technical education ('Focus on Birmingham', p. 400).

[3] Russell, 'Organisation of Secondary Education', p. 981. As we have seen, the grammar school provision was later increased.

[4] *E.D.*, 26 March 1945.

[5] Russell, 'Organisation of Secondary Education', p. 981.   [6] Ibid., p. 982.

[7] Russell, 'Education in Birmingham', p. 47.

[8] *B.M.*, 4 March 1944, editorial.

technical) school places that should have been available even to put us on a near parity with comparable cities further north.'[1]

Meanwhile, the demand for grammar school places was growing among Birmingham parents, and more and more children were staying on at school voluntarily beyond the official leaving age. In 1952 the *Birmingham Post* called for the provision of more grammar school places, and also for an improvement of standards in secondary modern schools, so that parents would not feel that their children were condemned to an inferior education if they failed to gain entry to a grammar or technical school.[2] These demands were supported by the Birmingham Conservatives.[3] The main shortage, of course, was of girls' places, and by 1955 their total had almost caught up with that of the boys.[4] Yet it proved impossible in the short term to increase the grammar school provision very much above what had been planned after the war, and the Education Committee concentrated instead on improving courses in the secondary modern schools. In 1954 the committee initiated a fifth-year course at twelve secondary modern schools, and by 1958 it had been extended to forty schools, over one-third of the total.[5] By this time Russell was claiming that the most striking feature of Birmingham education, after variety, was that the old distinctions between different types of school were quickly disappearing. He wrote: 'The system of secondary education that is evolving in Birmingham is going a long way towards securing a real measure of equality of opportunity as the success of children from all the different types of school bears witness. (. . .) This is well indicated by the way in which the modern schools with extended courses, for example, are accepted by parents as providing for their children a reasonable alternative to other types of school.'[6]

On the other hand, one Birmingham schoolmaster pointed out in 1960 that parity between grammar schools and secondary modern schools had not been attained because classes were still larger in the latter, and because they had a serious staffing problem.[7] There was, however, a gradual improvement in the 1960s as the staffing position eased, and by 1965 extended courses were provided in 90 per cent of the non-selective secondary schools.[8] By this time, the development plan's aim of providing selective places for about 29 per cent of the secondary school population had almost been realized; twenty-four grammar schools and eleven technical schools were in operation.[9]

[1] *B.M.*, 1 October 1949, editorial.   [2] *B.P.*, 1 January 1952, editorial.
[3] See, for instance, statement by Councillor S. E. Dawes in *B.P.*, 3 March 1953.
[4] *B.M.*, 14 July 1955.
[5] Russell, 'Organisation of Secondary Education', p. 983.
[6] Ibid., pp. 983–4.
[7] Bowker, *Golden Hillock Boys*, pp. 30–1.
[8] Russell, 'Education in Birmingham', p. 43.   [9] Ibid., p. 47.

A further aspect of the variety which was seen as a key element of the Birmingham educational system was the scope given to voluntary schools.[1] Before 1939 the Roman Catholic and Anglican educational authorities had been allowed to participate fully in the provision of education in Birmingham. In 1936 Birmingham had forty-eight Church of England, and twenty-four Roman Catholic, primary schools. Many of the Roman Catholic schools, and the majority of the Anglican schools, were in the older districts of the city. On the whole, the Church of England was content to see its educational role diminish in relation to that of the local authority, and between the wars it devoted much of its resources to church-building. The Roman Catholics, on the other hand, began in the 1930s to build new voluntary schools on the new housing estates, and in 1937 they opened Birmingham's first voluntary school to be built specifically for senior children.[2] The 1936 Education Act allowed local education authorities to subsidize church authorities which wanted to build or extend schools in order to accommodate senior pupils, and Birmingham agreed to make the maximum grant of 75 per cent of the cost of approved schemes. The Roman Catholics submitted ten projects, and the Church of England eight, but only two of them were completed before war interrupted building work.[3]

After the war, the voluntary schools had to face the financial responsibility of bringing their schools up to the standards imposed by the Ministry of Education's new building regulations, but the 1944 Act provided for greatly extended help to voluntary schools from public funds. It also allowed the renewal of agreements for the building of new schools under the 1936 Act. The Church of England decided that it did not wish to pursue the 1936 reorganization scheme, and the development plan therefore included provision for only two Church of England secondary schools. Both these projects involved the rebuilding of central schools on cramped sites. The Roman Catholics, however, wished to maintain their pre-war scheme, and it was agreed that the development plan should include eight new Roman Catholic secondary modern schools.[4] Both churches planned numbers of primary schools, but here again the Roman Catholics made the bigger effort. Because they did not have as big a legacy of slum schools as the Church of England, they were able to concentrate on providing for the needs of new areas. By 1969 the Roman Catholics were operating forty-four primary schools (compared to twenty-six in 1949), fifteen comprehensive or secondary modern, and four grammar schools, together with one

[1] See Russell, 'Organisation of Secondary Education', p. 982.

[2] Black, p. 292. For a tribute by the Archbishop, Dr. Thomas Williams, to Birmingham's fair treatment of the Roman Catholic schools, see *Alderman Byng Kenrick: Tributes and Appreciations* (1943), p. 29.

[3] Black, p. 292.   [4] Black, pp. 292–3.

college of education.[1] The Church of England had thirty primary schools (compared to thirty-three in 1949), and two secondary modern schools.[2]

In contrast to the general post-war expansion of educational facilities, the Education Committee's ambitious plans for nursery schools could be put into effect only partially. During the war the Public Health Committee established over seventy day nurseries to encourage mothers to work in industry. But it regarded them purely as a temporary expedient, and planned to close many of them as soon as peace was restored. It agreed with the Education Committee that nursery needs should be satisfied by the provision of nursery schools and classes, a view which coincided with a big public demand for nursery education after the war.[3] The development plan made provision for 158 nursery schools, and by 1950 twenty-two of them were operating, while thirty-one primary schools were running nursery classes.[4] But further progress was extremely slow. The Ministry of Education made it clear from the start that priority would be given to the provision of education for children of compulsory school age,[5] and that very few resources could be devoted to the building of nursery schools. In 1965, the Education Committee still had no more than twenty-three nursery schools.[6] In the following year, however, the Department of Education and Science approved Birmingham's proposal to establish extra nursery classes in order to encourage married teachers with young children to return to teaching.[7]

Much more successful were the committee's efforts to expand the school meals service. In 1939 the proportion of children receiving school dinners free in Birmingham had been lower than in Liverpool, Manchester, and Leeds.[8] As we have seen, the meals service developed greatly during the war, and was extended to all children whether or not they were classed as needy. Even so only 19·4 per cent of Birmingham children were taking meals at school shortly after the end of the war, and plans were made to extend the service greatly. The Ministry of Education suggested that a target of 65 per cent provision should be set.[9] By 1948, 36·3 per cent of children in Birmingham's maintained schools were taking school dinners, but this proportion was still lower

[1] *The Official Catholic Directory of the Archdiocese of Birmingham.*

[2] *Birmingham Post Year Book and Who's Who.*

[3] B.C.C., *Pro.*, 5 June 1945, p. 511 (Public Health Committee); *E.D.*, 19 October 1945.

[4] Black, pp. 277–8.

[5] *Development Plan for Primary and Secondary Education*, pp. 4–5.

[6] Russell, 'Education in Birmingham', pp. 43–4.

[7] *H. of C. Deb.*, 5th series, vol. dccxxv, col. *621*, 10 March 1966.

[8] *H. of C. Deb.*, 5th series, vol. cccxlvii, cols. *703–4*, 11 May 1939.

[9] *B.M.*, 22 January 1946.

than the county borough average, and lower than in big cities such as Leeds, Sheffield, and Manchester.[1] The expansion of the service was restricted, like so many other aspects of local authority endeavour, by the staffing problem.[2] By 1963 the proportion taking school dinners in Birmingham had risen to 49.2 per cent, which was almost as high as the county borough average, although it was still exceeded by Bristol, Leeds, Manchester, and Sheffield among the large cities.[3]

Another significant development, pioneered by Birmingham, was the home teaching service. It was designed to provide instruction for children who, for health reasons, were unable to attend school. Plans for the new service were announced in 1948,[4] and obtained Ministry of Education approval. By 1952 the service had expanded to include sixteen teachers, and their number rose to forty by 1958.[5] Birmingham's example was soon followed in other parts of the country.

Further education

We have already seen that the Education Committee attached great importance to technical education, in order to satisfy industry's demands for qualified personnel. Consequently, it laid very ambitious plans for the expansion of further education after the war.[6] These plans were designed to maintain the very close cooperation with local industry that had been developed before the war, and the Education Committee recruited prominent industrialists to serve on the governing bodies of technical colleges and on advisory committees.[7]

The interest of industrialists in technical education arose from their growing inability to train their own employees, owing to the increasing complexity of the skills and knowledge needed. Birmingham was one of the first cities to act on a recommendation made by the Royal Commission on Education in 1932, that college and workshop training should proceed concurrently.[8] In that year the engineering and allied industries in the Birmingham area set up an apprenticeship scheme under which entrants had to attend technical college courses for three years as well as obtaining practical experience. Although the scheme was said to be a success, only a few large firms made extensive use of it, and only 364 certificates had been awarded by 1938.[9] But it was a step in the right direction, and later in 1938 a similar scheme was set up for the building trades, after the building employers had approached the Education Committee.[10] Alderman Byng Kenrick, chairman of the

[1] *H. of C. Deb.*, 5th series, vol. cdliii, cols. *43–4*, 8 July 1948.
[2] 'Focus on Birmingham', p. 426.
[3] Ministry of Education, *Selected Statistics*.   [4] *B.M.*, 2 February 1948.
[5] 'The home teacher', *Education*, 9 May 1958, p. 875.
[6] 'Focus on Birmingham', p. 400.   [7] Ibid., p. 406; Black, p. 301.
[8] *B.G.*, 22 June 1938.   [9] *B.P.*, 22 June 1938.
[10] *B.P.*, 3 November 1938.

committee, thought that if the college could provide a more general
course of instruction than could be obtained at work, many employers
would make it possible for their apprentices to attend.[1] The principal
of the Central Technical College, Dr. Stirling Anderson, was already
advocating the release of young workers on one day a week to attend
a technical institution.[2] Progress was greatly stimulated by the war,
owing to the sudden growth of demand for skilled workers. In 1940
the Central Technical College organized intensive courses in such skills
as welding and gauging.[3] Even firms with their own training schools
began to see the advantages of integrating more closely with the
Education Committee's services; the head of the Lucas training school,
for instance, called in 1940 for the establishment of a chain of branch
technical colleges in the city, to allow the Central Technical College
to concentrate on advanced courses.[4] In 1944 the Chamber of Commerce approved the principle of part-time education for young people
over school age, and the day release of young workers.[5] Nevertheless,
when firms began to plan their training schemes towards the end of the
war, they rejected the idea of turning over all the training of their
young workers to outside institutions, because of the need for some
specialized instruction.[6] Most of the schemes incorporated a combination of college and works training. These ambitious training proposals
were not limited to the larger firms—even the jewellery industry
wanted such a scheme.[7] These local demands, combined with Government support for technical education, encouraged the Education
Committee to plan an expansion of further education in Birmingham to
bring it up to the standard of most other large cities.

Before the war Birmingham had three technical colleges: in the city
centre, at Aston, and at Handsworth. Their facilities were already
grossly overcrowded before the war, and the Central Technical College,
Suffolk Street, came in for particularly heavy criticism.[8] Towards the
end of the war the Education Committee began to plan for the extension
of technical college provision, and the result was a scheme for three new
central colleges of Technology, Commerce, and Art, and two new
suburban technical colleges.[9] However, in the early years after the

[1] B.G., B.P., 9 November 1938.

[2] B.M., 23 May 1938. A few firms were already releasing apprentices to attend
the Corporation's day continuation school at Bournville, which was one of the very
few in Britain at that time.

[3] B.M., 21 May 1940.

[4] B.P., 16 August 1940.

[5] Birmingham Chamber of Commerce, Journal and Monthly Record, May 1944,
p. 245.

[6] See, for instance, Dunlop and Birmid schemes, E.D., 13 June 1944; B.P., 26
August 1944.

[7] B.W.P., 13 December 1946.

[8] See, for instance, Town Crier, 12 August 1944.   [9] Black, p. 299.

war the Ministry of Education required Birmingham to concentrate on primary school provision, a policy which Alderman Martineau criticized as short-sighted,[1] and pressure built up on the existing buildings and such temporary accommodation as the Education Committee had been able to find. More and more advanced work was undertaken at the central college, and work at lower levels was transferred increasingly to the suburban colleges and to technical institutes. The first technical institute had been opened at Bordesley Green in 1936 and during the war industrial firms' growing practice of releasing younger employees on one day a week led to the development of further technical institutes at Erdington and Selly Oak. The report of the Percy Committee on Higher Technological Education in 1945 recommended that devolution from the senior colleges should continue, allowing them to be developed into colleges of technology where courses could be offered of a standard comparable with that of a university degree course.[2]

After the war, Birmingham was designated as the chief centre of technological education for the whole of the West Midlands, which was a further stimulus to specialization in the central college, although it accentuated congestion until new buildings could be made ready.[3] Birmingham was not allowed to start work on its new central colleges until 1950. They had been planned in the mid-1930s after the Board of Education had criticized Birmingham's provision for higher technical education,[4] and an architectural competition was held in 1937. The first section, accommodating the college of technology, was opened in December 1955.[5] By this time the Minister of Education had announced plans for the expansion of higher technological education in Birmingham, and although development was at first restricted to the university,[6] the Central Technical College was designated as a college of advanced technology in 1956. It was the first college in the country to receive this distinction. At the suggestion of the Ministry of Education, the City Council relinquished control and ownership of the college, which passed into the hands of an independent governing body in 1961.[7] In 1964 the college was promoted by the Ministry of Education to the status of a technological university, known as the University of Aston

[1] *E.D.*, 4 October 1945.

[2] Black, p. 300; *Y.B.* no. 25, January 1949, p. 4.

[3] See, for instance, criticisms made by the House of Commons Select Committee on Estimates of the limitations of Birmingham's provision for technical education, *B.P.*, 27 August 1953. See also Norman Wheeler, 'Further education in the "City of One Thousand Trades"', *School Government Chronicle*, vol. cxli, no. 3276, July 1948, pp. 5–6. In 1946–7 over 4,000 students from other authorities attended Birmingham colleges (*Y.B.*, no. 25, January 1949, p. 4).

[4] *E.D.*, 4 October 1965.

[5] *Y.B.*, no. 102, December 1955, p. 1.

[6] *H. of C. Deb.*, 5th series, vol. dccc, cols. *105–6*, 20 July 1954.

[7] *Y.B.*, no. 167, November 1961, p. 1.

z

in Birmingham. The College of Commerce moved in 1953 into a new building in Broad Street,[1] but later it was able to occupy much larger premises on the site of the College of Technology at Gosta Green. Work started on the first phase of the new College of Arts and Crafts at Gosta Green in 1962, and it came into use from 1965. In 1964 work began on a new College of Food and Domestic Arts in the city centre, which was opened towards the end of the decade. Good progress was also made on the scheme for twelve branch colleges of art, first announced in 1948.

Progress was made, especially after 1950, in the provision of branch technical colleges, four of which were in operation by 1955, in addition to the two older established colleges at Aston and Handsworth.[2] The city had fourteen institutes of further education, under a scheme that had originally been introduced in 1932. Enrolments at these institutions had dropped sharply during the first year of the war, but they began to increase again from 1941–2, owing mainly to a big increase in the number of junior enrolments, and in 1944–5 they exceeded the highest pre-war figures. Numbers continued to rise rapidly after the war, and by 1949–50, 46,350 people were enrolled for day and evening courses—twice as many as in 1944–5.[3] Enrolments also increased at the Birmingham Athletic Institute.[4] By 1957 the number of students enrolled for courses at institutes of further education had risen to 86,000.[5] The expansion of further education was given an additional stimulus by the White Paper on technical education published in 1961. Between 1961 and 1964 the number of full-time students at technical colleges rose from 2,190 to 3,810, and of part-time students from 16,170 to 19,790.[6] On the other hand, the number of students enrolled at evening institutes now began to stabilize, and in 1967–8 the total of enrolments for all further education courses was only about 90,000.[7] No progress was made on the scheme for county colleges which had been envisaged by the Government at the end of the war for day release courses. Birmingham drew up a plan to provide twenty-one county colleges, but Alderman Martineau admitted that they were 'very much a castle in Spain'.[8] By 1955 Birmingham had five day continuation colleges, but the overall scheme for county colleges was deferred by the Ministry of Education at the same time as it gave it formal approval in 1956.[9]

[1] City of Birmingham Education Committee, *City of Birmingham, College of Commerce: Official Opening* (1953), B.R.L. 639409.

[2] 'Focus on Birmingham', p. 406. The first two new branch technical colleges had been opened in 1953.

[3] Black, p. 313.   [4] *Y.B.*, no. 21, August–September 1948, p. 4.

[5] *Y.B.*, no. 121, August–September 1957, p. 1.

[6] Russell, 'Education in Birmingham', pp. 52–3.

[7] City of Birmingham Education Committee, *Higher Education*.

[8] *B.G.*, 7 December 1948.

[9] City of Birmingham, *Scheme of Further Education and Plan for County Colleges* (1956).

Universities

One of the major reasons why the City Council sought to build up its Gosta Green colleges into an institution capable of maintaining Birmingham industry's technical standards was that the University of Birmingham was becoming less and less suitable to perform such a role. When Joseph Chamberlain and his friends founded the university in 1900, they intended it not only as 'a school of general culture', but also as an institution that 'would practically assist the prosperity and welfare of the district in which it is situated, by the exceptional attention which it would give to the teaching of Science in connection with its application to our local industries and manufactures'.[1] Birmingham industry provided most of the money to found the new university, and its court of governors was dominated by industrialists.

During the first three or four decades of its existence Birmingham University developed very much along the lines envisaged by its founders. Government grants slowly increased, but as late as 1945 they still represented under one-third of the university's income, while the Corporation still provided nearly one-tenth.[2] Student numbers stabilized at around 1,500 between the First World War and the late 1940s, and the considerable development of the scientific departments which took place was largely due to the generosity of Birmingham and Midland firms in endowing lectureships and chairs, and in directly commissioning research. This picture began to change after the Second World War. The Government began to expand the university as part of the general development of higher education in the interests of the whole country rather than of the city alone. By 1967 the number of students had increased to 6,484, and Treasury recurrent grants had risen to 67·2 per cent of the university's annual income. The increase in the number of students was accompanied by a fall in the proportion of those who came from the Birmingham area, because the Ministry of Education thought that it was educationally more profitable for young people to live away from home. Whereas a majority of students were of local origin before 1939, under one-quarter lived in the West Midlands in 1967, and only about one in seven came from the city or from the county of Warwickshire.[3] Although a number of Birmingham and Midlands firms continued to make generous gifts to the university, and to use its research facilities, the proportion of its income provided by local sources fell steadily. The City of Birmingham increased its annual grant from

[1] Joseph Chamberlain, quoted in Eric W. Vincent and P. Hinton, *The University of Birmingham: its History and Significance* (1947), p. 34.

[2] Calculated from University of Birmingham, *Report of the Council . . . and Accounts* (1945).

[3] Calculated from University of Birmingham, *Digest of Statistics*, no. 4, 1966–7, pp. 45–7.

£20,000 to £48,000 between 1948 and 1964, but the rise failed to keep
pace with the growth of the university's turnover.

Meanwhile, the City Council became unhappy with certain aspects
of the running of the University in the 1960s. Not only were councillors
increasingly worried by the behaviour and appearance of some students;
they also resented the attacks on municipal policies launched by certain
members of the teaching staff, notably Dr. D. E. C. Eversley.[1] During
the war, prominent academics from the university had been invited to
share in the moulding of municipal policies, but the Council virtually
ignored them after the late 1940s. In frustration, Eversley and others
vented their criticisms, which related mainly to the City's town planning policies, in the Birmingham press. In 1964 City–university
relations were brought to their lowest ebb ever when the City Council
complained to the Press Council about one of Eversley's articles. The
City's annual grant to the university was suspended for one year, and
was resumed in 1965 at a much lower rate. Relations subsequently
improved (although student protest activities and carnival pranks
caused increasing annoyance to the City Council), but in 1970 the
university remained a long way from realizing its full potential as a
constructive element in the Birmingham community.

The irony of the situation was that so successful were the City Council's strenuous efforts to build up the Gosta Green colleges that they too
became a university in the mid-1960s. So began a process which seemed
likely in the long run to convert Birmingham's second major centre of
higher education from a local into a national institution. Certainly, in
1970 relations between the City Council and the University of Aston
were still very close, and the university's proportion of local students
remained much higher than that of its sister institution. But student
unrest had already broken out on a large scale, and there was every
chance that within a few years Birmingham would have two educational
foreign bodies in its midst.

Education in Birmingham and other cities

We have discussed the organization of Birmingham education principally in a local context. But how did educational provision in Birmingham compare with other large cities?[2]

As we have seen, Birmingham had been deficient in many aspects of
education before the war, and it took a long time to overcome this
backlog. Owing partly to the attractions of Birmingham industry, and

---

[1] See above, p. 145.

[2] The following information has been extracted from Ministry of Education,
Selected Statistics, and *Secondary Education in Each Local Authority Area*; Institute of
Municipal Treasurers, *Education Statistics*.

partly to the deficiencies of Birmingham's secondary educational system, with its shortage of teachers and of grammar and technical places,[1] relatively few children stayed on at school after the school leaving age. In 1957, the first year for which full comparative figures became available, only Nottingham among the large cities had fewer children staying on beyond the age of fifteen than Birmingham. Moreover, despite its low number of senior pupils, Birmingham's ratio of senior pupils to teachers was the highest of all the large cities, and it had more over-sized senior classes than any other large city. It is hardly surprising, therefore, that fewer Birmingham pupils won university awards than those of any other large city except Liverpool and Nottingham. Birmingham also made fewer awards to other places of further education than any other major city except Nottingham. Nottingham was also the only large city to produce fewer training college entrants than Birmingham. Even in terms of lesser awards, Birmingham did worse than any big city except Nottingham and Sheffield. By 1963 Birmingham was still more retarded than most of the large cities, despite a general improvement in educational provision, especially of secondary education. Its junior classes were still bigger than in any large city except Liverpool, and although its ratio of senior pupils to teachers was much improved, it was slightly higher than the county borough average, and only Bristol, Leeds, and Manchester were worse off among the large cities. It had more over-sized junior and senior classes than any other large city, and it now made fewer university awards than any other. On the other hand, as a result of its big development of further education, it now gave more lesser awards to places of further education than any other major city, and almost as many as the average county borough. But, clearly, the foundations of further education, the primary and secondary schools, still needed improvement.

By 1968 much of this necessary improvement had been brought about. Birmingham's ratio of primary pupils to teachers was now better than the county borough average. In secondary schools its ratio was almost up to average, and was not appreciably inferior to that of any of the large cities. Thus by the later 1960s Birmingham had made up all its lost ground, and had created an educational system which put it on a par with other urban areas in each of the three major spheres—primary, secondary, and technical education. This was a significant achievement. It was also an achievement which placed a heavy burden on the rate-payer. By 1958–9 Birmingham was spending more on education than

---

[1] In 1960 Birmingham's proportion of thirteen-year-olds at grammar school was lower than the county borough average, but among the large cities Bristol, Hull, and Nottingham had a lower proportion. On the other hand, the proportion in technical and comprehensive schools in Birmingham was above average.

the county borough average, and more than any of the large cities except Coventry, Hull, Manchester, and Nottingham. One effect of this high outlay was that as Birmingham's educational standards came to approach or equal those of other areas, the inevitable demands for economies in education expenditure became harder to resist. It was partly as a result of these demands that by 1967–8 Birmingham was again spending less on education than the county borough average, and less than any large city apart from Leeds, Nottingham, and Sheffield. By 1970 this freshening of the wind of economy had exercised no visibly harmful effect on educational standards; indeed they continued to improve during the 1960s. Nevertheless, it was a sufficiently important development to merit some attention here.

Expenditure

Education expenditure had long been a potential cause of controversy in Birmingham. During the early years after the war, when rates were still relatively low, there were few objections to the increased education outlay. Yet as early as February 1945 Alderman Martineau warned that if the higher Burnham salary scales were not offset by a larger Government contribution, there might be a public outcry in protest against the increased burden on the rates.[1] Such an outcry did indeed occur from the early 1950s when the rate poundage began to rise more rapidly. Education expenditure was particularly vulnerable to public criticism, because it made up such a high proportion of the Corporation's total outlay, and because the Education Committee had a lot of ground to catch up before Birmingham's education system reached a satisfactory standard. In February 1951 the *Birmingham Mail* launched a strong attack on the Education Committee's 'rather frightening' estimates for 1951–2. Attention should be devoted, said the *Mail*, to getting more value for money, and it went on to question the basic assumptions on which the committee's plans were based: 'But a good many educationalists think our plans and methods are too lavish, that much expensive and worthless experimentation could be cut out; and that we may be wasting academic instruction on thousands of adolescent boys and girls who would profit more and be happier as apprentices in industry.'[2]

There was not much danger of economy cuts while highly-respected educationalists such as Byng Kenrick and Sir Wilfrid Martineau were still members of the committee, and they effectively defended the principle of high investment in education.[3] The Education Committee fought hard against Government attempts to limit expenditure from revenue on education in the early 1950s, and protested strongly, though

[1] *B.G.*, 7 February 1945.   [2] *B.M.*, 23 February 1951.
[3] See, for instance, *B.G.*, 4 December 1951.

in vain, against restrictions on capital outlay which delayed the school building programme. Then, in 1953, one year after the Unionist Sir Wilfrid Martineau had been replaced as chairman by the Labour Alderman Mrs. Smith, the Conservative members of the Education Committee moved a token reduction in the estimates.[1] The amendment was rejected after Alderman Mrs. Smith had claimed that the estimates were, if anything, too low, although the Conservatives argued that the reductions would not affect the services, and would help to prevent a backlash of public opinion against high expenditure. Her attitude was strongly attacked, this time by the *Birmingham Post*, which accused Labour of spending irresponsibly without making sure that the education system was actually working.[2] Meanwhile, the *Mail* had been publishing feature articles on local affairs by the ex-alderman Norman Tiptaft, several of which had been devoted to rising education costs. In one of these articles, in December 1953, Councillor Neville Bosworth (Conservative) was quoted as saying '. . . our present expenditure is extravagant and can be considerably reduced', and '. . . the blunt fact is we cannot afford 8s. 4d. of our 25s. rate for education . . .'.[3] The Conservative attack on education expenditure grew stronger in the later 1950s as the Conservatives made finance the main plank of their local election platforms. It was resisted by Labour until the end of the decade, but after the abolition of nearly all specific grants and their replacement by a block grant in 1958 the Education Committee's estimates became very vulnerable.[4] Moreover, the Labour majority in the City Council was substantially reduced in the elections of 1959 and the two following years, until it almost disappeared in 1961. These two factors persuaded the Labour group to cut back education expenditure as much as possible. The biggest cuts were made early in 1961, when defeat was staring Labour in the face. Alderman Jack Wood, the chairman, made it clear that the reductions were being made purely for electoral reasons: 'It would seem that Birmingham has reached this financial crisis for education before other authorities, and I do not pretend to know why. I cannot see any possibility of the others escaping the necessity of choosing between cutting educational services severely

---

[1] *B.P.*, 3 March 1953.

[2] *B.P.*, 3 March 1959, editorial.   [3] *B.M.*, 2 December 1953.

[4] In 1957 the Chief Education Officer had written to the City Treasurer expressing concern about the depressive effect that the new general grant might have on educational expenditure. In the past, Birmingham's education expenditure had been lower than average mainly because it was short of teachers; but now that more teachers were becoming available it was inevitable that Birmingham's increase in educational expenditure should be greater than the national average. The Finance Committee was not able to provide adequate reassurance on this point (B.C.C., *Pro.*, 8 October 1957, pp. 408–12 (Finance Committee)). For the effect of the block grant on the sources of education expenditure, see Alan Peacock, H. Glennerster, and R. Lavers, *Educational Finance: Its Sources and Uses in the United Kingdom* (1968), esp. p. 28.

and raising rates to an extent that will arouse great fury among articulate ratepayers, and especially among owner-occupiers.'[1] Even the Conservatives claimed to be shocked by the extent of the cuts. They said that the reductions should have been spread over all committees, and Alderman Hall argued that small savings could and should have been made before: 'It is because the majority of councillors think we are an extravagant committee that we are now asked to bear more than our fair share.' The final word came from Sir Wilfrid Martineau, who said that the last thing he would have expected was that Birmingham should be the first local authority to apply savage cuts to education.[2]

The Labour group's new attitude was closely linked to the fact that Birmingham, which in the early 1950s had been spending less on education (per head of population) than the average county borough, was spending more than average at the end of the decade.[3] Even though it was still spending less than Coventry, Hull, Manchester, and Nottingham among the large cities, such a high rate of expenditure was so unusual for Birmingham that it needed a strong majority in the City Council to maintain it. Labour, however, never recovered in the 1960s, despite their better electoral fortunes between 1962 and 1964, that confidence in the administration of municipal affairs that had been a feature of their rule in the 1950s. Fearing Conservative attacks on the finance issue, they clamped down on expenditure, and particularly on the education estimates. Education Committee chairmen found it difficult to resist complaints by other chairmen that they were being given too much. A particularly strong opponent of high education expenditure was Alderman Denis Thomas, chairman of the Public Works Committee, who was often influential in obtaining reductions. In 1964, for instance, the Labour group officers decided on big additional cuts in the Education Committee estimates, arguing that the committee had been treated too generously in relation to other committees. But the reductions agreed by Labour still did not satisfy the Conservatives. In March 1966, when the committee's estimates represented a 16·3 per cent increase in expenditure over the previous year, the Conservatives threatened to reduce them as soon as possible, and Councillor S. Bleyer, a leading Conservative, stated that he was 'sick and tired of the sacred cow of education'.[4] Partly as a consequence of this pressure, Birmingham's education expenditure had again sunk below the county borough average by 1966–7, and five out of the eight

---

[1] *Guardian*, 28 February 1961.   [2] Ibid.

[3] Institute of Municipal Treasurers, *Education Statistics*. It was normal for education authorities with an above-average ratio of pupils to total population, of which Birmingham was one, to spend less per pupil than the average authority (D. S. Lees et al., *Local Expenditure and Exchequer Grants: A Research Study* (1956), pp. 240–1).

[4] *B.P.*, 29 March 1966.

other large cities now spent more. Although the Conservatives did not make the cuts that they had promised after May 1966, they continued the economical policies of their predecessors.

This picture, at first sight, is a depressing one. Yet it is important not to overestimate the effects of this strong pressure for economies in education expenditure during the 1960s. Birmingham's high expenditure in the late 1950s partly reflected the strenuous efforts then being made to bring the city's educational system up to the standards achieved by some other comparable areas. By the 1960s this goal had been reached, and it so became possible to reduce expenditure relative to other areas without incurring a decline of standards. To some extent, therefore, it is arguable that the Education Committee's estimates came in for heavy cuts precisely because reductions *could* be made there without causing serious harm. Educational provision was certainly better in Birmingham in the late 1960s, both in absolute terms and in comparison with other cities, than it had ever been. Time alone would tell whether the new, economical approach to education would have a major influence on the quality of the service provided.

It would inevitably take some years before the greatly improved standards of educational provision achieved in Birmingham by the 1960s began to be reflected in the educational qualifications of the city's population. Nevertheless, the 1961 census suggested that Birmingham citizens were already at least as well educated as those of most other comparable cities.[1] In that year, 76·98 per cent of Birmingham's male population aged twenty-five and over had left school before the age of fifteen. Of the females, 79·60 per cent had left school at this relatively early age. 10·26 per cent of males, and 9·46 per cent of females, had left school at the age of fifteen. Those who had ceased full-time education at sixteen years made up 6·48 per cent of males, and 5·62 per cent of females. 3·35 per cent of males, and 3·36 per cent of females, had stopped between the ages of seventeen and nineteen, whereas 2·75 per cent and 1·91 per cent respectively had gone on to the age of twenty and over. On this basis, Bristol, Coventry, and Leeds, among the large cities, appeared to be better educated than Birmingham, in that more of their people had remained longer in full-time education. Birmingham was, however, on a par with Nottingham, Liverpool, and Manchester, and its population was markedly better educated than that of Sheffield and Hull. In Hull, for instance, the worst educated city of the nine, 79·90 per cent of males and 81·30 per cent of females had left school before fifteen; only 1·80 per cent and 1·39 per cent respectively had gone on to the age of twenty and above. The best educated city of the

[1] *Census 1961. England and Wales. Education Tables* (1966), table 4.

nine was Bristol, with corresponding proportions of 71·89 per cent, 73·97 per cent; and 3·71 per cent, 2·84 per cent. To some extent, of course, these figures were affected by the age, class, and employment structures of the cities. It is, however, clear that Birmingham's population was relatively well educated in 1961, and it must have become even better educated during the 1960s. Birmingham's own education effort deserved most of the credit for this improvement.

XI

THE IMPACT OF COLOURED IMMIGRATION

COLOURED people formed only a minority of the total of immigrants into Birmingham in the years 1939–70.[1] They were, however, the most noticeable, and in some ways they created more problems than white immigrants from other parts of the British Isles and from abroad. Not only were they marked out by the colour of their skin, but frequently, too, by their language difficulties. The great majority of them were manual workers with little or no education, who came to live in a community which also had a majority of manual workers with limited education. In some parts of Great Britain, such as Notting Hill, Nottingham, and Smethwick, the coloured influx led to racial disturbances and political conflict. But in Birmingham it did not. Why it did not, and what its effects were on Birmingham, are the questions that this chapter sets out to answer.

Birmingham had some coloured people before 1939, but their numbers did not exceed a few hundred at the most.[2] Many were professional people, especially doctors from India who had trained in England and settled to work here.[3] They were accepted by their peers in the local English community. On the whole they kept well away from Indians further down the social scale, who found their way from the ports to manual jobs in Birmingham during the 1930s. Other coloured immigrants worked in skilled jobs; for instance, one big Chinese family produced Christmas decorations in a large house in central Birmingham, and, by all accounts, kept itself to itself. To judge from the local press, coloured people excited interest and curiosity, not hostility. People were amused to read of three Sikhs who refused to remove their turbans when being taught how to put on gasmasks during the Munich crisis in 1938;[4] and later they were sorry to hear of the death by suffocation of a whole Arab family in an air-raid shelter in Holloway Head after the collapse of a wall of sandbags.

New arrivals expanded the coloured community during the war, though nobody took much notice at the time. Many had deserted their ships at British seaports and found their way to Birmingham where

[1] See section on immigration, above, pp. 202 ff.

[2] The total has even been estimated at under one hundred (J. A. G. Griffith, J. Henderson, M. Usborne, and D. Wood, *Coloured Immigrants in Britain* (1960), p. 38).

[3] The best account of the early growth of the Indian community in Birmingham is Dhani R. Prem, *The Parliamentary Leper: A History of Colour Prejudice in Britain* (1965), pp. 6–7.

[4] *Prepared: Birmingham A.R.P. Journal*, no. 3, February 1939, p. 9.

work was easy to obtain and detection was difficult. By 1942 about a hundred Indian workers were living in Birmingham, most of them single men. Balsall Heath, Aston, and Saltley were the areas they favoured, because they could obtain cheap accommodation there. After the war many of these single men were joined by their families, and their numbers were increased by the arrival of demobilized coloured servicemen from the Indian divisions, who hoped for a better living in England than at home. Already a Birmingham Indian Association was in existence, catering for Indian doctors, businessmen, and students; and during the war Dr. D. R. Prem, the most politically active of the city's middle-class Indians, set up the Indian Workers' Association in an attempt to bring the working- and middle-class sections of the Indian community closer together.

Coloured people from the Caribbean and from the African colonies were less numerous at this stage than the Indians, and they were certainly not organized to the same extent.[1] But the picture began to change after the war, when West Indian travel agents organized cheap voyages to England. Boatloads began to arrive from about 1948. Some of these immigrants were attracted to Birmingham, even though the city's industries were not yet expanding as fast as they would begin to do in the early 1950s. Now, for the first time, there were signs of hostility to coloured people in Birmingham. Previously, disturbances between coloured and white people had been restricted predominantly to the ports, with riots in Cardiff and Liverpool as early as 1919, and brawls in Liverpool dance halls in 1934.[2] But in May 1948 a crowd of about 200 men besieged and stoned a Birmingham house where Indians were staying.[3] True, this was a very isolated incident, but it confirmed the fears of some citizens that discrimination against coloured people in housing and employment was developing. Indian residents had been aware of it since the last year or so of the war, when the local manifestations of the campaign for Indian independence, organized by Dr. D. R. Prem and other leaders of the Indian community, in cooperation with the Borough Labour Party, had aroused some hostility. Indian guests had even been banned from certain hotels.[4] But in the late 1940s discrimination seemed to be directed against coloured people in general, not just against Indians, and it was certainly exacerbated by

[1] Most of the small group of West Indians in Birmingham at the end of the war were former RAF men (Griffith, etc., *Coloured Immigrants*, p. 39).

[2] For a study of race problems in the 1940s, which significantly concentrates on traditional coloured areas like Liverpool and Cardiff, and completely ignores Birmingham, see K. L. Little, *Negroes in Britain: a Study of Racial Relations in English Society* (1947).

[3] John Montgomery, *The Fifties* (1965), p. 102; Ruth Glass, *Newcomers: the West Indians in London* (1960), p. 128.

[4] Prem, *Parliamentary Leper*, p. 7.

the shortage of accommodation in Birmingham after the war. In June 1948 Percy Shurmer, Labour M.P. for Sparkbrook, drew attention in the House of Commons to the problems faced by African and West Indian students and workers seeking accommodation in Birmingham.[1] He was assured by the Secretary of State for the Colonies that the numbers involved were very small, and that their problems were being taken care of, but the whole episode was a portent of what was to come.

The events of 1948 did at least ensure that coloured immigration was recognized as a political problem in Birmingham. Community and political leaders were prepared to face up to it squarely. The Borough Labour Party had had strong links with the Indian community ever since the campaign for Indian independence. Dr. D. R. Prem was invited to offer himself for election as a Labour candidate at the municipal elections of 1945, and was chosen by Perry Barr ward committee from a short list which contained six other nominees, all of them British.[2] He was elected and served a full term of three years on the Council. Although he declined to stand again, he maintained his strong links with the Labour Party, and his friendship with Labour members of the Council and Parliament such as Harrison Barrow, Albert Bradbeer, Julius Silverman, Denis Howell, and Victor Yates. It was largely thanks to this contact that the Borough Labour Party, and the Labour group, were very sensitive to the problems of the immigrant community. The Birmingham churches, too, showed an early awareness of the potential problem. Bishop Barnes's complaints about the moral standards of some coloured immigrants, and their likely effect on the ethnic purity of the British race,[3] at least had the merit of drawing the attention of other churchmen to coloured people. Most of them adopted a far more constructive attitude than did Barnes. In March 1950 the Birmingham protestant churches jointly set up a Coordinating Committee for Overseas Nationals, under the chairmanship of the Ven. S. Harvie Clark, Archdeacon of Birmingham.[4] Later in the year, on a report from the committee, the diocesan conference passed a resolution calling attention to the Christian duty of caring for the well-being of coloured people in Birmingham.[5]

Joint consideration of this problem by the Birmingham churches was stimulated when the Birmingham Council of Christian Churches was formed in 1951. The Christian Social Council, for its part, was particularly concerned with the dangers of a colour bar in employment, but when the churches began to pass from the stage of committees of

[1] H. of C. Deb., 5th series, vol. cdli, cols. 147–8, 9 June 1948. Shurmer referred significantly to 'the Colour Bar' in Birmingham.

[2] Prem, Parliamentary Leper, p. 8.

[3] See, for instance, B.G., B.P., 19 February 1949; B.P., 12 June 1952.

[4] B.C.C., Pro., 15 June 1954, pp. 44–5 (General Purposes Committee).

[5] B.P., 24 November 1950.

inquiry to that of positive recommendations, they concentrated on the housing problem. In the summer of 1952 the Council of Christian Churches suggested that the Corporation should provide a transit hostel for coloured newcomers to Birmingham,[1] and in 1953 it supported the suggestion that a welfare officer for coloured people should be appointed.[2]

The churches' initiatives were greatly encouraged when Barnes was replaced by Bishop Wilson in 1953. The new bishop was a strong opponent of South Africa's apartheid policies.[3] Although he usually tried to avoid making statements on secular and social issues, in order to avoid the public controversy that had often marked Barnes's episcopate, he was never afraid to speak out clearly on the colour question and to defend the right of immigrants to full acceptance in the community. The churches' efforts to mould public attitudes and to encourage the provision of adequate facilities for coloured people were multiplied in the mid-1950s as the inflow of immigrants increased. In 1955 the Council of Christian Churches intervened in a dispute over the employment of coloured people in the Transport Department.[4] In the following year it declared its support for the Friendship Housing Association, set up to provide accommodation for coloured immigrants.[5] In 1957 the Christian Social Council organized an afternoon conference on the problems caused by Commonwealth immigration.[6] However, there were now clear signs that the practical aspects of the problem were too much for the churches, although they could still help to influence opinion. In December 1956 the Christian Social Council was very concerned by various reports on social problems from the Coordinating Committee for Coloured People,[7] and in that year the diocesan conference again found it necessary to pass resolutions urging clergy and laity to show all the hospitality they could to coloured people.[8]

It was perhaps unfortunate that the appointment of a chaplain to coloured people by the only church that had the necessary means, the Church of England, was delayed until 1959. As early as 1955 the Bishop of Birmingham had planned to make such an appointment, and a coloured Jamaican priest was on the point of being selected when negotiations suddenly collapsed. The diocese's official explanation was that the candidate had been discouraged by problems of finance and

[1] Birmingham Council of Christian Churches, Minutes, 24 June 1952.

[2] Ibid., 28 April 1953. See below, p. 368.

[3] See, for instance, *B.P.*, 22 January 1955.

[4] Birmingham Council of Christian Churches, Minutes, 10 February 1955. See below, p. 391.   [5] Ibid., 26 June 1956.

[6] Birmingham Christian Social Council, Minutes, 11 May 1957.

[7] Ibid., 13 December 1956. This was the new title for the former Coordinating Committee for Overseas Nationals.

[8] Diocesan Conference Agenda, 1956.

accommodation, but there were strong indications that the Jamaican's own outspokenness had influenced Bishop Wilson's last-minute decision not to appoint him.[1] Strong protests were made by immigrant organizations in Birmingham, but in vain. The chaplain finally appointed in 1959, the Revd. J. Paul Burrough, was an Englishman who had previously worked in Korea.[2] But by this time there was very little that the churches could do through their religious activities to incorporate coloured immigrants. Very few West Indians ever went to church, and many of those who did attended minority denominations catering solely for coloured immigrants, like the Bethel Apostolic Church, or the Church of God of Prophecy, both of which began to found churches in Birmingham from the late 1950s.[3] The Asian immigrants rarely came into contact with the churches at all. So for the provision of practical assistance to the immigrant, we must return to the secular authorities.

The Borough Labour Party, as has already been noted, had built up links with the Indian community in Birmingham. Labour gave an early indication of their concern for the rights of coloured people when, in May 1945, Albert Bradbeer moved an amendment in the City Council calling for all Corporation departments to be informed that their services were available to people 'irrespective of race or colour'. No department, he urged, should discriminate on grounds of race or colour when appointing staff. This issue had arisen because the U.S. army had designated the Kent Street baths out of bounds for coloured servicewomen; and some Labour councillors believed that the Corporation's health department had refused to let a doctor take up his appointment on the discovery that he was coloured.[4] The Unionist leadership objected to what they interpreted as a limitation on a department's freedom to appoint the most suitable individuals, and the amendment was defeated. However, many Unionists abstained, and the Unionist Alderman Tiptaft joined the Liberal councillor Paul Cadbury in voting for the amendment.[5]

Despite this concern for principles, no positive steps were taken by Labour to help coloured immigrants when they were in control of policy, apart from the organization of experimental English classes at one evening institute from 1948.[6] The first significant decision in this

[1] *E.D.*, 13, 15, 16 September 1955; *B.G.*, 19 September 1955.

[2] *B.M.*, 6 October 1959.

[3] The proportion of churchgoers among West Indians in Britain has been estimated at 4 per cent (Clifford S. Hill, *How Colour Prejudiced is Britain?* (1965), p. 150). See also M. J. C. Calley, *God's People: West Indian Pentecostal Sects in England* (1965), esp. pp. 118–25; R. S. Moore, 'Religion and immigration in the urban twilight zone', *Advancement of Science*, vol. xxiii, no. 108, June 1966, pp. 65–8.

[4] *Ex inf.* C. J. Simmons.

[5] B.C.C., *Pro.*, 15 May 1945, p. 440 (General Purposes Committee).

[6] *Y.B.*, no. 57, November 1951, p. 3.

field was taken by the Education Committee in 1951 when the Unionists were in control. This was to open a Centre for Coloured Peoples at the Clifton Institute, Balsall Heath, an area which already had a high concentration of coloured residents. The centre, which provided both further education and social activities, was described as 'an official effort to break any racial distinctions which may exist in Birmingham'.[1] Yet it catered primarily for West Indians, who were still in a minority among the city's coloured immigrants,[2] and the premises were available only on a part-time basis. In the following year, however, the Education Committee began to hold English classes for Pakistanis and Indians at a number of evening institutes.[3]

In November 1952 the Archdeacon of Birmingham went to see the Lord Mayor, Alderman Bowen, about the problems of coloured people, and the matter was submitted to the General Purposes Committee. It was agreed to appoint representatives from a number of Council committees to the Coordinating Committee for Overseas Nationals. Pressure now began to build up on the City Council to take more positive action. In June 1953 the Coordinating Committee requested it to appoint a welfare officer for coloured people, and in July the Afro-Caribbean Association called for the establishment of a social centre for immigrants, and an inter-racial welfare council.[4] Both Alderman Bowen and Alderman Bradbeer, who had again become leader of the Labour group, were fully aware of the problem and eager to take action. Alderman Bradbeer was convinced, in particular, of the need for a special welfare officer, and he pursued this idea despite the Council's habitual unwillingness to set up new departments.[5] The decision to appoint a liaison officer for coloured people was finally made by the Council in January 1954 when it was also decided in principle to set up a social centre.[6] The appointment of the liaison officer, which set an example for the other local authorities, was an important step towards preventing overt racial conflict in Birmingham. Even though only limited financial resources were available the work of the department was much appreciated by individuals and immigrant organizations.[7]

[1] *Y.B.*, no. 50, March 1951, p. 3.

[2] In 1952 the city's coloured population was estimated as follows: Pakistanis 2,500, Arabs 400, Sikhs and Indians 500, Africans and West Indians 1,000, others 200. Total 4,600 (B.C.C., *Pro.*, 15 June 1954, p. 45 (General Purposes Committee)).

[3] *Y.B.*, no. 57, November 1951, p. 3.

[4] B.C.C., *Pro.*, 15 June 1954, p. 46 (General Purposes Committee).

[5] When Bradbeer was granted the freedom of the city in May 1960, it was stated that the appointment of a liaison officer for coloured people was largely the result of his perseverance (B.C.C., *Pro.*, 7 May 1960, p. 980).

[6] B.C.C., *Pro.*, 15 June 1954, p. 47 (General Purposes Committee).

[7] It has been suggested that if Smethwick county borough had taken similar steps to help immigrants in the mid-1950s, much subsequent trouble might have been avoided (Paul Foot, *Immigration and Race in British Politics* (1965), pp. 20–2).

The City Council's important new departure was clearly influenced by considerations of principle, which were again strongly reflected in its resolution, passed in April 1955, that appointments to Corporation posts should be made 'without any distinction as to race, creed, or colour'. Fittingly, the motion was proposed by Alderman Bradbeer, ten years after his original amendment to that effect.[1] Yet the decision to appoint a liaison officer was also prompted by the Council's growing awareness of the social problems resulting from coloured immigration into Birmingham. During 1954 those problems, as seen from the Council House, seemed to become more serious. In January 1954 the Council was given an estimate of the Birmingham coloured population which dated from 1952, and totalled a mere 4,600.[2] But a new estimate made shortly afterwards put the total at around 10,000.[3] This sudden increase in the estimate seems to have worried many Council members. Almost at the same time that the welfare officer was appointed, the Conservative Councillor Charles Collett began a campaign for the control of immigration. Neither group in the Council concurred officially with some of the more outspoken views of Councillor Collett, but a feeling grew up even in the Labour group that adequate welfare arrangements could be made for the immigrants only if their number were restricted.[4] Indeed, this feeling was shared by none other than D. R. Prem, who had already been to Delhi to urge Pandit Nehru to restrict Indian immigration to Britain.[5] By the end of 1954 the Labour group's mind was made up, and in January 1955 a delegation, led by Alderman Bowen, called on the Home Secretary to ask him to restrict coloured immigration into Birmingham. Bowen expressed 'extreme concern' at the pressure on services and especially on housing.[6]

The Government firmly rejected Birmingham's request. Its view, which was staunchly maintained until 1961, was that Commonwealth citizens had every right to enter Britain and settle where they wished. However, in order to defend this principle against those who wished to restrict Commonwealth immigration, the Government had to maintain that there was no difference between immigrant Commonwealth citizens and indigenous Britons. In consequence of this argument it could not logically continue to advocate the provision of special welfare

[1] B.C.C., *Pro.*, 5 April 1955, p. 1192.

[2] Prem, *Parliamentary Leper*, pp. 21–2. In the early 1950s the spokesmen of the immigrant communities reckoned that the number of coloured people in Birmingham was twice as high as the official estimates (J. A. G. Griffith, etc., *Coloured Immigrants*, p. 39).

[3] This figure was quoted by the Lord Mayor, Alderman Gibson, in October 1955 (Prem, *Parliamentary Leper*, pp. 21–2).

[4] Ald. Sir Wilfrid Martineau had expounded this view as early as 1952 (Norman Tiptaft, *My Contemporaries* (1952), p. 135).

[5] Prem, *Parliamentary Leper*, p. 18.

[6] Paul Foot, *The Rise of Enoch Powell* (1969), p. 44; *B.M.*, 19 November 1955.

AA

facilities for coloured immigrants, as it had begun to do in the early
1950s. From about 1954, in Nicholas Deakin's words: 'Official concern
with the needs of the new minorities, especially in accommodation and
employment, was superseded by the need to demonstrate, through
strict non-interference, the equality of citizens from all parts of the
Commonwealth.'[1] So in January 1955 Birmingham was told that it did
not have a coloured immigrant problem, and that no Government
intervention could be expected. This meant not only that immigration
would not be controlled, but also, by implication, that no Government
help could be expected in solving housing and other social problems.

From 1955 onwards the City Council began to take its cue from the
Government by gradually adopting a policy of strict impartiality and
non-interference in matters concerning coloured immigrants. The first
indication of this change of attitude came in October 1955 when
Birmingham took part in a conference of fourteen West Midlands local
authorities and other bodies, organized by D. R. Prem, on the welfare
of Indian immigrants in the region. Alderman A. L. Gibson, Lord
Mayor of Birmingham, told the conference that the main problem in
Birmingham was a shortage of housing. Birmingham declined to join
the regional welfare council set up by the conference on the ground
that it already had its own welfare officer.[2] Thus the City Council lost
the opportunity of establishing its leadership over the whole conurbation in the provision of welfare facilities for coloured immigrants.
One effect of the Council's call for immigration controls (which
appeared to many to contradict the Council's declared policy of strict
impartiality) was to break up the harmony which had existed until
1955 between the churches and voluntary associations, the Birmingham
Trades Council, and the Borough Labour Party. Immediately, in
January 1955, the Trades Council, which had consistently opposed any
discrimination against coloured people at work or outside, passed
unanimously a resolution opposing any move by Birmingham to obtain
restrictions on immigration.[3] It maintained this opposition until the
Commonwealth Immigration Act was passed in 1962. Once the Labour
group had broken with the Trades Council over this issue of principle,
it was less concerned about subsequent criticism from that quarter.
The same was true of the Council's relations with the voluntary bodies,
and full cooperation was never completely restored, especially as
criticism of the Corporation's attitude to coloured immigrants mounted
in the late 1950s and 1960s.

On the other hand, it must not be forgotten that the policy of strict
impartiality had its positive aspects, and with Bradbeer still leading the

---

[1] See Nicholas Deakin, 'The politics of the Commonwealth Immigrants Bill',
Political Quarterly, vol. xxxix, no. 1, January–March 1968, pp. 25–6.

[2] Prem, *Parliamentary Leper*, pp. 21–2.   [3] B.T.C., *Annual Report*, 1955–6, p. 5.

Labour group, the Council pursued its integrationist policies into the later 1950s. It was happy that the serious disturbances in 1958 in Notting Hill and Nottingham did not spread to Birmingham; the city police had taken special precautions to deal with any trouble firmly and promptly, but they were not needed.[1] However, the City Council was tempted to assume that the maintenance of calm in Birmingham indicated that its policies were adequate. Indeed, they had probably been very influential in avoiding racial strife, but so had the general climate of opinion in the city, influenced as it was by churchmen and voluntary associations, and the low rate of unemployment. The Labour group was deprived of Bradbeer's leadership when he fell ill towards the end of 1957, and although he had recovered by May 1958, he never re-established his old ascendancy over the group. During his illness he was replaced by the deputy leader, Alderman Watton, who in May 1959 challenged him for the leadership and won it. Alderman Watton did not have Bradbeer's contacts with the immigrant community; instead, he was closely in touch with the views of white citizens in Aston where he lived. And he was aware—indeed, everyone in Birmingham was aware—of a growing climate of opinion against the increase in the number of coloured people in Birmingham. Opinion polls relating specifically to Birmingham were infrequent, but in one such poll taken in about 1956, nearly 74 per cent of those questioned considered that there was a colour bar in Birmingham, and over 98 per cent said that they would be unwilling to take a coloured lodger. Over 80 per cent wanted Commonwealth immigration to be restricted, although only 13 per cent wanted it stopped altogether. Only 17 per cent considered that they had a special duty to ease the lot of the coloured worker in Birmingham.[2]

This big groundswell of opinion could not fail to encourage the activities of racialist organizations and right-wing political parties. One of the first to attempt to exploit it was Oswald Mosley's Union Movement. Mosley had few supporters in Birmingham, despite his great reputation there in the 1920s when he had won so many votes for Labour. He had not spoken in the city since 1935.[3] However, the Union Movement had been warning of the dangers of unrestricted coloured immigration since 1952,[4] and in 1956 Mosley saw the immigrant issue, together with industrial unrest, as an opportunity to gain popularity in the city. In March 1956 he spoke at a meeting in Sparkbrook, where he was quoted as saying: 'Our greatest hope lies in

---

[1] City of Birmingham, *Report of the Police Establishment*, 1958, p. 12.

[2] John Darragh, *Colour and Conscience* (1957), p. 21.

[3] According to John Darragh, the Union Movement had only 200–300 members in Birmingham (*S.M.*, 7 October 1956). For Mosley's political activities in Birmingham in the 1920s see Sir Oswald Mosley, *My Life* (1968), pp. 176–93.

[4] Mosley, *My Life*, p. 448.

Birmingham. It is there that I shall draw my strength.'[1] But he reserved his main effort for the autumn, when he planned a big rally in the Town Hall. As soon as news of the rally was announced in September, numerous Birmingham organizations and individuals demanded that Mosley be banned from using the hall. Prominent in this campaign were the Trades Council, the Communist Party, the Liberal Party, a large part of the Borough Labour Party, and all the immigrant organizations. But the Lord Mayor, Alderman E. W. Apps (Conservative), was adamant. Birmingham, he said, had a tradition of free speech, and it would be wrong to prevent a politician from speaking at the Town Hall because his views might be disagreeable. In truth, Alderman Apps could have said nothing else owing to the strong tradition in Birmingham that the Lord Mayor should be completely non-political. The *Birmingham Post* fully supported the Lord Mayor, and urged that Mosley's rally should be ignored, not disrupted. It also attacked leaders of the coloured community, such as Dr. Clarence J. Piliso, president of the Afro-Caribbean Association, who had called on people to demonstrate against the rally. Their language, said the *Post*, was 'calculated to inflame their followers to acts of violence'.[2]

The *Post*'s views were at first angrily rejected by the organizations planning to demonstrate against Mosley, but calmer counsels eventually prevailed. Shortly before the rally the Trades Council and the other protesting organizations decided simply to boycott it.[3] The Town Hall was half empty on the night of the rally, and although there were a few violent incidents, no general confrontation occurred between protesters and fascists.[4] The Union Movement did not plan another big meeting in Birmingham until 1958. This time the situation was more tense than in 1956, owing to the racial disturbances that had already taken place in Notting Hill and Nottingham.[5] The Trades Council again planned a counter-demonstration. It wanted to hold a meeting in the Town Hall just before Mosley's rally, to see what happened when the fascist supporters arrived. But the immigrant organizations approached the problem more calmly this time, and advocated another boycott. Dr. W. C. Pilgrim, president of the West Indian Association in Birmingham, appealed to all West Indians to stay away, reminding them that they had always been treated with 'sympathetic consideration' in the city.[6] A few days before the rally the Birmingham Trades Council abandoned its plan to hold a counter-demonstration, and the rally again passed off without major incidents.

---

[1] *E.D.*, 24 September 1956.   [2] *B.P.*, 2 October 1956, editorial.
[3] *B.P.*, 26 October 1956.   [4] *B.P.*, 29 October 1956.
[5] For an analysis of these disturbances, see James Wickenden, *Colour in Britain* (1958).
[6] *B.M.*, 30 September 1958.

One ominous note was struck, however, when Colin Jordan, a Coventry schoolteacher, and other members of his newly formed White Defence League, distributed leaflets outside the Town Hall. 'We shall be showing our hand before long in many towns and cities', Jordan told a reporter.[1]

The 1958 meeting marked the end of Mosley's challenge in Birmingham. More specialized organizations soon creamed off much of his racialist support. Another rally was organized for him at the Town Hall in November 1960, but it did not attract the same volume of protests as in 1956 and 1958. The attendance, estimated at 1,400, was about half as high again as on the two previous occasions, but many of them were students who went to heckle, and there was some fighting in the hall. It was this violence, and not the views expressed by Mosley, which at last forced the Corporation to ban Mosley from the Town Hall when he wanted to speak there in October 1962. A number of Union Movement meetings held in other cities earlier in the year had been disrupted by violent demonstrations.[2] The decision to cancel was taken by Alderman Watton, after he had obtained the agreement of the leader of the Conservative group, Alderman Pritchett.[3] Watton's initiative allowed the Lord Mayor to retain his non-political standpoint, and later decisions of this type were made by the majority group leader, not by the Lord Mayor.

Mosley's failure to obtain much support in Birmingham was partly due to his party's bad reputation in the city. His attempts to take advantage of industrial unrest in Birmingham in 1956 had been bitterly resented by workers, and had culminated in a violent incident in Calthorpe Park when hundreds of workers attending a strike meeting attacked a loudspeaker lorry manned by Union Movement members. Councillor Collett declared his strong opposition to the Union Movement in 1956 and planned to go to the October rally to heckle Mosley.[4] But Mosley's failure did not imply that Commonwealth immigration was not potentially a political issue in Birmingham. Indeed, Birmingham became from the late 1950s one of the most important centres of opposition to uncontrolled immigration.

The most important figure in the early years of the anti-immigration movement in Birmingham was the Conservative Councillor Charles Collett, a shopkeeper. The Council's decision to ask for the control of

---

[1] *B.P.*, 13 October 1958. Until 1954 Colin Jordan had been organizing the Birmingham Nationalist Club, but the failure of this venture was typical of the fate of most extremist organizations in Birmingham (George Thayer, *The British Political Fringe: a Profile* (1956), p. 16).

[2] Mosley later claimed that there were no incidents at any of his rallies until 1962, when, he insists, the Communists made a concerted attempt to disrupt them (Mosley, *My Life*, p. 453).

[3] *B.M.*, 31 July 1962.   [4] *B.G.*, 29 September 1956.

immigration into Birmingham was a victory for his point of view, but in the later 1950s his outspokenness and inability to compromise somewhat isolated him in the City Council. So he threw himself with vigour into the national campaign for control of immigration which developed at the end of the decade. In 1960 he was elected president of the Birmingham Immigration Control Committee (later, Association) which had been formed earlier in the year by a small group of enthusiasts who had begun writing letters to the Birmingham press calling for immigration controls from the late 1950s.[1] This association became the most powerful anti-immigration pressure group in the country, and several more splinter groups formed from it.[2] But the B.I.C.A. expressed its views moderately, and Collett prevented any association between it and more extreme neo-fascist organizations.[3] More overtly racialist breakaway groups, like the Argus Britons Rights Association,[4] made little progress in Birmingham. However, Collett was not entirely successful in his efforts to stop B.I.C.A. members standing for election to the City Council, which was bound to annoy his Conservative colleagues. The secretary of the association, Harry Jones, stood as an Independent for Sandwell ward in the elections of 1961, and beat the Labour candidate into third place. Although Sandwell was a safe Conservative ward, the result was an indication to both parties and especially to Labour that immigration as a political issue could be dangerous to them. And the clear growth of feeling in Birmingham against uncontrolled immigration[5] helps to explain the attitude to the problem adopted by the Labour group from the late 1950s.

We have already seen that in the mid-1950s the City Council considered the housing shortage to be the main obstacle to Commonwealth immigration into Birmingham. Housing was indeed a serious problem, but the accommodation shortage facing coloured people was different in character from the city's overall shortage. Coloured people's search for somewhere to live was complicated by the prejudices against them of some landladies, landlords of rented property, house agents, and owner-occupiers. Most coloured people came to live in decaying areas of the city where a steady decline in the white population left room for them.[6] In addition to the housing problem there was

---

[1] Foot, *Immigration and Race*, pp. 195–8.   [2] Ibid., pp. 195–200.

[3] For a typical B.I.C.A. statement, see John Sanders, *Immigration: The Incredible Folly* (1965).

[4] See Peter Griffiths, *A Question of Colour?* (1966), p. 218.

[5] John Sanders, chairman of the B.I.C.A., claimed that 100,000 signatures calling for control of immigration were obtained in the Birmingham area in the months before the Commonwealth Immigration Bill was introduced (*Immigration: The Incredible Folly*, p. 7).

[6] See above, pp. 210 ff.

the whole question of provision of social services in the areas which had a high concentration of immigrants. The City Council took some steps to expand social services in the immigrant areas, but on the whole its approach to the problem was a cautious one, based on the principle that coloured people should be treated no differently from anyone else in the city. Its policies from the mid-1950s, which we shall now go on to examine, were partly the result of respect for the demands of economy, and of an unwillingness to risk political discontent and possible racial conflict among the citizens of Birmingham by taking special measures to help the coloured immigrants.

Before and during the war the first coloured immigrants to Birmingham had gone to live in particular districts of the city. During the 1950s certain districts in the middle ring, such as Handsworth and Soho in the north-west, and Balsall Heath and Sparkbrook in the south, became recognized as areas with a high proportion of coloured people. They also contained a high proportion of the city's Irish population.[1] The development of these immigrant districts produced mixed reactions in the city. On the one hand, some feared that they would develop into ghettos as English people left them, thus hindering the process of integration, and perhaps leading to inter-area strife in the future between black and white districts.[2] On the other hand, the concentration of coloured people in a few areas meant that the great majority of English people in the city rarely came into contact with them, so that friction was limited. Moreover, from the Council's point of view the immigrant areas were convenient to administer; they allowed municipal services to be tailored to meet the special needs of the immigrant. But conditions became so bad in the immigrant areas that by the late 1950s they were beginning to pose special problems for the Council from the point of view of public health and overcrowding.

The Council had its attention drawn forcefully to the problem of the immigrant areas in May 1959. This was when the report of the Liaison Officer for Commonwealth Immigrants was printed in full for the first time in the report of the General Purposes Committee.[3] Until 1959 the Liaison Officer had been doing very useful work in smoothing over relations between the coloured people and the rest of the community in respect of employment, housing, and social problems. Few members of the Council had been very interested in what he was doing, and it was generally assumed that his efforts were sufficient to fulfil the Corporation's responsibilities. But now the Liaison Officer himself

[1] See E. Robinson, 'The Irish in Birmingham' (Birmingham University B.A. dissertation), 1969.

[2] See, for instance, *E.D.*, 5 October 1959; Report by the Liaison Officer for Commonwealth Immigrants, B.C.C., *Pro.*, 21 May 1959, pp. 16–20 (General Purposes Committee).

[3] B.C.C., *Pro.*, 21 May 1959, pp. 16–20.

came out in support of a growing feeling in Birmingham that integration was moving further away and that this trend, unless checked, was likely to have serious consequences. He announced that a recent survey had revealed 3,200 houses occupied by coloured people, and a sample check had suggested that there were eleven people in each house. This meant that there were about 35,200 coloured people in the city, of whom some 24,000 were estimated to be West Indians. Most of these coloured people were living in a few small districts in the middle ring of the city. The report went on:

From the nature of interviews which take place in the office, it is now certain that a large number of the coloured immigrants, particularly the West Indians, intend to settle in the city, but there is ample evidence to suggest that the integration desired by the Council is not taking place. The immigrants are living in tight pockets turning inwards to themselves and it would seem intent [sic] on creating a 'little Jamaica' or the like within the City. I believe that this trend, unless checked, will have serious consequences. (. . .) I would emphasize that the integration desired by the Council is not being achieved except in a small way at the places where coloured people work and, as it appears that at least fifty per cent of the coloured people now in the City are likely to stay, I am of the opinion that further action should be developed on the lines I have indicated.

The positive suggestion made by the Liaison Officer was that coloured people should be visited in their homes to help solve problems as they arose. As things were, problems were brought to him only when it was too late, and the coloured people involved were already convinced that they were being discriminated against. The General Purposes Committee authorized the establishment of an experimental visiting service, but large-scale visiting never became possible owing to the lack of resources for the appointment of staff. It was, in any case, clear to most councillors that more far-reaching steps would have to be taken.

In the autumn of 1960 the General Purposes Committee appointed an *ad hoc* sub-committee to inquire into the problem of overcrowding in Birmingham, after an amendment to this effect, moved by Councillor Collett, had been passed in October.[1] Towards the end of the year the *ad hoc* committee produced an interim report which concluded that over the city as a whole there had been a slight reduction in overcrowding during the decade, but that 'the intensity of overcrowding in individual units may have increased'.[2] The report went on to make clear that overcrowding in certain wards was due mainly to the intensive occupation of 'a considerable but unknown number of houses', 'mostly by newcomers', in areas such as Handsworth, Aston, Sparkbrook, and

[1] B.C.C., *Pro.*, 4 October 1960, p. 378 (General Purposes Committee). Councillor Collett had first proposed such a motion in 1956.

[2] B.C.C., *Pro.*, 6 December 1960, p. 571 (General Purposes Committee).

Balsall Heath. Conditions in these houses, it was admitted, had become much worse than in those commonly known as slums.[1] Evidence was produced of high infant mortality and a high incidence of tuberculosis and venereal diseases among coloured immigrants.[2] Reference was also made to the high birth rate among coloured women, who made up less than 5 per cent of the Asiatic population but some 40 per cent of the West Indian.

What was to be done about these problems? The committee suggested that if immigrants were required to obtain a certificate of health before entering Britain, the tuberculosis problem might be substantially solved. But this still left the housing problem. The committee's report made it very clear that, as things stood, coloured immigrants had little chance of obtaining a municipal house. In the first place, all applicants for houses had to live in the city for five years before they were eligible for consideration. This stipulation had been introduced in 1949, and had originally been directed against English and Irish immigrants to Birmingham, not coloureds. But as the 1950s wore on the 'five year rule' had been recognized as an effective barrier against a flood of applications for houses from coloured people newly arrived in the city. Even after five years, reported the committee, few immigrants could expect to be rehoused; they would become eligible for an offer '*if and when* they have enough points, which is not likely to occur in most cases for several years after they have satisfied the five year rule. Only the cases of exceptionally severe overcrowding are likely to acquire enough points for time on the list plus need to qualify for an offer in the sixth year after their arrival in the city, and the number of such cases is comparatively small.'[3] Of course, it was open to the Council to enforce the new overcrowding provisions of the 1957 Housing Act, which would have enabled many more coloured immigrants to qualify for rehousing. But to do so, said the committee, would throw an intolerable burden on the Housing Management Committee, which in 1960 had been able to allocate only 5 per cent of lettings to 'special priority groups' and just over 10 per cent to homeless families. Moreover, to attack multi-occupation in one twilight area would simply drive the problem into the next ward. So all that the committee could recommend positively was that a survey should be undertaken of houses let in lodgings, to establish the true extent of the problem. This proposal, and the suggestion that Birmingham should ask the Government to require a

---

[1] B.C.C., *Pro.*, 6 December 1960, p. 573.   [2] Ibid., pp. 575–9.

[3] Ibid., p. 582. The italics are those of the original report. The Corporation was clearly worried about the opinion prevalent among some citizens of Birmingham that coloured residents were given more favourable treatment in housing allocation than white people, and the General Purposes Committee's assurances to the contrary were prominently featured on the front page of the official news sheet (*Y.B.*, no. 157, December 1960, p. 1).

certificate of health from immigrants, were accepted by the Council.[1]

The Council's attitude at this stage did not suggest that it was prepared to take exceptional measures to provide housing for coloured immigrants. The General Purposes Committee confirmed this impression in October 1961, when, in reply to a memorial presented by Councillor Collett complaining that 'immigrants' were given more consideration than English residents, it stated that it had never been the Council's policy to give immigrants preferential treatment. However, the committee rejected a further demand in Collett's memorial that the City should press for control of immigration. It would not be appropriate, thought the committee, to make such a recommendation to the Government 'at the present time'.[2] But with the prospect of tight controls on immigration in the near future, the City Council was able to proceed confidently towards its goal of containing and controlling the problems raised by coloured immigrants in Birmingham.

Until 1954 Birmingham had enjoyed powers under its own bye-laws to register and inspect houses let in lodgings, but these powers were removed by the Housing Act of that year. Powers of inspection and control were restored by the 1961 Housing Act, but local authorities were not given powers to control the creation of lodging houses and their consequent overcrowding. Birmingham had done its best to persuade the Government to include such powers in the Act; a deputation had been to see the Minister of Housing on this point in November 1960,[3] and further representations were made after the Council had passed a resolution calling for powers of registration in July 1961.[4] The exclusion of these powers from the Act made it difficult to use it to prevent the spread of multi-occupation, for the City became liable to rehouse those displaced when overcrowding orders were made. To some extent the City was prepared to face up to this obligation, and displaced coloured families came to be rehoused in sub-standard properties acquired for redevelopment. However, action was taken only in the worst cases in order to avoid a big displacement of tenants.[5] By October 1962, the Health Committee had served notice in 141 cases of houses let in lodgings, out of a total of multi-occupied houses estimated at 3,600 at that time.[6] Even this cautious approach soon

[1] B.C.C., *Pro*, 6 December, 1960, p. 598.

[2] B.C.C., *Pro.*, 25 July 1961, p. 256; 10 October 1961, pp. 354-5 (General Purposes Committee). The Labour group would have embarrassed the parliamentary Labour Party if Birmingham had supported immigration controls at a time when Labour was strongly opposed to them nationally. But the Labour group was in fact strongly in favour of control, and some of its leaders would have liked the Commonwealth Immigration Bill to apply to the Irish Republic too.

[3] B.C.C., *Pro.*, 6 December 1960, p. 581 (General Purposes Committee).

[4] Ibid., 4 July 1961, p. 199 (General Purposes Committee).

[5] B.C.C., *Pro.*, 9 October 1962, pp. 307-10 (General Purposes Committee).

[6] Ibid., pp. 307-8.

began to create problems for the Housing Management Committee. The number of homeless families requiring assistance increased from 1962 onwards, and by 1964 the committee was planning to establish two further hostels in the near future. However, the committee was careful not to allow this growth in the number of coloured applicants to obscure the needs of English homeless families, and it told the Council that it was working closely with other committees to ensure 'a proper balance' in allocation.[1]

The City Council's disappointment at the exclusion of the powers it wanted from the 1962 Act was tempered by the hope that they might be included in subsequent legislation. But these hopes were again dashed. Representations were made to the Government in respect of the Housing Bill 1964, but all that the Government would do was to allow local authorities to require the registration of multi-occupied houses immediately on their creation, instead of after the three-year delay stipulated in the 1961 Act.[2] The situation was transformed, however, by the election of a Labour Government in October 1964. Discussions on the problem of multi-occupation were held with the Minister of Housing, Richard Crossman, when he visited Birmingham. It was made clear that the Corporation would now stand a good chance of obtaining the powers it wanted by putting a Bill of its own through Parliament. By December 1964 the Corporation had prepared a Bill to allow it to refuse applications for the registration of a multi-occupied house when the building, the area of the city, or the owners of the property were considered unsuitable. Secondly, the Corporation would have powers to require the provision of adequate facilities and the execution of necessary work before a house could be brought into multi-occupation. Thirdly, the Council could enforce the limitation of the total of occupants to a pre-determined figure.[3] The Bill was approved unanimously by the City Council, and after passing the hurdle of the town's meeting, it finally received the royal assent in 1965, substantially in the form in which it was deposited.

In the meantime, the City Council had decided to purchase one area of some 400 houses near Birchfield Road in order to preserve its character and prevent the spread of multi-occupation through it.[4] Registration was enforced throughout the city from January 1966. Only common lodging houses, houses under the control and management of the Corporation, and houses with less than three separate occupancies and five individual lodgers were excluded from registration.[5]

After 1966 these powers were used carefully by the Corporation.

[1] B.C.C., *Pro.*, 4 February 1964, p. 779 (Housing Management Committee).

[2] B.C.C., *Pro.*, 15 December 1964, p. 505 (General Purposes Committee).

[3] Ibid., pp. 505–6.   [4] Ibid., 15 June 1965, p. 136 (Public Works Committee).

[5] Ibid., 5 October 1965, pp. 361–74 (General Purposes Committee).

On the whole, the spread of areas of multi-occupation was checked, but no attempt was made to cut down the number of coloured people in the city by deliberately reducing the number of houses that could be let in multi-occupation.[1] Indeed, to attempt to do so would have increased the number of applications for municipal housing from homeless coloured families to an embarrassing extent. Those displaced by overcrowding orders continued to be rehoused predominantly in sub-standard properties, although after about 1965 increasing numbers of coloured people at last began to qualify for municipal houses via the housing list. Many of them found their way into new or inter-war dwellings. Exact figures cannot be obtained because the Housing Department did not keep figures for the numbers of its tenants of different nationalities or colour, but it would seem that the proportion of coloured people living in municipal houses in 1970 remained lower than the proportion of coloured people in the city as a whole.[2] The proportion, however, tended to rise owing to the redevelopment of immigrant-occupied areas, which by 1970 had begun in some cases.[3]

Although relatively few coloured people were directly rehoused by the Corporation until the later 1960s, they were given considerable help to acquire properties by the granting of Corporation mortgages. Local authorities were given powers to grant mortgages for house purchase under the Housing (Financial Provisions) Act 1958. Birmingham announced its plans to set up a mortgage scheme in December 1959, and wide interest was shown, with more than 2,300 inquiries made to the Corporation.[4] By September 1960, 830 advances had been made,[5] and a year later the total had risen to 2,518.[6] In July 1965 the granting of mortgages had to be considerably decelerated as part of the Government's new deflationary measures,[7] but the situation subsequently improved. Again, recent figures are not available of the proportion of mortgages granted to coloured people, but in 1964 the

[1] Elizabeth Burney, *Housing on Trial* (1967), p. 29.

[2] It has been estimated by outside sources that just over eight per cent of coloured immigrants in Birmingham live in local authority housing (E. J. B. Rose, etc., *Colour and Citizenship: a Report on British Race Relations* (1969), p. 190).

[3] For a suggestion that Birmingham's allocation procedure virtually excludes coloured people from rehousing on inter-war and post-war estates, see John Rex and Robert Moore, *Race, Community and Conflict: A Study of Sparkbrook* (1967), pp. 26–7. This view has been questioned by V. A. Karn in 'A Note on Race, Community and Conflict', *Race*, vol. ix, no. 1, p. 101. The Corporation was accused in the Trades Council of racial prejudice in the allocation of houses as early as 1951 (Birmingham Trades Council, *Annual Report*, 1951–2, p. 12).

[4] B.C.C., *Pro.*, 8 March 1960, p. 810 (Finance Committee).

[5] Ibid., 4 October 1960, p. 396 (Finance Committee).

[6] Ibid., 10 October 1961, pp. 684–5 (Finance Committee).

[7] Ibid., 5 October 1965, pp. 376–7 (Finance Committee).

Town Clerk told Dr. D. R. Prem that a glance at the names of mort-gagees suggested that hundreds, if not thousands, had been granted to coloured applicants.[1] By 1966 the number of such mortgages granted to coloured people since 1959 was tentatively estimated at 2,000.[2]

It would appear that most of the properties for which coloured immigrants obtained mortgages were small tunnel-back houses in the middle ring, in or near areas already occupied by a high proportion of coloured people. Most immigrants could not afford larger or more modern houses, so in granting mortgages the Corporation was not creating political problems for itself as it might have if it had rehoused a high proportion of coloured people on municipal estates. Moreover, by helping coloured people to purchase houses in the middle ring the Corporation prevented the rapid decline in property values there which might otherwise have taken place. And since lodgers were not allowed in houses bought with the help of Corporation mortgages, there was no danger that the multi-occupation problem would spread.[3] Indeed, the availability to immigrants of mortgages for cheap houses helped to reduce the pressure on municipal accommodation caused by the campaign against multi-occupation from 1962.[4] By 1969 it was estimated that some 40 per cent of coloured immigrants in Birming-ham were owner-occupiers, and that this proportion tended to increase in relation to the length of time spent in the city.[5] In 1968 some 40 per cent of the Corporation's mortgage advances were made to coloured immigrants.[6]

The concentration of the great majority of coloured people in a few small areas created a serious educational difficulty from the late 1950s. In 1959 some 1,000 coloured children were at school in Birmingham.[7] Most of them were West Indian, for there were still very few Indian and Pakistani women in the city. At that time it was still believed that many of the immigrants, especially the single men, would eventually return home. A survey of public opinion undertaken by the Westhill Training College in about 1960 suggested that there was no colour prejudice amongst teachers and primary school children, and that white parents did not object to their children being educated with

[1] Prem, *Parliamentary Leper*, pp. 51–2.

[2] J. Sibley, 'Immigrants in Aston', *Institute of Race Relations News Letter*, February 1966, p. 16.

[3] However, the 'no lodgers' rule was often broken, and the Corporation went to some trouble to detect offenders (B.C.C., *Pro.*, 16 July 1968, p. 161 (General Purposes Committee)).

[4] The effects of the granting of mortgages to coloured people are more fully dis-cussed in R. J. Smith, 'Migration in post-war Birmingham', History of Birmingham Project Research Paper no. 9, pp. 34–5.

[5] Nicholas Deakin, etc., *Colour, Citizenship and British Society* (1970), pp. 82–7.

[6] B.C.C., *Pro.*, 16 July 1965, p. 161 (General Purposes Committee).

[7] B.C.C., *Pro.*, 21 May 1959, p. 19 (General Purposes Committee).

coloured children.[1] It was not until 1961, when the Government's intention to restrict immigration accelerated the inflow and encouraged many immigrants to send for their families, that the problem of numerous coloured children was recognized as serious.[2] It became even more serious after 1962, when coloured immigrants already in Britain were allowed to bring over relatives even though the number of immigrants coming to find work was seriously cut back.

The education of large numbers of coloured children presented a triple problem. The first was purely technical. It had been noticed in the late 1950s that coloured immigrant children were less successful academically than indigenous white children. As most of the coloured children in school at that time were West Indian, this difficulty was not based on language, and it was suggested that overcrowded living conditions might be responsible.[3] In the 1960s, and especially after 1962, there was a steady increase in the number of Indian and Pakistani children. Most of them had severe language problems, for it was estimated that less than one-fifth of their parents had a working knowledge of English when they came to Britain.[4] Even after learning English, most of these parents spoke in their native language to their children at home. The danger was that such children would slow down the learning-rate of English children in the same class.

The second part of the problem was social. Because most coloured people lived in a few small areas, primary schools in these districts began to accumulate very high proportions of coloured children in the 1960s. So not only were the children deprived of contact with English people outside school, but they saw fewer and fewer of them inside. English parents were often tempted to move their children away from schools with high proportions of coloured children, or to move away from the district, thus accentuating the problem. It was generally agreed in Birmingham that young children were not colour-prejudiced, so that the integrating effect of mixed schools was considerable. If, therefore, schools developed very high proportions of coloured children, both white and coloured were deprived of perhaps the only opportunity in their lives to get to know each other.

The third aspect of the problem, which developed from the second, was political. As we have seen, the policy of the City Council towards coloured people was essentially to leave them alone. This policy was accepted by the majority of English citizens because coloured people and the problems they created were restricted to a few areas of the city.

[1] Fred Milson, *Operation Integration: An Enquiry into the Experience of West Indians Living in Birmingham, with Particular Reference to Children and Young People* (1961), p. 2.

[2] See, for instance, *The Times*, 12 April 1961.

[3] Milson, *Operation Integration*, p. 3.

[4] Clifford S. Hill, *How Colour-Prejudiced is Britain?* (1965), p. 197.

For the City Council to do anything other than leave the coloured child to register at the local primary school would have contradicted its basic policy, and might have led to political controversy and even racial strife. To disperse children daily from the immigrant areas to schools in other parts of the city would probably have caused opposition among English parents in the reception areas. And its corollary, the transfer of suburban white children to schools in immigrant districts, would have caused an even bigger outcry.

Concern about the growing education problem was reinforced in 1962 by the Minister of Education's report for 1961, which prophesied that in five years' time eight out of ten children in some Birmingham schools would be coloured. The chairman of the Education Committee, Councillor Nigel Cook, put the situation in perspective by pointing out that under 2 per cent of the total school population was coloured, and that only twenty-four schools had more than 10 per cent coloured children. The language problem, he said, affected only one coloured child in five, and teachers had already been appointed to teach English to them.[1] Alderman Hall, the Conservative spokesman for education, confirmed that the Education Committee had the matter well in hand, but he added a somewhat ominous remark: 'The difficulty which arises is in integrating these children. Where the proportion is under 10 per cent assimilation is relatively easy. It only becomes a problem when the proportion of coloured children gets to the 50 per cent mark.'[2]

In fact, by the end of 1962 the Education Committee was already discussing the integration aspect of the problem. A co-opted member of the committee, W. H. Poulton, suggested that congestion in central schools should be relieved by taking pupils every day to schools on the outskirts. Many of the children thus transported would be coloured. The committee decided to take no action but to keep the proposal in mind.[3] Certainly there were strong arguments against transportation, which disrupted the children's educational day, and prevented them from building up strong friendship links with children in the reception areas, whom they did not meet after school hours. The committee's decision was supported a few days later by a conference on the teaching of immigrants organized by the Birmingham Association of School-masters, the principal primary schoolteachers' union.[4] The delegates concluded that racial enclaves had come to stay, and that coloured immigrants could not be forced to integrate. So it would be unrealistic

[1] *B.M.*, 12 July 1962. In 1966 almost 23 per cent of coloured children needed special language help (Nicolas Hawkes, *Immigrant Children in British Schools* (1966), p. 16).

[2] *B.M.*, 12 July 1962.   [3] *B.P.*, 4 December 1962.

[4] Birmingham Association of Schoolmasters, 'The educational problem of immigration', report on a conference, 7–8 December 1962 (Birmingham University Institute of Education Library).

to spread coloured children among schools throughout the city. Not only would parents demand that their children attend local schools, but 'sharing the load' would simply transfer the problem of low academic standards to every school in the city. Even one illiterate child in a class, agreed the teachers, could reduce the standard of all. In any case, there would never be enough teachers willing to work with backward coloured children, so that it would be most useful to concentrate this type of teacher in schools where they would come into contact with large numbers of immigrant children.

The problem did not arise again with any force until 1964. In the meantime the committee had applied the policy outlined in 1962 with some success. Capitation allowances had been increased in schools with high proportions of coloured children, and intensive language teaching arrangements had been made in several schools which had spontaneously high numbers of coloured children. An increasing number of peripatetic English teachers, paid above normal rates, were employed to give tuition when needed at other schools. Attempts were made to reduce the proportions of coloured children in the schools where they were highest by modifying local catchment areas.[1] But there was no escaping the fact that some schools were fast approaching the proportion of coloured children which Alderman Hall had warned against in 1962. By the end of 1964 some ten or twelve primary schools already had more than one coloured child in three, and the proportion of coloured schoolchildren in the city had risen to 7 per cent.[2]

During that year Bradford education authority introduced a scheme for transporting children out of the immigrant districts into schools in white areas, and it was frequently discussed in Birmingham. The *Birmingham Post* supported the idea, in the interests of integration. J. Joshi, president of the Indian Workers' Association, gave qualified approval, but pointed out that the children would be inconvenienced. He wanted to see greater urgency devoted to the provision of more schools and teachers.[3] The Department of Education and Science, under the new Labour Government, was known to be in favour of dispersal on the Bradford pattern, but its circular advising local

[1] *B.M.*, 29 December 1964.
[2] Ibid. Two years later it had risen to 8 per cent (Hawkes, *Immigrant Children*, p. 20). For distribution figures, see Norman Pannell and Fenner Brockway, *Immigration: What is the Answer? Two Opposing Views* (1965), p. 86. In 1968 the proportion of non-European schoolchildren was 8·7 per cent and their number was expected to double by 1972 (B.C.C., *Pro.*, 16 July 1968, p. 159). Figures for other large cities, none of which had as high a proportion of immigrant children as Birmingham, can be found in Institute of Race Relations, *Colour and Immigration in the United Kingdom* (1969), p. 32.
[3] Ibid. However, the Indian Workers' Association was opposed to the grouping of coloured children in special classes where attention could be given to their English, on the ground that this amounted to segregation (*Guardian*, 11 January 1964).

Bull Ring metamorphoses, 1937 and 1941

Bull Ring metamorphoses, 1959 and 1967

education authorities to restrict the proportion of coloured children in any school to under 30 per cent did not arrive until the summer of 1965. By this time twenty-four schools in Birmingham, about 5 per cent of the total of primary and secondary schools, had passed this figure.

Two important factors prevented Birmingham from adopting the Department's advice. Firstly, the Education Committee had already put its effort into an alternative policy which it considered satisfactory, and it might have been dangerous to reverse it. Secondly, both the main political parties were opposed to dispersal. It had been discussed at the Labour municipal policy conference in March 1965, but Harry Watton declared strong opposition to the idea on the ground that it amounted to segregation.[1] The Education Committee, therefore, decided to ignore the Department's circular. The *Birmingham Post*, which by now had become one of the strongest forces in the city in the campaign against colour discrimination, was horrified: 'The fact is that the Birmingham Education Committee is taking the easy line, the line of least resistance.'[2] Some support for dispersal now came, too late, from the teachers, with the Birmingham Association of Teachers (N.U.T.) announcing proposals involving some dispersal in October 1965.[3] By now the teachers were claiming that one school already had 90 per cent coloured children, and that others were approaching that figure.[4] The main reason for the teachers' change of attitude was that so many schools now had a high proportion of immigrants—their number had doubled since 1963[5]—that the problems created could no longer be ignored by the majority as they had been in 1962. At a meeting between teachers' representatives and Councillor Cook, in November 1965, it was agreed that it was too late to do anything about schools in the main immigrant areas, but that some dispersal might be possible in the fringe districts. Cook, however, was still doubtful about the value of dispersal: 'In my view, general, natural dispersal of immigrants is the only final answer to this problem.'[6]

The parents were now beginning to take a hand. In October 1965 the first big confrontation had taken place when mothers of white children at the Grove primary school, Handsworth, had threatened to withdraw their children if its proportion of 80 per cent coloured children were not reduced.[7] Similar situations arose subsequently at other schools. Unfortunately, practical problems were also beginning to arise in the immigrant schools. In September 1966 the heads of several secondary schools in the immigrant areas were refusing to take any more non-English speaking children, because of the shortage of

[1] *B.P.*, 12 July 1965.   [2] *B.P.*, 21 October 1965.
[3] *B.M.*, 22 October 1965.   [4] Ibid.
[5] Russell, 'Education in Birmingham', p. 47; Institute of Handicraft Teachers and College of Handicrafts, *Conference Handbook* (1965), pp. 43, 53.
[6] *Guardian*, 5 November 1965.   [7] *Daily Telegraph*, 8 October 1965.

teachers.[1] Birmingham did its best to increase the resources devoted to schools with a high proportion of immigrants, and from 1968 it was able to obtain direct financial help from the Government to this end. But the problems remained serious. Short of rebuilding most of the schools in the immigrant areas, nothing could be done to remedy the fact that many of the buildings were out of date as well as overcrowded. And the social effects of allowing coloured children to build up huge concentrations in certain schools remained unassessed. During the late 1960s the call for dispersal by the Government, certain politicians and sections of public opinion became even stronger, and was supported by the teachers' organizations. However, the Education Committee always showed tact and consideration in dealing with parents and teachers, and was praised by some observers for avoiding a build-up of racial tension over education, and for its efforts to teach English to Asiatic children.[2] Birmingham's use of peripatetic English teachers and the grouping of coloured children into special classes for part-time language instruction were even hailed by one study as a more effective measure than dispersal.[3]

We have seen that by the time the Conservatives came to power in the City Council in May 1966, the Corporation had taken a wide range of practical steps to deal with the special problems associated with the presence of a large coloured minority in Birmingham. Because the City Council's policies in this sphere had been predominantly bi-partisan, the transfer of control did not lead to major changes. The Conservative group continued to adapt municipal services wherever possible to meet the special needs of coloured immigrants, while main-taining that positive discrimination in favour of coloured people, particularly in the allocation of municipal housing, would be against both common justice and the interests of the Birmingham community as a whole. Like their predecessors, the Conservatives were worried about the steady increase in the size of the Birmingham coloured community, and they consistently pressed the Government either to control the number of coloured people moving into the city, or to provide extra financial assistance for those services on which the coloureds made unusually heavy demands.

The Labour Government rejected the proposals for restrictions on movement, but showed some sympathy to Birmingham's case for

[1] S.M., 25 September 1966.

[2] See e.g. Clifford S. Hill, How Colour-Prejudiced is Britain? (1965), p. 203, and comments by the secretary of the Association of Teachers of English to Pupils from Overseas, N. Hawkes (B.M., 28 February 1966).

[3] By 1968 Birmingham had fifty-two full-time peripatetic English teachers and some part-time. For high praise of Birmingham's achievement here, see Nicolas Hawkes, Immigrant Children in British Schools (1966), pp. 33, 39–42; E. J. B. Rose, etc., Colour and Citizenship, p. 277.

extra financial help, which was being echoed by a number of other towns with big coloured populations. A first step was taken by the Local Government Act of 1966, under which Birmingham received a specific grant of 50 per cent in respect of the additional expenditure incurred in the employment of extra staff to deal with the problems of coloured immigrants. This contribution was most welcome, but the Corporation maintained that its *real* extra expenditure on coloured people was much higher. By 1968 Birmingham was spending an estimated £419,371 per year on the employment of additional staff, but the *full cost* of this extra effort was estimated at £801,023 per year.[1] So the Conservatives maintained their demand for further financial assistance, supported by frequent public exposures of the extent of the problems with which the Corporation had to deal.

During this campaign the Conservatives incurred some criticism from the Labour minority in the City Council, which argued that it was dangerous and unnecessary to draw attention to the coloured minority and to imply that they constituted a serious problem for the City. Labour now maintained that more could be done within the city to meet the special demands of coloured people. For instance, in April 1968 the leader of the Labour group, Alderman Sir Frank Price, strongly criticized recent statements on coloured immigration into Birmingham by Conservative leaders and added: 'It is just not good enough to blame the Government when the City Council has stuck its head in the sand and done nothing to alleviate the existing problem.'[2]

Although this difference developed into a raging controversy between the two groups in the early months of 1968, it bore fruit in the form of a more sympathetic attitude at Westminster towards Birmingham's special problems. It also coincided with a reappraisal by the Corporation of what had been achieved so far, and of what still remained to be done. On 14 May 1968 the General Purposes Committee organized a conference of interested committees on immigration and in July it reported at length to the City Council on the proceedings of the conference.[3] The report outlined the special steps taken so far, particularly in public health, housing, and education, but stated that much still had to be done. It admitted that 'poor progress' was being made in improving infant mortality rates in the inner areas of the city,[4] a

---

[1] B.C.C., *Pro.*, 19 July 1968, p. 164 (General Purposes Committee).

[2] *B.M.*, 29 April 1968.

[3] B.C.C., *Pro.*, 19 July 1968, pp. 158–71 (General Purposes Committee).

[4] Over the five years 1966–70 the infant mortality rate among non-white children averaged 28·9 per 1,000 births, compared to 18·8 among white children. Over the years 1961–5 the rates had been 26·3 (non-white) and 21·6 (white), indicating that the excess of the non-white infant mortality rate over the white was steadily increasing, both relatively and absolutely, during the 1960s ('Ethnic origins of Birmingham children born in 1970', report by Corporation Statistician, 1971).

situation which 'clearly points to the need for health education and improvement of facilities.' Consequently 'every effort' was already being made to increase the numbers of health visitors, and it was recognized that the shortage of general practitioners for 'these un-attractive areas' could be met only by the provision of good working conditions in the form of health centres.[1] However, the tendency of coloured people to concentrate in certain areas of the city, the report stated, greatly complicated the problem. The formation of immigrant communities, 'in a manner not dissimilar to the selection by individuals of the established population of neighbourhoods in which to live', made demands on local services. 'Some services', the report went on, 'tend to be overburdened by this concentration of immigrants in specific localities because of the above normal demands which they make.' The extra demand for education facilities was especially pronounced; the cost of school building undertaken to date specifically for immigrant children was estimated at £1,376,235. Without immigration, seven planned schools would not have been required, and two others would have been smaller.

Because the problem was seen largely as one of the distribution of existing services within the city, the report suggested that dispersal of the immigrant communities would help to solve it by spreading the load. However, it went on to say that 'by present methods', which involved relocation as and when coloured immigrants had to be rehoused from unsatisfactory accommodation, this process appeared to be a slow one. Meanwhile, the persistence of areas of housing in multi-occupation was seen as complicating the full integration of coloured people into the Birmingham community. 'The paramount and urgent need,' stated the report, 'is to avoid continuation of the situation of immigrants being an under-privileged class whose standards are readily identifiable as being inferior to those of the indigenous popu-lation.' It was extremely important, therefore, to up-grade physically the accommodation occupied by coloured immigrants. Landlords were unlikely to undertake improvements voluntarily, and compulsion would be needed in the case of multi-occupied houses deemed worthy of standing for a reasonable period. Meanwhile, there was a need for the 'urgent application' of slum clearance, comprehensive redevelop-ment, and improvement procedures to the immigrant areas. However, the report warned that such action would raise the problem of how to ensure that immigrants were integrated on the pre-war and post-war housing estates 'to which they will need to be moved in substantial numbers.' At the end of the City's long-term housing programme about half the citizens of Birmingham would be living in municipal pro-perties, and on current estimates 10 per cent of municipal tenants

[1] Some progress was by now being made towards this end. See below, p. 426.

would then be coloured immigrants. Consequently, the report stated, a continued influx of immigrants into Birmingham would reduce the chances of success of improving their housing conditions and effecting smooth social integration.

The report ended with four major recommendations. First, it reiterated that the number of persons moving into Birmingham should be restricted,[1] the extent of the restrictions depending on the area of land made available outside the city for peripheral housing development. Secondly, it called for an acceleration of urban renewal in the obsolete areas, and for the promotion of improvements to the standards of existing accommodation. Thirdly, it urged the Government to refund to local authorities the *full* additional costs, on both capital and revenue accounts, incurred in respect of immigrants. Finally, and in connection with the first recommendation, it called on the Government to recognize that Birmingham had an imperative need for more building land outside the city boundaries.

This report and its recommendations proved generally acceptable to both the major groups in the City Council, and the only amendment to it was proposed by the Liberal Councillor Tilsley. He called for the deletion of the recommendation relating to the restriction of the number of persons coming into the city, but his amendment was negatived. Just three days after the City Council had accepted the report, on 22 July 1968, the Home Secretary announced that the Government would soon introduce a special programme of financial assistance for cities like Birmingham, known as the Urban Programme. This programme came into being in the early summer of 1969, and the City Council took full advantage of the extra aid which it brought. In June 1969, for instance, the Council voted the enlargement of six day nurseries, approved by the Government as part of the initial phase (1969/70) of the Urban Programme.[2] Other new schemes soon followed. The City Council, however, continued to press for further financial help from the Government, particularly in respect of education outlay. For instance, the Conservative municipal election statement in May 1970 called for more financial support for children's homes, given that 31 per cent of children in care were coloured. It also wanted bigger education subsidies: 'The City is not getting a fair deal from the Government over the education problems arising from the increasing number of immigrant children.'

While services were being expanded, a major step forward was being achieved at the end of the 1960s when Birmingham's massive slum clearance and rehousing machine began to turn its attention to areas

[1] This recommendation made no distinction between coloured and English-born people.

[2] B.C.C., *Pro.*, 17 June 1969, p. 98 (Health Committee).

occupied by high proportions of coloured people. By 1968 about 250
coloured families were being rehoused each year from the waiting list
and under the clearance programme, and 16 per cent of the people
coming on to the housing list were coloured.[1] A substantial improvement
in the housing conditions of coloured immigrants was reflected in
figures published by the Corporation Statistician in 1971. In 1967,
70·6 per cent of West Indian children born into private families made
their appearance in dwellings where people were accommodated at
two or more persons to a room. By 1970, however, this proportion had
dropped sharply to 47·9 per cent. A marked fall was also noted among
people of Indian and Pakistani origin, where the proportion dropped
from 63·8 per cent to 51·3 per cent.[2] Much of this improvement could
be attributed to the Health Department's work in dealing with applications to convert houses to multi-occupation, and inspecting existing
multi-occupied houses. Between the coming into operation of the 1961
Housing Act and the end of 1970, the department enforced a limitation
of the number of occupants in 2,395 cases, and served 1,208 management
orders. 1,768 notices were served requiring the provision of facilities
under the 1961 Housing Act, and in 1,299 cases the department carried
out the improvement work itself. Resort was had to legal proceedings
in 3,121 cases, and fines totalling over £20,000 were imposed. By the
end of the decade the number of multi-occupied houses was in marked
decline, and only 4,350 were registered at the end of 1970.[3] Improvements to areas of newer and more substantial housing occupied by
coloured people were facilitated by the 1969 Housing Act. Birmingham
made full use of it, and in January 1971 the City Council approved the
designation of seven general improvement areas.[4] Large parts of these
areas had high coloured populations, and a considerable improvement
in environmental standards within them was foreseen for the 1970s.

We have discussed the ways in which coloured people found themselves grouped together and separated from the generality of the white
citizens of Birmingham. At work, however, the coloured immigrants
usually found a very different situation. From the early 1950s most
industrial employers welcomed them, for they helped to satisfy the
growing demand for unskilled labour and allowed Birmingham
industries to expand. The city's high rate of employment meant that
they were not normally resented by English workers who might otherwise have thought that the coloureds were taking their jobs away

---

[1] B.C.C., *Pro.*, 16 July 1968, p. 161 (General Purposes Committee).

[2] 'Ethnic origins of Birmingham children born in 1970'. The comparable proportions for the Irish were 34·0 per cent and 20·7 per cent, and for the indigenous
population, 14·5 per cent and 8·7 per cent.

[3] *B.M.O.H.*, 1970, pp. 242–5.

[4] B.C.C., *Pro.*, 5 January 1971, pp. 541–6.

from them.[1] The main difficulties found by coloured people seeking jobs were in those trades where they came into contact with the public or handled goods consumed by the public. For instance, there was already great prejudice in the late 1940s against the employment of coloured people in baking.[2] However, the immigrants had organized labour on their side. The Trades Council began to discuss coloured immigration in 1950, and consistently opposed all forms of discrimination, whether at work or outside. It urged that coloured workers should be fully integrated into the trade union structure, in order to make them feel at home, and to prevent their working for low wages, thus depressing general wage levels. This policy was a success, and by the late 1950s most immigrant workers had joined trade unions, which looked after their interests effectively.[3] There was no firm evidence that coloured workers were ever paid lower wages than the British for the same work.[4]

With the Trades Council giving the same clear lead as the clergy and other community leaders had given in the field of social relations, coloured immigrants were normally well accepted by their English workmates.[5] But there were a few exceptions, the most serious of which occurred in 1954, when a majority of Birmingham municipal bus workers objected to the employment of coloured men in the Transport Department. This was an exceptional episode in more ways than one, because most Birmingham bus workers were not English but Irish, recruited directly from Ireland by the Transport Department.[6] It was only because Irish sources could not completely satisfy the department's needs that it was decided to employ coloured people as conductors, even though the Transport Committee knew that it was 'a delicate matter'.[7] Local bus workers called for a ballot of all employees

---

[1] Clifford Hill detected a close correlation between racial tension and unemployment (*How Colour-Prejudiced is Britain?*, p. 25).

[2] *B.P.*, 21 January 1949.

[3] The Birmingham Transport Department, for instance, with a high proportion of coloured employees, had 99 per cent trade union membership in 1959 (John Darragh, *The Closed Shop and 100% Trade Unionism* (1959), p. 10). But for a more qualified view of the attitude of trade unions towards coloured workers, see Leslie Stephens, *Employment of Coloured Workers in the Birmingham Area* (1956), pp. 16–20.

[4] Stephens, *Employment of Coloured Workers*, pp. 13–14.

[5] It is generally agreed that English workers are prepared to accept coloureds at work, if not outside (Paul Foot, *Immigration and Race in British Politics* (1965), pp. 186–9).

[6] John Clews, 'The Irish worker in English industry with particular reference to the Birmingham district' (paper presented to the Belfast meeting of the B.A.A.S., 1952, B.R.L. 626439). It was suggested at about this time that tension between coloured people and the Irish was much higher in the Midlands than in the major seaports (Michael Banton, *The Coloured Quarter: Negro Immigrants in an English City* (1955), pp. 70–2).

[7] *T.B.*, no. 82, February 1954, p. 2.

to decide for or against admitting the coloureds, against the advice of
the national T.G.W.U. It was suggested at the time that they were
not racially motivated, and that they simply wanted to continue working a lot of overtime.[1] In any case, the Transport Committee (chaired
by Harry Watton) maintained a firm refusal to the imposition of a
colour bar, and began to take on coloured conductors (although for
the first few years the committee observed an agreement with the local
trade union branches not to employ more than 10 per cent coloured
bus workers). The committee's refusal to bow to pressure from transport
employees was strongly supported by the Labour group and by the
Birmingham Trades Council.[2] By 1958 the Transport Department was
able to announce that coloured employees were now fully accepted
by the public and their workmates.[3]

Opposition to coloured workers became more general in 1956, when
Birmingham industries were particularly hard hit by a trade recession
and petrol restrictions following the British invasion of Egypt. It was
suggested that coloured workers were more affected by dismissals than
whites, and some trade union officers began to favour the restriction of
coloured immigration into Birmingham for the time being.[4] But this
was only a temporary phase, and the Trades Council did not modify
its strong liberal position.[5] In 1957 the situation returned to normal,
and the problems of 1956 never recurred.

During the 1960s a growing proportion of coloured people seeking
employment in Birmingham were school leavers, and some observers
feared at first that they might raise special problems. These fears were
not justified by events. On the whole, the coloured youngsters found
little difficulty in obtaining work.[6] Many firms which had remained
all-white as a matter of policy in the 1950s were forced to take on
coloured workers by the severe labour shortage in the West Midlands
in the early 1960s.[7] It was occasionally suggested that they were sometimes arbitrarily excluded from certain jobs; for instance, some firms
which employed coloured people in the works were said to be reluctant
to take them into the office.[8] But the Youth Employment Department
considered that such cases were few, and that most coloured children

[1] *Observer*, 21 February 1954.   [2] B.T.C., *Annual Report*, 1954–5, p. 29.
[3] Ruth Glass, *Newcomers*, pp. 77–8.
[4] See *B.M.*, 15 May 1956; 23 June 1956; 13 July 1956; *B.P.*, 3 August 1956.
[5] Although several hundred coloured workers were laid off in Birmingham in
1956, they suffered less than other workers because of their high mobility. Most found
new employment in the north-west (Peter L. Wright, *The Coloured Worker in British
Industry* (1968), p. 55). The similarly high mobility of Indian immigrants is stressed
in Rashmi Desai, *Indian Immigrants in Britain* (1963).
[6] See statement by the Youth Employment sub-committee in *B.M.*, 16 September
1965.
[7] John Lenton etc., *Immigration, Race and Politics: A Birmingham View* (1966), p. 43.
[8] See also Nicholas Deakin, etc., *Colour, Citizenship and British Society* (1970), p. 310.

found employment suitable to their attainments.[1] This conclusion was supported by an independent study, which suggested that the frustration felt by many coloured school leavers was the result of unrealistically high job aspirations.[2] A small local survey, undertaken by Fred Milson and his students at Westhill College, found that although coloured youngsters were less likely than their white contemporaries to be in skilled manual or non-manual jobs, or to obtain apprenticeships, the majority were happy in their work, and few complained that their colour was an obstacle.[3] During the later 1960s jobs became harder to find for both white and coloured school leavers, but the Education Committee organized special further education classes to help coloured school leavers find employment.[4] Although it is still occasionally suggested that the Birmingham white worker has an underlying fear that a coloured man may take his job away,[5] the available evidence suggests that the integration of coloured people into the employment structure has proceeded with little difficulty.

The City Council's policy towards coloured immigrants was partly based on the assumption that to discriminate positively in their favour would produce racial strife. How far was this aspect of municipal policy justified by events? And how far did the political parties themselves refrain from touching on the immigrant issue?

Foreign immigrants were first recognized as a factor in elections in 1952 when the Unionist municipal candidate for Duddeston issued election addresses in Urdu and Hindustani.[6] This remained an isolated experiment until 1957, when a Labour candidate issued posters in Arabic in Market Hall ward.[7] Yet these candidates did not make a special appeal to the immigrants—they simply used translations of their standard election propaganda. Immigration did not begin to enter local politics as an issue until after 1959, when Harold Gurden and other Conservative M.P.s from Birmingham and nearby added their support to the growing campaign for the control of immigration. Even then, the issue did not arise on a large scale in city elections until 1961, when it was stimulated by the intervention of an independent candidate advocating controlled immigration in Sandwell.[8] The Conservative election manifesto of that year contained a guarded

---

[1] B.C.C., *Pro.*, 16 July 1968, p. 160 (General Purposes Committee).

[2] See David Beetham, *Immigrant School Leavers and the Youth Employment Service in Birmingham* (1967).

[3] Fred Milson, *Operation Integration Two: The Coloured Teenager in Birmingham*, Westhill Occasional Paper no. 13 (1966), p. 9. See also Lenton, *Immigration, Race and Politics*, p. 21.

[4] B.C.C., *Pro.*, 19 July 1968, p. 160 (General Purposes Committee).

[5] See e.g. *B.P.*, 5 August 1965.   [6] *B.M.*, 5 May 1952; *B.G.*, 6 May 1952.

[7] *B.M.*, 8 May 1957.   [8] See above, p. 374.

statement that immigration into Birmingham was causing concern, and that it should be controlled for the benefit of all the citizens, including the immigrants themselves. Neither of the party leaderships, however, wanted to encourage the issue, and although Alderman Sir Theodore Pritchett made a statement towards the end of the campaign promising that, if elected, the Conservatives would make further representations to the Government on the control of immigration, his intervention was designed principally to calm matters down.[1] Immigration did not figure at all in the 1962 campaign, because it seemed to have been taken out of the hands of local authorities by the Commonwealth Immigration Bill. Even in 1964, the year of the notorious Smethwick parliamentary election campaign, the issue did not come to the fore. In the later 1960s it was alluded to in election material, but on the whole it is true to say that both parties steered clear of immigration, and condemned independent candidates who promoted the issue.

The failure of immigration to develop as an election issue had three major causes. Firstly, and most important, the leaderships of all the established parties believed that to emphasize immigrant problems would adversely affect integration. Secondly, the parties were in general agreement over immigrant policy from the time the problem was first discussed in the mid-1950s. Even sections of the Birmingham Liberal Party, including the leader, Wallace Lawler, had come to favour restrictions on coloured immigration into Birmingham by 1968. Finally, any temptation that there might have been to make political capital out of immigration was outweighed by a strong suspicion in all parties that to use the issue might do them as much harm as good. Furthermore, the immigrants themselves, with only a few exceptions, did not stand for election. And those few who did so normally stood as independents, not as nominees of immigrant associations. There were no signs of the establishment of an 'immigrant party', partly because most politically active coloured people were embraced by the Labour Party. Handsworth Labour Party, in particular, built up a strong coloured element from the early 1960s, and issued much of its election material in Asian languages.

Immigration was an equally obscure issue in parliamentary election-eering in Birmingham, despite occasional alarms and excursions. The first Birmingham M.P. to campaign actively for immigration control, Harold Gurden, did not begin to do so until after the 1959 general election. So it did not become a potential campaign issue in the city until the general election of 1964. By this time the activities of the Smethwick Conservative Association, led by Peter Griffiths, which had been devoting much attention to immigration since the early 1960s,[2] appeared to some Birmingham Conservatives to offer a hope

[1] B.M., 9 May 1961.   [2] See Peter Griffiths, A Question of Colour?(1966).

of Conservative success in an election where the party seemed to be
facing certain defeat. On 23 July 1964 five of Birmingham's seven
Conservative M.P.s (the absentees were the liberal Sir Edward Boyle
and Aubrey Jones) met with prospective candidates and party officials
at a house in Chester Square, London, belonging to Geoffrey Lloyd
M.P., the president of the Birmingham Conservative and Unionist
Association.[1] The aim of the meeting was to draw up a plan of campaign
for the general election, and it was decided to make immigration one
of the main planks in the platform. At the time, the announcement of
this decision caused some alarm.[2] But two of the M.P.s, L. G. Seymour
(Sparkbrook) and J. H. Hollingworth (All Saints), later qualified the
press statement, and said that they would not fight their campaigns on
the issue of colour.[3] Conservative Central Office was embarrassed by
the statement, and asked the Birmingham M.P.s and candidates not to
use the issue.[4] Most of them accepted this advice, although colour
figured to some extent in Dr. Wyndham Davies's successful campaign at
Perry Barr which was assisted by officers and members of the Birmingham Immigration Control Association.[5] Even when Conservative
candidates or supporters used the issue, their Labour opponents
refrained from taking it up,[6] and Commonwealth immigrant organizations kept quiet after receiving assurances from the local parties that
immigration would not be made an issue.[7] So exploitation of race was
avoided for the most part, and the campaign remained quiet. Of course,
at the time the Conservatives did not know for certain that use of the
immigration issue could bring them votes. And even though the victory
of Peter Griffiths over Patrick Gordon-Walker at Smethwick suggested
that it might have done so, the Birmingham Conservatives were not so
dissatisfied with the result of the campaign that they were in danger of
panicking. They had lost only two seats overall to Labour, and the
swing to Labour in Birmingham had been considerably less than in the
country as a whole, without the use of the immigration issue.

During the next two years Conservative Central Office, worried by
the critical public reaction to the Smethwick campaign, discouraged
M.P.s and prospective candidates from using the immigration issue.
In any case they had little opportunity to do so owing to the Labour

[1] Paul Foot, *Immigration and Race in British Politics* (1965), p. 143.

[2] See e.g. Anthony Howard, 'The Chamberlain Legacy', *New Statesman*, 7 October
1964, p. 170.

[3] Rex and Moore, pp. 206–7.

[4] Paul Foot, *The Rise of Enoch Powell* (1969), p. 67.

[5] Foot, *Immigration and Race*, pp. 79–80. Griffiths claims that he refused the offer of
B.I.C.A. support in Smethwick (*A Question of Colour?*, p. 217).

[6] See e.g. a reference by Roy Hattersley to the self-control exercised by most
candidates in avoiding the immigration issue in 1964, in *H. of C. Deb.*, 5th series, vol.
dccix, cols. 379–80, 23 March 1965.

[7] Prem, *Parliamentary Leper*, pp. 90–1.

Government's rigid restriction of new immigration. The issue did not figure prominently in the 1966 general election campaign, in Birmingham or elsewhere.[1] Commentators such as Paul Foot detected a resurgence of it after 1966, but it had not created serious problems by 1970 and city politicians did not attempt to stir up feelings in Birmingham. On the other hand, many Birmingham M.P.s and other politicians repeated time and time again that coloured immigration into Birmingham should be controlled. But this demand had become by 1970 so much part of the accepted canon of Birmingham politics, supported by the municipal Conservative, Labour, and Liberal parties, and many of the city's M.P.s, that it no longer stirred up feeling among the white or coloured communities.

One beneficial result of the politicians' interest in race was the increased attention given to the problems and needs of the immigrant community after 1964. Towards the end of the 1950s it had seemed that the growing size of the coloured community in Birmingham was drowning the efforts of community leaders like the churches and the Trades Council to ensure its well-being. After about 1958 it became clear that what was needed was more practical help for the immigrants and new institutions to allow them to integrate more effectively with white people. In this area voluntary organizations greatly supplemented the Corporation's activities, which were extended to some degree after the acceptance of the Liaison Officer's report in 1959.[2] The most important voluntary effort was the Sparkbrook Association, founded in 1960 on the initiative of a Labour councillor, Mrs. Burgess, by a large number of middle-class Birmingham residents, many of whom were connected with the Faculty of Commerce and Social Science at Birmingham University.[3] It was set up principally as a community association, and it remained faithful to its multi-racial, integrationist aim despite occasional attempts by English residents of Sparkbrook to convert it into a purely white organization.[4] In 1962 it set up a multi-racial social club and an adventure playground in Sparkbrook.[5] The importance of its work was fully recognized by the Corporation, and it expanded its efforts after 1964, appealing for funds to build a special family centre for the area.[6] 1965 also saw the foundation of a new body dealing with problems of race relations, the Birmingham Voluntary

---

[1] D. E. Butler and Anthony King, *The British General Election of 1966* (1966), p. 117.

[2] Evidence from a number of places has suggested that the efforts of the welfare services and voluntary bodies can be very valuable in helping immigrants to adapt, and in informing public opinion. See Sheila Patterson, *Dark Strangers: a Study of West Indians in London* (1965), p. 354.

[3] Rex and Moore, p. 215.

[4] Robert Moore, 'Reluctant hosts', *New Society*, 9 February 1967, p. 192.

[5] *B.P.*, 31 March 1962.   [6] *Y.B.* no. 211, November 1965, p. 3.

Liaison Committee.[1] The BBC Midland Region now began to transmit special television programmes for Indian and Pakistani immigrants. In 1966 the West Midlands organization of the Government's new Race Relations Board was set up, although it took some time to work effectively. Other multi-racial community associations began to be founded; notably the Balsall Heath Association.[2] Immigrant areas to the north of the city centre had similar bodies by the late 1960s.[3]

We have discussed mainly the effects of coloured immigration on Birmingham. But what of the immigrants themselves? Did their lot improve as time went on, or did prejudice against them, and their living and working conditions, deteriorate? Firm evidence on the strength of colour prejudice is hard to come by, and very few polls were taken on this issue in Birmingham. Some pessimistic observers even suggested that race relations in the city were getting worse in the 1960s,[4] but the work of local researchers such as Fred Milson threw considerable doubt on their gloomy predictions.[5] Immigrant associations became more vociferous in their demands for equal rights, and there appeared to be a danger that direct conflict might develop between them and the immigration control associations. On the other hand, the increase in the proportion of women among the coloured immigrants from about 1958, and especially after 1962, helped to reduce tensions caused by competition for girls.[6] It is, however, almost certain that the weight of opinion in favour of restricting immigration grew during the 1960s. A survey of opinion among young people in Birmingham between the ages of fourteen and twenty-one, in 1961, showed that two-thirds of those interviewed did not believe that coloured people should be prevented from settling in England.[7] But in a similar survey carried out in 1964, nearly nine out of ten supported the control of immigration.[8] However, these views did not necessarily indicate prejudice against coloured people already in Birmingham. Much prejudice clearly

[1] *B.P.*, 3 November 1965.

[2] This association was first proposed in 1962, with the support of local clergy (*B.P.*, 12 December 1962).

[3] For the view that an active community association can do a lot to promote ntegrationist ideas among English residents, see Moore, 'Reluctant hosts', p. 194.

[4] See e.g. Mervyn Jones, 'Strangers and Brummies: immigration in Birmingham', *New Statesman*, 18 December 1964.

[5] See e.g. Milson, *Operation Integration Two*; Philip Cliff and Fred Milson, *Where it is Happening: A Study of Integration* (Westhill College, 1969).

[6] Hill, *How Colour-Prejudiced is Britain?*, p. 26. A colour bar imposed by the Mecca management in three Birmingham ballrooms after disturbances was removed in 1958 after protests from the Trades Council and others. It was never re-imposed (B.T.C., *Annual Report*, 1958–9, p. 12).

[7] Fred Milson, *Operation Politics* (1962), p. 8.

[8] Fred Milson, *Youth and the 1964 Election* (1964), p. 4.

existed in Birmingham, it is true, but it was not always expressed in an offensive manner and the almost complete absence of disturbances must be attributed to the general tolerance, as well as the passivity, of Birmingham citizens. Although the Corporation was overtaken in the 1960s by Bradford and Nottingham in terms of the practical help that it gave to immigrants, it continued to strive against the generation of racial conflict. The *Birmingham Post* also played an important role in controlling feeling by its objective reporting and frank comment.[1] The *Evening Mail* was less careful, and it frequently gave space in its correspondence columns to letters from prominent members of immigration control associations. Yet it never attempted to exploit colour problems in a sensational way, and in the later 1960s it adopted a strong integrationist and reformist policy similar to the *Post*'s.

Information on the incomes of coloured immigrants is also hard to come by, but a survey undertaken in Birmingham in about 1969 showed that although the household incomes of coloureds were lower than the average for the whole city, the differences were not normally excessive. Household incomes tended to rise with the length of time spent in Britain, and the average earnings of households established in Birmingham before 1960 were higher in some immigrant groups than the city average. This increase over time was, however, largely accounted for by increases in household size, and there was no increase in per capita real income over time.[2] Yet the figures did not suggest that the coloured immigrants, given their usually poor qualifications and their limited experience of Britain, could be regarded as an unfairly depressed class.

On the other hand, the living and health conditions of immigrants were far from satisfactory, and they caused alarm to the City Council as well as contributing to prejudice. Although their plight has often been exaggerated, the generality of the coloured population of Birmingham was clearly living in a far from ideal situation in 1970. Indeed, one authority expressed the fear that in Birmingham '. . . the potentiality for inter-racial conflict has probably reached its highest level to date'.[3] But the fact remains that race relations in Birmingham were still placid enough in 1970 to be envied by many other areas. Whatever criticisms may be aimed at the policies of the Birmingham authorities, they must claim at least some of the credit for the avoidance of serious racial strife.

[1] See e.g. *B.P.*, 25 September 1964.
[2] Nicholas Deakin, etc., *Colour, Citizenship and British Society* (1970), pp. 82–7.
[3] Ibid., p. 157.

XII

TRANSPORT, UTILITIES, AND HEALTH

MUCH attention in this book has been devoted to housing because it was the major determinant of the comfort and happiness of the Birmingham citizen. But several other important services and amenities contributed to his physical well-being, some more successfully than others. Public transport facilities, of which the municipal bus service was by far the most important element in terms of numbers of passengers carried, were a constant problem, owing to the rapid growth of new types of demand, and the need to adapt established services to changing circumstances. In complete contrast, the public utility services, several of which came to be administered by the State, did not normally face serious obstacles in supplying demands which the stability of the city's population and area rendered almost static. Public health services, too, were able to meet fully the demands made on them, even though their role changed substantially after 1939, and the establishment of smokeless zones was a major new departure. But the most spectacular example of adaptation to new conditions was Birmingham's creation of a new road system.

Roads

After 1945 Birmingham concentrated effort on road building to an extent unparalleled in the British provinces. By 1967 the City had accumulated a debt in respect of highways and bridges which amounted to £22·26 for every person living in Birmingham—more than twice as much as any other provincial city.[1] Birmingham was able to spend so much on roads because the City Council gave them a high priority, and because the Government was convinced that massive road improvements in the city were in the national interest. But how was this consensus reached?

The City Council first became aware of the need to improve its roads during the First World War, when the transport of munitions placed a growing load on the road system. With wheeled traffic likely to increase still further after the war, the Council foresaw that Birmingham's industrial prosperity might come to depend on the maintenance of easy road communications. In January 1918 the Council adopted a Public Works Committee proposal that all the main radial roads should be widened sooner or later to between 110 and 120 feet,

[1] Institute of Municipal Treasurers, *Return of Outstanding Debt (England and Wales)*. Birmingham was followed by Coventry (£9·54), and Leeds (£9·14).

by the purchase of the necessary land when existing buildings were demolished.[1] This method was economical, but took a long time to come to fruition. By 1952 some eleven miles of arterial road had been widened and provided with dual carriageways,[2] but most were in the outer areas of the city, and nearly all the radial roads remained very narrow where they approached the city centre. Central congestion became a very serious problem in the late 1920s and 1930s, because so many factories still operated on the fringes of the central business district. In 1933 a one-way scheme was introduced there, and it had to be extended in 1936.[3]

The Second World War allowed the City Council to look at its road problem afresh. Now, more than ever, it was concerned about the city centre. Although the one-way system normally kept the traffic moving,[4] it would have been saturated by 1941, had the war not intervened.[5] The Public Works Committee's advisory planning panel on traffic, set up in 1942, concentrated mainly on the city centre, and in March 1943 the Public Works Committee told the Council that the rapid completion of an inner ring road was 'an indispensable measure for alleviating the difficulties when traffic once again resumes a normal basis.'[6]

The origins of the inner ring road lie back before the First World War. It seems that the idea of building such a road first struck certain councillors and the City Engineer, Henry Stilgoe, in 1910, when a civic delegation was particularly impressed by Vienna's wide radial roads and 'ring roads' carrying tram tracks on special reservations.[7] The report on the arterial roads scheme in 1917–18 referred to an 'inner ring' or 'kind of loop' around the city centre, which would link up all the terminal points of the widened radial roads, and carry a circular tram track. Detailed proposals for this inner ring were not submitted, but its route was tentatively indicated following a girdle of existing streets which skirted the business district at a radius of about half a mile. The area enclosed by this ring of streets corresponded almost exactly to the built-up area of Birmingham in 1780.

Although the Public Works Committee never produced a detailed scheme for the inner ring road, certain widenings were carried out

[1] B.C.C., *Pro.*, 16 October 1917, pp. 503–53 (Public Works Committee).

[2] City of Birmingham, *Development Plan, Statement* (1952), p. 65.

[3] Black, p. 361.

[4] See e.g. H. M. Bateman, *On the Move in England* (1940), p. 56.

[5] B.C.C., *Pro.*, 6 July 1943, p. 419 (Public Works Committee). The number of motor vehicles registered in Birmingham had risen by 40 per cent in the 1930s (*Abstract*, vol. i).

[6] B.C.C., *Pro.*, 9 March 1943, p. 259 (Public Works Committee).

[7] City of Birmingham, *Report to the General Purposes Committee of the Deputation Visiting Germany and Austria, May 25–June 5, 1910, for the Purpose of Studying Town Development* (1911), p. 26.

The Bull Ring shop-
ping centre in 1971.

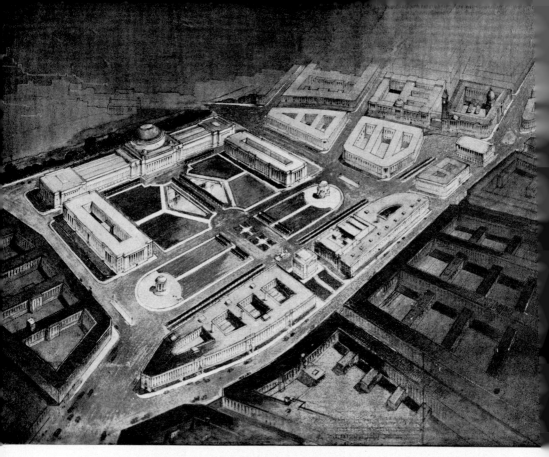

The pre-war scheme for the Civic Centre

Part of the replanned Civic Centre. The new central libraries building, designed by John Madin.

between the wars in thoroughfares, such as Great Charles Street and Suffolk Street, which seemed almost certain to be incorporated into the inner ring.[1] Further properties along the route were destroyed by bombs in 1940–1, creating what Herbert Manzoni called a 'uniquely favourable opportunity' to build the road.[2]

Although the traffic advisory panel suggested that a north–south tunnel would be 'much more effective' than a ring road in diverting traffic from the centre,[3] the Public Works Committee recommended the early construction of a ring road. The City Council approved the scheme in principle, in July 1943. The route differed hardly at all from that envisaged in 1917, but an additional street was planned to cut across the area enclosed by the ring, from Snow Hill to Moor Street. Furthermore, Colmore Row was to be widened throughout its whole length from Victoria Square to Steelhouse Lane, where it met the new 'chord' thoroughfare. These new elements were included to satisfy the Transport Department's request that buses should be allowed to penetrate into the centre, so that no part of it should be more than 300 yards from a bus stop. The Chamber of Commerce, too, had urged that too large an area should not be cut off from wheeled traffic. All the streets in the scheme were planned to be 110 feet wide, except Colmore Row (80 ft).[4]

To defray the cost of so ambitious a project, the Public Works Committee decided to follow the example of the Corporation Street improvement scheme in the 1870s by acquiring frontage land, to an average depth of eighty feet, and leasing to developers. This decision increased the area to be acquired to eighty acres, 14·3 of which were already in the hands of the Corporation. The total cost of acquisition was estimated at £12,088,000, with a further £2·5 million for the works. The City Council approved the detailed scheme in July 1944, despite an effort by Councillor J. C. (later Sir Charles) Burman (Unionist) to have it referred back on planning grounds.[5]

The Town Clerk and the City Engineer were agreed that special powers should be obtained to carry out the scheme,[6] and a Corporation Bill was drawn up and submitted to a town's meeting in December 1945. The vote in favour among the 1,500 people who attended was almost unanimous, and the press came out in strong support.[7] Almost

[1] House of Commons, Session 1945–6, *Minutes of Proceedings Taken Before the Select Committee of the House of Commons on the Birmingham Corporation Bill* (7–23 May 1946), p. 25.

[2] Public Works Committee minutes, 23 October 1941.

[3] Public Works Committee minutes, 25 June 1942.

[4] B.C.C., *Pro.*, 6 July 1943, pp. 418–27 (Public Works Committee).

[5] B.C.C., *Pro.*, 25 July 1944, pp. 469–71, 487 (Public Works Committee).

[6] Public Works Committee minutes, 11 January 1945.

[7] See e.g. *B.P.*, 20 December 1945.

the only objection came from the Birmingham and District Property Owners' Association, which complained that too much land was being acquired.[1] This solid support for the scheme in the city impressed the House of Commons, which hardly modified the Bill. The Lords were more critical; they excluded certain properties from acquisition, and insisted that the City pay full market value for properties acquired for streetworks carried out after 1949. But the essential parts of the scheme remained intact, and the Council was assured that the final form of the Bill was 'reasonably satisfactory'.[2]

Until then, the inner ring road scheme had followed a course similar to that of the central redevelopment areas. Both projects had been planned in outline before the war, but their implementation had been delayed by limitations of powers and finance. Then the war had allowed time for detailed planning, and had created, in both City Council and Parliament, a willingness to infringe individual property rights in the common interest. Birmingham took advantage of this new atmosphere to obtain the powers it needed immediately after the war, before a reaction set in both locally and nationally. But then followed years of frustration in which the City was not able to use its powers. In the Government's view, the national economic situation could not allow the allocation of materials, labour, and resources to schemes which were considerably more ambitious than those of any other provincial city. So Birmingham had to mark time, while the others caught up.

In the bleak years of the late 1940s Birmingham had enough trouble keeping its existing roads in repair. Surfaces had deteriorated badly during the war, and the press was full of complaints about potholes. In 1946 the City Council adopted an ambitious reconstruction scheme, but by the end of that year the programme was already badly delayed.[3] By March 1948 only £200,000 had been spent out of the £600,000 allocated for the first instalment of the works.[4] Shortages of labour and materials remained a problem even after Defence Regulation restrictions were relaxed in 1950. In 1951 16 per cent of the city's first-class roads, and 6·1 per cent of the secondary roads, were still in urgent need of reconstruction, and annual expenditure on maintenance was still below its pre-war figure.[5] Even now, only £600,000 had been spent of the £2 million approved by the Council in 1946.[6] This sum had been expended by 1954, but much work remained to be done, and the

[1] *B.G.*, 20 December 1945.   [2] B.C.C., *Pro.*, 30 July 1946, p. 756.

[3] 'Repairing Birmingham roads', *Municipal Review*, vol. xxviii, no. 330, June 1957, p. 263; B.C.C., *Pro.*, 3 December 1946, p. 71 (Public Works Committee).

[4] B.C.C., *Pro.*, 9 March 1948, pp. 374–6 (Public Works Committee).

[5] B.C.C., *Pro.*, 6 February 1951, pp. 788–90 (Public Works Committee).

[6] Article by Ald. G. H. Griffith, chairman of Public Works Committee, *B.P.*, 2 February 1951.

Council approved further annual maintenance programmes.[1] In 1957 the main roads were at last in sufficiently good condition to allow the Council to switch some two-thirds of its maintenance resources to the reconstruction of local roads.[2] By the following year 75·2 per cent of main and secondary roads were in good or fair condition, as were 86·7 per cent of local roads. At this stage the Council, which was now looking for ways to economize, resigned itself to seeing little further general improvement. The law of diminishing returns made it uneconomical to renew road surfaces which were in tolerable condition, but not of the highest standard.[3] In any case, Birmingham's massive redevelopment and road building schemes, which were now beginning to accelerate, resulted in the deterioration of many miles of road in the years before they were torn up, or totally reconstructed to meet new needs. So the city's road surfaces continued to cause some adverse comment, especially in the central areas, throughout the 1960s.

The only new roads to be built in the later 1940s were on or near municipal housing estates. However, the pressure of traffic began to build up again soon after the war. Despite petrol rationing and the priority given to the export of motor cars, the number of vehicles licensed in the city exceeded the highest pre-war total in 1947, and by 1951 it had risen to over 100,000. Fortunately, until the abolition of petrol rationing these vehicles were *used* less than before the war, and a traffic census in 1950 showed that congestion was hardly, if at all, worse than the late 1930s.[4] But from then on pressure mounted steeply, and the City Council became impatient to start on a number of improvement schemes. First priority was given to the widening of Digbeth, the city centre's main outlet to the east. The Minister of Transport responded to pressure from the Corporation by allowing preparatory work to be undertaken in the summer of 1951,[5] but he refused to allow a start on the widening for another two years. It was only after very strong representations by Birmingham that permission was at last granted in the summer of 1953,[6] and the new Digbeth was opened to traffic in July 1955.

During the years in which the Digbeth improvement was delayed, the Corporation had made a very strong case in favour of ambitious road improvements in Birmingham, with the help of the local Labour

[1] B.C.C., *Pro.*, 2 February 1954, p. 766; 1 February 1955, p. 859 (Public Works Committee).

[2] B.C.C., *Pro.*, 9 April 1957, p. 982 (Public Works Committee).

[3] B.C.C., *Pro.*, 1 July 1958, pp. 159–60 (Public Works Committee).

[4] *Abstract*, vol. iii, p. 115.

[5] B.C.C., *Pro.*, 10 March 1953, p. 858 (Public Works Committee); *H. of C. Deb.*, 5th series, vol. cdxc, cols. *1359–68*, 18 July 1951.

[6] B.C.C., *Pro.*, 10 March 1953, pp. 857–9 (Public Works Committee); *Y.B.*, no. 79, November 1953, p. 2.

M.P.s. It was frequently argued that the city had especially urgent needs. In 1951, for instance, Julius Silverman told the Minister of Transport that Birmingham's history and structure had given it a traffic problem quite different from that of any other large city.[1] Another common argument was that Birmingham was making a particularly valuable contribution to the well-being of the nation. In 1953, for instance, the Public Works Committee reported: 'Your Committee feel very strongly that the City, through the industry and craftsmanship of its citizens, is making a tremendous contribution towards the economic recovery of the country, but it is not receiving the support to which it is entitled by the allocation of capital expenditure.'[2] This argument received some official recognition in a speech by the Minister of Transport, John Boyd-Carpenter, when he opened the improved Digbeth in 1955: 'This scheme in this great city, the heart and centre of the industrial Midlands, will contribute directly towards providing an efficient transport system to serve the industry of this country, by which every man, woman and child in this country lives.'[3] But why did Birmingham put so much emphasis on its need for new roads? And were there any alternatives?

The strongest pressure for better road communications within the city came from Birmingham industry. Transport was one of the main policy interests of the Chamber of Commerce after the war, and it made frequent representations to the Council for better roads and parking facilities. Although nearly all Birmingham's factories were within easy reach of a railway line, most local products were light and could be distributed more easily by road than by rail. Moreover, the pronounced interdependence of Birmingham firms resulted in the extensive transfer of components and part-finished goods from one factory to another.[4] Finally, the growing importance of the vehicle assembly industry in the city after 1945 led industrialists to demand better facilities within the city for the distribution and use of vehicles. The Trades Council added indirectly to this pressure by calling for improvements in the municipal motor transport service, on which, owing to the shortage of attractive suburban railway services, the city was almost completely dependent.[5] Furthermore, the City Council was aware of the danger of political pressure from an increasingly motorized

[1] H. of C. Deb., 5th series, vol. cdxc, cols. 1359–68, 18 July 1951.
[2] B.C.C., Pro., 10 March 1953, p. 859 (Public Works Committee). The City claimed that in recent years only 0·2 per cent of the national road fund allocation had gone to Birmingham, although it represented over 2 per cent of Britain's population (Y.B., no. 73, April 1953, p. 1).
[3] Quoted in Black, p. 346 n.
[4] This point was strongly emphasized by Herbert Manzoni at a conference of the British Road Federation in 1956 (B.P., 20 September 1956).
[5] See John R. Kellett, The Impact of Railways on Victorian Cities (1969), pp. 125–49.

electorate—although this pressure never materialized, probably as a result of the clear priority given to roads by both the main parties. Concentration on roads also made sense to the Council from a financial point of view, because from 1946 approved schemes on trunk roads qualified for 75 per cent grant from the Ministry of Transport. If the Ministry was prepared to approve a large number of schemes in Birmingham, it was natural for the City Council to want to take full advantage of the situation. Until the mid-1950s the Government was clearly not prepared to give Birmingham roads significant priority over those of other cities and areas. But then the Government realized that the future national motorway network, which radiated from the West Midlands, would greatly increase traffic flows in the Birmingham area. It consequently awarded priority to trunk roads within Birmingham, nearly all of which were likely to serve sooner or later as motorway feeders.

The City Council's near-unanimous decision to concentrate on road building was not made without the discussion of alternatives. In January 1947 some councillors had urged the construction of a tube railway to serve north-east Birmingham, but the Public Works Committee reported that the patronage of such a line would not be enough to justify its cost, estimated at £13,750,000.[1] The subject was raised again in the Council in July 1950, when Councillor Frank (later Sir Francis) Griffin (Unionist) called for the provision of underground electric railways to relieve congestion and to provide shelter in an atomic war. The Council carried this amendment, seeing no harm in investigating the matter further at a time when all road improvements were still held up.[2] The Public Works Committee, however, saw no reason to alter its former attitude, and did not present a detailed report. Some members of the committee later had the chance to examine rapid transit systems in the United States in 1956, but they came away even more convinced that rapid public transport was not an alternative to motor roads.[3]

It was clear that underground railways in a city with as low a population density as Birmingham (some twenty people to the acre) could never pay their way. But it was not until the mid-1950s, by which time Birmingham was already largely committed to motor roads, that a surface rapid transit system was seriously considered. The proposal emerged from a conference of representatives of interested committees studying city centre traffic problems, which held regular meetings from early 1954. Its chairman was Alderman W. T. Bowen, a former leader

[1] B.C.C., *Pro.*, 27 July 1948, pp. 881–2 (Public Works Committee).
[2] B.C.C., *Pro.*, 4 July 1950, p. 172 (Public Works Committee).
[3] City of Birmingham, *Visit to America, 26 March to 6 April, 1956: Report of the Delegation by the Public Works Committee, 17 April, 1956*, p. 51.

of the Labour group. Bowen was an enthusiast for mass public transport, and on his own initiative he drew up a scheme in 1955 for an
electric railway to run along the central reservations of the Bristol and
Tyburn Roads, which until recent years had been used by trams.
Short tunnels were included under the city centre and other bottle-
necks. At the time Bowen's plan did not make much impression on the
traffic conference, which was dominated by the Public Works Committee. After a report by the City Engineer, minimizing the scheme's
effect on traffic congestion, the conference discarded it, fearing that it
might slow down progress on the inner ring road if adopted. Bowen
took his plan to the General Purposes Committee, where he had more
influence, and persuaded it to present the scheme to the whole Council.
This was done in April 1957.[1] But work was now beginning on the
inner ring road, and the Council accepted the traffic conference's
view that a decision on rapid transit should be postponed until it
became clear what sort of a traffic problem would remain after the
ring road's completion.[2]

The main defect of Bowen's scheme was that it came too late. Of
course, the Public Works Committee was right in its contention that
rapid transit was no alternative to road building. It would have contributed only very indirectly to industrial transportation, and would not
have qualified for Government subsidy. But it was unfortunate that
the scheme was so peremptorily dismissed, as was a similar suggestion
by Councillor Gilroy Bevan (Conservative) in 1965.[3] By the late 1960s
it was becoming clear that some form of rapid transit would be needed
even when the city's roads were fully modernized, especially if even
more peripheral housing was allowed. The Council undertook further
studies, but no decision had been taken by the early 1970s.

Although the Council emphasized the needs of the whole city and
even of the whole region in its campaign to persuade the Government
to allow road building to begin in the mid-1950s, it wanted to concentrate on the city centre. Clearly, congestion was at its worst there, and
there was no point in improving the radial roads if the central system
was to remain unable to handle bigger flows. True, plans had existed
in outline since the later years of the war for an intermediate ring road
to run through the five central redevelopment areas at a distance of
one or more miles from the city centre, but this was never seen as an
alternative to the inner ring road. The Public Works Department was
far from convinced that the intermediate ring road would remove all
through traffic from the city centre. Even if it did so, the increase of
traffic with business in the centre would alone have produced intoler-

[1] B.C.C., *Pro.*, 9 April 1957, pp. 913–27, 935–47 (General Purposes Committee).
[2] B.C.C., *Pro.*, 3 December 1957, p. 569 (General Purposes Committee).
[3] B.C.C., *Pro.*, 8 March 1965, p. 706 (General Purposes Committee).

able congestion there within a few years. The intermediate ring road could not be built until the central redevelopment areas were fully cleared, and its greater length would have made construction very costly. In contrast, the inner ring road had numerous advantages. The Corporation already possessed special powers to build it, and most of the property had already been acquired at surprisingly low cost.[1] Moreover, it was much more than just a road scheme; one of its biggest attractions was that it would bring about the extension and partial redevelopment of the congested central shopping district. Finally, the careful planning of the road and the favourable publicity that it had obtained greatly strengthened Birmingham's case for being allowed to start work. Any suggestion by the City Council that the road might not provide a complete solution to Birmingham's current traffic problems could well have given the Minister of Transport an excuse to postpone the work still further.

The City Council began its intensive campaign for permission to start the road in 1954, when work began on a service tunnel to link the new shops on the Big Top site to the inner ring road.[2] A conference of interested committees confirmed that it wanted the road and nothing but the road, and the abolition of building licences now made it possible for displaced firms to build alternative accommodation. First priority was given to the sections from Smallbrook Street to Moor Street, and from Snow Hill to Moor Street, in order to provide a complete ring of usable roads. A formal approach was made to the Minister in March 1955, and later in the year the Council agreed in principle to build a multi-storey car park in the Bull Ring, the first of several planned in connection with the road.[3] After a first rebuff, a civic delegation visited the Minister in November, and emphasized the road's importance to a city that was making a big contribution to the export drive: 'The Ring Road should, in the City Council's view, be treated for Government investment policy purposes, in the same way as a scheme for a large conveyor installation in one of our big motor works.'[4]

Unfortunately for Birmingham, Minister Boyd-Carpenter had already committed himself to a four-year programme consisting mainly of arterial road and motorway schemes. But he was soon replaced by

---

[1] In order to prevent the erosion of compulsory purchase powers by time, all notices to treat had been served by the end of 1951 (City of Birmingham, Public Works Committee, *Inner Ring Road Scheme* (1957), p. 9).

[2] See below, p. 443. Special powers to build the tunnel were obtained by the Corporation Act of 1954. See also *Y.B.*, no. 91, December 1954, p. 4.

[3] B.C.C., *Pro.*, 1 February 1955, pp. 855–8 (Public Works Committee); 20 September 1955, pp. 352–66 (Public Works Committee).

[4] City of Birmingham, 'Statement of case . . . to the Minister of Transport . . . in support of the application to proceed with . . . the Inner Ring Road Scheme, Birmingham', p. 33 (B.R.L. 660828).

Harold Watkinson, who was prepared to look at Birmingham's problem afresh. Alderman Frank (later Sir Frank) Price, the forceful chairman of the Public Works Committee, contributed to the Minister's reappraisal by making it clear that he would raise the issue at every conference and meeting that Watkinson attended, until Birmingham's urgent needs were recognized. By February 1956, when he visited Birmingham, Watkinson was considering a readjustment of priorities to allow the construction of more urban roads.[1] Shortly afterwards, he approved the commencement of the first section of the inner ring road, and it was soon confirmed that the work would qualify for a full 75 per cent grant.

In the meantime, the City Engineer and some members of the Public Works Committee had visited the United States. While seeing nothing which made them question the City Council's general road strategy, they were very impressed by the numerous flyovers and underpasses in American cities.[2] Immediately on the return of its delegation, the committee began to incorporate twin-level interchanges into the road. But this transition was not without its difficulties. In their eagerness to start work, the Public Works Committee decided not to include twin-level junctions in the first section to be built, from Smallbrook Street to the Bull Ring. The line of the road was altered to avoid the Market Hall, a building of historic interest which housed a large number of small traders who would have been difficult to re-locate. The resulting roundabout, though a marked improvement on the original wartime design for the crucial junction with Digbeth, was not entirely satisfactory from the point of view of traffic flow. Even Herbert Manzoni admitted that it would be unable to handle peak traffic flows.[3] Another feature inherited from wartime plans was the construction of shops and offices along the road so that it became a corridor shopping street. This arrangement made financial sense, but it generated extra traffic on a part of the ring road that was less well fitted than later sections to carry the load.[4]

While Smallbrook Ringway was under construction, the Public Works Department was reshaping its plans for the rest of the inner ring road. Not only were underpasses and flyovers inserted at all major junctions, but the whole strategy of the road was altered to take account

[1] B.M., 10 February 1956.

[2] See City of Birmingham, *Visit to America, 26 March to 6 April, 1956: Report of the Delegation by the Public Works Committee, 17 April 1956.*

[3] Sir Herbert J. Manzoni, 'The Inner Ring Road, Birmingham', *Proceedings of the Institute of Civil Engineers*, vol. xviii, January–April 1961, p. 271.

[4] The planning of frontage development along the ring road was criticized by the City Surveyor of Manchester as early as 1956 (Leslie B. Ginsburg, 'The Birmingham Ring Road: town planning or road building?', *Architect's Journal*, vol., cxxx, no. 3363, 1 October 1959, p. 290).

of the likely results of motorway construction in the Birmingham area and the provision of feeder expressways within the city. The northern section of the road, from Lancaster Place in the north-east to Holloway Circus in the south-west, now became the major route for through-traffic, and was designed to urban motorway standards. This allowed the southern sections, including Smallbrook Ringway, to perform more mixed functions. As the main weight of through-traffic ran along a north-east/south-west axis, this new strategy was a sensible one. This new scheme was fully planned by early 1960, and it remained substantially unmodified during the building of the whole of the rest of the road.

Once the first two sections had been started, in 1957 and 1959, Government approval and subsidies were soon obtained for the others. Meanwhile, several car parks were being built, and city-centre parking restrictions were tightened up, culminating in a parking meter scheme, approved by the City Council in February 1962.[1] Progress on the road was not unduly delayed by capital restrictions imposed by the new Labour Government from 1964. By 1970 most of it was in use, and work was almost complete on the ambitious northern section, which included two long tunnels and a multi-level interchange. Completion of the whole scheme followed in 1971, which was very close to the twenty-five-year schedule set by Herbert Manzoni at the end of the war.

Although shops and offices lined only Smallbrook Ringway and the chord section running across the city centre, the inner ring road was subjected to strong criticism from a number of architects, town planners, and traffic engineers in the 1960s.[2] But these people often failed to understand that the whole project had been *planned* as a multipurpose venture. Herbert Manzoni himself wrote of it: 'The Ring Road is a city street of novel character—it is not an urban motorway, nor principally a traffic street or a shopping street.'[3] And again: 'It should be quite clear that this basis of design was a consciously chosen compromise between the needs of traffic, cost and amenity. It was a compromise because the use of areas of land, for main junctions, of such size as to produce complete grade-separation, would have involved the purchase of very much more than was then possible; the cost would have been very substantially increased and the loss of land from development would have been so great as to diminish very severely the economic value of the centre for whose benefit the road was being constructed.'[4] The choice of a compromise solution was largely justified by the progress

[1] B.C.C., *Pro.*, 6 February 1962, pp. 746–51. Birmingham was the first British provincial city to adopt parking meters. Free parking schemes like those of Leicester and Paris were considered but rejected as impracticable.

[2] See e.g. article by John Lewis in *B.P.*, 31 May 1965.

[3] Manzoni, 'The Inner Ring Road', p. 267.

[4] City of Birmingham, *Inner Ring Road* (1965), p. 4.

made on the road and its associated redevelopment, which far surpassed similar schemes elsewhere.

The City Council's concentration on city-centre roads meant that few major improvements could be carried out on radial routes in the 1950s because of the prevailing limitations on capital expenditure stemming from central Treasury controls. But once work was under way on the inner ring road, the Public Works Committee began to turn its attention to the roads which ran into the city centre. Early in 1957 the committee presented a report on long-term traffic needs,[1] which envisaged the gradual improvement of the twelve main radial roads, linked by three ring roads (inner, intermediate, and outer). Extensive parking facilities were outlined, and the report referred to the possibility that some radial roads might be converted into expressways to link the city centre to the new national motorways. The committee also wanted to encourage Birmingham's development as a regional centre: 'Birmingham will benefit from this increased activity, and representatives of commerce and other interests and shoppers must not be dissuaded from bringing their cars into the City.'

Later in the year began a big expansion of Birmingham road building. Among the schemes now approved by the Council were the construction of a length of the intermediate ring road, and of two underpasses on the Walsall road, at Birchfield Road and Six Ways, Aston. Another underpass, on the Coventry Road at Yardley, was approved in 1959, and a flyover was planned at Hockley Hill, on the West Bromwich road. The Ministry of Transport urged the Corporation to carry out these projects rapidly if it wanted approval for improvements at other big bottle-necks.[2] Birmingham's schemes for the years 1962–6 were placed before the committee on roads in the West Midlands conurbation, set up by the Minister in 1958, which accepted all but one of them. In April 1961 the City Council authorized the consequent acceleration of the road programme.[3] By now, it was so enthusiastic that it approved a plan to build a £3·5 million overhead section on the Coventry Road, against the strong opposition of local councillors and residents.[4] On the other hand, the Council was also prepared to experiment with cheap expedients like the prefabricated flyover built at Camp Hill in 1961.[5]

With the opening of the Birchfield Road underpass, the first in the provinces, in March 1962, Birmingham began to win national recog-

[1] B.C.C., *Pro.*, 9 April 1957, pp. 986–1009 (Public Works Committee).

[2] B.C.C., *Pro.*, 21 July 1959, pp. 243–4 (Public Works Committee).

[3] B.C.C., *Pro.*, 18 April 1961, pp. 1015–17, 1023.

[4] B.C.C., *Pro.*, 6 December 1960, pp. 619–24, 634 (Public Works Committee). This project was later deferred pending the completion of motorway developments in the Birmingham area.

[5] B.C.C., *Pro.*, 10 January 1961, pp. 700–1 (Public Works Committee).

nition for its growing achievement in road-building. In the following year, however, the Ministry warned that the road programme would have to be decelerated.[1] For the next few years fewer new schemes were approved, and work on the Yardley underpass and the intermediate ring road did not begin until 1964. But work was again accelerated in 1966, when the Ministry of Transport confirmed its intention to accord priority in its motorway programme to the completion of the Midland links between the M1, the M5, and the M6. This decision made it particularly urgent to complete the Aston and Perry Barr (Walsall road) expressways by the early 1970s. The Aston expressway was especially ambitious. First announced in 1963, it was a completely new road running from Lancaster Place to a multi-level interchange on the M6 at Salford Bridge. Smaller schemes, such as the Coventry Road and Bristol Street widenings, also benefited from the new urgency. The year 1966 saw the approval of a major improvement on the western approach to the city centre, the underpass at Five Ways, Edgbaston.

By 1970 all these ambitious schemes were well advanced, and most were due to come to full fruition in the early 1970s. Congestion inevitably remained at many points, but Birmingham was demonstrating that a large British city could be adapted to the motor car provided that sufficient effort and enthusiasm were applied to the task. Despite the many gloomy prophecies emitted by the opponents of urban roads during the 1950s and 1960s, Birmingham's road schemes had contributed substantially to improving mobility within the city by 1970, as well as contributing to city-centre and inner-area renewal.

Public transport

Although the Birmingham road programme was designed principally to facilitate private transport, it was also intended to improve a public transit system based almost entirely on the motor bus.[2] The very great majority of passengers were carried by the municipal transport department,[3] which was incorporated into the West Midlands Passenger Transport Authority in 1969. Suburban areas near the city, and some of the fringe districts within the city boundary, were served by a private regional company, Midland Red Motor Services. British Rail operated passenger services on a handful of suburban lines terminating in the

---

[1] B.C.C., *Pro.*, 9 April 1963, p. 898 (Public Works Committee).

[2] In 1966 some 60 per cent of people working in the city centre travelled by bus. Some 27 per cent used private cars and only 7 per cent came by train (Colin Buchanan and Partners, *The Conurbations* (1969), pp. 35–6).

[3] See W. A. Camwell, *The A.B.C. of Birmingham City Transport* (1950); Michael H. Ford, *A.B.C. Birmingham City Buses* (1959); Prince J. Marshall, *A.B.C. Birmingham City Buses* (1960); City of Birmingham Transport Committee, *City of Birmingham Transport Department 1904–1954* (1954).

city centre. But to all intents and purposes public transport in Birmingham meant municipal road transport. Midland Red services were not normally allowed to compete with municipal buses and trams within the city boundaries. The railway services were never very attractive to people travelling within the city, even before the war.

Although the Corporation had not taken over responsibility for transport until the early twentieth century, the transport department had developed into one of Birmingham's major trading undertakings by 1939. It was already the largest municipal transport undertaking in the country, and its services covered a wider area, and served a bigger population, than any other. At a time when private cars were few, it provided a key link between the new housing estates and the industrial and commercial areas of the centre. The development of suburban areas was largely responsible for the greater use made of transport services in the 1930s, when the total of passenger journeys made each year rose from 357 million to 427 million.[1] However, the new estates were something of an embarrassment to the department even during the high noon of its prosperity. Densities were so low, and distances from the centre so great, that it was impossible to provide frequent services to many estates without making heavy losses. The cheap fares available to workers further depressed the return from these routes.[2] The great area of the city also meant that many people's journeys were very long. It was partly to speed up journeys that the transport department decided to allow tram services to run down and to replace them with motor buses.[3] The number of service miles run each year by trams fell from 19,476 to 14,284 during the 1930s, while the corresponding figure for motor buses rose from 12,864 to 27,448. But long journeys to work remained a serious cause of concern to working-class organizations in Birmingham and also to town planning groups like the Bournville Village Trust. The problems of municipal transport were an important factor in the City Council's growing realization in the 1930s that Birmingham was already big enough.

The Second World War placed a severe strain on the transport department. Petrol rationing greatly reduced the number of private motor cars on the roads, and shift work and dispersal of production made it necessary to provide extra services to new destinations at unusual hours.[4] After a slight fall in the first two years of war, owing

[1] *Abstract*, vol. i.

[2] B.C.C., *Pro.*, 4 July 1939, p. 733 (Transport Committee); Geoffrey Boumphrey, *Town and Country Tomorrow* (1940), p. 96; B.T.C., *Annual Report*, 1938–9, p. 9.

[3] Motor buses took thirty-five minutes to travel to Rubery from the city centre, whereas the trams took forty-three minutes (B.C.C., *Pro.*, 9 April 1957, p. 956 (General Purposes Committee)).

[4] See W. A. Camwell, *The A.B.C. of Birmingham City Transport, Part 2, Buses* (1950), p. 13.

mainly to evacuation and school closures, the number of passengers carried rose each year from 410,674,000 in 1941 to 479,402,000 in 1945. In order to conserve petrol, tram services were retained wherever possible, even though the tracks deteriorated considerably.[1] Nevertheless, petrol supplies were insufficient, and motor services had to be reduced in the middle of the day, during evenings, and at weekends.[2] On Government instructions, the number of stops was reduced by one-third,[3] and one motor bus in twenty was converted to use producer gas instead of petrol. Nevertheless, the war was a prosperous period for the transport department, and the committee looked forward with some disquiet to peacetime, when more frequent but less heavily loaded services would again be run.[4]

For some years after the war the transport department was in a parlous state. Many of its vehicles were obsolete and in poor condition, for only a handful of new buses had been delivered during the war. The trams and their tracks were particularly decrepit. Nevertheless, the number of passengers continued to rise until the end of the 1940s, when it began to stabilize. The Transport Committee courageously set up a network of all-night services in 1946, well in advance of most other large cities. New buses were delivered from 1947, but they were too few to allow the rapid suspension of tram routes. It was not until July 1949 that the City Council was able to approve a firm programme for the conversion to motor buses of the remaining tram and trolley-bus routes, by 1953.[5] This target was reached thanks to an improvement in deliveries from the late 1940s. By this time, however, the transport department was running into serious financial difficulties, which were to plague it for evermore.

The Transport Committee's end-of-war pessimism had not been borne out in the late 1940s simply because conditions did not return immediately to normal. Petrol rationing was maintained, and sales of new motor cars on the home market were severely restricted. Losses on the tram services were more than compensated for by a big motor bus surplus, which amounted to £495,000 in 1948–9.[6] The committee acceded to trade union pressure for better services, especially during the years when Labour controlled the City Council. So when the total of passengers fell in 1950 for the first time since 1941, the department found itself over-stretched. A further decline in patronage and an increase in fuel tax resulted in the huge deficit of £390,000 in 1951–2.[7] Fare increases failed to stop the rot, and in 1953 the committee began

[1] B.C.C., *Pro.*, 1 July 1941, pp. 405–6 (Transport Committee).
[2] B.C.C., *Pro.*, 2 July 1940, pp. 541, 545 (Transport Committee).
[3] B.C.C., *Pro.*, 6 July 1943, pp. 395–6 (Transport Committee).
[4] B.C.C., *Pro.*, 3 July 1945, p. 592 (Transport Committee).
[5] *Y.B.*, no. 32, August–September 1949, p. 1.
[6] Ibid.   [7] *Y.B.*, no. 66, August 1952, p. 2.

to curtail some unprofitable services, including all the routes running across Birmingham via the city centre.[1] By the following year the annual deficit had been wiped out, and the number of passengers remained stable until 1956. Shortage of staff, however, prevented any new improvement of services. So when the steady decline in passengers resumed in the later 1950s the committee found itself under fire from two sides. The trade unions and residents of suburban estates complained that services were inadequate, while the Conservatives in the City Council were ready to condemn any signs of the re-emergence of a deficit. Labour never dared to suggest a general rate subsidy, though the Corporation bore the cost of its unique free-travel scheme for old people, which was set up after many vicissitudes (and largely thanks to the perseverance of Harry Watton) in the mid-1950s. The shortage of staff not only restricted services, but forced the department into the costly expedient of paying above the national rate.[2] But when the committee introduced experimental new services, such as limited-stop routes, they had to be withdrawn owing to minimal public support.

During the 1960s the fall in passengers became faster still, and in 1968 only 334,000,000 were carried, compared to over 544,600,000 in the peak year of 1950. Fares continued to rise, although big efforts were made to cut costs, for instance, by the introduction of one-man buses from 1965. A few limited-stop services were resumed towards the end of the decade. But the department was never strong enough to provide the frequency, speed, and economy of service which alone might have discouraged the motorist from using his car. Experimental 'park-and-ride' schemes were failures. And growing congestion prevented the buses from benefiting fully from the city's new roads.

Because of the absence of a rapid transit system,[3] and the inability of Midland Red to make a major contribution to transport within the city, only the railways could supplement the ailing municipal bus services. But they were themselves in a much worse state. Although very few stations were closed after 1939, several had been discontinued in the previous twenty years, together with a number of suburban services.[4] Only one new station, Longbridge, was opened after the war (in 1954), and no new lines were built. During and shortly after the war the suburban lines benefited from the restriction of independent transport, but their use declined rapidly in the 1950s, and services were cut back. In the middle of the decade, in response to calls for the more intensive use of suburban lines and coordination with road transport,[5] British Railways introduced a number of frequent diesel services. But they failed to attract much support, and while the diesels

---

[1] *Y.B.*, no. 77, August 1953, p. 2.　　　　　[2] *Y.B.*, no. 147, January 1960, p. 1.
[3] See above, p. 406.　　　　[4] *V.C.H. Warcks.*, vol. vii, p. 42.
[5] See e.g. *B.M.*, 2 January 1952, editorial.

were retained, frequency was abandoned, despite protests from the City Council.[1] Nevertheless, the suburban services staggered on in very much their old form until the early 1960s, when drastic closures were announced. Most had been carried out by the end of the decade, although some were substantially delayed owing to protests from the City Council and local M.P.s.[2]

The loss of a number of stations and services led the City Council to take a new initiative, by calling for a comprehensive survey of conurbation traffic problems. The Ministry of Transport took up this idea in August 1963, and the Birmingham Corporation convened a meeting of local authorities and other interested parties. The survey began in 1964, with Birmingham contributing substantially to the cost, and Alderman Watton chairing the steering committee.[3] Shortly afterwards the new Labour Government announced its plans for regional transport authorities to direct the operation of all public transport. The West Midlands authority was set up in 1969, chaired by Birmingham's Alderman Griffin. By 1970 the authority had taken some important steps towards establishing a more integrated transport structure, but the problems of creating an efficient, economical public transport service still remained daunting. The authority had been refused permission to incorporate the Midland Red, and it seemed unlikely that it would be able to shoulder the crushing financial burden involved in subsidizing uneconomic railway services.

Electricity

The biggest problem facing public transport was a sharp fall in demand. Other utility services, in contrast, benefited from much more stable conditions of operation. But all had to face the problem of adapting their distribution systems to changing population and activity patterns within Birmingham.

Although electricity supply remained a municipal responsibility until the Birmingham undertaking was nationalized in 1948, the City Council had already lost much effective control over it before the war. The national grid had been set up as early as 1926, and the Central Electricity Board told Birmingham how much power to generate. The Board kept tight control of all capital works, and could also *require* the Corporation to extend its generating capacity. Moreover, the undertaking, which made no contribution to the rate fund, was self-financing, so that the City Council had little opportunity to interfere in its affairs.

[1] See e.g. B.C.C., *Pro.*, 9 April 1957, p. 999 (Public Works Committee); Colin Buchanan and Partners, *The Conurbations* (1969), pp. 35–6.

[2] See e.g. B.C.C., *Pro.*, 10 April 1962, p. 904 (General Purposes Committee).

[3] B.C.C., *Pro.*, 8 October 1963, pp. 335–7; 4 February 1964, pp. 726–8 (General Purposes Committee). The survey was published four years later. See Freeman, Fox, Wilbur Smith, and Associates, *West Midlands Transport Study* (1968).

It had close links with other electricity undertakings and supplied power to Solihull. However, the City Council's Electricity Supply Committee had power to fix its own charges, which were recognized as very low.

Rearmament and the war required a big increase in generating capacity, much of which was carried out during the hostilities.[1] Supply nearly always exceeded demand, and even during the heaviest raids linkages to damaged factories were usually restored almost immediately.[2] Demand began to fall from about 1943, leaving excess generating capacity which would be diverted after the war to new housing estates and the expanding export industries. Wartime experience not only confirmed the value of the national grid, but revealed a need for larger distribution areas. The result was the nationalization of electricity supply in 1948, under the control of fourteen area boards.[3] Nationalization was not ill-received in Birmingham; even the Unionists recognized that it was a logical step, though they complained about the terms of compensation.[4] The new area board pursued the Electricity Supply Committee's plans to improve transmission to the south-west and south-east of Birmingham, where the first new housing estates were going up. Power cuts and load reductions continued until the end of the decade owing to the coal shortage, but the new organization was not responsible for them; the Midlands Electricity Board had no more control over overall generating policy than had the old Electricity Supply Department.

During the late 1940s and early 1950s nearly all the Midlands Electricity Board's efforts to extend and improve the distribution system in Birmingham were related to new housing developments.[5] It was not until about 1953 that industrial development began to demand more than a very minor proportion of supply extensions. Yet by the middle of the decade new industrial demand was outstripping new domestic demand, as industry expanded and municipal building contracted. A further load was placed on the electricity system by the introduction of smokeless zones from the mid-1950s.[6] From about 1957 the office-building boom created demand for improvements to distribution in the city centre. Indeed, the board now had some difficulty in meeting the overall demand in the Birmingham area, though the relaxation of

[1] Black, pp. 73–4.
[2] B.C.C., *Pro.*, 3 July 1945, p. 626 (Electricity Supply Committee).
[3] Black, pp. 200–1.
[4] The Corporation received only £14 million in compensation, amounting to the undertaking's outstanding debt (*T.B.*, no. 50, March 1951, p. 2).
[5] This section is based on Midlands Electricity Board, *Report and Statement of Accounts*, 1948– ; annual figures of units sold and consumers in the Birmingham area in *Electricity Supply Handbook*.
[6] See below, pp. 421 ff.

Office building in the city centre. John Madin's *Post and Mail* building

High-density, low-rise housing at Chelmsley Wood, 1970. This development obtained an MOHLG Gold Medal Award for Good Design in
Housing, 1970.

capital controls allowed it to make up deficiencies very quickly. By the early 1960s this moment of difficulty was past, and although new requests for industrial supplies were frequent, they no longer embarrassed the board. From 1964 new housing again became the more important source of new demand.

So the effect of electricity nationalization on Birmingham was minimal. On the whole, the board kept up with demand, and it was certainly not responsible for any deceleration in the growth of local industry or of house-building. The power cuts of the late 1940s were repeated in 1962–3, but they resulted from the overloading of the national system. The pre-1948 Birmingham supply area retained its separate organization, with the addition of Sutton Coldfield, and local interests were still able to state their special needs through the board's users' consultative council.

Gas

The history of Birmingham's gas supply since 1939 is very similar to that of its electricity. But there are two important differences. Firstly, because coal gas is not usually distributed over very long distances, no equivalent of the national electricity system had been set up by 1939. Regional links, on the other hand, were extremely important. Secondly, demand for gas grew much more slowly than for electricity, so the Birmingham supply system was under much less pressure.

During the war the municipal gas undertaking increased its production by nearly one-quarter—this was much less than the Electricity Supply Department, which increased its generating capacity by nearly one-half, yet it was achieved only by the use of a number of temporary expedients, including the manufacture of carburetted water gas.[1] Although gas shortages and interruptions of supply were few, even during the bombing, the war emphasized the importance of links with nearby undertakings. The connections established as a precautionary measure before the war with Smethwick, Oldbury, and Walsall proved crucial on several occasions.[2] These links were extended after the war, when the Corporation signed agreements in 1945–7 to supply gas to five areas to the west of Birmingham. Because this new obligation proved a slight embarrassment, the Coventry Gas Department began to supply gas to Birmingham in 1948, helping to augment gas pressures in the east of the city. So gas flowed out of Birmingham to the west, and into it from the east.

Gas production was not taken over by the West Midlands Gas Board

---

[1] City of Birmingham Gas Committee, *The City of Birmingham Gas Department 1939–1945* (1945), p. 5; Black, pp. 70–3; B.C.C., *Pro.*, 3 July 1945, pp. 558–61 (Gas Committee).

[2] Black, p. 187.

until 1949, under the terms of the Gas Act 1948. The Unionists complained bitterly about compensation, but few other objections were made in Birmingham. Like its sister undertaking, the gas department had made no contribution to the rate fund. Until vesting the Gas Committee's problems had been very similar to those of the Electric Supply Committee—the national coal shortage which forced frequent reductions in pressure, and the need to improve distribution in the north and north-west of the city. New gasworks were planned, but because some schemes were delayed by capital restrictions, the committee had installed producer gas plant to safeguard its position.[1] The Birmingham gas undertaking, the second-biggest in Britain, fitted easily into the new regional organization, which amalgamated the smaller, less efficient units, but encouraged the large ones.[2] Indeed, the Birmingham undertaking had a considerable influence over the West Midlands Board's operations, for it was the only one in the area to have its own team of specialist officers. The Birmingham area, with the addition of Solihull and Henley-in-Arden, formed a separate division in the new regional organization.

Because Birmingham had almost over-reached its capacity before vesting, shortage of gas actually restricted the expansion of gas-using industries in the later 1940s and early 1950s. But supplies to housing estates were extended according to demand, although there remained some difficulty in the south-west of the city. From 1954 the completion of new gasworks at last established a safe margin between capacity and demand, and all requests for industrial supplies were now satisfied. By about 1957 industry was taking half the total output, compared to just over one-third after the war. Total domestic consumption began to *decline* after 1955, owing to the unpopularity of gas heating in new houses. The fall was not checked until 1960, when new gas appliances began to attract buyers. From 1963 domestic consumption again expanded rapidly owing to the proliferation of gas central heating systems.

In the late 1950s the West Midlands area was reorganized on 'functional' lines, with an area grid system and large 'regions' instead of divisions. Birmingham, however, remained the major element in the new central region. Thanks to new plant and the advent of natural gas in the 1960s, the problem of supply was completely solved. But growing domestic demand, which actually exceeded that of industry by 1966, required major improvements in the Birmingham distribution system. Industrial demand stabilized, with a tendency to decline, from 1965.

Post and telephones

Unlike the two services discussed above, postal and telephone provision

[1] *Y.B.*, no. 21, August–September 1948, p. 1.

[2] This section is based on West Midlands Gas Board, *Report and Statement of Accounts*, 1949– .

were never a potential limiting factor on the growth of the city, but they were a major element in its amenities. The administrative functions of post offices expanded rapidly after 1945, so that a growing number of people needed to have access to one. Working-class districts were very dependent on the provision of public telephones and their quick repair after damage. In middle-class areas, the private telephone was an essential link for people who often lived long distances from shops, administrative offices, and friends.

Until the Second World War, Birmingham enjoyed a high standard of postal services, perhaps unnecessarily high. Letters could be posted on buses and trams and most areas had four deliveries of mail a day. As soon as war broke out, shortage of manpower led to big restrictions. Facilities on buses and trams were withdrawn, and the number of deliveries was reduced.[1] Nevertheless, the G.P.O. performed admirably during the war, and people became so used to the restricted facilities that there was no outcry when the old standards were not resumed after the war. But the war interrupted plans to provide new post offices and sub-post offices, of which there were slightly fewer in the city in 1945 than in 1939.[2] Telephone services, on the other hand, were greatly expanded. The number of telephones in use in the Birmingham telephone area (which was slightly larger than the city) rose from 62,725 in March 1939 to 82,590 in March 1945; every year some three or four thousand new telephones were installed.[3] This growth was accelerated after 1946, and the 100,000 mark was passed during 1950. With one telephone for every eleven people, Birmingham was well provided by the standards of provincial cities, though London still had over twice as many telephones. During the 1950s the installation of new telephones was accelerated and from the middle of the decade the big backlog of applications was greatly reduced. A total of 200,000 telephones was reached in 1965. The demand for new lines expanded rapidly again from the mid-1960s owing to the big increase in house building, and the waiting list became even longer than it had been in the early 1950s. But by the last years of the decade there were signs that the G.P.O. was meeting this challenge and in 1968 the total of telephones had risen to over 235,000.

This expansion of the private telephone service was not accompanied by a similar growth in public facilities. The number of public telephones in Birmingham increased only from some 1,550 in 1954 to about 1,760 in 1967, and the provision of new post offices was even slower. In 1966 Birmingham had only forty-four branch offices, two less than in 1945,

[1] *B.P.*, 8 September 1939.
[2] Information and figures in this section have been kindly provided by G.P.O. Birmingham, except where otherwise stated.
[3] *Abstract.*

and 198 sub-post offices, only twelve more than at the end of the war. The number of posting boxes, on the other hand, was increased by about one-third between 1939 and 1966, from 780 to 1,025. Of course, the almost static total of offices resulted partly from the loss of many premises in the central redevelopment areas, and slow progress in providing shopping centres on new estates until the late 1950s. Nevertheless, the shortage of offices and public telephones was the cause of almost continuous complaints in the outer areas, especially in the 1950s. In the following decade the G.P.O. was at last able to provide some of the facilities requested, and complaints became less frequent. But the problem of providing adequate services in areas of low-density housing was never completely solved. Nevertheless, the numbers of letters and parcels posted in Birmingham increased by nearly half between 1946 and 1966.

Water

Unlike the services mentioned so far, water supplies and drainage services remained directly or indirectly under the control of the Corporation. Water was the responsibility of a Corporation department,[1] while drainage was handled by the Birmingham Tame and Rea District Drainage Board, the majority of whose members were nominated by the City Council. Although both these services had to expand and improve their networks in order to meet changing needs, they always kept ahead of demand, and never restricted the development of the city and its industries. The main work in establishing adequate systems for the city had been done in the late nineteenth and early twentieth centuries; subsequently it was a matter of keeping them up to scratch in a situation of slowly expanding demand and slow technical change. Nevertheless, the cumulative increase in demand for water made it necessary to undertake new supply schemes, which mostly took the form of extensions of the existing Elan system. Work on the Claerwen dam, which had been planned in the 1930s but interrupted during the war, began again in 1946. The dam was inaugurated in 1952, but by the early 1960s water supplies were again running short, and Birmingham took part with other authorities in a scheme to draw water from the Severn in Monmouthshire. Completion of this scheme was delayed until the late 1960s, but Birmingham was never seriously short of water. However, Birmingham had to be more hesitant in supplying water to other authorities, which it had started to do before the war. The Water Committee successfully opposed, for this reason, Government attempts to extend the Birmingham supply area by the incorporation of other undertakings.

The growing consumption of water inevitably increased the load on

[1] See *City of Birmingham Waterworks: a Short History* (1954).

the Birmingham Tame and Rea District Drainage Board. Before the war the Ministry of Health had extended the area covered by the board, so that it had come to serve a district twice the size of Birmingham. These extensions were not resisted by the City Council because they did not involve the risk of any deterioration of provision in Birmingham. After the war, the drainage system in the city had to be greatly extended to serve new housing and industry, but the work was done in good time, and did not delay building. The increase in industrial effluents caused serious, but never insurmountable, problems.

Clean air

Birmingham Corporation's efforts to provide efficient sewerage and pure water had begun in the nineteenth century, and it had won the battle against waterborne disease long before 1939. But the Council did not rest upon its laurels in the health field. During the Second World War it planned to attack another evil which had been recognized in the previous century, but which had been left almost unchecked. This was the curse of atmospheric pollution. Birmingham enjoyed an advantage in the implementation of smoke abatement because, despite its reputation as a 'dirty' city, its industries produced less smoke than those of many northern towns. Even more important, however, was the Birmingham City Council's determination to control smoke. The Labour group was strongly committed to the idea, and the enlightened industrialists and professional men who led the Unionist group ensured that there was little opposition from within their own ranks. If progress towards smoke abatement was held up in the early post-war years, it was not the result of any lack of motivation in Birmingham, but of the impossibility of finding alternative sources of power and heat.

The City Council began its campaign against smoke in 1949, attempting to use powers contained in the 1936 Public Health Act.[1] But these powers proved inadequate and the Corporation failed to persuade the Minister of Health to reinforce them.[2] In any case, the West Midlands Gas Board was already warning that it would be unable to meet extra demand for industrial supplies resulting from smoke abatement orders.[3] By 1953, however, the power shortage had been almost overcome, and as the Government showed no signs of introducing new legislation despite an energetic campaign by the Birmingham M.P.s,[4]

[1] The amount of soot in city centre air was estimated in 1948 at over nineteen tons per square mile per month (*Y.B.*, no. 53, June 1951, p. 4). The Birmingham press often published panoramic views of the city on August Bank Holiday Monday, emphasizing to readers that smoke control could make Birmingham look like that all the time.

[2] See *H. of C. Deb.*, 5th series, vol. cdlxv, cols. *165, 2297*, 2 June 1949.

[3] West Midlands Gas Board, *Report and Statement of Accounts*, 1949–50, p. 13.

[4] See e.g. *B.M.*, 20 September 1950.

the City Council decided to promote its own Bill. It became law in the following year, though it was substantially weakened by the House of Commons Select Committee after objections by Birmingham industrial interests. Nevertheless, in the summer of 1955 the Council designated the central business district and Shard End as smokeless zones.[1]

In the following year the Government followed Birmingham's lead by passing the Clean Air Act, which strengthened the powers available to the Corporation and allowed a more ambitious attack on industrial areas. First of all, however, the Corporation concentrated on extending the central smokeless zone, and creating new ones in the residential suburbs. Three such zones were created in 1958 and 1959. It was also in 1959 that the Council approved a plan of campaign to make Birmingham completely smoke-free within fifteen years.[2] In the 1960s smoke abatement orders were applied to increasingly large areas; that of 1964, affecting Sparkhill and Hall Green, was said to be the most extensive in the country.[3] By 1970 the Birmingham atmosphere was already extremely clear, in comparison with many northern cities. Undoubtedly, the advanced technical standards of most local industries, and the general prosperity of the city, had facilitated the conversion process. But the foresight and determination of the City Council had been principally responsible for making Birmingham Britain's cleanest major city.

Health

The Corporation's efforts to provide pure air and water and a cleanly environment undoubtedly contributed to the steadily improving general level of health in Birmingham after 1945. The substantial rise in average real earnings and the widespread renewal of housing also helped. But these general improvements could not alone ensure that everyone in Birmingham remained healthy. What, then, of the medical services and the work of the Corporation's public health department?

In 1939 the Birmingham City Council was responsible for a wide range of medical and local health services, including a number of hospitals and asylums which had been managed until 1929 by the poor law guardians. The city also had several voluntary hospitals and other medical institutions. Many of the buildings were old, poorly-equipped, and ill-designed, but in the straitened circumstances of the 1930s little could be done to improve them. Their deficiencies, and those of hospitals in other big cities, became a matter of national concern as war approached. The Ministry of Health established close control over them in order to ensure that air raid casualties were adequately catered for,

[1] *Y.B.*, no. 99, August–September 1955, p. 3.
[2] *Y.B.*, no. 145, November 1959, p. 1.
[3] *Y.B.*, no. 198, August–September 1964, p. 1.

and the need to reserve beds for indefinite periods in casualty wards accentuated the interdependence of Birmingham hospitals as patients were moved from one to another. Although the system stood up well to the raids, which caused far fewer casualties than had been anticipated, serious defects were revealed, and long waiting lists built up for ordinary surgical cases.[1] This experience pointed the way to post-war reorganization, which was foreshadowed by the White Paper of February 1944, 'A National Health Service'.

The City Council welcomed the Government's plans to provide free medical attention, but opposed the suggestion that local authority hospitals should be transferred to State control.[2] The voluntary hospitals, on the other hand, welcomed the White Paper. They had been receiving Government subsidies for some time, and recognized that incorporation into a national system was essential to their continued growth.[3] The national system was established by the National Health Service Act of 1946, and hospitals and out-relief were transferred to the State in July 1948. Local authorities were left to provide a number of important local health services, including day nurseries, child welfare, midwifery, health visiting, home nursing, vaccination, ambulances, mental health, and the prevention, care, and after-care of illness.[4] Like the nationalized gas and electricity services, hospitals were organized on a regional basis, but Birmingham was allowed some say in their administration through the individual notables, many of them members of the Council, who were invited to serve on the Birmingham Regional Hospital Board and the hospital management committees.

After 1948 Birmingham's hospitals were linked more closely to others in the region. More patients came in from outside the city while Birmingham citizens were often treated elsewhere. Regional organization brought many tangible benefits, such as the expansion of the blood transfusion service after 1950, and the establishment of a mass radiography unit. There were substantial economies of scale, and the whole service became more efficient.[5] But the regional board was severely handicapped by the defective state of many Birmingham hospitals at the time when they were taken over. Summerfield Hospital, for instance, which was used for geriatric services, continued in use for many years after the need for its complete demolition had been recognized, and it

---

[1] Richard M. Titmuss, *Problems of Social Policy* (1950), pp. 492–3, 502–5.

[2] B.C.C., *Pro.*, 10 October 1944, pp. 542–54, 562–5 (Public Health Committee). A Labour amendment in support of State control of hospitals was heavily defeated.

[3] This point emerges very strongly from Rachel Waterhouse, *Children in Hospital: A Hundred Years of Child Care in Birmingham* (1962).

[4] D. G. Watts, 'Public health', *V.C.H. Warcks.*, vol. vii, esp. pp. 348 ff; J. Parker, *Local Health and Welfare Services* (1965).

[5] National Health Service, *Birmingham Regional Hospital Board 1947–1966* (1966), esp. pp. 13–30.

was asserted in 1961 that the building had hardly been altered since its construction in the mid-nineteenth century.[1] Many city hospitals were severely congested, and the Birmingham M.P.s tried hard in the 1950s to persuade the Minister of Health to give priority to their improvement and extension. In some cases there was no doubt that shortage of accommodation caused acute suffering. In 1954, for instance, the Minister of Health admitted that over five hundred people in Birmingham were awaiting admission to tuberculosis sanatoria; 'I am by no means satisfied with the situation,' he said.[2] Even by the end of the decade there had been little improvement, and Percy Shurmer was telling the House of Commons that Birmingham hospitals, apart from the modern Queen Elizabeth Hospital, were 'a disgrace'.[3] By the early 1960s the completion of a number of major works had averted the crisis, but shortages and deficiencies remained in certain areas, such as dental surgery and maternity hospitals.[4] Many of these deficiencies were, however, remedied during the decade. The new dental hospital was opened in April 1965, and the gradual decline in the number of complaints made in the House by Birmingham M.P.s suggested that the city was at last beginning to enjoy adequate hospital services.

The shortage of maternity beds and the other deficiencies of the hospitals extended, though sometimes indirectly, the local authority's responsibilities. This extra burden was most unwelcome, but it encouraged the Corporation to maintain and improve a standard of health provision which had already won national recognition. Under the National Health Service Act, the new Health Committee, set up in 1947, concentrated on personal hygiene, and preventive and social medicine.[5] The role of the health visitor, who had previously been responsible for young children and mothers alone, was greatly extended to include responsibility for preventing the spread of infection among persons of all ages, including care of the elderly and the integration of hospital and domiciliary care. Significant among the services expanded to supplement the work of the hospitals was the domiciliary nursing service for infants and children, which was inaugurated in October 1954 as an extension of the home nursing service. Other innovations introduced by the department included the screening of children for metabolic diseases and for hearing defects. Screening services were extended during the 1960s, for instance by examining new-born babies for congenital malformation of the hip. From 1967 Birmingham followed

[1] J. H. Sheldon, *Report to the Birmingham Regional Hospital Board on its Geriatric Services* (1962).

[2] *H. of C. Deb.*, 5th series, vol. dxxv, col. *591*, 18 March 1954.

[3] *H. of C. Deb.*, 5th series, vol. dxcvi, cols. *825–6*, 1 December 1958.

[4] See e.g. *Y.B.*, no. 185, June 1963, p. 1; *H. of C. Deb.*, 5th series, vol. dclxxvii, cols. *11–12*, 6 May 1963.

[5] *B.M.O.H.*, 1952, p. 15.

Bradford in pioneering the screening of immigrant school-entrants for tuberculosis and other conditions. The City was also among the first to introduce fluoridation of water supplies as an aid to dental health, in 1964.

This development of health services after the war involved the Corporation in a very high outlay. In 1952–3 Birmingham spent far more than the county-borough average on all local health services except health visiting, mental health, and domestic help.[1] The City's per capita outlay on overall health services was higher than that of any other major city except Coventry; in some cases Birmingham's pre-eminence was spectacular. Subsequently Birmingham's pre-eminence in terms of outlay began to fade as other cities developed their own health services, and the Health Department suffered increasingly from that persistent Birmingham problem, the recruitment and retention of sufficient qualified staff. In 1958–9 Birmingham still spent much more than the county-borough average, but three major cities (Bristol, Coventry, Nottingham) now surpassed it, and others had almost caught up. By 1966–7 the City was spending only marginally more than the average county borough, and five major cities now spent more than Birmingham—in some cases (Bristol, Coventry, Hull), very much more.

To a very large extent this apparent relative decline in outlay on health provision was caused by manpower problems. By the late 1960s the home nursing, school health, and health visiting services were all operating below establishment. Health visitors and doctors were particularly difficult to obtain. Like the Education Department, the Health Department had set up its own training schemes, particularly for health visitors, district nurses, nursery nurses, and public health inspectors. Unlike some other authorities, Birmingham was unable to offer special inducements such as housing and motor cars. Salaries were increased in some cases, with beneficial effects on staffing, but the rates payable to many classes of employee, such as nurses and midwives, were tied to national scales. The training schemes and salary adjustments produced some improvement, without eradicating the fundamental shortage. As in other departments, however, the shortage of manpower helped to bring about a highly efficient utilization of available staff, and organization and equipment were frequently modernized to save labour. Public health inspectors, for instance, were based in a number of sectors of the city in order to reduce journey times, and in the 1960s many of the department's nurses and other employees were encouraged to provide themselves with motor transport by means of an assisted-purchase scheme for cars and a mileage allowance.

[1] Institute of Municipal Treasurers, *Local Health Services Statistics.*

A key element of wartime plans for the improvement of Birmingham's health had been the provision of a number of health centres, especially in the inner areas, where doctors could work together and share equipment and maintenance services. When the provision of health centres was designated by the 1946 Act as a local responsibility, Birmingham made enthusiastic plans, and by 1950 nineteen sites had been earmarked.[1] The Government, however, accorded very low priority to health centres after the war, and delayed approval for the building of Birmingham's first centre, at Nechells Green, until the later 1950s. The general practitioners, too, were for a long time unenthusiastic about health centres, despite the Health Committee's efforts to obtain their full participation. Fortunately, this situation began to change when the Nechells Green centre, opened in 1960, became a clear success. The opening of Birmingham's second purpose-built centre, in Newtown, was delayed for a while in the mid-1960s by the refusal of some doctors to work with others,[2] but once these difficulties were overcome there were no obstacles to the opening of further centres, though Ministry approvals were still tardy and many local doctors still showed some reluctance to work in health centres. Early in 1968 the Health Committee agreed on a five-year programme with the Birmingham Executive Council to provide a further eight health centres in the city. At the end of the decade one new centre was under construction, and others were being set up in existing buildings. By 1970 six health centres were housing twenty-seven doctors and providing for over 73,000 patients, and several more undesignated centres were in existence.

We have already seen that Birmingham remained an extremely healthy city in most respects throughout the years 1939–70.[3] To a large extent, of course, high health standards were the result of an improving physical environment and high living standards, but there can be no doubt that the national and municipal health services were playing their due part in maintaining this happy state of affairs.

[1] Black, p. 264.
[2] *H. of C. Deb.*, 5th series, vol. dccxxii, cols. *1680–3*, 20 December 1965.
[3] See above, pp. 192 ff.

XIII

URBAN DESIGN AND ARCHITECTURE

Between the later 1930s and the early 1950s Birmingham's abundance of land, which had long been a feature of the city, was gradually but decisively replaced by a serious land shortage.[1] Such a crucial change of fortune could not fail to exercise a radical influence on the city's future layout. Fortunately, Birmingham's planners were well equipped to meet this new challenge. The City of Birmingham's early town planning schemes had given it a national lead in urban design before the First World War, and during the inter-war years it had enhanced a reputation of good planning that was equalled by few other British cities. But the hallmark of Birmingham planning was spaciousness. Thanks to massive boundary extensions, suburban land was available in plenty for playing fields, parks, greenswards, and central reservations along major roads. Flats and tenements were almost non-existent, and even new industrial buildings were predominantly one-storey structures. Yet the central areas, which the planners hesitated to touch, remained congested, with high residential densities and almost no open space. The central business district was smaller in extent than those of many a less important city, and the density of traffic, office workers, and shoppers there made a strange contrast with the wide open spaces of the suburbs. After the Second World War the Corporation was at least endowed with powers adequate to deal with the central areas; but by this time nearly all reserves of land within the city had been used up in low-density development. So, could Birmingham's distinctive style of planning survive after 1945? And what effect would the new conditions have on the architectural mediocrity which had also been a feature of pre-war Birmingham?

Before the war, much of the responsibility for physical planning had already come to rest on the City. After 1945 the municipality was even more closely involved. Not only were its general planning powers greatly extended by the Town and Country Planning Acts of 1944 and 1947, but the Corporation itself carried out directly major schemes of housing, slum clearance, and city centre redevelopment on a scale which greatly exceeded anything undertaken between the wars. Private development of houses, on the other hand, was greatly restricted by the land shortage and the priority given to municipal building. The planning outlines for private developers' schemes for shops and offices were often determined by the municipal road-building and redevelopment schemes into which they were incorporated. The Calthorpe Estate was

[1] See above, ch. IV.

the only private agency allowed to carry out a major town planning scheme.

Housing

The first aspect of town planning to preoccupy the City Council during and after the war was the design of municipal housing estates. Building for general needs was the first major element of reconstruction to get under way after the war. Moreover, because the huge pre-war estates had attracted much interest and criticism, planning questions affecting new housing were thoroughly discussed.

Until the Second World War criticism of Birmingham's municipal housing estates had centred on their shortage of community facilities, and the great distances which separated many of them from the major centres of employment.[1] Their layout and appearance were rarely questioned, even though repetition of house types and uniformity of architectural detail made them extremely boring visually. During the war, the City was converted to the neighbourhood unit principle, and determined that, in future, shops should be better sited in relation to houses.[2] But the characteristic feature of the pre-war estate, low residential density, was questioned by few. The influential Bournville Village Trust produced evidence of a continuing big demand for gardens, and of the good condition in which most gardens were kept on municipal estates. It recommended that flats should be built only in central slum districts, and even there it wanted to see a proportion of maisonettes and terraced houses.[3] On the other hand, the Birmingham and Five Counties Architectural Association, which was asked to prepare a draft plan for the Shard End estate, suggested that a proportion of flats should be provided, partly in order to provide more architectural variety.[4] More flats were also advocated by the Birmingham Communist Party, which foresaw the need for more economical use of land.[5]

Plans for new estates published after the war revealed some deference to criticism of the layout of pre-war estates. The Tile Cross estate, plans for which were revealed in 1946, had an unusually open layout, and made use of existing landscape features. With a system of interlocking open spaces, the whole scheme was claimed to be a complete break from

[1] See, for instance, Bournville Village Trust, *When We Build Again* (1941), p. 119.

[2] See esp. B.C.C., *Pro.*, 9 March 1943, pp. 264–7; 12 October 1943, pp. 506–10 (Reconstruction Committee).

[3] *When We Build Again*, pp. 83–6, 122.

[4] Birmingham and Five Counties Architectural Association Reconstruction Committee, 'Extract from a memorandum on the planning of typical housing development in the outer area of the city', *The Architect and Building News*, vol. clxxix, 29 September 1944, pp. 195–8.

[5] (Birmingham Communist Party), *Homes for Birmingham: The Communist Party Plan* (1945), p. 6.

the pre-war geometrical and symmetrical tradition.[1] But in this case the more flexible layout was achieved only by incorporating very low densities. The estate was in fact planned to attract upper-income-group tenants, and, in any case, its development was not planned to start for some years. The Tile Cross plans contrasted sharply with the estates which were actually developed in the two or three years after the war. Many of the houses built were on partially completed pre-war estates, the layouts of which could not be altered. The only architectural variety resulted from the use of new materials and prefabricated sections. For a time, speed of construction was highest on the Council's list of priorities. Several thousand prefabricated houses were erected without much thought for layout or visual amenities, as it was hoped that they would be replaced by permanent houses within ten years. It soon became clear, however, that the construction of permanent houses would remain slow for some time, and the Public Works Department was able to devote more thought to visual planning. In July 1948 the City Council, stimulated by the publication of a Central Housing Advisory Committee report, *The Appearance of Housing Estates*, agreed to spend £7,000 on landscaping work at the Grove estate, Harborne.[2] Two years later, it decided to build a proportion of traditional (brick) houses on estates being developed with non-traditional houses, in order to relieve their monotony.[3] But these were very minor palliatives, and many council members grew increasingly unhappy about the appearance of the new estates. Some even began to suggest that Birmingham was placing itself at a disadvantage in relation to other local authorities by leaving all architectural work to the City Engineer and Surveyor, Herbert Manzoni.

In the past, the City Council had taken pride in the fact that Manzoni, a qualified architect, could take sole charge of engineering, town planning, *and* architecture. But when the building rate began to increase from about 1950, it became increasingly arguable that Birmingham's standards of design and layout were inadequate. Herbert Manzoni, with characteristic candour and humour, admitted as much himself in 1955 when he told the annual conference of the Institution of Municipal Engineers that the ideal of low densities had had some undesirable results: 'Tens of thousands of acres were developed to this standard between the wars to form the dreariest and most depressing monument erected to my generation—I plead guilty to over thirty thousand of them.'[4] Some council members also believed that a separate Architect's Department could do layout and design work more quickly, thus

[1] B.C.C., *Pro.*, 12 March 1946, p. 353 (Public Works Committee).
[2] B.C.C., *Pro.*, 27 July 1948, p. 889 (Public Works Committee).
[3] B.C.C., *Pro.*, 7 February 1950, p. 999 (Public Works Committee).
[4] *B.P.*, 23 June 1955.

speeding up the output of houses. The Unionists, who had controlled the Council since 1949, and who claimed the credit for the improved building rate, had introduced a number of changes into the organiza- tion of building. By 1951 they were prepared to countenance further changes in the administrative structure even if they implied a certain demotion of Herbert Manzoni. And they had the tacit support of the Labour group. In July 1951 the General Purposes Committee presented a report on the responsibilities of the Public Works Department.[1] It pointed out that Birmingham was the only large town in the country to entrust all planning, engineering, and architectural work to one officer: '. . . it is asking a great deal of any one man that he should be responsible (however good his staff may be) for the control of a Public Works Department so vast as Birmingham's has grown to be.' Great pains were taken to remove implications that there was lack of confi- dence in Herbert Manzoni: '. . . it is a very high tribute to Mr. Manzoni that he has so far been able so successfully to command so large an undertaking (. . .) a revision would have had to be proposed before now had the office of City Surveyor not been so ably filled.' It had been felt for some time, continued the report, that it would be necessary to separate the functions of engineer and architect when Manzoni retired, since individuals who were qualified in both branches were now very rare. As the City Engineer would reach a possible retiring age in 1959, it would be advisable to set up an Architect's Department well in advance. There would be no sudden changes; for a transitional period the new City Architect would work within the Public Works Department.

It was difficult to take exception to so carefully worded a proposal. The Labour group did not oppose it, and the only dissent came from a small minority of Unionist members, notably Alderman P. W. Cox, who objected to the new appointment mainly on financial grounds. The proposal was carried by a large majority.[2] It was welcomed by the Birmingham press,[3] and the new appointment was made in the follow- ing year. The man chosen was A. G. Sheppard Fidler, who had pre- viously been Architect at Crawley New Town. Although he was not allowed to set up a department separate from Public Works until 1954, he was able to build up a big staff, and to introduce many changes in the layout and design of buildings. He was helped by a decision which the Council had taken in July 1952, at the suggestion of Alderman Grogan (Labour), to set up a standing joint conference between the four committees responsible for housing. The object of this innovation was to establish closer liaison in fixing the layout of housing estates, and the standard, type, and design of the dwellings.[4]

---

[1] B.C.C., *Pro.*, 24 July 1951, pp. 287–91.   [2] *B.G., B.P.*, 25 July 1951.
[3] See, for instance, *B.M.*, 25 July 1951, editorial.
[4] B.C.C., *Pro.*, 8 July 1952, p. 209 (House Building Committee).

Even before Sheppard Fidler's appointment the Public Works Committee had begun to recognize that Birmingham was using up its available land too quickly by building at extremely low densities. Sheppard Fidler agreed that higher densities were essential, but he was also distressed by the uniformity of external design, and the lack of variety in house types.[1] The alternative he favoured was mixed development, with a variety of house types and designs, including flats and maisonettes, even on suburban estates. Mixed development would raise densities, help to provide a more balanced social structure, and improve the appearance of the estates. Moreover, it would offer the non-traditional builders more interesting work than the two-storey houses which they were building in Birmingham at the time.[2] The same principles, thought Sheppard Fidler, should also be applied to the central redevelopment areas,[3] though mixed development here actually involved lower densities than those previously achieved by the Public Works Department using multi-storey blocks alone: 'A great variety of accommodation should . . . be provided within the neighbourhood and this variety is welcomed by the architect as his great opportunity to create an interesting and satisfying living community.'[4] This variety of buildings should include a proportion of multi-storey flats, especially in the central areas, even though they were not strictly necessary to achieve the planned residential densities. Speaking to the conference of the Royal Institute of British Architects in 1955, Sheppard Fidler said, 'I think we need some [tall blocks of flats]. Variety in mass and outline of buildings, as well as variety of dwelling types, is an important element in the creation of vital living areas. We must avoid at all costs the creation of a new dullness, a new mediocrity like the old, outworn buildings we are replacing with such expenditure of money and effort.'[5]

Sheppard Fidler's defence of multi-storey flats came at a time when Birmingham was already being forced to modify its traditional opposition to vertical living. Owing to the almost complete absence of tenements in the nineteenth-century city, and the strong influence of low-density areas like Edgbaston and Bournville on the inter-war municipal estates, it had become an accepted orthodoxy that Birmingham citizens would not live in flats. A few experiments were made with flats between the wars in the central areas, and the Unionists had come to accept the

[1] 'Housing in Birmingham: City Architect's Address at Housing Centre', *The Builder*, vol. cxcii, no. 5960, 21 June 1957, p. 1136.

[2] 'Recent housing developments in Birmingham', *Municipal Journal*, vol. lv, no. 3356, 14 June 1957, p. 1286.

[3] See above, pp. 222 ff. For an exposition of the advantages of mixed development, see A. G. Sheppard Fidler, 'Planning problems of high density housing', *Municipal Journal*, vol. lxii, no. 3222, 19 November 1964, p. 2867.

[4] A. G. Sheppard Fidler, 'The building and development of flats', *British Housing and Planning Year Book*, 1953, p. 87.

[5] *B.P.*, 16 February 1955.

need for them in slum redevelopment by 1939. Unfortunately, the design of the experimental blocks was not wholly satisfactory, and most tenants remained strongly opposed to them. Their criticisms were taken up before and during the war by the Borough Labour Party: '. . . the working class people of Birmingham do not want to live in flats.'[1] The party even attacked wartime plans for the Duddeston and Nechells redevelopment area, because they included a high proportion of flats.

After 1945 the Labour group had the chance to abandon these war-time plans for flats in the central areas. But it did not do so. During the last years of the war the group, as distinct from the Borough Labour Party, had associated itself with Unionist policy and the ideas of the City Engineer, which favoured the rehousing of a high proportion of slum-dwellers within the redevelopment areas. A leading Labour alderman, Walter Lewis, became chairman of the Public Works Committee in 1943, and presided over the preparation of the high-density Duddeston and Nechells scheme. After the war opposition faded within the Borough Labour Party, as flats were represented as the *sine qua non* of rapid slum clearance. But Labour did not yet advocate multi-storey development in the suburbs, even though the rapid exhaustion of reserves of building land would clearly be accelerated when slum clearance got fully under way, and displaced many residents from the redevelopment areas.

When the Unionists reformed the City's housing machine after taking control of the Council in 1949, they brought into Birmingham a number of national building firms which had developed a variety of non-traditional techniques since the war.[2] Although they were at first asked to build two-storey houses, they were capable of erecting much bigger structures far more cheaply than would have been possible by traditional methods. Indeed, some of the contractors were already building flats for other local authorities, and could offer fully designed and tested blocks 'off the peg'.[3] By 1951 the House Building Committee had decided to take advantage of these offers, especially as the twelve-storey towers under construction in the Duddeston and Nechells redevelopment area were considered to be prohibitively expensive.[4] In the 1952 building programme, one-fifth of the dwellings were flats.

[1] *Homes for the People!: Labour's Policy for Birmingham's Need* (1945), p. 10.
[2] See above, p. 228.
[3] For instance, Wimpey's six-storey, three-winged blocks. See 'The first six-storey No Fines flats', *Municipal Journal*, vol. lxi, no. 3141, 1 May 1953, pp. 889–90.
[4] Because these were Birmingham's first high-rise flats, standards of safety and comfort had been set abnormally high in order to obtain the approval and support of tenants and the public at large. For instance, five emergency staircases were incorporated, on Fire Department advice, in addition to the two main staircases and lifts.

The Crescent wharf, Civic Centre, before (1957) and after (1969) improvement.

Most of the blocks were in the central redevelopment areas, and the Labour group made no objections to the proposals. But pressure was now growing in the Birmingham press for a general extension of flat-building to the suburbs,[1] especially now that the City Council had decided not to seek an extension of the city boundaries except in exceptional circumstances.[2] The injection of the City Architect's views into this argument greatly strengthened the case for multi-storey flats.

By 1953 Sheppard Fidler was already beginning to exercise some influence. When the Labour group returned to power in May 1952 it was eager to encourage the Architect's efforts to improve design standards, since it had so heavily criticized Conservative policies in this field. The mixed-development principle was already being applied to plans for new estates announced in early 1953.[3] Sheppard Fidler even planned to build multi-storey blocks on estates that had already been developed at low densities. The first steps were taken towards keeping traffic out of pedestrian areas such as shopping centres, and Radburn layouts were applied to some new residential districts. In other cases, such as the Ley Hill estate, road layouts were simplified to economize on space and resources.[4] The purchase of land in 1953 at Kingshurst Hall, just outside the city boundary, gave Sheppard Fidler his first opportunity to plan a large area from scratch.[5]

These early schemes were prepared in association with the City Engineer, but Sheppard Fidler had a free hand in the design of layouts from January 1954 when his department was made independent.[6] The Public Works Department continued to fix the pattern of roads on new estates, but the layout of minor streets, paths, open spaces, and buildings, and all architectural design work, now lay in the hands of the City Architect. Sheppard Fidler's plans remained subject to approval by the Public Works Committee, but interference from this quarter was minimal. His influence was further strengthened in March 1954 when all the Education Committee's architectural work was transferred to his department, despite the strong opposition of that committee and of the Conservative minority group in the Council.[7]

Although fully aware of the need to save land, Sheppard Fidler never departed from his policy of mixed development. High-density pockets

[1] See e.g. *B.P.*, 3 January 1952, editorial.
[2] See above, p. 128.
[3] *Y.B.*, no. 71, February 1953, p. 1; L. H. C. Jennings, 'Birmingham develops on the fringe', *Municipal Journal*, vol. lxi, no. 3130, 13 February 1953, pp. 329–35.
[4] A. G. Sheppard Fidler, 'Post-war housing in Birmingham', *Town Planning Review*, vol. xxvi, April 1955, p. 29.
[5] Ibid., p. 29; B.C.C., *Pro.*, 6 January 1953, pp. 657–8 (House Building Committee).
[6] B.C.C., *Pro.*, 1 December 1953, p. 597 (General Purposes Committee).
[7] B.C.C., *Pro.*, 2 February 1954, pp. 731–4, 748 (General Purposes Committee).

EE

were used to balance low-density areas like the Sheldon Hall estate.[1] Experiments were made with the joint usage of sites for dwellings and social amenity buildings in order both to economize on land and to integrate community provision with housing.[2] More and more Radburn layouts were applied, one of the best examples being the Primrose Hill estate, King's Norton, plans for which were announced in 1962.[3] Of course, the City Architect was aware that flats, especially those in tall blocks, were not popular with tenants. At first, many of the high density layouts incorporated low three-storey blocks of flats in an attempt to overcome some of the tenants' objections. But it was soon found that maintenance costs were as high as in bigger blocks, while the flats remained unpopular with their occupants. From 1954, therefore, the City Council started to build two-storey maisonettes in blocks of four storeys, and for a time these proved to be much more popular.[4] At the end of the decade, the bulk of the accommodation being built to house the average family was in the form of four-storey blocks of maisonettes. They were also being grouped in taller blocks, where one of their many advantages was that they reduced the cost of providing lifts.[5]

Meanwhile, major changes were being made in the internal and structural design of municipal residential buildings. There had been signs during the war that the new interest in neighbourhood planning would be accompanied by an improvement in the design of the dwelling units themselves. In Birmingham tenants were consulted for the first time, and in 1943 the Public Works Committee set up a committee of women, representing the wives of municipal tenants, to advise on the design of kitchens in post-war houses.[6] Birmingham was the first local authority to take such an initiative. Meanwhile the Government encouraged better standards with a series of building and design manuals published in 1944 by the Ministries of Housing and Works. The Dudley Report of the same year further strengthened the case for better design. Local authorities began to plan more space within their houses, to increase storage capacity, and to include upstairs bathrooms. There was also a trend, reinforced after the war by the labour shortage,

[1] See 'Low density housing: Sheldon Hall Estate, Birmingham', *Architect and Building News*, vol. ccix, no. 26, 28 June 1956, p. 732.

[2] See, for instance, A. G. Sheppard Fidler, 'Slum clearance and redevelopment from the design and economic point of view', paper given to the Town Planning Summer School, Oxford University, 4 September 1957 (notes communicated by A. G. Sheppard Fidler).

[3] *Y.B.*, no. 177, October 1962, p. 4. This estate was awarded a Ministry of Housing gold medal in 1966.

[4] *E.D.*, 11 June 1954.

[5] A. G. Sheppard Fidler, 'The New Birmingham', talk to Birmingham Council of Christian Churches, 30 November 1961 (text communicated by A. G. Sheppard Fidler).

[6] 'A post-war kitchen', *Town and Country Planning*, vol. xi, 1943, p. 29.

towards greater prefabrication, and the incorporation into traditional houses of whole kitchen and bathroom units completed off the site.[1]

Birmingham, with its unusually severe labour problems, at first moved further in this direction than most authorities, although the City Council expressed a marked preference for traditional houses (i.e. built of bricks and mortar) in normal circumstances.[2] The Public Works Department designed a steel-framed house, known popularly as the 'Manzoni', which could be covered with a variety of materials. The first houses of this type were erected, as an experiment, as early as 1944.[3] Other experimental houses were erected by private contractors. Within a few years of the end of the war the Council began to lose interest in these experiments, although it continued to develop the prefabrication of internal units. The Labour group had a marked preference for traditional methods, for prefabrication seemed to them to imply a degree of impermanency. In 1946 most of the experimental house designs were dropped, and a big programme of traditional building was approved. Not only did this decision slow down the building rate, but it discouraged further attempts at originality by the contractors and the Public Works Department.[4] For the time being design refinements had to be sacrificed to catching up on the backlog of building. One important casualty of this period of retrenchment was the Shard End district heating scheme, abandoned because of its high cost to tenants only a few months after powers had been obtained to establish it in the Corporation Act of 1948. The *Architectural Review* took no interest in any Birmingham municipal housing project from the end of the war until as late as 1954, when the twelve-storey blocks in Duddeston and Nechells received some attention.[5]

It took a change of majority in the City Council in 1949 to bring a little more variety into housing design. The introduction of big, national contractors into Birmingham revived the situation which had existed at the end of the war, when much of the drive towards innovation

[1] 'Towards an architecture: post-war housing in Britain', *Architectural Review*, vol. civ, July–December 1948, p. 179.

[2] B.C.C., *Pro.*, 6 February 1945, p. 118 (Public Works Committee).

[3] 'Birmingham experimental houses', *Architect and Building News*, vol. clxxviii, 19 May 1944, pp. 108–10. Similar experiments had been made after the First World War to accelerate house-building, with the same transitory results.

[4] For one explanation of the reasons for local authority conservatism in house building, see 'Towards an architecture', p. 188: 'The architect to the local authority is generally faced with the difficulty of having to satisfy a client who has little idea of good contemporary design, a client who, furthermore, is afraid of criticism by the even less enlightened mass of electors.' This decline of interest in industrial building methods was common to most local authorities in the late 1940s and early 1950s. See e.g. Anthony Jackson, *The Politics of Architecture: A History of Modern Architecture in Britain* (1970), pp. 169, 196.

[5] *Architectural Review*, vol. cxv, January–June 1954, p. 342.

had come from the builders. At first they had little opportunity to innovate, because priority was given to rapid building, but when the City Architect was appointed they were given every encouragement to cooperate in the design process. The City Council now realized that a more experimental approach could lead to reduced costs as well as higher standards.[1] The contractors were delighted because they hoped that designs tested in so influential a city as Birmingham would be adopted by other local authorities. At first, shortages of materials, especially steel, limited freedom to experiment,[2] but these difficulties eased considerably by the mid-1950s. For a time the contractors' biggest contribution was in developing new construction methods. One early experiment was in the 'lift-slab' method of building multi-storey flats. But soon close collaboration was established in the internal design of buildings. The City Architect's Department approached the builders to find out what they would build most easily and cheaply, and then designed dwellings to fit in with the builders' guidelines. This subordination of plan to structure[3] was accentuated in the 1950s and early 1960s as more and more prefabricated elements went into building. Gradually, the role of the Architect's Department in the design of many buildings was subordinated to that of the contractors' own architectural staffs. By the early 1960s the department was concentrating on layouts and special buildings; most blocks of dwellings were designed entirely by the contractors.[4] This trend was confirmed when the Corporation began to allow the introduction of industrialized building techniques. The financial saving was, of course, very great. On the other hand, architectural variety was sacrificed, both within the city, where most of the blocks built in the late 1950s and 1960s corresponded to no more than three or four basic designs, and also in comparison with other towns, where the same contractors were building to the same standard designs. Consequently, Birmingham's housing programme, unlike Sheffield's, attracted little attention for its architecture.

[1] For a graph showing increases in building costs between 1939 and 1954, see B.C.C., *Pro.*, 1954–5, p. 791.

[2] See e.g. a description of six-storey flats at Rubery which had to be built in load-bearing brick, in order to save steel ('Flats: Birmingham', *Architectural Review*, vol. cxv, January–June 1954, pp. 62–6).

[3] See, for instance, 'Birmingham puts structure before plan', *Architect's Journal*, vol. cxxiii, no. 3181, 16 February 1956, pp. 205–7; 'A new design principle for multi-storey flats, Birmingham', *Architect and Building News*, vol. ccix, no. 20, 17 May 1956, pp. 539–41; 'Flats at Birmingham', *Architect and Building News*, vol. ccxx, no. 16, 18 October 1961, pp. 583–8.

[4] There were, however, a number of important exceptions where multi-storey flats and other dwellings were designed by the City Architect's Department. Among them were the much praised Chamberlain Gardens, Primrose Hill, and Metchley Grange schemes, all completed in the 1960s. See e.g. *Architect and Building News*, 28 September 1966.

Layout, on the other hand, was widely admired, especially from the late 1950s. For instance, the Kents Moat shopping centre, arranged around a pedestrian precinct (1957), the Lyndhurst estate, Erdington, one of Birmingham's best examples of mixed development to date (1958), and the Primrose Hill estate (1963), were all featured in the pages of the *Architectural Review*.[1] In few of these cases was attention focused on the buildings, but the layouts were highly commended.

The high standard of these estates was achieved despite the fundamental division of responsibility between the Public Works Department and the City Architect's Department. During the early years of the Architect's Department's independent existence there had been few disagreements, particularly as the Public Works Committee was happy to concede the major responsibility for the planning of new estates to the City Architect. Yet there was always the possibility of trouble. The City Engineer, Herbert Manzoni, sometimes saw the City Architect as an unnecessary intruder, who had been foisted on him by a Council which did not appreciate the advantages of keeping all building, planning, and engineering under a single control. Sheppard Fidler, for his part, felt himself to be in an inferior position, in which his department's talents for planning were not fully utilized. Town planning of the city as a whole remained within the province of the Public Works Department, a situation to which the City Architect was totally opposed, and which he did his best to alter. But there was not much he could do to demonstrate his talent for planning outside lands owned or directly controlled by the Corporation. And as time went on, he felt that even here he was baulked by a Public Works Department, which, in his view, was behind the times in planning matters.

This potentially explosive situation finally blew up between 1960 and 1964. The purchase of Castle Bromwich airfield gave the Corporation its first opportunity for well over a decade to demonstrate what it could do with a really large area. However, the site presented severe constructional problems, and because it was totally flat and treeless, it contrasted strongly with those estates, rich in landscape features, on which Sheppard Fidler had done his best work.[2] The Public Works Department layout for the estate,[3] drawn up in 1960–1, divided it into nine irregularly shaped residential areas, separated by narrow strips of open space, with a winding dual-carriageway road running through the whole site from south-west to north-east. The plan also included a large shopping centre close to a big roundabout at the junction of Chester

[1] *Architectural Review*, vol. cxxi, January–June 1957, p. 18; vol. cxxiii, January–June 1958, p. 76; vol. cxxxiii, January–June 1963, pp. 40–1.

[2] See 'Birmingham: new residential area', *Architect's Journal*, vol. cxl, no. 5, 29 July 1964, p. 259.

[3] City of Birmingham, 'Castle Bromwich Airfield' (plan) (B.R.L. 662202).

Road and Kingsbury Road, at the west end of the site. This non-geometrical layout was clearly intended to combat the potential visual boredom of the flat site; the *Architect's Journal* called it 'a sort of miniature garden city effect with shops by the roundabout'.[1] At this stage, however, the House Building Committee, advised by the City Architect, took exception to the proposed plans. It criticized the layout of the residential areas, the planning of the major routes, and the siting of the shopping centre. Eventually, in November 1962, the chairman of the Public Works Committee, Alderman D. E. S. Thomas, felt it necessary to write an open letter to the chairman of the House Building Committee, Councillor Ernest Bond, pointing out that zoning was the responsibility of the Public Works Department.[2] In March 1963 a compromise plan was agreed by the two committees. The shopping centre was moved away from the roundabout and linked to a central spine of tall blocks of flats which ran from west to east across the site. Low-density areas consisting mainly of two-storey houses were sited to the north and south of this spine. In the southern section of the site were located more flats and a large area of open space. The main differences from the Public Works Department scheme were that the non-geometrical layout was abandoned, high-density areas were clearly separated from those of low density, the shopping centre was sited further away from the main roads, and most of the open space was no longer distributed in narrow strips between residential areas. The *Architect's Journal* thought that the compromise scheme was a great improvement, and that most of the credit for it should go to Sheppard Fidler. It also expressed amazement that planning functions should, in so important a city as Birmingham, be divided between two departments, and that the House Building Committee should have to tell the Public Works Committee how to do its job.[3]

This victory encouraged Sheppard Fidler to push forward his claims for control of all town planning throughout the city. However, after the Castle Vale episode the chairmen of the committees responsible for housing set up a liaison procedure which avoided further confrontations. Further, a planning advisory panel composed of the four interested chief officers was set up in 1963 to study general planning policy, and from 1966 the panel occasionally co-opted outside experts for special tasks.[4] So it seemed that all was well again, and Sheppard Fidler's claims were rejected by the Labour group early in 1964. Shortly after, he resigned and went into private practice.

After Sheppard Fidler's departure there was at first no fundamental change in the planning and design policies which had been worked out in association with the Public Works Department over the previous

[1] 'Birmingham: new residential area', p. 262.   [2] Ibid.   [3] Ibid.
[4] *T.B.*, no. 187, August–September 1963, p. 2; no. 216, April 1966, p. 1.

decade. But major pressure for change was steadily building up owing to increasing opposition among tenants to multi-storey flats. The proportion of dwellings completed in buildings of three storeys or more rose from 3·69 per cent in 1951 to 75 per cent in 1957. By this time the Council's policy was to provide 30 per cent of all housing in multi-storey blocks, with the balance in four-storey maisonettes, and a few houses and bungalows for large families and old people. Since 1945 very little had been heard of the Birmingham citizens' 'natural aversion to flats', but in the late 1950s a new reaction took place against them. Pre-war objections to flats had been based mainly on prejudice, but those which were expressed with increasing vehemence in the 1950s reflected the experience of Birmingham's growing army of flat-dwellers. Much of their dissatisfaction reflected more general defects of municipal housing, such as the lack of social facilities on the new estates, the high cost of living, distance from places of work, or the inevitable transfer of housing register applicants to areas which were totally unknown to them. But discontent seemed to crystallize around the flats, especially on the suburban estates. The tenants voiced their complaints in the press, and at Labour Party ward meetings and municipal policy conferences. They were supported by a growing body of informed opinion which was worried by the social implications of flat life. The most vociferous critic of Birmingham flats was the university lecturer and prophet of the new town, Dr. David Eversley, whom we last met during his attempt to thwart the City Council at the Wythall inquiry.[1] In 1957 Eversley began to publish a series of readable articles on Birmingham planning in the *Evening Mail*. Very little of what he had to say was at all complimentary to the Corporation, and one of his main targets was the municipal flat-building policy. Not only were flats expensive and bad from a social point of view, he suggested, but Birmingham's flats were worse than most because they were so badly designed.[2]

By now, council members and officials did not need Eversley to tell them that people did not like flats. In 1958 the Housing Manager, John P. Macey, admitted that at least 80 per cent of Birmingham flat-dwellers disliked their homes. Moreover, they were still more expensive than houses in terms of both capital and maintenance costs.[3] For the time being, however, the proportion of flats built could not

[1] See above, p. 145.   [2] See e.g. *B.M.*, 20 March 1957.

[3] John P. Macey, 'Problems of flat life', paper read at the Public Works and Municipal Services Congress, 12 November 1958. The average cost per dwelling in 1960 for blocks of over six storeys was £2,800; for buildings of three storeys and less it was £2,100. The nature of the subsoil made flats even more expensive to build in Birmingham than in most places (Long, *The Wythall Inquiry*, p. 14n; M. C. Madeley, 'A New Town for the Midlands', *Town and Country Planning*, vol. xxiv, no. 144, April 1956, p. 201).

be reduced, as there were so many in the pipeline, and it even rose still further to a peak of 84·86 per cent in 1961. But the Corporation managed to reduce the number of very high blocks built from the early 1960s. After 1961 the proportion of flats built began to drop, and by 1963 it had fallen to 62·20 per cent. The reduction was due partly to the growing shortage of sites on which high blocks could be built, though a high proportion of houses was planned for the huge Castle Bromwich airfield site.[1] However, the proportion of flats built rose again to 77·08 per cent in 1965, mainly because most of the sites still available were in the central areas, where high densities were essential and had rarely been questioned by the public.

After 1965 the proportion of flats built began to fall steadily. The granting of permission to build at Water Orton (Chelmsley Wood), and the strong possibility of more land to come, greatly eased the pressure on sites.[2] Secondly, changes in housing subsidies introduced by the Labour Government increased the financial unattractiveness of flats, which had previously been encouraged by the central Government to prevent wastage of land. Thirdly, Birmingham Corporation, in advance of most authorities, perfected methods of achieving high densities with low-rise housing alone. Plans for the Chelmsley Wood estate, finalized in the summer of 1965, included only 10 to 15 per cent of dwellings in tall blocks. This proportion was maintained in developments approved by the Council after the Conservatives took control in May 1966. As Birmingham's housing shortage eased in the later 1960s, many prospective municipal tenants became harder to please, and it was recognized that the main (or, perhaps, the only) attraction of the remote new peripheral estates was their high proportion of houses. In 1969 the chairman of the Housing Committee, Alderman Dark, went so far as to announce that no more multi-storey flats would be planned in Birmingham. Although it was clear that the occasional tall block would continue to be built, especially in the city centre, it seemed probable in the early 1970s that Birmingham's multi-storey flat-building days were over.

So the wheel had come full circle, and the Corporation was again building a predominance of two-storey houses, most of them in long terraces. But this was no step into the past. In the first place, Birmingham was now providing its citizens with the type of housing that they clearly preferred. Secondly, design standards continued to improve, and were adapted to the new demands and opportunities of low-rise housing.

One of the factors contributing to Sheppard Fidler's resignation in 1964 had been a growing lack of confidence among the leaders of the

[1] *Y.B.*, no. 190, December 1963, p. 3. Only 25 per cent of the dwellings at Castle Vale were to be in tall blocks.

[2] See above, p. 150.

Labour group in his department's ability to produce houses in sufficient numbers. The long delay in the development of Castle Bromwich airfield had done nothing to dispel these doubts. The quality of Sheppard Fidler's work was not in question, but it was clear that the new City Architect would be expected to produce quantity as well. This double requirement was increasingly satisfied by Sheppard Fidler's two successors. J. R. Sheridan Shedden, who was appointed City Architect in July 1964, played a key part in the big increase in the building rate which began in that year. In particular, he pushed ahead with building on the Castle Vale (Castle Bromwich airfield) site which, once under way, gave the municipal housing and design machine the impetus that it needed. After his death in the spring of 1966 his deputy, J. A. Maudsley, was appointed to succeed him as City Architect.

From then on, until the end of the decade, the department was greatly expanded. The number of staff employed rose from about two hundred in 1964 to more than double that number in the early 1970s. Landscape architecture, which had first been introduced into the department in 1958, was greatly expanded, and Maudsley established it as a separate branch within the department.[1] Experiments with a variety of building methods, materials, and house types were continued and extended. Close contacts were developed with the building contractors, allowing a big increase in productivity.[2] The quality of design also remained very high, and in some respects was substantially improved. This progress was reflected in the award of four Ministry of Housing gold medals for design in the later 1960s, and more followed in the early years of the next decade. Design of special buildings also developed and many attracted national attention; for instance, old and disabled people's housing.[3]

The department's interest in environmental planning continued to develop. Maudsley greatly increased the number of qualified architectural planners—men capable of designing both layouts and individual buildings. The Chelmsley Wood out-city estate, which eventually housed some 50,000 people, offered even more opportunities than Castle Vale for the development of an integrated community. The City Architect's work here was rewarded by a Ministry of Housing award in 1970.[4] More award-winning design work was carried on in the civic centre,[5] and the department also undertook planning for nearby towns such as Meriden and Tamworth. The preliminary planning survey for the proposed National Exhibition Centre was the work

[1] For some results, see 'Three landscaping schemes', *Building*, 2 April 1971, pp. 55–9.
[2] See e.g. National Building Agency, *Housing Productivity in Birmingham* (1969).
[3] See *Municipal Engineering*, 26 August 1970, p. 1749.
[4] See ' "Good design in housing" award', *Concrete Quarterly*, January–March 1971, pp. 26–8.
[5] See below, pp. 449–55.

of the City Architect,[1] and the department developed an interest in the recreational use of land adjacent to canals and under urban motorways. Although the fundamental division of planning responsibilities between the Public Works Department and the City Architect still raised occasional difficulties and tensions, the two departments worked well together, as was evidenced by the big improvement in environmental design standards in Birmingham by the later 1960s.

Town Planning

Although the Corporation of Birmingham was the first local authority to prepare a town planning scheme under the 1909 Act, and completed plans for all the suburban areas between the wars, like other cities it had not prepared a scheme for the central districts before 1939. It had been argued, to justify this omission, that too many interests would be disturbed for such a plan to be practicable under current legislation. But the problem had to be faced sooner or later, and in 1939 the City Council decided to prepare a town planning scheme for the central areas.[2] The task was facilitated by the Town and Country Planning (Interim Development) Act of 1943 which gave the Corporation planning control over all developments in areas not covered by existing planning schemes.[3]

By this time, the Public Works Committee had reached an advanced stage in planning a major scheme which would radically alter the city centre—the inner ring road. Its report to the City Council in July 1943 on the planning of the city centre was based on this ring road, which it hoped would extend Birmingham's cramped central business district, and bring about the redevelopment of much of the rest of the area under the Corporation's control. To this end, the Corporation would acquire extensive frontage sites along the road.[4] Extensive land purchase had been a feature of the improvement scheme for Corporation Street in the 1870s, and had not only allowed the Corporation to recoup much of the cost of the scheme, but had given it power to direct the building of a high-class shopping and business area.[5] The City had retained the freehold of all the Corporation Street land, and with the addition of sites along the inner ring road it would be able to control the evolution of most of the city centre. So the City Council decided, on the advice of the City Engineer, that it would be superfluous to prepare an overall plan for the central business district. In any case, very little building was done in the city centre until the relaxation of building restrictions in 1954. The area had not suffered concentrated

---

[1] See J. A. Maudsley, *National Exhibition Centre: An Appraisal* (1970).
[2] B.C.C., *Pro.*, 4 July 1939, p. 802 (Public Works Committee).
[3] Black, p. 375.
[4] B.C.C., *Pro.*, 6 July 1943, pp. 418–27 (Public Works Committee).
[5] See Briggs, pp. 77–82.

bomb damage, and so did not qualify for special Government approval for replacement shopping and office developments, as did cities like Coventry and Plymouth. So, above all, the Corporation wanted to avoid discouraging developers by laying down a rigid planning scheme; it preferred to attract them to Birmingham by the implied offer of freedom to build what they liked, and then to persuade them to introduce modifications into their schemes.[1] When work began on the inner ring road in 1957, and building sites were cleared along it, it was even more important to the City to encourage the developers. Left idle, the land would have involved the ratepayer in heavy loss. But once a developer's interest could be aroused in a site, he would often agree to extend the area of Corporation freehold land by acquiring adjacent privately-owned sites and passing them over to the Corporation. In return, he would receive a lease of the enlarged area. To reach such agreements the Corporation needed a very great flexibility of approach, and the existence of a three-dimensional plan for the city centre would almost certainly have ruled them out completely.

Apart from the blitzed Big Top site, which was rebuilt from 1954, the first major developments in the city centre were on inner ring road sites. The first of these sites was leased in 1954, three years before work began on the road.[2] However, developers showed little interest in other inner ring road sites, even after it became clear in 1956 that road construction work would soon be starting. Although the city's shopping centre was very cramped, department stores and business interests were very reluctant to move outside it. The advertisement of three large sites on Smallbrook Ringway in 1957 produced a total of only three offers in nine months. However, one of the bidders, John Laing & Son, proposed the joint development of all three sites. The Public Works Committee saw the opportunity of an impressive architectural scheme, and decided to negotiate with Laing's. Apart from stipulating that retail shops should be let to nominees of the Corporation and that a hotel should be included, the Corporation made few demands on the developer.[3] The design of the buildings was largely dictated by the shape of the sites, which were long and of limited depth, but the Public Works Department was happy with the scheme prepared by James Roberts, a local architect. The result was a continuous frontage of five storeys running along the whole of the southern side of Smallbrook Ringway, and buildings of similar dimension and design on the north side. This arrangement resembled the type of frontage develop-

---

[1] Coventry's very different methods and results are described in Kenneth Richardson, *Twentieth-Century Coventry* (1972), pp. 277–309.

[2] This was a site in Smallbrook Street, leased to a firm whose existing site was needed for the new road.

[3] B.C.C., *Pro.*, 5 November 1957, pp. 510–11 (Public Works Committee).

ment which the Public Works Department had envisaged for the road just after the war. The creation of continuous shopping frontages, with façades of several storeys above, had also been recommended by the department as suitable for a major shopping street junction to the architects of the Big Top scheme, now complete. Although the Public Works Department's partiality for corridor streets later came in for criticism, Laing's proposals attracted very favourable attention in the press in 1958, and offers multiplied for other ring road sites.[1] The property boom was already beginning to spread from London to the provinces, and Birmingham, which had been Jack Cotton's original operating area, was the first provincial city to benefit, thanks to its size and prosperity.[2]

The City Council was now able to release parts of its Corporation Street estate, for which the original leases were beginning to fall in. As early as 1957 the Council had granted a ninety-nine-year lease of a large site bounded by Corporation Street, Old Square, Upper Priory, and Steelhouse Lane. The redevelopment of this area was particularly important because one of its frontages faced the planned Priory Ringway, on the traverse section of the inner ring road.[3] The second such lease, of a larger area in the block bounded by Corporation Street, Union Street, High Street, and Bull Street, was approved in 1958.[4] By careful negotiation, the Estates Department was able to bring about the development of the whole block, and to extend the Corporation's freehold interest to almost all of it. The Council decided to widen Union Street, and later, Bull Street, in conjunction with this development.[5]

Another big success in 1958 was an agreement to lease three interlinked sites near the Bull Ring and the Market Hall to J.L.G. Investments Ltd. This was a local concern headed by Jo Godfrey, a developer who had worked closely with Laing's on Smallbrook Ringway. The scheme was a classic example of the Corporation's willingness to listen to developers' proposals without any preconceived ideas. The Public Works Committee had originally advertised a site at the junction of Moor Street and the Bull Ring for the construction of a multi-storey car park, with some shops and offices. Only two firm offers were received, but one of them, from J.L.G. Investments, went much further than the committee had envisaged. J.L.G. were worried that the site was too far away from the central shopping district, even though the

---

[1] Oliver Marriott, *The Property Boom* (1967), pp. 223–4.

[2] See Marriott, *The Property Boom*. The Birmingham-born Jack Cotton was, with Charles Clore, Britain's best-known property developer in the late 1950s and early 1960s.

[3] See above, p. 401.

[4] B.C.C., *Pro.*, 22 July 1958, pp. 376–8 (Estates Committee).

[5] B.C.C., *Pro.*, 22 July 1958, p. 435; 9 June 1964, p. 79 (Public Works Committee).

Public Works Committee planned to build a pedestrian subway under the new roundabout on the ring road, to link the site with the open-air market in the middle of the roundabout, and further on, with High Street and New Street. So J.L.G. asked for a ninety-nine-year lease (instead of the normal seventy-five-year lease which had until recently been the Corporation's maximum), permission to erect shops in the subway, the lease of part of the open-air market for the erection of more shops, and the lease (also for ninety-nine years) of a site at the western exit of the subway bounded by High Street, New Street, Worcester Street, and the inner ring road. The City Council agreed to these proposals, but stipulated in return that the developer should build a hotel on the westernmost site, or on one of the sites in Smallbrook Ringway.[1] The final agreement also required the developer to build a circular tower block of not less than twelve storeys on the New Street site. But the main innovations had been introduced by the developer; not only had the Corporation not previously considered putting shops in subways, but the new scheme substantially influenced the development of the rest of the Bull Ring. In fact, the Public Works Committee had to make an urgent call for a conference of interested committees to discuss the future of the whole area after the agreement with J.L.G. Investments had been finalized. The major decision taken at the conference, in November 1958, was to demolish the century-old Market Hall so that a much broader area would become available for redevelopment.[2]

The developers' hesitancy to undertake schemes in Birmingham was replaced by a mood of optimism as the property boom of the 1950s reached its height. But the developers who had shown faith in the Corporation a few years earlier, and who had worked with it on the first ringway developments, had a great advantage over their rivals. They and their architects had developed close contacts with the chairmen and members of interested committees, especially the Public Works Committee. This situation was responsible for some of the confusion that grew up over the development of the rest of the Bull Ring area.

Soon after the decision to demolish the Market Hall, the architect James Roberts, and the developer Jo Godfrey, approached the Public Works Committee with a scheme for a multi-level shopping centre, retail market, car park, offices, and bus station. The committee was delighted with these proposals, and approved them in principle in January 1959—the City Council was told that the development would be 'on a capital city scale'.[3] But complications arose. The chairman of the

---

[1] B.C.C., *Pro.*, 4 November 1958, pp. 651–67 (Public Works Committee).

[2] B.C.C., *Pro.*, 6 January 1959, p. 777 (Public Works Committee).

[3] B.C.C., *Pro.*, 10 March 1959, p. 963 (Public Works Committee).

committee, Frank Price, suddenly resigned in February 1959, on ground of pressure of work, before the financial details of the Bull Ring scheme had been fixed. His successor, Councillor D. E. S. Thomas, a firm supporter of the Godfrey–Roberts scheme, was scarcely in the saddle when he was faced by the opposition of the Estates Officer, R. F. H. Ross, to the financial arrangements proposed by the developers. Ross pointed out that the ground-rent offered was much too low, and when Godfrey refused to increase it, the Public Works Committee decided to withdraw from the negotiations. Meanwhile, in July 1959, the Council had established the principle, on the General Purposes Committee's recommendation, that leases of city-centre sites should normally be advertised, not negotiated.[1] When the Bull Ring site was advertised, eleven offers were received, some of them substantially more favourable than Godfrey's. But the Public Works Committee was more concerned to obtain a satisfactory development by a reliable developer than to squeeze the last drop of blood out of the site. Consequently, it accepted an offer of £110,500 gross per year—not the highest offer—from the Laing Investment Co.[2] The firm produced a scheme somewhat similar to James Roberts's, though by a different architect, and work began in the early summer of 1961. The Bull Ring Centre, one of the most advanced and successful indoor shopping centres in Britain, opened its doors towards the end of 1964.

Meanwhile, many sites had been let along other sections of the inner ring road and in the Corporation Street area. One of the Corporation's biggest successes was to negotiate the inclusion of another hotel in a development on Snow Hill Ringway in 1962.[3] But it had its failures too; one of the most disappointing was the long series of abortive attempts to negotiate the construction of a theatre in Smallbrook Ringway.[4] Then, in early 1965, the local property boom came to an end when the Labour Government's ban on new office building was extended from London to Birmingham.[5] Several schemes were completely dropped—notably an ambitious project for the redevelopment of the whole of the southern end of Corporation Street. But this relaxation of pressure on city-centre land allowed the Public Works Committee to formulate a new policy of including residential development wherever possible in central schemes, either by arrangement with private developers or by the building of municipal flats. Demand for sites began to increase again from about 1967, as Government restrictions were relaxed, and developers sought to take advantage of the City

[1] B.C.C., *Pro.*, 21 July 1959, pp. 214–15 (General Purposes Committee).
[2] B.C.C., *Pro.*, 2 February 1960, pp. 767–9 (Public Works Committee).
[3] B.C.C., *Pro.*, 9 January 1962, pp. 673–6 (Public Works Committee).
[4] See above, pp. 303 ff.
[5] Marriott, *The Property Boom*, p. 183.

Council's new willingness, under its Conservative majority, to sell the freehold of Corporation sites wherever it was possible to do so without prejudicing future redevelopment of the city centre. The glut of shops and offices which had already grown up in the city centre by 1964 was accentuated, but developers were confident that in the long run the expansion of the regional economy would lead to the occupation of all the vacant space.

From the point of view of the volume of new building, the Corporation's flexible attitude towards developers had been completely vindicated by the end of the 1960s. Far more of the city centre had been rebuilt than in other big provincial cities like Manchester, Liverpool, Leeds, and Glasgow.[1] There can be no doubt that Birmingham's prosperity, and the shortage of shops and offices in the cramped city centre after the war, had been largely responsible for the property boom. But the Corporation's willingness to help the developers as far as was possible without compromising essential planning standards had been a very important influence. However, given this order of priorities, it was inevitable that the quality of development should come in for criticism from outside the City Council.

Some of the strongest attacks were made by Leslie Ginsburg, director of the Birmingham School of Planning. In 1959, for instance, he strongly criticized frontage-development along the inner ring road, Birmingham's failure to impose plot ratios on developers in order to leave more space free at ground level, the lack of an overall plan for the city centre, and the priority accorded to the needs of traffic.[2] Ian Nairn joined in with criticism of Birmingham's pedestrian congestion, which led to 'pedestrian traffic jams' controlled by policemen on Saturdays, and which resulted partly from the Corporation's policy of retaining existing shopping frontages in all new developments.[3] Implied criticism also came, towards the end of the 1950s, from the City Architect, A. G. Sheppard Fidler, who was consulted on the architectural aspects of city-centre development schemes only after their principal design features had been agreed by the Public Works Department. For instance, Sheppard Fidler told the Birmingham Rotary Club in July 1959 that it was necessary to create a landscape by the use of trees and open spaces in city centres.[4] This view implied a measure of conflict with the Public Works Department's willingness to help the developer obtain a very large area of rentable floor space. In the same

[1] See plans in M. B. Stedman, 'Birmingham builds a model city', *Geographical Magazine*, vol. xl, no. 16, August 1968, pp. 1388–9.

[2] Leslie B. Ginsburg, 'The Birmingham Ring Road: town planning or road building?', *Architect's Journal*, vol. cxxx, no. 3363, 1 October 1959, pp. 288–94.

[3] Ian Nairn, 'Birmingham: Liverpool: Manchester', *Architectural Review*, vol. cxxviii, July–December 1960, pp. 114–15.

[4] Notes communicated by A. G. Sheppard Fidler.

year Sheppard Fidler launched an even stronger attack at the Conference of the Royal Society of Health, when he criticized the crowding of buildings into the main thoroughfares, and stressed the importance of pedestrian precincts.[1] He also called for the construction of a few towers in the city centre to add variety to the skyline.

To some extent the features recommended by Sheppard Fidler and others were included in schemes approved in the 1960s, but the Public Works Department still held out against the preparation of a master-plan for the city centre.[2] One of the main opponents of this proposal was the City Engineer, Sir Herbert Manzoni, who was distrustful of master-plans because they were often obsolete by the time they were put into effect. There was much to be said in defence of this point of view, yet close cooperation with the City Architect's Department might well have produced a coordinated architectural scheme for the city centre without excessive loss of flexibility. But this cooperation was lacking; the City Architect was not consulted about the overall planning of the city centre, and was not normally allowed even to vet the developers' individual proposals. Further difficulties arose from the division of responsibility for redevelopment between the Public Works Committee, which handled the leasing of inner ring road sites, and the Estates Committee, which looked after sites in Corporation Street and other lands previously owned by the Corporation.

However, despite its obvious defects, there was more to be said in defence of the new city centre than most of its detractors were prepared to admit. Many hard words were said about the forcing of pedestrians under the new roads, but warm and dry subways were preferable to elevated walkways and bridges like those on London Wall, so vulnerable to sweeping blasts of wind and rain. Above all, the association of central redevelopment with a road building scheme ensured rapid progress. Mistakes were certainly made in Birmingham, but by 1970 it possessed a city centre which was without question the most modern in Britain. Redevelopment led, it is true, to the disappearance of many small, specialist shops, and of some of the best-loved corners of old Birmingham. But without redevelopment Birmingham would have retained a cramped, dirty, overcrowded, inconvenient, and ugly centre, which had been recognized as totally inadequate long before the war.

Many critics of city-centre planning failed to recognize that the Corporation had prepared a master-plan for part at least of the central area—that reserved for the new Civic Centre. But the history of this project helps to explain why Sir Herbert Manzoni had such a low

---

[1] A. G. Sheppard Fidler, 'The redevelopment of urban centres'. Paper given to the Conference of the Royal Society of Health, April 1959, pp. 3–4.

[2] See also John Tetlow and Anthony Goss, *Homes, Towns and Traffic* (1965), p. 175.

opinion of master-plans. Indeed, the progress of the Civic Centre scheme, which lay entirely in municipal hands, makes an interesting contrast with the dynamic development of the rest of the centre by private enterprise.

The Civic Centre

One of the products of the renewed spirit of municipal enterprise which developed during the First World War was the decision, made shortly after the armistice, to build a Civic Centre for municipal offices and public buildings. The Council's choice fell on a large site lying to the west of Easy Row and fronting on Broad Street, near the Town Hall and Council House. From 1919 the Corporation began to buy up property in the area. There were hopes that an early start could be made, at least on new municipal offices. No further extension of the Council House was possible, and several departments were already housed in rented accommodation throughout the city centre.

In 1926 the City Council organized an open competition to obtain the best possible layout for the Civic Centre. Architectural competitions had been frequent in Birmingham since the success of the contest that had produced a design for the Town Hall in the 1830s, and they had generally produced satisfactory results. Indeed, this new competition was a great success in that it attracted entries from several countries, and that of the first prizewinner, Maximilian Romanoff of Paris, was generally agreed to be a magnificent conception. But when the General Purposes Committee came to study Romanoff's scheme in detail it decided that it was far too ambitious for a provincial city, as were the other winning designs. Finally, the City Engineer was asked to prepare a more modest scheme in consultation with James Swan, one of the competitors, and S. N. Cooke, a Birmingham architect whose Hall of Memory had already been built within the area in 1923-4. The resulting layout was approved by the City Council in 1934, together with a plan to acquire the whole area by compulsory purchase, and build a first block of municipal offices. In the following year another open competition was held—restricted this time to British architects—to obtain suitable building designs. The winner was the Nottingham architect, T. Cecil Howitt, who was engaged as architect for the first part of the scheme, a municipal office block. The City Council decided to make a start on building in 1936, and the new block, known later as Baskerville House, was ready for occupation early in 1940.[1]

Progress on the Civic Centre had been slow because of national economic difficulties and the Council's reluctance to sanction expenditure

[1] J. T. Jones, *History of the Corporation of Birmingham*, vol. v, pp. 570–4; N. Pevsner and A. Wedgewood, *The Buildings of England: Warwickshire* (1966), pp. 115–16.

on an expensive scheme which was mainly of amenity value. It was not by chance that the only section to be completed, apart from the Hall of Memory and its balancing colonnade, was a municipal office building, which was urgently needed. This slow progress, which was to become even slower after the Second World War, had two unfortunate results. One was that the City Council became so accustomed to not getting anywhere that it lost all sense of urgency. And the other was that the 1934 master-plan, based on a vast square surrounded by monolithic buildings, grew increasingly anachronistic.[1]

Despite previous disappointments, the City Council's hopes in the future of the Civic Centre were revived during the Second World War. In 1944 it approved a scheme for a central parade ground of over eleven acres, with a setting of formal gardens, prepared by another architect, William Haywood. Around the square would stand more offices, a city hall and two smaller halls, a planetarium and colonnade, and buildings suitable for use as a library, museum, or art gallery. All the buildings would maintain the style and scale of the block of offices that had already been built. In the middle of the square would rise a 140-foot civic column, on top of which would stand a sculpture 'intended to symbolize the traditional energy of the city in the form of a smith, carrying a wrought disc upon which would be shown in relief a mother and child standing against an oak tree to signify the rebirth of art in association with natural beauty.' This whole scheme had grown to look like an ancient monument by the late 1950s, but when approved it was fully in line with the Beaux Arts leanings of most British architects and town planners. And the central parade ground, with standing room for 12,000 people, seemed an essential feature in view of the massive public meetings which had been held in Victoria Square during the war.[2]

Although the Council formally approved the scheme in 1945, no estimate was made of its cost, and it was understood that it would be completed in stages over a very long period. Surprisingly, perhaps, the element of the scheme on which the most progress was made in the 1940s was the preparation of the sculpture for the civic column. William Bloye was commissioned to prepare this group while he was working on a memorial to Boulton, Watt, and Murdock. This latter memorial was erected near the Civic Centre site in 1956, but a decision on the civic column was postponed from 1948 until the whole idea was dropped in the early 1950s.

Progress on the actual buildings of the Centre was non-existent, partly because the Corporation had not yet acquired the whole area,

[1] See Bryan Little, *Birmingham Buildings: The Architectural Story of a Midland City* (1971), p. 39.
[2] Black, pp. 571–9.

but mainly because alternative arrangements were made for offices. In 1947 the Council decided to acquire the shell of a private office block, Bush House, in Broad Street, the construction of which had been interrupted by the war.[1] By coincidence, this block lay on the western fringes of the Civic Centre area, so that in theory it could be incorporated into the scheme. In fact, however, it diverted the Council's energies away from building the Civic Centre, for if the Corporation did not build offices on the site it clearly would build nothing at all there in the foreseeable future. The advantages of buying Bush House were that it would be easy to obtain a building permit and materials for completion because all the structural steel work had already been erected, and little capital outlay was involved at a time when loan sanction for office schemes was hard to obtain. However, the necessary permits and sanctions were not received until about 1954, and it became necessary to make further temporary arrangements. In March 1948 the Council decided to transfer some activities to temporary single-storey buildings in the Bath Row redevelopment area.[2] In October of that year it decided to build new offices for the Estates Department at the corner of Summer Row and Lionel Street, but this scheme was held up until 1950 by failure to obtain a lease of the site from the Colmore Estate, and subsequently by building restrictions.[3] In 1954 the General Purposes Committee had second thoughts about the plan, and decided to complete Bush House first.[4] In fact, Bush House was not ready until 1956, and although it greatly eased the office shortage, so great a back-log had built up that the Council had to agree to rent more offices in private blocks in October 1959.[5] Further expedients of this nature were agreed in the 1960s.

Although the Council was unhappy about spreading Corporation offices all over the city centre, its early decisions to do so had the effect of committing it to a policy which increasingly diverted it from building the Civic Centre. After the civic column had been abandoned nothing was done until March 1955, when the General Purposes Committee asked the new City Architect to prepare yet another master-plan. Sheppard Fidler presented an outline scheme in 1958.[6] Its flexibility contrasted strongly with the rigid monumentality of earlier schemes— Sheppard Fidler called it 'prophetic'. He recognized that because the Civic Centre could not be built as a single operation, the old 'axial and monumental solution' was out of place. Instead, the overall design

[1] B.C.C., *Pro.*, 14 October 1947, p. 1096 (General Purposes Committee).

[2] B.C.C., *Pro.*, 9 March 1948, p. 185.

[3] B.C.C., *Pro.*, 12 October 1948, p. 966; 14 March 1950, pp. 1062–3 (General Purposes Committee).

[4] B.C.C., *Pro.*, 27 July 1954, pp. 266–7 (General Purposes Committee).

[5] B.C.C., *Pro.*, 6 October 1959, pp. 252–9 (General Purposes Committee).

[6] B.C.C., *Pro.*, 10 June 1958, pp. 60–79 (General Purposes Committee).

would have to be adaptable to the requirements and functions of each new building as and when it was built. The architecture should not be predetermined, to avoid building in an out-dated style. Sheppard Fidler's proposed layout replaced the big, central square by a pattern of interlocking spaces, separated by buildings of varying size and scale. This conception was very similar to his designs for mixed-development housing estates, in which he tried to create a sense of enclosure, which he considered to be a typical feature of Birmingham. Of the new Civic Centre, he said: 'We need variety and changing views, interest and drama—architecture in the service of man, not his master.' He also proposed certain new elements—the inclusion of shops and an exhibition hall in order to vary the functions of the area, and the incorporation of the surrounding canals to add to visual amenities in a city centre which suffered from its lack of open space.[1]

The Council approved Sheppard Fidler's master-plan, and the Civic Centre now seemed to be moving more rapidly to a point where construction could begin. This new impetus was provided in part by the elaboration of a plan for the new exhibition hall. This scheme emerged after the Birmingham Chamber of Commerce's decision to discontinue the engineering and hardware sections of the British Industries Fair at Castle Bromwich after 1957, owing to the problems raised by the closure of the London branch of the Fair in the previous year, and the withdrawal of Government financial support. The Fair had been used principally by medium and small firms which, unlike larger concerns, could not provide adequate show facilities on their own premises.[2] The Chamber of Commerce's regrets at having to close the Fair were almost exceeded by those of the Birmingham Trades Council, which feared that it would have a depressive effect on Midlands industry.[3] The Labour group in the City Council recognized that there was a general demand for exhibition facilities in the city centre, especially in view of the patent inadequacies of the antiquated, crumbling Bingley Hall. Being at the height of its power and optimism, the group confidently announced plans to build a new exhibition hall, as the next stage in the Civic Centre scheme, in 1957.[4] The Conservative group, aware of the demand for such facilities from Birmingham industrialists, gave its full support after receiving an assurance from Labour that municipal trading within the hall would be kept to an absolute minimum. In November 1958 the chairman of the General Purposes Committee, Alderman Watton, announced that Birmingham would seek parliamentary powers

---

[1] This element of the scheme had first been suggested by students of the Birmingham School of Architecture in 1950 (*B.M.*, 4 April 1950; 'A scheme for the centre of Birmingham', *Architectural Review*, vol. cix, January–June 1951, pp. 90–7).

[2] *Birmingham Chamber of Commerce Journal*, August 1951, p. 706.

[3] B.T.C., *Annual Report*, 1957–8, p. 14; 1958–9, p. 5.　　　　[4] *B.P.*, 9 May 1957.

to build the £1 million hall on a site to the south of Broad Street, close to the Civic Centre area. It would be, he said, the City's first priority among the new civic buildings for which it was seeking loan sanction. Although it would be the largest single building project undertaken by the City in over fifty years, it had an excellent chance of success. Alderman Watton even held out the prospect of world-title boxing matches in the new hall.[1] The City Council approved the new Corporation Bill later in the month,[2] and both the main parties united to defeat the efforts of Gregory Prescott's Birmingham Rate-payers' Alliance to have the Bill thrown out by the town's meeting. The Bill passed rapidly through Parliament, and the royal assent was obtained in July 1959. The Broad Street site was acquired in May 1960.[3] The second impetus to progress on the Civic Centre was the inclusion of four fourteen-storey blocks of municipal offices in the Sheppard Fidler scheme. The Council was told in October 1959 that one of them could be ready in four years, and construction of this first block (known as Block 36) was approved in principle in January 1960.[4]

It was, however, from early 1960 that enthusiasm for both these important elements in the Civic Centre scheme was slowly dissipated. The re-elected Conservative Government's severe deflationary measures included restrictions on capital expenditure by local authorities, so that an immediate start was out of the question. But a more fundamental and insidious cause of delay was the City Council's basic reluctance to undertake expensive capital projects without Government subsidy, especially at a time of high interest rates. This caution was accentuated by the Conservatives' attack on high municipal expenditure and rates, which reached a peak in the early 1960s, and forced the Labour group to introduce stringent economy measures. Labour had wanted to pay for civic centre developments like the exhibition hall out of the Corporation's capital fund, but the group's decision to keep the rates down prevented the making of adequate contributions to the fund out of revenue. The first project to suffer was Block 36. Its construction was postponed from year to year until its eventual abandonment in 1965 on ground of high cost (£1·5 million).[5] This decision rang the death-knell of the other office blocks in the Civic Centre.

The exhibition hall took longer to kill. A private developer's proposal to build the hall at no cost to the Corporation was turned down by the Labour group leaders in 1960 because the applicant wanted rent-free sites and development rights over a very wide area. Two years later the Council decided to build a municipal multi-storey car park on one

[1] *E.D.*, 11 November 1958.
[2] B.C.C., *Pro.*, 24 November 1958, pp. 681–3 (General Purposes Committee).
[3] B.C.C., *Pro.*, 24 May 1960, p. 16 (General Purposes Committee).
[4] B.C.C., *Pro.*, 6 October 1959, pp. 252–9; 5 January 1960, p. 600.
[5] B.C.C., *Pro.*, 27 July 1965, p. 263 (General Purposes Committee).

corner of the site in order to free the rest of the area, most of which was
occupied by an open-air car park.[1] In August 1963 the Corporation
announced that it hoped to make a start on the hall within the next
two years, but finance, it admitted, was still a problem.[2] In November
1963 an outline scheme was submitted to the City Council, and
approval in principle was given.[3] But by 1965 no definite decision
had been made on a start, and the Lord Mayor, Alderman Price,
publicly expressed concern about rumours that the hall might be
delayed. Alderman Watton described the rumours as 'ridiculous and
completely untrue', but he was unable to predict a starting date for
the hall.[4] By the time Labour lost power in May 1966 there had still
been no decision, and the Conservatives, who since the original vote in
1958 had been lukewarm about the hall because of its high cost, continued to let the matter slide. In 1968 they decided to lease the site
that had been acquired for the hall to Associated Television for a
broadcasting and entertainment centre. The Labour minority was
furious, but they had only themselves to blame for having postponed
a firm decision for so long. The Conservatives made attempts to find
an alternative site for the hall in the city centre, but these were abandoned as hopes were aroused that a new national exhibition centre
might be sited at Birmingham. Fortunately, this story had a happy
ending, for in 1970 the Corporation persuaded the Government to site
their new national exhibition centre on the outskirts of Birmingham,
instead of in London. Not only was this decision a great success for the
brilliant advocacy of Birmingham's case by Alderman Griffin and other
Conservative leaders,[5] but it also had a good chance of coming to
fruition because part of the funds needed were to be provided by the
Government (though a much heavier load fell on Birmingham Corporation).

These long years of frustration and indecision, if they did nothing
else, at least proved the City Architect's wisdom in recommending a
flexible scheme for the Civic Centre. By 1964 it had been decided to
incorporate a new School of Music, the Birmingham Athletic Institute,
a drama centre and accommodation for youth organizations, in addition
to the new central library which had been in the master-plan of 1958.
Changes also had to be made after the decision to build a tunnel for the
inner ring road under the eastern end of the site. So a new master-plan
was prepared by the City Architect, J. R. Sheridan Shedden, with
major buildings designed by John Madin and James Roberts. The

[1] B.C.C., *Pro.*, 9 October 1962, pp. 355–7 (Public Works Committee).
[2] *B.M.*, *B.P.*, 28 August 1963.
[3] B.C.C., *Pro.*, 5 November 1963, pp. 428–32 (General Purposes Committee).
[4] *B.M.*, 16 March 1965.
[5] See *Sunday Times*, 1 February 1970.

main change outside the eastern section of the area was the replacement of the four blocks of offices along the northern boundary by multi-storey flats.[1] The inclusion of flats at least seemed to ensure that *something* would be built in the Civic Centre in the following few years, and, indeed, all four towers were in occupation by 1969. The City Architect's Department combined their construction with an award-winning layout for a public promenade on the banks of the nearby canal.[2] Moreover, rapid progress on the inner ring road stimulated building work at the eastern end of the site, where the inadequate central library was due to be demolished to make way for the road-works. So in 1967 the Council approved the building of a new central library over the tunnel carrying the road, together with the adjoining buildings planned by John Madin. The transformation of the central section of the site began in the following year, and work also started on the new repertory theatre to the west. So by the end of the decade the Civic Centre was considerably more advanced than it had been when its main proponents, the Labour group, lost power in 1966. Much of the credit for pushing the project along at last must go to the inner ring road. There was no better example than this of how the association of road-building with amenity developments could accelerate their completion.

Wholesale markets

One of the main objects of the city centre strategy, based on the inner ring road, was to exclude industry and other activities which, it was considered, had no place there. The application of this principle raised special problems in the case of the markets. Birmingham's wholesale markets were grouped in a series of buildings dating from the late nineteenth century to the south-east of the central shopping district, near the Bull Ring. After the war the Public Works, and Markets and Fairs, Committees drew up a plan for a new market precinct, to be built on the extended site of the existing markets. But it was agreed that the abattoir and meat market should be transferred to Castle Bromwich, on the eastern outskirts of the city, because their recon-struction in the city centre would be difficult and would require 50 per cent more space. Furthermore, the committees felt that the abattoir was a potential cause of nuisance, and unsuitable to a modern city centre. A large site was acquired at Castle Bromwich in 1948, but building was held up by Government restrictions on capital expendi-ture, and uncertainty over the Government's policy on the wholesale meat trade and slaughtering.[3]

[1] B.C.C., *Pro.*, 27 July 1965, pp. 258–69 (General Purposes Committee).
[2] See 'Canal side development', *Building*, 10 July 1970, pp. 67–70.
[3] *Y.B.*, no. 20, July 1948, p. 4.

This delay, together with the abandonment of a contemplated Government scheme for regional slaughtering centres, had undermined the Markets and Fairs Committee's belief in the value of decentralization by 1953. In that year, it decided to improve slaughtering facilities at the existing abattoir in Bradford Street. However, in July 1954, Government control of slaughtering and distribution came to an end, and the committee found that contrary to their expectations, less work came the way of the Bradford Street abattoir.[1] In this situation, the Markets and Fairs Committee was even more doubtful about the move to Castle Bromwich, even though it was now under pressure from the Public Works Committee to make the transfer so that the future of the rest of the Castle Bromwich site could be decided, and city-centre redevelopment accelerated. So the Markets and Fairs Committee, after consulting the meat trades, made a decision—to remain in the city centre. It asked the Public Works Committee for a new market and abattoir in the planned market precinct, even though this would involve extending the area of the precinct from fourteen to twenty-two acres.

The Public Works Committee remained worried about the possible nuisance from the abattoir, the generation of extra traffic, and the cost of acquiring further land so near the city centre. So the Public Works Committee suggested that the meat market should remain in the centre, but that the abattoir should be built at Castle Bromwich. The Markets and Fairs Committee, with strong support from the meat traders, turned this proposal down flat, insisting that the two elements must be adjacent to each other. While the matter was still being discussed, the Salvage Committee was allocated part of the Castle Bromwich site for a refuse destructor, and the Medical Officer of Health came out strongly against siting the abattoir in its vicinity.

By the late 1950s this affair was building up into one of the acrimonious inter-committee disputes which characterized the last few years of Labour's period in power. The Public Works Committee sent a delegation to visit modern abattoirs at Fareham and Lisbon to see if they were obnoxious, and the delegation returned from Portugal with evidence that a modern slaughterhouse was not necessarily a cause of nuisance. However, a majority of the Public Works Committee was still in favour of moving the abattoir, if not the market, to the outskirts. A report stating this preference was made to the City Council in July 1960, but the chairman, Alderman D. E. S. Thomas, freely admitted that the committee was not unanimous and invited the Council to decide the issue. The chairman of the Markets and Fairs

[1] *E.D.*, 3 June 1954. The chairman, Councillor T. Payton, had expected that the increased demand after the ending of meat control would force the City Council to accelerate the building of an abattoir and market at Castle Bromwich.

Committee, Councillor Mrs. S. A. Smith,[1] moved the reference back, and a majority of the City Council supported her amendment.[2] After further discussion between the two committees it was agreed that both the abattoir and the meat market should be located within the market precinct, but this and other changes of plan now made it necessary to extend the precinct to twenty-seven acres, about twice the area envisaged when the Development Plan was drawn up in 1952.[3] When, in 1964, it was decided to designate the precinct as an area of comprehensive development, it was increased to just over twenty-eight acres in extent.[4]

Very little progress had been made on creating the new markets precinct by 1970. Like central markets in other cities, Birmingham's were so inconvenient and inaccessible that they did less and less business as time went on. So redevelopment was postponed because it was no longer urgent on ground of congestion, even though the existing buildings were clearly obsolete. Capital expenditure on the precinct was re-phased from 1963 at the request of the Priorities Committee in order to conform to 'a more realistic pattern of expenditure'.[5] With the benefit of hindsight, it is perhaps arguable that the original decision to retain the various wholesale markets in the city centre was a mistake.

The Calthorpe Estate

We have concentrated on the municipal role in town planning. But in one very important case a private interest was given an almost completely free hand to plan a whole district.[6] When the Public Works Committee began to prepare a Development Plan for Birmingham in 1947, it had to make a decision on the future of the Calthorpe Estate, Edgbaston. This was a large area (1,625 acres) of low-density middle-class housing and open space, the eastern fringes of which lay about one mile to the west of the city centre. Its open residential character had been preserved since the eighteenth century by restrictive clauses inserted by the Estate in all building leases, and as late as 1958 it had a gross population density of only five persons to the acre.[7] All industrial

---

[1] Not to be confused with Alderman Mrs. E. V. Smith, sometime chairman of the Education Committee.

[2] B.C.C., *Pro.*, 5 July 1960, pp. 223–32 (Public Works Committee).

[3] B.C.C., *Pro.*, 3 July 1962, pp. 212–13 (Public Works Committee); *Y.B.*, no. 177, October 1962, p. 3.

[4] B.C.C., *Pro.*, 4 February 1964, p. 771 (Public Works Committee).

[5] B.C.C., *Pro.*, 4 December 1962, p. 514 (Priorities Committee).

[6] The Bournville village estate plan was almost complete before 1939. The only other major post-war private planning scheme, that of Birmingham University, is something of a special case and will be dealt with below in the section on architecture, p. 467.

[7] M. B. Stedman and P. A. Wood, 'Urban renewal in Birmingham: an interim report', *Geography*, vol. i, no. 1, January 1965, p. 16.

and commercial activity was at first forbidden, and the density of building was strictly controlled. In the nineteenth century the Calthorpe Estate had housed many of Birmingham's richest and most influential citizens, and it had exercised a substantial influence on planned suburban areas like Bournville, the Harborne Tenants Estate, and, later, the municipal estates, all of which tried in some measure to reproduce its arcadian environment. Furthermore, in a city where inner areas were very short of open space, Edgbaston had a considerable amenity value. So the question was, should the Calthorpe Estate be allowed to retain its character, or should it be required to conform to the higher densities which seemed to be necessary in other parts of the city?

In the late 1940s opinion within the City Council and in the city as a whole was strongly in favour of preserving the character of the area. Even the Labour group and the Borough Labour Party did not cast covetous eyes over Edgbaston with a view to using it for municipal building. They were strongly in favour of low residential densities, and still had high hopes of building a more beautiful city. Edgbaston, to them, was a model for other parts of Birmingham, not a shameful waste of valuable space. Moreover, the Calthorpe Estate had an excellent reputation for good management, unlike the estate companies which owned slum properties in the central redevelopment areas, against which Labour was very bitter. In any case, the land shortage within Birmingham was not yet severe, and it was possible that the eventual target population for the city might be fixed low enough to attenuate it. So both the parties were agreed on the future of the Calthorpe Estate.

In 1950 the Calthorpe Estate was asked to settle the lines of its future development for inclusion in the Development Plan. The Estate, significantly, commissioned the Bournville Village Trust to prepare a plan,[1] which was agreed by the City Council after the Estate had accepted a number of detailed modifications proposed by the Public Works Committee. As part of the agreement, the Estate agreed to sell four fringe areas (some 100 acres) to the Corporation for municipal housing. This arrangement was to the benefit of both parties, for these districts already had higher residential densities than the rest of the Estate, and had deteriorated more rapidly than its central zone, partly because they adjoined slum areas under the control of the Corporation. Their sale allowed the Estate to retire into an enclave bounded on the north by Hagley Road and on the east by Bristol Road, and to hand over to the Corporation what would have been a very difficult task of redevelopment. The Corporation, for its part, could extend its redevelopment schemes into these fringe Calthorpe areas, to the benefit of its overall replanning, and, by raising densities

[1] H. E. Greening, 'The redevelopment of a private urban estate', paper read to the Public Works and Municipal Services Congress, 16 November 1960, p. 10.

there up to central redevelopment area levels, compensate to some extent for the low densities (thirty persons to the acre) tolerated on the Estate. Even so, thirty persons to the acre was three times the Estate's current net density. This arrangement was ratified by the City Council on 8 November 1955.[1] By this time feeling within the Borough Labour Party, though not within the Labour group, had begun to veer in favour of making more use of the Calthorpe Estate for municipal housing, and the agreement helped the Labour group to answer criticism from within its own party that it was being too soft on the Estate. Further areas were acquired or leased from the Calthorpe Estate in the early 1960s.

No redevelopment at all was done on the Estate from the end of the war until 1954,[2] so the preparation of a detailed planning scheme did not become urgent until the late 1950s. In February 1957 John Madin, a leading Birmingham architect, was appointed to prepare redevelopment proposals and act as consulting architect. He was required to achieve the City Council's minimum density requirement while retaining and improving the character and amenities of the area.[3] It had already been decided that part of the Estate near Five Ways, close to the city centre, should be zoned for commercial development. Sir Patrick Abercrombie's West Midlands Plan had recommended that the cramped city centre should be allowed to expand into Edgbaston,[4] and the Estate had already allowed some houses near Five Ways to be used as offices during the war, after city-centre premises had been blitzed. This westward expansion fitted in closely with the City Council's policy of developing Broad Street as a business axis, which was pursued with moderate success from the early 1950s. The rest of the Estate had been zoned primarily as a residential area. Here, too, the natural development of the district was already pointing the way towards the higher densities agreed between the Estate and the Council, for some houses were converted into flats there from the early 1950s.[5]

Madin's plan divided the residential area into three density categories. The highest density was to be achieved in areas of multi-storey flats, and the lowest in districts of detached houses, some of them with very large gardens. The medium-density areas would have small blocks of flats and terraced houses. This arrangement had much in common with the mixed development introduced on municipal estates by the City Architect, A. G. Sheppard Fidler. Another common point was the separation of pedestrians from traffic, which Madin carried much

[1] B.C.C., *Pro.*, 8 November 1955, pp. 554–6 (Public Works Committee).

[2] *B.P.*, 22 October 1954.

[3] Greening, 'The redevelopment of a private urban estate', p. 10.

[4] *West Midlands Plan* (1948), p. 29.

[5] R. J. Smith, 'The changing housing stock of Birmingham 1945 to 1966', History of Birmingham Project Research Paper no. 7, p. 14.

further than was usual in private developments.[1] The business zone was also advanced in layout, compared with the development that the City Council was carrying out at the time along the inner ring road. Madin planned a series of tower blocks, with a plot ratio of 2·5, along both sides of Hagley Road where it approached Five Ways from the suburbs. This arrangement, which was very similar to parts of London's Barbican scheme, allowed two-thirds of the ground space to be left open, and ample parking space was provided. Other tower blocks were planned to the south of the Hagley Road frontage, interspersed by lower buildings.

The whole scheme, which was approved by the City Council in September 1958, was designed to revitalize Edgbaston to the benefit of the whole city. The inclusion of a high proportion of flats and small houses was intended to allow young middle-class couples to live near the city centre, instead of being forced to move to the outer suburbs. In addition to Five Ways, two neighbourhood shopping centres were planned to meet the needs of these new residents. Nevertheless, the Borough Labour Party was unhappy with the proposals, and at the municipal policy conference in 1959 a motion was passed attacking their acceptance by the Labour group.

Redevelopment proceeded rapidly from the late 1950s. By the summer of 1960, 120 flats and over 100 new houses had been completed.[2] Progress was hindered, however, in the mid-1960s by the Labour Government's proposals for leasehold reform and a levy on betterment value resulting from development. About half the houses on the estate were affected by the provisions of the Leasehold Reform Act,[3] which allowed occupants to purchase their freehold from the Calthorpe Estate. The Estate's redevelopment proposals were not radically affected, because most of the properties concerned were either very poor ones on the fringes of the estate, or small houses built in recent years under the development plan. The Estate was also allowed to retain general control of the environment even in areas where it had to give up the freehold. However, the Act substantially weakened the Estate's confidence in its ability to carry through a scheme so advanced from the point of view of layout and dwelling-types as Madin's. In particular, the growing public reaction against multi-storey flats brought Madin's high-density areas into question. Moreover, the Government's plans for a development levy seemed likely to reduce the profits made by the Estate, which, unlike a private developer, did not itself build dwellings. So from about 1964 the Estate abandoned its plans for further multi-storey flats, and some areas scheduled for

[1] John Tetlow and Anthony Goss, *Homes, Towns and Traffic* (1965), p. 147.
[2] Greening, 'The redevelopment of a private urban estate', p. 14.
[3] *Ex inf.* H. E. Greening, agent for the Calthorpe Estate Company.

mixed development were leased to a private building contractor for development with small, uniform houses. The advantage of this form of development was that the houses were certain to find purchasers, but it reduced the proportion of accessible open space and involved the removal of more trees than Madin had planned. However necessary this change of policy was for commercial reasons, it was certainly a disappointing step away from the ideals of John Madin. Nonetheless, by 1970 the redevelopment of Edgbaston, which was now far advanced, had succeeded almost everywhere in enhancing the beauty of the area.

Architecture

We have dealt so far with planning and layout rather than with the buildings themselves. But the appearance of all these new developments depended very much on vertical as well as horizontal designs. How far did Birmingham's architecture correspond to its planning standards?

The years 1939–70 were one of the more distinguished periods in Birmingham's architectural history, but this is not saying very much. The city had a very poor architectural tradition, mainly because of its relatively small size until the eighteenth century, and had shown little respect for its few buildings of architectural merit.[1] Birmingham had also failed to produce a strong local school of able architects in the early nineteenth century. Most of Birmingham's major buildings of notable architectural quality in the first half of the nineteenth century were designed by outsiders such as Joseph Hansom, Charles Barry, and Augustus Welby Pugin. Only Thomas Rickman, who came to Birmingham early in his career, can be claimed with some justification as a notable local architect.[2]

As the town expanded a number of Birmingham architects built up thriving practices in the second half of the century, but few apart from J. A. Chatwin produced much work of merit. Numerous older buildings of some distinction were torn down to make way for new shops and offices, and the Birmingham public grew accustomed to the loss of old buildings which happened to be in the way of necessary improvements. Other buildings, in the well-planned residential districts which had been developed to the north-west of the centre in the late eighteenth century, were converted into stores or workshops before their eventual deterioration and demolition. Nor were the new buildings which replaced them in the nineteenth century distinguished from an architectural point of view. So cramped was the town centre that maximum

---

[1] This section leans heavily on Nikolaus Pevsner and Alexandra Wedgewood, *The Buildings of England: Warwickshire* (1966); Douglas Hickman, *Birmingham* (1970); and Bryan Little, *Birmingham Buildings: The Architectural Story of a Midland City* (1971), but the value judgments it contains are predominantly ours, not theirs.

[2] Though to do so is like claiming Handel as an English composer; Rickman was a Liverpool product.

floorspace was the most important requirement in any new building. Large and ornate commercial structures were rare, owing to the absence of the big mercantile concerns which contributed a number of distinguished buildings to Liverpool in the later nineteenth century. Nor did Birmingham, with its small-scale industries and small firms, see many impressive factories or warehouses. Because wealth was shared more equally among the population than in Manchester and the other textile towns of the north, rich private patrons were rare, and the residential suburbs, of which Edgbaston was the best-known example, were very modest in their architecture, though often distinguished in layout and landscaping. The same was true of the garden suburb of Bournville, developed from the 1890s. Few dared contradict *The Builder*'s lament: 'There is no doubt that up to the present time Birmingham is one of the most architecturally depressing of all our large towns'.[1]

Even at the turn of the century, when architects in Glasgow and Liverpool, influenced by Art Nouveau and the Arts and Crafts movement, began to design buildings which were beginning to be valued in the 1960s, Birmingham lagged well behind. A few local architects such as W. H. Bidlake and W. A. Harvey produced important work, and in the Eagle Insurance (now Orion Insurance) building, Colmore Row, W. S. Lethaby designed what Pevsner regards as one of the most original buildings for its date (1900) in England. But this, and Bidlake's church of St. Agatha, Sparkbrook, are isolated gems. With the city going through a commercial eclipse, little money was available for the construction of impressive buildings, secular or religious. Birmingham's shortage of attractive churches was particularly serious. Apart from those built by Thomas Rickman at the beginning of the gothic revival, few had much distinction. The Church of England had always been too weak in Birmingham to afford large churches and brilliant architects, and the nonconformists, with no example to follow, had built little of note. Indeed, by 1914 several of the churches built in the attractive classical style of the eighteenth and early nineteenth centuries had been demolished, together with much of Rickman's work, owing to population movement to the suburbs and pressure on sites in the city centre.

In the absence of patronage by rich individuals, thriving commercial concerns, and prosperous religious denominations, much of Birmingham's more distinguished architecture had been communally financed. The example set by the Improvement Commissioners with their Market Hall (1828) and the Town Hall (1834) was not fully emulated by the Corporation of Birmingham after 1838, owing to an almost permanent respect for the demands of economy. In the 1860s and 1870s, however, when the purse strings were loosed for a time, the Borough Council showed what it could do, in building the central library (1863, rebuilt

[1] *The Builder*, vol. lix, no. 2491, 1 November 1890, p. 336.

1879) and the Council House (1874). Later, the granting of an assize to Birmingham led the Corporation to build the Victoria Law Courts (1887). Educational institutions were another important source of patronage. In 1833 the King Edward VI Grammar School in New Street was rebuilt in the gothic style by Charles Barry, who was later to design the new Palace of Westminster. The School Board commissioned numerous unpretentious but efficient buildings from the 1870s. And Sir Aston Webb, the architect of the Victoria Law Courts, was recalled to the city to design the first phase of the new university buildings at Edgbaston in 1900.

After the First World War the Corporation's reawakening to its responsibilities in housing, education, and social provision enhanced its role as a patron of architecture. But once again the results were modest. Private interests did not make a big contribution to Birmingham architecture in the inter-war years. High-class residential estates now grew up principally outside the city, in Solihull and Sutton Coldfield, where the more prosperous of Birmingham's middle-class citizens moved to escape smoke and high rates. Edgbaston, hemmed in by poorer districts, stagnated. Commercial building in the city centre, as in London, was undistinguished, and concentrated on making the fullest use of the sites available. Typical of the period was the demolition of Barry's grammar school in New Street in 1937 and its replacement by an anonymous office block, King Edward House, built by a youthful Jack Cotton. The limited resources of the church extension movement launched by the Church of England in the 1920s precluded the construction of buildings of great architectural interest.[1] Only in the field of cinema architecture did Birmingham come to the fore, under the aegis of Oscar Deutsch's Birmingham-based Odeon circuit.[2] A Birmingham architect, Harry W. Weedon, designed several cinemas in the city for Oscar Deutsch in a massive, but modernistic, brick style, and as the circuit expanded in the later 1930s Weedon's designs spread throughout the country.[3] Meanwhile, the brewers made a pleasant contribution to the townscape with a number of pastiche public houses in half-timbered and other exotic styles, many of them designed by a Birmingham architect, Holland Hobbiss.

Although the Second World War brought something new to Birmingham in the shape of bombing, the destruction of old buildings which it caused was no innovation. In fact, rather less was destroyed than the City Council might, after consideration, have hoped. But it was unfortunate that two of Birmingham's rare early nineteenth-century classical

[1] For examples of pre-war Birmingham church design, see *Fifty Modern Churches* (1947); Joseph Crouch, *The Planning and Designing of a Methodist Church* (1930).

[2] See Dennis Sharp, *The Picture Palace* (1969), pp. 126–44.

[3] Ironically enough, Weedon supervised the Odeon cinema designs of the Nottingham architect, Cecil Howitt, designer of the Birmingham Civic Centre.

buildings, the Market Hall and Thomas Rickman's church of Saint Thomas, Bath Row, should be so severely damaged during the raids. The destruction of part of the city centre and the deterioration of much of the rest reinforced the City Council's determination to carry out as complete a clearance as possible of the business district and the inner areas after the war, and to make a fresh start. Yet for some years after the war such redevelopment was largely out of the question. Until the early 1950s the only new buildings in Birmingham to attract national attention were industrial. One good example was a steel-frame and glass repair shop for machine tools in Wrentham Street, designed by Rudolf Frankel in the style of Mies van der Rohe, and built in 1948.[1] Good work at the Austin Motor Company's works at Longbridge by Harry Weedon and Partners was supplemented in the 1950s by an efficient and attractive extension designed by C. Howard Crane.[2]

As we have seen, municipal building in the late 1940s and early 1950s was concentrated on the low-density suburban estates, and was modest in scale and undistinguished architecturally. Even in the later 1950s, when the City Architect became influential, and the rebuilding of the central redevelopment areas got under way, the layouts rather than the buildings attracted praise. Even in the central redevelopment areas, where the City Architect was able to group large and small blocks with extensive open space, the results were, to Pevsner's eye, 'on the whole disappointing' from the architectural point of view.[3]

The relaxation of building restrictions in the 1950s released a flood of development in the city centre. As it was a key point of municipal policy that developers' architects should be interfered with as little as possible, the result was a stimulating variety of forms and architectural treatments, few of which possessed any striking merit. The first important building in the city centre, Grosvenor House, New Street, designed in 1951 by the Birmingham firm of Cotton, Ballard, and Blow, seemed promising. This standard was not maintained by City Centre House (1954–7), designed for the Big Top site by the same firm of architects. On this large site, split into several different ownerships, the original shopping frontages were retained, and offices were included above in two blocks of twelve and seven storeys. So many different interests had to be reconciled that the architectural result was inevitably 'a bad joke', as Pevsner called it.[4] Cotton, Ballard, and Blow produced similarly undistinguished results when the combined Woolworth Building and Winston Churchill House were built on the site of the demolished Theatre Royal in New Street in the late 1950s. Here

---

[1] *Architectural Review*, vol. cvl, January–June 1949, pp. 170–1.
[2] *Architectural Review*, vol. cxii, July–December 1952, p. 48.
[3] *Buildings of England: Warwickshire*, p. 50.
[4] Ibid., p. 125; *Architectural Review*, vol. cxxi, January–June 1957, pp. 24–5.

again, a variety of interests were involved, and Cotton, Ballard, and Blow had the ungrateful task of coordinating the work of two other architects. With further joint developments on the way, the architectural future of central Birmingham looked very bleak in the later 1950s.

Fortunately, the situation began to improve. The end of the decade saw the rise to prominence of two important new Birmingham architects, John Madin and James Roberts, who had been contemporaries at the Birmingham School of Architecture in the 1940s. Both had been stimulated by a major reform of courses at the School, involving a marked shift away from the arid historicism of pre-war days. Madin's first important building in the city was an attractive block of offices for the Engineering and Allied Employers' Association in Frederick Road, Edgbaston, in 1958.[1] His success here helped him to obtain the commission of the Calthorpe Estate development plan, and much of his subsequent work was in Edgbaston, where he designed a variety of highly praised shop, office, and residential buildings.[2] In the 1960s he worked more frequently outside the Edgbaston area, designing successively the A.E.U. offices in Smallbrook Ringway, the Post and Mail building at Colmore Circus,[3] and the Midland headquarters of the BBC in Pebble Mill Road. Madin also designed several buildings, including a big library, for the Civic Centre, in association with the City Architect. By the end of the decade he had built up one of the largest private architectural offices in the country.

James Roberts pursued a very different course via his association with the developers of Smallbrook Ringway and parts of the Bull Ring. He was fortunate that almost the whole of Smallbrook Ringway could be developed as one scheme, for it allowed him to design a continuous block of shops and offices along the south side of the road which won wide acclaim.[4] In 1962 he was able to add the Albany Hotel, on the north side of the road, in a corresponding style, and the other architects who built in Smallbrook Ringway, John Madin among them, respected his overall concept. Smallbrook Ringway was one of Birmingham's few examples of a conventional layout partially redeemed by satisfactory architecture—the reverse of the usual situation in the city. James Roberts went on to design the Rotunda and St. Martin's House, further along the ringway in the Bull Ring. As we have seen, he had a considerable influence over the design of the Bull Ring shopping centre itself, the final design for which was prepared by

[1] *Architectural Review*, vol. cxxiii, January–June 1958, pp. 236–9.

[2] For Madin's much-admired Chamber of Commerce building, see *Architectural Review*, vol. cxxix, January–June 1961, pp. 276–7.

[3] See *Architectural Review*, vol. cxxxi, January–June 1962, p. 61.

[4] See e.g. Ian Nairn, 'Birmingham: Liverpool: Manchester', *Architectural Review*, vol. cxxviii, July–December 1960, p. 112.

Sydney Greenwood and T. J. Hirst. Although much of James Roberts's work was done outside Birmingham from the mid-1960s, he was called in to add the final touches to Smallbrook Ringway, as consultant architect for two tower blocks of municipal flats at Holloway Circus, completed in 1970.

The city-centre work of architects from outside Birmingham was somewhat less successful than that of Madin and Roberts. The new Rackham's (Harrod's) store in Corporation Street, designed by T. P. Bennett and Son in 1957, was another attempt, just a short distance from the Big Top, to maintain existing shopping frontages and to combine a large department store, an arcade of independent shops, and a multi-storey office block above.[1] More satisfactory in this area was the work of another Birmingham firm, J. Seymour Harris and Partners, who in 1963 designed the Corporation Street Estate Company building, a thirteen-storey office block with ground-floor shops, on the other side of the road. Even better was a large shopping precinct just to the north, designed in 1963 by another Midlands architect, Frederick Gibberd. Certainly, the quality of city-centre architecture improved in the 1960s as the Corporation began to see the advantage of shopping precincts and pedestrianization, and encouraged developers to free a bigger proportion of the ground space of their sites.[2] The glut of offices which grew up in the early 1960s, and restrictions on office building in the middle years of the decade, helped to reduce the area of offices included in city-centre development schemes and greatly simplified the architects' task. Towards the end of the decade work began on several interesting new schemes, including the Bank of England offices near the cathedral, and the ATV Centre at Paradise Circus, the work of a London architect, Richard Seifert. By 1971 the reconstruction of New Street station, begun in 1964, was complete, as were the adjoining Exchange Buildings, pleasant but anodyne, by Cotton, Ballard, and Blow.

Church building was also held up in the early years after the war, but the success of Anglican appeals for church extension funds allowed rapid progress to be made from the early 1950s. The early post-war Anglican churches still showed a preference for Romanesque and Byzantine styles in brick, but their derivative character was not allowed to prejudice efficient internal planning, and many were of pleasant external appearance. The encouragement given by Bishop Wilson to modern design from 1953 also had some effect.[3] Yet a national exhibi-

[1] *Architectural Review*, vol. cxxv, January–June 1959, pp. 60–1. See also criticism by Ian Nairn in 'Birmingham: Liverpool: Manchester', p. 114.

[2] For a somewhat encouraging picture of the future of architecture in Birmingham, see articles by Leslie Ginsburg and Tim Rock in *Architectural Review*, vol. cxiv, no. 863, January 1969.

[3] See e.g. *B.P.*, 12 October 1957.

tion of church design in 1963 included no examples from Birmingham,[1] and it was not until the following year that ecclesiastical architecture in the city began to attract attention, with the consecration of St. Matthew, Perry Beeches. This church, designed by Robert Maguire and Keith Murray, was based on the principles of the Liturgical Movement, the aim of which was to achieve a relationship between the various functions of the liturgy by spatial relationships in church buildings. Hexagonal in shape, and with an undivided interior, it was intended to allow the whole congregation to participate fully in worship.[2] Other interesting Anglican churches followed, notably St. Michael's, South Yardley, designed by Denys Hinton and Associates,[3] and a combined church and community centre at Hodge Hill, designed by Birmingham University's Institute of Religious Architecture.

Owing to their straitened circumstances, the nonconformist denominations were restricted after the war to building utilitarian churches, none of which were very distinguished architecturally. The Roman Catholics concentrated most of their resources on building schools, and for many years after the war their church designs were cramped by a conservatism more pronounced than that of any other denomination in the city. But they too swung towards modernity in the 1960s. The Roman Catholics built Birmingham's first circular church, St. Catherine of Siena, Horsefair, against the wishes of many parishioners who wanted a gothic design.[4] Later, the archdiocese, stimulated by changes resulting from the papacy of John XXIII and Vatican II, planned even more adventurous designs.[5] The first of these, St. Dunstan's, King's Heath, another circular church, designed by Desmond Williams and Associates, was started in 1966 and consecrated in November 1968.[6]

With so much architecture of mixed quality being produced in Birmingham in the 1950s and 1960s, the buildings erected on the campus of Birmingham University attracted more attention than most. Until the late 1950s, new buildings erected on the site were designed to conform to the layout and style established by Sir Aston Webb in 1900, with particularly insipid results. The university went outside Birmingham to commission a new layout in 1957 from Sir Hugh Casson and Neville Conder, and it also sought architects for most of its individual buildings from outside the city. Opinions on the layout differed,[7] but most of the

[1] See *New Churches: Church Design Today* (catalogue) (1963), B.R.L. 662728.

[2] *Architectural Review*, vol. cxxxi, January–June 1962, pp. 28–9.

[3] *Architectural Review*, vol. cxxxvii, January–June 1965, p. 82.

[4] *Guardian*, 22 July 1961.

[5] See e.g. *B.M.*, 19 November 1965.

[6] *Architectural Review*, vol. cxxxix, January–June 1966, p. 76.

[7] Praised by Pevsner, it was criticized in *Building Design*, 17 April 1970, p. 10. See also Hugh Casson and Neville Conder, 'Proposed development for Birmingham University', *Town Planning Review*, vol. xxix, 1958–9, pp. 7–26.

new buildings, built as part of the university's rapid expansion programme from the late 1950s, were widely praised.[1] Special acclaim was
reserved for the Faculty of Commerce and Social Science, by Howell,
Killick, Partridge, and Amies, and the Arts and Commerce tower, by
Ove Arup in association with Sir Hugh Casson. Furthermore, the
arrangement of the halls of residence around a lake to the north of the
main campus won a Civic Trust amenity award in 1970. Rather less
building was done at the adjacent Queen Elizabeth Hospital, but
progress was made in preparing its comprehensive development plan.[2]
By the end of the 1960s the university and hospital area had become
Birmingham's main centre of architectural interest.

In 1970 Birmingham's architecture was still in a state of flux, with
demolition and new building proceeding apace, and the new city
centre still incomplete. Much of the city's attraction now lay in its
almost transatlantic modernity, which made a striking contrast with
many other provincial centres. Of course numerous old buildings had
been demolished to make way for the new, but very few of them had
been worth preserving. Indeed, it was the general lack of architectural
quality in the old Birmingham that had allowed the City Council to
plan a clean sweep. Occasions on which public opinion was stirred up
against demolitions were rare, and even rarer were those on which it
carried any weight. Modernity, of course, was not a substitute for
architectural quality. Many of the new buildings were built as economically as possible, and some of them inevitably looked cheap. But in
view of the speed of redevelopment it is hardly surprising that some
mistakes were made and some corners were cut. In Birmingham action
had replaced talk. That action had already, by 1970, laid the foundations of one of the most visually dynamic and exciting cities in Britain,
if not in Europe.

[1] See e.g. *Architectural Review*, vol. cxxiii, January–June 1958, pp. 34–5; vol.
cxxvii, January–June 1960, pp. 12–16; vol. cxxxiii, January–June 1963, pp. 24–5;
vol. cxxxiv, July–December 1963, p. 278; vol. cxxxv, January–June 1964, p. 38;
vol. cxxxix, January–June 1966, pp. 17, 210–14.

[2] *Architectural Review*, vol. cxxxvii, January–June 1965, p. 456.

XIV

BIRMINGHAM 1939–1970:
A BALANCE SHEET

THE first two volumes of this History of Birmingham charted the development of a city of which the population and area never ceased to grow. This third volume has covered a sharply contrasting phase in Birmingham's history. From the early 1930s onwards the city's municipal boundaries were virtually fixed, and as a consequence the number of people who lived in Birmingham remained almost static. Of course, municipal boundaries are mere conventions, and in this case they do not accurately reflect the reality of Birmingham's growth. Tens of thousands of Birmingham citizens moved out to homes beyond the boundaries, while continuing to work in the city. The continuous built-up area of Birmingham was extended, on both sides of the official boundaries, by construction on open land within the city and in neighbouring communities such as Solihull, Sutton Coldfield, and Water Orton. Until the very end of our period, members of the City Council were not required to live within the boundaries, and many, particularly on the Conservative side, lived in commuter suburbs outside Birmingham. From these points of view, Birmingham as an urban unit was still growing. Yet even in this more broadly defined Birmingham, growth was less spectacular than in some earlier periods of the city's history.

The rigidity of the city's municipal boundaries was the product of a nation-wide reaction against the unrestricted growth of large cities, which had begun in the 1930s. The residents of independent suburban communities began then to cherish their relatively low rates, which were no longer offset by a poor standard of local services. The central Government showed increasing concern about the social and aesthetic drawbacks of suburban sprawl, the vulnerability of large cities to air attack, and the unemployment problems of the depressed areas. Even within Birmingham growth was no longer seen as entirely beneficial to the city's interests, and the City Council began on its own initiative to purchase land to form a green belt. The Greater Birmingham ideal, which had stimulated a series of boundary extensions since the early 1900s, faded away. During and after the Second World War the central Government strengthened its resolve to limit big-city growth, in order to distribute employment more evenly and to protect scarce agricultural land. Birmingham and its neighbours found themselves held in by a Government-defended green belt, while new industries were effectively excluded from setting up there. In a more dynamic period for the national economy, or with quicker population growth, such policies might have been unsuccessful in restricting Birmingham's expansion. But the years 1939–70 were a period of crisis and uncertainty, rather than of growth and prosperity, for the British nation as a whole. The disruption of the war, the economic difficulties of the later 1940s, and the stagnation of the 1960s, were interrupted only by the intermittent and precarious growth of the 1950s. Even the modest industrial expansion achieved during this decade involved rapid inflation and a series of balance-of-payments difficulties whose effect on local government activity was particularly severe. Rapid growth would no doubt have burst Birmingham's boundaries; their rigidity consequently reflected more than blind administrative convention.

This relatively static condition of the Birmingham economy was most clearly reflected in its employment structure. The previous volumes of this History have described the introduction or development of major new industries in the city; guns, brassfounding, engineering, bicycles, vehicles, and numerous other new branches allowed Birmingham to take full advantage of changes in production factors and demand. One looks in vain for comparable new departures in the years 1939–70. Aero engineering, introduced into Birmingham in wartime, was of temporary duration. The newer, science-based industries did not even gain a foothold. True, the Government placed few restrictions on the expansion of Birmingham's established industries, especially as many firms made a key contribution to British exports. These industries enjoyed sufficient buoyancy to keep employment and earnings at a high level in Birmingham throughout most of our period, and local fears that the city economy was becoming precariously over-specialized were dismissed at Westminster. Yet the very end of our period was marked by a sharp rise in Birmingham unemployment until it exceeded the national average—an unheard-of state of affairs. It also saw the near-bankruptcy of a concern, Birmingham Small Arms, which had once epitomized the adaptability and enterprise of the city's industry. Only time would tell whether this change in Birmingham's fortunes would be lasting, and the city's overall prosperity had not been affected in the early 1970s. But too many voices in Birmingham had been warning for too long of approaching nemesis for this setback not to cause serious alarm.

A second marked feature of Birmingham's manufacturing industries was their tendency to employ fewer people as time went on. This was not in itself a cause of concern, for it reflected a growth in the capital-intensivity and general efficiency of Birmingham industry, and the decline of some of the older, labour-intensive trades such as jewellery manufacture. It was also offset by an increase in the volume of service employment, which in turn reflected higher living standards in Birmingham, and the further reinforcement of the city's role as a regional capital. It was not by chance that Birmingham became the major provincial centre of the office-building boom in the early 1960s; it could hardly fail to benefit from its position at the focus of Britain's most prosperous post-war provincial region. Before the war, Birmingham had been short of services in comparison with the nation as a whole. In 1970 it still had less than the national average, but it compared favourably with other major provincial cities. The establishment of a better balance between manufacturing and services not only made Birmingham a more pleasant and convenient place in which to live, but by increasing opportunities for female employment it contributed to a rise in household incomes.

Birmingham's emergence as a more effective regional capital made the political restrictions imposed by the central Government even harder to bear. Some of these controls were linked to Westminster's general policy of limiting the city's physical growth. Others were intended to make Birmingham's municipal services conform to national standards. Still more (and they were the most resented) aimed to hold down Corporation expenditure, especially on capital account, to a level consonant with the aims of national economic planning. Birmingham did not question the principle of these controls, nor did it refuse the massive financial aid provided by the central Government on both capital and revenue accounts. Their detailed administration, however, often caused annoyance in the city. Left to itself, and given a more flexible system of local taxation, Birmingham Corporation would almost certainly have spent more, especially on capital schemes, in the post-war years. In almost every chapter of this volume examples abound of central Government restrictions and directives which effectively transferred control of the city's local affairs to Westminster. Of course, in many respects central influence was positive. Massive subsidies for housing, roads, and schoolbuilding greatly helped the Corporation to modernize Birmingham. Yet here too the effect of central aid was to make Birmingham dependent on Westminster, and even small changes in subsidies could crucially influence such decisions as were still made in Birmingham.

In a period when coherent national planning became firmly established as a principal aim of government, it was both inevitable and desirable that big cities like Birmingham should conform to a national pattern. It must nevertheless be accepted that the years 1939–70 saw a diminishing of the status of Birmingham and other large cities. Central Government policy was dedicated to preventing a relatively prosperous and dynamic Birmingham from obtaining more than its share of scarce land and capital resources, without so damaging its productive capacity that the national economy suffered. Birmingham was vulnerable because it fell between two stools. From Westminster's point of view it was too large, too prosperous, and had to be held in check. From the point of view of its capacity to resist such restrictions, it was not large enough. In terms of population and area it formed less than half of a West Midlands conurbation which was governed by a number of separate local authorities. When even the central Government began to show concern, in the 1960s, that local authority autonomy might have been so far reduced as to undermine the very principle of *local* government, one of the most important proposals made by its Royal Commission on Local Government was that a single authority should be established to cover the whole conurbation. This proposal was incorporated into legislation, in the hope not only that the conurbation as a whole would be more effectively planned and administered, but that the new authority would merit a bigger allocation of decision-making power. This reorganization was not due to come into effect until 1974, and only time would tell whether the conurbation ('metropolitan area'), rather than the city (to be accorded the status of a 'district'), would be the urban unit of the future.

This uncertainty about the effects of such major changes helps to explain why hardly any effective progress was made towards conurbation integration during the years 1939–70. The other authorities feared domination by Birmingham in any new organization, while Birmingham was afraid of a dilution of its own initiative or even a fragmentation of its area. So it was left to the central Government, whose own recent record in local government reform was far from reassuring, to take the lead and in the end to impose solutions on Birmingham. In the early 1970s even the City Council had difficulty in defining its attitude to the coming changes; at best, they might well strengthen Birmingham's position both *vis-à-vis* the central government and as the leader of the conurbation. Nonetheless, the period which concerns us here, like many preludes to revolutionary changes, was a troubled and uncertain time in the City's affairs.

The major result of central restrictions and controls was that Birmingham was rather slower in modernizing herself than would otherwise have been the case. This effect is particularly evident in the field of housing and slum clearance, where a shortage of land, for which the Government was largely responsible, held back progress until the mid-1960s. That Birmingham made up its lost ground and more after 1964, when land was suddenly made available, suggests what might have been achieved earlier. It must also lead to speculation on how many thousands of Birmingham citizens suffered from poorer housing conditions than they might have done during earlier post-war years. The replacement of obsolete schools was also held back during most of our period, partly by capital restrictions, and partly by the slow rate of general slum clearance. The extra strain on municipal health and welfare services resulting from these survivals of poor conditions is impossible to calculate accurately, but extra strain there must have been. Only in the building of new roads was Birmingham allowed by the central Government to outstrip other large cities. Here, the city's position at the focus of the national motorway network gave it a fortuitous priority, and the spectacular progress made gave some indication of what might have been achieved in other spheres in the absence of central restrictions.

Before the central Government becomes too firmly cast as the villain of this story, two further points must be made. The first is that whatever speculations may be adventured on what might have been, the general condition of the Birmingham commonwealth substantially improved during the years 1939–70. In many respects the Corporation extended its activities, and for the average citizen Birmingham was a more pleasant place in which to live by 1970. So central control was associated with a steady improvement in conditions. The second point is that if municipal outlay had been allowed to run on unchecked by central restrictions, it would sooner or later have faced local opposition to high taxation. Even as things were, such opposition arose. It was certainly provoked by that crude and inflexible method of raising municipal revenue, the general rate on built property, but Birmingham's pre-1939 experience had shown that a popular demand for economy in local government is an almost permanent phenomenon. During the Second World War and the early years of peace Birmingham's rate poundage was artificially depressed, but when it began to rise rapidly from the early 1950s it became the principal local issue in city elections. Although it had very little effect on voting, the position of the Labour majority which controlled Council policy between 1952 and 1966 was often so precarious that it did not dare to ignore the issue. Major concessions were made to demands for economy in the late 1950s and early 1960s. The Conservatives, who were the party of economy when in opposition, continued their crusade in this cause after they took power in 1966.

Of course, there was a world of difference between what the parties said at election times, and what they did when in office. Neither party would have dreamed of cutting back or slowing the development of essential municipal services, though there are signs that some high-spending departments, of which education is the clearest example, were buffeted by a particularly strong wind of economy in the 1960s. It was the non-essentials which suffered most. Unfortunately, they often contributed to Birmingham Corporation's image among the less aware of its citizens and people from other areas. It was, for instance, of little real importance that Birmingham should be almost the only European city not to put up Christmas illuminations in the later 1960s.

Nor was it really significant that the City Council should refuse paltry sums to guarantee National Film Theatre operations in Birmingham, and to support a local radio station. But these decisions helped to give the City Council a reputation for parsimony which, even in the field of cultural provision, it did not deserve.

When one looks in detail at the effects of the economy drive on individual services, one has the impression that it principally promoted greater efficiency, rather than any reduction in standards of service. Even the most determined Parkinsonian would have been hard put to it to find local government employees with time on their hands in Birmingham. Some services, such as education and the police, were permanently understaffed (which was part of the explanation for the City's lower than average outlay on such services). High general wage levels in the city made local government employment unattractive, but the Corporation responded by developing labour-saving methods to an extent unparalleled in Britain. By 1970 the Birmingham citizen was being asked to date-stamp his own library books and to obtain his own ticket on buses, where one-man operation had long been familiar. City police had been so completely motorized that they were rarely to be seen walking about in the streets.

This great efficiency in the use of personnel was paralleled by marked organizing ability in the upper echelons of Corporation departments. As Britain's biggest single-tier authority, the City of Birmingham both needed and attracted able officers. To be a chief officer in Birmingham was to have reached the top of the tree, and, once appointed, departmental heads rarely left for posts elsewhere. Many built up national reputations. Sir Herbert Manzoni and Sir Lionel Russell were the best examples of such figures, but many other officers became well-known outside Birmingham in their own fields. With local government problems growing increasingly technical, many officers exercised a significant influence over the formulation of policy, as well as its execution. Again, Sir Herbert Manzoni's example springs first to mind, for the coherence and direction which he gave to Birmingham's post-war reconstruction, but others played similar roles in less spectacular ways. Birmingham had cause to be grateful to such servants.

Impressive though these senior officers were, Birmingham's elected representatives were not overawed. Before the war many Unionist committee chairmen, often members of local patrician families, had devoted much of their time to municipal affairs. After 1945 few men of this type remained in the City Council, but they were replaced by others who were prepared to sacrifice much of their working lives to municipal work. Alderman Harry Watton, a craft printer, chose to eke out a living by part-time lecturing during his years as Labour group leader. On the Conservative side a high proportion of chairmen came from professional groups, such as solicitors and estate agents, whose work allowed them flexible hours. Alderman Frank Griffin, leader of the Conservative group, retired prematurely from business when his party took power in 1966. There was occasional talk in Birmingham about a decline in the quality of council members compared to pre-war days, but there was no tangible evidence to support it. The Council certainly contained fewer big industrialists, and the proportion of white-collar workers and professionals rose in both party groups, but there was still no shortage of able and devoted committee chairmen.

Post-war municipal politics did, however, produce one remarkable phenomenon. This was the emergence of a new type of group leader. After 1945 Labour had rather the better of exchanges at municipal elections, and they came to determine the dominating ethos of Birmingham municipal politics as the Unionists had done before 1939. The affairs of the Borough Labour Party and of the Labour group were organized on a very democratic basis, and the group leader acted for some years as a *primus inter pares*. Changes of leader were frequent. Then, from the mid-1950s, Albert Bradbeer and his successor, Harry Watton, strengthened the role of the leader so that he could act as chief policy coordinator for the whole of the Corporation. Harry Watton made the most progress towards this goal, establishing himself in effect as the 'prime minister' of Birmingham. He strengthened discipline and organization within the group and even within the Borough Labour Party, with the twin aims of rationalizing municipal policies and keeping his party in power in the Council. With his establishment of a Priorities Committee, and his unending efforts to secure more building land, he was the major architect of Birmingham's resistance to central Government dictation. Democracy within the Birmingham Labour movement suffered to some extent, and disagreements within the Labour group were not entirely eradicated. Later group leaders on both sides repudiated some of his methods, but they maintained the centralized, coherent direction of policies which he had built up. Harry Watton was by no means a popular figure with everyone in Birmingham, but in his handling of the city's affairs he was the first Labour majority leader to bear comparison with Joseph Chamberlain.

The parallel with Joseph Chamberlain is even more striking in the history of the Birmingham Party machines. Chamberlain had founded the Birmingham Liberal caucus, in order to establish Liberal control over all the city's administrative bodies and its representatives at Westminster. From his time onwards, in step with the growing central influence over Birmingham affairs, local and national politics had become increasingly intertwined in the city. After 1945 they became so

inseparable that municipal election voting came to reflect almost
exactly the division of political opinion in the country as a whole.
Birmingham was dominated more than ever before by the local
machines of the two major national parties. The word 'caucus' was no
longer used, but the party machine over which Harry Watton presided
was firmly in the Chamberlainite tradition of efficient organization.
The only political group to seek votes on specifically local issues, the
Liberals, won a few seats in the 1960s, but they did not seriously
undermine the Labour and Conservative dominance.

The annual pitched battles between Labour and Conservatives at the
municipal elections, with predominantly national policies in contention,
were all the more incongruous in that over local issues the two parties
were often in agreement. Before 1939 Labour had openly defended the
interests of the Birmingham working class, but after 1945 they concentrated more on the well-being of the city as a whole. A marked consensus
had emerged in wartime between Labour and Unionists, in which the
Unionist willingness to envisage municipal infringement of private
property rights and a high level of municipal expenditure demonstrated
how much they still honoured their Chamberlainite heritage of 'municipal socialism'. For a few years after the war, during which neither party
secured a firm majority in the City Council, the consensus was maintained. However, the growing unpopularity of Clement Attlee's
Government was accompanied by a resurgence of the Conservative
ideals of free enterprise, low public expenditure, and the defence of
private property. Even the principle of the planned use of national
resources, unquestioned in wartime, fell into disrepute for a time. The
success of this Conservative programme at the general election of 1951
was reflected by a move to the right by the Birmingham Conservatives.
In the 1950s they began to attack high expenditure, municipal trading,
municipal control of land, and other aspects of what they called
'socialism by the back door'. Labour ignored these attacks for some
years, but the undermining of their majority in the later 1950s led
them to make major concessions to Conservative criticisms. These
concessions were most marked under the leadership of Harry Watton,
and to a large extent they re-established a consensus with the Conservatives, though its centre of gravity was to the right of the old wartime
understanding.

To a large extent this tendency towards consensus reflected the
precarious character of majorities in the City Council, owing to the
wild swings which low and declining turnouts often permitted. Labour
could not afford to alienate the Birmingham middle classes, who were
the most assiduous in their voting. Nor dared the Conservatives offend
the city's skilled working classes. The general party agreement also
reflected the loss of decision-making power to Westminster; after 1945

there were fewer topics about which the local parties *could* disagree. This general placidity of Birmingham local politics was not in itself a cause of concern, but the steady decline in turnouts at municipal elections after 1950, which was possibly not unconnected with it, could not be viewed without disquiet. And some people in the city worried about the apparent move to the right in Birmingham municipal politics in the 1950s and 1960s.

On the other hand, it is quite probable that the calm state of Birmingham politics was largely the product of the city's prosperous economy and generally good environment. Many of its better-off citizens, it is true, moved outside the boundaries to seek a standard of housing which was denied them by congestion inside the city. A high proportion of those who moved in to replace them were working-class people earning relatively low wages. This change was reflected in the growing proportion of semi-skilled and unskilled workers living in Birmingham, a city which had long prided itself on its high proportion of skilled workers. But this trend had not gone far enough by 1970 to undermine the widely-spread affluence of Birmingham's population. Despite the survival of many slum houses, overall housing standards were high in comparison with other big industrial cities during our period. Environmental standards greatly improved thanks to smoke control and better town planning, and were reflected in the city's generally good health record. A community in which personal success and contentment were so widely distributed was not likely to have a volatile political life. Extremists on both the right and the left of the political spectrum got short shrift whenever they sought support in Birmingham.

The general contentment of the great majority of Birmingham people helps to explain how a large foreign immigrant population was assimilated with so little difficulty in the 1950s and 1960s. Coloured and Irish immigrants frequently accepted unskilled employment which no longer attracted indigenous workers. They made their homes in decaying districts where the indigenous population was in decline. Consequently, they never came into intensive competition with the city population for housing or employment. The City Council's policies towards foreign immigrants varied over the years, but its key guiding principle was to avoid all positive discrimination in favour of coloured people, in order to prevent jealousy among the white population which might have led to political controversy and even racial conflict. Such conflict was indeed avoided, despite the gloomy forebodings of some observers from outside Birmingham. The corollary of this success was, however, the persistence of appalling housing conditions in the areas of coloured immigrant settlement. Although something was being done to reduce overcrowding by 1970, there were indications that the majority of

coloured people in Birmingham were still living more than two to a
room. Infant mortality rates among the coloured population remained
frighteningly high. Of course, history provides many examples of
foreign immigrants to cities who inevitably lived in poor conditions at
first, but who later prospered and dispersed. The Irish in Liverpool and
Manchester in the 1840s are one example. So are the European immigrants who flooded into the eastern seaboard cities of the United States
in the nineteenth century. But in 1970 it looked as though Birmingham's
coloured immigrants might follow a less auspicious precedent, that of
the southern negroes who moved into the industrial centres of the
American north from the 1920s. Many Birmingham blacks were
prospering in the later 1960s, but, in contrast to the Irish, they were not
dispersing. On the contrary, the proportion of coloured people living
in the major districts of black settlement was actually increasing, and
several observers predicted the rapid emergence of a ghetto situation.
This was a problem which would have to be faced in the 1970s and
1980s. Fortunately, there were indications by the early 1970s that the
City Council had recognized the problem and was prepared to take
steps to deal with it.

The growing coloured population formed one facet of a new popular
image of Birmingham, for so long regarded as a dull and conventional
city. The mushrooming of Chinese, Indian, and other exotic restaurants
and clubs contributed to the emergence of a more vibrant, more
cosmopolitan community. But Birmingham was changing in even more
spectacular ways thanks to the efforts of its native population. Much of
the 1940s and 1950s had been a difficult time for the city, with major
wartime disruption followed by years of somewhat disappointing
progress towards the creation of the New Birmingham that had been
glimpsed during the war. Then, in the 1960s, the city's fortunes began
to change, and the latter half of the decade saw rapid progress towards
the completion of a number of schemes that had long been delayed.
Some of the City's more ambitious wartime plans had been scheduled
for completion over a twenty-five-year period. In 1960 projects such as
the inner ring road and the rebuilding of the central redevelopment
areas were seriously in arrear. In 1970, thanks to a decade of rapid
progress, they were again on schedule, and almost complete. This
happy culmination to a quarter-century of uncertainty and difficulty
was no less than Birmingham deserved. It also deserved the major
growth in entertainment and cultural provision which occurred in the
1960s, much of it a result of municipal enterprise. By 1970 Birmingham
was looking forward to the early completion of a new repertory theatre
and central library, both of them wartime dreams. The year also saw
the opening of a new chapter, in the designation of Birmingham as the
site for a national exhibition centre. For the first time since the war,

Westminster appeared to be doing full justice to Birmingham's position as Britain's second city.

Modernity was the most striking feature of Birmingham 1970. Aesthetic and architectural standards were not consistently high, but Birmingham's gleaming new buildings and roads made a striking contrast with many less prosperous cities. It was modern in its outlook too; Birmingham industry eagerly awaited Britain's entry into the European Common Market. Birmingham was worthy of its place among the rebuilt cities of the new Europe, but an even more striking parallel was with the industrial cities of the United States. Its expressways, sprawling suburbs, tall buildings, and its air of bustle and enterprise all combined to make it Britain's most transatlantic city. It also shared many problems with American cities—traffic congestion even on new roads, noise, black ghettoes, a rising crime rate, and a certain materialism and acquisitiveness among its people. Whatever its faults, Birmingham was almost certainly a glimpse of the future, the shape of things to come. It was far from a discouraging glimpse; between 1939 and 1970 Birmingham strengthened its position as Britain's most pleasant and prosperous industrial city. Some in Birmingham, it is true, shook their heads at the disappearance of familiar landmarks, at a rate of physical change which reached frenetic heights in the later 1960s. But for most citizens Birmingham had become an exciting, dynamic place in which to live. In 1939 it was still possible for an outsider to be indifferent to Birmingham; in 1970 it could not fail to provoke a thrill, or perhaps a shudder, among all who beheld it.

The year 1970 provides a fitting termination for this third volume of Birmingham's History. In that year the New Birmingham, dreamed of in wartime, had come to pass. The city was already going on to face the problems, and take the opportunities, of a new age. But those who had participated in the city's life during thirty eventful years had a right to pause for a while, and consider with not a little pride the progress made during three of the most momentous decades in the whole long story of Birmingham.

APPENDIX A

LORD MAYORS OF BIRMINGHAM
(1939–1970)

1939 Theodore Beal Pritchett, M.C.
1940 Wilfrid Martineau
1941 Norman Tiptaft
1942 Walter Samuel Lewis
1943 Lionel George Helmore Alldridge
1944 William Theophilus Wiggins-Davies
1945 Alan Stewart Giles
1946 Albert Frederick Bradbeer
1947–8 John Charles Burman
1949 Hubert Humphreys
1950 Alfred Paddon-Smith
1951 Ralph Cyril Yates
1952 William Tegfryn Bowen
1953 George Henry Wilson Griffith
1954 Joseph Reginald Balmer
1955 Arthur Lummis Gibson
1956 Ernest William Apps
1957 John Joseph Grogan, M.B.E.
1958 Donald Johnstone
1959 John Henry Lewis, O.B.E.
1960 Garnet Benjamin Boughton
1961 Eric Edward Mole, O.B.E.
1962 Ernest Walter Horton
1963 Louis Glass
1964 Frank Leslie Price
1965 George Corbyn Barrow
1966 Harold Edward Tyler
1967 James Stephen Meadows, O.B.E.
1968 Charles Valentine George Simpson
1969 Neville Bruce Alfred Bosworth
1970 Stanley Bleyer

FREEMEN OF BIRMINGHAM (1939-1970)

26. Field-Marshal Jan Christiaan Smuts (1944)
27. Winston Leonard Spencer Churchill (1946)
28. Clement Richard Attlee (1947)
29. Sir William Joseph Slim (1947)
30. Sir Frank Henry Cufaude Wiltshire (1947)
31. Harrison Barrow (1949)
32. Mrs. Ann Marie Howes (1955)
33. Sir Barry Jackson (1955)
34. Sydney Vernon (1955)
35. Sir Albert Frederick Bradbeer (1960)
36. Sir Theodore Beal Pritchett (1960)
37. Sir Francis Griffin (1970)
38. Harry Watton (1970)

CHIEF OFFICIALS OF THE
CORPORATION OF BIRMINGHAM

Town Clerks

1918 Sir Frank Henry Cufaude Wiltshire
1946 Francis Cecil Minshull
1949 John Frank Gregg
1960 Thomas Harry Parkinson

City Treasurers

1922 J. R. Johnson
1948 James Percy Eames
1960 Francis Stephenson

Medical Officers of Health

1950 Dr. Matthew Burn
1961 Dr. Ernest Millar

*City Engineers and Surveyors**

1927 Dr. H. P. Newsholme
1935 Sir Herbert Manzoni
1963 Neville Borg

Education Officers

1919 Sir Peter Innes
1946 Sir Lionel Russell
1968 Kenneth Brooksbank

* In 1965 the title was changed to City Engineer, Surveyor, and Planning Officer.

STATISTICAL TABLES

Table 1. Industrial Structure of Birmingham Employment Area, 1951
(estimated insured employees, excluding ex-service persons
not industrially classified)

	(a) No. in labour force	(b) % of total labour force	(c) Location quotient
Primary			
AGRICULTURE, FORESTRY, FISHING	1,483	0·3	4
MINING AND QUARRYING	145	—	—
TREATMENT OF NON-METALLIFEROUS MINING PRODUCTS OTHER THAN COAL	4,505	0·7	47
Manufacturing			
CHEMICAL AND ALLIED TRADES	12,175	2·0	100
METAL MANUFACTURE	29,245	4·8	185
Iron and steel melting, rolling, etc.	465	0·1	10
Iron foundries	4,014	0·7	117
Iron and steel tubes	5,185	0·9	450
Non-ferrous metals, smelting, rolling, etc.	19,581	3·2	640
ENGINEERING, SHIPBUILDING, ELECTRICAL GOODS	81,355	13·3	168
Machine tools	12,330	2·0	500
Stationary engines	1,653	0·3	150
Ordnance and small arms	1,753	0·3	100
Constructional engineering	791	0·1	25
Other non-electrical engineering	17,666	2·9	126
Electrical machinery	17,353	2·8	400
Batteries and accumulators	3,430	0·6	600
Other engineering, shipbuilding and electrical goods (inc. agricultural machinery)	26,379	4·3	600
VEHICLES	98,703	16·2	345
Manufacture of motor vehicles and cycles	55,860	9·1	607
Motor repairs and garages	5,527	0·9	75
Manufacture and repair of aircraft	2,714	0·4	50
Manufacture of parts and accessories for motor vehicles and aircraft	29,127	4·8	800
Manufacture and repair of carriages, wagons and trams	4,359	0·7	233
Other vehicles	1,116	0·2	200
METAL GOODS NOT ELSEWHERE SPECIFIED	72,698	11·9	541
Tools and cutlery	3,582	0·6	200
Bolts, nuts, screws, rivets, nails	6,100	1·0	500

	(a) No. in labour force	(b) % of total labour force	(c) Location quotient
Iron and steel forging not elsewhere specified	2,083	0·3	150
Wire and wire manufacture	4,099	0·7	350
Hollow ware	4,399	0·7	233
Brass manufacture	17,638	2·9	1,450
Metal industries not elsewhere specified	34,797	5·7	570
PRECISION INSTRUMENTS, JEWELLERY, ETC.	12,983	2·1	300
Scientific, surgical and photographic instruments	3,460	0·6	150
Jewellery, plate, and refinery of precious metals	9,523	1·5	750
TEXTILES	4,865	0·8	18
LEATHER, LEATHER GOODS, AND FUR	1,931	0·3	75
CLOTHING	6,987	1·1	32
FOOD, DRINK, TOBACCO	28,972	4·7	147
Bread, flour, confectionery	5,702	0·9	128
Milk products	3,555	0·6	200
Cocoa, chocolate, sugar, confectionery	10,446	1·7	567
Brewing, malting	2,235	0·4	100
Wholesale bottling	895	0·1	100
Other food, etc.	6,139	1·0	100
MANUFACTURE OF WOOD AND CORK	9,230	1·5	107
Timber	1,404	0·2	67
Furniture, upholstery	4,000	0·7	100
Other manufactures in wood and cork	3,826	0·6	150
PAPER AND PRINTING	12,315	2·0	87
Cardboard, boxes, cartons and fibre bond packing cases	1,719	0·3	150
Other paper and prints	10,596	1·7	81
OTHER MANUFACTURING INDUSTRIES	19,847	3·3	275
Rubber	12,099	2·0	400
Other manufacturing industries	7,748	1·3	120

Services

BUILDING AND CONTRACTING	27,834	4·6	74
Building	21,341	3·5	67
Electrical wiring and contracting	1,973	0·3	100
Civil engineering contracting	4,520	0·7	117
GAS, ELECTRICITY AND WATER SUPPLY	9,980	1·6	94
Gas	4,153	0·7	117
Electricity	4,589	0·7	100
Water	1,238	0·2	100
TRANSPORT AND COMMUNICATIONS	27,857	4·6	61
Railways	10,297	1·7	74
Tramway and omnibus services	7,924	1·3	108
Goods transport by road	5,310	0·9	100

	(a) *No. in* *labour force*	(b) *% of total* *labour force*	(c) *Location* *quotient*
Postal, telegraph and wireless communications	2,836	0·5	33
Other transport and communications	1,490	0·2	11
DISTRIBUTIVE TRADES	54,113	8·9	74
INSURANCE, BANKING, FINANCE	10,534	1·7	85
PUBLIC ADMINISTRATION AND DEFENCE	17,282	2·8	35
National government service	4,738	0·8	16
Local government service	12,544	2·0	74
PROFESSIONAL SERVICES	35,612	5·8	85
Education	11,772	1·9	82
Medical and dental	15,962	2·6	93
Other professional services	7,878	1·3	81
MISCELLANEOUS SERVICES	30,316	5·0	54
Catering, hotels, etc.	14,778	2·4	60
Other miscellaneous services	15,538	2·5	47

Source: Board of Trade, given in *Birmingham Abstract of Statistics*, no. 2, p. 123.

Table 2. Comparability of Industrial Groupings, 1951, 1961

Industrial categories employed in the *1951* census		Equivalent or near-equivalent categories employed in the *1961* and subsequent censuses	
	I		I
	II		II
	XIII		III
	IV		IV
	V		V
VI	VII	VI	IX
IX	XVI	VIII	XVI
	VII		VIII
	X		X
	XI		XI
	XII		XII
	III		XIII
	XIV		XIV
	XV		XV
	XVII		XVII
	XVIII		XVIII
	XIX		XIX
	XX		XX
	XXI		XXI
	XXIII		XXII
	XXIV		XXIII
	XXII		XXIV

Source: Appendix D of Census 1961, Industry Tables, Pt. 1.

Table 3. Industrial Structure of Birmingham Employment Area, 1961–1970
(estimated insured employees, excluding ex-service persons not industrially classified)

	1961	1970	diff.	% diff.
AGRICULTURE, FORESTRY, FISHING	978	677	−301	−30·8
MINING AND QUARRYING	105	87	−18	−17·1
FOOD, DRINK, TOBACCO	28,268	27,360	−908	−3·2
Bread, flour, confectionery	(6,828)	(5,913)	(−915)	(−13·4)
Bacon curing, meat and fish products	(1,467)	(1,225)	(−242)	(−16·5)
Cocoa, chocolate and sugar confectionery	(12,799)	(10,859)	(−1,940)	(−15·2)
Fruit and vegetable products	(1,357)	(1,661)	(+304)	(+22·4)
Brewing and malting	(2,787)	(2,750)	(−37)	(−1·3)
CHEMICALS AND ALLIED INDUSTRIES	13,738	8,456	−5,282	−38·5
Paint and printing ink	(2,214)	(2,024)	(−190)	(−8·6)
Synthetic resins and plastic materials	(2,421)	(2,641)	(+220)	(+9·1)
METAL MANUFACTURE	29,637	32,006	+2,369	+8·0
Steel tubes	(6,345)	(5,020)	(−1,325)	(−20·9)
Light metals	(5,109)	(7,815)	(+2,706)	(+53·0)
Copper, brass, and other base metals	(16,901)	(17,368)	(+467)	(+2·8)
ENGINEERING AND ELECTRICAL GOODS	99,995	74,451	−25,544	−25·5
Metal working, machine tools	(9,785)	(7,382)	(−2,403)	(−24·6)
Engineers' small tools and gauges	(5,550)	(6,573)	(+1,023)	(+18·4)
Industrial engines	(1,355)	(137)	(−1,218)	(−89·9)
Industrial plant and steel works	(6,153)	(5,449)	(−704)	(−11·4)
Ordnance and small arms	(10,758)	(1,326)	(−9,432)	(−87·7)
Scientific, surgical and photographic instruments	(4,351)	(2,591)	(−1,760)	(−40·4)
Electrical machinery	(17,935)	(10,975)	(−6,960)	(−38·8)
Domestic electrical appliances	(3,939)	(1,464)	(−2,475)	(−62·8)
SHIPBUILDING AND MARINE ENGINEERING	8	0	−8	−100·0
VEHICLES	94,946	87,910	−7,036	−7·4
Motor vehicle manufacturing	(74,034)	(76,713)	(+2,679)	(+3·6)
Motorcycles, three-wheeled, vehicles and cycles	(12,866)	(6,118)	(−6,748)	(−52·4)
Aircraft manufacture and repairs	(2,930)	(3,047)	(+117)	(+4·0)
Railway carriages	(4,063)	(1,988)	(−2,075)	(−51·1)
METAL GOODS NOT ELSEWHERE SPECIFIED	82,198	74,253	−7,945	−9·7
Tools and implements	(1,966)	(2,200)	(+234)	(+11·9)
Bolts, nuts, screws, rivets, etc	(7,182)	(6,691)	(−491)	(−6·8)
Wire and wire manufactures	(4,614)	(3,139)	(−1,475)	(−32·0)
Jewellery and precious metals	(9,612)	(5,709)	(−3,903)	(−40·6)
TEXTILES	3,140	1,049	−2,091	−66·6
Weaving of cotton finery and man-made fibres	(2,065)	(30)	(−2,035)	(−98·5)
LEATHER, LEATHER GOODS, AND FUR	838	680	−158	−18·9

	1961	*1970*	*diff.*	*% diff.*
CLOTHING, FOOTWEAR	4,322	2,449	− 1,873	− 43·3
Dresses, lingerie, infants' wear, etc.	(2,012)	(1,263)	(− 749)	(− 37·2)
BRICKS, POTTERY, GLASS, CEMENT	3,132	3,045	− 87	− 2·8
TIMBER, FURNITURE	7,292	4,461	− 2,831	− 38·8
Timber	(1,136)	(784)	(− 352)	(− 31·0)
Furniture, upholstery	(2,049)	(584)	(− 1,465)	(− 71·5)
Shop and office fittings	(2,116)	(1,553)	(− 563)	(− 26·6)
PAPER, PRINTING, PUBLISHING	13,324	12,672	− 652	− 48·9
Cardboard boxes, cartons, etc.	(2,048)	(1,971)	(− 77)	(− 3·8)
Printing, publishing, newspapers, etc.	(1,705)	(1,720)	(+ 15)	(+ 0·9)
OTHER MANUFACTURING INDUSTRIES	18,413	17,545	− 868	− 4·7
Rubber	(13,132)	(11,748)	(− 1,384)	(− 10·5)
Toys, games, and sports equipment	(1,504)	(1,684)	(+ 180)	(+ 12·0)
CONSTRUCTION	34,858	36,644	(+ 1,786)	+ 5·1
GAS, ELECTRICITY, WATER	9,369	11,775	+ 2,406	+ 25·7
Gas	(3,996)	(5,789)	(+ 1,793)	(+ 44·9)
Electricity	(4,493)	(4,881)	(+ 388)	(+ 8·6)
TRANSPORT AND COMMUNICATIONS	23,555	20,032	− 3,523	− 15·0
Railways	(8,728)	(4,031)	(− 4,697)	(− 53·8)
Road passenger transport	(7,982)	(6,980)	(− 1,002)	(− 12·5)
Road haulage contracting	(4,503)	(4,386)	(− 117)	(− 2·6)
Postal services and telecommunications	(1,029)	(1,525)	(+ 496)	(+ 48·2)
DISTRIBUTIVE TRADES	71,744	58,854	− 12,890	− 18·0
Wholesale distribution	(16,659)	(14,673)	(− 1,986)	(− 11·9)
Retail distribution	(48,409)	(37,645)	(− 10,764)	(− 22·2)
Dealers in coal, grain, and agricultural supplies	(3,261)	(2,390)	(− 871)	(− 26·7)
INSURANCE, BANKING, FINANCE	14,664	22,996	+ 8,332	+ 56·8
PROFESSIONAL AND SCIENTIFIC SERVICES	54,136	70,284	+ 6,148	+ 29·8
Accountancy	(2,901)	(3,112)	(+ 211)	(+ 7·2)
Education	(25,704)	(35,372)	(+ 9,668)	(+ 37·6)
Legal services	(1,944)	(2,319)	(+ 375)	(+ 19·3)
Medical and dental	(19,829)	(25,031)	(+ 5,202)	(+ 26·2)
MISCELLANEOUS SERVICES	44,324	40,140	− 4,184	− 9·4
Cinemas, theatres, radio	(2,822)	(2,010)	(− 812)	(− 28·8)
Sport and other recreations	(1,364)	(1,844)	(+ 480)	(+ 35·2)
Laundries	(3,064)	(1,639)	(− 1,425)	(− 46·5)
Dry cleaning, etc.	(1,036)	(833)	(− 203)	(− 19·6)
Motor repairs, garages, etc.	(8,694)	(10,447)	(+ 1,813)	(+ 21·0)
Hairdressing and manicure	(2,532)	(1,789)	(− 743)	(− 29·3)
Private domestic services	(2,043)	(576)	(− 1,467)	(− 71·8)
PUBLIC ADMINISTRATION AND DEFENCE	13,351	14,883	+ 1,532	+ 11·5
National government service	(1,357)	(1,459)	(+ 102)	(+ 7·5)
Local government service	(11,994)	(13,424)	(+ 1,430)	(+ 11·9)

Figures in brackets refer to those industrial sub-categories which are specifically defined and which employ at least 1,000 persons.

Source: Board of Trade, given in *Birmingham Abstract of Statistics*, no. 6, 1960–1, p. 59; no. 15, 1970–1, p. 63.

Table 4. Women Workers in Birmingham, 1961 and 1970

	Number		Percentage of total women employed	
	1961	1970	1961	1970
Agriculture, forestry, fishing	168	243	0·1	0·1
Mining and quarrying	15	22	—	—
	183	265	0·1	0·1
Food, drink, tobacco	12,566	11,440	5·1	4·8
Chemicals and allied industries	4,769	2,979	1·9	1·3
Metal manufacture	5,565	6,048	2·3	2·6
Engineering and electrical goods	29,879	23,077	12·1	9·8
Shipbuilding and marine engineering	—	—	—	—
Vehicles	16,546	12,447	6·7	5·3
Metal goods not elsewhere specified	34,804	28,422	14·1	12·1
Textiles	2,319	628	0·9	0·3
Leather, leather goods, fur	562	439	0·2	0·2
Clothing and footwear	3,649	1,989	1·5	0·8
Bricks, pottery, glass, etc.	546	552	0·2	0·2
Timber, furniture, etc.	1,777	1,116	0·7	0·5
Paper, printing, publishing	5,628	4,678	2·3	2·0
Other manufacturing industries	5,928	5,359	2·4	2·3
	124,538	99,174	50·4	42·2
Construction	2,646	3,046	1·1	1·3
Gas, electricity, water	1,675	3,401	0·7	1·4
Transport and communications	4,329	4,331	1·8	1·8
Distributive trades	37,281	32,838	15·1	14·0
Insurance, banking, and finance	7,678	14,268	3·1	6·1
Professional and scientific services	36,899	47,512	15·0	20·2
Miscellaneous services	27,545	22,665	11·2	9·6
Public administration	3,799	5,156	1·5	2·2
Ex-service personnel	220	2,545	0·1	1·1
	122,072	135,762	49·5	57·7
	246,793	235,201		

Source: As for Table 3.

Table 5. Demographic Structure of Major Provincial Cities of England, 1951 and 1966

(a) Population Changes in England's Major Provincial Cities, 1951–1966

	Birmingham	Liverpool	Manchester	Sheffield
Pop. 1951	1,112,685	788,659	703,082	512,850
Pop. 1966	1,064,220	691,380	598,640	482,540
Decline	48,465	97,279	104,442	30,310
% Decline	4·4	12·3	14·9	5·9

(b) Sex Ratio in England's Major Provincial Cities, 1951–1966

Males per 1,000 females	Birmingham	Liverpool	Manchester	Sheffield
1951	922	882	891	927
1966	973	919	941	933

(c) Changes in Age Structure in England's Major Provincial Cities, 1951–1966

		0–14	15–24	25–44	45–64	65 +
Birmingham	1951	23·7	12·8	31·5	22·7	9·3
	1966	23·7	15·8	24·2	25·5	10·8
Liverpool	1951	25·9	14·7	28·8	21·7	8·9
	1966	25·9	15·8	23·5	23·7	11·1
Manchester	1951	22·8	12·9	30·8	23·9	9·6
	1966	23·9	15·5	23·7	25·5	11·4
Sheffield	1951	22·1	12·0	30·8	24·7	10·4
	1966	20·9	14·9	23·7	27·6	12·9

Source: Censuses of Population.

Table 6. Changes in the Definition of Birmingham's 'Rings'

At the dates stated, the rings were redefined as follows:

Definition in 1934
(a) *Central Wards:* Market Hall; St. Bartholomew's; St. Mary's; Duddeston and Nechells; St. Martin's and Deritend; St. Paul's; Ladywood.
(b) *Middle Ring:* Aston; Washwood Heath; Saltley; Small Heath; Sparkbrook; Balsall Heath; Edgbaston; All Saints; Rotton Park; Lozells.
(c) *Outer Ring:* Gravelly Hill; Erdington; Bromford; Yardley; Stechford; Sparkhill; Hall Green; Acock's Green; Moseley and King's Heath; Selly Oak; Northfield; King's Norton; Harborne; Soho; Handsworth; Perry Barr; Sandwell.

Definition in 1949
(a) *Central Wards:* St. Paul's; Duddeston; Ladywood; Market Hall; Deritend.
(b) *Middle Ring:* Soho; Lozells; Aston; Gravelly Hill; Washwood Heath; Saltley; Small Heath; Sparkbrook; Balsall Heath; Edgbaston; Rotton Park; All Saints.
(c) *Outer Ring:* Kingstanding; Perry Barr; Stockland Green; Erdington; Sandwell; Handsworth; Stechford; Yardley; Sheldon; Acock's Green; Sparkhill; Fox Hollies; Moseley; King's Heath; Selly Oak; Harborne; Weoley; Brandwood; Hall Green; King's Norton; Northfield.

Definition in 1962
(a) *Central Wards:* Aston; Newtown; Duddeston; Ladywood; Deritend.
(b) *Middle Ring:* Soho; Handsworth; Gravelly Hill; Washwood Heath; Saltley; Small Heath; Sparkbrook; Sparkhill; Moseley; Selly Oak; Edgbaston; Rotton Park; All Saints.
(c) *Outer Ring:* Sandwell; Perry Barr; Oscott; Kingstanding; Stockland Green; Erdington; Shard End; Stechford; Yardley; Sheldon; Acock's Green; Fox Hollies; Hall Green; Billesley; Brandwood; King's Norton; Northfield; Longbridge; Weoley; Quinton; Harborne.

Changes in the area embraced by the rings are shown in the following table:

AREA OF RINGS IN ACRES

	1934	*1949*	*1962*
Central Wards	3,023	3,488	4,016
Middle Ring	8,944	11,020	14,565
Outer Ring	39,180	36,639	32,566

Table 7. Demographic Change in Birmingham's Three Rings, 1951–1966

(a) POPULATION CHANGE

		Central Wards	*Middle Ring*	*Outer Ring*
	1951	132,000	344,000	637,000
	1961	96,000	331,000	680,000
	% change	−27·3	−3·7	+6·7
Population*	{1961	149,000	378,000	580,000
	{1966	120,000	360,000	584,000
	% change	−19·4	−4·7	+0·6

(b) AGE STRUCTURE (%)

	0–14	*15–24*	*25–44*	*45–64*	*65 +*
(i) 1951					
Central Wards	27·2	12·7	32·5	18·9	8·7
Middle Ring	22·6	12·2	32·3	22·0	10·9
Outer Ring	23·5	13·1	30·9	22·4	10·1
(ii) 1961*					
Central Wards	29·3	14·2	26·8	21·2	8·5
Middle Ring	21·3	15·3	27·3	24·6	11·5
Outer Ring	21·9	13·8	25·6	27·0	11·7
(iii) 1966*					
Central Wards	31·5	15·4	24·6	20·6	7·9
Middle Ring	24·0	15·7	25·0	23·8	11·5
Outer Ring	21·9	15·9	23·7	27·5	11·0

(c) SEX DISTRIBUTION. MALES PER 1,000 FEMALES

	0–14	*15–24*	*25–44*	*45–64*	*65 +*	*All population*
(i) 1951						
Central Wards	1,024	838	1,099	901	685	963
Middle Ring	1,040	832	1,037	831	643	914
Outer Ring	1,034	870	971	1,008	498	918
(ii) 1961*						
Central Wards	1,063	1,041	1,182	1,053	539	1,028
Middle Ring	1,066	1,000	1,160	948	550	975
Outer Ring	1,047	1,042	983	939	604	949

(iii) 1966*

Central Wards	1,126	1,066	1,209	1,109	566	1,073
Middle Ring	1,052	1,056	1,208	974	536	992
Outer Ring	1,047	1,037	978	960	581	943

* Post 1962 boundaries.

Source: Special ward statistics taken from Censuses of Population and given in *Birmingham Abstract of Statistics.*

Table 8. Birmingham's Changing Class Structure, 1951–1966

(a) Percentage Occupied and Unoccupied Males by Social Class, 1951

	Social Class		
	I/II	*III*	*IV/V*
Birmingham	13·7	59·0	27·3
Derby	11·8	59·4	28·8
Leeds	16·2	57·5	26·3
York	15·2	57·8	27·0
Manchester	14·2	55·4	30·4
Liverpool	12·1	50·3	37·6
Oldham	12·0	55·6	32·4
England and Wales	17·8	52·9	29·2

(b) Percentage Occupied and Unoccupied Males by Socio-economic Grouping, 1961 and 1966

1961	*1, 2, 3, 4, 13*	*5, 6, 8, 9, 12, 14*	*7, 10, 11, 15, 16, 17*
Birmingham	9·6	58·8	31·6
Derby	8·3	60·2	31·4
Leeds	12·1	61·2	26·7
York	9·5	57·8	32·6
Manchester	5·9	62·7	31·3
Liverpool	9·9	53·4	36·8
Oldham	9·2	54·9	35·8
England and Wales	14·1	54·6	31·2
1966			
Birmingham	9·9	58·4	31·7
Derby	7·6	60·4	32·1
Leeds	13·4	60·2	26·4
York	11·8	58·3	30·0
Manchester	10·2	58·5	31·4
Liverpool	9·3	53·3	37·4
Oldham	8·9	55·6	35·5
England and Wales	15·0	55·3	29·7

Source: Censuses of Population.

Table 9. Crude Birth and Death Rates in Birmingham,
1945–1970
CRUDE BIRTH RATES (per 1,000 population)

	Birmingham	*England and Wales*
1945	17·7	15·9
1946	20·8	19·2
1947	21·8	20·5
1948	19·4	17·8
1949	18·0	16·7
1950	17·0	15·8
1951	16·7	15·5
1952	16·5	15·3
1953	16·7	15·5
1954	16·4	15·2
1955	16·1	15·0
1956	16·7	15·7
1957	17·2	16·1
1958	17·7	16·4
1959	17·8	16·5
1960	19·1	17·2
1961	19·6	17·6
1962	20·1	18·0
1963	20·2	18·2
1964	20·4	18·4
1965	19·7	18·1
1966	19·5	17·7
1967	19·5	17·2
1968	18·9	16·9
1969	17·5	16·3
1970	16·7	16·0

CRUDE DEATH RATES

1945	11·2	12·6
1946	11·0	12·0
1947	11·2	12·3
1948	9·8	11·0
1949	10·7	11·8
1950	10·8	11·6
1951	11·5	12·5
1952	10·2	11·3
1953	10·7	11·4
1954	10·6	11·3
1955	11·3	11·7
1956	10·9	11·7
1957	11·2	11·5
1958	11·0	11·7
1959	11·6	11·6
1960	11·0	11·5
1961	11·3	11·9
1962	11·3	11·9
1963	11·4	12·2
1964	10·7	11·3
1965	11·1	11·5
1966	11·3	11·7

	Birmingham	England and Wales
1967	10·9	11·2
1968	11·7	11·9
1969	11·6	11·9
1970	11·1	11·7

Source: Registrar General's Statistical Reviews.

Table 10. Crude Illegitimacy Rates in Birmingham and Selected Cities, 1951–1966
(Illegitimate births per 1,000 population)

	Birmingham	Liverpool	Manchester	Leeds	Sheffield
1951	0·9	1·2	1·2	1·1	0·5
1961	1·9	1·3	2·1	1·4	0·9
1966	2·2	1·8	3·0	2·0	1·4

Table 11. Mortality and Morbidity Rates in Birmingham and England and Wales
(a) Deaths in Birmingham and England and Wales by various causes, 1936–1965

BIRMINGHAM

	1936–40	1941–5	1946–50	1951–5	1956–60	1961–5
T.B.	0·82	0·81	0·61	0·26	0·12	0·07
Influenza	0·22	0·14	0·08	0·11	0·10	0·06
Other infections	0·22	0·17	0·07	0·03	0·01	0·01
Cancer	1·62	1·80	1·45	1·98	2·21	2·21
Strokes	0·62	1·09	1·12	1·42	1·57	1·54
Heart Diseases	3·43	3·09	3·33	3·72	3·77	3·81
Bronchitis, pneumonia, other resp. diseases	1·44	1·56	1·37	1·37	1·44	1·60
Peptic ulcer	0·15	0·17	0·15	0·15	0·13	1·09
Nephritis	0·27	0·28	0·09	0·09	0·08	0·06
Maternal	0·04	0·03	0·01	0·01	0·01	0·01
Suicide	0·14	0·11	0·12	0·12	0·13	0·11
Other violence	0·68	0·50	0·31	0·31	0·37	0·43
Other causes	2·38	2·17	2·19	1·28	1·21	0·15
Crude Death Rate	12·03	11·92	10·90	10·85	11·15	11·15

ENGLAND AND WALES

	1936–40	1941–5	1946–50	1951–5	1956–60	1961–5
T.B.	0·67	0·66	0·48	0·22	0·10	0·06
Influenza	0·24	0·06	0·09	0·13	0·09	0·07
Other infections	0·19	0·13	0·06	0·02	0·01	0·01
Cancer	1·66	1·87	1·87	2·01	2·12	2·19
Strokes	0·79	1·30	1·36	1·93	1·66	1·65
Heart Diseases	3·87	3·59	3·90	4·12	4·29	4·38
Bronchitis, pneumonia, other resp. diseases	1·33	1·52	1·16	1·26	1·26	1·44
Peptic ulcer	0·12	0·12	0·14	0·13	0·11	0·10
Nephritis	0·36	0·31	0·26	0·13	0·09	0·07
Maternal	0·04	0·04	0·02	0·01	0·01	0·01
Suicide	0·12	0·09	0·11	0·11	0·12	0·12
Other violence	0·35	0·60	0·36	0·34	0·37	0·39
Other causes	2·81	2·82	1·94	1·25	1·36	1·28
Crude Death Rate	12·55	13·11	11·75	11·66	11·59	11·77

(b) Age specific mortality from tuberculosis in Birmingham and England and Wales, 1931–1966

(Deaths per 10,000 population)

BIRMINGHAM

		Ages			
	0–4	5–14	15–44	45–64	65+
1931	7·7	2·3	13·9	24·3	12·6
1951	2·4	0·4	3·9	11·6	9·8
1961	—	—	—	2·5	6·8
1966	—	—	0·2	1·1	6·0

ENGLAND AND WALES

	0–4	5–14	15–44	45–64	65+
1931	8·1	2·0	10·5	8·9	12·3
1951	2·5	0·6	2·8	3·1	2·2
1961	—	—	0·2	—	1·4
1966	—	—	0·2	0·4	0·9

(c) Tuberculosis rates in Birmingham, 1945–1970

(per 10,000 population)

	Notifiable Cases	Deaths
1945	13·5	7·5
1946	12·4	6·8
1947	13·1	6·9
1948	13·1	6·3
1949	11·3	5·9
1950	11·2	4·6
1951	11·9	3·8
1952	12·4	2·7
1953	12·4	2·5
1954	11·1	2·1
1955	11·4	2·0
1956	10·2	1·5
1957	8·8	1·3
1958	9·5	1·3
1959	7·3	0·9
1960	8·0	0·5
1961	7·3	0·8
1962	6·7	0·7
1963	6·5	0·8
1964	6·7	0·7
1965	6·1	0·5
1966	6·3	0·6
1967	5·9	0·4
1968	5·9	0·4
1969	5·4	0·3
1970	5·6	0·5

(d) Age specific mortality in Birmingham from influenza and infectious diseases, 1931–1966

(Deaths per 10,000 population)

(i) Influenza

		Ages			
	0–4	5–14	15–44	45–64	65+
1931	3·5	0·2	1·2	6·5	14·2
1951	—	—	0·4	4·1	17·9
1961	0·4	—	0·1	1·5	13·4
1966	—	—	0·1	0·8	5·1

(ii) Other Infectious Diseases

	0-4	5-14	15-44	45-64	65 +
1931	35·6	4·4	0·5	0·4	—
1951	1·8	0·2	0·1	—	—
1961	2·0	0·2	—	—	—
1966	0·6	0·1	—	—	—

(e) Age specific mortality in Birmingham from respiratory diseases, 1951–1966
(Deaths per 10,000 population)

	Ages				
	0-4	5-14	15-44	45-64	65 +
1951	13·9	0·2	1·5	28·3	161·8
1961	12·1	0·1	0·5	19·8	157·7
1966	11·4	—	0·8	21·3	191·7

Sources: Censuses of Population; Registrar General's *Statistical Reviews*; *B.M.O.H.*

Table 12. Birmingham Migrants

(a) Marital status of migrants

  (i) Immigrants of 5 years' and under duration in Birmingham in 1966

	Total	*Married, widowed, divorced*	*Single persons 15 +*	*Persons 5-14*
Male	23,790	56·5	28·8	14·6
Female	22,690	60·7	24·8	14·5
Total	46,480	58·6	26·8	14·6

  (ii) Emigrants who left Birmingham, 1961–1966

	Total	*Married, widowed, divorced*	*Single persons 15 +*	*Persons 5-14*
Male	65,010	70·9	14·7	14·4
Female	67,500	73·4	13·2	13·4
Total	132,510	72·2	13·9	13·9

(b) Age structure of migrants

  (i) Age at immigration

		Per cent			
		5-14 yrs	*15-44 yrs*	*45-64 yrs*	*65 + yrs*
Male	23,790	14·7	70·3	12·4	2·6
Female	22,690	14·5	68·3	8·9	8·3
Total	46,480	14·6	69·3	10·7	5·4

  (ii) Age at emigration

		5-14 yrs	*15-44 yrs*	*45-64 yrs*	*65 + yrs*
Male	65,010	14·4	64·2	15·4	6·0
Female	67,500	13·4	61·8	12·8	12·0
Total	132,510	13·9	63·0	14·1	9·0

(c) Occupation of migrants (as a percentage of economically active migrants) in 1966

	Immigrants of 5 yrs' or less duration		Emigrants of 5 yrs' or less duration	
	Male	Female	Male	Female
Engineering and allied trade workers n.e.c.	17·7	6·4	20·9	5·5
Labourers n.e.c.	6·2	0·3	3·8	0·3
Transport and communications workers	5·3	1·6	5·3	1·8
Warehousemen, storekeepers, packers, bottlers	2·6	2·4	2·2	3·7
Clerical workers	7·0	27·6	6·4	27·0
Sales workers	9·3	9·0	11·4	10·7
Service, sports, and recreational workers	8·8	13·3	5·2	15·7
Administrators and managers	5·6	1·1	7·7	0·8
Professional, technical workers, artists	22·1	32·6	17·8	16·6
Others	15·4	5·7	19·3	7·9

Table 13. Housing Conditions, Birmingham and Selected Cities, 1951
(Households lacking basic amenities, as a percentage of all households)

	Piped water		W.C.		Bath		Lacking one or more of: piped water, bath, W.C., sink
	shared	none	shared	none	shared	none	
Birmingham	16	11	21	1	8	38	48
Liverpool	20	1	17	—	12	36	51
Manchester	13	—	10	—	8	33	44
Leeds	10	—	31	1	5	28	42
England and Wales	14	6	13	8	8	37	48

Source: 1951 Census, Housing Report.

Table 14. Demolition and Construction of Houses by Birmingham Corporation, 1945–1966

	Houses demolished		Municipal dwellings built within city boundaries	
	Number	Index	Number	Index
1945	—	—	6	—
1946	—	—	413	—
1947	—	—	826	—
1948	160	13	1,400	53
1949	356	28	1,227	46
1950	411	33	2,016	76
1951	276	22	3,409	128
1952	320	26	4,733	178
1953	609	49	3,998	151
1954	911	73	2,913	110
1955	1,262	101	2,799	105
1956	1,298	103	2,328	88

	Houses demolished		Municipal dwellings built within city boundaries	
	Number	Index	Number	Index
1957	996	80	2,331	88
1958	875	70	2,201	83
1959	1,424	114	1,890	71
1960	1,403	112	1,882	71
1961	1,966	157	1,924	72
1962	1,590	127	2,116	80
1963	1,522	122	2,160	81
1964	2,093	167	2,407	91
1965	2,241	179	4,036	152
1966	4,075	325	4,702	177

Base 100 = average annual number of houses built or demolished, 1948–66

Source: City of Birmingham *Abstract of Statistics.*

Table 15. Housing Conditions, Birmingham and Selected Cities, 1966

(a) Dwellings by tenure (%) 1966

	Owner-occupier	Local Authority	Private	Others
Birmingham	39·9	40·5	16·9	2·7
Leeds	41·0	33·3	23·5	2·2
Sheffield	37·5	33·0	27·3	2·1
Liverpool	29·8	31·8	36·2	2·1
Manchester	34·2	30·2	33·2	2·4

(b) Persons per Room, by Household (%) 1966

	Over $1\frac{1}{2}$	1–$1\frac{1}{2}$	$\frac{1}{2}$–1	Less than $\frac{1}{2}$
Birmingham	3·0	6·1	55·8	35·1
Leeds	1·1	4·5	60·2	34·2
Sheffield	1·1	4·3	58·7	36·0
Liverpool	2·6	7·3	56·3	33·8
Manchester	2·1	5·7	56·4	35·9

(c) Households without certain amenities (%) 1966

	Hot water tap shared	Hot water tap none	Fixed bath shared	Fixed bath none	W.C. shared inside	W.C.—Outside exclusive use	W.C.—Outside shared	W.C.—Outside none
Birmingham	4·1	17·5	6·3	18·6	6·0	23·0	4·8	0·3
Leeds	1·6	7·5	2·7	12·0	2·8	8·2	11·7	0·2
Sheffield	1·7	14·3	2·6	26·5	2·4	32·0	1·4	0·3
Liverpool	4·0	20·2	6·0	25·6	6·4	30·6	1·0	0·3
Manchester	3·2	13·0	6·5	19·5	6·3	31·6	0·3	0·3

(d) No. dwellings in multiple occupation (%) 1966

	Purpose built	Converted
Birmingham	12·5	1·5
Leeds	11·0	2·1
Sheffield	8·9	1·1
Liverpool	12·0	1·9
Manchester	9·0	1·1

HISTORY OF BIRMINGHAM
PROJECT RESEARCH PAPERS

During the period of our research we produced a series of cyclostyled research papers on detailed aspects of our work which would not justify lengthy treatment in this volume. Copies have been deposited in the main library of the University of Birmingham, and in the Birmingham Reference Library. The titles of these papers are as follow:

1. The Blitz on Birmingham, 1940–1943
2. The provision of air raid shelters in Birmingham during the Second World War
3. The organization of civil defence in Birmingham during the Second World War
4. Housing in Birmingham immediately after the end of the Second World War
5. The production of municipal houses in Birmingham, 1939–1966
6. The two worlds: the University of Birmingham and the local community
7. The changing housing stock of Birmingham, 1945–1966
8. The tip of the iceberg: Birmingham M.P.s and local issues, 1939–1966
9. Migration in Birmingham, 1931–1966
10. Mortality in Birmingham, 1931–1966
11. Fertility in Birmingham, 1931–1966
12. The demographic structure of Birmingham, 1931–1966
13. Population and housing in Birmingham, 1931–1968
14. The changing housing environment: Birmingham, 1931–1967
15. Campaigns and policies: aspects of Birmingham municipal politics, 1939–1966

INDEX

Compiled by D. E. JONES